Linux® Hardware Handbook

Roderick W. Smith

A Division of Macmillan USA
201 West 103rd St., Indianapolis, Indiana, 46290 USA

Linux® Hardware Handbook

Copyright © 2000 by Sams Publishing

International Standard Book Number: 0-672-31918-7

Library of Congress Catalog Card Number: 00-100061

Printed in the United States of America

First Printing: July 2000

03 02 01 00   4 3 2 1

Trademarks

Warning and Disclaimer

ACQUISITIONS EDITOR
Neil Rowe

DEVELOPMENT EDITOR
Laura N. Williams

MANAGING EDITOR
Charlotte Clapp

PROJECT EDITOR
Carol Bowers

COPY EDITOR
Mary Ellen Stephenson

INDEXER
Sandra Henselmeier

PROOFREADERS
Katherin Bidwell
Daniel Ponder

TECHNICAL EDITOR
Roman Rochelt

INTERIOR DESIGNER
Anne Jones

COVER DESIGNER
Anne Jones

COPY WRITER
Eric Borgert

Overview

Contents

7   Optical Drives   191

B   Hardware Manufacturers 625

Index   649

Dedication

To John Kounios, mentor and friend.

Acknowledgments

I'd like to thank acquisitions editor Neil Rowe, development editor Laura Williams, project editor Carol Bowers, and copy editor Mary Ellen Stephenson. These are the people who worked with me before and during the book writing process to ensure that the end result would be worth all the effort. Without their contributions this book would not be possible.

A book like this doesn't just slide through the works without being checked for accuracy. Roman Rochelt deserves thanks for doing this generally thankless job. Any errors that remain are, of course, my own.

David King provided me with many useful leads and tips concerning information presented in this book. I would also like to thank all the many companies and individuals who have written device drivers for Linux. These people make working with Linux possible. Unfortunately, listing them all would take a chapter unto itself.

About the Author

Roderick W. Smith has been using computers since high school, including systems using operating systems as diverse as AppleDOS, MacOS, TOS, MS-DOS, Windows 95 and 98, Windows NT, OS/2, VMS, Ultrix, and, of course, Linux. He has been building and upgrading x86 PCs since 1992, and has experience with Linux running on both x86 and PowerPC hardware. Rod has used Linux since 1994, and has used it as his primary OS since 1996. This is Rod's fourth book, the first three being Que's *Special Edition Using Corel WordPerfect 8 for Linux*, Sams' *Linux: Networking for Your Office*, and Que's *Multi-Boot Configuration Handbook*. He holds a BA from Oberlin College, an MA from the University of Michigan, and a PhD from Tufts University. He currently resides in Malden, Massachusetts.

About the Technical Editor

Roman Rochelt is a Linux developer for a company in Vancouver, Canada. For the past four years, he has focused his energy on Linux. In his spare time he helps with the development section of the Linux.com Web site.

Tell Us What You Think!

As the reader of this book, *you* are our most important critic and commentator. We value your opinion and want to know what we're doing right, what we could do better, what areas you'd like to see us publish in, and any other words of wisdom you're willing to pass our way.

You can fax, email, or write me directly to let me know what you did or didn't like about this book—as well as what we can do to make our books stronger.

Please note that I cannot help you with technical problems related to the topic of this book, and that due to the high volume of mail I receive, I might not be able to reply to every message.

When you write, please be sure to include this book's title and author as well as your name and phone or fax number. I will carefully review your comments and share them with the author and editors who worked on the book.

Fax: (317) 581-4770

Email: linux_sams@macmillanusa.com

Mail: Mark Taber
        Associate Publisher
        Sams Publishing
        201 West 103rd Street
        Indianapolis, IN 46290 USA

Introduction

Linux began life in 1992 as a pet project of a college student named Linus Torvalds. Linus was familiar with the UNIX OS used at his university, and wanted something similar for his own use. He could not afford a dedicated UNIX computer, however. At the time—and still today—the sorts of computers that run most traditional UNIX OSs cost much more than a mass-market PC based on an Intel x86 or compatible CPU. Faced with this dilemma, Linus did what comes naturally to enthusiastic young programmers: He wrote his own UNIX. More specifically, he wrote the kernel for a reimplementation of UNIX, and relied upon a substantial installed base of UNIX utilities to provide a useable system atop that kernel.

Linux has grown and matured substantially since 1992, but today's Linux continues the original tradition: The OS runs on inexpensive x86 hardware. (It's also been ported to many other platforms.) To be sure, the x86 computers of 2000 are substantially more powerful than were those of 8 years earlier. Indeed, today's desktop x86 computers put the dedicated UNIX servers of 1992 to shame, in terms of basic characteristics like total RAM support and CPU speed.

Although x86 hardware is inexpensive, it has one important drawback compared to the hardware used in dedicated UNIX boxes from Sun, SGI, and others: The x86 hardware marketplace is chaotic. For most major component types—video card, modem, motherboard, and so on—there are dozens of competing models, which often require unique drivers to function correctly. This chaotic marketplace provides you, the consumer, with plenty of choices, but the choices can be bewildering when you first encounter them. Couple the large number of choices with the requirement for OS drivers, and a Linux user faces an additional challenge—locating hardware that works with Linux.

In the past, few hardware manufacturers supported Linux in any way. The most important Linux hardware drivers were written entirely by volunteers, who were generally motivated by a desire to use the hardware that they themselves owned. Recently, however, things have begun to change. An increasing number of hardware companies are supporting Linux by sponsoring Linux driver development, either by hiring programmers to write Linux drivers or by donating hardware and documentation to individuals and organizations who are willing to do the work. Still, not all hardware works under Linux. Some devices are simply quite rare, and some manufacturers obstinately refuse to divulge necessary programming information to willing developers. It's therefore vital that anybody considering using Linux or buying new hardware for an existing Linux system understand the challenges involved in creating or expanding the hardware in a Linux computer. I wrote this book to meet this need.

Who Should Buy This Book

Linux Hardware Handbook is intended for two overlapping audiences:

- People who want to run Linux on their computers, but who don't know if their hardware is compatible with Linux. If you fall into this category, you probably don't want to buy much new hardware; you just want to know how to get what you already have working.

- People who want to buy or build a new computer to run Linux, or upgrade or expand an existing Linux computer. Such people need information on Linux hardware compatibility in order to avoid making costly and time-consuming mistakes in hardware selection.

The needs of both groups are similar. In both cases, it's necessary to know what hardware Linux supports, where to look for drivers and supporting applications, and what caveats and limitations exist for that hardware. In some cases, a person may start in the first group, but find himself or herself in the second group because some hardware component is simply useless under Linux.

I've written this book with an eye towards typical Linux consumers, not hardware professionals. If you need to know the intimate details of how a hard disk's read/write heads work, another reference may be better suited to the task. If you want to know how Linux interacts with the hard disk in a general way, this is your book. In describing the various hardware components, though, I do cover some background information regarding how the devices work, and sometimes the history of a device in the marketplace. This information is often helpful in understanding the current marketplace and technological limitations.

Because computer hardware changes so rapidly, I can't cover most products by specific model numbers, although I do make reference to a few specific models where it seems appropriate or as examples. Instead, I provide information on how to locate information on current hardware and its support in Linux. In some sense, my goal is to teach you to fish, rather than giving you a fish.

How *Linux Hardware Handbook* Is Organized

This book is divided into six parts ranging from two to six chapters each. Each section covers one set of topics that are closely related to one another. These parts are

- Part I, "Core Systems," covers the most fundamental features of any computer, including the CPU, motherboard, memory, and case. All computers have these components, although some are unusual in one way or another. (For instance, the cases and mother-boards of notebooks are quite different from those of desktop computers.)

- Part II, "Storage," covers hard disks, removable disks, CD-ROM and related technologies, tape backup devices, and SCSI host adapters. All computers have at least some form of storage available, although not all computers sport all these specific storage types.

- Part III, "Audio/Video," discusses devices used for the input and output of sounds and visual information—sound cards, speakers and headphones, microphones, video cards, video capture hardware, and monitors. With the exception of video cards and monitors, none of these components is critical to a computer's functioning, and even video cards and monitors can be dispensed with in some cases. These components are nonetheless popular and important for home uses, and increasingly for business uses as well.

- Part IV, "Input/Output," describes various devices used to transfer data to and from a computer, such as keyboards, mice, parallel and serial ports, networking hardware, modems, scanners, and printers. In some sense, many other devices also qualify as input/output hardware, but these all fall into more tightly defined categories, such as data storage and audio/video devices.

- Part V, "Prebuilt Systems," covers purchasing new computers for running Linux. I break this task down into three chapters: "Store-Bought Non-Linux Systems," "Linux Workstations," and "Notebooks." Each chapter covers the unique challenges and opportunities you face with each type of computer.

- Part VI, "Appendixes," includes miscellaneous additional information. Appendix A is devoted to drivers—how to find them, how to match them to your hardware, and so on. Appendix B is a list of hardware manufacturers. You can use it to locate manufacturers of devices you seek, or to track down manufacturers' Web sites in search of drivers or support.

Chances are you'll read the book piecemeal, as you find the need to replace hardware. If you want to buy or build a new computer, though, or if you want to evaluate a system you already own for Linux compatibility, you can read the book straight through. If you want a (relatively) quick tour of the most critical and difficult-to-configure components, I recommend you read Chapters 1, 2, 7, 10, 12, 17, 18, and 20, plus whatever chapters relate to any additional unusual hardware you might have, such as Chapter 9 if you use SCSI devices or Chapter 13 if you have a digital camera or TV input card. If you want to buy a prebuilt computer, read Part V, or at least whichever chapters are relevant to the type of purchase you intend to make.

Conventions Used in This Book

This book uses certain conventions to help you get the most from the text.

Text Conventions

Various typefaces in this book identify terms and other special objects. These special typefaces include the following:

Type	Meaning
Italic	New terms or phrases when initially defined.
Monospaced	Information presented by the computer, including file-names, command names, and URLs for Web-based information. Examples from configuration files appear as entire lines of monospaced text.
Boldface Monospaced	Information that you type into the computer, such as commands entered at a command prompt.
Italic Monospaced	Information presented by the computer (or which you type, if the text is also boldfaced), which may vary from what's in the book. Such information could include command options, device filenames, and so on.
Capitalization	The capitalization of menu names, dialog box names, dialog box elements, and commands in the text matches the way they appear onscreen. Because Linux is a case-sensitive OS, you must enter commands in the case in which they're presented in this book (generally all lowercase).

Key combinations are represented with a plus sign. For example, if the text calls for you to enter Ctrl+S, you would press the Ctrl key and the S key at the same time.

I represent a series of selections in GUI programs by comma-separated lists of options. For instance, File, Enter means to select the File menu item, followed by the Enter item in the File menu.

Special Elements

Throughout this book, you'll find Tips, Notes, Warnings, and sidebars. These elements provide a variety of information, ranging from warnings you shouldn't miss to ancillary information that will enrich your networking experience, but isn't required reading.

TIP

Tips are designed to point out features, annoyances, and tricks of the trade that you might otherwise miss. Tips generally help you to make better use of Linux networking by providing a quicker or more effective way of doing something than might otherwise be immediately obvious.

NOTE

Notes point out items that you should be aware of, although you can skip these if you're in a hurry. Generally, I've added notes as a way to give you some extra information on a topic without weighing you down.

CAUTION

Pay attention to Warnings! These could save you precious hours in lost work. Don't say I didn't warn you.

Sidebars

You can think of sidebars as extended notes—information that's interesting but not vital to understanding the main point of the text. Information in sidebars takes longer to explain than information in notes, though.

Contacting Me

I welcome comments and suggestions concerning *Linux Hardware Handbook*. You can send me email at rodsmith@rodsbooks.com, or visit my Web page at http://www.rodsbooks.com.

Core Systems

IN THIS PART

The Central Processing Unit

IN THIS CHAPTER

You're presumably reading this book because you want to buy, build, or upgrade a computer to be used with Linux, or because you want to ascertain your existing computer's compatibility with Linux. Depending upon your needs, you might find it most convenient to skip directly to the chapter on whatever hardware is of most immediate interest to you. If you want a thorough grounding in the subject, though, you can start at the beginning and work through the entire subject. For computer hardware, the beginning is arguably the *central processing unit* (CPU).

At the core of every computer lies the CPU. This component is perhaps the most important *computing* component in a computer. Other devices, such as hard disks, RAM, and so on, can be extremely important in determining the speed and usability of a computer, but the CPU performs the bulk of the computer's computational tasks. Your choice of CPU, therefore, influences your computer's speed and, just as importantly, determines what operating systems you can run. Fortunately, Linux is available for many types of CPUs, although the OS is most popular on the Intel x86 line of CPUs and its clones.

> **NOTE**
>
> The term *CPU* is sometimes used to refer to the main "box" of a computer—the part that houses the motherboard, hard disk, and so on, as opposed to the monitor, keyboard, or mouse. Throughout this book, though, I use *CPU* in reference to the chip at the core of the computer, not the main system box.

CPU Architectures

Computers function by following instructions provided by humans. Typically, a human programmer writes instructions in a *high-level language* such as C, C++, Pascal, or FORTRAN. These instructions are then *compiled* into an entirely different form that the computer's CPU can use. (Some languages are *interpreted* rather than compiled. In an interpreted language, the computer does the translation as it reads the program code, resulting in slower execution.) The compiled code is generally referred to as an *executable, machine code,* or *binary code.* Machine code isn't very intelligible to humans, and, without the benefit of a compiler or interpreter, high-level language code is unintelligible to computers.

Just as there are several different high-level languages available, there are multiple types of machine code. If you want to program in several high-level languages, you need multiple compilers. If you want to use several types of machine code, though, you need multiple CPUs, because each CPU implements one set of machine code instructions. These instructions, together with other details of CPU design, are referred to as the CPU's *architecture.* CPU architectures all do more-or-less the same thing, and, in fact, there are mathematical proofs showing that any problem solvable by one architecture can be solved by another. Different CPU architectures vary in how easy they are to program and in their speed, however, so as a practical matter, one architecture might be better suited to some tasks than to others.

As a general rule, software that's been compiled for one architecture can't run on another. Most importantly, an OS designed for one architecture won't run on another. Fortunately, Linux has been recompiled to run on many different CPU architectures. Because so much Linux software is available with source code, you can usually recompile the software for any architecture on which Linux itself runs. (Commercial software is the most important exception to this rule.) The drawback to this state of affairs is that, if you want to run Linux but haven't bought hardware, you must first make a very basic decision: On what architecture do you want to run Linux?

Your choice of CPU architecture has consequences for other hardware, too. Most notably, different CPUs require different motherboards, and the motherboard in turn determines what types of memory and plug-in cards you can use. (I cover motherboards in Chapter 2.)

CISC Versus RISC

One meta-decision in your choice of CPU architecture is whether to use a *reduced instruction set computer* (*RISC*) CPU or a *complex instruction set computer* (*CISC*) CPU. Historically, CPUs developed prior to the early 1990s grew in complexity with each new generation. CPU designers added instructions to perform more and more complex functions with single instructions—hence they were CISC CPUs. This trend was great for anybody writing software in *assembly language* (a set of mnemonics that correspond very closely to machine code, but are more intelligible to humans). Complex instructions make assembly language easier to handle. The drawback is that complex instructions make the CPU larger, more complex, more difficult to manufacture, and slower.

The alternative was RISC, which gained in popularity among UNIX systems in the early 1990s. A RISC architecture eschews complex machine code instructions in favor of a simpler and faster core CPU design. This approach makes assembly language programs longer, but each instruction executes more quickly, so overall CPU speed is the same or faster. As a benefit, it's often easier to produce compilers for RISC architectures. The reduced number and complexity of instructions means there's less need to analyze the source code in search of ways to use the fastest available CISC instructions.

Towards the end of the 1990s, the line between RISC and CISC architectures became quite blurry, with CPUs from each camp taking on characteristics from the other. For instance, many x86-class CPUs (traditionally a CISC design) began using RISC cores in conjunction with circuitry to convert CISC instructions into multiple RISC instructions.

Among common desktop CPU architectures, the Intel x86 has traditionally been a CISC design, although, as I've just said, many current x86 CPUs use a hybrid RISC/CISC design. The PowerPC CPU line used in modern Macintoshes and the Alpha CPUs used in many UNIX boxes are RISC designs. Unless you intend to do assembly language programming, the RISC/CISC distinction isn't very important. Instead, you should focus on overall CPU speed, hardware availability, and software availability.

x86

The x86 CPU architecture invented by Intel is the most popular for desktop computers today. All computers that run the Windows 9x OS use x86 CPUs. The name *x86* comes from an abbreviation of the CPU names. In the 1980s and early 1990s, Intel gave its CPUs numbers, such as 80286 and 80386. CPUs in the x86 line varied only in the middle number, so *80x86* became an abbreviation for the entire line, and this abbreviation was further shortened to *x86*. The abbreviation *i386* is sometimes used for 80386 and later CPUs.

Intel x86 CPUs are immensely popular—so much so that in the past, several companies have produced x86 clone CPUs, and three companies (AMD, VIA, and Transmeta) continue to do so today. The x86 CPU line—or the 80386 CPU, to be more precise—was the CPU for which Linux was originally written. Most Linux computers today run on x86 hardware, so much of this book focuses upon hardware that's used on x86 computers, although a lot of this book's contents are also applicable to other architectures. In fact, most of this chapter is devoted to x86 CPUs.

The x86 CPU line is a good choice for most users; it provides performance that's more than adequate for most desktop and server applications. Because of its popularity, x86 hardware is inexpensive, and peripherals for the hardware are quite common. One drawback is that many x86 peripherals are low in quality, so you need to know enough to steer clear of the lemons—a task that should be much easier with the help of this book. x86 hardware is also not generally the fastest available, particularly in floating-point computations, and so might not be suitable if you want to use a computer for very demanding scientific or engineering simulations, graphics rendering, or other high-performance tasks.

Alpha

Digital Equipment Corporation (DEC) developed the Alpha CPU for use in high-performance workstations and servers. When it was introduced, the RISC Alpha CPU was faster than x86 CPUs, but the Alpha CPU had a hard time gaining market share because it lacked software. When DEC went out of business, Compaq (http://www.compaq.com) took over the Alpha CPU line, and still sells Alpha CPUs and computers, including the option to preinstall Linux.

If you want to do high-performance computing with Linux, an Alpha CPU can be a good choice. Current Alpha CPUs are faster than the best x86 CPUs, and the Alpha port of Linux is stable and well supported as such things go. In fact, the special effects for the film *Titanic* were done with a farm of Alpha-based computers running Linux.

Red Hat (http://www.redhat.com) dominates Linux distributions for the Alpha CPU, although you can find other Alpha distributions, most notably Debian GNU/Linux (http://www.debian.org). Both these distributions are quite stable.

SPARC

The SPARC CPU family is most commonly found in Sun's workstations. These computers come with their own variety of UNIX (SunOS or Solaris). Linux enthusiasts have ported Linux to the architecture despite this fact—in part because they like Linux, in part to avoid paying license fees, and in part because, like climbing Mt. Everest, facing the challenge is a reward unto itself.

The SPARC architecture includes both 32-bit and 64-bit CPUs, and Linux runs on both. The 64-bit CPUs use twice as many bits to represent numbers internally, which can speed processing of large values. The SPARC processors are quite fast, making SPARC hardware a good choice for CPU-intensive work.

You can learn more about the UltraLinux project (which hosts Linux development for the SPARC CPU family) at http://www.ultralinux.org. Red Hat (http://www.redhat.com) has a version of its Linux distribution for SPARC processors, as does Debian (http://www.debian.org).

PowerPC

The PowerPC CPU is the result of a collaboration among Apple, IBM, and Motorola. This CPU line is used primarily in Macintosh computers, but IBM and Motorola have both used PowerPC CPUs in some of their computers, and there are a handful of other computers that use them. For the most part, though, if you want to use a PowerPC CPU, you must purchase a Macintosh.

NOTE

Early Macintoshes used CPUs from Motorola's 680x0 family. 680x0-based Macintoshes haven't been manufactured for years, however, so any *new* Macintosh you buy will use a PowerPC CPU. If you're considering buying a used Macintosh or using one you already own for Linux, you must ascertain whether it has a 680x0 or PowerPC CPU. Linux is available for both CPUs, but the PowerPC distributions are more sophisticated.

The PowerPC uses a RISC architecture, and is quite speedy, particularly in floating-point operations. In early 2000, the latest PowerPC CPUs (the G4 line) outperform the best of the x86 CPUs, although not by so wide a margin as to make x86 CPUs an unwise purchase choice. In terms of Linux support, several distributions are available for PowerPC computers:

- LinuxPPC (`http://www.linuxppc.org`)
- Yellow Dog Linux (`http://www.yellowdoglinux.com`)
- Debian GNU/Linux (`http://www.debian.org`)
- SuSE Linux (`http://www.suse.com`)

The LinuxPPC and Yellow Dog distributions are both based closely on Red Hat Linux. Debian and SuSE both produce distributions that are popular on the x86 platform, as well as their PowerPC offerings.

At one time, Apple funded the development of MkLinux, a PowerPC Linux distribution that used the Mach micro-kernel in addition to the regular Linux kernel. MkLinux development has largely halted, however, so I recommend you use another Linux distribution on PowerPC hardware, if at all possible.

Before trying to install Linux on a PowerPC system, it's important that you ascertain your system's compatibility. Differences in ROMs, motherboard features, peripherals, and so on result in gaps in the capability of any given PowerPC Linux distribution to work with hardware.

Other Architectures

The preceding are only some of the most popular CPUs on desktop computers today. There are others, however, including

- **Palmtop CPUs**   Linux has been ported to several CPUs used on palmtop computers, such as the ARM CPU used in Psion computers (`http://www.calcaria.net`), NEC's VR-series CPUs used in many Windows CE palmtops (`http://www.linuxce.org`), and even the 3COM PalmPilot (`http://www.uclinux.org`). Some of these ports can also be used on embedded devices—computers built into cell phones, industrial robots, and so on.

- **Rare desktop and workstation CPUs**   Linux is available on the 680x0 line used in early Macintoshes, Amigas, and Atari STs (`http://www.linux-m68k.org`), the PA-RISC CPU used in some Apollo workstations (`http://www.linux.esiea.fr/APOLLO/`), MIPS CPUs used in some DECStation computers (`http://decstation.unix-ag.org`), and others.

- **Mainframe computers**   There's even a project underway to get Linux running on mainframe computers (`http://www.acude.org/roam.htm`), although it's not very far along.

You can find a set of pointers to many Linux porting projects at `http://www.linux.org/projects/ports.html`. Chances are, unless a CPU is particularly old or rare, there's a project underway to port Linux to it—if the task isn't already complete. In most cases, I don't recommend seeking out such exotic systems with the goal of running Linux. Unless you've found a real bargain, you can run Linux for less on an x86 system; or a PowerPC, SPARC, or Alpha workstation will get you plenty of computing power. If you have *very* intense CPU needs, look into a Linux cluster, a group of Linux computers linked together with fast networking technology to produce supercomputer-level computing power. One group working on this technology is the Beowulf Project (`http://www.beowulf.org`).

One potentially important development in the CPU arena is Intel's new 64-bit chip, known as *Itanium*. This CPU is brand-new for 2000, and although it's backward-compatible with earlier Intel x86 CPUs, it introduces substantially new capabilities that can only be used by a new OS—or by a new version of an old OS. Intel has been working with the Linux kernel programmers to ensure that Linux can quickly and easily be adapted to the new CPU.

Generations of x86 CPUs

Because most people run Linux on x86 hardware, that's what I focus on in this book. That's not to say that this book is useless to people who use Linux on non-x86 hardware, however; much of the information applies across architectures. x86 hardware is, however, both more popular and more varied than that of most other CPU architectures. Because of the importance of the x86 in the Linux community, I spend some time here to describe the development of the x86 CPU over the years.

> **CAUTION**
>
> When deciding on an x86 CPU, be sure your motherboard and CPU are matched. Most motherboards are designed to work with a narrow range of CPUs. You can't use a Pentium motherboard with a Pentium II CPU, for instance. Even within the realm of one CPU sub-class, there's substantial variability in compatibility. Some Pentium boards, for instance, only work with Pentium CPUs up to a certain clock speed, or might work with some clone CPUs but not others. Check the motherboard manufacturer's Web site for compatibility information.

The Stone Age: 8086 Through 80286

The earliest CPU that deserves to be considered part of the x86 family is the 8086, although the 8086 was itself derived from still earlier designs. A low-cost variant of the 8086, the 8088, was used in the first IBM PCs. The next Intel CPU development used in PCs was the 80286, which was used in the IBM PC-AT, among other computers. Aside from some experimental and limited ports, Linux can't run on computers of this vintage; the CPUs lack important features that Linux requires, such as 32-bit memory addressing.

> **NOTE**
>
> The 8086 and 80286 used 16-bit memory addressing, meaning that they could directly address 2^{16}, or 65,536 bytes. To address more memory, these CPUs used special extended addressing modes that allowed the CPU to specify which of several 64KB segments to use. Linux assumes it has direct access to at least a 32-bit memory space, giving a theoretical limit of 2^{32} bytes, or 4GB, for RAM. (Intel Pentium Pro and later CPUs use a 36-bit memory space, resulting in a theoretical 64GB address space, and some non-Intel CPUs have even larger memory spaces.)

If you have an 8086 or 80286 computer, the best advice I can give is to forget about using it with Linux, except perhaps as a "dumb terminal"—a text-based display you can use to run programs on another computer. Any of dozens of terminal programs can be used in this capacity.

80386: The Earliest Linux-Capable CPUs

Linus Torvalds wrote the first version of the Linux kernel on an 80386 computer in 1991. Today, many Linux distributions still run on 80386 CPUs, although some include optimizations for later CPUs, making it difficult or impossible to run the OS on 80386s. In practice, an 80386 running Linux is probably best delegated to running only very simple programs, or for use as an X terminal for a more powerful computer.

Architecturally, though, the 80386 added the features that are most important for running an advanced OS such as Linux. These features include 32-bit memory addressing and *protected-mode* operation, which makes multitasking much easier to implement. 80386 CPUs did not include math coprocessors (also known as *floating-point units*, or *FPUs*). These devices handle floating-point arithmetic, and greatly speed up mathematical computations. It was, however, possible to add FPUs to most 80386 motherboards. In theory, Linux requires an FPU; but the kernel has optional FPU emulation. In practice, you can run Linux even on a 386 without an FPU, if you've compiled the appropriate support into the kernel.

The 80386 was available in two major forms: the *SX* and the *DX*. The SX was a lower-level CPU with a pinout to match that of the 80286. The idea was to let computer manufacturers modify existing 80286 motherboard designs in order to bring a product to market more quickly and inexpensively than would be required with the 80386DX CPU, which had an entirely different pinout. Using the older 80286 interface, however, slowed the performance of the 80386SX relative to the 80386DX.

NOTE

The 80386 might be inadequate for most uses on modern desktop computers, but it's not completely useless. The 80386 continues to see life in certain embedded applications. The most spectacular of these might be on the International Space Station, which uses 80386 CPUs to control many of its components. NASA uses the 80386 rather than more sophisticated designs in part because it takes a long time to certify a product for use in space. NASA also favors the 80386 because the larger size of circuit traces on the 80386 (relative to those of more recent members of the x86 family) makes the 80386 more resistant to cosmic rays. A single hit by a high-energy cosmic ray can cause a CPU to malfunction—a real problem in orbit.

80486

The 80486 wasn't as radical a departure from the 80386 as was the 80386 from the 80286. The 80486 provided speed improvements over the 80386, so if you run both an 80386 and an 80486 at the same clock speed, the 80486 will perform more computations per second. Another feature of the 80486 is that it uses an internal memory *cache*—an 8KB section of very fast memory on the CPU itself that can greatly speed CPU operation when working on data that fits inside the cache. Intel also introduced a new pinout for the 80486 (see Figure 1.1), so it was impossible to use 80386 motherboards with 80486 CPUs. (Cyrix, one of Intel's competitors at the time, introduced a series of CPUs called the 80486SLC and 80486DLC that did fit on 80386 motherboards, and that provided performance in-between those of an Intel 80386 and 80486 CPU.)

Like the 80386, the 80486 came in both SX and DX varieties. The 80486DX, however, differed from the 80486SX in that the DX included a built-in FPU, whereas the SX did not. Placing the FPU on the CPU wafer greatly improved the speed of the FPU, as compared to placing it on a separate chip.

Many Linux distributions today run on 80486 CPUs. As with the 80386, some distributions include optimizations that make it impossible to install or run the OS on an 80486. By today's standards, the 80486 is pretty old, and it doesn't perform well with many modern programs, particularly those that are graphics intensive. If you've got an old 80486, you might still be able to use it with Linux in certain capacities, including

- **Small network router or firewall**   Set up an 80486 running Linux as a gateway between a small home or office network and a cable modem or digital subscriber line (DSL) system, in order to protect your network or attach several computers to one IP address. (For more on this type of configuration, see my book *Linux: Networking for Your Office*, from Sams Publishing.)

- **Dedicated X terminal**   Two people can use a single Linux computer simultaneously if you have a computer to function as an X server for the main system. An old 80486 can perform this task reasonably well.

- **Light use**   If your needs are modest, an 80486 can perform adequately. You might not like the way a huge package like StarOffice (http://www.sun.com) performs, but you can run an older or smaller word processor, text editors, and so on just fine on an 80486.

FIGURE 1.1
An 80486 CPU, shown here with a heat sink attached, has 168 pins.

Pentium-Class

Through the 80486, Intel had used numbers to identify its CPUs, but Intel found that its competitors used the same numbers for their compatible CPUs, and Intel could not legally trademark a number to prevent this practice. With the CPU that would have been known as the 80586, then, Intel changed to the name *Pentium*.

The Pentium CPU continued the evolution of the x86 line, with speed improvements and additional features, some of which were added late in the Pentium's lifetime. The *multimedia extension* (*MMX*) feature, for instance, appears only on late models of the Pentium CPU. The Pentium CPU is often touted as being 64-bit, but this refers to the number of bits it can transfer to and from memory in one operation, not to the size of its internal memory registers or the number of bits it uses to specify what memory address to fetch. The Pentium increased the size of the on-board cache relative to the 80486, and no Intel Pentium CPUs lacked an FPU. Intel introduced a new socket design for the Pentium, and that design went through a few minor revisions before settling on the popular Socket 7 layout (see Figure 1.2).

FIGURE 1.2
A Socket 7 CPU has more pins than a 486 CPU, and is physically larger as well.

Prior to the Pentium, Intel's competitors had used CPU designs that were nearly identical to those from Intel, used under license. With the Pentium, Intel's main competitors (AMD, Cyrix, and NexGen early in the Pentium life cycle, with IDT added later) began using unique re-implementations of the x86 design. Some of these designs were radically different from the Pentium's design. For instance, the AMD K5 and NexGen Nx586 CPUs were the first to use a RISC core surrounded by logic to process complex x86 instructions through multiple RISC instructions. These unique designs make it difficult to compare the relative speeds of Pentium-class CPUs with those of different manufacturers' CPUs; the CPU clock speed alone is inadequate for comparisons. Some manufacturers used a *P-rating* or *PR-rating* to express their CPU's speed relative to a Pentium. For instance, the Cyrix 6x86 P-166 could be expected to run at the speed of a Pentium clocked at 166MHz—or so Cyrix claimed. In practice, speed varies from one application to another. P-ratings have largely fallen by the wayside, although Cyrix CPUs are still labeled with P-ratings.

To sum up, Pentium-class CPUs include

- **Intel Pentium**   The "standard" for this class.
- **Intel Pentium MMX**   Available in faster clock speeds and with the addition of MMX instructions.

- **NexGen Nx586** The NexGen Nx586 was the first Pentium clone chip. It was unusual among Pentium clones for several reasons, including the fact that it used its own socket design and, therefore, required its own motherboard. The early versions of the CPU also lacked an FPU. NexGen was subsequently bought by AMD.

- **Cyrix 6x86** Cyrix named this CPU to suggest better-than-Pentium performance, and in integer arithmetic (the sort used by most programs), the 6x86 does outperform a Pentium at the same clock rate. This difference isn't great enough to make the 6x86 a competitor to the Pentium Pro or later Pentium versions, however. Cyrix did not have a manufacturing facility, and so the companies that manufactured the CPUs (mainly IBM) also sold them under their own names. Cyrix was bought by VIA in late 1999.

- **Cyrix MediaGX** The MediaGX was a variant of the 6x86 that incorporated many multimedia features into the CPU and motherboard chipset, rather than using add-on cards. MediaGX chips tend to appear in certain low-end motherboards from their day (mostly 1998). Although Linux can run on the MediaGX, the kernel doesn't support the advanced multimedia features of the chip, so you might have difficulty using these features of the computer. You might need to add a conventional video or sound card to use X or sound on Linux on a MediaGX computer, for instance.

- **AMD K5** AMD's Pentium competitor was late and, in its first pressings, slightly slower than a Pentium at the same speed. Later versions of the K5 brought it into approximate speed parity with the Pentium at the same clock speed, but by that time AMD had introduced the K6, which quickly overshadowed the K5.

- **IDT WinChip** The IDT WinChip appeared very late in the Pentium life cycle and was never very popular. IDT announced in late 1999 that it was selling its WinChip design to VIA.

All of these CPUs are compatible with Linux. For best performance, you might want to recompile your kernel and select the appropriate CPU in the kernel configuration options (see Figure 1.3).

In 2000, Pentium-class systems are still adequate for running Linux, although older Pentium systems can be quite sluggish and even fast Pentium systems can be inadequate for tasks that are particularly demanding of the CPU, such as scientific simulations. No Linux distributions yet include optimizations that prevent them from running on Pentiums.

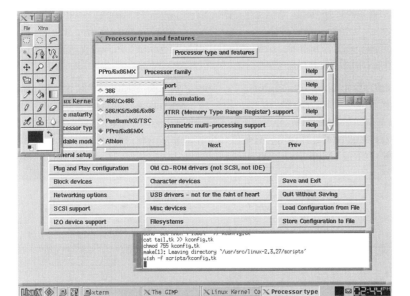

FIGURE 1.3
The Linux kernel configuration provides options to help you optimize your kernel for the CPU in your computer.

Pentium Pro Through Pentium III

After the Pentium, Intel released a series of upgraded versions of the Pentium CPU, known as the Pentium Pro, Pentium II, Pentium III, and Celeron. These CPU families differ from the Pentium in several ways, including

- **L2 cache on the CPU package**   *L2 cache* is a fast type of RAM that, on Pentium designs, resides on the motherboard. These CPUs place it on the CPU's package, although it's not part of the same microchip wafer as the CPU proper. This placement speeds up system performance because the cache can run at a faster speed than it could when placed on the motherboard. Early Celeron CPUs, however, lacked the L2 cache.

- **36-bit addressing**   These CPUs can access 2^{36} bytes, or 64GB, of memory, as opposed to the 4GB limit of the Pentium line.

- **Improved speed**   Although not as radical as the speed improvements in some early generation changes, these CPUs are generally faster than their predecessors when set at the same clock rates. The Pentium Pro is actually slower than the Pentium when running 16-bit code, but faster when running 32-bit code. (Linux uses 32-bit code exclusively, except when running emulators like DOSEMU.)

- **Improved clock speeds**   These CPUs can run at faster clock speeds than their predecessors, which is the source of the greatest speed improvement. Some models can also run at faster *bus speeds*, which is the speed with which the CPU communicates with other computer components.

- **Different packages**   Through the Pentium Pro, Intel's x86 CPUs have all used socketed designs, although the details of the sockets have varied from one CPU to another (see Figure 1.4). The Pentium II, however, introduced a different *slot* design, known as *Slot 1*. Some versions of the Pentium II and Celeron, however, are available in both socket (*Socket 370*) and Slot 1 formats.

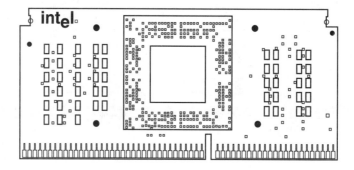

FIGURE 1.4

Pentium II and III CPUs attach to the motherboard using a circuit board encased in a plastic shell, rather than using a socketed design like earlier x86 CPUs.

If you plan to buy a new Intel CPU today, I recommend that you get a Pentium III, although high-end Pentium II and Celeron CPUs can be adequate for low-end systems. Pentium Pro CPUs are very hard to find and slow by today's standards. Celeron CPUs have small or no L2 caches, which hampers their performance. This isn't to say that anything less than a Pentium II is a poor CPU, of course; for many purposes, you don't need the fastest CPU available, and Linux runs fine on slower CPUs. For a new computer, you should purchase something that will remain viable for a while into the future.

TIP

You can get the most "bang for the buck" by purchasing a CPU that's a few notches below the fastest available. For instance, in early 2000, Pentium-III 700 CPUs were selling for about $850, but Pentium-III 600 CPUs were about $500 and Pentium-III 500 CPUs sold for about $300. The drop of the first 100MHz therefore saves $350, whereas the next 100MHz drop saves only $200.

The very latest of the Intel Pentium III line is called *Coppermine* (although it doesn't use the copper trace technology invented by IBM and now used in PowerPC CPUs). Coppermine incorporates several advancements over previous Intel CPUs, such as a 133MHz motherboard bus, integration of the L2 cache into the main CPU wafer, and smaller circuitry. Aside from allowing higher motherboard bus speeds, these enhancements are largely invisible to you as a consumer, except that they produce a faster CPU. In fact, Intel chose not to release Coppermine under a new name; it's still a Pentium III CPU.

Advanced Non-Intel x86 CPUs

Through 1999, Intel's competitors continued to use the Socket 7 design for CPU interface used in most Pentium CPUs. This meant that most competing CPUs used L2 caches on the motherboard rather than the CPU (the exception being AMD's K6-III), and these CPUs were limited to the 32-bit, 4GB memory address space of Pentiums. In terms of speed, though, some of these CPUs compete with CPUs through mid-range Pentium-IIIs. CPUs in this range include

- **AMD K6** The K6 was based largely on designs developed by NexGen for the never-released Nx686. It includes MMX technology and approaches Pentium II speed when run at the same clock rate.

CAUTION

Some early K6 CPUs contained a bug that caused occasional unreliable operation. This bug isn't Linux-specific, but for various reasons it manifested itself frequently when using the GCC compiler, and it could cause Linux kernel compiles to fail sporadically, among other problems. If you have an early K6 CPU, therefore, you might want to replace it rather than run Linux on it.

- **AMD K6-2 and K6-III** The K6-2 and K6-III are faster versions of the K6 CPU. They both run at faster clock rates and include changes to improve performance when the CPUs are run at the same clock rate.

- **Cyrix MII** The MII is basically a 6x86 run at a higher clock rate. The MII also incorporates MMX instructions. I include the MII CPU here rather than in the Pentium section mainly because it can run at faster clock rates than Intel's Pentium.

- **Transmeta Crusoe** Transmeta (http://www.transmeta.com) is the latest entrant in the x86 CPU sweepstakes. The Crusoe is distinguished by its low voltage requirements, which makes it well-suited for use in portable devices such as laptop and palmtop computers.

In addition to these CPUs that run in Socket 7 motherboards, AMD in 1999 introduced the Athlon, which uses a slot connector similar to (but incompatible with) the one used by Pentium-II and Pentium-III CPUs. The Athlon includes many advanced features, and competes directly against Pentium-III systems. In fact, in late 1999 and early 2000, the fastest x86 computers available were powered by Athlon CPUs. Like Intel's post-Pentium x86 CPUs, the Athlon includes an L2 cache on the CPU module and uses 36-bit memory addresses.

Mixed-Generation CPUs

Various manufacturers have produced CPUs that straddle the line between different CPU generations. Examples include

- **Cyrix 486SLC and 486DLC**   These CPUs host CPU cores that resemble those of ordinary 80486 CPUs, but that use the physical interfaces of 80386SX and 80386DX CPUs, respectively. They perform between the 80386 and 80486 lines, compared at the same clock speeds.

- **Cyrix 5x86 and AMD 5x86**   Both Cyrix and AMD produced CPUs bearing the *5x86* moniker. These CPUs are essentially souped-up 80486 CPUs, and fit on 80486 motherboards, but can perform similarly to low-end Pentiums. The Cyrix 5x86 included some features used in the Cyrix 6x86 CPU.

- **Intel Pentium Overdrive**   Intel released a stripped-down Pentium that fit into an 80486 CPU socket. It competed against the 5x86 CPUs from Cyrix and AMD.

In addition to these CPUs, various third parties, such as Evergreen Technologies (http://www.evertech.com), market modified versions of various CPUs. These modified CPU kits typically include the CPU permanently mounted on a special adapter that enables the CPU to be used on older motherboards that would not otherwise accept the CPU. For instance, Evergreen markets its Spectra line, which fits an AMD K6-2 400 CPU onto many motherboards that can accept Pentium-75 and later CPUs. Such kits can be very helpful in extending the life of an older motherboard.

Linux CPU Requirements

Linux is one of the most flexible OSs available when it comes to supporting CPUs. Although it was originally developed only for the x86 architecture, Linux has been ported to a wide variety of other CPUs, as described earlier. On the x86 line, mainstream Linux requires an 80386 or higher CPU, but there have been ports to lesser x86 CPUs as well. Linux can be made to perform better on older x86 CPUs than can many other x86 OSs, thanks to the fact that Linux can be stripped of advanced and performance-robbing features such as its GUI.

Supported CPU Architectures

Earlier in this chapter, I outlined many of the CPUs available on desktop computers today, and pointed out the Linux distributions available for these CPUs. In fact, it's the rare modern CPU for which Linux is not available. That's not to say that Linux works equally well on all these architectures. Some of the pros and cons of each include

- **x86**   Linux's first CPU was the x86, and given the dominance of the x86 in the small computer marketplace, this is where most of the emphasis is in the Linux community. x86 hardware is inexpensive and plentiful, but some of that hardware isn't compatible with Linux. The variety of Linux distributions for x86 hardware means you're likely to find a version of Linux to suit your needs. Many commercial Linux programs are available only for x86 CPUs.

- **Alpha**   The Alpha CPU is a good choice if you want to do high-performance computing with Linux. Red Hat's Alpha version is mature and popular. You can obtain Alpha-based Linux systems from a variety of vendors, although they are more difficult to find than SPARC computers.

- **SPARC**   The SPARC CPU is used mostly in Sun's workstations, so one drawback is its relatively limited and expensive hardware options. The SPARC CPU performs very well, however, particularly in floating-point operations, making it an excellent choice for high-performance simulations or other FPU-intensive tasks. Red Hat's SPARC port, like its Alpha version, is well supported.

- **PowerPC**   You're most likely to encounter a PowerPC CPU in a Macintosh, but Motorola and IBM both produce PowerPC computers, as well. Top-of-the-line PowerPC computers can edge out x86 computers in performance, particularly in floating point operations. The existing PowerPC distributions are somewhat less mature than the major x86 distributions, but not by much.

As a general rule, if you want to buy or build a computer to run Linux, I recommend going with an x86 CPU. Other architectures, although sometimes technically superior to x86 CPUs, limit your choice of software, cost more, and often limit your choices in terms of ancillary hardware. If you happen to have an unused computer that uses another CPU, however, you might want to load Linux on that computer. You might also want to buy such a computer if you need its specialized advantages, such as the best possible FPU speed, or if you want to dual boot with some other OS that's available for that hardware, such as MacOS for PowerPC systems.

Requirements for Minimum Functionality

On the x86 architecture, Linux requires at least an 80386SX CPU. Unless you're buying a computer from a yard sale, then, any x86 computer you purchase today will have sufficient CPU power to run Linux.

NOTE

The Embeddable Linux Kernel Subset (ELKS) project
(http://www.elks.ecs.soton.ac.uk) is dedicated to porting Linux to 8086 through
80286 and other old CPUs. This project has yet to produce a fully usable system, however.

Although the Linux kernel and most Linux software can run on an 80386SX CPU, some Linux
distributions impose higher minimum requirements. Generally this is because the distribution
includes a kernel or other critical components that have been compiled with optimizations for
later CPUs, rendering the distribution unusable on older models. Specific official requirements
for some popular Linux distributions in early 2000 include

- Caldera OpenLinux 2.3: 80386
- Corel Linux 1.0: Pentium
- Debian GNU/Linux 2.1: 80386
- Linux Mandrake 7.0: Pentium
- Red Hat Linux 6.1: 80386
- Slackware 7.0: 80386
- SuSE Linux 6.3: 80486DX (80386 is supported for "limited usage.")

As a general rule, if a distribution supports a given level of CPU, it supports all CPUs and
clones at that level. For instance, you can use a Cyrix 6x86 or AMD K5 with a distribution that
requires a Pentium CPU.

NOTE

If a distribution requires a Pentium CPU, it might not include FPU emulation. Because
early NexGen Nx586 CPUs lacked an FPU, you might not be able to use such distributions on early NexGen systems, unless they include the matching FPU chip. In theory,
you can get around this problem—and other Pentium requirements—by hacking the
install floppy or by installing using a different CPU, recompiling the kernel or other
components, and then replacing the CPU. In practice, this is almost always more
effort than it's worth.

Linux has yet to make much use of MMX or AMD's 3DNow multimedia extensions. Modern
CPUs all include MMX, however, and there's no reason to avoid CPUs with these extensions.

A handful of Linux programs, such as some MPEG playback software, can be to take advantage of these instructions.

Requirements for Adequate Performance

As a practical matter, most Linux systems today should have at least a Pentium-level CPU. If you're building a new computer, I recommend using an Intel Pentium-III or AMD Athlon for most systems, although a high-end Intel Celeron, Intel Pentium-II, AMD K6-III, or Cyrix MII can be adequate for a low-performance system.

If you have a computer that you'd like to upgrade, you have three choices for CPU upgrades:

- **Replace the CPU with a higher-speed supported model**   Most motherboards support a range of CPU speeds, such as Intel Pentium 100–233. If your current CPU is at the low end of the supported speed range, you can upgrade to a higher-speed model in the supported range without too much difficulty, assuming you can find a supplier for the higher-speed CPU. This is generally the safest and simplest approach, but it's also the one likely to produce the least speed improvement.

- **Replace the CPU with an aftermarket CPU kit**   Companies such as Evergreen Technologies (`http://www.evertech.com`) sell CPU kits that consist of a CPU mounted on a voltage regulator or other hardware to adapt a faster CPU to motherboards that expect slower models. Such kits generally work well, but occasionally don't work with some motherboards.

- **Replace the motherboard**   You can generally get the most speed improvement by replacing the entire motherboard and CPU. You can upgrade an 80486 to a Pentium-III or Athlon in this way, as an example. This approach is generally the most expensive, however, and it often requires that you replace other components. RAM is often incompatible across more than a generation or so of motherboards, for instance, and you might even need to replace video cards, SCSI host adapters, or other components, particularly if you want to upgrade an old EISA or VLB 80486 computer.

The x86 CPU Marketplace

The x86 CPU marketplace is quite dynamic, with new models being introduced frequently and old ones disappearing with equal ease. Because of publication delays, therefore, information presented in a book can't be completely up-to-date and accurate by the time you read it. This section covers the state of the CPU marketplace in early 2000, and includes information on up-and-coming CPUs, so it should remain relevant throughout 2000. For the most current information, however, you should consult the CPU manufacturers' Web sites.

Intel CPUs

In early 2000, Intel's (http://www.intel.com) x86 product line includes models in the
Pentium MMX, Pentium-II, Pentium-III, and Celeron lines. The Pentium MMX CPUs are dis-
tinctly outmoded, however. I recommend using them only as upgrades for older systems or if
you have some special need, such as if you've obtained a Pentium motherboard for free—and
even then, a CPU from the AMD K6 line is likely to produce better performance than an Intel
Pentium CPU. Pentium CPUs can be used in multi-processor motherboards, however, whereas
AMD and Cyrix Pentium-class CPUs cannot.

If you want a new Intel-powered system, a Pentium-III CPU is probably your best bet,
although a high-end Pentium-II or Celeron can be adequate for some purposes. Intel expects to
surpass 1GHz clock speeds with its Pentium-III CPU, and to support faster motherboard bus
speeds as well. These changes might be accompanied by a change in name to Pentium-IV.

Intel plans to introduce its Itanium CPU in mid-2000. This CPU, which went by the code name
Merced during development, is a true 64-bit CPU based in part on x86 technology. It represents a shift in CPU technology similar to that from the 8086 to the 80386. Just as the 80386
ran 8086 software, the Itanium runs older x86 software, but benefits from new OSs and software. Intel has been working with Linux kernel programmers to ensure that a 64-bit version of
Linux will run on Itanium soon after its introduction. How quickly this will translate into
actual Linux distributions remains to be seen. The fact that most software for Linux is available
in source code form, and that this source code has long been compiled on architectures as
divergent as x86, 680x0, PowerPC, and Alpha, suggests that Linux might be one of the first
full-fledged OSs available in 64-bit form for the Itanium.

AMD CPUs

AMD's Web site (http://www.amd.com) lists the K6-2, K6-III, and Athlon as being current
CPUs in early 2000. At this time, the K6-2 is available at higher CPU clock speeds than is the
K6-III, but the K6-III outperforms the K6-2 when clocked at the same speed. The K6-III therefore produces better overall performance. Both the K6-2 and the K6-III work on Socket 7
motherboards, and these CPUs produce the fastest available performance on such hardware. In
fact, in early 2000, the best K6-III systems compete with mid-range Pentium-III systems in
overall performance.

AMD's Athlon uses its own unique motherboard design, based around the *Slot A* CPU interface
method. AMD licensed this technology from Compaq, which uses it with its Alpha CPUs (but
the Athlon can't use Alpha motherboards). Like the Pentium-II and later versions, the Athlon
places its L2 cache on the CPU module itself, which results in faster overall system performance because the L2 cache runs at a faster speed than it could if it were on the motherboard.

According to most benchmarks, the Athlon performs similarly to the Pentium-III in integer operations when clocked at the same speed, and outperforms the Pentium-III in floating point operations. In early 2000, the Athlon is available at higher clock speeds than is the Pentium-III, meaning that the fastest available x86 PCs are powered by Athlon CPUs.

AMD is expected to continue developing the Athlon CPU through 2000, and will probably surpass 1GHz speeds with the CPU.

VIA/Cyrix/IDT CPUs

With VIA's (`http://www.viatech.com`) purchase of Cyrix and the designs to IDT's CPUs, the chipset manufacturer has become the third major player in the x86 marketplace in 2000. In early 2000, the major VIA CPUs on the market are the Cyrix MII line. (VIA is continuing to use the Cyrix name with these CPUs.) These CPUs lag well behind the Intel and AMD offerings in terms of speed. Therefore, I can't recommend an MII for anything but a very low-end system unless and until this situation changes. The IDT WinChip line is even slower than the MII series, and is much more difficult to find in stores.

Of more potential interest is the next-generation VIA CPU, code-named *Joshua*. This CPU will reportedly use the Socket 370 interface, which is used mainly by most Celeron variants. VIA appears to be positioning this CPU for mid-range systems, but it's unclear just how the CPU will perform when it's released. Joshua is an extension of earlier Cyrix designs, but may incorporate some features developed by IDT for the WinChip.

Transmeta CPUs

Transmeta (`http://www.transmeta.com`) is the newest entrant to the x86 CPU arena. In January 2000, Transmeta announced its Crusoe processor line, which is a series of x86 CPUs intended to be used in mobile applications such as laptop and palmtop computers. The Crusoe CPU uses a novel architecture in which much of the CPU's work is done by special low-level software, rather than by circuitry in the CPU itself. In part because of this design, the Crusoe CPUs can function on much less power than can other x86 CPUs, which translates into less heat and longer operating times in mobile devices. Another feature of these CPUs is that they can adjust their operating speed, and hence their power requirements, dynamically. The result is that the CPU can run at full power for a brief period, and then throttle back to 50%, 25%, or less, when the computer is idle. This saves energy with little or no impact on performance.

Of particular interest to Linux users, Transmeta employs Linus Torvalds, the original developer of the Linux kernel. It is as yet unclear whether mainstream Linux distributions will adapt to take advantage of Crusoe's unique features. If they do, these CPUs can present unique advantages over other x86 CPUs, in the form of improved speed or extra functionality.

Summary

At the heart of every digital computer is the CPU, and the choice of CPU can be felt through the rest of the computer. The CPU determines what OSs and software the computer can run and is a major factor in the speed of the computer as a whole. The CPU also determines what other hardware components can be used, most directly by determining the motherboards that are compatible. The motherboard's features determine what add-on cards, RAM, and other devices work with a computer, however, so the CPU has an indirect influence in this respect.

Linux works with a wide variety of CPUs, but is most strongly associated with x86 and compatible CPUs. Hardware for x86 computers tends to be inexpensive, and the combination of this inexpensive hardware with the open source Linux OS brings unprecedented power to low-cost computers.

Motherboards

IN THIS CHAPTER

If the CPU is the heart of a computer, the motherboard is its circulatory system. The motherboard functions as a means of connecting the CPU to all the other devices in the computer, either directly (as when the CPU accesses RAM plugged into the motherboard) or through another component (as when accessing a hard disk through a SCSI host adapter). The motherboard is generally the largest circuit board in a computer. It contains a slot or socket for the CPU, slots for memory, slots for expansion cards, connectors for hard disks, floppy disks, and external devices, and a power connector, among other features. These features are all illustrated in Figure 2.1, which shows a typical Socket 7 motherboard.

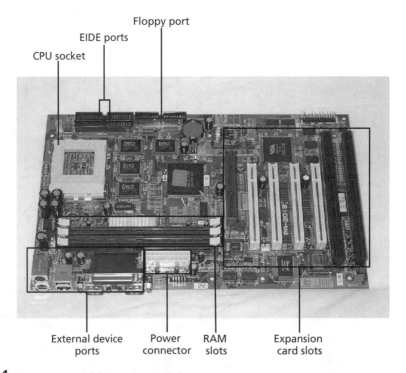

FIGURE 2.1

A typical motherboard contains a wide array of connectors of various types.

This chapter describes some of the most important characteristics of motherboards today, in order to help you decide what features you need in a motherboard. This chapter does *not*, however, go into any details about configuring your motherboard or integrating it into a complete computer system. For that information, consult your motherboard's documentation.

Matching the Motherboard and CPU

One of the most critical aspects of motherboard selection is in matching the motherboard to the CPU. As described in Chapter 1, "The Central Processing Unit," CPUs vary in many ways that require support on the motherboard. These variables include the physical interface of the CPU to the motherboard, CPU bus speeds, CPU voltage requirements, and BIOS support.

CPU Sockets and Slots

Until recently, each generation of CPU (80386, 80486, and so on) has used a unique CPU/motherboard interface method. These have generally come in the form of *sockets*, in which the CPU has a number of pins on its bottom that fit into a square connector on the motherboard (see Figure 2.2). More recent CPUs, including most Pentium-II, Pentium-III, and Athlon CPUs, use a slotted design more like that of plug-in cards. (Most Celeron CPUs continue to use a socketed design, but some varieties are available in a slotted form.)

FIGURE 2.2
A socket on motherboards for socketed CPUs contains many holes into which the pins on the bottom of the CPU fit.

Socketed Designs

Most CPU series have seen the coming and going of several socket variants. For instance, the very earliest Pentium CPUs used a pin layout that's incompatible with what later Pentium

CPUs used. Early 80486 motherboards used sockets that required great force to insert the CPU, but later 80486 motherboards used *zero insertion force* (ZIF) sockets, in which a lever on one side of the socket allows you to tighten it around an inserted CPU. (This lever is visible to the right of the socket in Figure 2.2.) The vast majority of Pentium-class motherboards use ZIF sockets. Popular sockets for 80486 and later CPUs include

- **Socket 1** 169-pin socket for 80486 CPUs.
- **Socket 2** 238-pin socket for 80486 and Pentium Overdrive CPUs.
- **Socket 3** 237-pin socket for 80486 and Pentium Overdrive CPUs. Includes support for 3.3v operation, which reduces heat generation by CPUs that also support this feature.
- **Socket 4** 273-pin socket for 60 and 66MHz Pentiums.
- **Socket 5** 320-pin socket for 75–133MHz Pentiums.
- **Socket 7** 321-pin socket for Pentiums of 75MHz and above, including Pentium clones from AMD, Cyrix, and IDT. Some motherboards use a *Super7* socket design, which is a Socket 7 layout with support for faster bus speeds, as described shortly.
- **Socket 8** 387-pin socket for Pentium Pro CPUs.
- **Socket 370** 370-pin socket used by Celeron CPUs.
- **Nx586** The NexGen Nx586 CPU used its own unique pinout. Most Nx586 CPUs were not socketed, however; instead, they were soldered directly to their motherboards.

NOTE

A Socket 6 design was developed, but never implemented on production motherboards.

It's critically important that you match the socket type to your CPU. You cannot use a CPU that requires one type of socket on a motherboard that uses another. Most 80486 CPUs can be used with Sockets 1 through 3, although some of the more advanced 80486 CPUs require the later Socket 2 or even Socket 3. All Pentium-class motherboards on the market in 2000 are Socket 7 designs (in fact, most implement Super7 features, as well). The motherboard shown in Figure 2.1 is a Socket 7 motherboard. One exception to the interface-matching rule is that Socket 370/Slot 1 adapter cards are available. These allow you to plug a Celeron CPU into a Slot 1 motherboard. Such an adapter might be useful if you want to build a low-cost Celeron computer but plan to upgrade it to a more powerful CPU at some time in the future.

Socket 7 motherboards are still viable in the marketplace, thanks largely to the AMD K6-2 and K6-III CPUs, which can perform competitively to low-end Intel Pentium-II and Pentium-III CPUs. With AMD's release of the Athlon CPU, though, AMD is likely to eventually abandon Socket 7 CPUs. Likewise, VIA (which bought Cyrix and IDT late in 1999) has announced that its next CPU wil use a Slot 1 interface. Intel now uses Socket 370 for most of its Celeron CPUs, but the most powerful Intel CPUs use l a slotted CPU interface.

Slotted Designs

In early 2000, only three types of CPU slots are in common use:

- **Slot 1** This 242-pin design is used by Pentium-II, Pentium-III, and some Celeron motherboards.
- **Slot 2** This 330-pin design is used by more recent Pentium-II Xeon CPUs. Most Slot 2 motherboards support at least two CPUs.
- **Slot A** This 242-pin design is used by AMD for its Athlon CPU. (AMD licensed the technology from Digital Equipment Corporation [now Compaq], which uses the design for its Alpha CPU.)

Each slot design is incompatible with the others. Also, although both the AMD Athlon and the Compaq Alpha CPUs use the same CPU bus, they require different motherboards.

CPU Bus Speeds

Modern CPUs run at two separate speeds: the *core* speed and the *bus* speed. The core speed is the number you probably associate most strongly with the CPU, and is the speed at which most of the CPU's internal circuitry runs. A Pentium-III 700 runs at a core speed of 700MHz. The core of the CPU can run at a higher speed than the motherboard can. The bus speed is the speed of the interface between the CPU and the motherboard. An 80486 motherboard typically ran at a bus speed of only 33MHz, although a few models went as high as 50MHz. Most motherboards used with Intel Pentiums run at 66MHz, although some CPU speeds require bus speeds of 60MHz or 50MHz. Super7 motherboards boost the bus speed to as high as 133MHz.

Among slotted designs, bus speed ranges from 66MHz up to a theoretical maximum of 400MHz for Slot A. In practice most Slot 1 and 2 designs in early 2000 run at 133MHz or less and most Slot A designs run at 200MHz.

Whatever interface type you choose, it's critical that the CPU and motherboard share a bus speed. In some cases, a CPU can run at several different bus speeds, but requires a particular speed to achieve its best performance. If you're building a new computer, you should be sure that the motherboard you purchase supports operation at the CPU's best speed.

CAUTION

CPU bus speed has an impact on other system components, most notably RAM. The PC100 and PC133 forms of RAM are designed to operate on 100MHz and 133MHz motherboard busses, respectively. You can safely run faster RAM on a slower bus (PC133 RAM on a 100MHz bus, for instance), but don't try to run slower RAM on a faster bus. In some cases it's possible to use slower memory on a faster bus, however, by inserting *wait states*—pauses in the motherboard's RAM access cycle. Slot A motherboards running at 200MHz use PC100 or PC133 memory in early 2000; they run the memory bus at 100MHz or 133MHz and the CPU/chipset bus (the *front-side bus*) at 200MHz. Faster motherboard speeds, expected to appear in 2000, may require faster types of RAM, such as RDRAM. For more information on RAM, see Chapter 3, "Memory."

In order to set the CPU core speed, motherboards include jumpers or BIOS settings to specify a *clock multiplier*. The CPU runs its core at the bus speed multiplied by the clock multiplier. For instance, a 100MHz bus combined with a 4x clock multiplier produces a 400MHz core speed. The exact meanings of the clock multiplier settings can vary from one brand or model CPU to another, however, so it's important that you consult your motherboard documentation to set the clock multiplier appropriately for whatever CPU you use.

CPU Voltage Requirements

Like all electronic devices, CPUs operate at specific voltages. Most 80486 and earlier CPUs, and even some Pentium-class CPUs, operated at 5v. As CPU speeds increased, however, it became desirable to reduce the CPU voltage, in order to reduce the heat buildup inside the chips. Reduced operating voltage also helps lengthen battery life on laptop computers. Therefore, a plethora of new voltage requirements emerged during the Pentium CPU's lifetime. In fact, many Socket 7 CPUs require the use of *dual voltages*—one setting for the CPU core and another for input/output (I/O) circuitry. Dual-voltage CPUs generally run the I/O voltage at 3.3v and the core voltage at some lower level, although in some cases the core voltage may be higher.

As with bus speed, it's critical that your motherboard supply your CPU with the voltage level it requires. In some cases, a CPU can work on a narrow range of voltages, so you may be able to get by with a setting that's slightly different from what the manufacturer recommends. In other cases, however, a slight deviation in voltage may cause your computer to operate unreliably; you may experience strange problems, memory errors, or even system crashes if you set the voltage incorrectly. In extreme cases, you might damage your CPU if you set the voltage incorrectly. I therefore recommend you pay careful attention to the voltage requirements of your CPU. In most cases, the motherboard's manual includes information on appropriate voltage settings for the CPUs the board accepts. Occasionally this information may be missing, often because the CPU is a newer model than the motherboard. In these cases, check your motherboard manufacturer's Web site for updated configuration information.

CPU BIOS Support

As a general rule, a BIOS does not need to include extensive support for specific models of CPU. Typically, if you use a CPU that's not supported by the BIOS, the worst that happens is that the CPU is misidentified when the system boots. There are exceptions to this rule, however, such as

- Some advanced 80486 CPUs support cache modes that can cause data corruption if they're not supported by the BIOS. For this reason, you should only use CPUs such as the AMD and Cyrix 5x86 on motherboards that are built for these CPUs.

- The Cyrix 6x86, 6x86MX, and MII CPUs support a special *linear burst* mode that can improve cache memory access times. This feature requires BIOS support. If this support is absent, the CPU still operates, albeit at a slightly slower speed than it would otherwise.

If your motherboard lacks support for a new CPU and you want to add that support, you should check with your motherboard manufacturer to see if an updated BIOS is available. Modern motherboards support a *flash BIOS* feature, in which you can update the BIOS by running a special DOS program. On older computers (mostly early 80486 systems and earlier), you may need to physically replace the BIOS chip, which is usually labeled with the distributor's name (see Figure 2.3).

TIP

BIOS flash utilities typically run under DOS. If you don't normally run DOS or Windows 9x on your computer, you can run the flash utility from a DOS boot floppy—in fact, this is the recommended procedure even if you have a DOS partition on your computer. If you don't have a DOS boot floppy, look into FreeDOS (http://www.freedos.org), an open source version of DOS. *Do not* attempt to flash your BIOS using DOSEMU under Linux!

BIOSes come from a variety of sources, but each BIOS is customized for a specific model of motherboard. You therefore should not attempt to use a BIOS for one brand or model motherboard in a different product, even if the BIOSes are from the same company. If you need help locating a BIOS for your motherboard, check with the motherboard manufacturer (the BIOS producer isn't likely to be able to help), or check Wim's BIOS Page (http://www.ping.be/bios/), which includes information on BIOSes for a wide variety of motherboards.

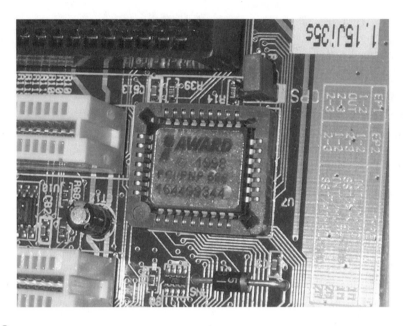

FIGURE 2.3

BIOS chips come in a wide variety of shapes and sizes, but in most cases they're clearly labeled with the BIOS distributor's name—Award, in this case.

CAUTION

Flashing a BIOS is a potentially dangerous undertaking. If there's a problem, such as a power failure during the operation or if you flashed the wrong BIOS, your computer may be rendered unbootable until you replace the BIOS chip with one that's been programmed by the motherboard manufacturer. I therefore recommend that you flash a BIOS only during normal business hours, and that you keep a backup of a working copy of your BIOS on a floppy. (Most BIOS flash utilities give you an option to create such a backup before flashing a new BIOS.) That way, you may be able to get help from a computer store if something goes wrong.

Motherboard Busses

The term *bus* has several different but related meanings in computer circles. Earlier in this chapter, I used the word in reference to the speed of the interface between the CPU and the motherboard. Another meaning relates to the physical and electrical interface between the motherboard and the various plug-in boards you can add to the motherboard. On most computers, you use such boards to provide a variety of both critical and less-critical functions, such as a video board, sound board, and so on.

There are half a dozen major bus types. Most motherboards implement two or three of them, but a few are restricted to just one bus type. A few motherboards, mostly those in specialized products and notebooks, contain no expansion bus slots at all. They usually implement the electronics involved internally in order to support features such as video and audio. Some busses are in common use today, but others are largely relics of the past. You might encounter these outmoded busses on 80486 and earlier motherboards, but seldom on Pentium-class models or above.

ISA Bus

The *industry standard architecture* (ISA) bus is the oldest in common use on x86 computers. The basic design of the ISA bus dates all the way back to the original IBM PC, although there have been some modifications to the design since that time. In the original PC, the ISA bus was an 8-bit design that ran at 4.77MHz—the same speed as the computer's CPU. Subsequent expansions allowed the bus to run at up to 8.33MHz, and boosted the width of the bus to 16 bits. These expansions were done in a backward-compatible way, so that older 8-bit ISA cards could fit into 16-bit ISA slots. Figure 2.4 shows ISA (and several other) slots in a modern motherboard. ISA slots are larger than other modern slot types, and their motherboard connectors are generally black in color, as compared to white for PCI or brown for AGP.

In theory, the ISA bus can transfer data at up to 8MB/s, which by today's standards is pretty slow—modern hard drives usually exceed this speed, for instance, as do many Ethernet adapters. The ISA bus is therefore of limited utility in today's systems, and, in fact, is on the way out. You can still buy motherboards that contain ISA slots, but the number of ISA slots on modern motherboards has been shrinking for several years, and many of the latest models have none.

Just as motherboards include fewer and fewer ISA slots, there's less and less need for them. There are still many ISA cards on the market, but there are almost always PCI alternatives. Sample applications for ISA cards include

- **SCSI adapters** Very low-end adapters, such as those that come with internal Iomega Zip drives, are generally ISA models. PCI SCSI host adapters are plentiful, however, and some models are quite inexpensive. I don't recommend buying a new ISA SCSI host adapter except under unusual circumstances.

- **I/O cards** Older 80486 and earlier computers used ISA cards for serial, parallel, floppy, and IDE ports. Such cards are still available today, and it's conceivable you'll want one if you want two parallel ports or more than two serial ports. PCI cards to fill these functions are also available. With the exception of modern EIDE hard disks, the ISA bus is adequate to handle the speed of these I/O devices, so if you do need an extra port and if you've got an ISA slot free on your motherboard, an ISA board is a good choice.

AGP slot   PCI slots   ISA slots

FIGURE 2.4

Each bus type uses unique size and positioning of connectors to prevent accidental use of one type of card in the wrong slot.

- **Ethernet adapters** If you need an Ethernet adapter to run at 10Mbps or slower, the ISA bus is adequate to the task, although an ISA card is likely to consume more CPU time than a PCI card. 100Mbps networking benefits from the PCI bus, so I recommend buying most new Ethernet adapters in PCI form.

- **Sound cards** Basic audio functionality doesn't require massive bandwidth, and so the ISA bus is adequate for this task. In fact, until 1998, PCI sound cards were poorly supported in Linux, and so ISA cards remained the best choice for sound. Today, however, Linux includes good support for a number of PCI sound cards, so you can use either bus type. The most advanced sound cards require additional bandwidth for advanced audio functionality, and so can benefit from the PCI bus. These functions are generally not implemented in Linux.

- **Specialized applications**   Some rare cards, such as certain scientific data acquisition cards, remain available only in ISA form. If you need to use such a card, you may be tied to the ISA bus. Given the decreasing prevalence of ISA in the marketplace, you would do well to shop for an alternative card if you're building a new system. This is especially true if the card is expensive and you intend to use it for several years. At some point in the future, ISA motherboards may become unavailable, so repairing a computer with a damaged motherboard may cause you serious problems if that computer contains a critical and expensive ISA component.

The computer industry would like to see the ISA bus vanish because supporting it requires circuitry on the motherboard that, if eliminated, would simplify motherboard designs. ISA cards are also more difficult to configure than are more modern cards. Older ISA cards typically required jumpers to configure properly. Newer models are generally *Plug and Play* (PnP), meaning that the motherboard's BIOS or utilities in the OS do the configuration.

In Linux through the 2.2.x kernel series, PnP configuration is done through the `isapnp` package, which comes with most Linux distributions. To configure your cards, follow these steps:

1. Run `pnpdump`, which scans the system for PnP devices and returns information on those devices. It's best if you redirect the output of `pnpdump` to an appropriate text file, as in `pnpdump > pnpinfo.txt`.

2. Edit the text file produced in step 1. The file contains a number of multiple-choice configurations for settings, such as interrupt request (IRQ) and direct memory access (DMA). You must uncomment *one* option for each setting by removing the pound sign (#) at the start of each line. For instance, you might see a line that reads `# (INT 0 (IRQ 5 (MODE +E)))`. Remove the leading # to activate the board using IRQ 5. For each device you want to use, you must also uncomment a line that reads `# (ACT Y)`; this is the activation line for that board. Some boards include more than one device. For instance, a sound board might include separate configurations for digital audio, wavetable sound, and a joystick port.

3. Move the text file you've edited to a convenient location. Traditionally, `/etc/isapnp.conf` is used. Be sure not to overwrite an existing file, or back up the existing file, in case it already contains configuration information for some other device.

4. Run the `isapnp` utility, and tell it to use the configuration file. If `isapnp` is in the `/sbin` directory, you could do this by typing **/sbin/isapnp/etc/isapnp.conf**. Normally, you'll configure your system to perform this step whenever it books, by placing the command in your `/etc/rc.d/rc.local` file, or in some other initialization script, depending upon your distribution. Some distributions include a command that performs this step automatically.

If your configuration changes don't cause any conflicts, you'll then be able to load appropriate drivers and use the ISA card. You do, however, have to load driver modules or load them into the Linux kernel; PnP configuration isn't sufficient to use the hardware under Linux.

The format of the `isapnp.conf` file is a bit intimidating to somebody who's never edited the file before, largely because it includes a large number of options, the vast majority of them commented out. Scan through the file once or twice, paying careful attention to the comments that begin `Card` *n* (where *n* is the card number) and to the `NAME` options, which identify the device. Once you've browsed through the file once or twice, you should have some idea of what the options are, and you can begin setting them. If your computer dual-boots between Linux and another OS such as Windows, you may be able to determine what resources to assign to the card by looking up the resources used in the other OS.

The Linux 2.4 kernel will include PnP support directly, which will change the way ISA PnP devices are configured in Linux. With 2.4.x kernels, there will be no need for an `isapnp.conf` file; drivers for ISA devices will auto-detect and configure PnP devices. In the event of conflicts, you may need to adjust settings in the `/etc/conf.modules` file or by passing parameters to the Linux kernel, as much as is possible today with PCI cards.

MCA Bus

The *Micro Channel Architecture* (MCA) bus was IBM's successor to the ISA bus. Used in the IBM PS/2 line of computers, MCA never caught on in the industry as a whole, although in its day it was a fine bus. MCA, like most other x86 busses, supports a width of 32 bits. Not all cards or MCA slots are 32 bits, however; some are only 16 bits wide.

For a long time, Linux didn't work with MCA computers, but the latest Linux kernels do include MCA support. Not all MCA cards are supported, however. To use Linux on an MCA computer, you must be sure that your kernel is compiled with MCA support, which is a kernel configuration option in the General setup area (see Figure 2.5). Most MCA computers don't support other busses, and you won't find MCA busses in modern computers.

EISA Bus

The *extended ISA* (EISA) bus was developed by Compaq and other x86 PC vendors as an alternative to IBM's MCA bus. Unlike MCA, EISA is backward compatible with ISA. You can plug an ISA card into an EISA slot, and it generally works. A 32-bit bus that runs at 8.33MHz, EISA is capable of maximum transfer rates of approximately 33MB/s. This speed is adequate even for many modern functions, although not all. Some SCSI host adapters, for instance, can transfer data at 40MB/s, 80MB/s, or higher; and some EIDE interfaces are capable of 66MB/s speeds.

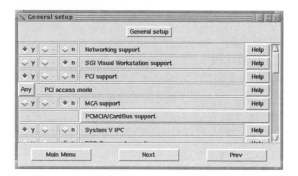

FIGURE 2.5

The General setup area of the Linux kernel configuration includes options relating to Linux's handling of busses, including the MCA and PCI busses.

EISA experienced a brief period of acceptance, if not gushing popularity, in the early 80486 era. EISA was most popular as a bus for SCSI host adapters, although other devices were also available in EISA format. The bus acquired a reputation for moderately difficult configuration, however, and it was more expensive than competing busses. In the end, other busses surpassed EISA in popularity, and it's not available on modern motherboards.

Linux supports the EISA bus, and includes drivers for a variety of EISA cards, including popular EISA SCSI host adapters such as the Adaptec 1742. If you have an old EISA computer on which you want to run Linux, you stand a good chance of getting it working.

VL-Bus

Seeing the need for a higher-speed bus than ISA for video cards, a video card trade group, the Video Electronics Standards Association (VESA), developed its own bus for 80486 CPUs. Known as the *VESA Local Bus* or VL-Bus for short, this bus was popular on many 80486 motherboards. Like the MCA and EISA busses, the VL-Bus is 32 bits in width. It gains further in the speed arena by running at the motherboard's bus speed—typically 33MHz for 80486 systems. Some computers ran it at speeds as high as 50MHz. (40MHz is the VL-Bus's maximum official speed.) Even when run at just 33MHz, the VL-Bus is theoretically capable of transferring up to 132MB/s, which is quite an improvement over ISA's 8MB/s. Physically, the VL-Bus uses an ordinary ISA connector (refer to Figure 2.4) with a special extension connector located in line with the ISA connector. This design takes up a lot of space on motherboards, but allows a VL-Bus slot to accept ordinary ISA cards.

The VL-Bus was very popular on 80486 motherboards, but it has its drawbacks, including

- **Ties to 80486 architecture**   Assorted limitations of the design make it difficult to implement on non-80486 CPUs. Although a few Pentium motherboards with VL-Bus were produced, they never became popular and were frequently troublesome.

- **Limited number of cards**   Most VL-Bus motherboards had only two or three VL-Bus slots, the rest being ordinary ISA slots. As the bus speed increases, the number of VL-Bus devices that can be added is reduced. At 50MHz, VL-Bus barely functions with a single card.

- **Finicky connectors**   The long dual connectors of VL-Bus make VL-Bus cards prone to working their way out of their connectors. When this happens, the system fails to boot or (if it happens when the computer is powered on) crashes.

In its heyday, the VL-Bus was used mostly by video cards, SCSI host adapters, and IDE controllers. Linux includes very good support for VL-Bus devices, although as with any device, you should check for Linux compatibility before trying to use Linux on a VL-Bus system.

PCI Bus

The *peripheral component interconnect* (PCI) bus was developed by the PCI Special Interest Group (spearheaded by Intel) to be a cleaner and faster bus than preceding x86 bus types. Where the VL-Bus was a more-or-less direct tap into the CPU's data lines, the PCI bus inserts an electronic "bridge" between the CPU and the bus. This design decouples the bus from the CPU, allowing it to be used with a wider array of CPUs. This design is known as a *mezzanine bus*. In the x86 world, the PCI bus has been used on all CPU types from the 80486 onward, and PCI busses have appeared on various other architectures as well, including PowerPC and Alpha. In fact, it's possible to use some PCI cards in more than one computer architecture. Some PCI cards contain ROMs or other design features that are specific to x86 CPUs, however.

The PCI bus is primarily a 32-bit bus, and it usually runs at 33MHz, leading to a 132MB/s maximum transfer rate. The specification allows for a 64-bit bus width (and hence 164MB/s transfer rate), but 64-bit PCI implementations have never made their way into the marketplace. PCI connectors are smaller than those for most other bus types (refer to Figure 2.4), so PCI cards are easy to insert and remove compared to VL-Bus cards.

One of the most important characteristics of PCI busses from a software point of view is the fact that the PCI specification includes PnP characteristics. Most PCI cards therefore lack the configuration jumpers that are common on older ISA and VL-Bus cards. In most cases, you insert a PCI card and the motherboard's BIOS detects it and assigns resources to it. Some Linux device drivers allow you to override these assignments by providing appropriate parameters on the Linux boot prompt or in the /etc/conf.modules file, but this generally isn't necessary.

> **NOTE**
>
> PCI's PnP is built in to the bus's specification, whereas ISA's PnP is a klunky hack on an older design. There's no need to use Linux's `isapnp` utility to configure PCI cards, even with 2.2.x-series kernels.

PCI was initially used mainly for video cards, SCSI host adapters, EIDE controllers, and network interface cards (NICs). More recently, PCI has become the bus of choice for sound cards, add-on serial and parallel ports, and other devices.

Linux's support for PCI is very good. There are a few kernel configuration options that relate to PCI, as shown in Figure 2.5. You should select *Y* for the PCI support configuration option if you have a motherboard with a PCI bus. (This option is the default.) For the PCI access mode option, Direct causes the Linux kernel to detect and configure PCI cards itself, whereas selecting the BIOS option passes the responsibility on to the BIOS. Setting this option to Any causes Linux to attempt the configuration itself, but defer to the BIOS if it has problems. For the most part, each of these options works well, although one or another may work better on any given system.

AGP Bus

Video cards have long required unusually high bandwidth, and this fact didn't change with the emergence of PCI. For a time, the PCI bus was adequate to slake video cards' thirst for speed, but in 1996 Intel released the specification for the *Accelerated Graphics Port* (AGP), which is a PCI variant designed for increased speed and used exclusively for graphics devices. The leftmost slot in Figure 2.4 is an AGP slot. AGP surpasses the speed of PCI by running at 66MHz, instead of 33MHz. In addition, AGP supports multiple transfers per clock cycle. In 2x mode, two transfers occur per cycle, and in 4x mode, four transfers occur. All told, a 4x AGP device can transfer up to 1GB/s—eight times PCI's typical speed. As video resolutions have increased over the years, from 640×480 to 1024×768 to 1280×1024 and beyond, the need for faster transfers has grown. Even assuming the same number of colors, a 1280×1024 display holds more than four times the amount of data as a 640×480 display.

Linux handles the AGP bus *per se* just fine. However, as I describe in Chapter 12, "Video Cards," Linux doesn't always work well with the very latest video cards. Video card manufacturers seldom bother to produce drivers for Linux (or, more precisely, for XFree86 [http://www.xfree86.org]), so it takes a while for the XFree86 developers to modify existing drivers or create new ones. SuSE (http://www.suse.com) helps develop new XFree86 video drivers. You may want to check there for the newest drivers. The commercial X servers Accelerated-X (http://www.xig.com) and Metro-X (http://www.metrolink.com) sometimes support newer video cards than does XFree86.

PC Card Bus

PC Card (formerly *Personal Computer Memory Card International Association*, or PCMCIA) is not really a motherboard bus in the same sense as the others I've described in this chapter. In fact, it more closely resembles the EIDE bus used by hard disks. Nonetheless, PC Card fills a role similar to that of motherboard busses, but for laptop computers. It's also possible to add a PC Card slot to a desktop computer. You can obtain a variety of devices in PC Card format, including modems, Ethernet adapters, SCSI adapters, serial and parallel ports, and video adapters. Related technologies include the Compact Flash (CF) and Smart Media cards commonly used on palmtop computers and digital cameras. In fact, inexpensive adapters exist to let you use CF or Smart Media devices in PC Card readers, thus giving you access to the files stored on palmtop computers or digital cameras.

Linux includes support for PC Card busses, although not all PC Card adapters or devices are supported. For more information, check the Linux PCMCIA Information Page, `http://pcmcia.sourceforge.org`. I cover PC Card in more detail in Chapter 23, "Notebooks," and particularly in the section entitled "PC Card Ports."

Motherboard Form Factors

Motherboards come in a variety of shapes and sizes. Just as importantly, motherboards have small holes through which you insert screws to attach the motherboard to the computer's case. These holes are often referred to as the *mount points* of the motherboard. Motherboards also require certain types of connectors for keyboards and other external devices. Finally, motherboards have differing requirements in terms of power supply connectors. Collectively, these characteristics determine the motherboard's *form factor*. In theory, motherboards of just about any form factor can be designed to use just about any CPU or bus type, although the size requirements of components make certain combinations impractical. In reality, certain combinations don't appear because certain technologies (like 80386 CPUs or the VL-Bus) died out before specific motherboard form factors (like ATX) came into being.

Linux isn't particularly concerned with the motherboard form factor *per se*, although Linux can work better with some specific models of motherboard than with others. Linux may not have drivers for a video or audio device included on a mini- or micro-ATX motherboard, for instance. Before buying such a motherboard, or a system built around such a board, you should research the chipsets used and consult the appropriate chapters of this book and current Linux driver availability information. If you have cause to use a specific motherboard form factor, you can do so with Linux. You must simply do the research to be sure that the motherboard's included peripherals are supported.

AT and Baby AT

One of the first standardized motherboard form factors was used in IBM's PC AT computer, and so the form factor is referred to as the AT form factor. AT motherboards are some of the largest around, measuring up to 12 inches wide and 13.8 inches deep. IBM needed more than one square foot to hold assorted components that today occupy much less space. For instance, RAM in those days was mounted flat on the motherboard, rather than on SIMM, DIMM, or RIMM modules perpendicular to the motherboard.

Over the years, it became possible to shrink components and make more efficient use of space on the motherboard. Therefore, the full 12×13.8-inch space wasn't required. Manufacturers began using a smaller form factor first used with the IBM PC XT computer. Rather than call this design the *XT form factor*, manufacturers called it *Baby AT*, in order to prevent customers from thinking that computers built around it were akin to the less-powerful PC XT computer. Baby AT motherboards can be up to 8.57 inches wide and 13.04 inches deep, although the exact dimensions of specific products vary.

Because of their smaller size, Baby AT motherboards can be used in smaller computer cases, such as *mini-tower* cases. Many larger cases can accept either full-sized AT or Baby AT motherboards, however.

Most AT and Baby AT motherboards have but a single external connector, a 5-pin DIN for the keyboard. (A few Baby AT motherboards use a mini-DIN connector.) The original PC AT, as well as most AT and Baby AT motherboards until the mid-1990s, relied upon plug-in cards to provide ports for other external devices, such as serial and parallel ports. These plug-in cards had their own external connectors, either directly on the card or attached via ribbon cables and mounted on the computer's case. Later 80486 motherboards, as well as Pentium and later boards, include circuitry for external devices such as serial ports and parallel ports (and, later, mouse ports and USB ports) on the motherboard itself. These motherboards used connectors on the motherboard to provide these services; external connectors were linked to the motherboard via ribbon cables.

AT and Baby AT motherboards used a pair of power connectors, which had to be attached to the case's power supply via cables permanently attached to the power supply (see Figure 2.6). The motherboard itself ran on 5v of current, which caused problems with some CPUs, particularly in the Pentium era, when 3.3v CPU voltage became common. Such motherboards required *voltage regulators*, which converted 5v to 3.3v. These voltage regulators produced heat, and depending upon the amount of current drawn by the CPU, could overheat and cause unreliable operation.

2

MOTHERBOARDS

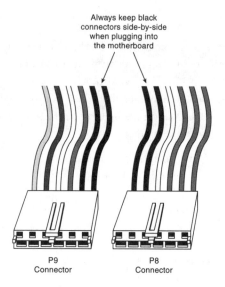

Always keep black
connectors side-by-side
when plugging into
the motherboard

P9
Connector

P8
Connector

FIGURE 2.6

AT-style power connectors come in pairs, which must be attached with the black wires together.

CAUTION

AT-style power connectors can be attached backward. Doing so is likely to *destroy* your motherboard, and perhaps destroy attached devices such as CPUs, video cards, and so on. Each power cable is made up of several wires, one of which is black. It's important that the black wires be seated *next to* each other when the power cables are attached to the motherboard.

Although popular through the 80486 and most of the Pentium eras, AT and Baby AT motherboards became quite rare beginning in 1998–1999. They still exist in 2000, but sales are mostly limited to the replacement and upgrade markets. New computers almost always use some variant of the ATX form factor. There are a few Slot 1 AT or Baby AT motherboards, but such designs are extremely rare.

ATX, Mini-ATX, Micro-ATX, and Flex-ATX

Beginning in 1996, ATX motherboards became available. Intel developed the ATX specification, and has revised it several times. The broad outlines remain constant across ATX revisions, although some details have changed. ATX was designed to address several deficiencies in the AT and Baby AT form factors, such as

- **Altered width/depth ratio** Baby AT designs are deeper than they are wide, forcing placement of CPUs or other components in line with the slots. This placement can limit options for the addition of large cards, particularly on CPUs like late-model Pentiums that require large heat sinks with fans. ATX motherboards, by contrast, are wider than they are deep. In an ATX design, the CPU goes to the side of the slots, as shown in Figure 2.1.

- **Addition of external I/O ports** With motherboards universally deploying external I/O ports, the ATX specification includes a standardized location for ports to be built into the motherboard, as shown in Figures 2.1 and 2.7. The keyboard uses a small mini-DIN plug, rather than the larger DIN connector used in AT and ATX motherboards. (Inexpensive adapters allow one type of keyboard to be used on the other type of mother-board.) Mounting external ports directly on the motherboard reduces cable clutter in the computer and improves computer reliability.

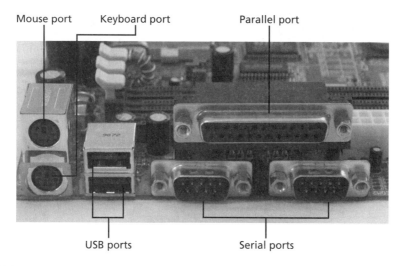

FIGURE 2.7
Some ATX motherboards include video or audio connectors in addition to those shown here.

- **Internal I/O connector locations** AT and Baby AT board designers tended to put I/O connectors for floppy, EIDE, and (when present) SCSI adapters anywhere they could. Occasionally these locations produced long and tangled runs of cables to disk drives. ATX boards tend to place these connectors close to where the matching devices end up in a computer's case (see Figure 2.8). This placement minimizes cable clutter.

- **Improved power connector** ATX motherboards use a single keyed power connector (see Figure 2.9), in contrast to the dual connectors of AT and Baby AT boards. The keyed ATX power connector makes it nearly impossible to destroy a motherboard by connecting the power supply incorrectly. In addition, ATX boards run on 3.3v, eliminating the need for a voltage regulator. ATX boards also host a series of power-related changes, allowing the computer to power itself off when the OS shuts down, power itself on in response to specified events, go into low-power mode, and so on.

Floppy and EIDE disk connectors

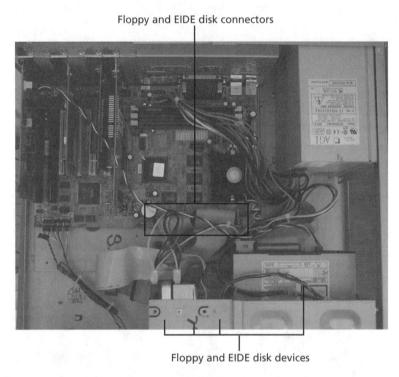

Floppy and EIDE disk devices

FIGURE 2.8

The design of ATX motherboards and cases places disk cable connectors near the matching disk devices.

FIGURE 2.9

The pins of the ATX power connector are keyed to make it impossible to insert the matching cable incorrectly.

- **Cooling changes** Although not a motherboard change *per se*, the ATX specification includes changes to the flow of air through the computer. The new placement of the CPU allows the power supply to blow air over the CPU, theoretically eliminating the need for a separate cooling fan for the CPU. In practice, however, many ATX systems retain a separate CPU cooling fan.

As you might guess, the ATX motherboard design includes enough changes to make it impossible to use an ATX motherboard in an AT case. There are a few hybrid cases available, which can be used with either Baby AT or ATX motherboards, but for the most part, use of an ATX motherboard necessitates use of an ATX case. Therefore, if you have an existing AT or Baby AT system you want to upgrade, you should either look for a Baby AT motherboard or plan to replace your computer's case, as well as the motherboard.

Overall, ATX boards represent a substantial improvement over the older Baby AT design. ATX motherboards typically measure approximately 9.6 inches deep by 12.0 inches wide; this width limits ATX use in small cases. The smallest case that's practical to use for an ATX motherboard is a desktop or mid-tower design. In order to help reduce case size, smaller ATX variants have been developed, including mini-ATX (8.2×11.2 inches), micro-ATX (9.6×9.6 inches), and flex-ATX (9.0×7.5 inches). As with other form factors, these represent *maximum* sizes. Individual boards can be somewhat smaller in one or both dimensions. The Micro-ATX form factor became quite popular in 1999 among PCs priced at less than $1,000. These smaller ATX variants typically have fewer than the 5–7 usable expansion slots present on full-sized ATX motherboards. Some such boards have only two or three usable slots. This lack of slots is compensated for to some extent by the inclusion of extra functionality on the motherboard. These boards typically include both video and sound features that would require the use of two plug-in boards on most full-sized ATX motherboards. Some such motherboards include modems, Ethernet adapters, SCSI host adapters, or other devices on the motherboard, as well.

2

MOTHERBOARDS

> **NOTE**
>
> Most motherboards with PCI slots place one PCI slot and one ISA slot very close to one another (refer to Figure 2.4). Because PCI boards mount components on the opposite side of the board as compared to ISA boards, only one of those two slots can be used. As a result, the number of *usable* slots is one less than the number of *actual* slots. The motherboard depicted in Figures 2.1 and 2.4, for instance, has seven slots, but only six are usable.

Inclusion of video, audio, and perhaps other functions normally handled by plug-in cards on the motherboard can be convenient, and—if it reduces the size of the computer—may be beneficial if available space is limited. There is a downside, however. Upgrading or replacing these components may be difficult or impossible. This factor can be particularly important for Linux users, because Linux remains incompatible with some devices. Suppose you purchase a computer that uses a micro-ATX motherboard, only to find that the video functions don't work reliably with Linux. You'll need to sacrifice one of your PCI slots for a video card, and you won't be able to select an AGP video card, because the motherboard won't include an AGP slot. After all, the video board is built into the motherboard, so why include an AGP slot? In some cases, it may not be possible to completely disable the unwanted hardware.

All in all, I favor purchasing a system built around a conventional full-sized ATX motherboard with a full complement of slots. If you're tempted by a system with extra functionality built in to the motherboard, do extra research to be sure that the components used are compatible with Linux.

NLX

Most motherboard designs place the CPU, RAM, bus slots, and other components all on one plane, which lies horizontally in a desktop case or vertically in a tower case. Because PCI and ISA cards require a certain amount of height, this design imposes a minimum height requirement on the resulting computer system. Particularly in desktop cases, however, a *low-profile* design has a certain appeal. A low-profile system is a desktop design that's shorter than normal for PCs. The current low-profile design of choice is known as NLX. To achieve this configuration, the motherboard includes no PCI or ISA slots. Instead, the motherboard supports a *daughter card,* or *riser,* on which the PCI and ISA slots reside, as shown in Figure 2.10.

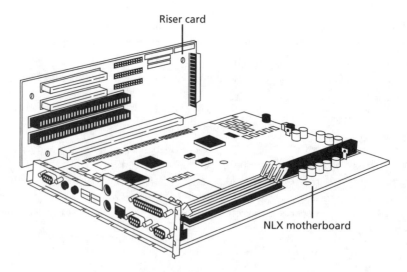

FIGURE 2.10

The riser in an NLX system contains little in the way of circuitry, and serves mainly as an attachment point for expansion cards.

In theory, an NLX motherboard offers a major advantage when you want to upgrade hardware, because the design allows you to remove the motherboard from the computer without disturbing the expansion cards or (assuming the case is designed properly) the disks. This fact makes a motherboard upgrade very easy, as compared to an upgrade of a conventional system. On the other hand, NLX systems tend to be quite small, which limits your ability to add internal devices like multiple hard disks, CD-ROM drives, and tape backup drives.

Proprietary and Rare Layouts

Over the years, a number of proprietary and little-used motherboard layouts have emerged. These designs include

- The larger PC manufacturers, such as IBM and Compaq, often design their own motherboards and use non-standard layouts for them. These designs limit your choices for upgrading or repairing an existing computer, so I recommend that you avoid buying a computer that uses such a unique motherboard form factor.

- A low-profile form factor used in years past was known as LPX. This design, like the newer NLX design, used a riser, but placed it in the middle of the motherboard. LPX boards weren't quite perfectly standardized, so it's not always possible to swap one LPX motherboard for another. If you want to buy or build a new low-profile computer, I recommend you use NLX rather than LPX.

- A new form factor, known as WTX, has been designed with an eye towards Itanium CPU requirements. WTX systems are quite rare in early 2000, but may become more popular once Intel releases the Itanium CPU. You can learn more about WTX at `http://www.wtx.org`.

I recommend you avoid proprietary and unusual motherboard form factors, with the possible exception of WTX, which has the potential to become more common in late 2000 or early 2001. Proprietary boards often require unusual cases, which in turn often require unusual face plates on floppy disks, unusual power supplies, and so on. Replacing such components can be an expensive and of proprietarytime-consuming proposition.

Motherboard Chipsets

All circuit boards in a computer owe their electronic identities to one or more chipsets they carry. A *chipset* is, as the name implies, a set of one or more chips that implement most or all of the functions of the board. In the case of a motherboard, the chipset provides functions such as

- Interface between the CPU and memory
- Interface between the CPU and expansion card busses (ISA, PCI, and so on)

2

MOTHERBOARDS

- System timers of various sorts
- Ports—serial, parallel, IDE, floppy, USB, and sometimes others

> **NOTE**
>
> Motherboards from the 80486 period and earlier typically didn't include most ports; these functions were performed by expansion cards. Even late 80486 and early Pentium systems used separate chipsets to perform these functions. These chipsets resided on the motherboard itself, but were separate from the main motherboard chipset.

With the exception of this final item, these functions are easy to overlook, but they're vitally important to the function of a motherboard. Details of how a given chipset implements these functions can influence the speed of a motherboard. In the case of features such as EIDE ports, Linux needs drivers to operate the devices. Linux includes generic IDE drivers that work with all EIDE ports, but optimized drivers for a particular chipset can improve the performance of EIDE devices. Therefore, it's important that you get a motherboard that uses a main or EIDE chipset that Linux understands, at least if you intend to use EIDE hard disks.

In the 80486 era, many manufacturers competed in the chipset marketplace, but Intel cornered most of the market for early Pentium motherboards. Alternatives arose again for Super7 motherboards, when Intel pushed its new Slot 1 design, leaving Socket 7 to AMD and Cyrix.

Each generation or type of CPU (80386, 80486, Pentium, Pentium Pro/Pentium-II/Pentium-III/Celeron, and Athlon) requires its own motherboard chipset designs. You can't use an 80486 chipset with a Pentium, for example (except for the Pentium Overdrive, which was intended to be used on 80486 motherboards). In the following sections, I focus on chipsets for Pentium and later CPUs, because those are the chipsets you're most likely to encounter in new and recent motherboards.

Identifying Your Chipset

If you have a motherboard already and aren't sure what chipset it uses, look at the largest chips that are permanently soldered to the motherboard. These should bear some identifying marks. For instance, Figure 2.11 shows one of the major chips on the motherboard depicted in Figure 2.1. This chip clearly identifies the chipset as being from VIA, and, in fact, it's part of the VIA MVP3 chipset. You may need to browse the chipset manufacturer's Web site to locate a reference to a particular chip ID code.

FIGURE 2.11

A motherboard's chipset can usually be identified by markings on the largest chips on the board.

2

MOTHERBOARDS

NOTE

Motherboards aren't the only computer components to use chipsets. Expansion card manufacturers often try to conceal the chipset manufacturer by placing a sticker over critical components or even by replacing the chipset manufacturer's silk screen with their own. Some chipsets, particularly on high-end video cards and some mother-boards, also run so fast that the board manufacturer places a heat sink over the component. *You should not attempt to remove a heat sink that's been bonded to a chipset component.* You can safely remove a sticker, but if you find a glass window in the chip, replace the sticker or put a new one over the window. Such windows are typically used on erasable programmable read-only memory (EPROM) chips, and are used to erase the memory by exposing the chip to ultraviolet radiation. Stray exposure to sunlight could conceivably erase such a chip, which you probably don't want to have happen.

Another way to identify a chipset is to examine files in the Linux /proc directory. If the motherboard has a PCI bus, the /proc/pci directory can be particularly informative.

For instance, among other entries the computer whose motherboard is shown in Figures 2.1 and 2.11 produces the following /proc/pci information:

```
Bus  0, device   7, function  0:
   ISA bridge: VIA Technologies, Inc. VT82C586/A/B PCI-to-ISA [Apollo VP] (rev
71).
  Bus  0, device   7, function  1:
    IDE interface: VIA Technologies, Inc. VT82C586 IDE [Apollo] (rev 6).
      Master Capable.  Latency=64.
      I/O at 0xe400 [0xe40f].
  Bus  0, device   7, function  2:
    USB Controller: VIA Technologies, Inc. VT82C586B USB (rev 2).
      IRQ 5.
      Master Capable.  Latency=64.
      I/O at 0xe000 [0xe01f].
  Bus  0, device   7, function  3:
    PCI bridge: VIA Technologies, Inc. VT82C586B ACPI (rev 16).
```

Note that the *82C586* identifier appears on both the chip and in several /proc/pci entries. The multiple occurrence of this same chip in /proc/pci indicates that it serves several functions.

ALi Chipsets

Acer Laboratories, Inc. (ALi at http://www.ali.com.tw) produces several chipsets used on an assortment of motherboards. These chipsets and their basic characteristics are summarized in Table 2.1.

The ALi Aladdin IV, V, and 7 chipsets are intended for Socket 7 motherboards. The Aladdin 7 is marketed specifically for the AMD K6-III and is unusual in that it includes extensive multi-media functionality, including audio and video features normally present on separate cards. At present, no Linux drivers are available for these features, unfortunately.

The Aladdin Pro II, TNT2, and Pro IV chipsets are ALi's entrants in the Pentium-II chipset race. The TNT2, like the Aladdin 7, includes video card chipset functionality, but not sound support.

The Linux kernel includes support for ALi's fast EIDE controllers, so you can get full speed from EIDE devices attached to an ALi-based motherboard.

TABLE 2.1 ALi Chipsets and Their Features

Name	Maximum Bus Speed	Supported CPUs	SMP Support	Memory Types	Memory Error Handling	Maximum Memory	Maximum Cacheable	AGP Support	IDE Support	USB Support
Aladdin IV	83.3MHz	Pentium-class	No	FPM, EDO, SDRAM	Parity, ECC	1GB	512MB	No	Ultra-33	Yes
Aladdin V	100MHz	Pentium-class	No	FPM, EDO, SDRAM	Parity, ECC	1GB	1GB	1x and 2x	Ultra-33	Yes
Aladdin 7	133MHz	Pentium-class	No	SDRAM	Parity, ECC	1GB	1GB	1x–8x	Ultra-33	Yes
Aladdin Pro II	100MHz	Pentium-II	Yes	FPM, EDO, SDRAM	Parity, ECC	1GB (FPM) or 2GB (EDO or SDRAM)	N/A	1x and 2x	Ultra-33	Yes
Aladdin TNT2	100MHz	Pentium-II	No	EDO, SDRAM, VC-SDRAM	Parity, ECC	1.5GB	N/A	1x and 2x	Ultra-33 or Ultra-66	Yes
Aladdin Pro IV	100MHz	Pentium-II, Pentium-III, Celeron	No	EDO, SDRAM, VC-SDRAM	Parity, ECC	1.5GB	N/A	1x–4x	Ultra-66	Yes

2

MOTHERBOARDS

AMD Chipsets

AMD (http://www.amd.com) is a newcomer to the chipset marketplace. Aside from an abortive partnership with VIA to produce a near-clone of the VIA Apollo VP-2 Pentium-class chipset under the name *640*, AMD's first chipset product is the 750 (a k a *Irongate*), which was developed to support the AMD Athlon CPU. The 750 features a 200MHz bus speed; 768MB of SDRAM memory; AGP, PCI, and ISA busses; two Ultra-66 IDE ports; and four USB ports. As a chipset for the Athlon CPU, the AMD 750 can't be used on Pentium or Pentium-II/III motherboards.

Intel Chipsets

Intel (http://www.intel.com) offers a plethora of chipsets, as outlined in Table 2.2. In fact, Intel dominates the market for Pentium-II chipsets. Until Intel stopped developing new Pentium-class chipsets, the company dominated that market as well. With its shift away from the Pentium CPU, however, Intel has left the market for Socket 7 chipsets to its competitors.

Intel's chipsets are quite popular on all classes of computers. The 810 chipset is particularly popular on notebooks, because it includes integrated graphics. Intel distributes a Linux X server for this chipset at http://support.intel.com/support/graphics/intel810/linuxsoftware.htm, in both RPM and tarball formats. The Linux kernel includes support for the advanced EIDE controllers integrated into recent Intel chipsets, so you can get full benefit of these controllers' speed. The ISA interface is optional with 800-series chipsets, and, in fact, many motherboards based on these chipsets lack ISA slots. This change reduces the cost and complexity of the chipset, but limits your choices for expansion cards. Recent Intel chipsets, including the 820 and 840, also use *RDRAM* (see Chapter 3) rather than the older RAM technologies. RDRAM increases the memory access speed, but RDRAM is still relatively new.

SiS Chipsets

Silicon Integrated Systems (SiS at http://www.sis.com.tw) was a very strong force in 80486 chipsets. Eclipsed briefly early in the Pentium era, SiS nonetheless remains a viable chipset manufacturer; its chipsets are described in Table 2.3.

TABLE 2.2 Intel Chipsets and Their Features

Name	Maximum Bus Speed	Supported CPUs	SMP Support	Memory Types	Memory Error Handling	Maximum Memory	Maximum Cacheable	AGP Support	IDE Support	USB Support
430LX (Mercury)	66MHz	P60/66	No	FPM	Parity	192MB	192MB	No	None	None
430NX (Neptune)	66MHz	P75+	Yes	FPM	Parity	512MB	512MB	No	None	None
430FX (Triton)	66MHz	P75+	No	FPM, EDO	None	128MB	64MB	No	Bus master	None
430MX (Mobile Triton)	66MHz	P75+	No	FPM, EDO	None	128MB	64MB	No	Bus master	None
430HX (Triton II)	66MHz	P75+	Yes	FPM, EDO	Parity, ECC	512MB	512MB	No	Bus master	Yes
430VX (Triton III)	66MHz	P75+	No	FPM, EDO, SDRAM	None	128MB	64MB	No	Bus master	Yes
430TX	66MHz	P75+	No	FPM, EDO, SDRAM	None	256MB	64MB	No	Ultra-33	Yes
440FX (Natoma)	66MHz	Pentium-II	Yes	FPM, EDO, BEDO	Parity, ECC	1GB	N/A	No	Bus master	Yes

continues

TABLE 2.2 Continued

Name	Maximum Bus Speed	Supported CPUs	SMP Support	Memory Types	Memory Error Handling	Maximum Memory	Maximum Cacheable	AGP Support	IDE Support	USB Support
440LX	66MHz	Pentium-II	Yes	FPM, EDO, SDRAM	Parity, ECC	1GB (EDO) or 512MB (SDRAM)	N/A	1x and 2x	Ultra-33	Yes
440EX	66MHz	Celeron	No	EDO, SDRAM	None	256MB	N/A	1x and 2x	Ultra-33	Yes
440BX	100MHz	Pentium-II/III, Celeron	Yes	SDRAM	Parity, ECC	1GB	N/A	1x and 2x	Ultra-33	Yes
440GX	100MHz	Pentium-II/III, Xeon	Yes	SDRAM	Parity, ECC	2GB	N/A	1x and 2x	Ultra-33	Yes
450NX	100MHz	Pentium-II/III, Xeon	Yes	FPM, EDO	Parity, ECC	8GB	N/A	No	Ultra-33	Yes
440ZX	100MHz	Celeron, Pentium-II/III	No	SDRAM	None	256MB	N/A	1x and 2x	Ultra-33	Yes
810 (Whitney)	100MHz	Celeron, Pentium-II/III	No	SDRAM	None	256MB	N/A	Integrated	Ultra-33 or Ultra-66	Yes
820	133MHz	Pentium-II/III	Yes	SDRAM, RDRAM	ECC	1GB	N/A	1x-4x	Ultra-66	Yes
840	133MHz	Pentium-II/III	Yes	SDRAM, RDRAM	ECC	2GB	N/A	1x-4x	Ultra-66	Yes

TABLE 2.3 SiS Chipsets and Their Features

Name	Maximum Bus Speed	Supported CPUs	SMP Support	Memory Types	Memory Error Handling	Maximum Memory	Maximum Cacheable	AGP Support	IDE Support	USB Support
5511/ 5512/ 5513	66MHz	Pentium-class	No	FPM, EDO	Parity	1GB	256MB	No	Bus master	No
5581/ 5582	75MHz	Pentium-class	No	FPM, EDO, SDRAM	None	384MB	128MB	No	Ultra-33	Yes
5591/ 5592	75MHz	Pentium-class	No	FPM, EDO, SDRAM	Parity or ECC	768MB	256MB	1x and 2x	Ultra-33	Yes
530	100MHz	Pentium-class	No	SDRAM, SGRAM (for video)	None	1.5GB	256MB	Integrated 2x	Ultra-66	Yes
540	100MHz	Pentium-class	No	SDRAM	None	1.5GB	512MB	Integrated 2x	Ultra-66	Yes
600	100MHz	Pentium-II/III, Celeron	No	FPM, EDO, SDRAM	ECC	1.5GB	N/A	1x and 2x	Ultra-33	Yes
620	100MHz	Pentium-II/III, Celeron	No	SDRAM, SGRAM (for video)	None	1.5GB	N/A	1x and 2x	Ultra-66	Yes
630	100MHz	Pentium-II/III, Celeron	No	SDRAM, VC-SDRAM	None	1.5GB	N/A	1x–4x	Ultra-66	Yes

2

MOTHERBOARDS

Several SiS chipsets feature integrated video functions. Specifically, the 5581/5582, 530, 540, 620, and 630 chipsets integrate video features. The 540 and 630 also incorporate audio and Ethernet features. XFree86 drivers exist for the SiS video features in most chipsets, but support for the SiS audio and Ethernet features is as yet missing from Linux. You may need to use recent XFree86 servers from SuSE for some SiS chipsets. Linux currently doesn't include explicit support for the EIDE controllers in recent SiS chipsets. You can still use EIDE devices under Linux, but you won't get the fastest possible speed.

VIA Chipsets

VIA Technologies (`http://www.via.com.tw`) is currently a very popular supplier of chipsets for x86 computers (see Table 2.4). VIA's product line is also one of the most diverse, including chipsets not just for Pentium and Pentium-II systems, but for AMD's Athlon. VIA chipsets occasionally appear under other names. For instance, AMD briefly sold the VIA VP-2 under the name *AMD 640*, and Soyo motherboards contain VIA chipsets sold under the *ETEQ* name.

Among Pentium-class CPUs, the VIA Apollo MVP3 chipset is one of the most popular. The MVP4 is based on the MVP3, but adds video functionality based on the Trident Cyber3D chipset, for which drivers exist in XFree86 3.3.4 and later. The MVP4 also includes audio functionality for which Linux drivers exist in late 2.2.x kernels. VIA's Apollo Pro and Apollo Pro 133 chipsets are used in a respectable array of Slot 1 and Socket 370 motherboards. Linux includes support for the VIA chipsets' IDE controller, so you can use it in full DMA mode.

2

MOTHERBOARDS

TABLE 2.4 VIA Chipsets and Their Features

Name	Maximum Bus Speed	Supported CPUs	SMP Support	Memory Types	Memory Error Handling	Maximum Memory	Maximum Cacheable	AGP Support	IDE Support	USB Support
Apollo VP1	66MHz	Pentium-class	No	FPM, EDO, BEDO SDRAM	None	512MB	512MB	No	Bus master	Yes
Apollo VP2	66MHz (75MHz unofficially)	Pentium-class	No	FPM, EDO, SDRAM	Parity or ECC	512MB	512MB	No	Ultra-33	Yes
Apollo VPX	75MHz	Pentium-class	No	FPM, EDO, BEDO, SDRAM	Parity	512MB	512MB	No	Ultra-33	Yes
Apollo VP3	66MHz	Pentium-class	No	FPM, EDO, SDRAM	Parity or ECC	1GB	1GB	1x and 2x	Ultra-33	Yes
Apollo MVP3	100MHz	Pentium-class	No	FPM, EDO, SDRAM, DDR SDRAM	Parity or ECC	1GB	512MB	1x and 2x	Ultra-33	Yes

continues

TABLE 2.4 Continued

Name	Maximum Bus Speed	Supported CPUs	SMP Support	Memory Types	Memory Error Handling	Maximum Memory	Maximum Cacheable	AGP Support	IDE Support	USB Support
Apollo MVP4	100MHz	P5-class	No	FPM, EDO, SDRAM, DDR SDRAM	Parity or ECC	756MB	512MB	Integrated	Ultra-66	Yes
Apollo Pro	100MHz	Pentium Pro, Pentium-II/III, Celeron	No	FPM, EDO, SDRAM	Parity or ECC	1GB	N/A	1x or 2x	Ultra-33 (Ultra-66 in Plus version)	Yes
Apollo Pro 133	133MHz	Pentium-II/III, Celeron	No	FPM, EDO, SDRAM		1.5GB	N/A	1x or 2x	Ultra-66	Yes
Apollo KX133	200MHz	Athlon	No	EDO, SDRAM, VC-SDRAM	ECC	2GB	N/A	1x-4x	Ultra-66	Yes

Onboard Ports

All motherboards contain at least some onboard ports. At a bare minimum, a motherboard must have a keyboard port—and, in fact, many 80486 and earlier motherboards had nothing *but* the keyboard port. Since late in the 80486 period, however, all motherboards have included more than a keyboard port. For the most part, the ports on a motherboard work well with the standard drivers included with Linux, although there are some exceptions. For instance, not all SCSI or Ethernet ports built in to motherboards are supported in Linux.

Keyboard and Mouse

AT and Baby AT motherboards typically came with a large 5-pin DIN connector for the keyboard. More recent motherboards use a smaller mini-DIN connector for this purpose. The two types of connectors are electrically compatible, so if you have one keyboard type and the wrong connector on the motherboard, you can obtain an inexpensive adapter. Figure 2.12 depicts an older keyboard connector and an adapter with the newer mini-DIN end visible. Keyboard handling is quite standardized, so you need no special drivers in Linux for the keyboard.

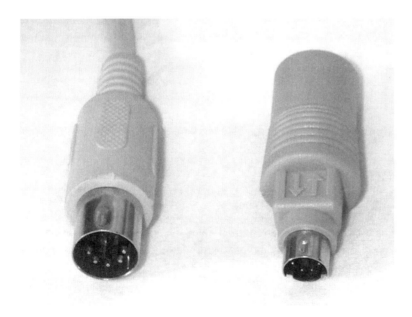

FIGURE 2.12

The large DIN connector on the left can be attached to a newer motherboard by using an adapter like the one on the right.

NOTE

Two exceptions to the uniform nature of keyboard handling exist. First, pre-AT computers used a different type of keyboard electronics. If you've got a very old keyboard from a PC XT or similar computer, therefore, you won't be able to use it with a modern computer. Some keyboards from that era have a switch to let you use the keyboard with either type of computer. Set the switch to *AT* and you should be able to use it with a modern computer. Second, USB keyboards have recently begun to appear, and a few systems now ship with USB keyboards. Linux can use USB keyboards, but you may need to compile a kernel with USB support. In early 2000, most Linux distributions didn't ship with this support enabled. Until this support ships with Linux distributions, I recommend avoiding USB keyboards.

Several types of mice exist for x86 hardware. (I use the word *mouse* to refer to both conventional mice and alternative pointing devices, such as trackballs and touch pads.) The two most popular mouse interfaces are serial and PS/2, with PS/2 mice being the more popular type on recent hardware. Linux supports both mouse types, and most Linux installers auto-detect and auto-configure your mouse. Most modern motherboards include a PS/2 mouse port on the back panel (refer to Figure 2.7). If you don't use a PS/2 mouse, some motherboards' BIOS utilities allow you to disable the mouse port, which frees up an IRQ for use by another device.

As with keyboards, USB mice have been gaining in popularity recently, but you need Linux support in the kernel to use USB mice, and this support is not yet a standard part of most distributions.

Chapter 15, "Keyboards and Mice," includes more information on keyboards and mice.

Serial and Parallel

Most motherboards include one parallel and two serial ports. Typically, you use the parallel port to attach a printer, and possibly also a Web camera, external zip drive, or scanner. The serial ports can be used for a mouse, an external modem, a digital camera, a personal digital assistant (PDA), or other devices. A few motherboards, particularly those on computers from large manufacturers such as Compaq, contain only one serial port.

Modern motherboards invariably support standardized modern parallel and serial port protocols. Linux support for these devices is quite mature, so you should have no problems using any motherboard's parallel or serial ports, assuming the hardware isn't defective.

Motherboards from the 80486 era and earlier typically did not include serial or parallel ports. On these computers, you had to add these ports on an ISA card. If you're refurbishing an older system and don't see these ports on the motherboard, this is why.

Chapter 16, "Parallel and Serial Ports," covers these ports in greater detail.

2

Floppy

80486 and earlier motherboards often placed floppy ports on expansion cards—often on the same cards that contained serial and parallel ports, or sometimes on a card with a SCSI host adapter. Modern motherboards, however, invariably include a floppy port, as shown in Figure 2.13. As with parallel and serial ports, floppy controllers are very well standardized, and don't vary much in modern computers. Most x86 computers today use 1.44MB floppy disks, but most controllers are capable of handling 2.88MB floppy drives. These higher-capacity floppies never caught on and are quite rare today.

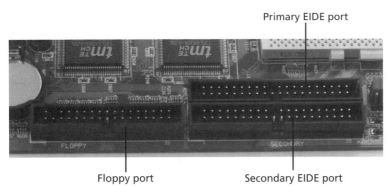

Primary EIDE port

Floppy port   Secondary EIDE port

FIGURE 2.13

One pin is missing from the floppy and each EIDE connector shown here. This is normal, and prevents backward insertion of the connecting cables, if they're properly keyed.

> **NOTE**
>
> Some computers ship with an LS-120 disk rather than a conventional floppy disk. These disks are available in EIDE and SCSI versions, and can read and write both conventional 1.44MB floppy disks and special 120MB disks. On a system with an LS-120 disk instead of a regular floppy disk, the motherboard's floppy disk controller will go unused unless the system also contains a 5.25-inch floppy drive or a floppy-interfaced tape unit.

EIDE

Next to the floppy port on most modern motherboards is a pair of EIDE ports (refer to Figure 2.13). Of the ports that are standard on modern motherboards, the EIDE ports are the most variable in design, and they're the only ports that benefit from specialized Linux drivers. These ports *do* work with a uniform EIDE driver, but this driver was written with the IDE ports of the early 1990s in mind. The standard Linux IDE driver doesn't support direct memory access (DMA) or high-speed operation. Using this standard driver, in sum, produces EIDE disk access speeds that are well below the level attainable by modern hard disks.

In order to take full advantage of a given motherboard's EIDE controller, you must typically activate options for that controller in the Linux kernel configuration, as shown in Figure 2.14. The Block devices kernel options window includes many options for specific EIDE devices. Some of these are for motherboard chipsets (such as the Intel PIIXn option near the bottom of the window in Figure 2.14), while others are for EIDE expansion boards.

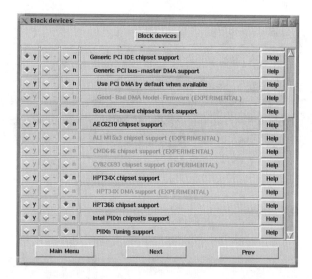

FIGURE 2.14

The list of EIDE devices is long and confusingly organized, so you may need to hunt a while to find yours.

Some Ultra-66 EIDE controllers don't work well with the stock Linux 2.2.x kernels. If you have such a board and want to install a 2.2.x-based Linux distribution, you may need to install Linux with an older EIDE controller card, then recompile a more recent kernel or apply kernel patches. Once that's done, you should be able to remove the older EIDE controller and use the Ultra-66 controller to run Linux. This problem will disappear as Linux distributions based on the 2.4.x kernel series become available sometime in 2000.

Most motherboards include two EIDE connectors. Each connector is capable of handling up to two EIDE devices on a single *chain* (that is, connected to a single cable). Thus, a typical motherboard is capable of controlling up to four EIDE devices. Each EIDE chain consumes one IRQ, however, so using even three devices takes two IRQs. Using EIDE for more than four devices requires adding a separate EIDE controller, and consumes at least three IRQs. For a large number of devices, SCSI (discussed in Chapters 5, "Hard Disks," and 9, "SCSI Host Adapters") is a better choice.

USB

The universal serial bus (USB) is the latest development in common use for external devices. Most modern PCs contain two external USB ports, and you can attach more than two USB devices by using a USB *hub*, which effectively turns one USB port into several. Devices available for USB include mice, keyboards, digital cameras, scanners, printers, and modems.

USB is capable of much higher speeds than conventional serial ports—12Mbps, as compared to 115kbps for most conventional serial ports. USB's speed is close to that of an EPP/ECP parallel port (about 16Mbps). USB is an appealing connection method for another reason: It's possible to connect up to 127 devices to a single USB controller. In practice, of course, 127 devices would most likely overload USB's bandwidth, unless most or all of these devices were very slow or seldom used. Nonetheless, with the explosion of external devices like scanners, digital cameras, and so on, USBs' appeal is substantial.

The Linux 2.2.x kernel series picked up USB support very late in its lifetime. Fortunately, the Linux developers have been working on substantially expanding USB support, and by the 2.4.x kernel will have substantial USB support. If you want to use a USB device, you may want to check the main Linux USB development page at `http://www.linux-usb.org`. Where applicable, I also describe Linux's support for specific USB devices in appropriate chapters of this book.

Optional Extras

In addition to the standard motherboard ports just described, some boards contain additional adapters. Video and audio features are common on motherboards intended for low-cost home PCs. SCSI and Ethernet adapters are common on high-end motherboards. A small number of motherboards include modem functionality. In theory, other types of adapters can be included on motherboards, as well, but in practice these are quite rare.

No matter what optional features you're considering, you should be sure that the chipset used is supported in Linux. Without Linux support, the feature is essentially dead weight on your motherboard, and may conceivably cause problems if it can't be completely disabled. Also, consider that you can often keep an add-on card when you upgrade your motherboard. If you buy a motherboard with integrated functions, you must buy another such motherboard or buy separate products for the integrated features if you later decide to upgrade the motherboard.

2

MOTHERBOARDS

SCSI Host Adapters

SCSI functionality in x86 motherboards is rare. When present, it's implemented by including a separate SCSI chipset on the motherboard; the SCSI features aren't implemented in the main motherboard chipset. Most boards that include SCSI features use chipsets from Adaptec (http://www.adaptec.com) or Symbios Logic (http://www.symbios.com). Both companies' products are well supported in Linux. In most cases you won't have problems with SCSI support built in to a motherboard. You should check to be sure that the specific SCSI chipset used on the motherboard is supported by Linux, however.

In order to boot from a SCSI host adapter, whether that adapter is on a separate board or built in to the motherboard, the SCSI adapter must have its own boot BIOS. In the case of SCSI adapters built in to the motherboard, this BIOS is generally integrated into the motherboard's main BIOS, although the SCSI BIOS may have its own user interface separate from that of the main BIOS. If you intend to boot from a SCSI hard disk attached to a host adapter on the motherboard, you should check to be sure that the motherboard includes an appropriate SCSI BIOS (most do). It might also be worth investigating BIOS upgrade procedures. In most cases, upgrading either the SCSI or the main motherboard BIOS on a computer with an integrated SCSI host adapter entails upgrading *both* the SCSI and the core motherboard BIOS. Because upgrading a motherboard BIOS is such a dangerous proposition, I recommend not doing so unless you're reasonably certain the upgrade will fix a problem you're experiencing.

One drawback to having a SCSI adapter on the motherboard is that there's often no *external* SCSI connector. Therefore, you can only connect *internal* SCSI devices. You can get around this limitation by using an internal/external adapter plug (shown in Figure 2.15). You mount the adapter in the computer's case, and then plug the *last* connector on an internal SCSI cable into the internal plug. The external plug then serves as a continuation of the SCSI chain for external devices. There are several different types of internal/external SCSI adapter plugs, providing access for a variety of internal and external cable types.

Network Ports

Like SCSI adapters, Ethernet network ports are rare on motherboards, but some motherboards contain this feature. In most cases, the Ethernet functionality is provided by a separate Ethernet chipset on the motherboard. In some cases this functionality is built in to the main chipset. Whatever the case, you should check to be sure that Linux drivers exist for the Ethernet chipset in use. Fortunately, Linux supports the vast majority of Ethernet devices, although the Ethernet features built in to some SiS chipsets is unsupported by Linux at the moment. You can read more about Linux's Ethernet support the "Ethernet Adapters" section of Chapter 16.

2

MOTHERBOARDS

FIGURE 2.15
An internal/external SCSI connector consists of two SCSI plugs and a small circuit board to connect them.

Modems

A few motherboards, mostly used on low-cost pre-built PCs, include modem functionality. These modems are generally of the "Windows-only" variety, meaning that no Linux drivers are available for them. Unless you're convinced that the modem is usable under Linux, I recommend you avoid such motherboards. Although you can probably use another modem, the motherboard may lack a second serial port, and the unused circuitry could conceivably interfere with any modem you might add to the system.

Video Adapters

Video adapter support is common on many low-end motherboards. Placing the video adapter on the motherboard can reduce the complexity of the assembled computer by eliminating an expansion card. Many motherboard manufacturers produce at least one or two models that include video and audio functions on the motherboard and reduce the number of available slots by two or so as compared to their other models, thus reducing the size of the motherboard. Some motherboards that feature integrated video do so by using a main motherboard chipset that incorporates video functionality directly. Others add a video chipset to the motherboard that would otherwise appear on a separate video card.

Although convenient in many ways, adding the video support onto the motherboard does have its drawbacks. For one thing, such designs generally take some of the main system memory and give it to the video functions. For instance, on a 64MB system, you might end up with only 60MB of main memory and 4MB of video memory. (Most such motherboards let you use the BIOS to set the amount of video memory. Typical values range from 2MB to 16MB.) An integrated design also robs you of flexibility. It's harder to upgrade to a new video card in the future, because motherboards with integrated video typically have fewer available expansion slots and usually no AGP slots.

If you're considering a motherboard with integrated video support, you should be absolutely certain that Linux (or, more precisely, XFree86) supports the video chipset in use. You can learn more about such support from the main XFree86 Web site, `http://www.xfree86.org`. SuSE (`http://www.suse.com`) is a Linux distributor that works on developing new XFree86 drivers, so you may want to check its Web site, as well, for the latest information.

Audio Features

Like video features, audio features often appear on low-end motherboards in order to save space and reduce total system cost. Audio functions are usually, but not always, implemented by way of a secondary chipset, so the section titled "Sound Card Chipsets" in Chapter 10, "Sound Cards," may be of interest in evaluating Linux compatibility of such motherboards.

Integrated audio generally doesn't rob you of any system memory. This feature is therefore less detrimental than is integrated video in this respect. Integrated audio still suffers from the drawback of inflexibility, however; upgrading to a new sound card may be more difficult because of the reduced number of expansion slots on motherboards with integrated audio.

Memory

All motherboards include some sort of memory support. The main memory sockets on most motherboards are dual inline memory module (DIMM) sockets, shown in Figure 2.16. Older motherboards may include single inline memory module (SIMM) sockets, as well as, or instead of, DIMM sockets. Some very recent motherboards use Rambus inline memory modules (RIMMs), which look much like DIMMs. Chapter 3 discusses memory in more detail.

FIGURE 2.16
Most modern motherboards include three DIMM or RIMM sockets.

Summary

The motherboard you choose for a Linux computer determines many aspects of how your system functions. You must match the motherboard with the CPU, and this combination together determines your system's overall computational speed. The motherboard determines how expandable your system is, in terms of the number and type of expansion slots. Integrated features, such as SCSI host adapters or video ports, may make a motherboard more appealing or reduce its cost, but these features can be added to motherboards that lack them by using plug-in expansion boards.

At the core of each motherboard is its chipset, which implements the electronic functions required by the CPU. The chipset determines much of a motherboard's personality, including limits on its speed, total memory supported, and so on. Two motherboards based on the same chipset are likely to perform similarly, although there may be differences because of divergent implementation details (the number of PCI slots, for instance). In some cases, motherboard manufacturers may impose limits more stringent than those of the chipset itself, as when a motherboard features only 512KB of cache when the chipset supports 1MB of cache.

2

MOTHERBOARDS

Memory

IN THIS CHAPTER

Most of the hardware components discussed in this book require special drivers or present unusual challenges on Linux than on other OSs. This isn't normally the case with memory. Assuming the memory is compatible with the motherboard, you can plug it in and use it under Linux just as you would under any other OS. Of course, Linux does require a certain minimum amount of memory, but Linux's requirements are no higher than those for most other modern OSs—indeed, Linux can get by on less memory than can many other OSs.

> **NOTE**
>
> Particularly on some older computers, Linux might present memory errors when other OSs (especially DOS and Windows 3.1) don't. This is because Linux is a 32-bit OS, meaning that it treats memory as one continuous space. DOS and Windows 3.1, by contrast, use 16-bit memory addressing modes, in which memory is broken down into 64KB chunks. 16- and 32-bit access methods impose different stresses on memory, and so it's possible for a given memory chip to work with one but not the other. Prior to the release of Windows 95, some memory and motherboard vendors tested their chips under DOS, but not under 32-bit OSs like Linux. These chips sometimes failed under 32-bit OSs. If you find that your computer is reliable under DOS but not Linux, it's possible that you're seeing this phenomenon at work, particularly if it's an old 80486 or earlier computer.

Linux Memory Requirements

In discussing the memory requirements of Linux—or of any OS—what's important is the total amount of random access memory (RAM). The *type* of memory, as described later in this chapter, generally isn't very important, although it might have a modest influence on the speed of the computer. The total amount of memory has a more substantial influence on system performance.

Minimum Memory Requirements

Most OSs include a minimum RAM requirement on their box or specifications Web page. Linux distributions are no different in this respect, and Table 3.1 summarizes the official minimum memory requirements for assorted popular Linux distributions.

TABLE 3.1 Official Memory Requirements of Linux Distributions

Distribution	Minimum RAM
Caldera OpenLinux 2.3	32MB
Corel Linux 1.0	24MB

Distribution	Minimum RAM
Debian GNU/Linux 2.1	4MB
Linux Mandrake 7.0	16MB
Red Hat Linux 6.1	16MB
Slackware Linux 7.0	16MB
SuSE Linux 6.3	8MB

You might think from Table 3.1 that the different Linux distributions are radically different OSs. In fact, they're not. The differences derive from several factors, including

- **Different default configurations**   Most distributions set themselves up by default with flashy X Window System (a k a X) graphical user interface (GUI) environments such as the K Desktop Environment (KDE) or the GNU Network Object Model Environment (GNOME). These environments require a great deal of RAM to operate smoothly. Distributions like Debian, which set up default configurations that don't automatically start X, can specify lower minimum RAM values. (SuSE specifies 8MB as its minimum without X, and 16MB as its minimum when running X.)

- **Different use assumptions**   Each distribution builds its minimum RAM requirements around assumptions of how the OS will be used. If those assumptions entail running many large programs, the minimum RAM requirement goes up.

- **Different tolerances for speed loss**   If you're willing to endure excruciatingly slow operation, you can run Linux in very small amounts of RAM, even with GUI desktops and many large programs. All other things being equal, more RAM improves system speed when running many programs. To a large extent the RAM requirements in Table 3.1 reflect nothing but a decision concerning how much slowdown users will tolerate because of low RAM.

- **Installation requirements**   Installation programs require a certain amount of RAM in order to hold a RAMdisk image as well as programs. If the distribution includes a flashy installation program that uses a large RAMdisk or bulky programs, RAM requirements go up simply for the installation program. Once the OS is installed, it might be possible to run it on less than the minimum amount of RAM.

Once installed and configured in similar ways, all Linux distributions require similar amounts of RAM. With the possible exception of the Caldera OpenLinux estimate, all the estimates in Table 3.1 are on the skimpy side for comfortable and practical use of Linux when using a GUI environment. Most computers today ship with at least 32MB of RAM, so it's not difficult to meet this minimum requirement on modern hardware. If you're trying to adapt an older computer to new duty using Linux, however, you might want to consider a RAM upgrade if the

3

MEMORY

computer has less than 32MB. Don't upgrade if the system will be used in a specialized and limited fashion, such as an IP masquerading router between a small network and a cable modem.

Adjusting Memory Estimates for Your System's Uses

Rather than rely on some blanket minimum RAM requirement, you should attempt to estimate how much RAM you need for any particular use of the OS. To do this, it's useful to start with a figure, such as 8MB, and add or delete RAM as required for each task you expect to perform *simultaneously*. That is, if you expect to run both an office suite and a graphics editor simultaneously, add values for both packages. If you expect to run these programs sequentially, add only the larger value. Table 3.2 presents adjustments for some common applications.

TABLE 3.2   Adjustments to Memory Requirements for Common Applications

Application	Amount of RAM to Add
X Window System	10MB
Desktop environment	15–20MB
Office suite	10–20MB
Basic graphics editing	5MB
Advanced graphics applications	10–30MB
GUI Web browser	10MB
Scientific or engineering applications	5–500MB
Low-volume server	5MB for *each* server
High-volume server	50MB for *each* server

As an example, suppose your Linux computer is directly connected to the Internet (via a corporate LAN or cable modem, for example), and you want to run a small Web site on which you expect to receive a few hits every hour (5MB for a small server). You also intend to use this computer for writing using a GUI word processor in X (10–20MB for an office suite, plus 10MB for X), and you want to use the GNOME desktop environment (15–20MB). Adding these figures, along with the 8MB base RAM requirement, yields an estimated minimum of somewhere between 48MB and 63MB. To be sure, you *can* run all these processes on less than 48MB, but performance is likely to be sluggish. Adding memory beyond 63MB might improve performance slightly, but not by as much as you get by moving up to 48MB.

You can probably fine-tune these values based on the particular programs you intend to use. For instance, WordPerfect 8 for Linux lists its minimum RAM requirement as 9MB. If you want to run a scientific or engineering application, you can almost certainly use your knowledge of the application to narrow the range to something tighter than the 5–500MB I've listed. Also, Table 3.2 is only a rough guideline. Specific programs might impose requirements outside of the range I've presented.

Using Virtual Memory

Linux, like all modern OSs, can make use of *virtual memory*, also known as *swap space*. The idea is that it's better to run a program slowly than not at all. Instead of having the OS fail to run a program because of insufficient RAM, Linux can make use of disk space to store information that normally goes in RAM. The Linux kernel includes rules for *swapping* information from RAM onto the hard disk. Ideally, Linux swaps out information that's seldom accessed, such as RAM used by a program that's still open but that you're not currently using. Of course, sometimes Linux guesses wrong, or you're really using all the programs, and all your programs make heavy and active use of memory. In such situations, the system can become quite slow as Linux constantly accesses the swap space on disk. This situation of constant swap space access is known as *thrashing*, and when Linux thrashes, it can take a *long* time to perform even very simple tasks.

Adding Swap Space

Linux supports two forms of swap space: a swap *partition* and a swap *file*. UNIX systems traditionally use swap partitions, which are entire hard disk partitions devoted to swap space. Because it's a contiguous areas of the hard disk and doesn't require the use of ordinary disk filesystem drivers to operate, a swap partition can be slightly faster than a swap file, which is an ordinary disk file used for swap purposes. Most Linux distributions prompt you to create a swap partition when you install the OS. Once installed, you can see how much swap space you have available by using the `free` command. This command produces output like the following:

```
              total      used      free    shared   buffers     cached
Mem:          95772     91916      3856      7040     24912      39452
-/+ buffers/cache:      27552     68220
Swap:        136512      3132    133380
```

The `Swap` line indicates that this computer has 136,512KB (133MB) of swap space, of which 3MB are used and 130MB is available. The `free` command also provides information on how much conventional RAM is present, used, and available.

If you find that you need more swap space, follow these directions:

1. If you want to permanently add swap space, you might want to create a new swap partition. You can use a utility like PowerQuest's (`http://www.powerquest.com`) PartitionMagic to dynamically repartition your hard disk in order to enlarge an existing swap partition or create a new one. Creating a new swap partition without the benefit of a dynamic partition resizer is quite tedious, because you must normally back up, repartition, and restore at least one partition.

2. If you want to temporarily add swap space, or if you don't want to repartition your disk, you can create a swap file. You can use the `dd` command to create an empty file of an appropriate size. For instance, **`dd if=/dev/zero of=/swap-file bs=1024 count=65536`** creates an empty file that's 64MB in size (bs×count bytes). This file is called `swap-file` and is located in the root directory, but you can place the file on any Linux filesystem on which you have enough free space.

3. Use the `mkswap` command to initialize the file or disk space as a swap file. For instance, use **`mkswap /swap-file`** for the swap file created in step 2 or `mkswap /dev/hda7` for a swap partition on `/dev/hda7`.

4. If you've created a swap file, change its permissions so that only root can read or write it. For instance, use **`chown root.root /swap-file; chmod 600 /swap-file`** to do this with the file created in step 2.

5. Use the swapon command to add swap space, as in **`swapon /swap-file`** or **`swapon /dev/hda7`**.

6. If you intend to use the swap space you've added in the preceding steps on a permanent basis, add an appropriate line to `/etc/fstab`, for instance

   ```
   /dev/hda7        none        swap        sw
   ```

7. When you're done using temporary swap space, you can stop using it by issuing the `swapoff` command, as in `swapoff /swap-file`.

NOTE

Linux, unlike Microsoft Windows or IBM OS/2, doesn't expand a swap file dynamically. If you have 64MB of RAM and a 64MB swap file, Linux has a maximum of 128MB of memory, and, if your programs attempt to use more than 128MB of RAM, some programs are likely to crash, or at least be unable to perform certain actions.

The Optimum Amount of Swap Space

In years past, it was generally recommended that swap space equal twice the amount of physical RAM available on a UNIX-like computer. This recommendation was based upon typical multiuser usage patterns, however, and it's not clear that this rule of thumb is as useful when applied to single-user Linux computers. Many desktop Linux users have swap space equal to or even less than the amount of physical RAM and seem quite happy with this configuration. In the end, an appropriate amount of swap space depends on how you use the computer; if you regularly, or even just occasionally, run enough programs to substantially exceed the RAM available on your computer, a large amount of swap space is beneficial. If you have enough RAM that its limits are seldom stressed, however, you might need little or no swap space.

The `free` command's listing of used RAM includes RAM used by Linux as disk cache—hard disk contents stored in RAM to improve disk access speed. Disk cache is the opposite of swap, and balancing swap and disk cache is a tricky art practiced by kernel programmers; you need not concern yourself with it. You should be aware, however, that your programs actually consume far less RAM than you might think from looking at the first line of `free`'s output. For this reason, `free` also reports the amount of RAM used *excluding* disk caches, on the `-/+ buffers/cache` line. Use this value, rather than the `Mem` value, when estimating how much RAM your programs consume.

Memory Module Types

RAM is built from silicon wafers, just as CPUs and other computer chips are. The silicon wafers, however, are quite delicate. In order to safely handle and transport RAM, it's necessary to embed the silicon wafers inside a plastic or ceramic package. This package is what we typically think of as a computer chip (see Figure 3.1).

FIGURE 3.1

A typical memory chip uses a number of metallic pins to interface the silicon wafer within the package to a motherboard or other device.

Early x86 PCs generally included RAM chips soldered directly onto the motherboard, or placed in individual sockets. This approach consumed a great deal of space on the motherboard, however, and made it difficult to upgrade memory or replace defective memory.

Therefore, various forms of *memory modules* were developed to hold the memory chips. These memory modules could be easily attached to the motherboard. The most popular memory module types through much of x86 history have been *single inline memory modules* (SIMMs) and *dual inline memory modules* (DIMMs). An example of each is shown in Figure 3.2. In late 1999, a new type of memory module began to appear: the *Rambus inline memory module* (RIMM). RIMMs are used by a new type of RAM, *Rambus dynamic RAM* (RDRAM), described later in this chapter.

FIGURE 3.2
The 30-pin SIMM (top) is largely obsolete today, but 168-pin DIMMs (bottom) are still used in many computers in 2000.

> **NOTE**
>
> Memory modules vary in height. If you purchase memory modules to expand your computer, don't be concerned if the modules you buy are taller or shorter than the ones you already have. On rare occasions, however, a memory module might be too tall for a given computer—there might not be enough clearance between the module and some other component, such as a hard disk bay. Sometimes you can get around the problem by relocating the other component or by putting the memory module in a different memory slot. Other times you might need to return the module and get one that's physically shorter.

SIMMs

SIMMs were the preferred method of memory distribution for 80386, 80486, and many Pentium-class systems. Physically, two forms of SIMM were popular at various times: 30-pin and 72-pin.

30-Pin SIMMs

The earliest SIMMs used 30 contact points, known as *pins*, to interface the memory to the motherboard. 30-pin SIMMs were common in 80386 and 80486 motherboards, but are quite rare today. You're more likely to encounter them in devices like printers or sound cards than in modern motherboards, but even in these secondary functions they've been largely supplanted by more recent types of memory module.

As described in the section titled "Generations of x86 CPUs" in Chapter 1, x86 CPUs vary in the width of their memory busses—that is, in how many bits they transfer to and from memory in a single operation. 80386SX CPUs employed 16-bit memory transfers, 80386DX and 80486 CPUs used 32-bit memory transfers, and Pentium-class and later CPUs transfer 64 bits in a single operation. This fact is important to a discussion of memory modules because each design can transfer a fixed number of bits per cycle. Therefore, to transfer more bits than the memory module supports, it's necessary to use multiple identical modules. For example, if a memory module design supports transfer of 8 bits, then to use the module with the 80386SX, it's necessary to use two identical modules to achieve the 16-bit transfer used by the CPU. A collection of memory modules that meets the transfer requirements of a CPU is known as a *bank*. Because CPUs vary in the width of their memory accesses, the bank size varies from one CPU to another. Likewise, memory modules vary in their access widths, so the number of modules per bank changes with module type.

30-pin SIMMs support 8-bit access, meaning that a bank is two SIMMs for the 80386SX, four SIMMs for the 80386DX and 80486, and a whopping eight SIMMs for Pentium and later CPUs. A typical 80486 motherboard included two banks of 30-pin SIMM sockets, although some supported three or even four banks. The eight-SIMM bank size of 30-pin SIMMs when used with Pentiums was a primary reason for the abandonment of the 30-pin SIMM design. Even two banks would have required 16 SIMM sockets, which would have consumed an exorbitant amount of motherboard real estate. Nonetheless, a few Pentium motherboards did support 30-pin SIMMs, usually in conjunction with 72-pin SIMMs. That is, such motherboards typically included one bank of 30-pin sockets and two banks of 72-pin sockets.

3

MEMORY

> **NOTE**
>
> In the mid-1990s, *SIMM-saver* modules gained modest popularity. These cards allowed you to plug four 30-pin SIMMs into a single 72-pin SIMM socket. These cards usually worked, but had their drawbacks, including a rather unwieldy size and reduced reliability. Today there's little reason to use a SIMM-saver module, because such modules cost more than most 72-pin SIMMs.

30-pin SIMMs are available in sizes of 256KB, 1MB, 4MB, and 16MB. Because a typical 80486 system uses 30-pin SIMMs four to a bank, this translates into bank sizes of 1MB, 4MB, 16MB, and 64MB.

72-Pin SIMMs

72-pin SIMMs are larger than their 30-pin counterparts, but not as large as the DIMM depicted in Figure 3.2. The memory access width of 72-pin SIMMs is 32 bits, meaning that a single 72-pin SIMM constitutes a complete bank for 80386DX and 80486 CPUs. You can therefore add 72-pin SIMMs singly to such motherboards. (In practice, however, 72-pin SIMMs were introduced after the heyday of the 80386 CPU, and you won't find 72-pin SIMMs on any but very late 80486 motherboards.) The Pentium CPU's 64-bit memory accesses create a bank size of two for 72-pin SIMMs, so you must add 72-pin SIMMs in pairs to most Pentium motherboards.

> **NOTE**
>
> A few Pentium chipsets supported breaking up the Pentium's 64-bit memory accesses into a pair of 32-bit memory accesses. Such chipsets allowed adding 72-pin SIMMs singly, or 30-pin SIMMs in groups of four. The cost was speed: Such split memory accesses take twice as long as a single 64-bit memory fetch, thus reducing overall system performance. Going in the opposite direction, some 80486 chipsets allowed combining two 32-bit memory accesses into a single 64-bit memory access, producing a small speed boost when adding 72-pin SIMMs in pairs.

72-pin SIMMs come in capacities ranging from 1MB to 128MB, with each higher capacity being twice that of the one immediately below it. The end result is substantially greater flexibility in memory configuration as compared to 30-pin SIMMs.

Pentium motherboards typically included 2–4 banks of two 72-pin SIMM sockets. Even considering the increased size of 72-pin SIMMs as compared to 30-pin SIMMs, this represents substantially reduced motherboard space consumption for memory, and added convenience—only 1/4 the number of SIMMs must be inserted or removed. Nonetheless, it would be more convenient still to be able to add memory one module at a time with Pentium and later CPUs, and that's where DIMMs come into the picture.

DIMMs

DIMMs use a 168-pin double-sided design—that is, each side of the DIMM has a separate contact point, as opposed to SIMMs, in which the contacts on both sides are treated as one. DIMMs also support 64-bit memory transfers, so a single DIMM constitutes a complete bank for Pentium-class and above CPUs, including Pentium Pro, Pentium-II, Pentium-III, Celeron, and Athlon. This fact makes DIMMs the memory module of choice for Pentium and above CPUs, and by 1998 DIMMs were the standard form of memory on all new x86 computers.

The 168-pin DIMMs used in x86 motherboards aren't the only variety of DIMMs available. For instance, some Macintosh computers use other types of DIMM, as do some printers. If you want to buy a DIMM for your motherboard, be sure it's for an x86 computer. You must also match the type and speed of memory to your motherboard, as described later in this chapter.

168-pin DIMMs come in capacities ranging from 8MB to 256MB. As with 72-pin SIMMs, each DIMM size is twice that of the next-lower size.

As with the transition from 30-pin to 72-pin SIMMs, the move from 72-pin SIMMs to 168-pin DIMMs saw a period in which motherboards supported both types of connectors. Such motherboards were usually Pentium-class boards, although some Slot 1 motherboards have both types of connectors. In early 2000, most motherboards include 2–4 DIMM connectors and support for no other RAM modules. A few motherboards in early 2000 support the new RIMM memory, however, and this technology is expected to become quite popular as 2000 wears on.

RIMMs

The latest memory module format is the RIMM. Previous memory module types have been largely independent of the design of the memory chips that populate the modules. RIMMs, however, were designed specifically for one type of memory, RDRAM, which will be discussed later.

RIMM modules look very much like DIMMs, although they have 184 pins and differ in details such as the placement of notches among the connecting pins.

Odd as it might sound, RIMMs transfer data at a width of only 16 bits. The RDRAM technology, however, allows data to be transferred at a much higher rate of speed than is possible with other memory types, so a motherboard designed to use RIMMs can buffer 16-bit transfers and feed them to the CPU at whatever width it requires. It's therefore possible to add memory one RIMM at a time. Overall RAM speed with RDRAM RIMMs can be close to three times that achieved with most DIMMs.

RIMMs are or will soon be available in capacities ranging from 32MB to 256MB, with still larger capacities to come. Most RIMM-based motherboards ship with three RIMM sockets.

One of the advancements of RIMMs is that the modules contain small flash ROMs. These ROMs contain information on the RIMM's capacity, timing requirements, and so on. The result is that there's less guesswork involved in matching a specific RIMM to a motherboard; the motherboard can read the RIMM's requirements and adjust itself to match.

3

MEMORY

RIMMs are also unusual in that empty RIMM sockets on a motherboard must be filled with a *continuity module*. With earlier memory types, empty sockets were—well—empty. The design of RIMMs, however, requires an electrical connection between certain pins, even when the socket isn't in use, and this connection is provided by a dummy RIMM continuity module. If you get a motherboard that takes RIMM memory, don't remove the continuity modules except to insert RAM, and don't discard modules you've removed—you might need them should you trade in two or more low-capacity RIMMs for a single higher-capacity model.

Error Detection and Correction

SIMMs and DIMMs support two major forms of error handling: Error detection (*parity*) and *error correcting code* (ECC). Parity memory allows the computer to detect an error, but it can't do anything about that error, so the result is usually a system crash. In some cases this can be worse than using corrupt data, but the problem is that without parity, you can't *trust* your data—the spreadsheet that contains your income tax information, the raw data for your dissertation, or whatever might or might not be accurate if you have no error detection circuitry.

ECC goes one step further; it can not only detect, but also correct, 98% of memory errors. This results in smoother computer operation and little doubt concerning the veracity of the data on your computer—or at least, little need to worry that it's been scrambled by a memory error.

Both parity and ECC require *more* memory, however. Specifically, parity requires one extra bit per byte. Rather than using 8 bits to store one byte of information, 9 bits are required—8 bits for the data, 1 bit for the parity information. For ECC, the equation is more complex, and depends on the width of the memory bus. For 80486 systems, ECC requires 7 bits per 32-bit transfer, but in Pentium-class systems and above, 8 bits per 64-bit transfer are required. Thus, ECC in Pentium-class and later systems takes the same amount of extra memory as does parity, and, in fact, you can use parity SIMMs or DIMMs in either parity or ECC modes, assuming your motherboard supports both options.

Although parity imposes no special speed penalty, ECC does. Reads from ECC RAM are as fast as reads from ordinary RAM, but writes require computations that slow memory access slightly—by a few percent at most.

Unfortunately, most SIMMs and DIMMs sold today don't support parity, and many motherboard chipsets don't support parity or ECC (see Tables 2.1 through 2.4 for information on parity and ECC support in many chipsets). If you're building your own system or buying a new one built to specification, it's well worth seeking out parity or, especially, ECC. This is particularly true if you use the computer in some critical capacity or in a role where you expect it to run without crashing for a long period, such as a server.

RDRAM, and hence RIMMs, support an optional parity bit, which can be used for either parity or ECC. RDRAM technology is new enough that it's unclear how common use of parity or ECC will become with RIMMs.

Memory Electrical Types

The preceding section described the various physical characteristics of assorted memory types—SIMMs, DIMMs, and RIMMs. With the exception of RIMMs, each memory module type can hold any of several different RAM chip variants. These variants differ in their electronic characteristics, their maximum access speeds, and so on.

FPM DRAM

One of the earliest types of RAM was *fast page mode* (FPM) dynamic RAM (DRAM). *FPM* refers to the capability of RAM to make consecutive accesses to the same area (that is, the same *page*) of a RAM chip more quickly than the first access. This timing is often represented by a series of numbers indicating the number of cycles for each access. Typical FPM memory operates on 5-3-3-3 timing. Assuming a 66MHz system bus (and hence 1/66,000,000 = 15ns cycle time), the first access takes 5×15ns, and each subsequent access takes 3×15ns, for a total of 210ns. Without taking advantage of FPM timing, the total would be 4×5×15ns, or 300ns.

FPM DRAM was used on most 80486 and Pentium systems from 1995 and earlier. It has become quite rare since then, because more advanced memory types are no more expensive to produce, and might be less expensive to purchase because of supply and demand forces in the marketplace. FPM DRAM is available in 30- and 72-pin SIMM formats.

EDO DRAM

Extended data out (EDO) DRAM was the next major advance in memory technology that found its way onto x86 motherboards. EDO's speed improvement derives from the fact that EDO allows consecutive memory accesses to overlap each other slightly. Expressed in terms of memory timing, EDO allows 5-2-2-2 timing, rather than the 5-3-3-3 typical of FPM DRAM. This translates into 165ns per four memory accesses, versus 210 for FPM DRAM.

EDO DRAM requires specific support in the motherboard's chipset, so you can't simply drop EDO DRAM memory modules into a motherboard designed to use FPM DRAM. EDO DRAM is most commonly found in 72-pin SIMM format, but early DIMMs also used EDO DRAM. This memory format was most commonly used between 1995 and 1997.

One variant on EDO DRAM is *Burst EDO* DRAM. Burst EDO never caught on in the marketplace, although a few chipsets did support it.

SDRAM

In early 2000, the most common type of memory used on computer motherboards is *synchronous DRAM* (SDRAM). SDRAM runs in synchronization with the system bus, unlike earlier memory types, which relied on *wait states* to allow the memory system to catch up with the system bus. Therefore, SDRAM allows memory access times of 5-1-1-1, or 120ns for four accesses on a 66MHz bus.

With the advent of motherboard busses run at speeds higher than 66MHz, SDRAM speeds had to increase. That is, SDRAM used on a 100MHz bus (as an example) has to be able to complete its accesses faster than SDRAM on a 66MHz bus—four accesses in 80ns, rather than 120ns. These faster SDRAM versions aren't different from 66MHz SDRAM in any fundamental way, but they do have special names: *PC100* and *PC133*. Each name includes a number corresponding to the maximum speed of a motherboard bus on which the RAM can be used. There's no problem in using PC133 SDRAM on a 100MHz or even a 66MHz system bus, so if you're in the market for SDRAM, it might make sense to buy the PC133 variety—but you'll pay a little more for it than for PC100 SDRAM.

SDRAM is usually sold on DIMMs. In fact, most DIMMs sold in 2000 are SDRAM; the older EDO DRAM DIMMs are quite rare today. Because most computers that accept DIMMs can use SDRAM, this doesn't pose compatibility problems when outfitting a motherboard with entirely new RAM.

> ### CAUTION
>
> Most motherboards don't allow you to mix SDRAM and EDO DRAM. Therefore, if you have a computer that uses older EDO DRAM DIMMs, you must either replace those DIMMs with larger SDRAM DIMMs or track down and purchase EDO DRAM DIMMs if you want to expand your computer's memory.

One potentially important variant of SDRAM is known as *double data rate SDRAM* (DDR SDRAM). DDR SDRAM operates by allowing *two* transfers per clock cycle, effectively doubling the speed of RAM. An assortment of chipset and CPU manufacturers, including AMD, SiS, and VIA, are promoting DDR SDRAM. Intel, by contrast, is promoting RDRAM, which offers a slightly greater speed increase. RDRAM is a patented technology requiring license fees, whereas DDR SDRAM is not so encumbered.

RDRAM

RDRAM is the latest form of memory to make its way onto x86 motherboards. As described earlier in this chapter, RDRAM is used exclusively on RIMMs; these memory modules were designed specifically for RDRAM.

RDRAM is unusual in that it incorporates its own bus. Previous memory technologies linked the RAM chips more-or-less directly to the memory bus controlled by the motherboard's chipset, which in turn linked fairly seamlessly to the CPU's memory bus. RDRAM adds another bus to the equation. This bus transfers 16 bits at a time, but operates much faster than the CPU's RAM bus. In early 2000, most CPUs run at an external clock rate of 100MHz and transfer 64 bits per memory access. RDRAM's Rambus, by contrast, operates at 800MHz. Even with only 16 bits per transfer, RDRAM is twice as fast as conventional SDRAM. In fact, RDRAM incorporates additional tricks to bring effective RAM speed close to three times that of PC100 SDRAM.

An RDRAM RIMM has its own internal structure, consisting of a 128-bit wide bus split into eight 16-bit banks. Each bank itself operates at 100MHz, hence the 800MHz total speed (8 banks × 100MHz = 800MHz). The internal operation at 100MHz means that the RAM chips used by RDRAM need not be substantially more technologically advanced than SDRAM; they're simply harnessed in parallel to produce greater net speed.

RDRAM is rare in early 2000, but is expected to become more common as the year wears on. Its greater speed will be a virtual necessity as CPU bus speeds increase. Recent Intel motherboard chipsets use RDRAM (refer to Table 2.2 for details). Because RDRAM requires support for the Rambus technology in the motherboard chipset, it won't become common until most motherboards support it.

Exotic and Non-Motherboard RAM Types

In addition to these mainstream RAM types, others exist. Some, such as Burst EDO DRAM, are variants on these common types. Others are used in specialized applications. For instance, video cards require their own RAM, and various forms of RAM specialized for this application have emerged, as discussed in the section titled "Video RAM" in Chapter 12.

Matching Memory to the Motherboard

If you're looking to upgrade the memory on an existing computer, you might think you now know enough to do the job. Sadly, this might not be the case, because additional RAM characteristics can disrupt an otherwise sound RAM match. Typically, if you mismatch some additional factor, you get unreliable computer operation, although in some cases the computer fails to recognize the RAM. In rare cases, you might even damage the motherboard or the RAM.

Checking Supported Memory Speed

Until PC100 and PC133 SDRAM came along, memory speed was measured in nanoseconds (ns). Indeed, even PC100 and PC133 RAM speed is measured in ns; it's just that the names

PC100 and *PC133* are designed to make it easier to match the memory type to the mother-board. If you're using a motherboard that supports SDRAM but that doesn't specify PC100 or PC133 memory, either type is probably fine, assuming you're not expanding existing EDO DRAM. Alternatively, you can purchase SDRAM that's slower than PC100, if you run your motherboard bus at less than 100MHz.

Whether you're using slower-than-PC100 SDRAM, EDO DRAM, or FPM DRAM, you should check your motherboard's manual for information on the speeds in nanoseconds of memory supported by the motherboard. For instance, a motherboard might support EDO DRAM with speeds of 70ns or less, or SDRAM with speeds of 15ns or less. Note that, when expressed in nanoseconds, lower values are faster, and therefore better. If a motherboard requires 70ns EDO DRAM, you can install 60ns EDO DRAM and you should encounter no timing-related prob-lems. This contrasts with the PC1*xx* labeling, in which a higher value is faster—PC133 SDRAM is faster than PC100 SDRAM.

If you've got an existing FPM or EDO RAM module and want to determine the speed of the chips it contains, you can often do so by examining the codes on the chips themselves. For instance, consider Figure 3.3, which shows a 30-pin SIMM. Two of the chips on this module contain the code *V53C404FK70*, while the third chip contains the code *VT531000AJ-60*. The early part of each code is unimportant for determining the speed of the module; it's the final two digits which are important. In the case of Figure 3.3's SIMM, two of the chips are 70ns parts, while the third chip (which provides the parity bit) is a 60ns part. The SIMM as a whole is only as fast as its slowest component—70ns. RAM chips rated at 100ns or slower omit the final digit of the speed, so a 100ns chip has an ID number that ends in *10*, not *100*. SDRAM chips use a different numbering scheme, and most modules containing such chips have stickers identifying them as PC100 or PC133 DIMMs.

FIGURE 3.3
The speeds of individual chips on a RAM module are printed as part of the chips' part numbers.

Mixing Memory Types

Most motherboards don't cope well with a combination of SDRAM and other RAM types. Therefore, if you use any SDRAM on a motherboard, you can't normally use other memory types. As a general rule, mixing FPM DRAM with EDO DRAM doesn't pose as many problems, but you should check with your motherboard's manual to be sure.

Some motherboards don't work well with mixed SIMMs and DIMMs, even when both module types contain the same type of RAM. You should therefore consult your motherboard's manual before adding RAM of one type to a system that contains another type of memory. Even when mixing types is allowed, it might not be possible to use all the RAM sockets. For example, a Pentium motherboard might contain two 168-pin DIMM sockets and four 72-pin SIMM sockets (two banks of two sockets). The motherboard might support only three banks of memory total, however, meaning that you must leave either one DIMM socket or two SIMM sockets unoccupied. Once again, you should consult your motherboard's manual for details.

Miscellaneous Additional Factors

Particularly with older memory types, there are additional factors that can influence the reliability of specific memory modules in specific motherboards. These factors include

- **Jumper settings**   Early 80486 and earlier computers often used jumpers on the motherboard to identify the amount of RAM installed. Later 80486 and later computers generally auto-detect the amount and, where applicable, type of memory. If you have an older motherboard, you might need to adjust jumper settings when you add or remove RAM.

- **Number of chips**   In the mid-1990s, there was a great deal of discussion about 2- or 3-chip 30-pin SIMMs as opposed to 8- or 9-chip 30-pin SIMMs. The 2- or 3-chip SIMMs used higher-capacity chips than did their 8- or 9-chip counterparts of the same capacity, and this difference resulted in some subtle electronic differences. The 2- and 8-chip SIMMs lacked parity, whereas the 3- and 9-chip variants were parity SIMMs. In general, it's best to keep the number of chips on each SIMM the same, particularly within a single bank, on motherboards of this era. More recent motherboards that use 72-pin SIMMs and 168-pin DIMMs are less troubled by such effects.

- **Sidedness**   Memory modules can have chips mounted on one or both sides. This characteristic is correlated with electronic differences, and some motherboards have specific requirements for single- or double-sided SIMMs or DIMMs. These requirements are usually documented in the motherboard manual, so you should check there for further information.

- **Parity**   If you plan to expand your memory, try to use parity memory if your system currently uses it, or non-parity, if not. Most computers report whether the memory is parity or non-parity in a brief display during bootup.

> **TIP**
>
> You can see the BIOS's hardware information display, including a summary of the memory type, by placing a blank formatted but not bootable floppy disk in the floppy disk drive and rebooting the computer. Be sure the BIOS is set to boot from the floppy disk before doing this, or the computer might try the hard disk first and boot Linux. Normally, when the BIOS encounters an unbootable floppy, it prints a short message on the screen and then stops, leaving the hardware information on display for you to read at your leisure. (The unbootable floppy message is actually contained on the floppy disk itself, and so varies depending upon how you formatted the floppy disk.)

- **Memory holes** Some motherboard BIOSes can be set to create or not create *memory holes* at particular locations, such as 16MB or 64MB. These memory holes are discontinuities in the memory map—small areas that aren't usable as RAM. Linux generally works with or without the memory holes, but if you experience problems in which Linux doesn't recognize all your RAM, you might want to check and change such settings in your BIOS.

- **Kernel parameters** Linux kernels prior to the 2.2.x series couldn't automatically detect the amount of memory past 64MB, so if you have an older kernel and a lot of memory, you might need to tell Linux how much memory you've got. You do this by adding a line like the following to your /etc/lilo.conf file and then rerunning lilo to reinstall the Linux boot loader:

  ```
  append="mem=nnnM"
  ```

The *nnn* value is the number of megabytes, as in *128* for 128MB of RAM. In some cases, it's necessary to use this command even with 2.2.x kernels, although these kernels can usually detect the memory correctly.

As a general rule, you should read your motherboard's manual to learn about any further peculiarities it might have with respect to memory. A few boards require peculiar RAM variants, and you should be careful to track down appropriate RAM for such computers.

Cache Memory

When you think of a computer's memory, you probably think first of the large chunk of RAM that's installed in SIMMs, DIMMs, or RIMMs. This isn't the only type of memory in a computer, however. As I mentioned earlier, video cards usually have their own stores of RAM, as do various other components, including CD-ROM drives, hard disks, and even some sound cards. In addition, another type of memory, known as *cache*, is associated with the CPU, and often the motherboard. Understanding what cache memory is, what types of cache exist, and how cache interacts with the main RAM storage is important when you build or buy a new computer or expand an existing one.

What Is the Cache Memory?

When applied to computermemory, the term *cache* refers to a type of memory that's used to hold a duplicate of a larger memory store. A cache memory is invariably faster than the corresponding main memory. By placing the most often accessed data in the cache memory, overall system speed can increase, because the CPU can perform many of its memory accesses using the cache memory rather than the slower main memory.

In fact, caches go further than memory accesses. On most OSs, including Linux, a portion of RAM is set aside as a *disk cache*—RAM that holds the contents of a portion of a hard disk. The RAM I mentioned earlier on CD-ROM and hard drives is a cache that's built in to those devices.

For the moment, though, let's consider only the caches that exist on the motherboard and the components that attach directly to it: the CPU (L1) cache and the L2 cache.

L1 Cache

Closest to the CPU is the *level 1*, or *L1*, cache. Since the 80486, an L1 cache has been built in to the CPU itself. This cache runs at the CPU's internal speed, and so is very fast. On most CPUs, however, the L1 cache is also quite small. Table 3.3 summarizes the cache sizes used on some of the most common x86 CPUs.

TABLE 3.3   x86 CPU Cache Sizes

CPU	L1 Cache Size
80386	0KB
80486SX, 80486DX, 80486DX/2	8KB
80486DX/4	16KB
80486 Pentium OverDrive	16KB + 16KB
Pentium	8KB + 8KB
Pentium MMX	16KB + 16KB
Pentium Pro	16KB + 16KB
Pentium II	16KB + 16KB
Celeron	16KB + 16KB
Pentium III	16KB + 16KB

continues

TABLE 3.3   Continued

CPU	L1 Cache Size
AMD K5	16KB + 8KB
AMD K6	32KB + 32KB
AMD K6-2	32KB + 32KB
AMD K6-III	32KB + 32KB
AMD Athlon	128KB
Cyrix 6x86	16KB
Cyrix 6x86MX & MII	64KB
NexGen Nx586	16KB + 16KB
IDT WinChip	32KB + 32KB

Some CPUs feature a single *integrated* L1 cache, in which both data and program code is stored in just one cache area. Other CPUs use separate code and data caches, which are generally of the same size. This second type of CPU cache is indicated by two values in the *Cache Size* column of Table 3.3.

All other things being equal, a larger L1 cache is better. All other things are not always equal, of course, so cache size isn't the only measure of CPU performance. It can be an important one, however, particularly if you regularly run programs that perform most of their operations using compact computational loops. The most important portions of the code can sit entirely within the L1 cache if it's large enough, thus improving performance substantially. With a smaller cache, not all of the relevant code fits in the L1 cache, slowing performance.

Because the L1 cache is part of the CPU, it can't be expanded or replaced except as part of a CPU swap. For most people, it's best to think of the CPU as an integrated whole and to make a decision concerning what CPU to buy based on overall CPU performance. If you know that your uses of the computer will involve compact but intensive computational loops, however, you might want to favor a CPU with a large cache.

L2 Cache

A *Level 2*, or *L2*, cache is more copious than an L1 cache, but it's also slower. Its location varies depending upon the CPU. In 80486 and most Pentium-compatible (Socket 7) systems, it's located on the computer's motherboard. On Pentium Pro, Pentium-II, Pentium-III, AMD K6-III, AMD Athlon, and some Celeron processors, it's located on the CPU package, although it's not part of the same wafer that gave rise to the CPU itself. Table 3.4 summarizes the L2 cache sizes of those CPUs that incorporate an L2 cache. Some CPUs are available with differing cache sizes, either as different variants at the same CPU speed or with differing cache sizes at different CPU speeds. Early Celeron CPUs had no L2 cache, which greatly reduced their performance relative to Pentium-II CPUs, but more recent models include 128KB of an L2 cache.

TABLE 3.4 x86 L2 Cache Sizes

CPU	L2 Cache Size
Pentium Pro	256KB–1MB
Pentium-II	256KB–512KB
Pentium-III	256KB–512KB
Celeron	0–128KB
AMD K6-III	256KB
AMD Athlon	512KB

Placing the L2 cache on the CPU module improves performance relative to putting it on the motherboard largely because the cache can operate at a faster speed. An L2 cache on the motherboard operates at the motherboard bus speed (typically 100MHz today), whereas a cache on the CPU module has the potential to operate at much higher speeds.

NOTE

The NexGen Nx586 CPU required special motherboards, largely because it used a separate bus for its L2 cache. Like the cache of Pentium Pro and later Intel CPUs, the Nx586 cache ran at the CPU's internal clock rate, rather than the motherboard bus speed. The Nx586's L2 cache was physically located on the motherboard, however.

Pentium-class CPUs, including faster Socket 7 models from Cyrix and AMD, place the L2 cache on the motherboard. Most 80486 and Pentium-class motherboards include a certain amount of cache soldered to the board, and some allow you to increase the motherboard's cache by adding chips or special cache memory modules. There is no standardized form for such modules, although a number of attempts have been made to create such a standard. In the end, you should consult your motherboard's documentation for details.

3

MEMORY

> **NOTE**
>
> The AMD K6-III CPU includes an L2 cache in the CPU's package, but it's used on Socket 7 motherboards that contain L2 caches themselves. When used with a K6-III CPU, the motherboard's cache becomes a *Level 3* (L3) cache. Its importance is reduced relative to its importance when used with other CPUs, but the presence of three levels of cache does improve performance marginally. In theory, an L3 cache could be added to a Slot 1, Slot 2, Socket 370, or Slot A motherboard, but few such motherboards include a cache because the benefit is relatively minor.

When considering Socket 7 motherboards, it's quite important that you consider the maximum cacheable RAM supported by the motherboard. With many products, it's possible to install more RAM than can be cached. The end result is frequently *reduced* overall system performance. Suppose, for example, that a motherboard can cache up to 64MB of RAM, but that you install 128MB on that motherboard. In this scenario, only half the memory accesses can benefit from the cache. If you happen to run some important piece of code (such as the Linux kernel or a heavily-used program) from the uncached 64MB of RAM, that program performs worse than it would if run from the cached 64MB of RAM—or if only 64MB were installed in the computer. To be sure, adding RAM can still improve matters if you routinely run so many programs that you would otherwise make heavy use of swap space, but, in general, it's wise not to extend your RAM beyond that which can be cached by the motherboard. If necessary, buy a new motherboard that can support more cacheable RAM.

Tables 2.1 through 2.4 list the total cacheable RAM for Pentium-class motherboard chipsets. The actual cacheable RAM on any given motherboard, however, depends in part on how large a cache is installed in the motherboard. The details of how large a cache is needed to support a given amount of RAM vary with the motherboard chipset and the type of cache it uses, so you should check your motherboard's manual, or contact the motherboard's manufacturer, for details.

ROM

In addition to RAM and cache memory, both of which allow both reading and writing, computers contain various forms of *read-only memory* (ROM). ROMs are used to store seldom- or never-changed data on a computer. (When the data consists of program code, it's referred to as *firmware*.) On the motherboard, a ROM stores the *basic input/output system* (BIOS), which controls the computer's boot process and is used to set various important motherboard parameters. Various other devices also contain ROMs, such as sound cards, video cards, SCSI host adapters, hard disks, modems, and printers. I focus on the motherboard ROM in this chapter, although much of this information applies to the ROMs on other devices, as well.

Motherboard ROMs and ROM Variants

There are several different types of ROM chips that have been used in various capacities over the years. These include

- **Ordinary ROMs**   The most basic type of ROM is known simply as a ROM. This form of ROM is truly read-only; the information it contains is programmed at the factory and cannot be changed. Ordinary ROMs tend to be slow and expensive, and they're not favored for use on modern equipment because if a bug is found in the firmware contained on the ROM, the only way to correct that bug is to physically replace the ROM chip. You're most likely to find ordinary ROMs on very old computers.

- **PROMs**   *Programmable ROMs* (PROMs) are a step-up from ordinary ROMs because their contents can be altered. PROMs arrive from the factory with no information, and data can be stored on them with the help of special equipment. Once programmed, however, a PROM cannot be erased and reused. They're therefore not used much in modern computers.

- **EPROMs**   An *erasable PROM* (EPROM) is a step up from a PROM in that the EPROM's contents can be erased by exposing the chip to ultraviolet light. Because of this method of erasure, EPROMs have clear windows in their ceramic or plastic packages. Manufacturers usually place stickers over these windows in order to prevent accidental erasure. Reprogramming an EPROM requires removing it from the device and using a special EPROM programmer, so EPROMs are not used on most modern equipment. They were still common in the mid-1990s, so you might still find EPROMs in devices from that era.

CAUTION

If you pull a sticker off a chip and find a clear window in it, replace the sticker or put a fresh one over the window. Although you're unlikely to accidentally erase an EPROM, particularly if the EPROM resides inside a computer's case, there's no sense in taking any chances.

- **EEPROMs**   *Electronically erasable PROMs* (EEPROMs, also known as *flash ROMs*) are the most common type of ROM in modern computer equipment. As the name implies, EEPROMs can be erased and reprogrammed electronically. This feature allows a user to update a motherboard's (or other device's) ROM without removing any chips or even opening the case. (Some motherboards do require you to set a jumper before updating the system's ROM, so you must open the case on such computers.) EEPROMs represent a vast improvement in terms of ease of use, although they also pose certain dangers, because it's easy for an end user to make a mistake in reprogramming the EEPROM. If that happens the device generally becomes useless until the EEPROM chip is replaced. A few devices contain a backup ROM with just enough information to flash new data into the EEPROM. Consult your documentation to determine if your motherboard or other device has such a backup ROM.

With each step along this progression from ordinary ROMs to EEPROMs, the *only* portion of the name *read-only memory* has become less and less accurate. Even EEPROMs, however, are not easily erased. It's necessary to run a special program to send extra current through an EEP-ROM to erase or reprogram it; an ordinary write operation to the EEPROM won't change its contents.

TIP

If you need to reprogram a flash ROM, you should take two precautions. First, make a backup copy of the ROM's original contents and put it on a floppy disk. Most EEP-ROM update utilities let you do this. Second, perform your update during normal business hours. If something goes wrong and you render your device unbootable, you'll then be able to take the computer and the backup floppy to a computer repair shop, where a technician can use the backup you made to create a fresh EEPROM chip, or reprogram your existing EEPROM with the older but working contents. You might want to look into preparing a backup EEPROM chip, if your motherboard's EEPROM is removable. That way, you won't need to take the computer to a repair shop to fix it in case of a reprogramming error, assuming you're comfortable with replacing a socketed chip. Check your motherboard manual for information on the type of EEPROM chips accepted by your motherboard. You can buy blank EEPROM chips from electronic supply shops, and then program them yourself with an EPROM burner, or take the chip and a copy of the computer's BIOS to a computer repair shop to have them do the job. Some motherboard manufacturers will also sell spare EEPROM chips pre-programmed with the BIOS for your motherboard model. If your motherboard contains a non-flashable backup BIOS, creating a backup BIOS EEPROM chip isn't necessary, although you should still copy a full working BIOS to a floppy disk before flashing the BIOS.

Most motherboard flash utilities are written for DOS. You can run such a program from a floppy disk, even on a computer that contains only Linux partitions. If you don't own a license to DOS, look into FreeDOS (http://www.freedos.org). This free reimplementation of DOS is adequate for running a BIOS flash utility.

The Importance of the System BIOS

The computer's BIOS is the most low-level code that it contains, and some of the most important. Without a BIOS, a computer cannot boot. Every CPU looks to some particular portion of
memory for instructions when it's first turned on. The x86 PC architecture, like that of most
computers, is designed so that ROM resides at the CPU's start-up location. That ROM contains
code to help the computer boot from a floppy disk, hard disk, or some other device. The details
are complex and vary from one computer to another, but a series of operations starting at the
BIOS and ending with high-level programs in your OS leads to a running computer.

The x86 BIOS was originally designed to provide services to a running OS. For instance, the
BIOS contains routines that an OS can use to read data from a hard disk and to display information on the screen. Linux doesn't use these routines in ordinary operation, though, because
Linux is a 32-bit OS and these BIOS routines are 16-bit in nature. Aside from a transfer of
control during the boot process, Linux makes little use of the BIOS. As I've said, that BIOS
boot code is critically important.

The BIOS also contains routines to help you configure how your hardware operates. This portion of the BIOS is known as the *CMOS setup utility* because it sets options that are stored in
complementary metal oxide semiconductor (CMOS) memory. This is a small area of non-
volatile memory on the motherboard. Options you can set in the CMOS setup utility include
the order in which the BIOS looks for boot devices, memory timing characteristics (particularly on older motherboards), and what motherboard devices (EIDE ports, parallel ports, and
so on) are active. Most CMOS setup utilities are broken down into a number of sub-sections.
For instance, Figure 3.4 shows a typical main screen. Each option along the top (Main,
Advanced, and so on) corresponds to a screen full of options.

Some CMOS setup settings affect how Linux handles the hardware in question, and so are
important even in Linux. The details of CMOS configuration vary a great deal from one
motherboard to another, both because the BIOSes come from different producers and because
different motherboards support different features. Indeed, how you enter a BIOS's CMOS
setup utility varies from one BIOS to another. Typically, you press a special key or key combination (Del and F3 are two common options) early in the boot process, typically while the
motherboard is checking its RAM. (Most BIOSes present a prompt at the appropriate point in
the boot process, so look for it, or consult your motherboard's manual.)

ROMs on Plug-In Boards

As I mentioned earlier, many plug-in boards have their own ROMs. On modern boards, these
ROMs are generally EEPROMs, although they can be other types on older products. Like the
motherboard's ROM, expansion card ROMs contain code that's used by the device to help control itself. Some expansion card ROMs are also used in conjunction with the motherboard's
ROM. For example, SCSI host adapters and some network adapters include *boot BIOSes* that

latch into the computer's boot sequence. Because SCSI host adapters vary so much in their design, the standard motherboard BIOS can't control SCSI devices, including SCSI hard disks. The SCSI boot BIOS provides expansion BIOS code to allow a computer to boot from a SCSI hard disk. The SCSI adapter's BIOS can also provide a user interface similar to the CMOS setup utility. This utility typically provides a way to configure the SCSI host adapter, and can include options to configure or modify SCSI devices. For instance, many such utilities let you perform a low-level format on a SCSI hard disk. Similar comments apply to network adapters that allow you to boot from a networked hard disk.

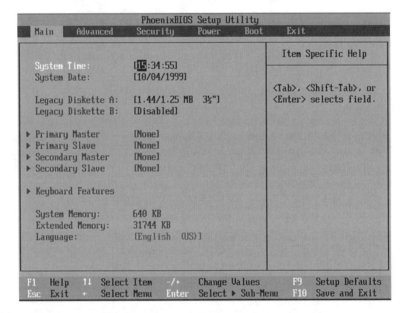

FIGURE 3.4
You adjust items in CMOS setup utilities using simple keyboard actions, which are summarized at the bottom of the screen.

NOTE

If you're running Linux on a non-x86 computer, you might be able to use PCI devices sold primarily for x86 computers. Some such devices, however, include ROMs that latch onto the x86 BIOS, and corresponding code for other platforms might not be available. In such cases, the device might not be usable on non-x86 hardware, or might present reduced functionality (such as an inability to boot from a SCSI hard disk). In other cases the device might not be usable on non-x86 hardware because the Linux driver doesn't compile properly on that hardware.

ROMs on most other devices, such as video cards, sound cards, and modems, don't interface so directly with the system BIOS. (Video card BIOSes do provide some limited services to the system BIOS, but these aren't used by Linux.) For the most part, these BIOSes provide firmware code that's used internally by the device in question. For example, the modulation techniques used by telephone modems are quite complex, and, in fact, many modems today are small computers in their own right. These modems require their own software, which is contained in ROMs. Upgrading the card's firmware can often improve the performance of the device. In extreme cases, you might be able to gain added functionality. For example, many modems sold in 1997 and 1998 used proprietary protocols for communicating at speeds up to 56Kbps. Eventually, the industry settled on the open v.90 protocol for such communications. Most modems using the earlier X2 and K56Flex protocols could be upgraded to support v.90 via a ROM upgrade alone.

> **NOTE**
>
> Some modems contain their important software in drivers rather than on the modem itself. Such modems are often called Windows-only modems or some abbreviation of that term. In general, these devices aren't usable under Linux, although there are exceptions to this rule. Chapter 18, "Modems," covers modems in much greater detail.

3

MEMORY

As with motherboard BIOSes, flashing an updated BIOS for an expansion card can generally only be done from DOS, or sometimes from Windows. FreeDOS (http://www.freedos.org) is very useful for Linux users who might need to run an update utility for such boards.

Summary

A modern computer can easily contain more than half a dozen different types of memory, including two or three types of cache RAM, the main system RAM, the motherboard BIOS ROM, RAM on a video card, and ROMs on a variety of expansion cards. Many of these memory types are best understood in the context of their specific devices, such as the ROM and RAM on video cards.

The main system memory itself is a fairly complex topic, because so many different types of memory have been used over the years—FPM DRAM, EDO DRAM, SDRAM, and RDRAM; distributed on SIMMs, DIMMs, and RIMMs; with varying speeds, sizes, and so on. Matching the RAM to the motherboard is one of the most important tasks you can undertake when you build a computer or upgrade the RAM in an existing computer. The most important thing you can do in making this match is to read your motherboard's manual.

Case and Power Supply

IN THIS CHAPTER

A computer's case is its most visually obvious feature. Computer cases vary substantially in size, shape, color, and decorative features. Just as important, cases vary in how easy they are to open, how many disk drives they can hold, what materials they're composed of, how well they're constructed, and how convenient their internal fixtures are to reach, repair, and replace. Some of these characteristics are obvious when looking at a case, or even just a photograph, but others require closer inspection. This chapter is devoted largely to these case features, in order to help you locate the optimal computer case when you want to build a new computer or give an old one a whole-body transplant from an original case that's become too small for your needs.

A component that's usually sold with the case is the power supply. The power supply converts your wall outlet's power source (120v AC in North America) to the 3.3v, 5v, and 12v DC required by the motherboard and disk drives. An inadequate or cheap power supply can make an otherwise fine computer behave erratically, so it's important that your computer have a good power supply.

Both the case and the power supply are tightly tied to the motherboard. The motherboard must mount properly in the case, which means that these two components must share a common *form factor* —the standards regarding the layout of mounting holes and overall motherboard size and shape. Similarly, the power supply must be able to provide the appropriate voltage levels to the motherboard. Fortunately, there are only a handful of common form factors, so matching the motherboard and the case isn't a difficult task. You should be aware of it from the beginning, however, because your choice of a form factor impacts all three components—the motherboard, case, and power supply.

Case Designs

One of the first questions you'll probably ask yourself with respect to a computer case is what overall design you want. Several possible designs exist. Most of these, and the most popular, can be classified into three categories: desktop cases, tower cases, and slimline cases. There are some exotic, specialized, and less-popular forms for cases, as well.

Desktop Designs

The original IBM PC XT and IBM PC AT computers were desktop designs. Cases of this form are relatively short but wide, as shown in Figure 4.1. They therefore consume a great deal of desk space, but it's often possible to place other objects, such as a monitor, on top of these cases.

Power Supply

Vertical 3.5-inch Horizontal 5.25-inch
drive bays   drive bays

FIGURE 4.1

Desktop cases can be convenient to work in because the motherboard lies horizontally.

CAUTION

Many desktop cases aren't designed to support the weight of today's large 19- and 21-inch monitors. Even a 17-inch monitor might be too heavy for some cases. Be sure to consult the case's documentation (generally just a single sheet of paper) or contact the case's manufacturer for information on how much weight the case can support.

4

CASE AND POWER SUPPLY

Modern desktop cases are fairly uniform in size, and therefore have similar capacities in terms of the number of disk drives they can support—about two 5.25-inch and three 3.25-inch devices. Their power supplies invariably lie in the right rear corner, and drive bays are in the right front corner (refer to Figure 4.1). Most desktop cases mount 5.25-inch drive bays horizontally, and 3.25-inch bays vertically, although some designs place the 3.25-inch bays horizontally as well. It's often important that the 5.25-inch drive bays lie horizontally, because CD-ROM drives that use trays often don't work well when the drives are vertical. Floppy disks, 3.5-inch hard disks, zip drives, and tape drives are usually less fussy about their orientation, so vertical positioning of these devices poses no problem.

The original IBM PC XT and AT computers had power switches attached directly to the power supply, positioned near the back of the right side of the case. This switch position was awkward, of course, and more recent models place a power switch somewhere on the front panel. Near this power switch is usually a reset button, one or two LEDs to indicate power status and hard disk activity, and occasionally other switches or LEDs. Through the mid-1990s, LEDs to indicate the CPU clock speed were not uncommon, as were key locks, which prevented the computer from running unless a key was inserted and turned. A turbo switch would often toggle some speed-enhancing feature of the motherboard. These last three features are quite uncommon on ATX cases.

Tower Designs

Because the desktop design consumes so much desk space, the tower configuration was developed. At its core, the tower design is nothing more than a desktop design turned on its side, with the power supply and drive bays at the top (see Figure 4.2). In fact it's often possible to simply turn a desktop case on its side to use it as a tower case. Doing so poses a few problems, the most important of these being that it's difficult or impossible to load many CD-ROM drives when they're mounted vertically. (CD-ROM drives that use caddies don't have difficulties with vertical orientation, and some tray-loaded CD-ROM drives include tabs that help retain a CD-ROM when the drive is mounted vertically.)

Tower cases include the same assortment of switches and front-panel LEDs as do desktop cases—a power switch, one or more LEDs indicating the computer's power status and hard disk activity, and on older cases, LEDs indicating the CPU speed and a keylock switch.

Tower cases can be difficult to work in if left in their vertical configuration, because inserting and removing expansion cards requires applying force that tends to topple the tower. It's therefore usually best to set a tower case on its side when working on it.

One advantage of the tower design is its flexibility; it's possible to create larger or smaller tower cases without adjusting the computer's footprint—it's just necessary to make the tower taller or shorter. Figure 4.2 shows a *full tower* case, meaning that it's larger than most. A *mid-tower* case is roughly the size of a desktop case, but turned on its side. *Mini-tower* cases are quite popular among lower-priced computers. These cases are shorter than a mid-tower case and typically have very limited room for expansion. The lines between these sub-varieties of tower case are blurry at best; one person's full tower might be another's mid-tower. Some companies might even use different names or break a range into more or fewer sub-styles. In the end, what's important is the size of the case and the number of drive bays it includes, not the name applied to it. Some tower cases, particularly the larger varieties, are available in variants with differing numbers of 3.5-inch drive bays.

Power Supply

5.25-inch
drive bays

3.5-inch
drive bays

FIGURE 4.2
A full tower case like this one provides a great deal of room for expansion and internal devices.

Slimline Cases

If you like a desktop design but prefer a case that's shorter, a slimline design might be just
what you need. These cases, as shown in Figure 4.3, are shorter than ordinary desktop cases—
note that the case has only one 5.25-inch and one 3.5-inch disk bay, one atop the other, with
less space beneath these bays than beneath the 5.25-inch bays in the case depicted in
Figure 4.1.

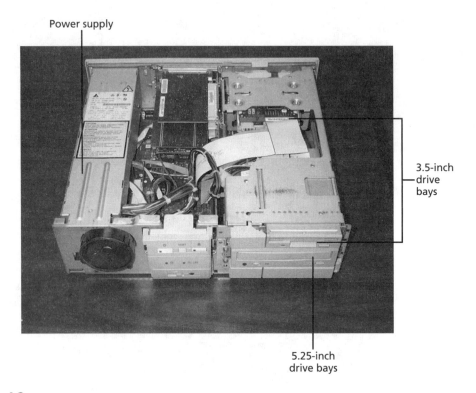

Power supply

3.5-inch drive bays

5.25-inch drive bays

FIGURE 4.3

A slimline case, such as this LPX model, tends to be more crowded than a conventional case.

Slimline cases require special motherboards that use the LPX or NLX form factors. (I recommend NLX because it's more standardized and newer.) You can't move a motherboard from a conventional desktop or tower case into a slimline case, or vice-versa. Most slimline computers come as prebuilt units from major manufacturers. These computers are often marketed for business desktop use, but of course there's no reason you can't buy such a computer for use at home, if you like. Unless the reduced height of these systems is of critical importance, I tend to favor ordinary desktop or tower designs, because they're more common and they typically give you more room for expansion.

Outside of the x86 arena, computers sometimes come in unusually slim slimline cases. These are sometimes referred to as *pizza box* designs, because they're little larger than a pizza delivery box. Pizza box computers generally offer a maximum of one or two expansion slots and few onboard amenities. x86 pizza box computer cases are quite rare, and when they exist, they generally use nonstandard motherboard designs.

Specialty Cases

If you buy or build a new computer, chances are you'll get one of the case types described previously. It's important to realize that there are variants on these common types, as well as more specialized designs.

Custom Variants of Standard Types

As described in the later section "Matching the Case to the Motherboard," most computer cases are designed to be mated with one of the standard motherboard types described in Chapter 2, "Motherboards." A few companies develop and sell their own unique designs. The cases used for these designs generally look much like ordinary desktop, tower, or slimline designs, but they use non-standard mounting holes for the motherboard and often use non-standard power supply types and case front plates. Such computers can be difficult to upgrade or repair. If you plan to buy a pre-built computer, I recommend asking about this aspect of the design. If the computer follows a standard form factor such as ATX, you'll have better options for future expansions and replacements than you will if the computer uses a proprietary form factor.

Many computers that don't use x86 CPUs follow their own unique form factors. Apple computers, for instance, don't use standard x86 PC layouts. If you want to use such a computer, you might have little choice but to use the designs supported by the company that controls that architecture.

Unusual Case Types

In rare circumstances, the usual assortment of case types doesn't suit your needs. In such a situation, you might want to investigate alternatives, such as

- **Notebooks**   Laptop and notebook computers need cases, of course, but they're even more miniaturized than are slimline cases. You don't generally buy a laptop case separately from the rest of the computer, as you can if you assemble a desktop computer yourself. Chapter 23, "Notebooks," covers notebook computers in greater detail.

- **Rack mount**   In some situations, a *rack mount* computer is desirable. In this design, the motherboard and other components are mounted in an open metal case, much like a workshop shelf system. These designs allow many computers to be housed together in one convenient location. Rack mount designs permit quick and easy access to the components of all the computers. They're of most interest for installations that require a large number of computers in a small space, such as a multi-computer cluster (see http://www.beowulf.org for information on one popular Linux cluster project).

- **Server**   A server case is typically much larger than the average case, in order to hold many hard disks. Such cases are also rather expensive.

- **One-piece**   From time to time, one-piece computers have appeared and become moderately popular. Most recently, this design was popularized by Apple's iMac in 1998 (see
Figure 4.4). The eMachines eOne uses a very similar design with x86 hardware. One-
piece computers generally leave little room for expansion and might require non-standard
motherboards, but they're more portable than most computers and they're generally more
compact, as well. Modern one-piece computers place most of the components in the
same case as the monitor, but some one-piece units from years past put the critical
components in the same case as the keyboard.

FIGURE 4.4

A one-piece computer places the motherboard, disk drive, and similar components in the same case with the monitor.

CAUTION

Unusual case designs can be quite convenient at times, but they can prove to be troublesome when it comes time to upgrade. This is especially true of one-piece units, but
less true of rack mount and server systems. You should carefully consider the costs
and benefits of any specific unusual design you consider.

Matching the Case to the Motherboard

The computer's case holds a number of additional components—a floppy disk, one or more hard disks, a CD-ROM drive, and so on. Indirectly, the case holds various expansion cards like video cards and sound cards. All of these components are available in one or two standardized sizes, so there's little chance that a component won't fit in a case unless you've simply filled all the available mounting points. The critical component that I haven't mentioned in this list is the motherboard. Matching the motherboard to the case presents the greatest potential for trouble. There are, of course, standardized form factors for motherboards, but it's critical to note the plural—there are *several* different motherboard form *factors*, as I described in Chapter 2. Even when you select a motherboard and case that follow the same form factor, it's possible for some detail to cause problems in fitting the motherboard and the case together.

Motherboard Layouts and Cases

Each of the major motherboard layouts described in Chapter 2 requires a different case type, although a few cases are designed to support more than one motherboard form factor. The form factors you're most likely to encounter include

- **AT and Baby AT**   The AT and Baby AT form factors were the most popular in desktop and tower designs through 1995. The AT motherboard form factor is larger than the Baby AT form factor, and requires a larger case. Cases capable of holding full AT motherboards tend to be mid-size or full towers or desktop designs. Cases that can hold full AT motherboards can also almost invariably support Baby AT motherboards. These motherboards can also be used in compact mini-tower cases. I don't recommend buying a new AT or Baby AT case today unless you already have a matching motherboard. In this case, because the AT and Baby AT designs are now obsolete, I recommend you locate a case that can handle either AT or ATX motherboards, so that you don't restrict your choices should you decide to upgrade the motherboard in the future.

- **ATX, Mini-ATX, Micro-ATX, and Flex-ATX**   As with the AT and Baby AT designs, these four designs represent variants on the same layout, with each one in succession representing a smaller design. Because ATX motherboards are wider than they are deep, whereas Baby AT motherboards are deeper than they are wide, most ATX cases are desktop, mid-tower, or full tower designs. Mini-tower ATX cases mount the power supply sideways, leaving space to the side of the power supply for the motherboard. This arrangement leaves little clearance for components on that side of the motherboard, typically including the CPU and memory modules. Mini-tower designs are more common for the smaller ATX variants. Full ATX cases can often accept smaller ATX variants, but not always.

- **LPX** LPX was the slimline case design common in the mid-1990s and earlier. Figure 4.3 shows an LPX computer. The details of LPX aren't perfectly standardized, so it can sometimes be difficult to match an LPX motherboard to an LPX case. I recommend avoiding such cases and their associated motherboards except under extraordinary circumstances, such as if you acquire a complete system at low cost.

- **NLX** NLX is LPX's replacement. Incorporating many of ATX's features, such as software-controlled power supplies, NLX is better standardized than is LPX, and is therefore a better choice than LPX for a new computer.

- **WTX** WTX is a new layout designed with Intel's new Itanium processor in mind. Unlike most earlier case designs, WTX includes specifications relating to required case features, case cooling, and so on. WTX cases are virtually non-existent in early 2000, but might become more popular after Itanium's release. You can learn more about WTX at `http://www.wtx.org`.

Once you've decided upon a form factor for your motherboard and case, you should consider some further factors to help make sure your case and motherboard match.

Ensuring Adequate Case Size

In theory, any case advertised for a specific size motherboard should be large enough to hold that motherboard. Sometimes, however, the case and motherboard combine to make an unusually tight fit, or some case component might block an important part of the motherboard. Such difficulties are more common in AT and Baby AT cases than in later designs, and they're more common in small cases than in large ones. Ideally, you should buy your case and motherboard from the same dealer, so that if you have problems you won't have dealers pointing fingers at each other, each refusing to accept a return. If you have the luxury of examining the motherboard you're considering buying mated to your case of choice, watch for some features in particular:

- **Power supply clearance** On some cases, the power supply overhangs the motherboard. Be sure that there's adequate clearance for any components that might reside under the power supply.

- **Drive bay clearance** Sometimes, 3.5-inch drive bays abut the motherboard, much as a power supply might. As with the power supply, be sure the drive bay leaves enough clearance for any components under the bay. Similarly, you must run cables from the motherboard or cards connected to it to the drives you mount in the bays. Be sure you can do so without too much difficulty. Some cases, particularly slimline designs, place one or two hard drive bays in peculiar locations, so don't restrict your check for drive bay clearances to the usual location at the front of the case.

- **Motherboard clearance**   I've seen cases in which a motherboard literally scrapes one or more components (typically a power supply) when inserted. This usually doesn't pose a serious problem, but it can impose stresses on the motherboard you might prefer to avoid.

- **Mounting hole locations**   Try to confirm that the case and power supply contain sufficient overlap in mounting hole locations to mount the motherboard safely. I've seen a few combinations, particularly in Baby AT cases and motherboards, in which a particularly small motherboard only has three or so mounting holes in common with a case. Such a situation can lead to instability and, therefore, unreliable operation.

Expansion Room

A new computer should be like a new home—big enough for all your belongings. As time goes on, though, your belongings are likely to expand to fill the available space. In a computer, this expansion takes two forms: disks and other disk-like devices and expansion cards you plug into the motherboard. If you buy or build a new computer that has insufficient room for expansion, you must make difficult choices to work around these limitations.

Free Drive Bays

One of the primary characteristics of any desktop computer case is the number of *bays* it contains for drives of various types—hard drives, floppy drives, CD-ROM drives, tape backup drives, zip drives, and so on. For most desktop cases, each bay can be classified into one of four categories:

- Visible 5.25-inch
- Hidden 5.25-inch
- Visible 3.5-inch
- Hidden 3.5-inch

Hidden bays are recessed into the computer's case so that the devices they hold aren't exposed to the outside. Hidden bays are therefore useful mainly for hard disks. Hidden 5.25-inch bays are rare in today's computers, because the vast majority of 5.25-inch devices work with removable media such as CD-ROMs and tapes. Most cases today have at least one representative of each of the remaining three categories, although there are exceptions to this rule.

4

NOTE

Cases come with panels you can snap into place in front of unused visible bays. You can also use a hard disk in a visible bay and use these panels to block access to the hard drive. If you leave off this panel, you can disrupt air flow patterns in the case, and make it easier to accidentally jar the hard disk.

In years past, bays were commonly classified by *height*. *Full-height* bays could hold the large hard drives of the mid-1980s. In time, *half-height* bays and devices came into being, and today the vast majority of 5.25-inch devices are half-height. *Third-height* devices are, as you might imagine, one-third the height of full-height devices. Most 3.5-inch devices are third-height. Some cases are designed in such a way that you can add devices of any height to at least some bays, or consolidate them as necessary. For instance, a bay might take a single full-height drive or two half-height drives.

All other things being equal, you should maximize the number of available drive bays in any case you buy. As a general rule, visible bays are more flexible than are hidden drive bays, and 5.25-inch bays are more desirable than are 3.5-inch bays.

TIP

It's possible to mount 3.5-inch components in a 5.25-inch bay by using an adapter like the one shown in Figure 4.5. Some of these adapters (like the one shown in Figure 4.5) are designed for hard disks. Some of these include a fan to help cool a hard disk (one of these appears in a bay near the top of Figure 4.2). Others contain openings to let you insert tapes, floppy disks, or other 3.5-inch media.

FIGURE 4.5

You can mount a 3.5-inch device inside the inner rails of an adapter, and then mount the adapter in a 5.25-inch drive bay.

In tower cases, the main thing you gain as you move from mini-tower to mid-tower to full tower is drive bays. Because 3.5-inch devices are generally third-height, whereas 5.25-inch devices are usually half-height, adding 5.25-inch bays adds more in the way of size to a case.

As a general rule, I suggest getting a case with at least two free drive bays beyond those you intend to use in the near future. At least one of these bays should be a visible 5.25-inch bay. This gives you the flexibility to add two devices, at least one of which can be a removable device.

One final consideration relating to bays is the method of drive mounting. Disk devices contain mounting holes intended for attaching the drive to a computer case. Many cases, however, use mounting *rails*. You attach the rails to the device, and you can then slide the device into the computer. An example is shown in Figure 4.6. Sometimes these mounting rails are designed so that you don't need a screwdriver to remove the device from the computer.

Mounting rail screws or
snaps into place

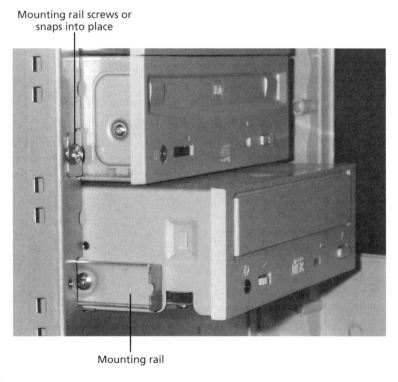

Mounting rail

FIGURE 4.6

Mounting rails let you slide a device in and out of a drive bay with relative ease.

4

CASE AND POWER
SUPPLY

Back Panel Cutouts

Most cases are designed to let you attach external devices, such as printers, external modems, and mice, via connectors on the back panel of the case. There are three types of connectors commonly used, from the point of view of the case:

- **Motherboard-mounted connectors**   As described in Chapter 2, all x86 motherboards have at least one connector permanently attached: the keyboard connector. Motherboards based on ATX and its variants support additional connectors, typically including serial, parallel, USB, and PS/2 mouse ports. The case includes appropriate openings to allow these connectors through, provided the case is designed for the motherboard type you use.

- **Card-mounted connectors**   Plug-in adapter cards, such as video cards, sound boards, and Ethernet cards, often include external connectors, or ports, as illustrated by the sound card in Figure 4.7. The vast majority of ATX cases have sufficient cutouts on their backs to accommodate all ATX motherboards, but on occasion you'll find an AT-style case with insufficient space for the slots on its motherboard.

FIGURE 4.7
When inserted in a case, the four connectors in the foreground of this card are accessible from the rear of the computer case.

- **Cable-linked connectors** Many cases include regions on their back panels that you can punch out to accommodate external connectors that link to internal connectors via ribbon cable. Such punch-out areas are particularly common on older AT-style cases, because the matching motherboards used ports that linked to external connectors via ribbon cables. Such punch-out openings are sometimes useful even on ATX systems, however. For example, the internal/external SCSI adapter described in Chapter 2 and shown in Figure 2.14 can connect through such a punch-out adapter. If your case lacks such openings, you can use an adapter that fits into an opening intended for an expansion card slot that you're not using.

Most motherboards have adequate back-panel cutouts, although the punch-out areas for cable-linked connectors are most common on larger case sizes. A few cases, particularly custom designs for major computer manufacturers, move one or more adapters to the front panel of the computer. USB and game port adapters are most likely to find their way to the front of such computers.

Beware of Non-Standard Designs

I've already warned you against non-standard motherboard and case form factors. Some cases, however, are non-standard in a more subtle way. Such cases might support standard motherboard sizes but use other non-standard components. For instance, many computers from large computer companies use front panels that curve in interesting ways. These curves often necessitate the use of unusual curving front panels on CD-ROM drives and other removable media devices. If you need to replace such a drive, you might be faced with a difficult job when it comes time to add the new drive, because it might not fit, or at least ruin the aesthetics of the case.

4

CASE AND POWER
SUPPLY

Expansion in the Face of Insufficient Space

So what happens if you've filled your computer case and you want to add one more device? You have several options:

- **Consolidate devices**   Sometimes you might be able to consolidate two or more devices into one. For instance, if you have two hard drives, you might be able to replace both drives with a single larger drive, thus freeing one drive bay. If you have an LS-120 drive, you probably don't need a 3.5-inch floppy drive. Similarly, there are Ethernet cards that support two Ethernet ports, combination Ethernet/SCSI cards, and other multifunction expansion cards that can let you squeeze more life out of your available back-panel space and motherboard slots.

- **Add an external case**   External cases are available for some devices. SCSI devices are particularly amenable to external placement, and you can purchase many SCSI devices in either internal or external varieties. You can convert an internal SCSI device into an external device by moving it into an external SCSI enclosure. There are even kits for converting EIDE devices for use externally. Unfortunately, external enclosures cost almost as much as a complete computer case, so this solution becomes quite expensive quite rapidly.

- **Replace the case**   Perhaps you're reading this chapter because you're considering this course of action. It's often the least expensive solution to a lack of space, especially if you need to add two or more devices and lack space for either of them.

Evaluating Computer Cases

Once you've settled on the basic characteristics of a case—AT, ATX, NLX, WTX, or some other design; desktop, slimline, or tower; and number and types of bays—you can begin shopping. I recommend shopping for cases in person, because so many details don't find their way into ads. Some case vendors, however, make life easier for Web shoppers by posting numerous clear photos, including close-ups of critical features, on their Web pages.

Construction Materials

In years past, most computer cases were made almost entirely from metal, the main exception being the front panel, which was usually plastic with a partial or complete metal backing. Today, many cases are built from plastic, usually with a metallic lining on the inside to block radio frequency (RF) transmissions.

In the United States, the Federal Communications Commission (FCC) has jurisdiction over just about anything that emits RF radiation. Computer circuit boards generate such transmissions as a side effect of their operation, and these transmissions can and do interfere with devices like televisions and radios. A poorly designed case can leak RF interference, and, if a neighbor traces the problem to your computer, you can be legally required to shut down your computer until it's fixed. Some case vendors claim their cases are "FCC Class A" or "FCC Class B" devices, meaning they comply with RF emissions standards for business or home use, respectively. These claims are false, however; the FCC doesn't rate individual components, only complete computers.

So long as a case with a plastic exterior has a solid metallic interior to block RF emissions, there's little reason to favor one type over another from a performance point of view. Plastic cases are increasingly available in a wide array of colors and shapes, which you might (or might not) find appealing.

Checking for Cut Corners

Computer cases vary substantially in price. In their most basic form, cases are metal boxes with some shaped metal parts to hold hard disks and other computer components. Therefore, one of the ways manufacturers sometimes reduce costs is to perform less complete finishing on the metal edges of the case. Unfortunately, this cost-cutting measure can cut other things as well, such as your fingers. The best cases fold the edges of metal components, particularly along the edges of case lids, as shown in Figure 4.8. A less expensive safety measure is to sand metallic edges until they're smooth—or at least less rough than they are when first cut. Some cases employ both techniques, generally reserving the folded-edge technique for removable lids and panels, and sanding interior edges smooth. All other things being equal, a case that makes heavy use of folded edges is preferable.

Most cases have one or more weak links—components that are unusually cheap and subject to breakage. For example, Figure 4.9 shows a broken plastic hinge on the front panel of one tower case. The hinge was designed to allow the front panel to swing away and then detach from the bulk of the case. The problem is that it had a tendency to scrape and catch against the metal components with which it was mated. The end result was severe wear along the top edge (to the left in Figure 4.8) and a complete break along the bottom edge (to the right in Figure 4.8). You should examine case parts, and particularly plastic parts that are involved in any movement, for signs that they might break prematurely or stop doing whatever they're designed to do.

FIGURE 4.8
The folded edges of this case panel won't cut your fingers.

FIGURE 4.9
A plastic latch or hinge is likely to break.

Evaluating Ease of Access

If you ever have cause to open a computer to remove, replace, or add components, you must be concerned with ease of access to those components. Here are some things to look for:

- **Ease of opening**   Cases from the mid-1990s almost invariably required 4–6 screws to hold the case together. You would remove these screws before pulling the lid off the case. Some cases use thumbscrews in place of conventional screws, and it's possible to purchase aftermarket thumbscrews that replace conventional screws for older cases. Some designs use fewer screws, or use latches instead of screws, so that it's not necessary to unscrew anything to open the case.

- **Number of panels**   Some cases have but a single opening, which is generally a large piece of metal bent to cover three sides of the case. These panels can be difficult to remove and replace, particularly in full tower designs. Other computers use separate panels for each side of the computer, which can be convenient when you only need access to one side of the computer. Some cases require that you open one panel before removing another; for instance, you might need to remove the front panel before opening the main case lid. These designs can be inconvenient.

- **Access location**   Most cases require that you manipulate something at the rear of the case in order to gain access to the interior. The manipulation can be removing screws or simply squeezing a latch. Other cases let you gain entry by performing similar actions at the front of the computer. Front access is generally easier than rear access, all other things being equal. Some tower cases now have sides that swing out or down, which can be quite convenient if you have sufficient clearance to the side of the computer.

- **Blocked motherboard components**   Particularly on small cases, drive bays, the power supply, and other case components sometimes block access to motherboard components. For instance, memory sockets might lie hidden behind drive bays. Try to avoid such designs.

- **Motherboard trays**   Sometimes it's difficult to fit a motherboard into a case. Some cases help ease this access by using a removable motherboard tray. You mount the motherboard to a case component that can be easily removed by sliding or lifting it out of the case. In the best of these designs, the motherboard tray includes the external slots for expansion cards, so you can remove the motherboard and its cards without removing the cards from the motherboard. This design allows for easy access to motherboard components that might be blocked by parts of the case or by cables within the case.

- **Access to drive bays**   If the case requires bolting drives directly to their bays, be sure you've got clear access to both sides of the bays. This access is awkward on some computers, because it might require removal of the motherboard or drive bays located to the side of the one you want to access. Cases that use rails generally provide easier access to drives.

4

CASE AND POWER SUPPLY

As you examine a case in a store, try to imagine where the various computer components will go in it, and what steps will be necessary to perform common upgrades on the computer— adding RAM, adding a hard disk, adding an expansion card, or replacing a CPU, for example.

Cooling

Most x86 computer cases include some provision for cooling. Most power supplies include a fan, but this fan is designed more for cooling the power supply than for cooling the interior of the case. On AT-style cases, the power supply fan blows out from the case, so air is drawn into the case through whatever openings it has. Ideally, the cool air drawn into the case flows over expansion cards, hard drives, and other components to help keep them cool. ATX-style cases reverse this air flow; the power supply draws air from outside the case and vents it within the case, typically directly over the CPU. The air then finds its way out of the case through vents provided for this purpose.

Each ventilation method has its advantages. AT-style cooling has the advantage that the air drawn over the computer's components is cool, as opposed to the ATX design, in which the air blown into the case has been heated by the power supply. ATX-style cooling, on the other hand, tends to build air pressure within the case, which is good for cooling, and allows a filter to remove dust particles.

Some components, such as the CPU, fast hard drives, and some high-end video chipsets, produce a great deal of heat. It's often beneficial to add cooling to these components. The most basic type of cooling is a *heat sink*. This is a metallic component with a number of fins, as shown in Figure 4.10. Because metal is a good conductor of heat, the heat sink warms up along with the component to which it's attached. Air can then flow around the heat sink's fins, drawing it away from the heat sink and the device that generates the heat. To improve the cooling effect, a fan can be attached to the heat sink to increase air flow around the fins.

CAUTION

Heat sinks with fans are particularly common on CPUs. Be sure your heat sink and fan are adequate for the CPU you use. A heat sink/fan combination that cools one CPU quite well might not cool another one. It's also important that you use *heat sink compound* between the heat sink and the CPU. This is a paste that conducts heat better than air. The goal is to use just enough heat sink compound to fill air gaps between the CPU and heat sink. When properly applied, the heat sink compound should be barely discernible as a greasy-looking film before you attach the heat sink to the CPU. You can obtain heat sink compound at most electronics stores, including Radio Shack (catalog #276-1372).

FIGURE 4.10
A heat sink's fins radiate heat away from the object to which it's attached.

It's not uncommon for large computers to have one or more auxiliary fans, in addition to the one in the power supply and any CPU heat sink fan. Two types are most common:

- **Whole-case fans**   A typical whole-case fan is a 3-inch square fan mounted on the front or rear panel of a case. Depending upon how it's mounted, the fan can either force air into or out of the case. Some include filters to keep dust out of the case. A variant design plugs into an unused PCI or ISA slot and vents through the rear port. This variant is particularly useful on smaller cases, which have no mount point for a 3-inch box fan.

- **Hard drive fans**   As hard drives have increased in speed, they've also increased in the heat they generate. In fact, the fastest modern hard drives, if run without adequate cooling, quickly destroy themselves from the heat buildup. 5.25-inch mounting brackets for 3.5-inch drives, like that shown in Figure 4.5, are therefore available with fans in the front. These fans are designed to cool modern 3.5-inch hard drives. You should consult your hard drive's manual concerning the need for such a fan, but, as a general rule, all 10,000rpm hard drives should be so cooled. Many 7,200rpm models can benefit from it, as well.

4

CASE AND POWER SUPPLY

Power Supply

Most cases come with power supplies. Each variety of case—ATX, AT tower, AT desktop, and so on—uses a power supply that's a different size and shape. In addition, each motherboard type uses a different power connector. Most importantly, AT and related boards use two power connectors that supply 5v, whereas ATX and related boards use a single connector that supplies 3.3v.

You should consider the features of a case's power supply when you buy a case. If a power supply fails or is inadequate, you can buy a new one to replace the one that came with the case. When you do so, you need to consider the features of power supplies.

Estimating Required Capacity

Computer power supplies aren't infinite founts of power for a computer. It's possible to overload a power supply, which can lead to erratic behavior. Each power supply also has a limited number of internal power connectors, and, if you run out of these connectors, it's necessary to add more by using special power splitter cables.

Power Supply Electrical Capacity

To understand power supply capacity, it's important to start with a fundamental relationship between three measures related to electricity: volts (v), watts (W), and amperes (amps). This relationship is

$$\text{Watts} = \text{Volts} \times \text{Amps}$$

For instance, if a 5v device draws 10 amps, it consumes 50 watts. Power supply capacity is measured in watts. For instance, a power supply might be rated at 235W. To understand how this translates into volts and amps, however, it's necessary to know the voltage drawn by the devices in question. In fact, various devices attached to modern computers each draw different quantities of power in 3.3v, 5v, and 12v amounts. To understand the capacity of a power supply, therefore, it's necessary to understand how many watts or amps it can provide at any given voltage. For example, a power supply might be capable of providing 14 amps at 3.3v, 22 amps at 5v, and 8 amps at 12v, for a total of 252.2W. Many power supplies, however, include a maximum combined output for combinations of voltages. For instance, there might be a 125W maximum for 3.3v and 5v operation, resulting in an adjusted total wattage of 221W.

If you want to be meticulous about acquiring an adequate power supply, you should seek out specifications on the power requirements of every component in your computer. Unfortunately, such information is hard to come by for some components, such as most expansion cards. Table 4.1 summarizes typical power consumption required by various types of devices.

TABLE 4.1 Power Consumption in Amps for Various Devices

Device	+3.3v	+5v	+12v
ISA card	0	2.0	0.175
EISA card	0	4.5	1.5
16-bit MCA card	0	1.6	0.175
32-bit MCA card	0	1.6	0.175
VL-Bus card	0	2.0	0
PCI card	7.6	5	0.5
3.5-inch floppy disk	0	1.5	1.5
3.5-inch hard disk	0	0.5	1.0
CD-ROM drive	0	1.0	1.0
Fan	0	0	0.1

Expansion card figures are maximums; those for other devices are typical values.

The motherboard's power draw varies with the CPU. Note that voltage regulators, which are required when using anything but one of the voltage levels provided by the power supply, result in some loss, so actual watts consumed is greater than you would expect by multiplying volts by amps.

As an example, consider a computer with one ISA card, two PCI cards, a 3.5-inch floppy disk, two 3.5-inch hard disks, a CD-ROM drive, and two extra cooling fans. Adding up these values, this computer requires 50.16W from 3.3v, 77.5W from 5v, and 70.5W from 12v, for a total of 198.16W. The motherboard consumes a few more watts, as well—perhaps 25W or so, depending on the board and CPU.

Of course, not all devices require their maximum amounts of power at the same time. Typically, for instance, hard disks require a great deal of power when they start up, to overcome the inertia inherent in stopped disk platters. A tape backup unit consumes little power unless it's in operation; likewise, for a floppy disk. This fact means that a power supply can be adequate most of the time but still fail at certain times, such as when the hard disks power up or when you use a tape drive and CD-ROM drive simultaneously. If you experience problems when you use a device, it's possible that an inadequate power supply is to blame.

4

CASE AND POWER SUPPLY

TIP

If you have several SCSI hard disks, you can reduce the startup power drain by configuring your SCSI drives to start up only when they're told to do so by the SCSI host adapter. Most drives can be configured in this way with a jumper setting, typically called *remote start* or something similar. The drives then power up after the motherboard has finished its initial tests, and the SCSI host adapter signals each drive to start in sequence, so they don't all start up at once.

As a general rule of thumb, a 235W power supply is adequate for small systems. If you add more than a handful of disk devices or loads of high-drain expansion cards, you might need to boost the capacity of your power supply. 300W and 400W power supplies are available for ATX systems, and are quite desirable for tower systems filled with devices.

Power Connecting Cables

One other aspect of power supply capacity is the number and types of power connect cables provided by the power supply. Most devices, including hard disks, CD-ROM drives, and tape backup drives, use standardized four-wire power connectors that are keyed to plug into the device in only one way. 3.5-inch floppy drives use smaller connectors, and motherboards use either one or two connectors, depending upon the type of motherboard.

CAUTION

AT and Baby AT motherboards use a pair of power connectors that must be inserted into the motherboard with the black wires next to each other. If you insert the power connectors backward, you can destroy the motherboard!

If you add more devices than the power supply has connectors, you can use one or more power splitters (shown in Figure 4.11) to increase the number of connectors. Instead of inserting a power supply power plug into a disk drive or other device, you plug it into the splitter, which then lets you deliver power to two devices rather than just one.

While internal power splitters can be extremely useful things, you should not over-use them, for two reasons:

- If you need lots of power splitters, that might be a sign that you're exceeding the capacity of the power supply. One or two splitters probably does not constitute a problem, but if you need half a dozen, it might be time to consider a more capable power supply.

- Each power splitter represents a potential failure point. If the power splitter's connection is weak, both attached devices can fail, sometimes mysteriously. I once traced a strange hard disk problem to a flaky power splitter.

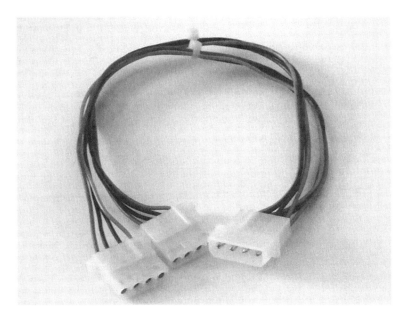

FIGURE 4.11
A power splitter lets you add devices to a computer even if the power supply doesn't have enough power leads.

On/Off Switches

Three types of on/off switch are common on x86 PCs:

- **Integrated into the power supply**   These switches, common on desktop AT-style cases, are part of the power supply. They are accessible from the outside of the case—in desktop systems, on the right side of the case near the rear. Some ATX power supplies also include on/off switches accessible from the back of the computer, but such switches are auxiliary to the main ATX power switch.

- **Remote switch on power supply**   Most AT-style tower systems include a toggle switch mounted on the front of the case. These switches are connected to the AT power supply by a cable. The switch itself is matched to the computer's case, and connecting the cables to the switch can be a nuisance, which makes replacing these power supplies a bit more trouble than replacing other types of power supply.

- **Remote switch through motherboard**   ATX and related motherboard designs are built to draw a tiny amount of power at all times. This current feeds circuits that watch for various events, which can result in the system powering itself up, such as a telephone ringing or the user pressing the power button on the front of the case. In these systems, the power button is therefore connected to the motherboard, not to the power supply, and the motherboard mediates all power-ups. ATX cases generally come with power buttons rather than toggle-type power switches.

Your case type determines the variety of power switch you get. Because of the prevalence of the ATX form factor today, your power switch is likely to be a motherboard-mediated design. Some ATX power supplies have switches on their backs. This feature is quite desirable, because it allows you to cut all power to the computer's circuits without actually unplugging the computer. This makes it safer to work on the computer, both for you and for the computer.

CAUTION

If your ATX power supply lacks a power switch, you should unplug the computer from the wall outlet before working inside the computer's case, in order to eliminate the possibility of injury from stray current on the motherboard. Unfortunately, this practice removes the most convenient means of grounding yourself—touching a metallic portion of the case—and therefore makes it more likely that you'll damage the computer through a static discharge. To reduce this risk, use an anti-static wrist strap or work where you can ground yourself frequently by touching a plumbing fixture or radiator.

If you have an AT-style case with a remote power switch, you must connect the power supply to the switch when you replace the power supply. Most power supplies have a diagram that indicates how you make these connections, but, in case yours is missing this diagram, make the connections as follows:

- The green wire, if present, is a grounding wire. Attach it to any convenient metal part of the case.

- The black and white wires connect to the angled tabs on the power switch.

- The brown and blue wires connect to the tabs that are parallel to one another on the switch.

> **CAUTION**
>
> The brown and blue wires always carry current when the power supply is plugged in! Therefore, you should only try to connect or disconnect these wires *after* unplugging the computer from the wall!

Power Supply Quality

Like all products, power supplies vary in quality, although it's hard for a consumer to detect this variation. Power supply quality differences manifest in terms of the stability of power delivered to devices inside the computer's case, even through power fluctuations in the current delivered to the computer. Over time, power fluctuations can damage or destroy the components inside the computer. In extreme cases, a power supply might conceivably deliver far too much power, or power at the wrong voltage, quickly destroying the computer.

To some extent, you can rely upon certifications to assure a minimum level of quality. In the United States, Underwriter's Laboratory (UL) certifies electrical products, including power supplies, for safety. Equivalents in other countries include the Canadian Standards Agency (CSA), Germany's TÜV Rheinland and VDE, and Norway's NEMKO.

A few manufacturers, most notably Astec (`http://www.astec.com`) and PC Power and Cooling (`http://www.pcpowerandcooling.com`) are noted for producing power supplies of unusually high quality. If you want to get the highest-quality power supply possible, you won't go far wrong with a product from either firm, assuming the power supply you purchase meets your wattage requirements.

If your power supply dies, you can obtain a replacement from a variety of local or mail-order computer parts suppliers. Generally speaking, any store that sells cases also sells power supplies. Be sure the replacement power supply you purchase matches the form factor of the one it's intended to replace (AT, ATX, and so on). You must typically unbolt the power supply from the case by removing four screws from the outside rear of the case—but be sure you get the correct screws, because some power supplies place their own screws in locations that are also accessible from the rear of the case. You must then disconnect all the power leads from the power supply to all the internal devices—the motherboard, hard disks, floppy disks, and so on. If it's an AT power supply, you must disconnect the power supply from the case's main switch. You can then remove the power supply and reverse the operation with the new unit.

4

Power Protection

A computer is an expensive product, and you're likely to want to protect it from mishaps. Power-related mishaps are particularly relevant to computers, and come in two forms: too little power (brownouts or blackouts) or too much (power surges). In the United States, electricity comes through your wall outlet at 120v, but there's always some small fluctuation to that value. While electrical appliances, including computers, can cope with some amount of fluctuation, larger fluctuations can prove to be quite damaging. There are several different types of devices you can buy to protect your computer against power problems:

- **Surge suppressors**   A *surge suppressor* (also known as a *surge protector*) is a device that blocks large power surges. These devices typically redirect dangerous voltages into the ground wire of your home or office, keeping your computer out of the loop. In the process, surge suppressors usually trip an internal circuit breaker, thus cutting off power to all devices. Really large surges can damage or destroy a surge protector. The theory is that it's better that it destroy the $50 surge suppressor than the $5,000 of computer equipment to which it's attached, so the surge suppressor is designed to sacrifice itself for the computer. UL has developed a standard, known as *UL 1449*, which outlines characteristics of an adequate surge suppressor. You should definitely look for this in any new surge suppressor you buy. Some surge suppressors also include jacks for telephone cords, and this is a valuable addition if you use a modem. A few models include similar jacks for cable TV cables, and if you use a cable modem, you should definitely consider such a model. (You're more likely to find cable-equipped surge suppressors in the television section of a department store than in the computer section.)

> **NOTE**
>
> The phone line protection of some surge protectors might or might not work with digital subscriber line (DSL) modems. The surge suppressor might or might not need to have four-line support to work with DSL modems, depending upon your wiring. Even if the appropriate wires are connected, surge protectors designed for telephones and conventional modems sometimes interfere with DSL operation, reducing connect speeds or preventing connections altogether. You can buy specialized DSL surge suppressors, or Ethernet surge suppressors to fit between the DSL modem and the computer, if you use an external DSL modem.

- **Line conditioners**   Surge suppressors are great for protecting your equipment from massive fluctuations, but smaller power fluctuations can take their toll as well. Most computers can weather events such as minor brownouts, typical power fluctuations, and even very brief power outages without too much difficulty. Such events can cause a power supply to fail earlier than it might, however, and can even cause your computer to malfunction. A *line conditioner* prevents these problems by forcing the power to more closely meet the desired specifications. This device can compensate for a mild brownout and turn a voltage level that fluctuates over a range of several volts into one that's much steadier. The end result is less wear and tear on your computer and a reduced chance of errors as a result.

- **Standby power supplies** A *standby power supply* (SPS) takes the line conditioner one step further, by adding a battery backup. If the power delivered to the SPS fails or drops below a certain level, the battery kicks in and continues to deliver power for a certain period of time. With any luck, the battery lasts long enough to let you safely exit from all your programs and shut down the computer. There is, however, a very brief interruption in power as the SPS shifts over to its battery. Most computer power supplies can weather the shift without too much difficulty, but the brief gap in coverage is undesirable and could conceivably cause memory errors or other problems, particularly if your computer's power supply is low in quality.

- **Uninterruptible power supplies** An *uninterruptible power supply* (UPS) is like an SPS in concept, but the design is different. Rather than detect a failure and switch over in the event of a failure, a UPS always operates from its battery, simultaneously charging and discharging it. In the event of a power failure, therefore, your computer experiences no interruption whatsoever; the UPS's battery simply begins draining without being charged. Some companies advertise their SPSs as if they were UPSs, so terms such as *true UPS* are often used for UPSs.

At a minimum, you should purchase a surge suppressor for your computer system. In fact, I use surge suppressors on all my expensive electrical appliances, such as my television, stereo, and so on. The drawback to a surge suppressor is that it offers no protection against a power outage. A UPS or SPS is an extremely useful device if you live in an area that experiences frequent power outages; you can weather an outage of a few minutes as if nothing happened, and power down safely in case of a longer problem. As you might expect, the cost of these devices rises as you move up the scale from a surge suppressor to a UPS.

All but the lowest-level UPSs contains an interface to the computer. This interface is generally a serial cable, and you can run a Linux program to monitor the UPS's status. In the event of a power failure, the daemon can order a safe shutdown of your Linux computer, thus saving you the bother, or doing it even if you're away. UPSs vary in how they communicate with the computer, however, so you should look into available UPS software. Some UPS manufacturers provide Linux software for their UPSs, but for others you might need to rely upon generic Linux software that works with several models, or you might be entirely out of luck. The Linux UPS HOWTO document (included with all major Linux distributions) has pointers to more specifics on UPS models and UPS software.

Summary

A computer's case is the most externally visible component of a computer, with the possible exception of the monitor, keyboard, and mouse. The case houses all the major computational devices of most computers—the motherboard, CPU, hard disks, expansion cards, and so on. A poor choice in a case can cause you grief for months or years to come, as you struggle against it whenever you upgrade some other component or curse its ungainly size. Checking a case out in person and looking for a few key features can go a long way towards ensuring that you have a computer with which you can live.

One of the most important components of a case is the power supply. The most important issue in picking a power supply is to get one that supplies adequate wattage to the components that reside in the computer's case. The 235W power supplies that are common today are adequate for most modest computers, but if you expect to load your system up with lots of hard disks, internal tape drives, half a dozen expansion cards, and so on, you might want to look into a larger power supply.

Storage

PART

II

IN THIS PART

Hard Disks

IN THIS CHAPTER

Hard disks use a fairly mature technology and are well standardized in their interfaces. Therefore, you're unlikely to encounter Linux-related difficulties with specific models of hard disks. (SCSI host adapters are another matter, however. Chapter 9, "SCSI Host Adapters," covers this matter in more detail.) When you purchase a hard disk, therefore, there are few Linux-specific issues you must consider. For the most part, a hard disk that's good for use in any other OS is good for use in Linux.

How you *use* a hard disk is somewhat different in Linux than in other OSs. Linux uses its own filesystem (currently ext2fs, although at least four new filesystems are in the running to become the next standard Linux filesystem). You probably want to partition a hard disk for Linux differently than you would partition it for most other OSs. There are also Linux utilities available that can help you get improved performance out of a hard disk. This chapter covers these issues, as well as the basics of hard disk technology.

Linux Disk Space Requirements

As with RAM requirements, official Linux disk space requirements vary from one distribution to another, but similar configurations of two distributions will require similar amounts of disk space. As with RAM requirements, most minimum disk space requirements are on the skimpy side. Making adjustments for your particular usage patterns can be tricky in some cases, particularly if you're unfamiliar with Linux.

Minimum Space Needed

Table 5.1 summarizes official disk space requirements for various popular Linux distributions.

TABLE 5.1   Official Disk Space Requirements of Linux Distributions

Distribution	Minimum Disk Space
Caldera OpenLinux 2.3	170MB
Corel Linux 1.0	500MB
Debian GNU/Linux 2.1	35MB
Linux Mandrake 7.0	500MB
Red Hat Linux 6.1	250MB
Slackware Linux 7.0	80MB
SuSE Linux 6.3	300MB

It's usually not possible to install a distribution on less than the official minimum amount of disk space because the installation routines won't let you remove packages to bring the disk space requirements down. It is often possible, however, to install the official minimum and then strip it down by removing packages after they've been installed. Therefore, if you've got the disk space to *temporarily* install 500MB of packages, you can install a big distribution like Corel or Mandrake and then remove unneeded software.

As with RAM, some distributions' minimum requirements are based, in part, on more generous assumptions about what programs will be installed and used. The 35MB and 80MB minimums for Debian and Slackware, for instance, are based upon text-only Linux installations. Although the X Window System (X) *can* be installed in under 100MB, by the time you add useful utilities—especially a desktop environment like the GNU Network Object Model (GNOME) or the K Desktop Environment (KDE)—the disk space requirements for X alone are likely to exceed 100MB.

As a general rule of thumb, I consider 200MB to be a bare minimum disk space requirement for a text-only Linux installation, and 500MB for a configuration that includes X and a reasonable assortment of X-based programs. With today's hard disks routinely exceeding 10GB in capacity, these minimums aren't difficult to meet, even when the hard disk is split between Linux and some other OS.

Estimating Space for Your Needs

New users of Linux frequently post on Usenet newsgroups asking for advice on how much disk space to devote to Linux. The answer is almost always "it depends," and justifiably so. Minimum disk space requirements such as those printed on Linux distribution boxes can tell you how much space a minimal Linux system, or even a Linux system configured to perform certain specific types of tasks, requires. These estimates aren't generally very helpful when it comes to deciding how much disk space *you* need on *your* computer. Even more difficult is the task of determining how to *partition* your disk space—that is, how to break it up into smaller chunks for ease of management, security, and other purposes.

The best way to determine how much disk space you need, short of installing everything you want on a really big disk and then checking free disk space, is to consider the needs of individual applications and users. Here are some considerations:

- **Basic Linux tools**   For most desktop users, a minimal Linux installation consumes about 500MB of disk space. This total includes tools and utilities like X, GNOME or KDE, mail clients, editors, the GNU C Compiler (GCC), a few basic games, and so on.

- **Additional major applications**   If you plan to run specific programs, like the StarOffice or WordPerfect office suites, check their disk space requirements. Sometimes these requirements are quite substantial. For instance, Activision's (http://www.activision.com or http://www.lokigames.com) Civilization: Call to Power game for Linux requires 320MB of disk space.

- **Additional minor applications**   Small tools also require disk space, and these requirements can add up quickly. It's difficult to enumerate all the little tools you might want to
  add, so it's best to just take a wild guess, based on your expectations of how many such
  programs you'll install. Assume each small program will consume 1–5MB of space, and
  multiply that by the number of extra programs you intend to install.

- **Program operating files**   Some programs generate large files, or numerous small files,
  as part of ordinary operation. For example, if you intend to run your own news server
  locally, that program will store news articles on your hard disk. If you only handle a few
  small newsgroups, the disk space required might be small. If you're configuring a news
  server to handle even a tenth of the thousands of newsgroups available, however, plan on
  devoting multiple gigabytes of disk space to it. You must have a fairly complete understanding of your programs to know what they'll generate in the way of operating files.
  Fortunately, most end-user programs don't generate huge temporary or operating files,
  only the files they're designed to create, such as spreadsheet or word processor document
  files. (Many programs do create one or more *temporary* files, but these are seldom much
  larger than their final data files.)

- **End user files**   Unless you're operating a server to handle limited tasks (such as an
  Internet router or news server), your computer will have one or more user accounts, and
  your users will generate files. If you're the only user of the computer, you can probably
  estimate the size and type of data files you'll generate. Will they be business letters,
  spreadsheets, program source code, graphics files, full-motion video, or something else?
  The types of files you generate will determine how much disk space to allocate for user
  files. If more than one person uses the computer, you must make estimates for each user.
  If you expect the users to generate similar file types, you can make one estimate and
  multiply by the number of users.

Once you've reached an estimate for the amount of space you'll need, multiply that estimate
by at least 3 to determine how much disk space you'll need. People frequently underestimate
how much disk space will be needed, and even when that doesn't happen, the tendency of files
to accumulate and fill all available space guarantees that disk space *will* be filled, sooner or
later.

Tips for Disk Partitioning

The x86 PC supports a method of dividing disk space into several segments, known as *partitions*. Partitions can be used to separate different OSs' files from one another, or to divide a
single OS's files into logical groups. In Linux and other UNIX-like OSs, partitions are used for
several reasons:

- **Security**   Placing critical files on separate partitions can give you fine control over mount options that can influence how users can access the partitions' files. For example, you can mount a partition that contains critical files (such as system software files) as read-only to prevent users from writing to the filesystem even in the event of an error in a directory's permissions.

- **Protection from runaway file creation**   Sometimes a program creates a file or files that are much larger than expected. For example, if you operate your own mail server, and if some inconsiderate or malicious individual sends a 1GB email message, that file could end up consuming a huge amount of disk space—possibly enough to overrun your available disk space and cause problems in other programs. If you split critical directories into separate partitions, you can reduce the damage such an overrun can cause, thus keeping the system mostly operational. The downside is that each partition is smaller than it would be otherwise, so you're more likely to encounter a problem as the disk space consumption rises.

- **Protection from filesystem damage**   Disk errors are a fact of life. When an error damages a disk partition, you're better off if that partition holds only a fraction of your data. In the event of a complete and unrecoverable error, a single small partition can be easier and quicker to restore than a larger partition containing all your data. In the event of a non-catastrophic error, a small partition is usually quicker to check for errors than is a large partition.

- **Speed**   Particularly if you have more than one hard disk, creating separate partitions can improve your system's speed, by spreading disk accesses across two hard disks. I cover this aspect of disk partitioning later in this chapter in the section titled "Using Multiple Disks for Better Performance."

- **Easier system upgrades**   When you want to upgrade your Linux system, it's sometimes desirable to completely wipe your existing installation and start again. When you do so, it's easier if your users' home directories—and perhaps directories containing programs that aren't part of the OS itself—reside on separate partitions. That way, you can leave those partitions alone, completely wipe the Linux partitions, and install a new version of the OS.

On the other hand, creating many partitions has its downside, as well:

- **Uncertainties about partition size**   Unless you're an experienced administrator, it can be difficult to judge how large to make each partition. A wrong guess can cause a great deal of trouble as you resize partitions or use symbolic links and strange directory structures to get around the problem.

- **Reduced performance**   If you lay out partitions on the disk in a less-than-optimal order, you can hinder your overall disk speed.

- **Reduced ability to create hard links**   A *hard link* is a way to create two directory entries that point to the same file. Such links can only exist when both directory entries are on the same partition as the file in question. You can, however, create a *symbolic link* from one partition to another. Symbolic links operate more slowly than do hard links.

If you're new to Linux, I recommend you make do with just two to four of the following partitions:

- **The swap partition**   The swap partition, which I describe shortly, serves as an expansion area for RAM.
- **The root (/) partition**   All Linux distributions require a root filesystem, and this resides on a hard disk partition. All other partitions are mounted at some point on the root partition, or on a partition that is itself mounted on the root partition or another partition. Figure 5.1 illustrates this integrated directory tree structure.

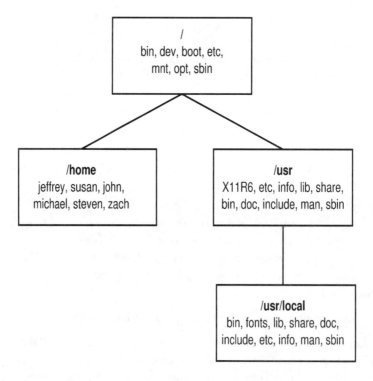

FIGURE 5.1

Linux allows you to mount a partition at almost any location in its unified directory tree.

- **A /home partition**   Most Linux distributions place user files in a directory called /home; each user has a subdirectory under this /home directory. For instance, in Figure 5.1, each of six users has a subdirectory in which to store files. Isolating user files from the rest of the OS is one of the best uses of partitioning, because it provides some of the greatest benefits. Also, most new administrators find it easier to estimate space required for user files as opposed to space required for various subdirectories in the Linux directory tree.

- **A /usr/local partition**   Traditionally, /usr/local is used for programs you build yourself, as opposed to installing from a pre-built package file. These files are therefore customized for your local installation. It's common to want to keep these files when you upgrade your OS, so putting them on a separate partition makes sense.

> **NOTE**
>
> Figure 5.1 shows /usr/local mounted onto a separate/usr partition. This arrangement isn't required, however; /usr/local can mount directly onto the root partition. Figure 5.1 is drawn the way it is to illustrate the fact that partitions *can* mount onto partitions other than the root partition, and to illustrate the desirability of a separate /usr partition for more advanced administrators.

If you've used Linux before and want to create a more advanced configuration, you might want to consider creating additional partitions for one or more of the following directories:

- **/usr**   The /usr directory contains many program and configuration files. In fact, the bulk of a Linux distribution resides in the /usr directory.

- **/usr/X11R6**   This directory contains files related to X, including the X server and most X programs.

- **/opt**   Many recent third-party programs have taken to installing in /opt by default. It can be a good candidate for splitting into a separate partition for many of the same reasons /usr/local is. Some people prefer to create one partition for both /opt and /usr/local, and have one be a symbolic link to a subdirectory in the other.

- **/var**   The /var directory stores operating files for a variety of system tools and servers. For instance, most Linux systems store operating logs in /var/log and print jobs are typically stored in /var/spool/lpd until they can be printed. Mail and news servers also store files in this directory tree. Systems that function primarily as servers for these protocols often benefit by separating this directory into a separate partition.

- **/tmp**   Linux programs typically store temporary files in the /tmp directory. Using a separate partition for this directory can protect the rest of the OS from problems should a program create a temporary file that's too large.

- **/boot**   Many Linux distributions place the Linux kernel in the /boot directory. If your hard disk has more than 1024 cylinders (as do all hard drives of more than 8GB capacity), it can be convenient to create a small (~5–20MB) /boot partition that resides near the beginning of the hard disk. In this way, you can be sure you can boot even from a large hard disk and when the rest of Linux falls partly or completely above the 1024-cylinder limit.

- **Other OS partitions**   If your computer hosts both Linux and some other OS or OSs, you can create mount points specifically to access files from those OSs. For instance, you might create a /win2k partition to access Windows 2000 files, and a /beos partition to access BeOS files.

Even advanced Linux administrators probably don't want to create all the partitions I've outlined here, although some might. Most administrators use somewhere between two and six partitions, plus a swap partition, and find this to be quite adequate.

Swap Space Requirements

Chapter 2, "Motherboards," describes the process of creating and using swap space in some detail. When you partition a hard disk for Linux, you should probably devote some of that space to a dedicated swap partition. The rule of thumb in years past was to devote space equal to twice your physical RAM to swap space. For instance, if your computer has 128MB of RAM, you would devote 256MB to swap space. This advice is overkill for most desktop computers today, however. A value approximately equal to the amount of RAM is adequate in most cases. Your need for swap space might be higher or lower than this, however. If you find that you generally don't make much use of swap but occasionally need to use massive amounts of RAM to run a particular program, you might want to create a very large swap partition to fill that occasional need. Alternatively, you could create a swap *file* and activate it only when you run your RAM-hungry program. I describe creating a swap file in Chapter 2.

You'll get the best system performance if you place your swap partition somewhere near the center of your disk or the center of your Linux partitions. For instance, if you create a 1GB root partition and a 1GB /home partition, you should place the swap partition between these two partitions. This placement minimizes the average disk head seek times to the swap partition, thus improving overall system performance.

EIDE Versus SCSI Disks

One of the biggest debates concerning hard disks is that between proponents of *Enhanced Integrated Device Electronics* (EIDE) drives and those who favor *Small Computer Systems Interface* (SCSI) devices. All modern x86 motherboards include EIDE controllers, but to attach a SCSI drive, you must normally purchase a separate SCSI host adapter (see Chapter 9 for more information on SCSI host adapters). Each technology has its advantages and disadvantages, and I describe these in this section.

> **NOTE**
>
> The terms *EIDE*, *Advanced Technology Attachment* (ATA), and *ATA Packet Interface* (ATAPI) refer to closely interrelated technologies, as does *Integrated Device Electronics* (IDE). As a general rule, *IDE* and *EIDE* refer to hard disks, whereas *ATA* and *ATAPI* refer to non-disk devices. *ATA* is sometimes used in conjunction with a number to describe the revision number of the ATA interface, as in *ATA-2* (ATA revision 2) or *ATA/33* (a 33MBps version of ATA).

EIDE Controllers

Because EIDE controllers are built in to all modern motherboards, it's important to pick a motherboard that supports the fastest form of EIDE possible. The interfaces you're most likely to see in the motherboards of 2000 are 33MBps and 66MBps variants. These variants can be referred to in various ways—for instance, a 33MBps EIDE interface can be referred to as *ATA/33*, *Ultra-33*, or *UltraDMA 33*.

The History of EIDE

IDE was EIDE's predecessor in the marketplace, and EIDE is, as the name implies, an enhancement to IDE. IDE, in turn, was a successor to older hard disk technologies. These older technologies used hard disks with very little electronic circuitry in conjunction with a separate interface board. IDE integrated these two components into one, hence the name. From the motherboard's point of view, an IDE controller looks just like a controller for an older drive type.

As late as the mid-1990s, plain IDE drives were quite common. IDE controllers from this period and earlier used a method of control known as *programmed input/output* (PIO), in which the computer's CPU fetched every byte transferred to or from the hard disk. PIO mode requires a great deal of CPU time, and so is not desirable with complex multitasking OSs like Linux. Eventually, however, the limitations of PIO mode gave way to *direct memory access* (DMA) EIDE controllers. DMA controllers have the capability to transfer data to and from memory directly, without CPU intervention. This design greatly reduces the CPU load when performing disk accesses, thus improving overall system performance in multitasking OSs.

Today, all motherboard EIDE controllers can operate in both older PIO modes and in newer DMA modes. The DMA modes typically require unique access methods for each chipset, whereas the PIO modes can be used with more standardized interface methods. You need customized Linux drivers to get the most out of an EIDE controller.

Linux EIDE Options

When you compile a Linux kernel, you're given options relating to EIDE chipset support, as shown in Figure 5.2. These options are scattered about the Block devices kernel options menu. Many devices are only available if you select Generic PCI IDE chipset support and Generic PCI bus-master DMA support. Some of these drivers are considered experimental, and are only available if you select *Prompt for development and/or incomplete code/drivers* in the *Code maturity level* options menu.

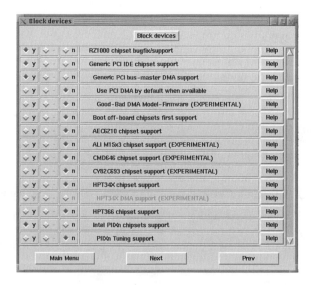

FIGURE 5.2

Linux includes support for a wide array of EIDE controllers.

CAUTION

Experimental drivers are potentially unstable, which means you might lose data if you attempt to use them. Some of these drivers are nonetheless quite reliable, but you should exercise caution when using them. If you enable experimental DMA support by turning on the appropriate kernel options and enabling DMA transfers using hdparm (as described later in this chapter), and if you subsequently begin experiencing mysterious disk errors or system crashes, turn off DMA support or try a newer kernel to see if the bugs have been fixed.

These EIDE drivers might or might not be available in any given Linux distribution as delivered. To be sure about this matter, you should recompile your Linux kernel. Doing so offers additional benefits, such as the ability to remove drivers you're *not* using and the ability to optimize the kernel for your CPU and other hardware.

Some of the EIDE drivers listed in the Block devices section of the kernel configuration utility are for EIDE support in common motherboard chipsets, including chipsets from Intel (Intel PIIXn chipsets support), ALi (ALI M15x3 chipset support and ALI M14xx chipset support), and VIA (VIA 82CXXX chipset support). Other drivers are for chipsets used on expansion cards, which you might use on older motherboards to improve EIDE speed. Some chipset manufacturers (such as ALi) offer more than one EIDE chipset, and so have more than one entry. In some cases, such as that of ALi, these entries aren't located close to each other, which can be confusing.

In addition to enabling support for the EIDE controller you use, you need to enable support for specific EIDE devices. These can include

- **Include IDE/ATA-2 DISK support**   Set this option to Y (not M for modular compilation) if you intend to boot off an EIDE hard disk.
- **Include IDE/ATAPI CDROM support**   Set this option to either Y or M if you have an ATAPI CD-ROM drive.
- **Include IDE/ATAPI TAPE support**   Set this option to either Y or M if you have an ATAPI tape drive.
- **Include IDE/ATAPI FLOPPY support**   Set this option to either Y or M if you have a removable ATAPI disk drive, such as an LS-120 or Iomega zip drive.

- **SCSI emulation support**   This option allows you to access EIDE devices as if they were SCSI devices. This feature can be particularly convenient when using certain types of software that are designed for SCSI devices when you have an ATAPI variant. For example, some versions of *CD recordable* (CD-R) software for Linux work only with SCSI devices. This software can be made to work with ATAPI CD-R drives by enabling the SCSI emulation support option in the Linux kernel.

As a general rule, Linux support for EIDE through Ultra-33 is very good, although some controllers aren't supported at this (or their maximum) speed and so can operate only at lower speeds. Support for Ultra-66 EIDE has been integrated into the 2.2.13 and later kernels. Many distributions that ship with earlier kernels by default won't install onto systems that use Ultra-66 EIDE controllers. If you find yourself in such a situation, you have several options:

- Install an Ultra-33 or earlier EIDE controller and attach your hard disk to it. Install Linux, then compile a more recent kernel. When that's done and you've configured your system to boot from the new kernel, remove the Ultra-33 controller, and reattach the EIDE cable to the Ultra-66 controller. Your system should now boot.

- Swap in an Ultra-33 EIDE controller and install using it. Leave this controller installed and continue using it without compiling a more recent kernel. This option might be necessary if your Ultra-66 controller is particularly uncooperative with the Linux Ultra-66 drivers.

- Switch to a Linux distribution that uses a 2.2.13 or later kernel, or even an earlier kernel with appropriate Ultra-66 support patches applied. Mandrake 7.0 and SuSE 6.3 both work with Ultra-66 controllers, and other distributions are likely to follow as 2000 wears on.

Characteristics of EIDE Disks

The basic technology behind all modern hard disks is quite similar, and, in fact, a few models are available in both EIDE and SCSI variants. (This practice used to be much more common than it is today.) Nonetheless, EIDE disks have certain unique characteristics, or at least tendencies:

- **Low cost**   On average, an EIDE hard disk of a given capacity costs less than a SCSI hard disk of the same capacity.

- **Low performance**   The reason for the low cost of EIDE hard disks lies, at least in part, in the fact that they perform worse than SCSI drives of similar capacity. On average, EIDE drives have smaller caches, spin at lower rates, and have higher seek times. (I describe these characteristics later in the section "Evaluating Disk Performance.") This performance deficit has nothing to do with EIDE and SCSI technologies *per se*; rather, it's a factor of which interfaces the hard disk manufacturers pair with their best drives.

- **Low command latency** Because of the simplicity of the EIDE interface, EIDE drives respond quickly to commands. The result is that EIDE drives can sometimes return the first data packet more quickly than can equivalent SCSI models. This characteristic is due to the difference between EIDE and SCSI, but it's generally swamped by other performance factors.

- **Low capacity** At any given moment in time, EIDE hard disks cover a lower range in capacities than SCSI hard drives. For example, Figure 5.3 represents the capacities advertised at a major Internet computer retailer in February of 2000. Note that there's considerable overlap in available capacities for both EIDE and SCSI, but the EIDE range is lower than that of SCSI devices.

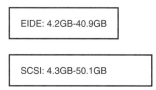

FIGURE 5.3

EIDE hard disks aren't available in capacities as high as those for SCSI hard disks.

- **CHS or LBA modes** IDE hard disks have traditionally used a three-number identifying code for each sector on the disk. Known as *cylinder/head/sector* (CHS) addressing, this code is a remnant from the days when hard disks had almost no onboard electronics. More recently, EIDE drives have added *logical* (or *linear* by some definitions) *block addressing* (LBA) mode, in which a single number is used to identify a sector on the hard disk.

In addition to these characteristics of EIDE drives, the EIDE interface itself possesses several characteristics of interest to this discussion:

- **Two-device limit** Each EIDE *chain* (that is, devices attached to a single port) is limited to just two devices. Most motherboards include only two EIDE ports, so the total number of EIDE devices supported per motherboard is just four. This isn't many on modern systems sporting devices like hard disks, CD-ROM drives, CD-R burners, and LS-120 or zip drives.

- **Non-concurrent communication** The two devices on each chain can't communicate simultaneously; one or the other monopolizes the EIDE bus.

- **Interrupt consumption** Each EIDE chain requires the use of one interrupt (IRQ). Because IRQs are a *very* limited resource on modern PCs, the use of one IRQ per two devices can be a very serious problem, particularly if you exceed the four devices supported by modern motherboards.

5

HARD DISKS

On the whole, EIDE is a good choice for low-cost computers that have just one or two hard disks and a single CD-ROM drive. When you begin adding more devices, EIDE's limitations start adding up fast, resulting in a serious liability. The fact that EIDE drives aren't typically the fastest available also makes EIDE a less than ideal technology for applications requiring the best disk performance, such as file servers or high-performance computing.

Characteristics of SCSI Disks

SCSI has always been the choice for high-speed hard disk operations. Characteristics of SCSI hard disks are the complement of EIDE characteristics:

- **High cost**   SCSI drives are typically more expensive than EIDE drives of the same capacity. Some of this is due to the SCSI interface, some is due to economic factors, and some of it relates to drive performance.

- **High performance**   SCSI hard disks have larger caches, faster rotation rates, and lower seek times, on average than EIDE drives of the same capacity.

- **High command latency**   The SCSI protocols impose greater overhead on commands than do the EIDE protocols. SCSI drives are therefore a bit slower to respond to commands than are EIDE drives.

- **High capacity**   You can obtain EIDE drives as large as most SCSI drives sold, but a few SCSI models exceed the capacity of the highest-capacity EIDE models.

- **LBA mode only**   SCSI disks have always communicated with their host adapters by presenting a view of the disk using a single linear block of addresses. This greatly simplifies matters for the computer if the computer understands this view of things. Unfortunately, x86 OSs have traditionally used CHS addressing, so SCSI host adapters translate LBA to CHS mode.

At least as important as the differences between EIDE and SCSI hard disks are the differences between the EIDE and SCSI busses. Characteristics of the SCSI bus that set it apart from the EIDE bus include

- **A 7- or 15-device limit**   In theory, you can attach up to 7 or 15 devices to each SCSI host adapter, depending upon the SCSI variant in use. (*Wide* SCSI variants support up to 15 devices, whereas *narrow* varieties support only 7.) In practice, cable length limits make it difficult to add more than 5 or 6 devices to a narrow chain. Each SCSI device has a unique ID number, which is set by a jumper or, in recent SCSI variants, can be assigned by the host adapter.

- **Device re-use**   Because the limit on SCSI devices is much higher than the limit on EIDE devices, it's more practical to add hard disks to a SCSI system than it is to add hard disks to an EIDE system. This means your initial investment in hard drives can last longer.

- **Concurrent communication** The SCSI bus was designed from the beginning to support concurrent communication. You can begin a transfer with one SCSI device and then start a second transfer with another device on the same chain. Both transfers can proceed at full speed, provided the sum of the speeds of the individual devices don't equal more than the speed of the SCSI bus. This factor alone gives SCSI a huge advantage when you need a high-performance disk system.

- **Interrupt consumption** Each SCSI host adapter, like each EIDE controller, requires one IRQ. Because you can attach many more SCSI devices to a SCSI chain, however, the SCSI devices tend to consume fewer IRQs.

- **Termination** A SCSI bus consists of several SCSI devices, including a SCSI host adapter, strung in a line. The device on each end of the line must be appropriately *terminated*, which is accomplished by setting a jumper or by adding a special terminating resistor pack to the SCSI cable. Termination problems account for many of the difficulties that arise with SCSI devices.

- **Driver issues** Unlike EIDE, SCSI controllers don't operate as clones of the early PC hard disk interfaces. Therefore, Linux needs specialized drivers for any SCSI host adapter you choose; there is no fallback compatibility mode as there is with EIDE. (Chapter 9, "SCSI Host Adapters," covers this matter in more detail.)

If costs were no object, SCSI would be the bus of choice for hard disks. Unfortunately, using SCSI rather than EIDE typically adds over $100 to the cost of a PC, and often $300–$500, depending upon the size of hard disk, number of SCSI devices, and so on. You do get more performance for this money, but the expense might not be justified for low-end or mid-range systems. I do strongly favor SCSI on systems that require several disk-like devices, such as tape backup units, CD-R drives, zip drives, and so on. These three devices alone, in conjunction with a CD-ROM drive and a single hard disk, require three IRQs and an add-on EIDE controller if bought in EIDE form. In SCSI form, all five devices can be attached to a single host adapter and consume a single IRQ. The latest SCSI host adapters, however, work best with the latest disk devices when only other high-speed SCSI devices are in use. It's sometimes therefore helpful to have two SCSI host adapters in such systems.

Using EIDE and SCSI in a Single System

In Linux, you access raw devices through entries in the /dev directory. EIDE devices are accessed as /dev/hdxy, where x is a letter (a, b, c...) and y is a partition number for hard disk partitions, or is absent for devices such as CD-ROM drives that don't have partitions. SCSI devices are more varied. SCSI hard disks are identified much like EIDE hard disks, except that the device filename takes the form /dev/sdxy. SCSI CD-ROM device filenames take the form /dev/scdx, where x is a number from 0 up.

5

It's not difficult to use a system with both SCSI and EIDE devices under Linux; you must simply use the appropriate device identifiers when you mount or use devices. The /etc/fstab file usually contains these identifiers for the most commonly used partitions and devices. As an example, consider a system with a SCSI hard disk and an EIDE CD-ROM drive. The /etc/fstab file might contain the following entries:

```
/dev/sda6   /          ext2    defaults      1  1
/dev/sda5   /home      ext2    defaults      1  2
/dev/hda    /mnt/cdrom iso9660 ro,user,noauto 0 0
```

These entries specify that two SCSI disk partitions (/dev/sda6 and /dev/sda5) will be mounted as / and /home, respectively. The EIDE CD-ROM drive, /dev/hda, is mounted as /mnt/cdrom.

Most computers' BIOSes are configured to boot from EIDE devices before SCSI devices. You can mix both EIDE and SCSI hard disks, but you'll need to install LILO on the EIDE disk, if you leave this boot order intact. On most systems, you can still install Linux on the SCSI disk, even when the system begins its boot process and loads LILO from the EIDE disk. If you change the BIOS boot order, you might need to modify your /etc/lilo.conf file to reflect this fact by using lines like the following:

```
disk=/dev/sda
  bios=0x80
```

These commands inform LILO that the BIOS treats /dev/sda as the first disk (code 0x80). Without this command, you likely won't be able to boot Linux using LILO if you set your BIOS to boot from SCSI disks before EIDE disks.

The 1024-Cylinder Limit

Both EIDE and SCSI disks suffer from what's known as the *1024-cylinder limit*. The difficulty is that the old CHS addressing mode uses a 10-bit number to identify the cylinder number of a hard disk. A 10-bit number can hold a value of between 0 and 1023, so the number of cylinders accessible by the BIOS is limited to 1024. Assorted systems have been developed to get around this problem. Many OSs, including Linux, aren't bothered by the 1024-cylinder limit once booted. The problem arises when booting the OS, because the ancient x86 BIOS *is* bothered by the 1024-cylinder limit. Given limits on the number of sectors and heads, the 1024-cylinder limit works out to a bit under 8GB with modern hard disks. Earlier BIOSes lacked features to raise it that high, and the limit could be as low as 504MB on these drives.

Whatever the exact value of the 1024-cylinder limit, it's necessary to put the Linux kernel below that limit in order for Linux to boot. That's because the BIOS loads the kernel (under direction from LILO). Once the kernel is loaded, it can use its own disk drivers, which aren't bothered by the 1024-cylinder limit, to continue booting the OS.

As I mentioned earlier in the chapter, one good way around the 1024-cylinder limit is to create a small /boot partition that falls below this limit. You can then place the Linux kernel in that directory and be assured you can boot. Another way around the limit is to use a floppy disk for boot purposes. Put the Linux kernel along with a copy of LOADLIN.EXE on a DOS boot floppy, or write the kernel to the floppy without a filesystem by using the Linux dd command. You can then boot Linux without using the hard disk to load the Linux kernel.

Another way around the 1024-cylinder limit is to use GNU GRUB (http://www.gnu.org/software/grub/grub-faq.en.html) to boot Linux rather than LILO. GRUB lets you boot an OS from above the 1024-cylinder limit, but only from EIDE hard disks. It uses its own EIDE driver to bypass the BIOS, and therefore can't be used with SCSI hard disks.

Evaluating Disk Performance

When you shop for a hard disk, you need to consider several different measures of hard disk performance. The three most important measures are the disk head seek time, the data transfer rates, and the disk's cache size. Depending upon how the drive is used, one or another of these might be the most important—generally the seek time or transfer rate. Seek time is most important when you frequently access several files, possibly on different partitions, as when several users read and write multiple files simultaneously. Transfer rate is most important when you routinely read a single large file straight through, as for instance when you play back a large audio or video file. As a rule of thumb, seek time is more important for multitasking OSs than for single-tasking OSs.

Disk Seek Times

The interior of a hard disk is built from one or more circular disk *platters* on which data are stored. These platters spin at high speeds, and the disk heads ride over and between the platters on arms that can pivot, bringing the heads over any point on the data storage surface (see Figure 5.4). The time it takes to move the head is referred to as the *seek time*. In fact, there are several possible measures of seek time, such as time to seek from the center to the outer edge (or vice versa), time to seek to the mid-way point, and so on. The seek time measurement that's most often used is the *average* seek time, which is the average time to move the head from one location to a randomly-selected other location. Statistically speaking, this is very close to the time to seek one-third of the head's range.

Another measurement closely related to seek time involves a second component beyond the head movement: latency. *Latency* is the time it takes the desired sector to come up under the read/write head after a seek operation, and averages out to half the time it takes for a rotation of the disk platter. The combination of seek time and latency is known as *access time*.

5

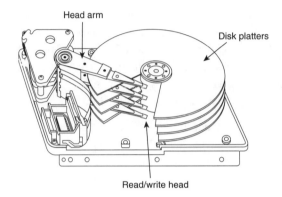

Head arm

Disk platters

Read/write head

FIGURE 5.4

Latencies involved in the movement of hard drive components are responsible for hard disk data transfer rates.

Seek time, latency, and access time are all measured in milliseconds (ms). Hard disks in 2000 have seek times of 5ms–10ms and spin at between 5,400 and 10,000 rpm, for average latencies of 3ms–6ms (lower latencies being associated with higher spin rates). The main point to keep in mind with respect to seek time, latency, and access time is that smaller numbers are better. Keep in mind the difference between seek time and access time, too. Sometimes you'll find one vendor advertising seek time while another promotes access time, but these values are not directly comparable. If you know the spin rate of the two drives, you can convert one to the other quite easily, of course, but you must be aware of the difference in the first place.

Disk Transfer Rates

The second major statistic of importance in comparing hard disks is the disk transfer rates—how quickly the disk can transfer data to and from the computer. Note that I referred to disk transfer *rates* (plural). There are two reasons for this:

- The disk spins at the same rate no matter what cylinder is being read, but modern hard drive designs place more sectors along outer cylinders than along inner ones. This means that data read from the outer cylinders transfer faster than do data read from inner cylinders. Hence, the internal data transfer rate is variable.

- The data transfer rate from the platters is potentially different from the data transfer rate between the hard disk and the computer. The latter rate is determined by the computer's interface type, such as 66MBps for an Ultra-66 interface. The former is determined by data density on the platter and the speed with which the platter spins.

Hard disk manufacturers generally try to emphasize the external transfer rate—the speed of the hard disk's interface. This transfer rate, however, is far less important than the *internal* transfer rate—that rate of information transfer from the disk platters to the drive electronics.

To further complicate matters, hard disk manufacturers often quote internal data transfer rates in megabits per second (Mbps), but external transfer rates in megabytes per second (MBps). The abbreviations for these terms vary only in the case of the letter *b*, but the difference is a factor-of-eight value. When the internal rate is reported as 240Mbps and the external rate is 66MBps, it's easy to become confused and believe that the external rate is the bottleneck. It's not—expressed in MBps, the internal rate is only 30MBps.

Disk Data Density

Early hard disks used a fixed number of sectors per cylinder, no matter where on the disk that cylinder was located—an inner cylinder or outer one. This design resulted in a lower density of data on outer tracks than on inner ones. In the quest for increased disk storage capacity, engineers began squeezing more sectors onto outer cylinders than on inner ones, resulting in higher data capacity per platter (see Figure 5.5).

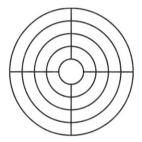
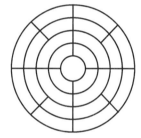

Fixed Sectors/Cylinder
16 Sectors Total

Variable Sectors/Cylinder
24 Sectors Total

FIGURE 5.5
Actual hard disks use far more sectors and cylinders than are depicted here, but the basic principle still holds.

> **NOTE**
>
> Floppy disks still used a fixed number of sectors per cylinder. Some exotic disk formats, such as the 400KB and 800KB formats used by early Macintoshes, varied the number of sectors per cylinder, but x86 floppies have never used such schemes.

In absolute terms, the number of bytes stored on each disk platter has increased substantially over the years. Hard drives sold in 2000 store tens of gigabytes in two or three 3.5-inch platters, as compared to a tenth the capacity on the same number of platters in the mid-1990s. This increase in data density translates into an increase in disk transfer speed, even when the rotational speed stays the same. When more data pass under the read/write head in any given period of time, more data are transferred to or from the hard disk.

Disk Spin Rate

The faster a hard disk spins, the faster it can transfer data. For this reason, disk spin rates have crept up over the years, from 3,600 rpm in the early 1990s to a minimum common speed of 5,400 rpm today. Indeed, 10,000 rpm hard disks are gaining in popularity today. All other things being equal, a faster hard disk is preferable to a slower one; however, all other things might not be equal. For instance, two 30GB hard disks might achieve their capacities in different ways. One might use three platters and spin at 10,000 rpm, whereas another might use two platters and spin at 7,200 rpm. With the greater data density on the latter drive, its 7,200 speed might actually result in faster data transfers than could be achieved from the 10,000 rpm drive. Another factor is the distribution of data in sectors as compared to in cylinders. A drive with fewer cylinders but more sectors per cylinder will be faster than one with more cylinders and fewer sectors per cylinder, all other things being equal.

In the end, to determine a disk's data transfer speed, you must rely upon transfer statistics provided by the manufacturer, or on test results printed in magazines or online. (Most such tests are conducted under Windows, but if you can find raw data transfer rates, those should not be much different than what you can obtain under Linux.)

Heat Generation and Dissipation

As hard drives have spun faster, they've developed increasing problems with heat. The faster spin rates produce increased waste heat from friction and from the increased demands placed on electronic circuits that process the data. Not all drives that spin at the same rate generate the same amount of heat, however. I've owned 5,400 rpm drives that generate more heat than some 7,200 rpm drives. Nonetheless, as a general rule of thumb, you should at least consider extra heat dissipation measures for drives that spin at 7,200 rpm or faster. A 10,000 rpm drive almost always requires such special cooling.

The most common method of providing extra cooling to extra-hot drives is to add a hard drive cooling fan to your system. These devices mount in a 5.25-inch drive bay and allow you to mount a 3.5-inch drive within adapter rails. The front bezel incorporates two or three small fans that blow air onto the hard disk, thus keeping it cool. If you use a SCSI hard disk, you might want to consider mounting it in an external case with its own independent cooling system. This practice can help isolate the heat generated by the hard disk from other components of the computer, and isolate the hard disk from heat produced by other disks.

Disk Cache Size

The final hard disk performance factor is the size of the built-in disk cache. As described in Chapter 3 (in the section "Cache Memory"), a *cache* is a type of memory that's smaller but faster than another type of storage. The cache holds frequently-accessed data so that the computer can access the data from the cache rather than pull it from the slower storage medium. In the case of hard disks, there are two common types of cache and one less common type:

- **Disk cache on the hard drive**   All modern hard drives incorporate a disk cache, typically between 512KB and 2MB in size. This cache is composed of RAM chips. When the computer tells the hard drive to read some set of sectors, the drive reads those sectors plus the sectors that immediately follow, and places it all in the disk cache on the theory that the computer is likely to ask for the following sectors next. This assumption is often correct, and so the hard drive need not access the hard disk for the next transfer, thus greatly improving both latency and transfer speed. The disk cache can therefore help performance when transferring small files in sequence. It's less helpful on sustained transfers, because the data go immediately to the computer. Disk caches can also hold data briefly as it's written. Instead of waiting until the write operation is complete, the hard disk can report that it's finished writing data, when, in fact, the data reside in the cache chips. In such cases, the disk writes data to its platters very soon thereafter; the write cache is used mainly to let the OS get on with its business as soon as possible after sending data to the hard disk.

- **In-computer disk cache**   Most OSs, including Linux, maintain their own disk caches in the computer's RAM. The OS-maintained disk cache operates much like a hard disk's built-in cache, except that it's even faster. In the case of Linux, the disk cache can grow and shrink as necessary. The Linux kernel implements rules that determine how much RAM to devote to disk cache, as compared to RAM devoted to programs and their data. The kernel must determine when to give up cache space as opposed to when to swap data out to a swap file. As a user, or even as a system administrator, you need not concern yourself too much with these details, but you should be aware of the existence of this form of cache.

- **On-controller cache**   The third type of disk cache, and the rarest, exists in the hard disk controller or host adapter. This cache type is most popular on high-end SCSI host adapters, some of which can be outfitted with RAM chips to function as a cache. Such host adapters were once moderately popular, but their popularity has faded recently. As a general rule, it makes more sense to increase the computer's main store of RAM than to add RAM to a SCSI host adapter, because RAM on the motherboard can be applied to whatever task is most appropriate.

Considered as a purchase criterion for a hard disk, the on-disk cache is a minor factor compared to the transfer rate and seek time. Nonetheless, a large cache can produce a small performance boost compared to a small cache.

Hard Disk Form Factors

The physical sizes of hard disks are fairly well standardized today. These sizes are generally measured in inches, and refer to the diameters of the platters contained within. The physical dimensions of the boxes you install in a computer are somewhat larger than this. Because of the standardized sizes of hard disks, you should have little or no trouble installing a hard disk in a computer case, provided the case has an appropriate bay available to receive the drive.

The form factor used doesn't matter to Linux, so you can purchase or use any hard disk form factor you like. The different form factors do vary, however, in their performance characteristics, price, and availability.

2.5-Inch Disks for Portables

The smallest hard disks in common use today are 2.5-inch units. These drives measure 2.75 inches wide by 3.94 inches deep. Their small size makes them ideally suited for use in laptop and notebook computers, and they're almost never found in desktop computers. The reason for this segregation is that 2.5-inch hard drives are more expensive, megabyte for megabyte, than are physically larger hard disks.

A 2.5-inch hard disk is small enough that it often pulls its power directly from a data cable, which is smaller than a typical EIDE or SCSI cable. Because these drives are normally used in portable computers that are purchased as a unit, you don't normally need to concern yourself with the details of this interface.

3.5-Inch Disks for Desktops

By far the most popular form factor for hard drives today is the 3.5-inch design. These models measure 4.02 inches wide by 5.77 inches deep. These drives contain two connectors on one end: a SCSI or EIDE cable connector and a power connector (see Figure 5.6). They also usually have jumpers that are used to set various options, such as a SCSI ID number or EIDE master/slave status.

When mounted in a case, the end of the hard disk with the power and EIDE or SCSI interface connectors faces toward the appropriate motherboard or expansion card, so that the cables can be easily connected. Unfortunately, this placement often makes it difficult to access the jumpers on the opposite end of the drive, and units with side-mounted jumpers can be even more difficult to configure. You should be sure that you've set all the jumpers correctly before mounting a hard drive in the case.

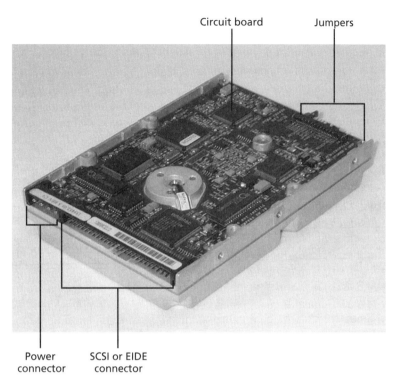

Circuit board   Jumpers

Power   SCSI or EIDE
connector   connector

FIGURE 5.6

A hard disk resembles a featureless slab of metal, except for a circuit board on the underside, a pair of connectors, and a few jumpers.

5.25-Inch Disks for Desktops

In the 1980s and even the early 1990s, 5.25-inch hard drives were common. These units measure 5.75 inches wide by 7.6 inches deep. True monsters compared to 3.5-inch drives, 5.25-inch hard drives were largely abandoned by the mid-1990s, although a few models, such as Quantum's Big Foot line, persisted through the late 1990s. Compared to 3.5-inch models, 5.25-inch models consume more power, have higher seek times, and vary more in their transfer rates. Their platters use lower data densities, which can make them less expensive to manufacture than 3.5-inch drives.

Like 3.5-inch drives, 5.25-inch models use separate power and data cables, which follow the same standards as those used on 3.5-inch drives. These drives are essentially larger versions of 3.5-inch drives—or perhaps it would be more accurate to say that 3.5-inch drives are miniaturized 5.25-inch drives, because the 5.25-inch design predated the 3.5-inch design.

5

HARD DISKS

Disk Heights

The preceding discussion omitted mention of the height of various drive types. This is because each of the disk varieties comes in an assortment of heights.

- 2.5-inch drives are available in heights ranging from 0.33 inch to 0.492 inch, to fit an assortment of notebook computer sizes.
- 3.5-inch drives are most commonly available in third-height form, which is 1.02 inches. A few half-height (1.64 inch) models are also available. Typically, the highest-capacity drives in a model line fit the half-height form factor, whereas small- and medium-capacity drives come in third-height form.
- 5.25-inch drives typically come in half-height form (1.64 inch), although a few ancient full-height behemoths measure more than 3 inches in height.

Be sure to check on the height of any drive before you buy it, particularly if you're low on expansion bays. If you buy a half-height 3.5-inch drive but don't have room for it in your case, you'll have to return the drive, remove some other component, or use an external drive housing to add the drive to your system. Your options are even more limited if you buy a 2.5-inch drive to replace a notebook computer's built-in drive.

Tuning Disk Performance in Linux

You probably want to get the best performance possible from your hard disks. If you have a hard drive capable of transferring 30MBps, you don't want to get only 8MBps speeds from it. Especially when using a laptop computer, you also want to configure your hard drives to *spin down* when not being actively used—that is, to go into an inactive state in which the hard drive platters don't spin, but the drive watches for data transfer requests and powers up the drive when one occurs. You can use an assortment of Linux utilities and configuration features to help improve your overall system performance with respect to hard disks.

Using `hdparm` to Activate Advanced Features

The most important Linux utility for handling advanced hard disk features is `hdparm`. This utility lets you set an assortment of options relating to hard disk performance, as well as run tests to find out how your hard disk is performing. You can learn more about `hdparm` by typing **man hdparm**. I present some highlights here.

> **NOTE**
>
> You must be running as root to use most of hdparm's features.

Testing Disk Speed

You can use the -t option to hdparm to test the read speed of a hard disk. For instance

```
hdparm -t /dev/sda
```

This command tests the speed of reading data from /dev/sda (the first SCSI hard disk). Substitute other device files (such as /dev/sdb or /dev/hda) to test other disks. The result of this command resembles the following:

```
/dev/sda:
 Timing buffered disk reads:  64 MB in  4.32 seconds =14.81 MB/sec
```

Linux is a multitasking, multiuser OS. Any given run of hdparm is therefore likely to produce results that are slightly inaccurate because of varying system load and disk accesses during the run. You can improve the accuracy by running the test several times—three is probably enough. If the results of each run are similar, then they're probably accurate. If one result is wildly divergent from the others, discard that result, or run additional tests to be sure it's the one you should discard.

> **NOTE**
>
> You'll never see hdparm -t test results that match the transfer rates advertised by the drive manufacturer. Advertised rates are theoretical abstractions, based on no head seeks, no overhead for EIDE or SCSI commands, and so on. In my experience, 75% of claimed disk speed seems to be a common result when using hdparm -t.

> **TIP**
>
> If you have several partitions on a disk, you can test performance for different portions of the disk by specifying the partition number, as in **hdparm -t /dev/hda1** or **hdparm -t /dev/hda9**.

The -t option has a variant, -T. This uppercase speed test command tests performance reading and writing from and to Linux's internal disk cache. This action tests the CPU and memory speed of the computer, not the speed of any hard disks attached to the system. You can combine the -t and -T options by specifying them both, as in **hdparm -tT /dev/sda**. When you do so, you get two reports, one of cache reads and one of disk reads.

5

HARD DISKS

Be sure that you've got at least 2MB free memory on your system to support disk cache operations when you use the -T option; if all your RAM is occupied by programs, hdparm won't be able to use disk cache, and so results will be inaccurate. You can check on free memory by using the free command. The output looks something like this:

```
                  total       used       free     shared    buffers     cached
Mem:              62136      59848       2288          0       2292       6744
-/+ buffers/cache:           50812      11324
Swap:            120452      15036     105416
```

The value of interest is on the -/+ buffers/cache line, under the free column—11,324 in this case. The free command reports memory values in kilobytes, so 11,324 is approximately 11MB—well over the 2MB minimum required for hdparm's cache memory test.

Setting DMA Options

If you use an EIDE hard disk with a controller capable of DMA transfers under Linux, you can set the controller to use appropriate DMA modes using hdparm. The relevant commands are -d, which programs the controller to use DMA mode, and -X, which sets the specific DMA mode to use. Each of these options takes its own subparameters. In most cases, something like the following will have the desired effect:

```
hdparm -d1 -X34 /dev/hda
```

The -d1 parameter sets DMA mode on (*1*, as opposed to *0*, to turn it off). The -X34 parameter sets the system to use the fastest available DMA mode (*34* is a code number for this mode).

CAUTION

If you use an EIDE controller for which Linux includes only experimental DMA support, activating DMA mode and high-speed DMA transfers can be dangerous. If you experience problems with these transfer modes, disable them by issuing an hdparm -d0 command.

Most modern Linux distributions include an appropriate call to hdparm to configure the hard disks for optimal performance. If yours doesn't, or if it's not working correctly, you can usually include an appropriate call in /etc/rc.d/rc.local or some similar startup script.

NOTE

The DMA mode-setting commands are only relevant to *EIDE* hard disks. If you use a SCSI hard disk, the SCSI driver uses DMA mode automatically, if the host adapter supports DMA.

If you don't know if your drive is set to use DMA, you can use the `-v` option to `hdparm` to find out. For instance

```
# hdparm -v /dev/hda

/dev/hda:
 multcount     =   0 (off)
 I/O support   =   0 (default 16-bit)
 unmaskirq     =   0 (off)
 using_dma     =   1 (on)
 keepsettings  =   0 (off)
 nowerr        =   0 (off)
 readonly      =   0 (off)
 readahead     =   8 (on)
 geometry      = 784/255/63, sectors = 12594960, start = 0
```

This command displays a summary of information about the drive and how it's being used. For the purposes of this discussion, the `using_dma` line is the most important.

Powering Down a Disk to Save Energy

If you routinely use a portable computer that's not directly connected to a wall outlet, you're probably concerned about the power consumption of all components, including the hard disk. You can save some power by telling Linux to set the hard disk into a low-power mode when the disk isn't being used. Having the system power down the hard disk as soon as disk accesses stop probably isn't a good idea. Powering down causes the system to consume a great deal of power when returning the drive to an active state, and it could result in a substantial reduction in performance. Instead, you probably want to instruct the system to power down the hard disk after some period of inactivity. Once again, you use the `hdparm` command to achieve this effect, with the `-S` parameter.

The `-S` parameter's settings are peculiar, and are summarized in Table 5.2.

TABLE 5.2   `-S` Options for Hard Disk Spindown Times

Values	Meaning
0	Energy-saving power-down disabled. (Drive is always fully active.)
1–240	Multiples of 5 seconds; for instance, *6* means 30 seconds.
241–251	1–11 units of 30 minutes, for times ranging from 0.5–5.5 hours.
252	21 minutes.
253	Vendor-defined timeout value.
255	21 minutes and 15 seconds.

5

HARD DISKS

Suppose you want to set your hard disk to power down after 10 minutes of inactivity. You could use the command hdparm -S120 /dev/hda to accomplish this effect. You can also combine this command with the ones you use to set DMA mode transfers, as in hdparm -d1 -X34 -S120 /dev/hda.

> **NOTE**
>
> You can't use hdparm's -S option to set a power-down time for SCSI hard disks.

Using Multiple Disks for Better Performance

If you want to improve your hard disk performance, you can get some benefit by using several disks. Suppose that your system engages in a series of disk operations like the following:

```
Read File 1
Read File 2
Read File 1
Write File 2
Read File 3
Write File 2
Write File 3
```

Note that, in this example, the even and odd file accesses are interleaved. Now, suppose that the even files are located early on the disk, whereas the odd files are located late on the disk. The result of this string of disk operations will be a series of long head seeks, which slows access to the files. If instead the even files are on one physical disk and the odd files are on another physical disk, then there will be little in the way of head seek operations, and overall performance will improve.

You can't guarantee that every other access uses a different physical disk, but you can improve the odds by using partitions on separate disks for a single Linux installation. For example, you might put your root or /usr directory on /dev/hda and your /home directory on /dev/hdb. This arrangement guarantees that accesses to Linux system files won't disrupt ongoing accesses to users' files, and vice versa. Precisely how you should break up partitions across disks varies with your needs and configuration, including what other OSs are present and the speeds of your hard disks. As a general rule of thumb, you should aim to equalize drive access across your hard disks. Putting little-used directories like /boot on one drive and everything else on another won't help your system's speed much, but putting frequently-accessed directories like /usr and /home on separate drives generally does help. Precisely what directories are frequently used varies from one installation to another.

Splitting Linux across two or more disks can be slightly more beneficial in a SCSI system than in an EIDE system, because of SCSI's capacity to support multiple simultaneous transfers. This is a speed boost in addition to the boost provided by reducing the need for head movements, however. The basic principle is beneficial for EIDE drives as well as SCSI drives—it's just *more* beneficial when used with SCSI drives. You can gain some of the same benefit by placing your EIDE hard drives on separate channels.

Linux RAID Support

Linux supports a technology known as *redundant array of independent disks* (RAID). This technique allows you to split your files across two or more hard disks in a seamless way. Rather than configure your system with partitions containing different data on different disks, you use RAID to combine two partitions on different disks into one virtual partition. By doing so, the computer can add redundancy to improve data security, split data across two disks to improve speed, or both. Two forms of RAID exist: hardware and software. Hardware RAID is supported by a special RAID SCSI host adapter, and is transparent to Linux. Software RAID must be implemented by the OS—the Linux kernel, to be precise.

Linux's software RAID is enabled by the Multiple devices driver support under the Block devices kernel configuration option, as shown in Figure 5.7. Once you've selected this option, several sub-options become available to let you select the type of RAID support you want to use.

Each variety of RAID supported by the Linux kernel has different characteristics and purposes:

- **Linear (append)**   This mode simply appends one partition to another. It can be useful if you need more space in a single partition than is available on a single hard disk. It provides no speed or robustness benefits.
- **RAID-0 (striping)**   RAID-0 fills disk partitions evenly, by writing pieces of data to the disks in an interleaved manner. The end result is as if you had one large partition, with alternating stripes of data coming from each disk. RAID-0 provides no redundancy, and

hence is no safer than conventional partitions. If the partitions used in striping are on separate physical disks, a speed benefit results. This speed benefit can be particularly large if you use EIDE disks on separate channels or SCSI disks.

- **RAID-1 (mirroring)** RAID-1 provides data redundancy; any information written to one partition is written to one or more others. This option reduces the likelihood that you'll lose data, but it provides little or no speed benefits.

- **RAID-4/RAID-5** This option works much like RAID-1, but in addition to redundant storage of data, the system allows you to store checksum information so that you can detect and correct errors. Ordinarily, you use three or more disks in place of one disk with RAID-4/RAID-5 support. One disk provides checksum storage, while the remaining disks store the data. In case of an error, the system can determine which disk is in error and can correct that error.

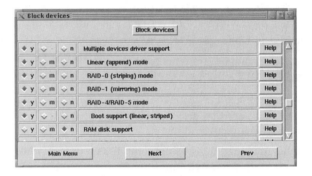

FIGURE 5.7
Linux's RAID support includes several sub-options for different varieties of RAID.

Once you've added appropriate RAID support to your Linux kernel, you need to use a set of tools to define meta-partitions. These tools are

- `mdadd [options] [mddev] [p1] [p2]` This command adds two conventional partitions (*p1* and *p2*) to a multi-disk device (*mddev*). For instance, `mdadd -p1 /dev/md0 /dev/sda3 /dev/sdb3` adds the third partition on each of the first two SCSI hard disks together to create `/dev/md0`. The most critical options take the form `-pn`, where *n* is a number from 0–1 or l, representing RAID levels 0–1 or linear mode.

CAUTION

Order counts when specifying conventional partitions! Always list the partitions in the same order when using `mdadd`.

- **mdrun** *[options]* *mddev*   This command activates the new RAID partition bundle. Without using this command, you can't access the RAID meta-partition.
- **mdstop** *[options]* *mddev*   This command turns off the RAID feature for the specified meta-partition. Use this command if you want to unmount a set of RAID partitions and reuse the partitions "raw."

You can also store information on RAID device assignments in the /dev/mdtab file. Each line takes the form

```
mddev   options   dev1 dev2 ... devn
```

The most important options are linear, raid0, and raid1, which correspond to the RAID levels. If you specify your RAID devices in /dev/mdtab, you can specify the -a option and omit the device list.

RAID can be a good way to improve performance or disk reliability, but it's not trivial to administer. Unless you select Boot support (refer to Figure 5.7), you can't boot from a RAID partition. It's generally best to reserve RAID for high-traffic data directories, such as the /home directory or (on certain servers) /var.

CAUTION

An error configuring RAID can result in serious problems, including lost data or difficulty recovering data.

For more information on RAID, see the Software-RAID HOWTO document, which comes with all mainstream Linux distributions.

Summary

The hard disk you choose plays an important role in the speed and usability of your computer. All hard disks sold today are large enough to hold Linux itself, but you might have extraordinary data storage needs that require larger disks. Of more interest to most people is the speed of the hard disk, which is measured in terms of sustained throughput, head seek times, and to a lesser extent cache size. The type of interface—both the contrast between SCSI and EIDE and the specific level of each interface type—is also quite important in determining the speed of your disk system.

Removable Disks

IN THIS CHAPTER

Hard disks are an indispensable storage medium for modern computers, but they're not the only storage medium, nor are they the best one for all purposes. One area where hard disks fall short is in portability. Although there are enclosures that allow you to quickly and easily remove a hard disk from a computer, the removed hard disk is just a bit on the bulky side. Carting an entire hard disk around is also risky, because the devices are delicate, and you probably don't want to risk all the data on your hard disk just to transport a few files from one location to another. For this reason, a wide assortment of specialized media have arisen to help you move files from Point A to Point B. These devices are typically permanently mounted in your computer, or attached to it as an external drive. Their *media*, however, are removable, and can be transported easily.

NOTE

Although I cover them in Chapter 7, "Optical Drives," optical media such as CD-ROMs certainly qualify as removable disk media. Until recently, however, it wasn't possible to record on these media, and even now creating a CD-R is more involved than is writing a few files to most removable media. For this reason, I cover CD-ROMs and related devices in Chapter 7.

One alternative to using removable media is using a network. With more and more computers permanently attached to the Internet, it's often possible to use Internet protocols to move files from one location to another. In fact, Linux excels as a file server for this purpose, as described in my book, *Linux: Networking for Your Office*, published by Sams Publishing. Chapter 17, "Network Hardware," covers hardware required to link two or more computers into a network, and Chapter 18, "Modems," covers devices to connect an isolated computer or small network of computers to an Internet service provider (ISP).

Types of Removable Disk

Removable media come in several different varieties, each of which has its unique strengths and weaknesses. These media can all be used in Linux, although configuration details vary substantially. The technologies used in these devices also vary. Most are based on magnetic recording principles similar to those used in hard disks, but some use technologies that are partly based on optical principles.

Table 6.1 summarizes the characteristics of the removable media technologies I describe in this chapter. Note that this list is not comprehensive; a number of devices have come and gone from the marketplace, or are currently available but fill relatively small niches.

TABLE 6.1   Common Removable Media Technologies

Drive Type	Capacity	Average Seek Time	Data Transfer Rate	Interfaces
Floppy Disk	180KB– 2.88MB	66ms	30KB/s[1]	Floppy, USB
Iomega Zip-100	100MB	29ms	0.6– 1.4MB/s	EIDE, SCSI, USB, parallel, PC-Card
Iomega Zip-250	250MB	29ms	0.9– 2.4MB/s	EIDE, USB, SCSI, PC-Card
LS-120	120MB	70ms	4.0MB/s	EIDE, USB, parallel, PC-Card
Magneto-Optical[2]	128MB– 5.2GB	25ms	2– 6MB/s	SCSI
Iomega Jaz	1GB– 2GB	12ms	5.4MB/s	SCSI
Castlewood Orb	2.3GB	10ms	12.2MB/s	EIDE, SCSI, USB

1. *Floppy disk transfer rates vary with drive capacity. The 30KB/s figure is for 1.44MB, 3.5-inch media.*

2. *MO disks have existed for a long time, and performance has improved over the years. The seek time and transfer rates cited here are typical values for drives sold in 2000.*

Floppy Disks

The humble floppy disk is one of the oldest recording devices used on x86 computers. (A primitive tape drive was actually used by the very first IBM PC, instead of a floppy disk, however.) Today's x86 computers almost invariably support a 3.5-inch floppy disk, but 5.25-inch disks were common as late as the mid-1990s. (Figure 6.1 shows both types of disks.) Earlier computers sometimes used 8-inch floppy disks, but these were never used on x86 hardware. The 8-inch and 5.25-inch floppy disks used flexible outer casings, hence the term *floppy disk*. The 3.5-inch variety incorporated a harder plastic shell, greater precision in disk mounting, and a shutter to cover the disk read/write access hole. These characteristics contributed to greater reliability and higher data densities in 3.5-inch floppies compared to earlier varieties.

FIGURE 6.1

Floppy disks have come in several sizes over the years. This picture depicts a 5.25-inch floppy on the left and a 3.5-inch floppy on the right.

Floppy disks have several important advantages as storage media for x86 computers:

- **Cost** Both floppy disks and their drives are inexpensive. This characteristic is particularly important when you want to send a file to somebody and you can't send it via the Internet. It's also important in shared computing environments, such as computer centers on college campuses. The low cost of floppies also means you can afford to lose or destroy a few—provided the data they contain aren't too important, or are backed up elsewhere!

- **Universality** Almost every desktop computer today has a 3.5-inch floppy disk drive, so you're almost guaranteed interoperability if you use floppies and a common filesystem, such as the *File Allocation Table* (FAT) filesystem.

- **Portability** 3.5-inch floppies fit into a shirt pocket, or you can pack a few into small cases or wallets designed for them and tote them around in a backpack, coat pocket, or purse without too much difficulty.

Floppy disks are an old technology, however. They simply have not kept up with increases in storage capacity and speed available on other media, both fixed and removable. These two factors—speed and capacity—constitute the floppy disk's Achilles' heel. The maximum floppy disk capacity in common use is 1.44MB, which is nothing compared to a typical hard disk in

2000, the capacity of which can be more than 10,000 times greater than the floppy's. Floppy disks are also notoriously slow, a fact which is mitigated merely by the low capacity of the medium. Table 6.2 summarizes the capacities available on floppy disks today. Note that, although double-sided high-density 1.44MB floppies are the largest in common use, they're not the highest capacity available. The higher-capacity 2.88MB floppies never caught on, and are nearly impossible to find today. Single-sided floppies use only one side of the disk to record information, whereas double-sided drives use two read/write heads to record on both sides of the disk medium.

TABLE 6.2   Floppy Disk k k Capacities

Floppy Type	Single-Sided Capacity	Double-Sided Capacity
5.25-inch, double-density	180KB	360KB
5.25-inch, high-density	600KB	1200KB
3.5-inch, double-density	360KB	720KB
3.5-inch, high-density	720KB	1440KB
3.5-inch, extra–high-density	1440KB	2880KB

Almost all floppies are double-sided, although a few very old systems used single-sided floppies.

In addition to the capacities outlined in Table 6.1, a number of non-standard capacities exist. Various floppy disk formatting programs let you place more sectors on each cylinder, or put more than the usual number of cylinders on a disk. Both methods increase the capacity of the floppy, but at the cost of reliability and interoperability—some systems can't read such non-standard floppy formats.

Most floppy disk drives interface through the floppy port on the motherboard, but a few USB-interfaced floppy drives are available. These are marketed primarily to Macintosh users, because some Macintoshes (notably the iMac) come without a floppy drive.

Iomega Zip Disks

Seeing a need for a higher-capacity removable storage medium, Iomega (http://www.iomega.com) introduced the Zip drive. This device uses proprietary disks that are slightly larger and thicker than standard 3.5-inch floppy disks (see Figure 6.2). The drive mechanism itself is small enough to fit into a 3.5-inch drive bay. The original Iomega Zip drives stored 100MB per Zip cartridge, but 250MB drives are now also available. These new drives can read old 100MB cartridges. Unfortunately, Zip drives aren't compatible with floppy disks, so if you want to read standard floppy disks, you need a separate floppy drive to do so.

FIGURE 6.2
Zip disks (left) are slightly larger than 3.5-inch floppy disks (right).

<blockquote>

CAUTION

Never insert a standard floppy disk into a Zip drive! Doing so can damage the Zip drive, possibly bringing on the notorious Zip drive "click of death." This is damage to a Zip drive that manifests in a clicking noise when trying to read a disk. Unfortunately, this phenomenon can damage a Zip disk, which in turn can damage another Zip drive, so this phenomenon can spread much like a contagious disease. If you encounter this phenomenon, discard or repair the Zip drive immediately, and discard any affected disks.

</blockquote>

The Zip drive is among the most popular medium-capacity removable disk formats. Available in ATAPI, SCSI, parallel-port, and USB variants, it's easy to attach a Zip drive to your computer. In fact, many new computers come with Zip drives preinstalled.

Zip disks support a few features in software that either aren't available or work by hardware on most other removable media. The most important of these is write protection. Under Linux, you can access the write protect feature or send an eject command using the ziptool package, which comes with many distributions or can be obtained from package distribution sites such as http://rufus.w3.org/linux/RPM/.

LS-120 SuperFloppies

The LS-120 SuperFloppy, pioneered by Imation (http://www.imation.com), is the Zip drive's main competitor in the medium-capacity removable disk market. Although the LS-120 fills a similar niche in the marketplace, it's distinguished from the Zip drive in two main ways:

- **Technology** When recording a 120MB disk, the LS-120 uses a hybrid magnetic/optical technology. The drive uses a laser to write an optical reference track to the disk, which enables the main magnetic read/write heads to position themselves more precisely than on standard floppies, hence producing higher capacity.

- **Compatibility** LS-120 disks are the same size as standard 3.5-inch floppy disks, and the LS-120 drive can read and write standard 3.5-inch floppies. This means that an LS-120 drive can replace a standard floppy disk on an x86 computer. In addition, an LS-120 drive can read standard floppies about three times faster than can a conventional floppy drive.

The vast majority of LS-120 drives come as internal ATAPI units. SCSI-based LS-120 drives are available, but difficult to find. USB and parallel-port models also exist.

Magneto-Optical Disks

Magneto-optical (MO) disks, like LS-120 disks, use a hybrid magnetic/optical technology. MO disks, however, rely more heavily on the optical portion of the technology. These drives use a laser to heat a special recording medium to high temperatures. At these high temperatures, a magnetic read/write head can alter the magnetic property of the disk, much like what happens in purely magnetic recording technologies. When reading the disk, no heating is required. The heating action of the laser is required to alter the magnetically encoded data on the disk. The result is that data stored on MO disks tend to be more resistant to change than data stored on purely magnetic media. This characteristic makes MO drives appealing for long-term storage. (More recently, CD-R drives have become still more appealing for long-term storage, because CD-R media cost much less than do MO media on a per-megabyte basis.)

MO drives cover a wide range of capacities and media form factors. They're available in both 3.5-inch and 5.25-inch styles, with capacities ranging from 128MB up to 5.2GB. Models that can read higher capacities can generally read media of lower capacity which use the same form factor. The 3.5-inch media resemble ordinary floppies, but are somewhat thicker. 5.25-inch MO media are constructed like the 3.5-inch media, complete with rigid plastic casing, but are larger. If you slide the metal cover away, the MO disks shimmer much like CDs.

MO drives are almost always sold as SCSI devices. MO drives tend to be expensive— $300–$2500, compared to $75–$200 for most Zip and LS-120 drives. MO media aren't much pricier than Zip and LS-120 disks, however, at least not for the lower-capacity media that compete with these disks.

If you're not concerned with exchanging data with others, an MO drive can be a good choice for medium- or high-capacity removable storage. This is especially true if you favor a SCSI interface over other interface types.

High-Capacity Removable Disks

As I've just mentioned, MO drives are available in some very high capacity forms, as removable drives go. Other technologies compete at the high end of the scale, as well, although none reaches quite as high as the highest-capacity MO drives. Most of these technologies are built on hard disk principles; they use hard disk technology, but with removable disk platters. The two most common of these at the moment are Iomega's Jaz (available in 1GB and 2GB varieties) and the Castlewood (http://www.castlewood.com) Orb drive (2.3GB). In their latest incarnations, these drives are comparable in terms of features and capacity, although the Orb has the edge in speed. The `ziptools` packagehelps you access Jaz drive features—eject and software write protection.

Like most MO drives, Jaz drives are available only with SCSI interfaces. Orb drives are available in a wider variety of interfaces. You can often purchase these drives in a bundle with a SCSI host adapter, but the quality of such bundled adapters tends to be low. You're probably better off buying a SCSI host adapter separately.

High-capacity removable disk drives are fairly rare, so don't count on using such drives for exchanging media with others unless you know what type of drive your counterpart uses. Because of the expense of the cartridges, these drives tend to be poor choices for data exchange with randomly selected individuals. If you need to distribute large files widely, a CD-R drive, as discussed in Chapter 7, "Optical Drives," is a better choice.

Choosing an Appropriate Interface

As detailed in Table 6.1, many removable media drives are available with a variety of interfaces. Which interface you choose has several consequences, including

- **Speed**   Some interfaces are faster than others. Speed differences for a single drive type in Table 6.1 are largely because of speed variation among interfaces.
- **Portability and mounting**   Some interfaces can be used only for internal devices, others only for external devices, and one (SCSI) for both internal and external devices.
- **Expense**   SCSI interfaces tend to be more expensive than the other varieties.
- **Linux drivers**   Linux supports all the major interface types, but some are easier to get working than others.

The Floppy Interface

Floppy disk drives are the only removable medium devices to have their own interface type. The floppy interface is a standardized part of all modern x86 motherboards. Many 80486 and earlier computers, however, placed the floppy interface on expansion cards along with EIDE or SCSI interfaces. Nonetheless, the standardized nature of the floppy interface guarantees that there are few incompatibilities between Linux and any floppy drive or floppy controller. It's therefore a safe interface, albeit a very slow one.

EIDE/ATAPI Interface

As described in Chapter 5, "Hard Disks," the terms *Enhanced Integrated Device Electronics* (EIDE) and *Advanced Technology Attachment Packet Interface* (ATAPI) both apply to the same interface, but they're generally used in reference to different devices. Specifically, ATAPI devices follow a set of protocols that are useful for controlling non-disk devices, such as CD-ROMs and tape drives. A few removable disk devices that attach to the IDE port don't include full ATAPI support, but most do. Table 6.1 refers to all such devices as EIDE drives for simplicity's sake, and I use that term in this discussion as a more inclusive term than ATAPI.

By whatever name, the EIDE interface is a reasonably good one for removable media devices. Designed for high-speed disk devices, EIDE has no trouble keeping up with the speed of removable-media drives, which tend to be substantially slower than modern hard disks. With support for booting from these drives in most BIOSes, these drives can be a convenient means for generating emergency Linux boot systems. You can install Linux to an appropriate removable medium, and then boot directly from that device in case of an emergency.

> **TIP**
>
> The Debian and Slackware distributions are particularly easy to strip down to the bare essentials for installation on a small removable drive such as a Zip or LS-120 disk. Even if you don't normally use one of these distributions, you might want to consider creating an emergency disk with one of them.

The EIDE interface does have its drawbacks for removable disks, however. One of these is that it's most suitable for internal drives. If you want the flexibility to move a drive from one computer to another, it's best to look elsewhere. (Kits for using EIDE devices externally do exist, however, so if you really must do it, it can be done.) Just as important, the limit of two devices per EIDE chain can be quite restrictive, particularly if you want to load your system up with additional devices like a CD-R burner and tape backup unit.

SCSI Interface

All other things being equal, the *Small Computer Systems Interface* (SCSI) bus is the best one for removable media. Even in its oldest SCSI-1 incarnation, SCSI is plenty fast for most removable media drives, and more recent versions can handle even the speedy Orb drives without trouble. Unlike EIDE, SCSI enables drives to be mounted either internally or externally, so you can move a single SCSI removable media drive from one computer to another—provided both computers have SCSI host adapters. SCSI also allows up to 7 or 15 devices (depending upon the SCSI variant) to be attached to a single host adapter, so it's easier to build a system with numerous SCSI devices than one with numerous EIDE devices.

SCSI does have its downside. One disadvantage is cost—the SCSI host adapter costs money, and SCSI versions of most removable media devices generally cost more than their EIDE counterparts. If you don't already have one, you'll need to add a SCSI host adapter, and the adapters that come with some removable media drives are rather low-end. Some can't be used with Linux.

Parallel-Port Interface

In the mid-to-late 1990s, the parallel port was the most common method of interfacing external removable media drives to computers. Such devices typically use splitter cables of one variety or another, so that you can attach the removable media drive along with a regular printer.

The parallel interface on these drives usually serves as a parallel-to-IDE or parallel-to-SCSI interface, and the drives then use IDE or SCSI internally. You therefore find Linux drivers for some of these devices in the EIDE or SCSI section of the Linux kernel configuration. I describe both types of configuration in greater detail later in this chapter.

In practice, the parallel port tends to be a weak interface for removable drives, for several reasons:

- **Speed**   Even at its best, the parallel port attains speeds of only about 2MB/s. In practice, it can't keep up with even a Zip-100 drive's speed, which is why parallel-interfaced versions of many drives are slower than their EIDE or SCSI counterparts.
- **Reliability**   Getting any sort of disk device working via the parallel port can be tricky. In most cases, it can be made to work reasonably well, but the rate of difficulties is higher than for most other interfaces.
- **Drivers**   It takes a hierarchy of Linux drivers to get a removable media device working on the parallel port. Although much rarer today than a few years ago, it's still possible that you won't find appropriate drivers for whatever parallel-port technology the drive manufacturer used.

- **Interference** Particularly prior to kernel 2.2, interference between a parallel-port disk drive and a printer was common. With the increasing demand for external devices (printers, removable disk drives, scanners, and so on), this problem can get quite bad if you want several external devices. Such systems generally do better with SCSI or USB interfaces.

Nonetheless, if you must have an external drive and SCSI is out of the question, a parallel-port device might be a reasonable choice. You might want to consider a USB device instead of a parallel device, however. Each interface has its drawbacks, but USB shows greater potential for the future.

USB Interface

The *Universal Serial Bus* (USB) interface is the latest craze among computer hardware manufacturers. Although USB is capable of still slower speeds than the parallel port (1.5MB/s versus 2MB/s), USB is a better choice for removable media drives because USB was designed to support several devices. I only recommend using USB for relatively low-end removable media devices, such as Zip and LS-120 drives, where the speed penalty from using USB won't be too great. Although Orb drives are available with USB interfaces, the speed drop (from 12MB/s to 1.5MB/s) is just too great to be tolerated except under extraordinary conditions.

Linux support for USB was nonexistent early in the 2.2.x kernel series, but has grown substantially since then, particularly late in the 2.3.x development series. This makes the choice of a USB removable media device tricky if you're currently using a 2.2.x-series kernel; you'll need to upgrade your kernel, or at least apply the latest USB patches to your existing kernel and recompile. As I write these words, USB Iomega Zip drives work well with 2.3.40 and later kernels, but LS-120 support appears to be spottier. I therefore strongly recommend that you check Deja News (`http://www.deja.com`) or the Linux USB development Web page (`http://www.linux-usb.org/`) for more information on Linux USB support for the specific drive you're considering.

NOTE

You can obtain the latest kernels from many general-purpose Linux FTP sites, such as `ftp://sunsite.unc.edu`, or from `http://www.kernel.org`. The Linux USB site, `http://www.linux-usb.org`, has patches for 2.2.x-series kernels to let them support most USB devices supported by 2.3.x-series kernels.

FireWire

FireWire (aka IEEE-1394 or i.Link) is the latest external connection technology. FireWire resembles USB in many respects—it's a serial technology that enables adding or removing devices while the computer is powered up. It's much faster than USB, however—it runs at up to 50MB/s, compared to 1.5MB/s for USB, with faster versions under development. These characteristics make FireWire an appealing technology for use with external disk devices.

Unfortunately, in early 2000, FireWire is largely vaporware. A few FireWire devices exist, but they're quite rare. FireWire drivers have appeared in late 2.3.x series kernels, but these drivers aren't yet available for 2.2.x kernels. Check `http://eclipt.uni-klu.ac.at/ieee1394` for more details.

PC-Card Interface

The PC-Card interface is used primarily by notebook computers to support assorted devices, including removable media drives. Some drives come with, or support as accessories, converters that let you use some other type of interface via a special PC-Card. Others let you plug a removable media device directly into the PC-Card slot.

Some notebook computers provide an option to use a Zip or LS-120 drive instead of a floppy disk or as a swap-out option in the same bay as a CD-ROM drive. These interfaces are likely to be faster than a PC-Card interface, and so are preferable in many cases to a PC-Card drive. Nonetheless, you might want to use a PC-Card interfaced drive for some reason, such as a greater ability to use the drive with other systems, such as a desktop computer.

Linux Compatibility with Removable Disks

Using removable disks with Linux is no more complex than is using a conventional fixed disk, although you do need to understand the rules for device files, mount options, and so on. Configuring your system to use a removable device sometimes poses challenges, however, because you must add appropriate devices drivers to the kernel, and it might not be obvious which drivers you need to add.

Kernel Options for Accessing Drives

When you configure your kernel for removable devices, you might need to check in several locations for appropriate device drivers. If you configure your Linux kernel by issuing the `make xconfig` command in the Linux source code directory (generally `/usr/src/linux`), you deal with two windows, which are shown in Figure 6.3. The first is the Linux Kernel Configuration window, which lists various broad classes of drivers and configuration options, such as *General setup* and *Block devices*. The second is the window you get when you click on any of these options, such as the General setup window in Figure 6.3. It's here that you set the options for your specific removable devices, although you set options for specific devices in several different windows.

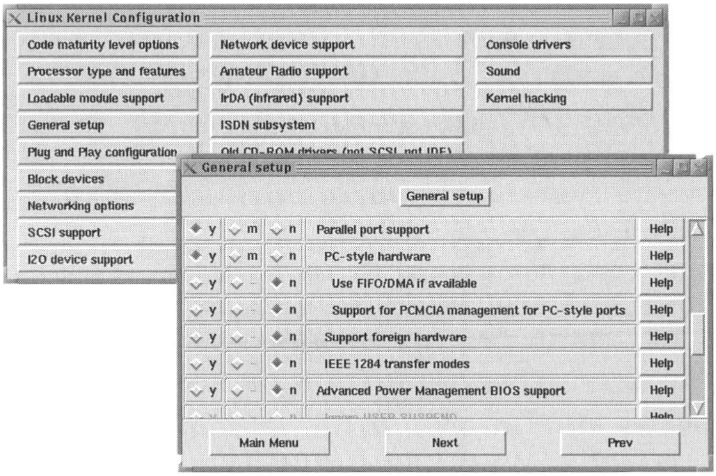

FIGURE 6.3

Open a specific kernel option's window, such as the General setup window, by clicking its matched button in the Linux Kernel Configuration window.

If you configure your kernel using a non-GUI tool, such as make menuconfig or make config, you make the same selections, but you use a text-based configuration tool, rather than the windows shown in Figure 6.3.

In most cases, you have a choice between three options for each device:

- Y Builds the driver into the main Linux kernel file. The driver will always be ready and available, but will also always consume at least some RAM.

- M Builds the driver as a separate module file, which you can load and unload as you see fit. This option saves RAM, but causes a slight delay when accessing files, especially if you don't configure your system to automatically load kernel modules as needed. This option isn't available for all devices, although it is for most.

- N Omits the driver from the kernel. You won't be able to use this device or feature.

Kernel Options for Floppies

Because of its simplicity, there's not much to be said about the options for floppy disks. On x86 computers, you must answer Y or M to the Normal PC floppy disk support option in the Block devices area to use the built-in floppy disk port. I generally use the modular compilation option to save a small amount of RAM, because I don't use floppies at all times.

If you have an external USB floppy, check the section on kernel options for USB devices. If you want to use an LS-120 drive to read conventional floppies, you do so through whatever interface your LS-120 drive uses.

Kernel Options for EIDE/ATAPI Drives

EIDE/ATAPI options are in the Block devices area. There are several options you might need or want to activate, in order to use an EIDE/ATAPI removable disk:

- **Enhanced IDE/MFM/RLL disk/cdrom/tape/floppy support**   This option must be set to Y or M to use EIDE/ATAPI devices of any sort. If you boot from an EIDE hard disk, it must be set to Y. If you use a SCSI hard disk but have an EIDE removable disk, you can set it to M if you like.

- **Include IDE/ATA-2 DISK support**   You must set this option to Y or M to use removable disks. Like the main EIDE support, this option must be Y if you boot from an EIDE hard disk, but can be either Y or M if you boot from a SCSI hard disk.

- **Include IDE/ATAPI FLOPPY support**   You must activate this option (Y or M) to use a removable EIDE disk.

- **EIDE chipset options**   Assorted options on the Block devices window relate to the specific EIDE chipset you use, either on your motherboard or on an add-on card. To get the best performance, you should activate appropriate options.

Kernel Options for SCSI Drives

SCSI options reside in one or two setup windows available from the Linux Kernel Configuration window. In the 2.2.x-series kernels, these options are spread across the SCSI support and SCSI low-level drivers items; in 2.3.x and 2.4.x kernels, the SCSI low-level drivers item has been moved into the SCSI support window as a sub-option. The options required for removable drives are:

- **SCSI support**   You must activate SCSI support. A Y response is required if you boot from a SCSI hard disk, but M is adequate if you boot from an EIDE disk.

- **SCSI disk support**   Like SCSI support, SCSI disk support is required, and must be Y only if you boot from a SCSI hard disk.

- **SCSI low-level drivers**   You must locate and activate the driver for the SCSI host adapter used by the removable disk drive. (See Chapter 9, "SCSI Host Adapters," for more information on SCSI host adapters.) If you boot from a SCSI hard disk, this option must be set to Y; otherwise it can be Y or M.

Kernel Options for Parallel Port Drives

Parallel-interfaced devices use a wide variety of drivers, many of which are tied to specific products. Options which you might need include

- **General setup, Parallel port support** This option is required for all parallel port removable disks, as well as all other devices that attach to parallel ports. Although you should be able to answer either Y or M to this option, I recommend Y, because so much depends on it and I've encountered cases where the kernel module auto-loader has problems with the parallel-port drivers.

- **General setup, PC-style hardware** If you use an x86 PC, respond Y or M to this option. If you use some other architecture, you might need to select another option, such as Support foreign hardware.

- **General setup, Use FIFO/DMA if available** Although not strictly required, answering Y to this option has the potential to improve performance, or at least reduce the CPU overhead when you access a parallel-interfaced disk drive.

- **Block devices, Parallel port IDE device support** This option is required (Y or M) for many such devices, but not for all them.

- **Block devices, Parallel port IDE disks** This option is used to support parallel-interfaced devices that use IDE without using the ATAPI protocols. If you're uncertain about it, build this support, at least as a module.

- **Block devices, Parallel port ATAPI disks** This option is like the previous one, but incorporates ATAPI protocols for devices that use them. Again, if you're uncertain, include this support.

- **Specific block devices** Below the last couple of options are a number of drivers for specific devices, such as the MicroSolutions backpack protocol. You *must* select at least one of these devices to use an IDE-style parallel port drive. If you don't see your device listed, try doing a search on http://www.deja.com for help, or simply select all the devices. The file /usr/src/linux/Documentation/paride.txt can also be helpful in determining what driver to select.

- **SCSI low-level drivers, IOMEGA parallel port (ppa - older drives)** Activate this option if you have an older parallel-port–interfaced Iomega Zip drive. You do *not* need the parallel-port IDE drivers for this device.

- **SCSI low-level drivers, IOMEGA parallel port (imm - newer drives)** Use this driver if you have a newer Zip Plus drive with a cable labeled "Auto Detect." You don't need parallel-port IDE drivers for this device.

> **TIP**
>
> If you have a SCSI hard disk and a parallel-port Iomega Zip drive, I recommend building the Iomega parallel-port drivers as a module and the driver for your main SCSI host adapter into the kernel. This guarantees that the kernel won't become confused and try to boot from the Zip drive instead of the SCSI boot disk.

When you use a parallel-interfaced device, how you access the drive depends on the sub-variety of interface used, SCSI or IDE. An Iomega Zip drive turns up as an ordinary SCSI device, whereas the IDE drives use special device files. The file `/usr/src/linux/Documentation/paride.txt` contains a script you can run to create appropriate device files, if they don't already exist on your system. (Most distributions include these device files.)

Kernel Options for USB Drives

USB kernel options are changing rapidly with the 2.3.x Linux kernels, and will probably vary somewhat from what I describe here for the 2.4.x kernels. If you want to use USB devices with a 2.2.x kernel, you must use a very recent 2.2.x kernel or apply a set of patches to add USB support to the older kernel. Options relevant to USB removable disks include

- **USB drivers, Support for USB** This option is required to use any USB devices.
- **USB chipsets** Two USB low-level drivers exist, UHCI and OHCI. You must select whichever one is appropriate for your computer.
- **USB drivers, USB SCSI (mass storage)** This option includes support for some USB disk devices, treating them as if they were SCSI disks.
- **SCSI options** The Linux USB support for disk devices relies upon SCSI drivers, so you must activate SCSI drivers as if you were using a SCSI host adapter. You don't need to use drivers in the SCSI menu for any particular SCSI host adapter, however.

Linux kernel support for USB storage devices is weak in the 2.2.x and 2.3.x kernels, but is rapidly improving. With any luck, the support will be reliable early in the 2.4.x series kernels. For the latest information, check `http://www.linux-usb.org/`.

Using Appropriate Device Files

To access a removable medium device, you normally mount it somewhere in the Linux filesystem using the `mount` command. For example, `mount /dev/fd0 /mnt/floppy` mounts a floppy disk at `/mnt/floppy`. You can also use these device files to create a filesystem on a removable disk, as in `mkfs -t ext2 /dev/fd0`, which creates a Linux ext2 filesystem on a floppy disk. What device files do you use, though? It depends on the type of interface, such as

- **Floppy port**   You use device files with filenames of the form `/dev/fd*`. In most cases, `/dev/fd0` suffices, but there are a large number of device files designed to force access to the drive using a particular capacity, such as `/dev/fd0h1440` and `/dev/fd0h720`, which force access as 1.44MB and 720KB, respectively. You can use these variants to force the Linux `fdformat` program to format a disk to an unusual capacity, as in **`fdformat /dev/fd0h1494`** to format the disk for a capacity of 1,494KB. If your computer has more than one floppy, the second is accessed as `/dev/fd1` or appropriate variants.

- **EIDE port**   An internal EIDE removable disk is accessed just like an internal EIDE hard disk, as `/dev/hdxy`, where *x* is a letter from a–d (or possibly higher in some cases) and *y* is a number from 1 up. The *x* value represents the device position—a for the master drive on the primary controller, b for the slave drive on the primary controller, and so on. The *y* value represents the partition number, and is omitted if you access the disk without partitions, as if it were a very large floppy disk, or when you use `fdisk` to partition the disk. (I describe partitioning shortly, in the section titled, "Removable Disk Partitioning Schemes.")

- **SCSI port**   SCSI drives take on device filenames similar to those for EIDE drives, but the SCSI drives take the form `/dev/sdxy`. The SCSI device *x* code is assigned differently; a is always the first SCSI drive, no matter what its SCSI ID, b is always the second SCSI drive, and so on.

TIP

If you have an external SCSI removable disk drive that you sometimes detach from your computer, give it a SCSI ID higher than that of any SCSI hard disks. That way, when you move the removable drive to another computer, it won't disrupt the device assignments of the fixed disks.

- **Parallel port**   Parallel port devices that use parallel-to-SCSI converters, such as the parallel version of the Iomega Zip drive, receive SCSI drive assignments, as just described. Parallel port devices that use parallel-to-IDE converters, by contrast, acquire entirely new drive identifiers, of the form `/dev/pdxy`. As with EIDE and SCSI devices, *x* is a letter representing the device, and *y* is an optional number representing the partition.

- **USB port**   Because the USB support uses the Linux SCSI features to handle disk devices, USB drives take on SCSI device filenames.

Exchanging Media with Other OSs

One of the key advantages to removable media is that they make it easy to exchange data with other computers—even those that don't run Linux. Fortunately, Linux's support for foreign filesystems is excellent, so you should have few troubles exchanging data with non-Linux computers, when you have your removable disk device working properly.

Removable Disk Partitioning Schemes

Unlike hard disks, floppy disks are so small that it makes little sense to break them up into separate partitions. Floppy disks are therefore never partitioned; you access the filesystem on the floppy disk using the main disk device file, such as `/dev/fd0`. This isn't always the case with higher-capacity media, however. These devices are sometimes partitioned just like hard disks, although they usually hold but a single partition. Common partitioning schemes include

- **No partitioning**   It's possible to use high-capacity removable media devices without partitions, just like floppy disks. You then create and mount filesystems using the device identifier without any partition number, as in **mount** `/dev/sdb` `/mnt/modisk` to mount an MO disk. This practice is particularly common with some low-capacity devices, such as older MO disk types.

- **Partition #1**   A reasonable choice for partitioning is to use partition #1 (`/dev/sda1`, for instance). This is the first primary partition entry on a disk. Many Linux users create Linux ext2fs partitions in this location when they use removable media drives.

- **Partition #4**   By default, Iomega partitions its Zip disks to use the standard x86 partition #4 (`/dev/sda4`, for instance). The partition is just as large as `/dev/sda1` would be; only the identifying number is different. If you use a Zip drive, you might want to use partition #4, in order to facilitate the exchange of data with other Zip drive users.

- **Non-x86 partitioning**   On rare occasions, you might encounter a removable disk that's partitioned, but not in a way that's common on x86 computers. For example, removable media from a Macintosh can use the Macintosh partitioning scheme, which is different from the x86 partitioning scheme. Linux's Hierarchical Filesystem (HFS) support includes support for simple Macintosh partition tables, so you can treat such disks as if they were unpartitioned. If you add Macintosh partition support to your kernel, you can also mount the disk using the partition number, which is likely to be #4.

I suggest using whatever partitioning scheme is most common for your type of drive. For example, on Zip disks, I recommend partitioning the disk into a single large partition 4. This practice allows you to create a single mount point and use a single entry in `/etc/fstab` to mount Zip disks from almost any source.

Filesystem Drivers for Foreign OSs

As I mentioned, Linux includes support for a wide variety of filesystems, which makes exchanging data with foreign OSs easy. The four filesystems you're most likely to encounter on removable media are

- **FAT**   The FAT filesystem is used natively by DOS, Windows, and OS/2, and is supported as a non-native filesystem by just about every other OS. It's therefore extremely common on removable media. In Linux, you can mount such a device using any of three filesystem types: msdos, umsdos, and vfat. The first provides access to traditional MS-DOS style filenames, which are limited to eight characters in length, plus a 3-character extension. The umsdos filesystem adds support for UNIX-style long filenames, permissions, and so on, but in a way that's only readable in Linux. The vfat option is generally the most useful today, because it supports Windows-style long filenames.

- **ext2fs**   Linux's native filesystem, ext2fs, can easily be used on removable media disks. It includes more overhead than FAT, so it tends not to be as efficient a choice on small- and medium-sized disks. If you want to preserve UNIX-style ownership and permission information, however, ext2fs is an excellent choice.

> **TIP**
>
> To maximize available space on an ext2fs removable disk, use the -m 0 parameter to the mke2fs command when you create the filesystem, as in **mke2fs -m 0 /dev/pda**. This parameter sets the *reserved space* to 0%. Ordinarily, ext2fs reserves a certain amount of space (5% by default) for the root user. The idea is that, if a filesystem fills up, the superuser should still have some disk space to use in cleaning up the problem. This logic isn't as applicable to a removable disk, however, so it's safe to set the reserved space to 0%.

- **Minix**   The Minix filesystem is moderately popular in the Linux community on floppy disks. This filesystem was designed for the Minix OS, which served as a partial model for Linux. In fact, the very earliest Linux systems used the Minix filesystem on hard disks. This filesystem is limited in its maximum size, however, and even Zip drives exceed its reach. It remains useful on floppies, however, because it requires less overhead than does ext2fs.

- **HFS**   If you regularly exchange files with Macintosh users, there's a good chance you'll get disks that use the Macintosh's native HFS. Linux kernels 2.2.x and later include HFS support, so you need only ensure that it's included in your kernel. Linux's HFS support is, as of the 2.2.x and 2.3.x kernels, still considered experimental, and it's been known to damage HFS disks. Therefore, I recommend only reading from HFS disks, if at all possible. Writing to small disks, and those that contain few or no files, is safer than writing to larger disks that contain many files.

NOTE

The floppy interface chips in x86 computers are incapable of reading the low-level encoding used by old Macintosh 400KB and 800KB floppies. You therefore can't read such floppies on x86 computers that run Linux, even if you've included HFS support in the kernel. Macintosh 1.44MB floppies, however, use the same low-level encoding format as do x86 1.44MB floppies, so you can read these newer Macintosh floppies.

NOTE

As of yet, there is no Linux driver to handle Apple's new HFS+. Fortunately, HFS+ is used almost exclusively on hard disks; you're unlikely to encounter it on a removable disk. It's possible you'll run across it on an unusually high-capacity disk, however, in which case you won't be able to read it in Linux until somebody releases a Linux HFS+ driver.

Linux uses the /etc/fstab file to indicate what partitions and other disk devices to mount at boot time. You can also use this file to tell Linux that ordinary users should be allowed to mount removable media. Here are some sample entries from an /etc/fstab file:

```
# Device filename   Mount point   Filesystem   Options            Dump   Fsck
/dev/fd0            /mnt/floppy   auto         user,noauto         0      0
/dev/sda            /mnt/maczip   hfs          ro,user,noauto      0      0
/dev/sda4           /mnt/zip      auto         user,noauto         0      0
```

Each entry consists of several columns, separated from one another by one or more space or tab characters. Lines beginning with a pound sign (#) are comments. The meaning of each column is

- **Device filename**   The name of the device file to be used, which can include a partition identifier. The preceding examples relate to a floppy drive and a SCSI Zip drive.

- **Mount point**   The location in the Linux filesystem where the device will be mounted. This is also the portion that an ordinary user uses to mount the device, as I describe shortly.
- **Filesystem**   You can specify a filesystem in this column, or use auto to tell the computer to attempt to auto-detect the filesystem type.

> **TIP**
>
> Specifying a filesystem of auto is a useful way to simplify your configuration. Both the /mnt/floppy and /mnt/zip mount points in the preceding example can be used to mount FAT, ext2fs, or various other filesystem types, so you don't need to know what filesystem is on a disk to mount it. Linux often has trouble auto-detecting HFS disks, though, which is one reason the preceding example has a separate entry for Macintosh Zip disks.

- **Options**   You can specify mount options, as described in the mount man page, in the next column. The most important of these for this discussion are user and noauto, which enable any user to mount a disk and prevent the system from trying to mount the disk at boot time, respectively. Chances are you want to include both these options for all your removable devices.
- **Dump code and fsck order**   The final two codes relate to whether to back up a partition using the dump utility and the order in which the kernel should check partitions at boot time. Neither is terribly useful for removable disks, and so both should be set to 0.

After you've made appropriate changes to your /etc/fstab file, you can type **mount -a** as root to activate those changes. You can then mount a removable medium as an ordinary user by typing **mount /mount/point**, where /mount/point is the mount point, such as /mnt/zip or /mnt/floppy. When you're done, use the umount command to unmount the disk in much the same way. (Yes, that command is spelled correctly; it's spelled without the first n.)

Direct-Access Tools and Miscellaneous Utilities

In addition to mounting a removable disk onto the Linux filesystem structure, you can perform other actions or access the disk in other ways. One of the most important of these is to use the mtools package, which lets you access a removable disk with commands modeled after DOS commands. For example, **mdir a:** shows a directory listing on the floppy disk, and **mcopy** **filename a:** copies a file called *filename* to the floppy disk. As a general rule, the mtools commands work like DOS commands of the same name, but the mtools counterpart commands prepend an *m* to the command names. The mtools package can be a very convenient way to access a floppy disk quickly, but it doesn't provide access to the disk from other programs. If you want to directly read or write a file using, say, a word processor, you must mount the disk in a conventional way. More information on mtools is available from the project's Web page, http://mtools.linux.lu/.

The hfsutils package is similar to mtools, but provides access to HFS disks. This package includes a program called xhfs that provides a GUI interface to let you copy files back and forth, as shown in Figure 6.4. You can learn more at http://www.mars.org/home/rob/proj/hfs/.

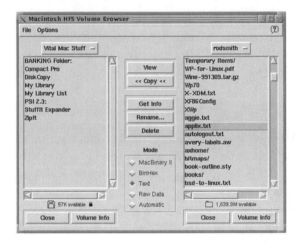

FIGURE 6.4
The xhfs utility lets you copy files to and from Macintosh disks using a GUI environment.

In addition to these specialized tools for accessing specific filesystems, you can use a number of standard Linux tools to manipulate disks in a variety of ways:

- **mkfs** The mkfs command creates a filesystem on a disk or partition. In actuality, mkfs simply calls another program, depending upon the filesystem type you specify with the -t option; for instance, mkfs calls mke2fs if you type **mkfs -t ext2 /dev/hdc4**, to create an ext2 filesystem on an EIDE removable disk. Most Linux systems come with mke2fs and mkdosfs (to create a FAT filesystem), but others are available as well.

- **fsck** This command checks a filesystem for integrity. As with mkfs, fsck relies on other programs to do most of the work. Of most interest, e2fsck checks an ext2 filesystem, but there's also a dosfsck to check DOS filesystems, and others for more exotic filesystems.

- **tune2fs** This program lets you adjust ext2fs parameters after the filesystem has been created. For instance, you can adjust an existing partition so that it has a smaller or larger reserved space area.
- **fdisk** If you decide to use your removable disks as hard disks, with partitions, you might need to use Linux's fdisk utility to create or modify partitions. You can use Linux's fdisk to change a partition type code to 0x83 ("Linux native") on a disk that's preformatted for FAT, for example.

Check the man pages for the appropriate utility to learn more about these tools.

Summary

Removable media disk drives can be a very useful tool for storage of seldom-used files and for the exchange of data between computers. Linux includes good support for such drives, but support for some drives is better than for others. As a general rule, you'll find it easiest to use a SCSI or EIDE/ATAPI drive. Devices based on parallel-port interfaces can be finicky, but can usually be made to work. Support for USB devices is improving rapidly as the Linux kernel moves towards a 2.4 release. The venerable floppy interface is quite usable in Linux, of course, but the only disk device to use that port is a conventional floppy disk. In years to come, FireWire might be an excellent interface for removable media, but in early 2000, the technology is too new, and the Linux drivers are still quite immature.

Optical Drives

IN THIS CHAPTER

Chapter 6, "Removable Disks," covered most removable disk media. There is one notable gap in Chapter 6's coverage, however: *compact discs* (CDs) and related media, which I refer to as *optical drives*. The reason for the gap in Chapter 6 is simple: These media are important enough that they deserve a chapter of their own. The importance of these media derives largely from their ubiquity. It's almost impossible to buy an x86 computer today that doesn't include some form of optical media drive. Optical media are also the media of choice for installing and distributing Linux, with the possible exception of installing via a network connection.

> **NOTE**
>
> Some media aside from those I describe in this chapter use optical technologies. For instance, magneto-optical (MO) drives use lasers as part of their recording process. CD-ROMs and related devices are the most common optical drives, however, and are the only devices in common use that rely exclusively upon optical technologies for data recording. MO drives, for example, use magnetic principles in addition to optics in reading and writing data.

Optical Media Overview

Optical drives can be classified along two dimensions: capacity and read/write capability. Low-capacity drives are CD-ROM, CD-R, and CD-RW devices, whereas the newer DVD devices are CD-ROMs' high-capacity relations. CD-ROM and plain DVD-ROM drives are read-only, but CD-R, CD-RW, DVD-R, and DVD-RAM devices add the capability to write data to discs.

CD-ROM: The Granddaddy of Optical Media

The CD-ROM is the oldest of the major optical media types, and it's still in common use today. All the more advanced drive types described in this chapter can read CD-ROM media, so you need not discard existing CD-ROM discs when it comes time to upgrade to a more capable drive type.

CD-ROM Design

The *compact disc* (CD) was developed in the 1980s as a medium for storing music. This fact had certain consequences that have influenced the way the CD medium was subsequently adapted as a computer data storage device. Most importantly, a music CD requires that data come off the disc at a constant rate. Two ways to accomplish this goal using a circular medium are in common use, assuming data are stored in *sectors* of fixed size:

- **Fixed number of sectors per rotation**   Consider a medium that is broken down into sectors and cylinders (or *tracks*), as shown in Figure 7.1. Suppose the disc is spun at a constant rate, no matter what portion of the disc is being read. This design is known as *constant angular velocity*, and it causes data to be read at a constant rate. Most floppy disks use this approach, as do some older hard disks and one format used by video laserdiscs. In some sense, so do old-style LP records, although they use a single spiral track rather than multiple cylinders, as depicted in Figure 7.1. The drawback to this approach is that it doesn't make optimal use of the recording medium. In order to record data reliably on the inner cylinders, the data density on the outer cylinders is much lower than the medium is capable of maintaining. Packing more data into the outer cylinders allows the storage of more data on the medium, but when the disc is spun at a constant angular velocity, the data transfer rate becomes variable from one cylinder to the next. This trade-off is acceptable for hard disks, but not for an *audio* recording medium.

- **Fixed linear sector size**   In order to pack more data onto a circular medium, it's possible to vary the number of sectors per cylinder. This approach is taken with modern hard disks. For absolutely optimum data storage capacity, it's useful to adjust the number of sectors for *each* cylinder. In CDs, in fact, the concept of a cylinder is eliminated, in favor of a single spiral track. Imagine a long track wound around a central core, as shown in Figure 7.2. This is the approach used by CDs. The difficulty with this design is that, to play music from the CD, it's necessary to spin the disc at a variable speed (in terms of rotations per minute), faster for reading the inner areas and slower for the outer areas. This requirement increases the complexity of the drive's design.

This spiral track design works well for audio CDs, but it's less than optimal for use as a more general-purpose data recording medium. The reason is that it can be difficult to locate specific tracks without precisely defined cylinders and sectors that begin at precisely-defined positions in the medium's rotation. For this reason and to add error-correction codes for increased reliability, data storage formats for CD-ROMs devote some space used for data in audio CD formats to other purposes. Audio CDs use a sector size of 2352 bytes. For data CDs, this 2352-byte sector is broken up into 2048 bytes of data plus 304 bytes of error correction and other codes.

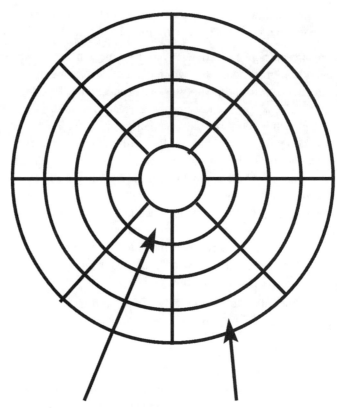

Variable Sector Size

FIGURE 7.1

Sectors on outer cylinders are physically larger in size with a fixed number of sectors per cylinder, but sectors retain the same capacity on inner and outer cylinders.

A standard 4.72-inch CD can hold 74 minutes of audio data as an audio CD or 650MB of data as a CD-ROM. It's also possible to wind the tracks slightly more tightly than normal in order to increase the CD's capacity, but CDs that can store more than 700MB, or 80 minutes, are quite rare. Increasing the disc's capacity past 650MB runs the risk that the disc won't be readable on some CD players or CD-ROM drives.

7

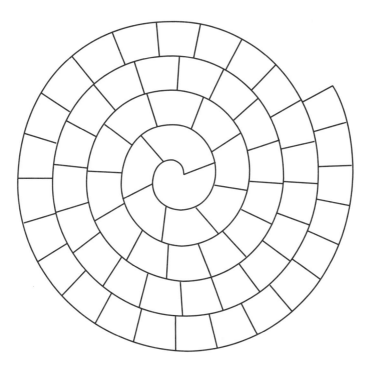

FIGURE 7.2
A spiral track with constant linear size of the sectors can fit more data on the medium, but requires a variable number of rotations per minute to achieve a constant data transfer rate.

Types of CDs

CDs come in many varieties, based largely on the way data are encoded on the disc. (There are mini-discs, however, which are physically smaller than conventional CDs.) Most of the CD classifications are referred to by the color of the book used to describe the specification. The most common CD types are

- **Red Book**   The format used by audio CDs. Also referred to as *CD-DA* (for *CD digital audio*).

- **Yellow Book**   The format used by data CDs. The term *CD-ROM* (for *CD read-only memory*) is often used in reference to Yellow Book CDs, although it's sometimes used in reference to other data-format CDs, as well.

- **Green Book**   The format used by *CD-interactive* (CD-i) discs. This format never became popular, but was a way to fit both computer data and audio-visual information on a single medium.

- **Orange Book**   The format used by recordable CDs. The Orange Book includes sections relating to some MO technologies. Part III refers to CD-R and CD-RW devices, which I describe later in this chapter.

- **CD Extra**   A format that contains separate audio (CD Extra format) and data (Yellow Book format) sections.

- **CD-ROM/XA**   *XA* stands for *extended architecture*. This format is another mixed audio/data format.

In addition to these low-level data formats, a number of high-level formats exist for laying out data, as described in the section "Optical Filesystem Options," later in this chapter.

CD-R: Making Your Own CD-ROMs

CD-ROMs are excellent media for unchanging data that can be distributed *en masse*, such as Linux distributions, clip art collections, and music. Because these are read-only media, however, you can't create your own CD-ROM. This deficiency is addressed with *CD recordable* (CD-R) technology. Where a CD-ROM uses a series of pits in a substrate to signal binary data, a CD-R uses a light-sensitive dye. When a CD-R drive's laser is turned on high power, it can alter the reflectivity of the dye, thus simulating the effect of a pit in a conventional CD. The result is that you can create your own CD-ROMs—or at least something very similar to a CD-ROM. The CD-R creation process is often referred to as *burning* a CD-R. Most CD-ROM drives can read CD-R discs, although there are occasional incompatibilities. CD-R drives can read ordinary CD-ROM discs, although their speed is generally slower than that of dedicated CD-ROM drives. CD-R drives are also more expensive and more delicate than CD-ROM drives, so many people who use CD-R drives have separate CD-ROM drives they use for reading both conventional CD-ROMs and the CD-R discs they burn themselves.

The compatibility of CD-R media with CD-ROM drives is something of a mysterious art. Different CD-R drives produce burned CD-Rs with different optical characteristics, even when using the same media. Table 7.1 summarizes hypothetical compatibility between different CD-R drives, media, and CD-ROM drives. Note that, depending upon the brand of media used, the compatibility patterns for CD-ROM drives 1 and 2 are completely reversed, whereas CD-ROM drive 3 can read anything. The only way to know what works well is to experiment. Fortunately, compatibility is better with recent CD-ROM drives, and recent media are better than those from just one or two years ago. If you buy a CD-R drive and experience problems reading the discs you burn, try switching media brand.

TABLE 7.1   Hypothetical CD-R Media/Drive Compatibility

	CD-R Recorder X		CD-R Recorder Y	
Reading Drive	*Media A*	*Media B*	*Media A*	*Media B*
CD-ROM 1	Y	N	N	Y
CD-ROM 2	N	Y	Y	N
CD-ROM 3	Y	Y	Y	Y

NOTE

There are three major types of CD-R media: green/gold (cyanine dye on gold substrate), gold/gold (phthalocyanine dye on gold substrate), and blue/silver (azo dye on silver substrate). Most drives work fine with each type of media, and any failures are brand-specific, and aren't predictive of the capability of a drive to cope with other media of the same type. Because the media are so new, longevity tests are tentative at best, but indications are that gold/gold and blue/silver media can last longer than green/gold media (100 years for gold/gold or blue/silver versus 10–50 years for green/gold are typical estimates).

7

OPTICAL DRIVES

To a CD-R drive, there's little difference between an audio CD and a data CD-ROM. It's therefore possible to create your own audio CDs using a CD-R drive. You can extract digital audio data from a CD or use a sound card to capture sound from another source—a microphone or an input from a stereo system, for instance. In this way you can transfer music from old analog LP records to CD, or create CDs of music you perform yourself.

CD-RW: Erasable CD-Rs

CD-Rs let you create your own CDs, but they suffer from a problem: They can't be erased and re-used. Suppose you download your favorite Linux distribution and burn it to a CD-R. A week later, you find that a newer version has been released. You must now burn a *new* CD-R, if you want to keep up to date; you can't erase and write over the one you just created. Fortunately, CD-R media are inexpensive, but a better solution is to use media that can be erased. This is the goal of *CD rewritable* (CD-RW) technology. CD-RW drives function like CD-R drives, but when used with CD-RW media, the results can be undone. Typically, it's necessary to first erase the CD-RW media, and then burn a new disc. Various drivers in Windows allow you to use a CD-RW disc much like a Zip, LS-120, or other conventional removable disk. Such support is still lacking in Linux, but it's likely to materialize eventually.

CD-RW technology does have a drawback: It's more expensive than CD-R technology. When they were first introduced, CD-RW drives cost several hundred dollars more than CD-R drives, but today that cost difference is less than $100. Likewise, CD-RW media were once much more expensive than CD-R media, but the price difference has shrunk substantially since 1998. Another drawback is that CD-RW media are readable only on a small fraction of the installed base of CD-ROM drives, although most new models can cope with CD-RW discs.

TIP

The term *MultiRead* applies to CD-ROM and related drives that can read CD-ROM, CD-R, and CD-RW discs. It's worth looking for a MultiRead CD-ROM drive if you're in a market for a new one.

Fortunately, CD-RW drives can write both CD-RW and CD-R media. You can therefore get the best of both media types by purchasing a CD-RW drive and using CD-R or CD-RW media, as seems best for any given disc.

DVD: The Next Step in CD-ROM

A typical CD-ROM disc (or a CD-R or CD-RW disc) is limited to about 650MB of data. In a pinch, the capacity can be pushed up a bit from this limit, but not by a lot. With the ever-increasing need for high-capacity storage, CD-ROMs have become inadequate for many purposes. Enter the *digital versatile disc* (DVD). A DVD can hold between 4.38GB and 7.95GB of data per side, and DVDs can be produced in a double-sided manner, so as to hold up to 15.90GB. Future DVD developments are likely to increase these limits further, although such changes will be incompatible with current DVD hardware.

The term *DVD-ROM* (DVD read-only memory) is often applied to data DVD discs or to DVD drives for computers, much as *CD-ROM* is used to refer to data CDs. Even video DVDs, however, use the new DVD filesystem; it's just that video DVDs encode the data in a highly structured way that allows the simple computers in TV-top DVD players to play a movie. The distinction between video DVDs and DVD-ROMs is therefore not as great as the distinction between audio CDs and CD-ROMs. I use the term *DVD-ROM* only in reference to discs that contain computer data, or to drives for computers. I use the term *DVD* in reference to the technology more generally.

DVD-ROM drives can read CD-ROM discs, and recent DVD-ROM drives can also read CD-R and occasionally CD-RW discs as well. In Linux, a DVD-ROM drive can automatically be used as a CD-ROM drive. The filesystem used on most DVD discs is fairly new, but support for it in Linux exists in a preliminary form, and will soon become a standard part of the Linux kernel. In fact, SuSE Linux 6.3 is available either on several CD-ROM discs or on a single DVD-ROM disc.

> **CAUTION**
>
> Early DVD drives couldn't read CD-R discs. In fact, some DVD equipment bears a warning that the DVD drive can damage CD-R discs. I therefore don't recommend using a DVD drive with CD-R discs unless the drive's manufacturer explicitly supports such use.

Recordable DVDs

As with CD-ROM, DVD is a read-only technology. There are, however, read/write variants. *DVD recordable* (DVD-R) is akin to CD-R. It actually comes in two sub-variants, known as *authoring* and *general*. *DVD-RAM*, *DVD-RW*, and *DVD+RW* are read/write formats that allow erasure and reuse of the media, much like CD-RW. Each is incompatible with the others. DVD-RAM, DVD-R, and DVD-RW are available today, whereas DVD+RW is expected in 2001.

DVD-R, DVD-RW, and DVD+RW are closely related technologies. DVD+RW is essentially an improved version of DVD-RW, capable of storing more data per disc. All three have the potential to create media that are readable by ordinary DVD players, although it's unclear how real this potential is, particularly for the unreleased DVD+RW format.

Recordable DVD technology has historically been quite expensive, but prices are dropping fast. DVD-RAM, in particular, is now becoming affordable, with prices for drives under $1000, and some under $500. Media created in DVD-RAM drives can't be played on ordinary DVD drives, however. DVD-R drives that can create media readable on read-only DVD players still cost several thousand dollars in early 2000.

As with CD-R and CD-RW drives, it's possible to download a Linux distribution onto a recordable DVD format and install from that DVD. In early 2000, most distributions are available in downloadable image files sized for CD-R media, however, so there's little to be gained from DVD media over CD media for this function. This situation is likely to change in the future, however.

Drive Interfaces

Like most other data storage devices, optical media drives come in a variety of interface types. Today, EIDE/ATAPI and SCSI drives dominate the market, but that wasn't always the case, and it might not be the case in the future. In particular, USB and especially the new FireWire interfaces have the potential to acquire market share, although they're both rare today—especially FireWire.

SCSI Interfaces

Some of the earliest CD-ROM drives used SCSI interfaces, and many optical drives continue to do so. As with other devices, the SCSI interface has an edge over others in flexibility. With its 7- or 15-device capacity per chain, it's possible to add more devices to a SCSI system than to an EIDE system. This fact is particularly important if you want to use both a CD-ROM or DVD-ROM drive and a recordable device; these two devices alone consume a complete EIDE chain.

Until recently, SCSI CD-ROM drives seldom transferred data at higher than SCSI-1 transfer rates. These drives could frequently be used with inexpensive ISA SCSI host adapters with little speed degradation. Many modern SCSI optical drives, however, are capable of transferring data at much higher speeds. A 40x drive, for example, can transfer data at a theoretical maximum of 6MB/s, which requires at least Fast SCSI-2. In practice, many such drives come with UltraSCSI interfaces (20MB/s), which allows for faster burst transfer rates. A few drives also come in Wide variants, which makes adding them to SCSI chains with Wide hard disks easier.

Because SCSI standards since SCSI-2 include standardized CD-ROM commands, there's no need to add device-specific drivers to Linux. You do need to add support for SCSI CD-ROMs, however, in the SCSI support section of the kernel setup options (see Figure 7.3). You can add the support either compiled into the kernel (Y) or as a module (M). A few CD-ROM drives support unique extensions to the standard SCSI commands. You can add support for these by selecting Y under the Enable vendor-specific extensions (for SCSI CDROM) option. Selecting this option unnecessarily does no harm, aside from a slight increase in the size of the driver. In addition to the SCSI CD-ROM support, you must add support for your specific model of SCSI host adapter.

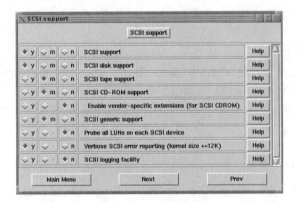

FIGURE 7.3

Add support for SCSI CD-ROM drives from the SCSI support kernel configuration area.

EIDE/ATAPI Interfaces

The popularity of the Enhanced Integrated Device Electronics (EIDE) interface for hard disks has spread to other media, including optical drives. Even fairly low-end EIDE interfaces are capable of handling fast optical drives. The main drawback to the EIDE interface is the severely limited number of EIDE devices that can fit on a single chain. In a system that includes several storage devices, this limitation can be a serious problem.

EIDE-based optical drives tend to cost substantially less than their SCSI counterparts. This makes the interface appealing even for those who use SCSI for hard disks. Because a CD-ROM drive is less likely than a hard disk to be in constant use, the loss of SCSI's multitasking features isn't so important to a CD-ROM drive. There's no problem in using SCSI hard disks and an EIDE-based CD-ROM drive. Recordable devices tend to have strict timing requirements, and so SCSI does offer some benefit for these drives, but modern EIDE recordable drives tend to be fairly reliable.

The Advanced Technology Attachment Packet Interface (ATAPI) specification includes a standardized set of commands for EIDE-interfaced CD-ROM drives. All but the very oldest EIDE optical drives support ATAPI, and, in fact, they're usually referred to as ATAPI drives.

Adding support for ATAPI optical devices is as easy as it is for SCSI optical devices; only the location of the relevant options is different. Specifically, you need to select Y or M under the Include IDE/ATAPI CDROM support option in the Block devices area of the configuration. As with SCSI, you must also add support for the underlying controller, which is done from the same menu. In the case of recordable drives, you might also want to select Y or M to the SCSI emulation support, and then add support in the SCSI section for SCSI CD-ROM and SCSI generic devices. Most Linux CD recording software only works with SCSI devices, or works best with SCSI devices, so providing this emulation helps a great deal when recording CDs on ATAPI recordable CD drives.

Older Proprietary Interfaces

In the early 1990s, CD-ROM drives were a luxury for most computer users. SCSI offered a standardized set of commands for CD-ROM drives, but IDE (EIDE's predecessor) did not; ATAPI had yet to be invented. IDE-based optical drives therefore did not exist. Because SCSI host adapters were quite expensive, manufacturers developed low-cost alternatives. Unfortunately, each manufacturer's alternative was incompatible with those offered by other manufacturers. These proprietary CD-ROM interfaces appeared on standalone ISA cards and on sound cards of the era. The matching CD-ROM drives were slow by today's standards; most were 1x or 2x drives, but a few 4x drives appeared as well.

If you have an old computer or have picked up an antiquated drive for use in a low-cost or temporary capacity, you might need to add support for these drives to your kernel. You can do this from the Old CD-ROM drivers (not SCSI, not IDE) configuration menu shown in Figure 7.4. You must select Y under the first option, Support non-SCSI/IDE/ATAPI CDROM drives, and select at least one drive type using a Y or M compilation option. Unlike with the SCSI and EIDE/ATAPI configuration, it's necessary for you to specify the exact model of CD-ROM drive you have. In some cases, you might need to specify additional options to help the driver locate the hardware.

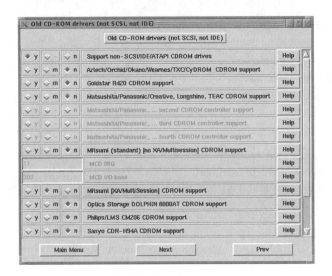

FIGURE 7.4
Linux includes support for many older proprietary CD-ROM interfaces.

Most Linux distributions ship with support for all proprietary CD-ROM drives enabled as modules. If you're not certain what model you've got, but you know it's an older proprietary device, you might want to do the same when you compile your kernel.

Parallel-Port Interfaces

A few CD-ROM drives use the parallel port. These devices are typically marketed for older portable computers that lack CD-ROM drives, and they're quite rare. In most cases, they use a parallel-to-IDE converter, and are handled in the same way as parallel-port removable media drives, described in the section "Parallel Port Interfaces" in Chapter 6.

As a general rule, I don't recommend using parallel-port CD-ROM drives, because they're not as reliable as their counterparts that use other interfaces. The parallel port also isn't capable of handling today's fast CD-ROM drives, although it's adequate for older drives.

USB Interfaces

The Universal Serial Bus (USB) is being used for a wide variety of devices today, including optical drives. USB optical drives currently have weak support in Linux, but that situation is likely to change in 2000 and 2001, as Linux's USB support matures. The Linux USB support maps disk devices, including optical media, to the SCSI protocols, so you must enable basic SCSI CD-ROM support in addition to appropriate USB options when you compile your kernel.

Although USB is a convenient interface for external devices, it's a weak one for optical media because of speed limitations. USB is restricted to 1.5MB/s transfer rates, which is far slower than that of typical drives today (such as 6MB/s maximum speed for a 40x CD-ROM drive). Nonetheless, USB speed is adequate for many CD-R and CD-RW drives, which typically use speeds of less than 1MB/s for burning. These drives can often attain higher speeds when *reading* data. Therefore, there is still a performance hit when using USB CD-R drives to read existing media.

CD Versus CD-R Versus DVD

If you're buying or building a new computer, you must decide which type of optical media drive to add to the computer. You must make the same choice if you decide to upgrade an existing drive or replace one that's broken. Note that these choices aren't mutually exclusive; you can have two or even more optical drives in one computer, assuming it's large enough and has enough resources such as IRQs or available SCSI IDs.

Choosing CD for Speed or Cost

The main advantages of CD-ROM drives are their speed and cost. Most CD-ROM drives today cost less than $100, although high-end SCSI models might cost a bit more, but still usually less than $200. These prices are coupled with excellent performance when reading conventional CD-ROM, CD-R, and often CD-RW media. In early 2000, it's difficult to find a drive that claims less than 24x performance, and 32x and 40x drives are more common. Some drives achieve speeds of up to 72x, or 10MB/s—as fast as some hard disks!

In practice, however, these speeds are never attained in the real world, for several reasons:

- **Head seeks** CD-ROM drives, like hard disks, use a moving head to seek to any area of the disc platter. These heads take time to move, and the seek times degrade overall performance, particularly when reading small files. Fortunately, most CD-ROM filesystems are inherently free of fragmentation, so there's typically no degradation because of fragmented files.

7

OPTICAL DRIVES

- **Filesystem overhead**   Although most CD-ROM filesystems reduce the need for head seeks caused by fragmented files, these filesystems are not entirely free of performance-robbing features. It's still necessary to check for file locations and perform other operations. As with head seeks, this factor is more important when reading small files than large ones.

- **Variable speed**   The earliest CD-ROM drives changed the rotational speed of the drive to read inner and outer portions of the disc. This design maintained a *constant linear velocity* of the laser beam over the media, and so such devices are known as *CLV* drives. Most recent designs don't vary their speed so much, and might not vary it at all, and are known as *partial constant angular velocity* (partial CAV) or *CAV* drives, respectively. These designs produce variable data transfer rates over different parts of the disc, and manufacturers typically quote their best speeds in advertising. Unfortunately, data on CD-ROM discs start at the innermost portion, which is the slowest, so a less-than-filled disc ends up being much slower to read than you might think by looking at the drive's specifications.

These principles all apply to other types of optical media, although CAV operation is most common with CD-ROM drives.

CAUTION

Some of the fastest CD-ROM drives available today use the *TrueX* technology, which uses multiple lasers to extract data at a higher speed than could otherwise be achieved. These drives tend to be CLV devices, and they spin at lower rates than other models, so they're quieter and less prone to speed-related errors. On the other hand, some people have reported problems using some TrueX drives with CD-R and CD-RW media, and some of these models are difficult to get working with Linux. Therefore, I suggest you check carefully on Linux and CD-R disc compatibility before buying a TrueX drive.

Choosing CD-R or CD-RW for Capability to Record

Recordable drives have an obvious advantage in their capability to record discs. This feature is particularly handy to Linux users with fast Internet connections, because it allows you to download your favorite Linux distribution and burn it to disc in a matter of hours. Recordable drives can also be useful as backup devices.

Using Recordable CDs for Backup

The low cost of CD-R and CD-RW media, and the high speed, random-access nature of these media, make them an appealing choice for backup media for many people. These drives weren't intended as backup media, however, so there are several obstacles to be overcome—or at least, questions you must answer.

One problem is the limited capacity of the media. 650MB is not much space for backing up most Linux systems today. One solution is to plan your Linux installation so that no partition contains more than 650MB of data, or at least no more than is likely to fit in that space, given compression. You can then back up one partition at a time. Another solution is to use backup software that supports splitting your backup across multiple archives. Unfortunately, most such programs were designed for tapes and floppies, not CD-R discs, so integrating the backup software with the CD-R software can sometimes be a nuisance. Probably the best solution is to use DVD-RAM (or perhaps some other recordable DVD technology), which has higher capacity than CD-based drives.

Another challenge comes in the choice of backup software. The usual CD-recording formats can give you true random access to your data, but they alter filesystem characteristics. Most importantly, they remove write access (which is meaningless on a read-only medium). Another option is to use tar or some similar archive program, and burn the resulting archive file to the CD-R. You then lose some of the random-access characteristics of the medium, but you preserve your filesystem information just as if you'd used a tape drive.

My own preference is to use a tape backup drive for most backup functions. I do, however, use a CD-R drive to create backups of critical and seldom-changing configurations, particularly when I want the archive to be readable on a variety of computers. For instance, I back up Windows boot partitions using my CD-R drive under Linux.

Recordable drives do have their downsides, however, including

- **Speed**   Although the read speed of CD-R drives is good enough for many purposes, it's not as good as the best CD-ROM drives. Recording speed is invariably slower than is reading speed, so speeds are generally given as two numbers, such as 8x/24x, which is quite fast by the standards of early 2000. CD-R seek times are also higher than are those of CD-ROM drives, because the recordable heads are heavier and therefore take more time to safely move.

- **Expense**   CD-R and CD-RW drives cost more than CD-ROM drives—usually between $200 and $400 in early 2000, although there are a few drives that cost more or less than this.

- **Delicacy**   Recordable drives are more sensitive to damage than are CD-ROM drives, and are therefore more likely to break.

Because of these factors, many people like to have both a CD-ROM or DVD-ROM drive and a CD-R or CD-RW drive. The combination of a DVD-ROM drive and a CD-RW drive gives a great deal of flexibility, provided the DVD-ROM drive is capable of reading CD-R, and ideally CD-RW, discs.

Choosing DVD for Access to New Media

At present, DVD-ROM drives are most useful if you want to play DVD films on your computer; however, it's only a matter of time before software comes to be routinely distributed on DVD-ROMs. In fact, this trend has already begun. SuSE Linux 6.3 is available either on six CD-ROMs or on a single DVD-ROM.

Unfortunately, as I write these words, the utility of DVD-ROM drives for viewing films in Linux is uncertain. Although a program known as DeCSS has been written for this purpose, the Motion Picture Association of America (MPAA) and the DVD Copy Control Association (DVD-CCA) have filed lawsuits to stop DeCSS's distribution. The claim of the MPAA and DVD-CCA is that DeCSS is a piracy tool. This is because DVD films include an encryption technology that makes their files useless except when viewed using decryption software, but DeCSS necessarily breaks that encryption, and as Open Source software, it's possible to use it to create an unencrypted file on a hard disk. DeCSS's proponents argue that because of the size of the files and cost of recordable DVD media, DeCSS's only *practical* use is as a means to view legally purchased DVDs, so the claim of intent to pirate is spurious. How these legal issues will be resolved remains to be seen, but you can check http://www.opendvd.org for the latest information.

> **NOTE**
>
> A few DVD drives come with a special decoder card that performs the work of decoding the video. In theory, such a card can be used in Linux to do the video decoding, but drivers for the card are necessary—and vanishingly rare. In early 2000, the only such card to have Linux drivers is the Creative DXR2, for which drivers are available from http://opensource.creative.com/.

Fortunately, DVD-ROM data discs aren't encumbered by the DVD-CCA's encryption technology, so Linux's capability to handle DVD-ROM discs isn't in danger. Many of these discs do use a new filesystem, however, as described later in this chapter, in the section "Optical Filesystem Options."

DVD-ROM drives are slightly more expensive than are CD-ROM drives, but not by a lot. Typical prices are in the $100–$150 range, although packages that include hardware decoders for DVD films cost about $100 more. In terms of speed, DVD-ROM drives are not quite as speedy as are CD-ROM drives, on average, although they're faster than most CD-R and CD-RW drives. DVD-ROM drives have speed ratings that are similar to those for CD-ROM drives (1x, 2x, and so on), but these ratings aren't relative to the same standard. For example, a 1x DVD-ROM drive is faster at reading CD-ROMs than is a 1x CD-ROM drive. Most drives' specifications include an equivalent performance rating for reading CD media. In early 2000, drives in the 5x–10x DVD-ROM speed range (32x–40x CD-ROM speed range) are common.

Evaluating Optical Drive Performance

As I mentioned earlier in this chapter, CD-ROM drives vary substantially in their performance characteristics. The specifications for CD-ROM drives are similar to those for hard disks. The key features are data transfer rate (which is determined by the rate at which the disc spins in the drive) and seek or access time. Like hard disks, CD-ROM drives also have on-board caches, and these can speed performance somewhat, so you should favor a larger cache over a smaller one, all other things being equal.

Spin Speed

The rate of spin of an original 1x CD-ROM drive varied, in order to achieve a constant data transfer rate of 150KB/s. Subsequent speed increases used the same CLV methods through approximately 10x speeds, depending upon the manufacturer. Most manufacturers then used CAV or partial CAV technology to increase maximum transfer speeds substantially, while improving minimum transfer speeds less dramatically. For instance, Plextor's (http://www.plextor.com) UltraPlex 40Max CAV drive achieves 40x transfer speeds at its fastest point, but only 17x at its slowest. You can expect similar speed disparities in other CAV drives, but less speed disparity in partial CAV drives.

TrueX drives, which use multiple laser beams rather than higher transfer rates to improve performance, generally use CLV operation, so they can achieve uniformly high transfer rates. As mentioned earlier, however, some of these drives don't work well under Linux, and some can damage CD-R or CD-RW media. Be sure to check with the manufacturer or on the comp.os.linux.hardware and comp.sys.ibm.pc.hardware.cdrom newsgroups about these details before buying one.

In years past, the fastest drives available typically used *caddies* (shown in Figure 7.5). These devices hold CDs in order to protect them and position them more precisely in the drive than can be done using a more typical tray-loading design. Ideally, you place each CD in its own caddy as soon as you get the CD, and don't remove it. You insert the caddy, complete with its passenger CD, into the drive when you want to read a data CD-ROM or listen to an audio CD. This procedure protects the CD from scratches and dirt, but can become expensive if you collect a large number of CDs. Today, caddies are rare, although a few recordable CD drives still use them.

FIGURE 7.5
A caddy's lid flips up to allow you to insert or remove a CD.

Head Movement Times

Optical drive head movement times are measured in the same ways as for hard disks. Two types of measurements are in common use:

- **Seek time** Seek time is the time it takes to move the head a given distance. The most common seek time measurement is the average seek time, which is statistically equivalent to the time to move the head one-third of the distance from its outermost position to its innermost position. Seek times for modern CD-ROMs are almost invariably under 100ms, and are typically in the 85ms range. Seek times for CD-R and CD-RW drives are typically about twice this. DVD seek times are typically about 100ms. CD-ROM seek times haven't improved much in the last couple of years.

- **Access time** Access time is the seek time plus the *latency*—the time for the desired data to rotate under the read head. On CLV drives, the latency varies from one position on the disc to another, but on CAV drives, the latency is constant from one position on the disc to another. As an example, consider the Plextor UltraPlex 40 I mentioned earlier. It's a CAV drive that rotates the disc at 8590 rpm, which means that one rotation of the disc takes 7ms, for an average latency of 3.5ms. Compared to the drive's seek time (85ms), this value is quite small, which is typical of modern CD-ROM drives.

> **NOTE**
>
> In a normal horizontal orientation, an optical disc is actually read from the bottom (the side with no writing, or the colored side of CD-R or CD-RW discs). Despite this fact, it's common to refer to the data on the disc passing *under* a read head.

For comparison, consider a modern hard disk, which typically has a seek time in the 9ms range, with disk rotation of 5400–10,000 rpm, resulting in latencies of 3–5.6ms. The high seek times of modern CD-ROM drives account for much of their speed deficit compared to hard disks. You should therefore not overlook the importance of seek time when evaluating different optical drives.

Digital Audio Extraction Capability

One feature of drive performance that doesn't show up in specification sheets is in drives' differing capabilities to perform *digital audio extraction* (DAE; also sometimes referred to as *ripping*). DAE is the process of reading audio data from a music CD into digital form that can be played on a computer's sound card, edited, and even recorded on a CD-R. All but the oldest CD-ROM drives are capable of performing DAE, but some drives do it far better than do others.

> **CAUTION**
>
> DAE, particularly in conjunction with a CD-R drive, provides the means to produce flawless copies of original music CDs. Such use, however, might be a violation of copyright laws. You should be sure that your use of DAE is legal before you use this feature. For instance, it's legal to copy music that's in the public domain, but it's not legal to copy the latest pop music CD for your friends. Copyright laws give you the right to copy copyrighted material for so-called *fair use* purposes, but precisely what constitutes fair use is debatable at best. Selling copies of music CDs or giving away copies to friends certainly falls outside of fair use, but very short excerpts (usually considered to be less than 10 seconds), backups, and in some cases limited copies created for use in scientific research or education are usually considered to fall within the fair use realm. Consult a copyright attorney if you're in doubt about your use of DAE—or copying data CDs, for that matter.

DAE is a challenging task for an optical drive because the audio CD medium was not designed for targeted data extraction. Specifically, the individual data sectors on an audio CD aren't labeled with indexes, so if you randomly seek to some sector and read it, you can't know what sector you've just read. This fact makes it difficult for a drive to seek to a specified location on an audio CD (say the start of a song) and extract audio data. In the event of a read error, the problem is exacerbated because the drive must try to locate the problem location a second time to re-read it. Even continuous reading isn't immune to the problem, because the program must read data in small chunks, in order to alternate between reading from the CD and writing to the hard disk. Data CDs overcome this problem by encoding a sector number among the error correction data as part of the sector overhead. (Recall that audio CDs use sectors of 2352 bytes, but data CDs devote 304 bytes of this to error correction and control data.) Using the sector numbers encoded within surrounding sectors, the drive can seek to a precise sector on the disc.

In DAE, the inability to reliably seek to a precise sector causes samples to overlap. For instance, if a DAE program extracts data in 8KB (four 2048-byte sector) chunks, then these chunks might overlap slightly or leave gaps, as shown in Figure 7.6. In reality, sample sizes in DAE are larger than 8KB, so the problem is seldom as severe as Figure 7.6 might suggest; but even a small gap or overlap can produce audible effects.

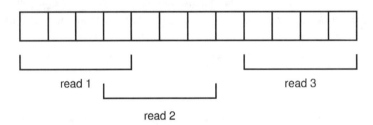

FIGURE 7.6
DAE reads often aren't well synchronized, resulting in overlaps and gaps in the data stream.

The flaws in an extracted audio file that result from these problems are known as *jitter*. (This term has another meaning with reference to non-CD audio.) Jitter typically sounds like small pops, cracks, or static in the extracted audio signal. When it's particularly bad, it can seriously disrupt the quality of music. Minor jitter might not be audible, however, particularly in loud passages or when the source was low in quality (such as a CD mastered from an old LP record).

Optical drives vary in the quality of their DAE. Some use above-average timing, special circuitry to assign sector numbers to extracted sectors, or other techniques to improve the reliability of the DAE. As a general rule, Plextor and Pioneer drives do better than most, but there are exceptions to this rule. (Plextor 6x drives aren't as reliable as most other Plextor models, for instance.) You can obtain some information on DAE jitter from the "Results" section of the Compact Disc Digital Audio Web page (http://www.tardis.ed.ac.uk/~psyche/cdda/). You might also want to check Deja News (http://www.deja.com) or post to the comp.publish.cdrom.hardware newsgroup with a specific query.

In Linux, you can use the `cdparanoia` or `cdda2wav` programs to perform DAE functions. Both programs include anti-jitter routines that can retrieve a clean audio file even from a drive that's weak at DAE. This jitter correction works by reading overlapping samples and then using the overlap to match up the samples without missing or duplicate sectors. This technique is effective, but time-consuming. Because of the overlap in sampling, DAE using anti-jitter techniques often extracts audio data at less than 1x speeds; it can take 7 or 10 minutes to extract a 5-minute track, for instance.

> **NOTE**
>
> Even when you don't use anti-jitter software, DAE often proceeds at less than the drive's rated data speed. For instance, a 32x CD-ROM drive might perform DAE at a maximum of 4x speed. Plextor drives are unusual in that they can generally perform DAE at or close to their normal data speeds.

> **TIP**
>
> If it's critical that you obtain flawless DAE, perform the operation twice, and then compare the files. The Linux `diff` command is extremely useful for determining whether two files differ. If they differ, perform another extraction and find which two match; chances are those two are both clean, and the third has a flaw. This technique is occasionally rendered ineffective, however, when the start and end points of the DAE vary. Two extractions could both be flawless, but differ because they begin and end at slightly different times.

As a general rule, CD-R and CD-RW drives have better DAE capabilities than do CD-ROM drives, but there are exceptions. As I've already noted, for instance, most Plextor and Pioneer CD-ROM drives have very good DAE capabilities, and some CD-R drives are poor at DAE.

Choosing a Recordable Drive

When you shop for a CD-ROM drive, the drive performance features I've just described—transfer rate, seek time, and DAE performance—are the most important considerations. There are some additional factors to consider when buying a recordable drive, however. Some of these, such as rewritable functionality, are drive performance factors. It's also important to consider Linux compatibility, however, because standardization in recordable command sets is comparatively new. It's possible to buy a drive that's incompatible with Linux CD recording software, particularly if you buy on the used market or from a dealer's closeout bin.

Do You Need Rewritable Functionality?

The first question you should ask yourself is whether you need the ability to handle rewritable discs. In some cases, you might not need this ability. For example, if your main goal is to create audio CDs from your collection of 78 rpm albums, you don't need rewritable functionality, because most audio CD players can't read CR-RW discs, and you presumably won't be changing these discs after you create them. Similarly, if you want to archive accounting or scientific data for long-term storage, a CD-R drive is quite adequate. On the other hand, if you want to create discs that you're likely to erase or modify in the near future, such as collections of updated packages for your Linux distribution, then the rewritable feature can be beneficial.

All CD-RW drives can also create CD-R discs, so you need not sacrifice compatibility with older CD-ROM drives and audio CD players in order to gain rewritable functionality. In fact, because CD-RW drives cost little more than otherwise equivalent CD-R drives, there's very little reason to favor a CD-R drive. The main exception would be if you saw a CD-R drive on sale for a particularly good price.

In the DVD realm, DVD-R drives are still quite expensive, but they produce DVDs that can be played on ordinary DVD drives. If you have the need to store more than 650MB of data on media that are at least somewhat commonly readable, DVD-R is the way to go. If you only need to read the media back on your own system, however, DVD-RAM drives cost much less. DVD-RW drives are still quite rare, but might become less so in the future. It is as of yet unclear where they and DVD+RW drives will fit into the marketplace.

Disk-at-Once Versus Track-at-Once

Another characteristic of recordable drives that bears mentioning is the distinction between *disk-at-once* (DAO) and *track-at-once* (TAO) recording modes. In DAO recording, the recording laser is turned on at the start of the disc and turned off only after the entire disc has been recorded. In TAO mode, the laser is turned on at the start of each track, turned off at the end of the track, and turned on again at the start of the next track. The laser is also turned on and off to write specialized control regions, such as the *table of contents*, *lead-in*, and *lead-out*—areas that control access to individual tracks and the CD as a whole. Most data CD-ROMs contain only a single track, so the difference between the two modes is minor (although using separate laser burns for the control areas does cause problems on a small number of CD-ROM drives and for some purposes such as mass duplication). Most audio CDs contain several tracks, so DAO and TAO modes produce slightly different results. On rare occasions, TAO CDs can't be played on some audio CD players, or produce peculiar effects such as causing a player to pause or stop between tracks. TAO also produces a very slight snap noise at the start and end of each track, although it's soft enough that you're not likely to notice it. Perhaps most important, most CD-R drives produce a minimum gap of two seconds between tracks in TAO mode, so you can't easily create a CD with no gap between tracks, as is desirable when creating a CD from concert performances.

For both audio and data CDs, most CD duplication services require original CD-R discs mastered in DAO mode. Therefore, if you plan to create CD-R masters for mass production, you should be sure to get a drive that can create DAO discs.

Fortunately, most modern CD-R and CD-RW drives can produce both DAO and TAO discs. A few older models support only TAO mode. If you think you'll want to produce concert-style audio CDs, or if you intend to send a CD to a duplicator for mass production, be sure the drive you purchase has DAO capability.

NOTE

The most commonly used Linux CD creation program, cdrecord, uses TAO mode by default, and only supports DAO mode on recent drives. The cdrdao program is an alternative designed explicitly for DAO support. I describe these programs, and GUI front-ends for them, in the section titled "Burning a CD-R or CD-RW Disc in Linux," later in this chapter.

Checking Compatibility with Linux CD-Creation Tools

The most important feature of any recordable CD technology for Linux is its compatibility with Linux CD-creation tools. Unlike most other recordable media (such as Zip disks, floppies, and tape drives), the command set for handling CD-R and CD-RW drives isn't quite completely standardized. The *multimedia command* (MMC) standard represents an attempt to change this state of affairs. Even drives that claim to be MMC drives aren't always 100% compatible, however, because they might contain bugs or deliberate deviations from the MMC standard. Nonetheless, your single best bet for compatibility is to purchase an MMC drive, which shouldn't be difficult because MMC has become nearly universal since 1999.

If you're considering a used or closeout non-MMC drive or if you want to further increase your chances of trouble-free operation under Linux, you should check these drive compatibility listings for Linux CD recording packages:

- **cdrecord** The README file for cdrecord (at ftp://ftp.fokus.gmd.de/pub/unix/cdrecord/) includes a list of supported drives.

- **cdrdao** Check http://www.ping.de/sites/daneb/drives.html for drive compatibility.

Linux GUI CD-creation tools generally use one or the other of these programs to do the "dirty work" of recording a CD, so even if you want to use a GUI tool, you should check the compatibility of these text-mode utilities.

Accessing Optical Media in Linux

Those who are new to Linux frequently have difficulty using a CD-ROM drive, simply because Linux's methods of CD access are foreign to them. Even experienced users can have trouble when installing a new CD-ROM of a different type (say, replacing an EIDE/ATAPI CD-ROM with a SCSI model), or when using a new type of device (say, adding a CD-RW drive). This section presents some tips relating to locating your optical devices and using the data on these devices.

Accessing Optical Devices

You access the vast majority of Linux hardware through *device files*—special files that are typically located in the /dev directory. In most cases, though, you don't access the device file for an optical drive directly; instead, you pass the name of the device file to a program such as mount, which uses it to make the device accessible in some way.

Locating the Appropriate Device File

If you installed Linux from an optical drive, chances are it created a link to the appropriate device file under the name /dev/cdrom. In such a case, you can use that name or examine the link to find what the underlying device is. For instance:

```
$ ls -l /dev/cdrom
lrwxrwxrwx   1 root      root            8 Dec 29 02:12 /dev/cdrom -> /dev/hda
```

This transaction indicates that the /dev/cdrom file is a symbolic link to /dev/hda, which is the true device file.

If for some reason your Linux distribution didn't create an appropriate symbolic link, or if you have replaced a drive of one type with another or reconfigured your EIDE bus, you might need to locate the device file in some other way. Each interface style has its own associated device files, as follows:

- **SCSI devices** SCSI CD-ROMs are assigned device names of the form /dev/scd*n*, where *n* is a number from 0 up. A computer with a single SCSI CD-ROM drive uses /dev/scd0, whereas a system with two optical drives also has a /dev/scd1. Typically, the device with the lower SCSI ID acquires the /dev/scd0 designation. Most SCSI CD-R drives can be accessed for reading using this same designation, but some don't show up as CD-ROM devices. Some drives have a jumper or switch you can set to alter the way they report themselves to the computer; you can change this jumper setting to make the drive appear or disappear as a /dev/scd*n* device. For write purposes, SCSI CD-R and CD-RW drives are accessed through the *generic SCSI* interfaces, /dev/sg*n*, where *n* is either a number from 0–15 or a letter from a–h, corresponding to the SCSI ID number. Do *not* attempt to use the generic SCSI identifier to mount a CD for reading. The /dev/scd*n* devices use major number 11 and minor numbers starting from 0. The /dev/sg*n* device files use major number 21 and minor numbers starting from 0.

- **EIDE/ATAPI devices** EIDE/ATAPI drives are accessed through device files named in the /dev/hd*n* pattern, where *n* is a letter from a–d (or occasionally higher). The letter is an indication of the EIDE chain and position on the chain. a is for the primary chain's master device, b for the primary chain's slave device, c for the secondary chain's master, and so on. Note that these identifiers are the same as those used for other disk devices. Therefore, you can't tell from the device filename alone whether a device is a CD-ROM, a removable disk, or a hard disk. In the case of recordable drives, it's best to compile SCSI emulation support into your kernel. You can then access the drive for writing using the generic SCSI device files. /dev/hd*n* devices use major numbers 3, 22, 33, and 34 for the primary and subsequent controllers, with minor numbers 0 and 64 for master and slave devices, respectively.

- **Proprietary devices** Old proprietary interfaces are assigned unique identifiers depending upon the specific device. For instance, /dev/mcd*xn*, where *n* is a number from 0–1, represents Mitsumi drives; and /dev/aztcd0 is the device file for Aztech CD-ROM drives. Check the appropriate documentation files in /usr/src/linux/Documentation/cdrom for further details.

- **Parallel-port devices** Most of these devices use the parallel-port IDE drivers, and acquire device identifiers of the form /dev/pcd*n*, where *n* is a number from 0–4. These devices use major number 46 and minor numbers starting at 0.

- **USB devices** The USB support for CD-ROM drives, such as it is, maps these drives into the SCSI device tree, so USB CD-ROM drives use SCSI identifiers.

7

OPTICAL DRIVES

NOTE

Device files aren't created automatically by the device's driver; they're created by scripts run during system installation. You'll therefore find device files for devices that aren't present on your computer. All modern Linux distributions create appropriate device files for all CD-ROM device types, and, if you accidentally delete a device file, most include a script in the /dev directory to create the device files anew. Alternatively, you can use the mknod command to create a single device file manually, but you must know the identifying characteristics—the *major* and *minor* device numbers mentioned in the interface descriptions earlier.

Using an Optical Device

After you've identified a device file, you can use it. The usual way to do this is to mount the device using the `mount` command, as in

```
mount /dev/scd0 /mnt/cdrom
```

You can then access the disc's files in the `/mnt/cdrom` directory tree. (For this command to work, you must have a *mount point*—an empty directory—at `/mnt/cdrom`.) You can automate this process to some extent by including an entry in `/etc/fstab`, such as

```
/dev/scd0      /mnt/cdrom      iso9660      ro,user,noauto    0 0
```

This entry identifies the device file (`/dev/scd0`), the mount point (`/mnt/cdrom`), the filesystem (`iso9660`), the mount options (`ro,user,noauto`), the backup frequency for the `dump` program (`0`), and the order for filesystem checking (`0`). The last two options should always be `0` for CD-ROM devices. If you include `user` in the comma-separated list of mount options, then normal users can mount and unmount the device. The `noauto` option indicates that the drive won't be mounted automatically at system startup, and `ro` specifies that it's a read-only medium.

> **TIP**
>
> Linux sometimes won't let an ordinary user unmount a CD-ROM that you mounted via an `/etc/fstab` shortcut if that shortcut specifies a symbolic link as the device file. I therefore recommend using the true device filename in `/etc/fstab`, rather than a `/dev/cdrom` symbolic link.

With an entry like the preceding one in `/etc/fstab`, an ordinary user can mount a CD-ROM by specifying the mount point with the `mount` command, as in

```
mount /mnt/cdrom
```

This is a very desirable option, so I recommend configuring your computer in this way, unless you have security reasons to not do so.

In some cases, you might need to access the raw device file more directly. For instance, if you want to copy a CD-ROM, you can use the `dd` command to extract the CD-ROM's contents into a file, which you can then burn to a CD-R using `cdrecord` or some other program. To extract the existing CD-ROM's contents, you use a command similar to the following:

```
dd if=/dev/scd0 of=cdrom.iso
```

This command creates a file called cdrom.iso that contains the data from the CD-ROM. When you burn that file to a CD-R, the result is an identical copy of the CD, even if it includes unusual filesystems such as the Macintosh's HFS.

> **NOTE**
>
> Discs that use CD-ROM XA or other mixed data/audio formats can't be extracted intact in this way; you'll get only one part of the CD's contents, such as the data tracks. Multi-session CD-ROMs might also not be extracted intact using this method.

> **NOTE**
>
> The dd command, when applied to extract an entire CD-ROM's contents as I've just described, exits with an error status. This is normal. You can compare the size of the resulting file with the size of the mounted CD-ROM filesystem. The extracted file should be slightly larger than the mounted filesystem, unless the CD includes multiple filesystems (such as ISO-9660 and HFS), in which case the extracted file *might* be substantially larger than the mounted filesystem—or the file might only be slightly larger than the mounted filesystem.

7

OPTICAL DRIVES

To extract data from an audio CD, you must use special DAE software, such as cdparanoia or cdda2wav. These programs operate on raw device files, not mounted CDs. Programs that play audio CDs through your computer's speakers also operate on raw device files. These programs frequently go directly to /dev/cdrom, so it's important that this file be a link to the appropriate device file on your system. This means you don't need to mount an audio CD in order to listen to it.

All these direct-access methods require that you have read and, usually, write access to the device file. Most Linux distributions include some mechanism to provide this access. For instance, Red Hat and its variants (such as Mandrake) include code that changes the ownership of the CD-ROM device files whenever somebody logs into the console. Some other distributions give full read/write access to all users in a certain group, or to all users. If you don't like the method that your distribution uses, you *might* be able to change it by altering the permissions on the device file, possibly in conjunction with other actions, such as creating scripts to change device file permissions or altering group membership of various users. The device file permissions are mostly irrelevant to the mount command, which runs with root privileges.

Optical Filesystem Options

Most CD-ROM, CD-R, and CD-RW discs use the *ISO-9660* filesystem. This is a filesystem that was designed for CD-ROMs, and there are three versions of it in common use:

- **Level 1**   This is the basic version of ISO-9660, and it contains many limitations. The most noticeable of these is the filename length limit, which is eight characters plus a three-character extension (the same as in MS-DOS). ISO-9660 further restricts legal characters, however; only uppercase alphabetic characters, numbers, the underscore (_), and a period (.) to separate the main filename from its extension are allowed. (Linux usually converts the uppercase to lowercase transparently, however.) Some CD creation programs violate some of ISO-9660 Level 1's restrictions. For instance, some place illegal characters in filenames, which usually causes no problems, but poses the risk of causing problems on some OSs.

- **Level 2**   Level 2 is much like Level 1, but extends the filename length limit to 32 characters. Filenames are still all uppercase, however, which Linux converts to all lowercase when you mount the CD-ROM in Linux.

- **Level 3**   Level 3 extends Level 2 to make it easier to create CD-R *packet writing* software. This software provides access to CD-R media in a fashion more like that used to access other disk devices. Packet writing software for Linux is still essentially nonexistent, but Linux can read Level 3 CD-ROMs.

Because of the severe filename length and other limits imposed by ISO-9660, two extensions to the filesystem have come into common use on CD-ROMs:

- **Rock Ridge**   The Rock Ridge extensions add UNIX-style mixed-case long filenames, ownership, permissions, and other features to ISO-9660. Rock Ridge builds on the existing ISO-9660 framework in a backward-compatible way. OSs that don't understand Rock Ridge can still read Rock Ridge CDs; they simply can't read the long filenames or other features. Rock Ridge is the format of choice when creating a CD-R for use on Linux systems.

- **Joliet**   Joliet is technically a complete filesystem specification, although it relies upon an ISO-9660 pointer to an alternative disc descriptor to function. In practice, therefore, it appears in conjunction with ISO-9660 filesystems. It's possible for a disc to make different files available in its ISO-9660 and Joliet portions, but most point to the same files on both filesystems. The result is much like using Rock Ridge. The difference comes in terms of filesystem details. Rock Ridge was designed for UNIX and UNIX-like OSs, and so supports the filesystem features used by these OSs. Microsoft designed Joliet for use with Windows 95 and later, and so Joliet supports the filesystem features used by the Windows family of OSs. For example, Joliet doesn't support UNIX-style file ownership and permissions, but it does include support for Unicode filenames.

The Linux `mkisofs` program can create a CD image file that uses ISO-9660 with both Rock Ridge extensions and a supplementary Joliet filesystem. You can even add the Macintosh HFS to the mix if you use the `mkhybrid` program. In this way, you can create a CD-R that's readable, and that has long filenames, on the widest possible array of OSs. The Linux kernel supports all these filesystem types, although HFS support isn't included in many distributions by default, and Joliet and HFS support appeared late in the 2.0.x kernel series, so if you've got a particularly old Linux installation, you *might* not have that support.

A new filesystem has recently appeared in the optical world: the *Universal Disk Format* (UDF). This format is designed for use both on larger DVD media and on read/write optical media like CD-R and DVD-RAM. (The read/write features appeared in the UDF 1.5 specification.) UDF isn't supported in the Linux 2.2.x kernels, but does appear in the 2.3.x development kernels and will be standard when 2.4 is released. You can read more about Linux UDF development at `http://trylinux.com/projects/udf/`.

Burning a CD-R or CD-RW Disc in Linux

If you've purchased a recordable drive, chances are you want to use it to record data. To do so, however, you need special tools. At the moment, it's not possible to simply mount a recordable disk as you do a regular CD-ROM or floppy disk and copy files to that disk using Linux commands like `cp` or GUI environments like KDE. Instead, you must use special software that creates a disk image and copies that image to the recordable CD in a single operation. (It's also possible to create *multi-session* discs to which you can add files at a future date.) The basic tools for creating a CD are text-based, but there are several GUI front-ends to these tools that can make the process much easier.

Using Command-Line Tools

I've already mentioned some of the text-based tools you can use to create a CD. Those that I've mentioned, and some that I haven't, include

- **mkisofs** This tool, which comes with most Linux distributions, takes a set of files that you specify and creates from them a *CD image file*, which is a file that contains the data that will ultimately go onto the CD. The image file includes an ISO-9660 filesystem (along with Rock Ridge and Joliet, if you so specify) and all the files that you indicate. You can find `mkisofs` at `ftp://ftp.fokus.gmd.de/pub/unix/cdrecord`, if you want an update or if your distribution doesn't include it.

- **mkhybrid** This is a variant of `mkisofs` that adds the ability to create a Macintosh Hierarchical Filesystem (HFS) in addition to ISO-9660 and optional Rock Ridge and Joliet extensions. Like `mkisofs`, `mkhybrid` creates a file; you need another program to burn that file to disc. If your distribution doesn't include `mkhybrid`, you can find it at Linux repository sites like `http://rufus.w3.org/linux/RPM/` or `http://www.debian.org/distrib/packages`.

- **cdwrite**   This program is no longer being maintained, but it remains useful for some older CD-R drives. It takes an image file and burns it to CD using any of its supported drives.

- **cdrecord**   This program performs the same function as does cdwrite, but it's being maintained, and is the most commonly-used CD-recording software for Linux. Read more at its home page,
  http://www.fokus.gmd.de/research/cc/glone/employees/joerg.schilling/private/cdrecord.html.

- **cdrdao**   Yet another file-to-CD program, cdrdao is distinguished by its use of DAO recording mode, rather than TAO, which is still favored by cdrecord. Read more at its Web site, http://www.ping.de/sites/daneb/cdrdao.html.

Recording a CD using these tools is a two-step process: You first create an image file and then burn it to a CD. The number of options supported by each of these programs is quite large, so you should consult their respective documentation for details. As an example, however, consider creating a CD using mkisofs and cdrecord, the most common combination.

To make a CD that you'll use under Linux, you should probably create an image that uses ISO-9660 with Rock Ridge extensions. This task can be accomplished using the following command:

```
mkisofs -r -o image.iso ./
```

The program outputs a number of messages, possibly including several lines of text describing the processing it's doing. The result is an image file called image.iso that contains the files in the current directory and all its subdirectories. You should check the size of the image file to be sure it will fit on a standard 650MB CD-R or CD-RW. If it's too large, you *might* need to trim some files or use a special high-capacity blank—700MB CD-R media are somewhat common. If you want to check that the image file contains reasonable data, you can mount it using the Linux loopback interface, as follows:

```
mount image.iso /mnt/cdrom -o loop
```

You can then check the files against the originals, verify the functionality of any programs you've included, and so on. When you're done, use the umount command to unmount the CD image file just as you would an ordinary CD.

When you're satisfied with the state of the image file, you can burn it to a CD-R with cdrecord:

```
cdrecord dev=6,0 speed=4 image.iso
```

This command writes the `image.iso` file to the CD-R device at SCSI ID 6, logical unit (LUN) 0 (most SCSI CD-R drives use a LUN of 0) at 4x speed. The program then prints information about the drive and recording options you've selected, ending with

```
Last chance to quit, starting real write in 1 seconds.
```

> **NOTE**
>
> You must run cdrecord as root or run it suid root. To do the latter, issue the command **chmod 4711 cdrecord** (adding an appropriate path if you're not in cdrecord's directory). Thereafter, cdrecord acquires root privileges even when an ordinary user runs it.

The write process then begins, but unless you've selected verbose reporting, you won't see any indication of this fact on your screen. Depending upon your recordable drive, however, you should see lights blink or change color to indicate that a CD is being recorded. When the process completes, you can mount the CD to check that it was recorded properly.

> **TIP**
>
> You can combine the filesystem creation and CD creation phases of this operation by using Linux pipes. For instance, **mkisofs -r ./ | cdrecord dev=6,0 speed=4 -** will create a CD from the contents of the current directory without the need to create an intermediary disk file. The downside is that you need more RAM, and the chance of a write error occurring because of an inability to feed data to the CD-R drive quickly enough is greatly increased, particularly if you record at a high speed.

Using X-CD-Roast

If you prefer to avoid command-line tools, you can use a GUI front-end to these programs, such as X-CD-Roast (`http://www.fh-muenchen.de/home/ze/rz/services/projects/xcdroast/e_overview.html`) or BurnIt (`http://sunsite.auc.dk/BurnIT/`). These programs can help in the CD-creation process by obviating the need to remember commands, particularly those relating to obscure options. As an example, consider X-CD-Roast. After configuring X-CD-Roast for your system by letting it detect your CD-ROM and CD-R or CD-RW devices, you can create a data CD by following these steps:

1. From the main X-CD-Roast screen, click Master CD. This produces the Master From/To window, shown in Figure 7.7.

Directory selection list

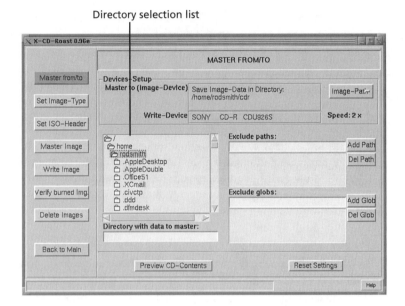

FIGURE 7.7

Use the Master From/To window to set the source directory from which you want to master a CD.

2. In the directory selection list, locate the directory you want to use as the base of your CD. Be sure it's listed in the Directory with data to master field.

3. Click the Set Image-Type button to get the Set Image Type window shown in Figure 7.8. You can set filesystem creation options here, such as whether to use Rock Ridge, Joliet, or both.

4. Click the Master Image button to get the Master Image window, shown in Figure 7.9. You can change the name of the image file you want to create, or, if you've configured X-CD-Roast to use a partition for this purpose, tell it to use that partition.

NOTE

X-CD-Roast uses the .raw filename extension for CD image files. .iso is a more common extension, but you shouldn't use this if you expect X-CD-Roast to be able to write the image file you create. If you've downloaded an image file that uses an .iso extension, you can rename the file to let X-CD-Roast see it and burn it to CD without re-creating the filesystem.

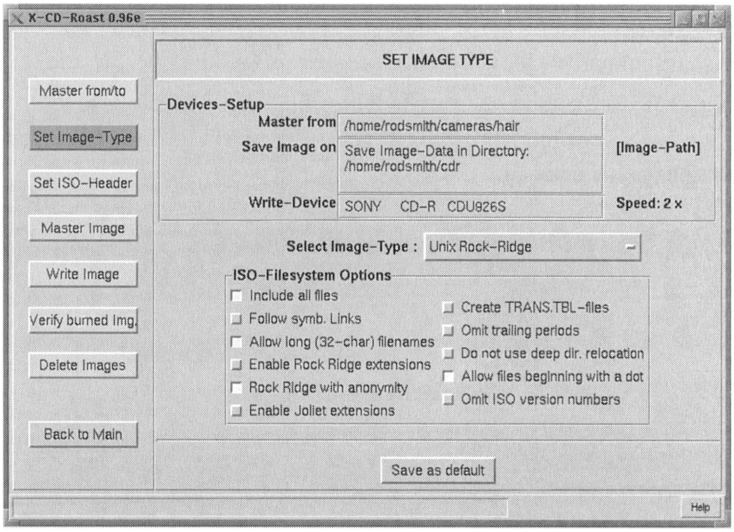

FIGURE 7.8

You can select from a set of predefined options using the Set Image-Type option button or select individual options using the ISO-Filesystem Options area.

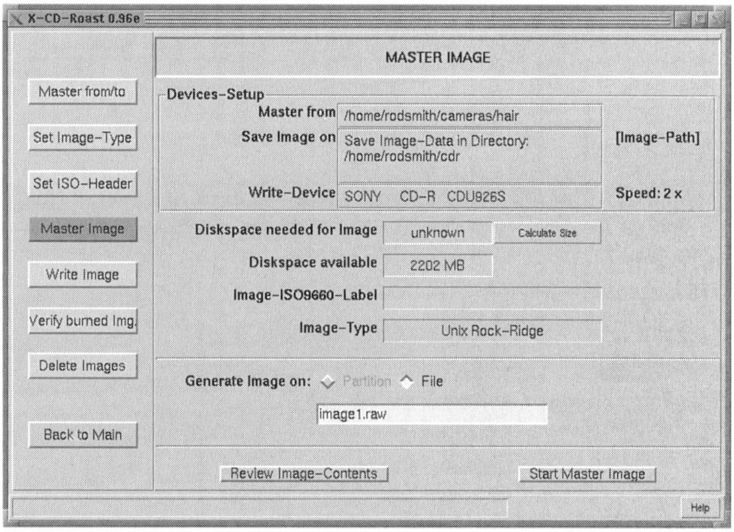

FIGURE 7.9

Change the name of the image file you create using the Master Image window.

5. After you've selected a filename, click Start Master Image. The program displays a dialog box that summarizes the program's progress in creating the CD image file.

6. After X-CD-Roast has generated a CD image file, click Write Image to display the Write Image window shown in Figure 7.10. If necessary, select the image file you want to write using the image file selector.

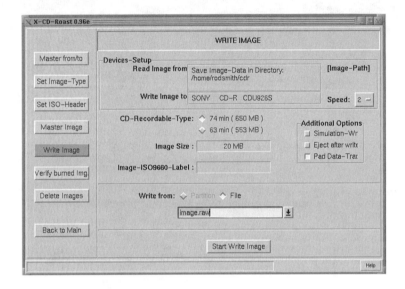

FIGURE 7.10

The Write Image window provides a GUI interface to the cdrecord *program.*

7. Insert a blank CD-R or CD-RW into your drive and click Start Write Image to begin the process. As with creating an image file, X-CD-Roast displays a progress dialog box, shown in Figure 7.11.

FIGURE 7.11

You can adjust the view of the progress dialog box to show more or less information about the write process.

8. When X-CD-Roast has finished writing the disk, you can use the Verify burned Img. button to check the disc against the image file on your hard disk. If you have a CD-ROM drive in addition to a recordable drive, you can configure X-CD-Roast to use the CD-ROM drive as the source for verification operations, so you *might* need to swap the disc into the other drive. Because modern CD-ROM drives are faster than modern CD-R and CD-RW drives, using the CD-ROM drive is generally faster than using the recordable drive.

X-CD-Roast contains many additional options I've not covered here. Most of its features are reasonably clear, so if you know what you want to do, browsing its menus should turn up the appropriate option. As of version 0.96e, however, X-CD-Roast does *not* support DAO recording, so that's one option you won't find on its menu. Because DAO support has been added to the underlying cdrecord, it's likely to turn up in X-CD-Roast eventually, though. X-CD-Roast also has yet to support creating bootable CDs, although mkisofs contains this functionality.

Summary

Optical media present some unusual characteristics to a Linux computer. They're normally read-only in nature. Recordable technologies provide a means to write data, albeit not in as seamless a way as can be done with other removable media. Because CD-ROM drives are an almost universal fixture on modern computers, however, recordable CD technologies provide an excellent means of distributing large amounts of data to a few sites. They're also a very useful means of backing up your own data—either data files generated by your applications or your entire system.

7

OPTICAL DRIVES

Tape Backup

IN THIS CHAPTER

A data backup device is an indispensable accessory for serious computing. Hard disks are very delicate instruments that can be easily damaged. More importantly, humans are error-prone beings who have a tendency to mistype important commands or click on the wrong files or program options. When your computer loses its data because of mechanical or human error, a backup device can let you recover your data—a few files or your entire system—with minimal fuss.

Note that I used the word *when* in the preceding paragraph with respect to data loss, not *if*. It's possible you've been lucky so far and have never experienced the need for backup, but, if so, that state of affairs will change. Thinking otherwise is—to put it bluntly—deluding yourself. A backup device is therefore a requirement for any but the most trivial Linux installations.

What *type* of backup, though? Several data storage devices I've covered in previous chapters have merit:

- **Hard disks**   You can add a second hard disk at low cost and periodically back up your system to this disk. Hard disks are fast and convenient, but unless you purchase twice or more of your main disk's capacity, you can usually only store a single backup on a disk. Worse, they're usually stored in the same case as the main disk, so a physical trauma that destroys the main drive will most likely destroy the backup, too. If you decide to use a hard disk, I recommend using an external Small Computer System Interface (SCSI) model, or buying a kit that lets you easily remove the backup disk when it's not in use.

- **Removable disks**   Disk devices like an Iomega Zip drive, LS-120 drive, or magneto-optical (MO) disk can be used for backup. Most of these devices are fairly low in capacity, however, or are quite expensive as backup media. If you have a large MO disk, however, it can prove to be a convenient and reliable backup medium if you don't mind the cost.

- **Optical discs**   Some people favor CD-R and CD-RW drives for backup purposes. The media are inexpensive and durable, and reading the data back is a snap. Recordable CD technologies impose low capacity limits, however (650MB), and the CD-creation process can sometimes be awkward. Recordable DVD technologies are better suited to this purpose, and are an increasingly realistic option as the price and availability of recordable DVD drives and media improve.

All things considered, another technology is often best suited for backup purposes—tape. Unlike the media I've just described, tape is a *sequential-access* medium, which means you must read the beginning of the tape before you can get to the end. (There are exceptions to this rule, however.) This characteristic makes tapes unsuitable for use in most data storage capacities, but it's not too great an obstacle for a backup medium, which is usually accessed in sequential write mode. Tapes are also inexpensive on a per-megabyte basis when compared to most other potential backup media. The tapes themselves are compact and removable, so you can easily store a tape backup away from the computer. (The ideal location is at another site, so that your data are safe in case of a fire or other major disaster.) Tape devices are also common and well supported in Linux, so they pose few unique Linux challenges, although there are exceptions.

Evaluating Your Tape Backup Needs

The first step in purchasing a tape backup device is to evaluate your needs. Tape drives come in a wide variety of speeds and capacities. It's also useful to know something about how frequently you'll be using the drive; a drive that's slightly slow or noisy can be a minor nuisance if you use it just once a month, but a major problem if you use it daily.

Knowing Your Capacity Requirements

The capacity of tape drives ranges from a few megabytes for obsolete models from a decade or more ago to tens of gigabytes for single-tape units or hundreds of gigabytes for *changers*— drives that can accept several tape cartridges and change between them, presenting the illusion of a single larger tape to the computer. Naturally, the higher capacity drives and media generally cost more than do the lower capacity units and tapes.

Factoring in Compression

Most tape drives today are sold with two capacity estimates: *raw capacity* and *compressed capacity*. Because tape drives are generally used to store data for archival purposes, it's common to apply compression algorithms to the data when writing to tape. These algorithms typically achieve an average of approximately 2:1 compression, so a 4GB tape can hold 8GB of data. Manufacturers generally use this 2:1 ratio when computing the compressed data storage capacity.

> ### CAUTION
>
> When evaluating tape drives, be sure to consider whether the capacity quoted for the drive is compressed or uncompressed. Some models use the compressed capacity, and others the uncompressed capacity, in advertising or model names. As a hypothetical example, one model might be advertised as the BigTape 20, and another as the UltraTape 10, but both might use the same tape with a 10GB uncompressed capacity.

Precisely how much compression you can achieve, of course, depends upon what type of data you store on your tapes, and perhaps also what backup software you use. If your hard disk is filled with uncompressed graphics or text files, chances are you'll achieve far greater than 2:1 compression; a 4GB drive might suffice to store 12GB–16GB of data. If your hard disk is

8

TAPE BACKUP

filled largely with precompressed files, such as GIF graphics or Linux RPM files, then you'll gain little storage space from compression. The same 4GB drive might then store only 4.5GB of data. In extreme cases, applying compression to precompressed files can actually *increase* the size of the files. In such a case, you should turn off the compression features of the drive or software.

Compression is achieved by one of two means:

- **Hardware**   Some drives include small CPUs and firmware that can apply compression to data as it comes from the computer. With such drives, your backup software doesn't need to support compression; in fact, applying such compression just slows down the backup and can reduce the capacity of the tape. As far as Linux is concerned, such a drive has a variable capacity that's larger than the raw capacity of the tape.

- **Software**   Some drives don't contain compression algorithms in their firmware, and so rely on the Linux backup software to do the compression. This software chews up CPU time and can slow down the backup, depending upon the CPU speed, the tape drive's bus speed and type, and the tape's speed.

NOTE

Applying both software and hardware compression produces no benefit. The hardware's compression algorithms won't be able to achieve any better compression than was achieved by the software compression. When using a drive that supports hardware compression, therefore, it's generally best to disable software data compression. In some cases, such as if you'll need to read the tape on a drive without hardware compression, you might prefer disabling the hardware compression. This process is described in the section titled "Using mt to Control a Tape Drive," later in this chapter.

Typically, hardware compression algorithms are the same for different models of drive that use the same media. For example, Travan NS drives all use the same compression algorithms. Therefore, a compressed tape created in one drive should be readable in another drive, provided both drives accept the same form and capacity of tape. There are exceptions to this rule, however, so using hardware compression can cause inter-drive compatibility problems. When you use software compression, no such problem arises, although you must use compatible software on both computers (as is true when using hardware compression). These factors are of interest mainly when you need to use a tape as a data transport mechanism or when you replace one drive with another.

As a general rule, I favor drives with hardware compression. Using hardware compression removes some computing burden from the host computer and can often speed up backups. When necessary, you can disable compression using jumpers or the Linux mt command, described in the section "Using mt to Control a Tape Drive." One of the prime advantages of hardware compression, though, relates to Linux backup software. Some Linux backup programs, such as tar with its gzip compression, use compression algorithms that render all the data after an error unreadable. This flaw makes using software compression a risky prospect. If you decide to buy a drive that relies upon software compression, you should definitely look into more sophisticated backup programs than tar, or use it without compression, in order to avoid these problems.

Estimating Your Space Requirements

Whether or not you use compression, it's important to know how large a tape drive you need to get. As a general rule, it's best to buy a tape drive with enough capacity to hold all your data on a single tape (or a single set of tapes, in the case of a changer). If you're backing up a single desktop computer, finding your capacity requirements is relatively straightforward; you can use the Linux df command to find how much space your files consume. For instance

```
$ df
Filesystem           1k-blocks       Used Available Use% Mounted on
/dev/sda6            2679650     1449936   1118867  56% /
/dev/sda8             676435      202258    439238  32% /usr/local
/dev/sda5            5135482     2879989   2255493  56% /home
/dev/sda3             31077       11530     18906  38% /boot
```

The Used column indicates the space consumed by files (in bytes) on each partition. In the preceding example, the system's files consume 4.3GB. What's more, the total capacity of the computer's disk is 8.1GB, so files could conceivably expand to fill that much space.

In theory, a 2GB uncompressed capacity drive might be able to back up the entire hard disk. I recommend, however, buying a drive with enough capacity to handle your entire hard disk's filled capacity, preferably without compression. The reason is simple—expansion. As you install more software and generate new data files, your needs for backup capacity will expand. A tape drive that's barely adequate today will become inadequate tomorrow. Upgrading to a higher-capacity tape format can be expensive, because either the drives or the tapes will cost a fair amount of money. If you buy a drive with capacity to spare, you won't need to upgrade it or resort to multi-tape backups for some time to come. In practice, therefore, to back up the preceding hard drive, I would recommend a drive with an 8–10GB uncompressed capacity. That drive will be adequate for the present and probably for at least another year or two.

If your system dual boots between Linux and one or more other OSs, you can modify this rule to one of purchasing a drive that's adequate to back up any one OS. For instance, if 5GB were

8

TAPE BACKUP

devoted to Linux and 3GB to Windows, then a 5GB uncompressed tape backup might be adequate. The reason is that it's generally not too inconvenient to back up two OSs separately; in fact, it can be necessary in order to preserve important filesystem information.

In a pinch, you can also back up separate Linux partitions independently or in two or more groups. For example, given a 3GB tape unit, you might back up the preceding system in two chunks: one for /home and one for /, /usr/local, and /boot. Independently backing up partitions can sometimes be convenient because it keeps data separated in a way that might be handy in case of an emergency restore. For example, if the /home partition were damaged, you could restore it without having to read through other partitions' data. This procedure increases the work involved in backing up, however, which can be inconvenient. This inconvenience is particularly irksome if you want to run unattended backups—for instance, scheduling a backup to run at night.

If necessary, a backup can be split arbitrarily across multiple tapes. Most backup programs support this feature. Unless you use a changer, though, you'll need to be present to swap tapes when you do this.

If you're buying a tape backup to serve as a backup device for an entire network of computers, you must estimate the space requirements for the entire network, and consider tape speed and backup scheduling requirements. For example, you might not be able to perform a backup of your entire network in a single day because of network bandwidth limitations. If so, using multiple smaller tapes makes sense; you can then back up a few machines each night over the course of a week, as opposed to backing up everything one time each week.

Whether you back up a single computer or a network, you might also want to factor your backup strategy into the equation. So far, I've emphasized the need to back up an entire computer. This is known as a *full backup*, and it's the most important type of backup when it comes to true disaster recovery. It's often desirable, however, to mix full backups with smaller *incremental backups*, in which only files that are new or that have changed are backed up. For example, you might perform a full backup once a month and incremental backups once a week. If you rely heavily upon incremental backups, you can reduce the need for high capacity, because the full backup doesn't occupy most of your backup time. You might find it acceptable to swap tapes for a three-tape full backup once a month, for example, but to perform unattended incremental backups once a week, or even once a day. The flip side is that incremental backups can make recovery from a complete disaster more complex, because you need to restore the full backup and then one or more incremental backups. If you regularly create and delete large files, you might need to delete these files after each restore operation, or you'll run out of disk space when doing the incremental restores.

Knowing Your Speed Requirements

Modern tape backup devices claim speeds of between 33–720 MB/min. High-end drives usually include hardware data compression, and these drives' manufacturers often include the compression in their speed estimates. If you're comparing two drives, one with compression and one without, be sure to take this fact into consideration. The slower drive might actually be faster, because when your computer compresses the data, the computer transfers less data to the backup unit. For example, with 2:1 software compression, a 66MB/min drive can store data at 132MB/min, assuming the computer can compress the data quickly enough.

> **NOTE**
>
> Most manufacturers quote speeds in megabytes per minute, but some quote speeds in other units, such as megabytes per second or megabytes per hour. Most manufacturers quote speeds for disk drives in megabytes per second or sometimes megabits per second. Be sure you compare equivalent units.

In practice, of course, few drives achieve their rated speeds in real life. Delays on the interface bus, a slow CPU with a drive that relies upon software compression, slow hard disk performance, and other factors can all slow down a drive. One potentially important factor is *shoe-shining*, the tendency of a drive to seek back and forth over the same area several times. Shoe-shining occurs when the computer can't keep up the rate of data flow to the tape drive to keep the tape running at its full speed. This might happen because compression slows things down or because head seeks or a slow hard disk reduce data throughput from the hard disk. The result is that the tape drive runs out of data, but the tape keeps rolling. When this happens, the tape drive must back up the tape to write to the area that was unwritten for lack of data. Because of the reversal of direction of the tape, shoe-shining takes a lot of time. If it happens frequently, it can cut the data throughput to a fraction of what it might be. Good tape backup software can help reduce the occurrence of shoe-shining by buffering large amounts of data, thus preventing the bottlenecks from affecting transfer to the tape drive. Even if the system takes a while to refill the buffer every now and then, the result can be a substantial improvement in throughput.

Your own personal data transfer rate requirements depend on your patience and how much data you must back up. Try computing the amount of data you must back up on a regular basis and set a goal for how quickly you want to back up the data. That estimate then produces a minimum tape backup speed requirement. For instance, suppose you have 6GB of data, and want to back it up in no more than two hours. This results in a minimum transfer rate of 51MB/minute. Keeping in mind that no drive achieves its maximum rated speed for more than a few seconds at a time, you should probably look for a drive capable of 100MB/min or so. If the drive's speed rating doesn't include compression, though, a 50MB/min drive can be adequate, because with compression, you'll really be transferring only 3GB of data, assuming a 2:1 compression ratio.

Keep in mind that factors other than the tape drive can present bottlenecks to your data transfers. For example, suppose you want to use your Linux computer to back up a network of Windows computers using a 10BaseT network. 10BaseT network cards can only transfer data at 10Mbps, or about 75MB/min in the speed terms most often used for tape drives. Network protocols will also take their toll, as well, reducing performance to less than this value—perhaps 30–40MB/min. A drive capable of 132MB/min is therefore overkill for such a network. In fact, the slow network transfer rates can result in shoe-shining, thus reducing the transfer rates to well below even 30MB/min. Good network backup software can buffer the transfers, thus keeping performance at close to the maximum allowed by the network. (To learn more about using Linux as a backup server for Windows or UNIX computers, see my book, *Linux: Networking for Your Office*, Sams Publishing, 1999.)

Knowing Your Backup Frequency Requirements

What might seem a minor inconvenience at first can become quite a major problem if you need to use the drive very frequently. As I mentioned earlier, for example, the need to swap tapes can be unacceptable if you need to back up in an unattended manner every night. It might not be so onerous if you only need to do so once a month, though. It's therefore important that you have some idea of how often you need to back up your data, and how much data you need to back up.

Unfortunately, there are no hard-and-fast rules for what constitutes an appropriate backup schedule. A system that's used infrequently, or that contains only seldom-changing data (such as a firewall computer), might need to be backed up *very* infrequently—perhaps once every six months. A computer that contains frequently-changing data, however, such as a file server, might need daily backups. You might even need different backup schedules for different parts of the computer. For example, the file server's system files might not change very often, but the user files might need daily backups. Similarly, you must assess your own tolerance for the plusses and minuses associated with incremental backups.

As a starting point, consider weekly backups. On infrequently-used systems, the weekly backup might be an incremental backup, with a full backup reserved for a monthly event. On a more heavily used system, the weekly backup might be a full backup, and you might consider adding incremental backups on a daily basis. A multi-OS computer or a network backup server might require a more complex arrangement, perhaps involving rotating full or incremental backups of particular OSs or hosts. For example, you might back up Linux one week and Windows the next, with incremental backups of each on alternating days.

Try to design your desired backup schedule before settling on a tape drive. This way, you'll be able to narrow your search to drives that are well suited to this schedule. You can rule out drives with insufficient capacity or speed, for example. If you plan to do nightly backups of a home computer in a room adjacent to your bedroom, you might want to favor quiet drives, so as to reduce the likelihood that you'll be disturbed by the sound of the backup. (Some Travan drives sound disturbingly like a dentist's drill.)

Tape Backup Interfaces

As with other data storage devices, the type of interface used on a tape drive is of critical importance to the drive's operation, and to how it interacts with other devices on your system. It should come as no surprise that SCSI and EIDE/ATAPI are the two major interfaces used on tape drives today, although a few other interfaces are also available.

SCSI Interfaces

As with many other devices, the SCSI interface is the interface of choice for tape backup drives. There are several reasons for this, including

- SCSI allows both internal and external devices, so it's possible to use one external SCSI tape backup device to back up several computers, even without using network backup tools.

- A SCSI bus can support up to 7 or 15 devices, depending upon the SCSI variant, as compared to only 2 devices for EIDE. This advantage is reduced, however, when mixing Ultra2 or faster SCSI devices with lesser SCSI variants, because Ultra2 or faster devices work best on SCSI busses that don't have slower varieties.

- The SCSI bus supports fully multitasking operation, which can reduce the likelihood of shoe-shining. If you put an ATAPI tape drive on the same chain as an EIDE hard disk, the computer must stop sending data to the tape drive in order to read data from the hard disk. This can cause the tape drive's buffer to run dry, necessitating a reversal in tape direction. This scenario is less likely when using SCSI devices because SCSI supports simultaneous access to two or more drives.

- As a general rule, the variety of tape drives is greater for SCSI than for EIDE or other interfaces. In particular, the highest-performance drives are available only in SCSI form. Even at the low end, SCSI drives aren't rare, except for drives of such low capacity that they're obsolete.

8

TAPE BACKUP

Before you can access a SCSI tape drive, you must ensure that your kernel includes appropriate support, as described here:

- You must enable SCSI support in the SCSI support area of the kernel configuration (see Figure 8.1).

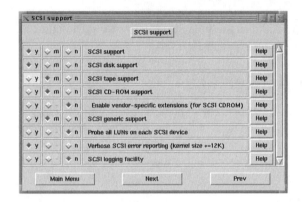

FIGURE 8.1

You must enable both SCSI support and SCSI tape support to use SCSI tape devices.

- You must select either Y or M to the SCSI tape support option in the same SCSI support kernel configuration area. I favor using modular tape support, because the tape drive is a device that's seldom accessed.
- You must add support for your SCSI host adapter in the SCSI low-level drivers configuration area. If you don't boot from a SCSI hard disk, you can enable this support as a module; otherwise, it must be compiled directly into the kernel. If your only use of SCSI is for the tape backup, modular compilation is adequate.

Major Linux distributions generally ship with SCSI tape support enabled, at least as a module. You can therefore use these devices without recompiling your kernel, if you like.

You access a SCSI tape drive in Linux using the /dev/stx (major device 9, minor device 0–1) device files, where x is a number from 0–1, or the /dev/nstx device files (major device 9, minor device 128–129). For a given x, the /dev/stx and /dev/nstx device files access the same tape drive, but in different ways. Specifically, /dev/stx causes the tape to rewind after every operation, whereas /dev/nstx leaves the tape wound to the position of its last access after every operation. Therefore, /dev/stx is useful when you want to write a backup to tape and be done with it, whereas /dev/nstx is useful when you want to write two or more backups to the same tape. You can write one and then another to the same device, without overwriting the first backup. I describe the use of tape backup software in more detail later in this chapter, in the section titled "Using a Tape Drive in Linux."

There are several varieties of SCSI bus, ranging in speed from 5MB/s (SCSI-1) through 160MB/s (Ultra3 Wide SCSI). Translated into MB/min figures, these speeds mean that even the slowest SCSI-1 interface is capable of handling all but the fastest SCSI tape drives. Tape handling commands were only finalized with SCSI-2, however, so most SCSI tape drives support at least Fast SCSI-2. In practice, most SCSI tape drives today also support UltraSCSI (20MB/s, or 1200MB/min).

EIDE/ATAPI Interfaces

The *Advanced Technology Attachment Packet Interface* (ATAPI) protocols are a command set extension used on *Enhanced Integrated Device Electronics* (EIDE) busses. The ATAPI protocols include commands for tape devices, based on the command set used by SCSI tape drives. Therefore, tape drives that hook up to an EIDE bus are typically referred to as *ATAPI drives*, although the term *EIDE drive* is also sometimes used.

As a high-speed interface designed for hard disks, EIDE is well suited to handling tape backup devices, at least in terms of speed requirements. Therefore, EIDE has become quite popular in recent years for low-end tape devices. Indeed, if your capacity requirements are modest, an ATAPI tape drive can be a good choice. There are two major caveats to using ATAPI tape drives, however:

- Because the EIDE bus supports only two devices per chain, and because most motherboards support only two EIDE chains, it's inconvenient—and sometimes impossible—to use more than four EIDE devices on a single computer. As the popularity of devices such as CD-R drives, removable media disks, and tape drives grows, it becomes increasingly easy to run out of space for EIDE devices.

- Because the EIDE bus doesn't support fully multitasking operations, it's important that you put your ATAPI tape drive on the EIDE chain that does *not* host your main hard disk. Putting the hard disk and tape drive on separate chains enables the computer to perform simultaneous access to both devices, which can reduce the chances that your transfers will be slowed down because of shoe-shining.

Kernel compilation options for ATAPI tape drives are similar to those for SCSI tape drive, but they're accessed from the Block devices configuration menu, as follows:

- You must enable the Enhanced IDE/MFM/RLL disk/cdrom/tape/floppy support option, either as a module or compiled into the kernel, as shown in Figure 8.2. Compiling this support directly into the kernel is necessary if you boot from an EIDE hard disk.

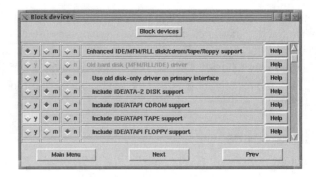

FIGURE 8.2
ATAPI tape kernel options are similar to those for SCSI devices.

- You must select Y or M to the Include IDE/ATAPI TAPE support option to add support for tape devices. It's generally safe to compile this option as a module, because you seldom access a tape drive for more than a small percentage of the time the computer runs.

- For best performance, locate your EIDE chipset from the list later in the Block devices menu, and activate it, along with the DMA transfer options. Doing so can improve tape performance. This factor is particularly important if you also use EIDE hard drives.

Most Linux distributions ship with ATAPI tape support compiled as modules. You therefore might not need to recompile your kernel merely to add this support.

You generally access an ATAPI tape drive through the /dev/ht0 or /dev/nht0 devices (device major 37 and minor 0 and 128, respectively). As with SCSI tape drives, the first device is a rewinding device file; any access to the drive is followed immediately by a rewind. The /dev/nht0 device file, however, results in no rewind, which can be convenient if you want to put more than one backup on a tape.

Floppy Interfaces

In years past, the floppy interface was a popular one for low-end tape drives. In fact, this interface remained popular through 1998, but it's now seldom used for tape devices, having been supplanted by ATAPI drives.

The floppy interface has many negatives and few positives as an interface for tape drives. The interface is highly sensitive to software timing, and data transfers are highly critical, so floppy-interfaced drives tend to be tricky to configure. Drivers for floppy-based tape drives are also sensitive things, and for quite some time they were very primitive in Linux. Today they're reasonably mature, at least for most floppy-based drives. You can find out more about the latest developments at http://www.instmath.rwth-aachen.de/~heine/ftape/. For most people, the version of these drivers included in the Linux kernel will suffice. To configure these drivers, you need to activate several kernel options. These are located in the Ftape, the floppy tape device driver configuration area, which is located in the Character devices menu. Options you must set include

- **Ftape (QIC-80/Travan) support**   This option is necessary to activate the more specific features.
- **Zftape, the VFS interface**   This feature has historically been optional, but is a requirement for 2.2.x and later kernels.
- **Floppy tape controllers**   This option should usually be left at the default value of Standard. Some floppy-interfaced drives, however, come with optional ISA cards that enable them to operate more quickly. If you use such a card, select it from the list.

The Ftape device files usually contain *ft* in their names, such as /dev/rftx and /dev/nrftx for rewinding and non-rewinding devices, respectively, where *x* is a number from 0–4. Device numbers for these devices files are major 27 and minor 0–3 for /dev/rftx and minor 4–7 for /dev/nrftx. Ftape versions in the 3.0x range supported separate compression devices that typically used device filenames of the form /dev/zqftx and /dev/nqzftx, but this feature was removed from Ftape 4.0x in order to support improved error recovery features. If you use a 3.0x version of Ftape along with the compression devices, the effect is much like using a tape device with built-in compression, except that your computer's CPU does the compression. Using the 4.0x version of the driver requires that you use backup software that supports compression, assuming you want to compress your data as you back it up.

Parallel Port Interfaces

As with many other external devices, the parallel port has long served as an interface method for removable tape backup drives. The parallel port was never intended for this function, however, and the results aren't as reliable as can be achieved with SCSI or ATAPI drives. If you want an external tape backup device, therefore, I favor using a SCSI drive. In the future, USB and FireWire might fill this niche, as well.

For all parallel-port tape devices, you must select Y or M to the Parallel port support option in the kernel's General setup area. You must also activate additional options, depending upon the type of parallel-port drive you have.

The Ftape driver, which is generally thought of as a driver for floppy-interfaced devices, supports a fair number of parallel-interfaced tape drives. When used with these devices, the Ftape driver uses the same kernel compilation options and device filenames, so check the section of floppy-based drives for more information.

Some newer parallel-port tape drives use the EIDE parallel-port support, which you activate by selecting the Parallel port ATAPI tapes kernel configuration option in the Block devices area. You access these devices through the /dev/ptx and /dev/nptx device files (major number96, minor numbers 0–3 and 128–131, respectively).

Proprietary and Unusual Interfaces

In addition to the major tape interface devices described earlier, a variety of proprietary interface cards and matching tape drives have been developed. These devices are largely obsolete now, and many have no support in Linux. One of the few exceptions is the QIC-02 tape interface, which is supported by a driver of the same name in the Character devices configuration area of the Linux kernel. As I mentioned earlier, the Ftape driver also includes support for a number of proprietary interfaces that can be used instead of a floppy interface with some floppy-interface drives.

A small number of USB tape drives have come onto the market, largely targeted at iMac users. In theory, it should be possible to add support for these devices under Linux's USB system. As of kernel 2.3.46, no explicit support is present, although it's possible the USB SCSI driver will work. (This driver maps USB mass storage devices onto Linux's SCSI system.) Check http://www.linux-usb.org for the latest information if you would like to use a USB-based tape drive.

Popular Tape Technologies

Differing formats often compete for dominance in the marketplace. In audio tape technology, 8-track tapes and cassettes competed for several years, and in videotapes, Beta and VHS formats competed. Likewise, different computer backup tape technologies exist. Unlike the audio and video tape formats, however, several formats are alive and well today. These formats are theoretically independent of the drive interface types I've just described, but, in practice, some tape formats are associated with only one or two interface types.

QIC

The *Quarter-Inch Cartridge* (QIC) tape format has been around for years. In fact, QIC cartridges come in two cartridge sizes, each of which hosts a large number of encoding variants. The two cartridge sizes are 4×5×0.625-inch and 3.25×2.5×0.6-inch. QIC tape model numbers begin in either *DC* or *MC*. The DC tapes use the larger form factor, whereas the MC tapes use the smaller one.

The first QIC tape standard, QIC-02, used a proprietary interface card, for which Linux drivers exist in the standard kernel. Most subsequent forms used the SCSI or floppy interfaces, with the larger form factor designs generally favoring SCSI interfaces and the smaller ones using floppy interfaces.

Two of the most popular QIC tape formats in the mid-1990s were QIC-40 and QIC-80. These two formats stored 40MB and 80MB of data per tape, respectively, although longer tapes could increase those values by 50%. These drives were popular because they were affordable to home users. By today's standards, these drives and their immediate successors are woefully short on capacity, but the most modern MC QIC formats can store several gigabytes of data. As a general rule, MC QIC drives can read from lower-capacity MC QIC tapes, but the capability of a drive to write to a lower-capacity tape varies. Like floppy disks, most MC QIC tapes require formatting by appropriate software before they can be used. The Ftape package includes a tape-formatting utility.

The DC drives have traditionally stored more data per tape than their MC cousins, which is not surprising given the physically larger size of the media. The largest DC drives can store a respectable 25GB uncompressed. Like MC drives, DC drives can usually read from lower-capacity tapes. Write capability varies, but is generally better than that of MC drives. Most DC tapes come preformatted, and don't need any special attention before being used.

Although still competitive in terms of capacity, QIC drives have fallen out of favor in recent years. Instead, Travan drives have taken over the low-end and mid-range market, whereas DAT, DLT, and others compete in the mid-range and high ends. Nonetheless, if you have a QIC drive that's adequate to your needs, or if you can buy one at a good price, there's no reason to avoid doing so, except perhaps for a scarcity of media.

Travan

3M (now Imation; `http://www.imation.com`) developed its Travan technology as a proprietary offshoot of QIC drives. Most Travan drives aren't manufactured by Imation, though; they're made by other companies. Imation dominates the market for blank Travan media, however. Travan drives and media come in several variants:

- **TR-1** The first Travan format stores 400MB of data, uncompressed. These drives generally use floppy-based interfaces.

- **TR-2** This improved Travan version stores 800MB uncompressed. Most TR-2 drives use the floppy interface.

- **TR-3** TR-3 doubles the capacity again, to 1.6GB uncompressed. These drives continue to use the floppy interface.

- **TR-4** TR-4 represents a more substantial improvement in capacity, to 4GB. Most manufacturers switched from floppy interfaces to ATAPI and SCSI interfaces with their TR-4 models.

- **TR-5** TR-5 increases the capacity to 10GB uncompressed. TR-5 drives use ATAPI or SCSI interfaces.

- **NS-8**   NS-8 is the name given to TR-4 drives that include built-in compression. These drives also support read-after-write operation (which I describe later in this chapter, in the section "Read-After-Write Verification"). Most NS-8 drives use SCSI interfaces.

- **NS-20**   NS-20 is the compressed variant of TR-5. Like NS-8 drives, NS-20 drives generally use the SCSI interface and support read-after-write verification.

> **NOTE**
>
> NS-8 drives use TR-4 tapes, and NS-20 drives use TR-5 tapes. Some tapes are marketed for one line or another, but marketing aside, there's no difference between TR- and NS- tapes.

In addition to these versions, a few companies offer nonstandard Travan-like drives. These drives have peculiar capacities, such as 5GB. The media for these drives often look just like ordinary Travan media, but they're incompatible. I recommend sticking with a standard Travan format, in order to increase your choice in media.

Unfortunately, most Travan drives cannot write to lower-capacity Travan media, although they can usually read lower-capacity media. This fact can make upgrading a Travan drive difficult, because you must replace the (expensive) media along with the drive.

Modern Travan drives generally use the EIDE or SCSI ports on your system, but a few models use unusual interfaces, such as the parallel port or even the USB port. It's best to stick with the EIDE or SCSI interfaces.

As a general rule, Travan drives are inexpensive ($200–$500 for TR-4 or TR-5 drives in early 2000, for example), but the media are costly ($20–$40 for TR-4 or TR-5 tapes). This fact makes Travan drives an economically good choice if you expect to purchase few tapes, but if you expect to buy many tapes, you might want to consider DAT instead.

Travan drives have a reputation for noise; they make a loud whirring sound, not unlike that of a dentist's drill, when in operation. Because the tapes spin at such high speed, they also tend to generate a substantial amount of heat, so you should place the drives away from other heat-generating components whenever possible, to avoid exacerbating heat stresses on all components.

DAT

Digital Audio Tape is a tape format that was developed for the storage of audio data, but that's been adapted for use as a computer data storage medium. DAT cartridges are physically smaller than QIC or Travan cartridges, but they store a lot of data. This feat is accomplished, in part, by the use of more advanced head technology. QIC and Travan drives record data in a handful of linear tracks on the drive. A DAT drive's read/write head resembles that of a VCR— it's tilted at an angle and spins, so that the data tracks cut crosswise. This recording method is known as *helical scan* recording (see Figure 8.3 for a comparison of these data storage methods). DAT drives also use a different encoding method than do linear drives like QIC and Travan devices. This more advanced design allows more data to be stored per square inch on a DAT tape than on a QIC or Travan tape, all other things being equal.

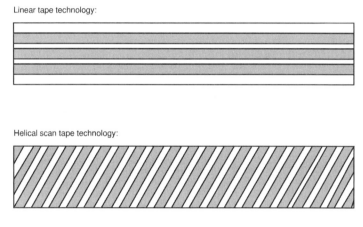

Linear tape technology:

Helical scan tape technology:

FIGURE 8.3
The rotating DAT head design yields a more efficient data storage pattern on the tape.

Like Travan, DAT drives are available in several variants:

- **DDS-1** The *digital data storage* (DDS) format is used by most DAT drives, and DDS-1 is the first incarnation of that format. DDS-1 drives have an uncompressed capacity of 2GB.
- **DDS-2** DDS-2 doubles the capacity of DDS-1, to 4GB uncompressed.
- **DDS-3** DDS-3 drives have a 12GB uncompressed capacity.
- **DDS-4** These drives have a 20GB capacity, uncompressed.

It's possible to vary these capacities (generally downward) by using shorter tapes. For instance, 1.3GB DDS-1 tapes are not uncommon. Almost all DAT drives support hardware data compression, which produces an average 2:1 compression ratio, thus doubling DAT capacity.

Compared to Travan drives, DAT drives are expensive ($650–$1000 for DDS-2 and DDS-3 drives, and around $1000 for DDS-4 drives), but their tapes are inexpensive ($8–$25 for DDS-2 and DDS-3 tapes, and $30–$35 for DDS-4 tapes). This pricing scheme makes DAT a cost-effective solution if you plan to buy many tapes. DAT drives can usually both read and write earlier DAT versions. You therefore don't need to abandon your old media if you replace a drive with a newer version, but the new drive is likely to be expensive.

DAT drives almost invariably use the SCSI interface, and always have. The drives are much quieter than are Travan or QIC drives, and they usually generate less heat. Their head mechanisms are extremely delicate, however, so you must be careful not to damage a drive, particularly if it's an external unit which might be dropped or receive other shocks.

Other Tape Drive Types

Although Travan and DAT drives dominate the marketplace for low-end and mid-range tape units, other technologies do exist, and might be of interest to you if you need to back up large quantities of data. Most of these drives are very expensive, costing $1000–$5000 or even more, but if you need to do regular backups of a 60GB server, this cost can be quite well justified. Keep in mind that these are only a few of the high-end tape backup formats. If you have a serious need for ultra-high-capacity backup, you should investigate the market more thoroughly.

DLT

Digital Linear Tape (DLT) is a high-capacity linear tape technology. DLT drives are marketed for servers and other high-capacity markets; they can store 20GB–35GB uncompressed. The drives themselves are quite expensive, unfortunately, costing upward of $3000.

8mm

One technology that's related to DAT is the 8mm tape drive. These tapes resemble those used in 8mm video cameras, although the tapes are formulated differently and so shouldn't be interchanged with 8mm videotapes. Exabyte (http://www.exabyte.com) is the only supplier of 8mm tape drives. Like DAT, 8mm uses helical scan recording. Some models of 8mm drive can store up to 60GB uncompressed, making these drives well suited for very high-capacity installations (at least by the standards of PC storage).

AIT

The *Advanced Intelligent Tape* (AIT) format (http://www.aittape.com/) uses cartridges that are superficially similar to 8mm cartridges, but the two are incompatible. Like DLT, AIT tapes can currently store up to 35GB uncompressed.

Tape Drive Features

No matter what variety of drive you choose to purchase, there are certain features you should look into. Some of these features are more common on some types of drives than on others.

Compatibility with Prior Standards

As I described earlier, some types of tape drives, such as DAT drives, are usually compatible with previous versions of the same format. A DDS-3 DAT drive, for example, can usually both read and write DDS-2 and DDS-1 tapes. This characteristic can be useful for two reasons:

- **Using old media** If you have an older drive of the same basic type, replacing that drive with a newer and higher-capacity model of the same basic type enables you to continue to use your existing media, while providing room for greater capacity when you buy new tapes. Similarly, future variants of the same drive type will likely be able to use the tapes you buy for your present drive, which might become important at some point in the future.

- **Low-cost media** Lower-capacity tapes of a given type typically cost less than their higher-capacity counterparts. You might therefore want to purchase tapes of a mix of capacities if you need to make some backups of large amounts of data and others with less data. For instance, full backups are typically quite large, but incremental backups are usually much smaller.

Some tape drive types, such as most Travan drives, support read, but not write, access to older media of the same type. This characteristic can be useful if you keep tapes for archival purposes, or if you need to replace a drive that's broken unexpectedly. It's not useful if you want to purchase lower-cost and lower-capacity media for smaller backup jobs.

Of course, if you have one tape drive and purchase one of a different type entirely, you'll have no compatibility with your current media. (The capability of most Travan drives to read some QIC MC tapes is an exception to this rule.)

Hardware Data Compression

Most low-end tape drives write data to tape in the form in which they receive it. The problem with this approach is that some backup software, such as `tar` in conjunction with `gzip`, creates a backup that's very sensitive to errors. If even a single bit of the recorded data is flawed, all the subsequent data on the backup becomes useless. Other backup packages, such as the commercial Backup and Recovery Utility (BRU—see `http://www.estinc.com`), don't suffer from this problem. Hardware data compression is another way around this problem. Instead of using `gzip`, you set the drive to use compression, which is usually the default configuration.

8

TAPE BACKUP

Read-After-Write Verification

Many of the more advanced drives support a feature known as *read-after-write verification*. In this configuration, a read head is placed so that it can read the data immediately after it is written by the write head, as depicted in Figure 8.4. The drive can then read the data immediately after it's been written, and if the drive detects an error, it can rewind the tape and write the data again. This feature can add substantially to the reliability of a tape drive.

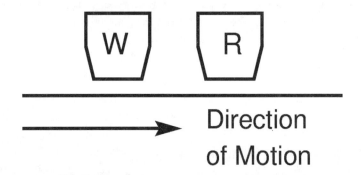

FIGURE 8.4

A given point on the tape passes under the write head, and then under the read head, enabling the drive to verify that the data were written correctly.

If you don't have read-after-write verification, it's important that you perform a verify pass on the tape immediately after you create it. This operation reads the tape's data and compares what's on the tape to what's on your hard disk. In the event of a discrepancy, you might need to perform the entire backup again, or at least back up those files that were written incorrectly.

> **TIP**
>
> For added safety, perform a separate verify pass even if your tape drive supports read-after-write verification.

> **NOTE**
>
> If you perform a separate verify pass, it's possible that some files won't match because they've changed between the time the backup was made and the time the verification is performed. This fact can make it difficult to determine whether the backup is of good quality, particularly if your system's contents are prone to change during the backup period.

> **CAUTION**
>
> A tape that passes a verify operation isn't guaranteed to function properly during a restore. The recording can fade over time, introducing errors that weren't present on the original. Also, if you replace one drive with another, it's possible that the new drive won't read a tape written by another drive as well as the original did. This lack of 100% reliability is one of the prime reasons you should keep at least two backups of your data. For instance, you might back up once a week, but keep two or more weeks' worth of backups on hand. That way, if your most recent backup fails to restore correctly, you can resort to an older one, which is still probably better than having no backup at all.

Changers

A tape *changer* is a tape drive variant that accepts several tapes at one time. The result is a tape device that appears to the computer to have a higher capacity than can be achieved by a conventional single-tape drive of the same type; the drive seamlessly directs the backup process from one tape to the next.

Changers are most often employed in high-capacity backup situations, such as backup devices for entire networks. As such, they're often used in conjunction with high-capacity media such as DLT drives. There are Travan changers available, though. You might want to consider such a device if you have an existing Travan drive but find that your backup needs have expanded past single-tape capacities.

Using a Tape Drive in Linux

You can't use a tape drive in the same way you use a hard disk or removable disk. Like record-able CD drives, tape drives require that you use special software to access the drives. You use this software in conjunction with one or more tape device files to perform a backup or restore operation.

Fortunately, the program interface to tape devices doesn't vary much from one drive to the next, so basic tape drive operation is identical across models and types of drive, although the details of what device file you use vary. This commonality of function means that you don't need to be concerned with Linux compatibility for any given tape drive. A few drives, though, support special features, such as tape partitioning, that might not be usable with all software. The Linux mt command includes support for many of these proprietary features, but you'll need to consult the mt man page for details.

Understanding Tape Device Files

Tape device files vary from one tape device type to another. The descriptions of various tape drive interfaces earlier in this chapter, in the section titled "Tape Backup Interfaces," provides information on the tape device files you should use to access your tape device.

> **TIP**
>
> If you administer several Linux computers that use different types of tape backup units, you might want to create a symbolic link from /dev/tape to the tape device files on each of your computers. That way, you can create scripts for backup that can be used on all the computers you administer, no matter what variety of tape drive each one uses.

Linux tape device files come in two varieties: *rewinding* and *non-rewinding*. The non-rewinding device filenames are the same as the rewinding device filenames, but begin with an *n*. For example, /dev/st0 is the rewinding device file for the first SCSI tape device, whereas /dev/nst0 is the non-rewinding variant of this device file.

When you want to perform a backup as a single operation and don't need to preserve any data that already exists on a tape, the rewinding tape device is the most convenient, because you can perform the backup using a single command. The non-rewinding device, however, enables you to store more than one backup on a single tape. For example, you can issue a series of tar commands, as in

```
tar cf /dev/nst0 /home1
tar cf /dev/nst0 /home2
tar cf /dev/nst0 /home3
```

This series of operations creates three backups on a single tape. Much the same effect could be achieved by using a single backup of all three directories:

```
tar cf /dev/st0 /home1 /home2 /home3
```

The use of the non-rewinding device is especially useful when you want to use a single tape for backups that occur at different times. For instance, you might want to put a week's worth of incremental backups on one tape. You can't do this with the rewinding device file, but you can with the non-rewinding file; you merely need to read past the previous days' backups using the mt command prior to issuing a new backup, as described in a later section.

Using tar for Basic Backups

Linux comes with several backup programs, such as cpio and dump. One of the most basic backup programs, however, is tar. Many of the principles I describe here apply to the use of other backup programs, but the details of how to apply these principles varies from one program to another.

tar takes various commands and parameters. Table 8.1 summarizes the most important commands. To use tar, you must use precisely one of the commands in Table 8.1. When you perform a backup, that command will normally be --create (c), possibly followed by --diff (d). restoring data, that command will be --extract (x).

8

TAPE BACKUP

TABLE 8.1 Main tar Commands

Command	Effect
c or --create	Creates an archive
t or --list	Displays the contents of an archive
x or --extract	Extracts files from an archive (for restore)
d or --diff or --compare	Compares archive contents to disk

In addition to the main tar command, you issue one or more supplementary parameters (some of which are listed in Table 8.2) to tell tar what else must be done. For instance, you can use --file (f) to tell tar to what file to back up the data (normally to your tape device file).

TABLE 8.2 Supplemental tar Parameters

Parameter	Effect
f or --file=*file*	Use the specified file for the archive
v or --verbose	Display filenames as they're processed
g or --listed-incremental=*file*	Perform an incremental backup
l or --one-file-system	Restrict backup to one filesystem
W or --verify	Perform a verify immediately after creating a backup
z or --gzip or --ungzip	Use gzip for compression
--exclude=*file*	Exclude the specified file or directory from a backup

These are only some of the most commonly used supplementary tar parameters. Consult the tar man page for more.

As an example of these parameters in use, consider the following command:

```
tar cvzWlf /dev/st0 / /home
```

This command backs up the root (/) and /home partitions. It shows a list of files as they're being backed up (v), uses gzip compression (z), performs a verify operation immediately after the backup is complete (W), doesn't back up partitions that are mounted on either of the specified partitions (l), and backs up to the rewinding SCSI device (f /dev/st0). Note that it's possible to string the parameters to the tar command together in a single mass. If you prefer a less compact but more intelligible form, you could issue the same command as follows:

```
tar --create --verbose --gzip --verify --one-file-system --file=/dev/st0 /
➥/home
```

The --one-file-system (l) parameter is particularly important, because it prevents any attempt to back up the /proc filesystem. This is a filesystem that Linux maintains in order to provide easy access to information about the computer, including a complete image of the computer's memory. Its files don't reside on any disk, and should never be restored from a tape backup. It's therefore important that you either include the --one-file-system parameter or explicitly exclude the /proc directory from your backup by using the --exclude=/proc parameter. If you fail to do this, you'll waste a lot of tape, and could cause your system to crash when you restore the /proc filesystem. If you've accidentally backed up /proc already and need to restore from that tape, you can use the --exclude=/proc parameter during restore to avoid problems.

If you use the --one-file-system parameter, you must specify each partition separately. For instance, in the preceding example, root (/) and /home are presumably two separate partitions. If any other partition is mounted under either of these (such as /usr/local or /opt), it won't be backed up by the preceding command. You can back up only certain directories by specifying the appropriate directory name—even if it's not a partition of its own. For instance, you can back up the /home directory even if it's not on a separate partition by giving its name in tar command:

```
tar cvlzf /dev/st0 /home
```

The tar command can be used to create on-disk archives of files. You must provide the name of the file you want to create instead of a tape device file. For instance

```
tar cvlzf home-backup.tgz /home
```

It's traditional to give the resulting files .tar extensions if compression has not been applied. Use .tar.Z extensions if they've been compressed with the old compress program, or .tar.gz or .tgz extensions if they've been compressed with gzip. Such *tarballs*, as they're often called, are often used for distributing programs, source code, and other files in the Linux community.

Using mt to Control a Tape Drive

In order to use the non-rewinding tape device most effectively, you must have some means of controlling the tape—a way to seek past one backup set to access or create another, rewind the tape, and so on. This functionality is provided by the mt command in Linux. The basic syntax of this command is

```
mt -f device operation [count] [arguments]
```

where

- *device* is the device file, such as /dev/nst0.
- *operation* is the operation to be performed, as detailed shortly.
- *count* is an optional count of how many times to perform the operation.
- *arguments* constitute any additional information required by the operation.

Table 8.3 summarizes the most important operations you can perform with mt. For more information, consult the mt man page.

TABLE 8.3 mt Operations

Operation	Effect
fsf	Space forward *count* files.
bsf	Space backward *count* files.
fss	Space forward *count* setmarks.
bss	Space backward *count* setmarks.
eod or seod	Seek to the end of valid data.

8

TAPE BACKUP

continues

TABLE 8.3   Continued

Operation	Effect
rewind	Rewind the tape.
offline or rewoffl	Rewind and unload the tape (unload is not meaningful on some drives).
retension	Rewind the tape, wind it to the end, and then rewind it again.
eof or weof	Write *count* EOF marks.
wset	Write *count* setmarks.
erase	Erase the tape.
status	Display information about the tape drive.
tell	Display the current read/write position on the tape.
seek	Seek to a new read/write position on the tape.
load	Load a new tape into the drive.
compression	Enable or disable hardware compression, by passing an *argument* of 1 or 0, respectively.
datcompression	Another compression-setting command. If used without an argument, reports the compression status (on or off).

Not all mt *operations work with all backup devices. For instance, the operations that work with setmarks work only with SCSI devices; and the* compression *and* datcompression *commands work only on drives that support hardware compression.*

The mt command, in conjunction with tar or some other backup program, enables you to control functions of the tape backup device and perform more sophisticated backups than can be done with tar and the rewinding device alone. For instance, suppose you want to store a series of incremental backups on one tape. For the first backup, you could issue a series of commands like the following:

```
mt -f /dev/nst0 rewind
tar cvlf /dev/nst0 / --listed-incremental=backup-info.txt
mt -f /dev/nst0 rewind
```

If the file backup-info.txt doesn't exist, this action backs up the entire root partition. If backup-info.txt exists and is of the correct format, this action backs up only those files that have changed since backup-info.txt was created. The next day, you could perform the following operations:

```
mt -f /dev/nst0 rewind
mt -f /dev/nst0 fsf 1
tar cvlf /dev/nst0 / --listed-incrental=backup-info.txt
mt -f /dev/nst0 rewind
```

This set of commands backs up files that have changed since the previous day's backup. On subsequent days, you can perform the same series of actions, just incrementing the value of the `fsf` operation in the second line from 1 to 2, 3, and so on.

When it comes time to restore data, you can do so in a similar way. Suppose you want to restore the third and fourth backups on a tape. You would perform these actions:

```
mt -f /dev/nst0 rewind
mt -f /dev/nst0 fsf 2
tar xvlf /dev/nst0
mt -f /dev/nst0 fsf 1
tar xvlf /dev/nst0
mt -f /dev/nst0 rewind
```

The second line skips over the first two backups, and the subsequent three lines restore the next two backups—the third and fourth. In this way, you can restore whatever files you want to restore.

> **CAUTION**
>
> The preceding restore operations assume that the current directory is the root (/) directory, or that you want to restore files under whatever the current directory is.

When you want to perform a new full backup, you can delete the `backup-info.txt` file from your hard disk. The next time you run the `tar` command with the `--listed-incremental` option, `tar` will create the `backup-info.txt` file anew and back up all files. You can maintain several different levels of incremental backups in this way, as well. For instance, you can keep two incremental backup files, a monthly and a weekly. Once a month, you delete the monthly file and create a fresh monthly backup file by performing a backup. You can then copy the monthly backup file to serve as the starting point for the weekly file. Every day of the week, you can perform a new daily incremental backup, the contents of which are tracked in the weekly file. At the start of a new week, you can copy the monthly file back over the weekly file and switch to a new incremental tape. The first incremental backup of each week therefore becomes larger as the month progresses, because it contains all the changes from the previous week's backup. The result of this backup strategy is depicted in Figure 8.5.

Although Figure 8.5 depicts a backup procedure that involves five tapes per month, at restore you'll only need two tapes if you use a two-tier incremental backup approach, even for a full disaster recovery: the monthly tape and the latest weekly tape. In principle, you could therefore get by with just two tapes. Using five, however, provides you with added protection in case a weekly tape goes bad, or in case you need to recover a file that was created and then deleted in a previous week.

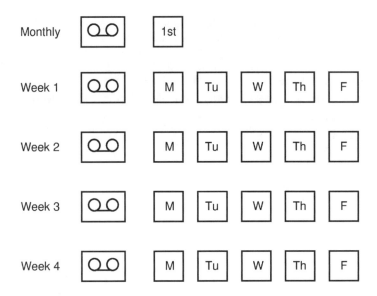

FIGURE 8.5
The monthly full backup is larger than any given incremental backup.

Of course, there are other ways to arrange an incremental backup strategy. If you use tar or a similar command-line tool, all rely upon mt to enable you to space past previous days' backups. Integrated backup packages often include scripts or GUI options to perform these actions in a more automated fashion.

Using GUI Backup Packages

Some tape backup programs use GUI environments. This is particularly true of commercial packages like BRU (http://www.estinc.com; shown in Figure 8.6) and ARKEIA (http://www.arkeia.com). There are also GUI front-ends to open source programs like tar. The KDat (http://sunsite.auc.dk/qweb/kdat/) program, for instance, adds a GUI front-end to tar. The operation of these programs varies substantially from one program to another, but the basic principles are the same.

In most GUI backup packages, you select the files and directories you want to back up using a file browser of some type. (In Figure 8.6, the file browser is the listing in the left panel.) You then specify that you want to back up the files you've selected. In BRU, you do this by clicking the Add button. In most programs, the selected files and directories then appear in a separate field (the right panel in Figure 8.6), so you can verify that you're backing up the files you intended. You can usually set a variety of options, such as the use of compression or incremental backup options. In BRU, you do this by clicking the Options button.

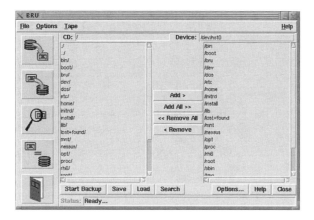

FIGURE 8.6
GUI tape backup utilities provide a friendlier interface than do text-based utilities like tar.

Summary

Tape backup devices can save you from untold difficulties. Chances are you have spent—or will spend—dozens, hundreds, or even thousands of hours configuring your computer and preparing data to be stored on the computer. If you're in charge of a Linux server that's used to store others' data, the data stored on that server might represent tens or hundreds of thousands of hours of labor. Data backup is therefore extremely important. Fortunately, most tape backup devices work well under Linux, and Linux provides many tools to help you perform backups. I recommend using SCSI tape backup devices, particularly for very high-capacity needs, but ATAPI devices are adequate for smaller workstations. Older floppy-based backup devices are generally inadequate to back up today's hard disks, although if you have one, it might still find a home backing up a firewall, router, or other small system. USB devices are becoming available but are as yet unsupported in Linux. In the future, FireWire devices might become a viable backup option.

8

TAPE BACKUP

SCSI Host Adapters

IN THIS CHAPTER

The *Small Computer System Interface* (SCSI, pronounced *scuzzy*) is a high-performance data bus intended for use by hard disks, CD-ROM drives, tape drives, and other data storage devices, although other devices are sometimes attached to SCSI busses, such as scanners and even an occasional printer. The SCSI protocols include many features useful in handling data storage devices, so it's possible to design a new SCSI device (such as a new removable media drive or a new tape drive) without re-inventing any protocols. If it follows the SCSI standards, the new device is also immediately compatible with existing software, such as Linux's mt and tar for controlling and accessing tape drives.

The protocol that most directly competes with SCSI is EIDE, which has adopted some of SCSI's strengths in its ATAPI protocols for handling CD-ROM and tape drives. As described in Chapter 5, "Hard Disks," EIDE hardware lacks some of SCSI's best features, such as the capability to string 7 or 15 devices to a single SCSI host adapter, and the multitasking SCSI bus. Nonetheless, EIDE is a popular interface because it's included with all modern x86 motherboards and is less expensive than SCSI. In fact, if your needs are modest, EIDE might be quite adequate. If you want to build a very high-performance computer, though, SCSI is the protocol of choice.

Characteristics of SCSI

It's important to understand some of the characteristics of a SCSI host adapter—and of the SCSI bus generally—before delving too far into the realm of SCSI devices and SCSI variants. Like other busses designed for disks, SCSI devices connect to each other via cables. It's also necessary to configure SCSI devices, often via jumpers, and some of these configuration options are specific to SCSI.

Cables and Connectors

Unlike most computer interfaces, SCSI supports both internal and external devices. That is, you can attach a SCSI device either inside the computer's main case or outside that case. (When mounted outside, the device normally resides in its own case.) To support this operation, most SCSI host adapters have at least two connectors, one of which is accessible from outside the computer (see Figure 9.1). Some host adapters have three or even four connectors in order to support both inside and outside connectors and two bus widths, as described later in "Varieties of SCSI."

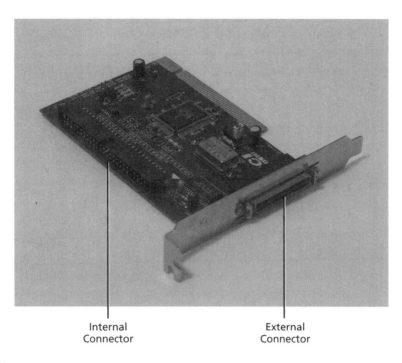

Internal
Connector

External
Connector

Figure 9.1
The internal and external SCSI connectors enable you to attach both internal and external devices to a single SCSI bus.

Caution

Although some SCSI host adapters have three connectors, you should *never* attach devices to all three connectors of most adapters. SCSI chains should be one-dimensional, each device falling along a single line. It's OK if the SCSI host adapter falls midway along this line, but the line must not split into a Y-shape. Adapters with four connectors usually support two separate SCSI busses, so you can attach devices to all four connectors.

SCSI cabling comes in a confusing array of options. Figure 9.2 shows just two types of SCSI cable: An internal 50-pin ribbon cable and an external 50-pin high-density–to–25-pin cable. Internal SCSI cables usually have enough connectors to link several SCSI devices using just one cable. External cables, by contrast, are two-device items. Most external SCSI devices include two connectors, so it's possible to link devices one after another.

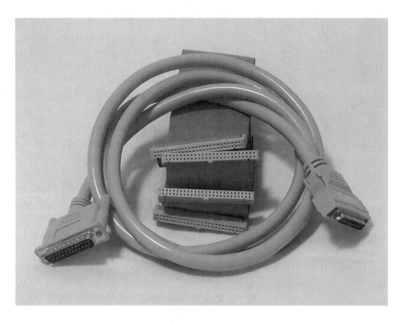

FIGURE 9.2

SCSI cables come in a wide variety of lengths and connector types. This figure shows two types of SCSI cable: an internal 50-pin ribbon cable and an external 50-pin high-density–to –25-pin cable.

If you have a SCSI cable that has the wrong connector type on one end, it's often possible to purchase a converter, such as the one shown in Figure 9.3. These converters are usually less expensive than a new SCSI cable, but they can also be awkward. In some cases, they add enough weight to the connection that they can come loose or even fall off completely. I therefore recommend avoiding such converters whenever possible.

Some of the most common SCSI cable and connector types include

- **50-pin ribbon cable**   Shown in Figure 9.2, 50-pin ribbon cable is the workhorse of older SCSI implementations. It's used for internal connections to older SCSI hard disks, and is still used for non-disk devices such as tape backups and CD-ROM drives.
- **68-pin ribbon cable**   68-pin ribbon cable is physically narrower than 50-pin ribbon cable, and uses connectors with pins spaced closer together. It serves the same basic function as 50-pin ribbon cable, linking internal devices. Most recent SCSI hard disks use 68-pin connectors.

FIGURE 9.3
SCSI converters let you plug one type of cable into a mismatched socket.

- **25-pin external cables**   25-pin cables should never have happened, but they did. 25-pin connectors are common on some inexpensive external SCSI devices, and some low-end SCSI host adapters have 25-pin external connectors. The connector on the left side of the external cable shown in Figure 9.2 is a 25-pin external SCSI connector.

- **50-pin Centronics cables**   50-pin Centronics connectors look like oversized parallel-port connectors on printers (see Figure 9.4). They're used on many external SCSI enclosures, and some older SCSI host adapter cards used them as well. They're a good choice for connecting 50-pin external SCSI devices.

- **50-pin high-density cables**   50-pin high-density connectors are commonly used as external connectors for SCSI host adapters. (The external connector in Figure 9.1, the right end of the external cable in Figure 9.2, and the visible end of the converter in Figure 9.3 all use these connectors.) Note that high-density connectors tend to be smaller than conventional connectors with fewer pins. These connectors are easy to use, but they sometimes work themselves loose, particularly when paired with an adapter like the one shown in Figure 9.3.

- **68-pin external cables**   These cables use connectors that look much like the 50-pin high-density connectors, except that they include 18 more pins. They're used to link external versions of modern hard disks to SCSI host adapters.

9

SCSI HOST
ADAPTERS

FIGURE 9.4

50-pin external devices often use Centronics-style SCSI connectors.

Which cable type you need depends on the devices you intend to link. Also, be aware that some SCSI variants require special characteristics in their cables. For instance, Ultra2 SCSI devices require special cables, although the connector types are the same as I've just described.

Termination

A SCSI chain must link devices in a linear arrangement; there can be no fork in the SCSI chain. The device on each end of the chain must be *terminated*, meaning that it must have a set of resistors attached to it to stop the SCSI signals from echoing back and forth across the SCSI chain. Without terminators, a SCSI bus tends to become unreliable.

Figure 9.5 shows two types of SCSI terminators. The comb-like objects on the right are terminating resistor packs for an old SCSI device. The terminators are inserted into sockets on the SCSI device to terminate it, and removed to unterminate the device. You won't see such resistor packs on most modern SCSI devices, however. Today's models incorporate termination that can be enabled or disabled by setting a jumper.

External SCSI devices are sometimes terminated by a switch or slider, similar in principle to a jumper on an internal device. Other times, it's necessary to use an external SCSI terminator on the end of the chain. The object on the left in Figure 9.5 is such a device. It attaches to one of the SCSI connectors on an external SCSI device, thus terminating it.

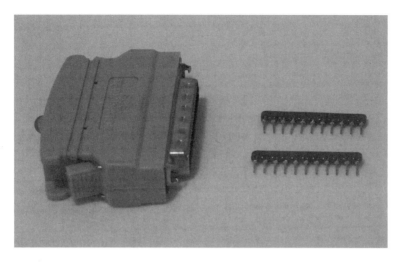

FIGURE 9.5
SCSI terminators, like SCSI cables, come in a variety of shapes and sizes.

SCSI terminators come in three varieties: passive, active, and low-voltage differential (LVD). Each is more advanced than the one before. Passive terminators are acceptable for low-end SCSI-1 devices, but most more advanced SCSI devices require at least active termination. Ultra2 and Ultra3 SCSI devices require LVD terminators when they're run at Ultra2 speed or above.

SCSI IDs

With up to 15 devices on a SCSI bus (plus the host adapter), SCSI requires some way for devices to identify themselves. This is done through SCSI ID numbers. You assign each device an ID, typically by setting jumpers on an internal device or by setting a dial of some sort on an external device. It's important that every SCSI device, *including the host adapter*, have its own unique ID. For SCSI devices that use 25- or 50-pin cabling, the SCSI ID can range from 0–7 (a 3-bit number, set by three jumpers). For 68-pin devices, the upper end is raised to 15 (a 4-bit number, set by four jumpers).

If two or more SCSI devices try to use the same SCSI ID, the results are unpredictable. Typically, one device "masks" the other, and the one that can be accessed frequently suffers severe performance degradation. Sometimes one or the other device appears to occupy *every* SCSI ID.

When you boot from a SCSI hard disk, the SCSI host adapter tries to locate the boot device by following a simple rule. The most common rule is to boot from the SCSI hard disk with the lowest SCSI ID. For this reason, it's traditional to give hard disks low SCSI IDs, usually starting with 0. Some host adapters start looking for the boot device at the other end of the scale, though. The SCSI host adapter itself typically acquires an ID of 7, although most host adapters let you change this assignment in one way or another.

If you have several computers and want to share an external SCSI device between these computers by moving it back and forth as the need arises, it helps if you can assign that device one ID and use that same ID on all computers. For this reason, when you work with several SCSI-equipped computers, I recommend standardizing on some set of common IDs, such as 0 and 1 for hard disks, 4 for CD-ROM drives, 6 for tape backup devices, and so on.

> **NOTE**
>
> Access to SCSI devices is prioritized by SCSI ID, with higher numbers having higher IDs on a Narrow bus. (On a Wide bus, the priority hierarchy goes 7-6-5-4-3-2-1-0-15-14-13-12-11-10-9-8.) For this reason, it's a good idea to give high IDS to devices that are very sensitive to timing, such as CD-R drives (but not higher than 7). Hard disks normally have low IDs not just so they can boot, but also because, if they're given high IDs, they tend to monopolize the SCSI bus over their slower SCSI neighbors. SCSI ID numbering is far from the most important SCSI performance characteristic, however; factors like incorrect termination or poor cable quality are much more likely to degrade performance than a poorly chosen SCSI ID choice.

SCAM

Modern SCSI devices support a protocol known as *SCSI Configured Automatically* (SCAM). SCAM is a way for the devices to negotiate SCSI options—most notably SCSI IDs and termination—automatically, without human intervention. Unfortunately, if you still use many pre-SCAM devices, this feature might not do you much good. If you run a computer with all new SCSI devices, though, there's a good chance you can simply plug them in and they'll configure themselves automatically.

Varieties of SCSI

Some of the differences in cables and termination I've just described relate to different varieties of SCSI. Since its introduction in the mid-1980s, SCSI technology has improved, leading to the introduction of multiple levels of SCSI, each of which improves on the previous level in various ways. Table 9.1 summarizes the most popular of these SCSI variants. Table 9.1 isn't complete, though; it omits rare technologies such as high-voltage differential (HVD) and seldom-used variants such as Narrow Ultra2 SCSI.

TABLE 9.1   Common Varieties of SCSI

SCSI Type	Speed	Cable Type	Maximum Cable Length in Meters
SCSI-1	5MB/s	25- or 50-pin	6m
SCSI-2	5MB/s	50-pin	6m
Fast SCSI-2	10MB/s	50-pin	3m
Fast/Wide SCSI-2	20MB/s	68-pin	3m
Ultra SCSI	20MB/s	50-pin	3m or 1.5m[1]
UltraWide SCSI	40MB/s	68-pin	3m or 1.5m[1]
Ultra2 Wide SCSI (LVD)	80MB/s	68-pin	12m
Ultra3 Wide SCSI (LVD)	160MB/s	68-pin	12m

[1]*Maximum cable length is 3m for three or fewer devices, 1.5m for more than three devices.*

One important characteristic of SCSI is that each variety is compatible with those that came before it. (One exception is HVD, which is incompatible with other SCSI signaling methods.) You can use a Fast SCSI-2 or even a SCSI-1 device on the latest host adapters supporting Ultra3 SCSI, for instance. In the case of 50- and 68-pin devices, either your host adapter must support both interfaces, or you must use an adapter to connect a 50-pin device to a 68-pin host adapter.

SCSI-1

SCSI-1 was the original SCSI standard. Approved in 1986 but used on some systems earlier than that, SCSI-1 was capable of 5MB/s speeds using 25- or 50-pin cables. As I mentioned earlier, however, 25-pin cables are not recommended. A normal 50-pin SCSI cable includes a large number of separate ground wires, but to reduce the number of pins, a 25-pin cable combines these all into one pin. The resulting cable usually works, but is less reliable than a 50-pin cable, particularly as the cable length grows. Today, few devices are limited to SCSI-1 speeds.

SCSI-2 and Fast SCSI-2

At its core, SCSI-2 is largely a clarification and extension of SCSI-1 protocols. The original SCSI-1 addressed the needs of hard disks but little else. Manufacturers found the SCSI bus appealing for CD-ROM drives, tape backup drives, and other devices, however, and so the manufacturers improvised, using proprietary extensions to the SCSI-1 protocol. Many of these were adopted for the SCSI-2 standard, and future devices followed the new standard.

With the introduction of SCSI-2 came several additional features, including

- **Fast SCSI**   10MB/s transfers, versus 5MB/s for SCSI-1 or non-Fast SCSI-2. In practice, the vast majority of SCSI-2 devices support Fast speeds.

- **Wide SCSI**   An 18-pin extension cable to the standard 50-pin cable enables still faster transfers (20MB/s for Fast/Wide SCSI-2). The 50-pin connector (sometimes called *Narrow SCSI*) uses an 8-bit parallel interface, and the extra 18 pins allow for a doubling of the width of this interface to 16 bits, hence the matched speed increase.

- **High density connectors**   The high-density connector was introduced with SCSI-2, enabling a 50-pin connector to take the space of the 25-pin connectors used on some products.

- **Active termination**   SCSI-2 introduced active termination as an option. Active termination provides more reliable termination of a SCSI bus, and should be used instead of passive termination whenever possible.

- **Command queuing**   This feature enables a device to receive several commands and then decide how best to execute those commands. For instance, if you tell a hard disk to retrieve sectors 57, 43,293, and 17,239, a device that supports command queuing can re-order those commands to reduce head seek time.

Unfortunately, SCSI-2's improvements come at a cost: reduced cable length. SCSI-1 cables can stretch as far as 6 meters (about 18 feet), but Fast SCSI-2 cables are limited to half that amount.

All in all, SCSI-2 represents a substantial improvement over SCSI-1. In fact, many SCSI devices today continue to use no more than SCSI-2 protocols. Modern hard disks, however, require faster transfer rates than can be provided by SCSI-2, particularly in its 50-pin form.

Fast/Wide SCSI-2 and SCSI-3

SCSI-2 added support for 68-pin transfers by using two SCSI cables. Such an arrangement is inconvenient, however, so the vast majority of Fast/Wide SCSI-2 devices use a 68-pin cable standard developed for the next SCSI version, SCSI-3. The SCSI-3 standard became more and more ambitious as time wore on, and soon manufacturers became impatient and started advertising their Fast/Wide SCSI-2 devices as SCSI-3 devices. Today, most of the features of SCSI-3 have become known by other names, as I describe shortly. If you see a device advertised as being SCSI-3, chances are it's really Fast/Wide SCSI-2 with a SCSI-3 68-pin cable. In its purest form, SCSI-3 incorporates all the features described in the next few sections.

UltraSCSI and UltraWide SCSI

Just as Fast SCSI-2 doubles speeds in comparison to SCSI-1, *UltraSCSI* doubles speeds in comparison to Fast SCSI-2—to 20MB/s for the 50-pin variety and 40MB/s for the 68-pin version. Even in early 2000, few hard disks exceed the 40MB/s speed of UltraWide SCSI, so in theory this interface is still adequate. In practice, however, most manufacturers have moved on to still faster SCSI versions for hard disks, in order to provide faster disk cache transfer speeds and to take advantage of higher speeds in multi-disk configurations. Some non-disk devices, such as CD-ROM drives, continue to use UltraSCSI, often in its 50-pin version.

Cable length shrinks again with the UltraSCSI variants, at least for SCSI chains with more than three devices. An UltraSCSI bus with fewer than three devices can use a cable length of up to three meters, but this value is halved with more devices. In practice, this makes it very difficult to use an UltraSCSI bus with many devices.

Ultra2 SCSI and Ultra2 Wide SCSI

The next major leap in SCSI speed is known as Ultra2, or *low voltage differential* (LVD), SCSI. Like UltraSCSI, Ultra2 drives are available in both 50-pin and 68-pin varieties, although in practice the 68-pin versions are far more common. This variant represents another doubling in speed, to 40MB/s and 80MB/s for the Narrow and Wide versions, respectively. Ultra2 Wide is a popular format for SCSI hard disks in 2000.

The LVD name for this interface refers to a variant form of SCSI signaling. The advantage of LVD over the *single-ended* (SE) signaling used in previous SCSI incarnations is that it allows for longer cable lengths, thus reversing the trend of shrinking maximum cable length and extending the limit to 12 meters. Most LVD devices can optionally be used in SE mode on older host adapters, but you might run into termination problems. LVD drives require LVD terminators when run in LVD mode, and they don't come with standard active SE terminators. Instead of setting a jumper to terminate the drive on an SE chain, you must locate a separate SE active terminator and use it. When you use an LVD drive with an LVD host adapter, it's also important that you use LVD cabling, which is made to higher standards than are conventional SCSI cables.

CAUTION

Prior to the introduction of LVD drives, HVD drives and host adapters existed. Unlike LVD drives, HVD drives cannot be safely mixed with SE devices or host adapters. Because HVD predated LVD, the documentation for these devices often refers to them merely as *differential SCSI*, although LVD drives also use differential technology, just at lower voltages. Do not attempt to mix such devices with standard SE or LVD SCSI devices, or you might damage some or all of your SCSI devices.

Ultra3 and Ultra3 Wide SCSI

The Ultra3 SCSI variants represent yet another doubling of SCSI bus speed, to 80MB/s and 160MB/s for the Narrow and Wide variants, respectively. As with Ultra2 SCSI, however, Ultra3 devices are available almost exclusively in Wide format, which is often referred to as *Ultra 160*. In fact, 160MB/s exceeds even the theoretical maximum 132MB/s transfer rate of a standard 32-bit PCI bus, so some Ultra3 host adapters use 64-bit PCI busses rather than the more common 32-bit variant. Be sure you can use such a host adapter on your motherboard before buying one.

The Future of SCSI

Ultra3 Wide SCSI's maximum speed of 160MB/s is certainly adequate for today's hard disks, but hard disk speed is always increasing, and it won't be long before 160MB/s is inadequate, especially for large servers running RAID configurations. Much of the future of SCSI is likely to lie in moves away from the traditional parallel SCSI architecture. Although a parallel interface allows the transmission of 8 or 16 bits of information at once, it poses problems as the speed scales up. The cause is tiny differences in the lengths or electrical characteristics of different wires in a cable. These differences can produce noticeable variations in the times at which signals arrive on different pins. This problem becomes worse as the bus speed increases, hence limiting future expansions of parallel SCSI bus speeds.

There might be future increases in SCSI speed using today's cabling designs, but it seems likely that SCSI will shift to a serial interface. This interface will probably use one or more of the interfaces that are already in development, such as IEEE-1394 (see the section "FireWire" in Chapter 6) or *Fiber Channel*. When this happens, you won't be able to continue using a SCSI device on older SCSI host adapters, unless the device maintains a dual interface.

SCSI and Motherboard Busses

Most SCSI host adapters plug into a computer's motherboard using one of the motherboard's expansion card slots, as described in Chapter 2, "Motherboards." Although most busses are adequate for very low-performance SCSI devices, it's important that you use a high-performance bus such as PCI when you use modern SCSI hard disks. In the following pages I describe some of the key considerations for using SCSI on various busses.

ISA Bus

The *Industry Standard Architecture* (ISA) bus is the oldest motherboard bus in common use on x86 PCs. In its earliest incarnation, the ISA bus was an 8-bit bus, but the one or two ISA slots that are still common on modern motherboards are invariably 16-bit slots that can accept either

8- or 16-bit cards. Although a few early SCSI-1 adapters worked in 8-bit ISA slots, these devices were very slow and undesirable even a decade ago. Today's ISA SCSI cards almost invariably use 16-bit ISA connectors.

CAUTION

Don't confuse the 8- or 16-bit nature of the ISA bus with the 8- or 16-bit (a k a Narrow or Wide, respectively) versions of SCSI. Most ISA SCSI cards use 16-bit ISA interfaces, but implement an 8-bit (Narrow) SCSI bus.

ISA SCSI cards are best classified as belonging to one of two categories:

- **PIO boards**   The least expensive ISA SCSI boards use *programmed input/output* (PIO). Like early IDE controllers, these boards require the computer's CPU to supervise every data transfer. PIO circuitry is inexpensive to produce, but the resulting CPU load causes these boards to impose a substantial performance penalty in a multitasking OS such as Linux.

- **DMA boards**   More expensive ISA SCSI cards implement *direct memory access* (DMA), in which the SCSI host adapter can transfer data directly from the SCSI bus to the computer's RAM. DMA boards reduce the CPU load when performing SCSI operations, and so are preferable to PIO boards. Unfortunately, the ISA bus limits DMA transfers to the lower 16MB of RAM, so on computers with more RAM, Linux might need to move data around in memory after a transfer. DMA boards usually implement a feature known as *bus mastering*, in which the expansion card takes over the motherboard's bus during its DMA transfer. These boards are therefore sometimes referred to as *DMA bus mastering,* or *bus mastering,* boards.

There's very little reason to purchase a new DMA ISA SCSI card today, because such cards are not much less expensive than PCI SCSI cards that often perform much better. Most of the ISA SCSI cards in today's market are PIO models that are bundled with low-end SCSI devices, such as scanners and CD-R drives. If you acquire such a package and have no other SCSI host adapter, you might want to try using it under Linux. You can then evaluate the device's performance and, if you notice an unacceptable slowdown of your system when using the SCSI device, replace the ISA board with a better PCI model.

A few of the very low-end ISA boards include only an internal or only an external SCSI connector. If you have only an internal connector but want to use an external device, you can attach an internal/external connector (see Figure 9.6) to the end of an internal SCSI cable, thus extending the chain outside the case.

9

SCSI HOST ADAPTERS

FIGURE 9.6

An internal/external SCSI connector lets you use external devices with a SCSI host adapter that has only an internal connector.

Few or no ISA boards implement any SCSI standard more advanced than Narrow Fast SCSI-2. Indeed, the ISA bus's theoretical maximum transfer speed is only 8MB/s, which is slower than Fast SCSI-2's maximum transfer speed of 10MB/s. There really is no point in supporting higher speeds than this in an ISA card.

EISA Bus and VL-Bus

Many 80486 computers used the EISA bus or the VL-Bus as a higher-speed alternative to the ISA bus. SCSI adapters were common on such busses, and, if you have such a computer and a matching SCSI host adapter, there's a good chance that you can use the host adapter in Linux.

DMA boards were the most popular type of EISA and VL-Bus SCSI host adapters, but a few PIO models were produced. Like ISA cards, few EISA or VL-Bus boards implement anything more sophisticated than Fast SCSI-2. These motherboard busses are capable of higher speeds, and a few models did include support for Wide devices.

Both EISA Bus and VL-Bus SCSI host adapters are very difficult to locate in the marketplace today, because of the demise of the bus type. If you must purchase such a board, your best bet is to look in used computer shops or on auction Web sites such as eBay (http://www.ebay.com). You might want to consider upgrading the entire computer, or at least the motherboard and components, to a more modern design.

PCI Bus

The PCI bus is by far the most popular one for SCSI host adapters today, or at least for host adapters that are used for hard disks and other high-performance SCSI devices. You can purchase PCI SCSI boards that implement everything from Fast SCSI-2 through Ultra3 Wide SCSI in PCI form, although choices on the low end of the performance scale are slim.

The vast majority of PCI SCSI cards are DMA bus mastering devices, so you can generally count on these cards to produce little in the way of CPU load. How much you should spend on a PCI SCSI card depends largely on your needs. A low-end card, such as the Adaptec 2910, might be adequate for devices such as SCSI zip drives and scanners. Boards of this class support Fast SCSI-2 and typically cost less than $100. If you intend to ever attach a hard disk to your SCSI bus, however, I recommend buying something that supports at least Ultra2 Wide SCSI for 80MB/s transfers. A device of this type also offers the advantage of longer cable lengths, assuming you use LVD devices exclusively. Host adapters capable of supporting Ultra2 Wide SCSI typically cost more than $100, and sometimes as much as $400. One drawback to the high-end adapters is that they frequently don't support the older 50-pin SCSI interfaces. Adding adapters to your SCSI chain can degrade performance and, perhaps just as important, reduce SCSI cable length limits. One solution to this dilemma is to use two SCSI host adapters. That might be unpalatable unless you need to use so many SCSI devices that one host adapter is inadequate to the task. Another alternative is to use a *dual-interface* SCSI host adapter, such as the ASUS SC-896. Such a product enables you to run two independent SCSI chains from a single SCSI host adapter.

Most PCI SCSI host adapters on the market are designed for use on x86 computers, but some can be used on other architectures as well, or come in variants for other architectures. If you want to use such a board on a Macintosh, Alpha PC, or some other system, be sure to check with the board manufacturer about compatibility. It's also important that you check whether the Linux drivers for the product work in your target architecture; some drivers include assumptions specific to the x86 architecture.

Oddball Connectors

Aside from the usual form of a SCSI host adapter on an expansion card, there are other forms the interface can take. These include

- **Motherboard SCSI support** Some high-end motherboards include SCSI support. Such support actually does fall into one of the categories I've described earlier; instead of using a physical expansion card socket, the SCSI host adapter circuitry resides on a virtual expansion card socket. Think of it as an expansion card that you can't unplug. Today, such SCSI support invariably uses the PCI bus, although some earlier motherboard might use the EISA or VL-Bus instead.

- **Parallel-port SCSI**   A few parallel-to-SCSI converters are available. These enable you to use external SCSI devices on computers that don't have their own SCSI host adapters. Unfortunately, the speed of these interfaces is quite limited, so they're not useful for anything but the slowest SCSI devices. Linux support is also limited; one of the few such devices supported by Linux is the one built into parallel-port Iomega zip drives.

- **USB SCSI**   As with parallel-port SCSI host adapters, some adapters are available in USB form. Speed is likely to be poor when using these devices, and Linux support is uncertain at best. I recommend you check `http://www.linux-usb.org/` for information on such devices before buying one.

- **PC-Card SCSI**   Yet another adapter enables you to connect SCSI devices through a notebook computer's PC Card slot. This is a better option than a parallel-to-SCSI or USB-to-SCSI adapter for most notebook computers. Linux includes support for most PC-Card SCSI adapters. Check the PCMCIA HOWTO (included with all major Linux distributions) for details.

SCSI Adapter Boards and Chipsets

When you know what sort of SCSI host adapter you want to buy, it's time to decide on a *specific* product. As with many hardware buying decisions for Linux, this task often boils down to one of deciding what *chipset* you need, and then locating a product that uses the chipset. Some of the largest names in the SCSI world, however, manufacture both chipsets and SCSI host adapters, so in some cases this task is easier than it is with some other products. No matter what chipset you select, you should also check on the BIOS support included on the SCSI host adapter. This support determines whether you can boot from a SCSI hard disk, and also determines some of the extra features available in the host adapter, such as cylinder/head/sector (CHS) geometry options and low-level disk formatting options.

Popular Products in Linux

SCSI host adapters and chipsets from a handful of manufacturers are most popular in Linux, and seem likely to remain so in the near future. These products are all well supported in Linux, and some of these manufacturers help with Linux driver development, either by providing information to Linux developers or by developing drivers in-house. These products include

- **Adaptec boards**   Most Adaptec (`http://www.adaptec.com`) host adapters work well in Linux. The Adaptec product line ranges from low-end ISA host adapters to top-of-the-line Ultra3 Wide SCSI products. Some motherboards that host integrated SCSI host adapters use Adaptec chipsets. Adaptec used to be stingy with Linux driver development support, but switched to a more supportive policy in 1998.

- **Advansys boards**   Advansys (`http://www.advansys.com`) has written its own Linux drivers, which have been incorporated into the Linux kernel. The Advansys product line isn't quite as broad as is Adaptec's; current Advansys products are all PCI-based, and only go as far as Ultra2 Wide SCSI, although future products might exceed this limit.

- **Initio chipsets**   Initio (`http://www.initio.com`) has developed a series of PCI SCSI chipsets that it uses on its own boards, and that are used on products from other manufacturers, such as SIIG (`http://www.siig.com`) and ASUS (`http://www.asus.com`). Initio's chipsets don't currently support the fastest SCSI standards, but they do support up to Ultra2 Wide SCSI. Initio wrote its own Linux drivers, which are now part of the standard Linux kernel.

- **Mylex boards**   Formerly known as BusLogic, Mylex (`http://www.mylex.com`) products have long been favored in Linux because of the stability and completeness of the Linux drivers. (Third parties wrote the drivers with support from Mylex.) To reach Ultra3 performance levels with Mylex products, it's necessary to purchase a host adapter with built-in *redundant array of independent disks* (for more information on RAID, see Chapter 5) technology.

- **Symbios chipsets**   Symbios (`http://www.symbios.com`), which used to be a division of NCR, sells a set of SCSI chipsets that are very popular in low-cost SCSI host adapters available from a wide variety of manufacturers, such as ASUS (`http://www.asus.com`) and J-Bond (`http://www.jbond.com`). Symbios also sells host adapters based on its own chipsets, and its chipsets find their way into some SCSI-equipped motherboards. The Symbios PCI chipsets have long been supported in Linux by *two* independent SCSI drivers, although only one (the `sym53c8xx` driver) is being maintained. Some Symbios chipsets are designed for ISA products, but these chipsets are rare; it's the Symbios PCI products that are of most interest to the Linux community. These products range all the way through Ultra3 Wide devices.

You should check for Linux compatibility before purchasing a product from any of the preceding companies. A few more obscure chipsets from these companies might not be supported, and it's also possible that the latest product might not work with an older driver.

Checking for Linux Compatibility

One way to check for Linux compatibility with a specific chipset is to do a kernel configuration and examine the boards and chipsets listed as options for SCSI host adapters, as shown in Figure 9.7. In some cases, the name of the driver corresponds exactly to the name of the product you are considering, in which case the decision is easy. In other cases, however, you must determine what chipset you use, or you must check the driver source code file (in `/usr/src/linux/drivers/scsi`). Somewhere in the source code file you can generally find a list of the specific boards or chipsets handled by the driver.

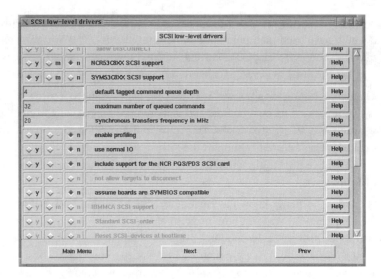

FIGURE 9.7
The list of SCSI host adapters is mostly alphabetical, although there are some exceptions.

In order to determine what chipset your product uses, you might need to examine the board closely. Look at the largest chip on the board and examine it for a logo or identifying number. In some cases you might need to peel back a sticker that the board manufacturer placed over the main chip in order to obscure the chipset manufacturer's name.

> **CAUTION**
>
> Board manufacturers occasionally change the chipsets used on their products, sometimes without altering the product name or packaging. Therefore, the fact that you've used a product in the past doesn't guarantee that you'll be able to do so in the future.

BIOS Support

The SCSI *basic input/output system* (BIOS) serves as a supplement to the motherboard's BIOS. The most important function of the BIOS is to enable the computer to boot from a SCSI device—primarily a hard disk, but also sometimes a removable disk or CD-ROM drive. In addition, most SCSI BIOSes provide services that enable you to configure various aspects of SCSI host adapter operation, including features such as

- **Host adapter termination**   Most modern host adapters let you set termination, using the keyboard. This can be extremely convenient if you have an external SCSI device that you regularly move between two or more computers.
- **Host adapter SCSI ID**   The host adapter needs its own SCSI ID, and the BIOS utility usually lets you set the ID to be used.
- **Disk geometry options**   SCSI uses a single linear address mode for its hard disks, but the x86 BIOS, and hence many programs, requires a CHS triplet. There are many ways to convert from one to the other, and some SCSI host adapter BIOSes support multiple translation methods, which you can set using the SCSI BIOS.

CAUTION

If you partition a disk using one SCSI host adapter and subsequently use the disk with another host adapter, it's possible that the second adapter won't support the first one's CHS mapping mode. If this happens, it might be impossible to recover data from the disk using the second host adapter. Your only choice in a case like this might be to back up the disk using the first host adapter, and then re-partition the disk and restore the data using the second host adapter. Most modern host adapters can recognize a wide range of CHS mappings, however, and adapt themselves automatically on a disk-by-disk basis.

- **Boot options**   You can often tell the SCSI BIOS to allow or forbid booting from non-hard disk devices such as removable disks and CD-ROM drives. Similarly, some host adapters allow you to set a limit on the number of potentially bootable hard disks (typically between 1 and 4), or specify which hard disk is the boot device.
- **Low-level disk formatting**   Most modern SCSI BIOSes include an option to perform a low-level format on hard disks. Such a format wipes out all data on the drive, and there's usually no need to perform such a format. If you do need to do so, the option is there.

TIP

If you've used a hard disk on one host adapter or computer and want to use it on another, but don't need the disk's data, doing a low-level format is one way to ensure that the disk's CHS geometry mapping won't cause problems on the new host adapter. You can accomplish the same goal more simply, however, by wiping out the hard disk's *Master Boot Record* (MBR). You can do this in Linux by issuing the command `dd if=/dev/zero of=/dev/sda bs=512 count=1`. (Change `/dev/sda` to the identifier for another disk, if desired.) When you re-boot, the host adapter assigns a new disk geometry to the drive based on whatever algorithms the host adapter favors.

You can enter most host adapters' SCSI BIOSes by entering a keystroke at some point during the computer's boot process. You usually need to enter this keystroke shortly after the motherboard's BIOS has done its memory check. Most host adapters provide a prompt for the appropriate keystroke during the boot process, so watch carefully.

Some SCSI host adapters, particularly models from the mid-1990s and earlier, include BIOSes but lack keyboard-accessible BIOS utilities. You can often set options similar to those I've just described on such boards using jumpers. These boards also often include utility programs (typically run from DOS) that let you check the SCSI bus, low-level format a hard disk, and so on.

Very low-end host adapters lack BIOS support. Such a lack does *not* mean that you can't use the host adapter with SCSI hard disks; however, it *does* mean that you can't boot from a SCSI hard disk attached to that host adapter. You can still use these host adapters for SCSI hard drives on a system that contains an EIDE boot disk, or a boot disk on another SCSI host adapter. You can even boot Linux using a Linux boot floppy on such systems, but you must ensure that the boot floppy contains a kernel with the appropriate SCSI driver compiled in, as opposed to compiled as a module. (The same is true when booting from a hard disk connected to a host adapter that has a BIOS.)

Some Symbios-based host adapters reside in a limbo land with respect to the boot BIOS. These host adapters don't contain BIOSes themselves, but some motherboards do include the Symbios SCSI BIOS. When mated with such a motherboard, the SCSI host adapter acts as if it had a boot BIOS installed. In some cases it's possible to add the Symbios SCSI boot BIOS to your motherboard's BIOS, even if it wasn't present to begin with. I only recommend trying this if you're familiar with flashing motherboard BIOSes and if you have a backup BIOS of one form or another. A mistake can render your system unbootable. Many modern motherboard flash BIOS utilities include options to add a Symbios boot BIOS image, which you can obtain from the Symbios Web site. You should check the documentation that came with your motherboard's flash BIOS utilities for details. Some motherboard EEPROM chips aren't large enough to support the Symbios boot BIOS in addition to the regular BIOS, however. On these boards you have little choice but to do without the SCSI BIOS.

Summary

SCSI can be a confusing subject for those who haven't dealt with it before. The various levels of SCSI, along with issues such as termination, SCSI IDs, and SCSI BIOSes, can be intimidating. The rewards of using SCSI devices can be considerable, however, particularly in a high-performance server environment. Today's fastest SCSI devices are faster than today's fastest EIDE devices. SCSI is inherently better suited than EIDE to communicate with several devices simultaneously, and to use a large number of different SCSI devices. These benefits can be mitigated by the need to mix modern, high-speed hard disks with older, lower-speed SCSI devices such as removable disks or scanners. Such a mixture might necessitate the use of two host adapters or shorter SCSI cables and lower transfer rates.

Fortunately, Linux support for SCSI host adapters is quite good. Aside from a few just-introduced models, most major SCSI host adapters and chipsets are supported by Linux, some with official support from the SCSI host adapter manufacturer. Support is actually worse at the low end of the scale, among bottom-of-the-line PIO ISA SCSI host adapters, particularly those from small manufacturers. Fortunately, you can usually replace such boards with better low-end PCI host adapters for under $100, and get a performance boost in the bargain.

Audio/Video

IN THIS PART

Sound Cards

IN THIS CHAPTER

Sound cards have traditionally been an important adjunct to home computer systems. Sound adds substantially to games and educational software, but legitimate business uses for sound have been sparse. Today, however, sound is becoming more important for serious computer productivity applications. Videoconferencing, for instance, normally requires sound, unless both parties can use sign language. (Videoconferencing also requires a camera on each end. I cover cameras in Chapter 13, "Video Capture and AV Input Hardware.")

No matter what your intended use for sound in Linux, it's important that you purchase a supported sound card. There are few real standards in audio hardware, so it's easy to purchase a product that's useless in Linux. Some computers—particularly low-cost desktops and notebooks—include audio hardware on the motherboard. With these designs it's especially important that Linux works with the sound hardware out of the box, because replacing the default sound hardware can be difficult or impossible. With most computers, you can swap the sound card without affecting other components, so a poor sound card in an otherwise good computer need not be too difficult a problem to overcome.

Board Busses

One of the first tasks in deciding on a sound card is to determine which motherboard bus to use: *Industry Standard Architecture* (ISA) or *Peripheral Component Interconnect* (PCI). As described in the "Motherboard Busses" section of Chapter 2, ISA is an old bus that's being phased out, whereas PCI is a newer bus that will likely be with us for some time to come. Audio hardware is one of the final remaining viable uses for the ISA bus, and you might want to give serious consideration to using an ISA sound card, even with the bus on the decline.

NOTE

If you have a Microchannel (MCA) computer, you must use an MCA sound card. Linux drivers for such cards are rare, however, so be especially careful in choosing an MCA sound card. Sound cards for the EISA and VL busses were never produced in anything even remotely resembling large quantities.

NOTE

Motherboards that have built-in sound support put that support on one or another type of bus. The sound hardware doesn't plug into an ISA or PCI slot, but it's treated electronically as if it were a separate card. If you're considering such a motherboard, don't concern yourself too much with whether the sound hardware behaves as an ISA or PCI device. PCI devices can be a bit easier to configure, but both types are adequate, and, because it's built into the motherboard, the sound hardware doesn't consume a slot. (This is a major consideration when buying a separate sound card.)

ISA Cards

The ISA bus is capable of transferring data at a theoretical maximum rate of 8MB/s. CD-quality stereo sound requires a data transfer rate of only about 0.17MB/s, so it should come as no surprise that the ISA bus is perfectly adequate for conventional sound tasks. Until recently, the ISA bus also had the advantage of being present on virtually all x86 computers, whereas competing busses were present on a minority of computers. Today, though, PCI exists on all new x86 computers, and PCI has existed for several years, so the PCI bus is present on most of the installed base of x86 computers, as well. Linux's driver support for ISA sound cards is excellent; you can get most ISA sound cards to work, using one driver or another.

Despite the fact that the ISA bus is capable of handling conventional audio tasks, it does have certain drawbacks, most notably

- **Unconventional audio**   Some sound cards support audio extensions that increase the bandwidth requirements. For example, Surround Sound lets you hook up additional speakers for movie theater-style sound. Assorted audio effects can help the computer simulate acoustic properties of various environments, such as concert halls or stadiums. Such effects can add substantially to the bandwidth requirements of the sound card. The OpenAL project (http://www.openal.org/home/) is dedicated to bringing such effects to Linux. This project started life in early 2000, however, so it has, as yet, produced little working software.

- **Buffer locations**   The ISA bus supports only 24-bit memory addressing, meaning that sound cards can transfer data to and from only the lower 2^{24} bytes (16MB) of memory. On systems with more than 16MB of RAM, therefore, Linux might find itself unable to allocate memory for sound operations. This problem can be overcome by a kernel option that allocates an appropriate buffer for sound card operation at boot time and locks that buffer in place.

- **PnP considerations**   The ISA bus wasn't designed for plug-and-play (PnP) operation. Nonetheless, all recent ISA cards incorporate PnP functionality. These features don't always work well, unfortunately, so it can be a bit tedious to configure Linux to work with these cards. I describe PnP configuration in Linux in the "ISA Bus" section of Chapter 2.

- **Shrinking ISA availability**   Some of the latest motherboards lack ISA support entirely. Others have only one or two ISA slots. If you have a board without ISA support, or if you need to use your available ISA slots for other devices, you might have no choice but to use a PCI sound card.

10

SOUND CARDS

If your motherboard has an available ISA slot, and if you have no immediate plans to replace that motherboard, then an ISA card can be a good choice. The main risk in purchasing an ISA sound card is that you might not be able to use it in your next computer. By contrast, if you purchase a PCI sound card but have available ISA slots, you might run out of PCI slots if you later choose to add devices like PCI Ethernet or SCSI adapters. Because sound cards need the speed of the PCI bus less than most other devices do, it makes sense to hoard your PCI slots for more bandwidth-hungry applications. On the other hand, the relative ease of configuration of PCI boards is a strong point in their favor.

PCI Cards

Before 1998, Linux support for PCI sound cards was extremely weak. This situation has changed, fortunately. You can find Linux drivers for many PCI sound cards from a variety of sources, as described later in this chapter, in the section "Linux Audio Drivers." You shouldn't take this support for granted, however; drivers for any given PCI sound card might or might not exist.

The primary advantages of PCI cards over ISA cards lie in the future viability of PCI and in PCI's easier configuration. The ISA bus is on its last legs, and can be quite rare on new motherboards in 2001 or 2002, so investing in an ISA sound card might not make much sense if you hope to use the card in the future. Unlike ISA, PCI was designed from the beginning with PnP operation in mind. PCI devices don't require any awkward Linux configuration tools, as do PnP ISA cards.

On the whole, I recommend buying a PCI sound card if your motherboard has few or no ISA slots, and if a PCI sound card won't rob you of your last PCI slot.

Sound Card Bitness and Sample Rates

To a physicist, sound is a series of changes in air pressure. One way of representing this effect visually is as a waveform, as shown in Figure 10.1. A stereo sound, such as the one depicted in Figure 10.1, can contain subtly or not-so-subtly different waveforms in each channel.

The more accurately a waveform is recorded and reproduced, the better the sound quality. Many features can influence the quality of reproduction, such as the quality of speakers, the quality of amplifiers built into the sound card, and so on. Two of the most important, however, are the *sample bit size* and the *sample frequency*. All modern sound cards are capable of recording sound at CD quality—16-bit sample size and 44,100Hz sample frequency on two independent channels. If you have an older sound card, however, your capabilities might be more limited, and some Linux drivers don't support the full capabilities of a card. You might also want to reduce the sample size or frequency in order to produce smaller sound files, even when your hardware supports better quality.

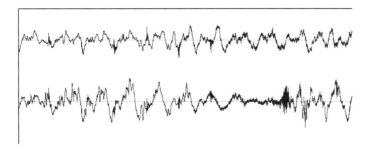

FIGURE 10.1

A waveform is translated into movements of membranes in a speaker, which creates pressure changes in the air that we hear as sound.

Bits on the Bus

Before proceeding further, it's important to distinguish between the *sample* bit size and the *bus's* bit size. The ISA bus comes in 8- and 16-bit variants, and the PCI bus comes in 32- and 64-bit variants (although 64-bit PCI busses are extremely rare). These bus bit sizes are completely irrelevant to the size of the samples used by the sound card. For instance, suppose you've got a 32-bit PCI sound card. You can play 8- or 16-bit sounds on this device; the card simply transfers four or two samples with each operation, or possibly transfers one with some wasted space in the transfer. In theory, an 8-bit ISA sound card could handle 16-bit sounds by using two transfers for each sample. In practice, however, ISA sound cards that use 16-bit sound samples also use 16-bit ISA bus interfaces.

The size of the bus (8–64 bits) is important to data transfer speed, although it's not the only factor in determining that speed. As described earlier, however, the 16-bit ISA bus's 8MB/s speed is quite adequate for most sound functions. Indeed, even the slower 8-bit ISA bus is more than adequate, especially for the slower 8-bit sound samples generally used on such cards.

Bits in the Sample

When used in reference to a sound card, the card's "bitness" generally refers to the number of bits in the sound sample. At any given moment in time—represented by a position on the X-axis of Figure 10.1—a sound waveform can be described by a single value—represented by a position along the Y-axis of Figure 10.1. (Figure 10.1 includes two waveforms, for left and right channels. Each has its own value at any given time.) This value is almost always either 8 or 16 bits in size. An 8-bit sample size allows for 2^8, or 256, distinct values. A 16-bit sample size allows for 2^{16}, or 65,536, distinct values. An 8-bit value is a bit deficient, but a 16-bit value is large enough that most humans would hear little or no difference if the sample size were increased to 24 or 32 bits. Some audiophiles claim to be able to hear the difference between 16-bit and 24-bit sound, though. As I mentioned earlier, CDs use 16-bit audio.

In the mid-1990s, sound cards were easily broken into two categories: 8-bit and 16-bit. The 8-bit cards were unable to record or play back 16-bit sounds. Sound card names frequently included the number *8* or *16* to distinguish the quality of the product. Some later products put higher values into the product name, such as *32*. This practice led some people to believe that these sound cards could record 32-bit samples, but, in fact, the value *32* referred to some other characteristic, such as 32 MIDI voices. Aside from very high-end audiophile products, few sound cards today use better than 16-bit sound.

All 16-bit sound cards are capable of playing and recording 8-bit sounds. In fact, some Linux drivers only support 8-bit sound, even on 16-bit cards. For example, as of kernels 2.2.14 and 2.3.47, the Linux kernel drivers for the VIA MVP4 chipset only support 8-bit sound, although the chipset is capable of 16-bit operation, and can achieve this performance with the commercial OSS drivers or the ALSA project drivers. As a general rule, enforced 8-bit operation under Linux arises because the sound drivers run the sound card in a mode that emulates the old 8-bit SoundBlaster Pro. It's a good idea to check the drivers for any sound card you're considering to be sure that the drivers run the card in its native 16-bit mode rather than in an 8-bit compatibility mode.

Sample Frequency

At least as important as the sample size is the sample frequency. This characteristic refers to the number of samples taken per second. Audio CDs are recorded at 44,100Hz—that is, 44,100 samples per second. Most sound cards sold today can record at up to that rate, if not higher. Some can go to 48,000Hz, which is the sample rate used by digital audio tape (DAT) recorders.

TIP

If you want to manipulate sound files that originated on, or will be transferred to, DAT, be sure your sound card can handle 48,000Hz sample frequency. This advice doesn't apply if you're using a DAT drive only for backup purposes. It only applies if you intend to use DAT as an audio platform.

Sample frequency affects how high a tone can be recorded. As a general rule, you need a sample rate of at least twice the frequency of the tone you want to record. For instance, consider Figure 10.2, which shows a pure tone of 20,000Hz. This means that a peak or valley occurs 20,000 times a second, or once every 0.00005s. Now, consider a digital sample frequency of

0.00005s (20,000Hz). The result might be Samples 1 and 3 shown in Figure 10.2. Because these samples occur at two peaks of the same height, the result would be interpreted by a sound card as a flat line—the sound card wouldn't know that a valley existed between the two samples. To reproduce the 20,000Hz tone with any accuracy, it's necessary to double the sample frequency to 40,000Hz, which adds Sample 2 to the mix. Now the sound card can reproduce a reasonable facsimile of the waveform, with both peaks and valleys intact.

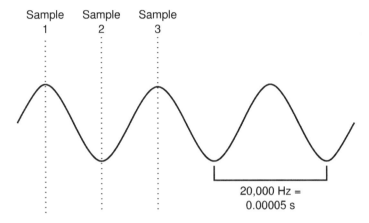

FIGURE 10.2

To reproduce a sound, a digital reproduction method must sample the signal frequently enough to detect both the peaks and the valleys of the original signal.

Note that I said you need to sample a sound using a sample rate of *at least* twice the sample frequency, in order to reproduce the sound. Consider what would happen if Figure 10.2's samples occurred at points slightly offset from the peaks and valleys, as shown in Figure 10.3. The result is a greatly attenuated sound—the volume will be reduced. In a worst-case scenario, the volume will be so low that the sound will be inaudible.

Matters are complicated still further by real-life sounds, which usually don't consist of the pure tones depicted in Figures 10.2 and 10.3. Real-life sounds consist of several different frequencies overlaid upon one another, which creates complex waveforms, such as those shown in Figure 10.1. Fortunately, it's the highest-frequency tones that are most important in determining the requirements for digital audio sample rates. For instance, if a 20Hz tone were overlaid upon the waveform shown in Figures 10.2 and 10.3, these figures would barely need to be modified, because 1000 of the 20,000Hz waves would fit within a single 20Hz wave. On the scale used in Figures 10.2 and 10.3 (just three 20,000Hz waves), the shifts associated with the 20Hz tone would be minor.

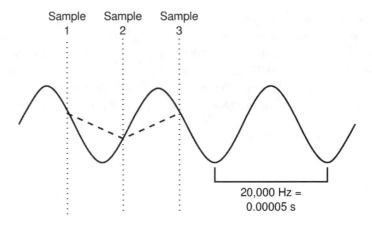

Sample 1   Sample 2   Sample 3

20,000 Hz =
0.00005 s

FIGURE 10.3

If a digital sample at twice a pure tone's frequency is offset from the sound's peaks and valleys, its apparent volume will be reduced in the reproduction.

As a result of these considerations, you can see that the maximum 44,100Hz sample rate produces a maximum best-case accurate reproduction for most sound cards of about 22,050Hz, with the potential for some attenuation of volume at more than 11,025Hz. It's no coincidence that the range for adult human hearing is approximately 20–20,000Hz. (Children can often hear somewhat higher than this, and some animals, such as dogs and dolphins, can hear much higher tones.)

Many of the sounds we hear in everyday life contain little in the way of high-frequency components, however. For recording a person speaking normally, a much lower sample rate might suffice. You should have no trouble understanding speech recorded at 8000Hz, for instance. If you want to accurately reproduce most music, though, a 44,100Hz recording rate is an absolute must.

All sound cards support setting a variety of recording and playback sample rates, and most sound software offers you a choice of several standard rates—generally power-of-2 fractions of 44,100Hz or multiples of 8,000Hz. You can therefore adjust your recording sample rate to fit the type of audio you're recording.

Channels

Most sound cards support both mono and stereo recording and playback. Just as in other audio equipment, mono operation records just one audio signal, whereas stereo operation records two—one for each of the two speakers you probably have connected to your computer.

A few sound cards support Surround Sound, which is a sound system that uses additional speakers—and hence recording channels—to provide a more realistic aural phenomenon. Surround Sound is used by many films, and so might be of interest if you want to play DVDs on your computer. Linux driver support for Surround Sound features is weak at best, however, so the investment in Surround Sound audio gear might not be worthwhile at the moment. This situation might change in the future, however, so check with the manufacturer or sound driver distributors for the latest information if you're interested in Surround Sound hardware.

MIDI Sound Production

The preceding discussion has focused upon what's generally known as *digital audio,* or *pulse code modulation* (PCM), recording—the exact reproduction of actual sounds by digital means. Most general-purpose sound cards today support another type of sound production, as well: *Musical Instrument Digital Interface* (MIDI). MIDI is just as digital as is digital audio, so the term *digital audio* is a bit misleading in some ways. The two forms of reproduction are radically different in their characteristics, as described in the following pages.

What Is MIDI?

MIDI is actually a simple networking protocol, although it's not something that's used on standard network hardware like Ethernet. Instead, MIDI uses its own specialized hardware and communications protocols to enable electronic musical instruments to communicate with one another. You can link MIDI-equipped keyboards, drum machines, and so on, in order to record music one piece at a time, and then play it all back at once. Most sound cards include a MIDI port (which generally uses the same external connector as the joystick port). You can therefore connect your computer to one or more MIDI instruments and control them from the computer, or record the music you perform as MIDI files on the computer.

Even if you don't have any external MIDI instruments, most sound cards include MIDI functionality in the form of a capability to play back MIDI files. These files are the electronic equivalent of sheet music. They contain information on the notes to be played, the instruments that are to play them, and so on. As such, MIDI files are much smaller than digital audio files of the same music. MIDI files are typically a few tens of kilobytes in size, whereas digital audio files of the same music, recorded at CD quality, consume tens of megabytes of disk space. MIDI is therefore an extremely compact format for music.

Because MIDI files rely upon external musical instruments or specialized MIDI circuitry in a sound card to produce sounds, however, the quality of MIDI playback varies substantially from one device to another. If a MIDI file calls for a trombone, you must have a device that can synthesize the trombone sound. An inexpensive sound card will likely do a poor job emulating a trombone. You'll hear the music, but you might not even realize that it's supposed to be a trombone playing. A more sophisticated sound card or external MIDI keyboard, however, is likely to produce sound that more closely resembles a real trombone. Similarly, except for the simulated sound of choirs singing individual notes, MIDI files don't include vocals. Therefore, your computer might play "It's a Wonderful World," but to hear Louis Armstrong's words, you must play a CD or some digital audio format, not a MIDI file.

External MIDI Devices

Some of the best MIDI sound comes from external MIDI devices. At the low end, electronic keyboards can do a good job of simulating the sounds of pianos and other instruments, but you must normally play an electronic keyboard as you would a piano keyboard, using the keys. Except for very expensive units, electronic keyboards don't respond with the subtlety of a real piano, and the nature of the keyboard interface can make it difficult to simulate some instruments. An assortment of other external MIDI devices exists to help get around the keyboard's limitations, although generally only professionals and serious hobbyists purchase such devices.

When connected to a computer's sound card, external devices can be controlled from the computer. You can therefore download MIDI files from the Internet, create or edit them with MIDI editing utilities—or create them by playing your external MIDI device—and then play the files back on your external device. This option can be particularly appealing if your sound card produces poor MIDI sound, as so many do.

FM Synthesis

Within the limits of each instrument's range, any two instruments can play the same notes, but each instrument's sound is nonetheless unique. You're unlikely to mistake a piano for a saxophone, for instance. In terms of the waveforms of instruments, this uniqueness derives from the unique combinations of different tones produced by each instrument. No acoustic instrument produces a *pure tone*, such as the one depicted in Figure 10.2. Instead, the tones produced by real instruments deviate from this pure form by the addition of higher- and lower-frequency *harmonics* and other characteristics. Thus is each instrument's unique sound produced.

One of the two major types of MIDI sound production within a computer's sound card is *frequency modulation* (FM) *synthesis*. FM synthesis works by combining two or more pure tones in an effort to simulate the sound of a real instrument. Pure tones are easy to generate and combine through electronic means, so FM synthesis is easy to implement in sound card chipsets. All that's needed is a set of tone generators and a table of rules for combining them to simulate each instrument.

Unfortunately, FM synthesis, although easy to implement in hardware, produces poor results. You're unlikely to mistake an FM synthesis piano for a real piano, or even a poor recording of a real piano. At best, the sound is vaguely piano-ish. The quality of FM synthesis varies from one sound card to another, however. One of the prime variables in determining the quality of a given card's FM synthesis MIDI production is the number of tones that can be combined. Some of the oldest and least expensive FM synthesis boards combined just two tones. More recent products generally use four or more.

Wavetable Synthesis

A more sophisticated method of simulating musical instruments is known as *wavetable synthesis*. Rather than rely upon the combination of several pure tones to simulate an instrument's sound, wavetable synthesis uses a recording of the instrument in question. The manufacturer digitally records an instrument playing a single note. A tiny snippet of that recording is then isolated, and circuitry in the sound card can play it back in a loop to reproduce the continuous note. Furthermore, the recorded note can be changed in volume, compressed to produce higher tones, or expanded to produce lower tones. Between these manipulations, it's possible to simulate the sound of the instrument playing any note at any volume.

Wavetable Quality

Even the worst wavetable synthesis sound cards usually sound better than the best FM synthesis cards when playing MIDI files. The variation among wavetable boards is quite wide, however. Variables that can affect wavetable quality include

- **Sample length**   All other things being equal, a larger sample is better than a smaller one.
- **Sample rate**   Just as with digital audio, wavetable synthesis samples are recorded at some specific sample rate. If the sample rate is too low, the sample can lose some of the higher-frequency harmonics that help to define the nature of a sound.
- **Number of samples**   When you play two notes on an instrument, their waveforms resemble one another, but they aren't identical, even when you adjust for the different frequencies. Therefore, many wavetable products actually record two or more samples for each instrument. Each sample handles a different range of notes. All other things being equal, more such samples are better than fewer.
- **Source**   Manufacturers use different instruments for their source samples. If the source instrument was poorly built or maintained, the resulting wavetable suffers.

Aside from the last factor, these variables all affect the ultimate size of the complete wavetable, as stored in ROM or RAM on the sound card. For instance, one product might have a 2MB wavetable, and another might have an 8MB wavetable. Chances are the second product will sound better than the first, although other factors might intervene. The first card might use better source instruments, for instance, or it might devote more space to instruments important to you, whereas the second might devote a great deal of space to accurately reproducing bizarre instruments you never use.

Wavetable Storage

Wavetable sound cards store their samples in one of three locations:

- **Sound card ROM**   Information might go on a ROM chip on the sound card. This location is convenient for the user because it requires no intervention on your part—simply plug the board in and it's ready for use. The drawback is that the ROM isn't easily upgraded, so you can't change to a better wavetable sample set.

- **Sound card RAM**   Some sound cards include RAM, either built into the card or on SIMM sockets, as shown in Figure 10.4. This design provides flexibility, because you can download updated wavetable samples, or even maintain several dozen megabytes of samples and download only those instruments you're using at any given time. The drawback is that you must use drivers or auxiliary software that supports the wavetable download function.

FIGURE 10.4

Some wavetable sound cards include SIMM sockets for storing wavetable samples.

- **Computer RAM**   A recent trend, particularly with PCI sound cards, is toward what's known as *software wavetable*. In this design, the wavetable functions are handled in software. Effectively, the computer generates a digital audio file from the MIDI file and a set of wavetable samples, and then plays that file on the sound card like any other sound file. Linux includes software wavetable support for all sound cards, as described shortly, so don't favor a sound card that advertises this feature over one that doesn't. Definitely don't consider such a sound card equal to any form of hardware wavetable support.

Some sound cards include both a ROM-based wavetable and RAM chips or SIMM sockets for expansion or replacement of the samples included on the ROM. This design provides the best mix of convenience and flexibility, all other things being equal.

Linux Software Wavetable Support

There are two main packages available for performing software wavetable operations in Linux: TiMidity and SoftOSS. The former is a user-space program, which means you're restricted to playing MIDI files from TiMidity itself. You can't normally use TiMidity to handle MIDI music from games or MIDI editors. SoftOSS, on the other hand, is a kernel module that replaces access to your sound card's normal MIDI devices with a software wavetable device.

Both TiMidity and SoftOSS rely upon patch sets for the Gravis UltraSound sound card, such as MIDIA (`ftp://archive.cs.umbc.edu/pub/midia/instruments.tar.gz`). You can often find MIDI patch sets packaged along with TiMidity, as well. Most Linux distributions come with such a patch set, in a package called `timidity-patches` or `midi-samples` or something similar.

Using TiMidity

TiMidity is included with most Linux distributions, or you can locate it at file archive sites such as `http://www.debian.org/distrib/packages` or `http://rufus.w3.org/linux/RPM/`. The trickiest aspect to using TiMidity is configuring it. The program relies upon a configuration file called `timidity.cfg`, which can reside in the `/etc` directory or in some other directory that tends to vary from one distribution to another. This file specifies the association between individual samples and the instruments to which they correspond. For example, a configuration file might begin something like this:

```
dir /dos/ultrasnd/midi
bank 0
0 acpiano.pat
1 britepno.pat
2 epiano1.pat
3 honky.pat
```

The first line specifies the location of the patch files—`/dos/ultrasnd/midi`. The second line indicates that the following specification applies to instrument bank `0`, which handles most instruments. Subsequent lines assign a patch file to each numbered instrument—instrument 0 is an acoustic piano (`acpiano.pat`), for instance. (MIDI includes a standard set of assignments, so instrument 0 should always be a piano, unless you want to achieve some instrument-changing effects.)

The `timidity.cfg` file can also contain a similar definition for drums, which begins `drumset 0` rather than `bank 0`. Some default configuration files use the `source` directive to push most of the configuration details into other files.

When your TiMidity configuration is complete (as, with any luck, it will be upon installation), you can play a MIDI file:

```
timidity midifile.mid
```

The result will be a wavetable rendition of the MIDI file, albeit at high CPU use. On the AMD K6-2/475 system I use, TiMidity consumes 10%–20% of the available CPU time, depending upon the complexity of the MIDI file.

If you want a user interface that's a bit more appealing than the command line, you can use the -ic option to start TiMidity with a particular user interface. Type **timidity -help | less** to get a list of c values available on your system. (TiMidity can be compiled with many different interfaces, but chances are the binary you have supports only a few of them.) Figure 10.5 shows TiMidity using the Athena widget set interface.

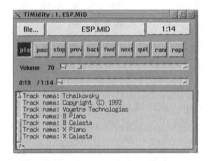

FIGURE 10.5
A GUI interface to TiMidity lets you control the MIDI playback dynamically.

On the whole, TiMidity can be a very useful utility if you lack a wavetable sound card and want to play an occasional MIDI file with better quality than you can achieve with FM synthesis. If you want high-quality MIDI playback from games or other utilities, though, you might be better off with SoftOSS—or better yet, a genuine hardware wavetable sound card.

Using SoftOSS

The Linux kernel includes a feature known as *SoftOSS*, which is a software wavetable function modeled after the wavetable features of the Gravis UltraSound (GUS) board. To use this feature, follow these steps:

1. Obtain an appropriate patch set for SoftOSS. SoftOSS uses GUS patch sets, such as the public domain MIDIA set (ftp://archive.cs.umbc.edu/pub/midia/instruments.tar.gz). Many Linux distributions include such patch sets, often as an adjunct package to TiMidity.

2. Place the sound samples in the directory /dos/ultrasnd/midi. (Chances are you'll have to create this directory.) If you've obtained the samples by installing a package along with your Linux distribution, creating a symbolic link from this location to the default location will work.

3. Enable the SoftOSS software wave table engine support in the Sound area of the Linux kernel configuration, as shown in Figure 10.6. You can adjust the quality of the software wavetable by changing the sample rate and number of voices.

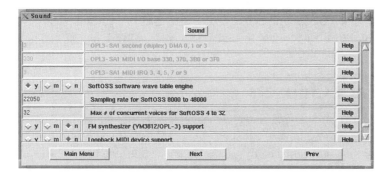

FIGURE 10.6

The SoftOSS feature turns any 16-bit sound card into a software wavetable sound card.

> **NOTE**
>
> I describe other sound card kernel configuration options later in this chapter, in the section "Linux Audio Drivers." You must use the standard kernel drivers to use SoftOSS.

4. Recompile your kernel or kernel modules with the SoftOSS support enabled and, if necessary, reboot to activate these changes.

If you use the commercial OSS drivers, configuration is simpler; you must merely select the SoftOSS driver as if it were a separate sound card device. There are several versions available for different CPU types. Among the x86 kernel options, these different types correspond to different quality settings. Higher quality produces better sound, but at the cost of greater CPU use—enough so that a lesser CPU might be overwhelmed and produce *poorer* quality, hence the categorization by CPU type.

SoftOSS, like TiMidity, is a rather resource-hungry feature. The minimum recommended CPU speed is a 133MHz Pentium, with MMX features recommended. The module stores samples in

RAM, so the RAM requirements can be quite large, especially if you use a large sample set. (The MIDIA set is 9MB uncompressed.) Note that SoftOSS allocates RAM for its own use and then doesn't relinquish that RAM, so you're effectively deprived of that RAM whenever you boot your system with SoftOSS enabled. You can reduce the resource requirements of SoftOSS somewhat by reducing the sample rate or number of voices in the kernel configuration step, but this will reduce the quality of the resultant sound. In addition to the general system resources, SoftOSS requires a 16-bit sound card.

When you're done configuring SoftOSS, you will be able to play MIDI files with MIDI utilities that work with the GUS card, such as `mplay` or `playmidi -g`. Games and sound utilities that use MIDI playback can also use the SoftOSS system, without any special configuration options.

Sound Card Chipsets

Like most expansion cards, sound cards rely upon their chipsets to perform most functions. It's therefore usually necessary to know what chipset a card uses if you want to use it in Linux. If you're shopping for a new sound card, you should pay careful attention to what chipset any new board you buy uses. A poor choice of sound card chipset can leave you with limited or no Linux sound support.

The Meaninglessness of SoundBlaster Compatibility

The Creative Labs (`http://www.creative.com`) SoundBlaster card was one of the first truly popular sound cards for x86 computers. By today's standards, the original mono SoundBlaster and its stereo variant, the SoundBlaster Pro, were truly primitive. They were limited to 8-bit sound and featured very minimal FM synthesis MIDI. These products, however, gained popularity over competing products with similar characteristics. Subsequent sound cards usually featured SoundBlaster compatibility, meaning that DOS programs expecting to find an 8-bit SoundBlaster could work with the competing sound cards. In most cases, these SoundBlaster-compatible products achieved the compatibility through hardware, but the compatibility mode often had to be activated by a small utility at boot time. Some products used special software drivers to achieve SoundBlaster compatibility.

As time went on, Creative Labs released the SoundBlaster-16, which produced 16-bit sound, and other companies released competing products. In most cases, these products continued to be compatible with the original 8-bit SoundBlaster, but not with the 16-bit functions of the SoundBlaster-16. Instead, these products relied upon their own native 16-bit sound modes. By this time, Windows was becoming popular on x86 hardware, so these boards could use custom-designed drivers; compatibility with the SoundBlaster-16's 16-bit functions was not critical. Nonetheless, the words *SoundBlaster compatible* continued to hold enough market sway that they appeared on most products' boxes.

In Linux today, SoundBlaster compatibility is next to useless. Linux relies upon its own native drivers for all sound functions. Linux does, of course, include drivers for most SoundBlaster models, but because most SoundBlaster-compatible sound boards require proprietary commands to enable SoundBlaster mode, these drivers don't do much good unless the board has already been initialized in SoundBlaster mode. Even then, because most SoundBlaster-compatible cards only emulate the 8-bit SoundBlaster Pro, you won't be able to use the card's 16-bit functionality.

> **TIP**
>
> If you've got a SoundBlaster-compatible card that has no native Linux driver, you might be able to get it working by running DOS and whatever DOS utilities the board manufacturer provides to initiate SoundBlaster compatibility mode. When you've done this, you can press Ctrl+Alt+Del to reboot to Linux, or use LOADLIN.EXE to boot Linux directly from DOS. If all goes well, Linux will then detect the board as a SoundBlaster Pro and you can use it as such. You won't be able to use 16-bit sound features, but 8-bit sound might be preferable to none. You might even want to set up a small (1MB–2MB should be adequate) DOS boot partition that includes a call to LOADLIN.EXE in its AUTOEXEC.BAT file in order to boot Linux automatically. You can then boot Linux regularly via this small DOS partition. A better solution is to replace the sound card, unless it's integrated into the computer (in a laptop, for instance).

In sum, ignore the words *SoundBlaster compatible* in any advertising or on any product boxes you might see. Instead, focus on the chipsets used by the sound cards, and look for boards that use the chipsets for which Linux drivers exist and are stable.

Common ISA Chipsets

Through the mid- and late-1990s, dozens of audio chipsets emerged on ISA sound cards. Most of these chipsets are used by several sound card manufacturers, although some are used by just one or two. Most have support in Linux. Some of the more popular chipset manufacturers and models include

- **AMD**   AMD (http://www.amd.com) produced one major ISA sound chipset, the Interwave. This product included a Gravis UltraSound compatibility mode and, in fact, was used on the UltraSound PnP model, among others.
- **Aztech**   Many low-cost boards from Aztech (http://www.aztechca.com) and others in the mid-1990s used Aztech chipsets, often with the names *Sound Galaxy* and *Washington*. Aztech products are less common today. Linux drivers exist for most Aztech products.

- **Creative Labs**   Creative Labs' (http://www.creative.com) products were long the standard, and so are very common. Creative Labs initially used custom chipsets reserved for the company's own use, but eventually Creative Labs' Vibra chipset and its successors found their way onto motherboards and occasional competing products. Creative Labs has also bought up other companies, and so some Creative Labs products use other companies' chipsets. As a general rule, Creative Labs products are well supported by Linux, but you should check on driver availability and features for any specific product.

- **Crystal Semiconductor**   Crystal Semiconductor (CS; http://www.crystal.com), which is now a division of Cirrus, has long been a major supplier of sound card chipsets. The CS ISA line is well supported in Linux, although a few individual products sometimes have problems for one reason or another.

- **ESS**   ESS (http://www.esstech.com) is another major sound chipset manufacturer. ESS products are the exception to the rule concerning SoundBlaster compatibility; products based on ESS ISA chipsets generally use Linux's SoundBlaster drivers.

- **Gravis**   The Gravis(http://www.gravis.com) UltraSound was a long-lived competitor to the SoundBlaster line. Unusual in that it did *not* include SoundBlaster compatibility, Gravis used its own proprietary chipset in the UltraSound. Gravis later joined with AMD to develop the Interwave chipset used in the UltraSound PnP model. The Linux kernel includes support for Gravis products.

- **IBM**   IBM (http://www.mwave.com) produced a very sophisticated digital signal processor (DSP) chip line known as the Mwave. These products appeared on a variety of combination modem/sound cards in the mid- and late-1990s, and were used on some IBM laptop computers. Unfortunately, no Linux drivers have been developed for the Mwave as of early 2000, although the 2000-series Mwave chips can be made to function in SoundBlaster Pro compatibility mode by first running the Mwave DOS SoundBlaster initialization program, as described earlier.

- **OPTi**   OPTi (http://www.opti.com) is another major ISA sound card chipset manufacturer. As with CS, Linux includes excellent OPTi ISA driver support.

- **Yamaha**   Yamaha's (http://www.yamaha.com) best-known ISA products are its OPL2 and OPL3 FM synthesis chipsets and its OPL4 FM synthesis and wavetable chipset. The OPL3-SA line is a variant of the OPL3 that includes digital audio capabilities. The OPL2, OPL3, and OPL4 chipsets are commonly used on sound cards along with chipsets from CS, ESS, OPTi, or other companies. Linux supports all these chipsets.

Developments in ISA chipsets in 2000 are modest, because manufacturers have shifted their attention to the growing PCI marketplace. This fact is good for Linux driver availability and stability; without the need to adapt to ever-changing product lines, the Linux drivers for ISA boards can mature and stabilize. For this reason, most ISA sound cards are good choices when it comes to Linux driver support.

Common PCI Chipsets

Most new sound card designs today are implemented on the PCI bus rather than the ISA bus, for reasons I've outlined earlier in this chapter. Therefore, both the PCI sound card marketplace and the Linux PCI sound card support change rapidly. Some of the more common chipsets available in 2000 include

- **Aureal**   Aureal (`http://linux.aureal.com`) has produced and distributes Linux drivers for its Vortex chipset, but the drivers have yet to be incorporated into the Linux kernel or the ALSA project drivers.

- **Creative Labs**   Creative Labs has released a number of PCI sound cards, some of them originally produced by other companies that Creative has purchased, such as the Ensoniq AudioPCI. Creative has been actively developing Linux drivers of late; you can check on the latest at `http://opensource.creative.com`.

- **Crystal Semiconductor**   CS has been active in producing PCI chipsets, just as they have produced many ISA chipsets. Some of these products are supported by one or another Linux driver, but you should check on support for the specific chipset before making a purchase.

- **ESS**   ESS has produced several PCI chipsets, most of which have support in Linux, mostly in the Linux kernel, but also in other drivers.

- **S3**   S3 (`http://www.s3.com`) produces a PCI chipset known as the SonicVibes, for which Linux drivers exist.

- **Trident**   Trident (`http://www.tridentmicro.com`) has entered the sound chipset market with a product known as 4D-Wave, which is also integrated into some SiS (`http://www.sis.com.tw`) motherboard chipsets. Support for this chipset exists in the 2.3.x-series kernels and in the ALSA project drivers, but not in the 2.2.x kernels.

- **VIA**   The motherboard chipset manufacturer VIA (`http://www.via.com.tw`) includes unique audio functionality in some of its motherboard chipsets. This product is supported by the Linux kernel, but only in 8-bit mode as of the 2.3.47 kernel. Better support is available in the commercial OSS drivers and open source ALSA drivers.

As a general rule of thumb, Linux audio support for PCI sound card chipsets is less mature and complete than that for ISA sound card chipsets. It's therefore doubly important that you research the Linux drivers for PCI sound cards before making a purchase.

Linux Audio Drivers

For most low-level hardware devices, drivers come with the Linux kernel, and are available from no other source. On occasion, you might want to track down a development driver or a driver provided in binary-only form by a hardware manufacturer, but for the most part, your first and last stop in locating a driver is the Linux kernel configuration script. Sound cards are an exception to this rule. Sound card drivers are available from three main sources:

- **The Linux kernel** Most of these drivers are derived from the Open Sound System driver set of several years ago, and are known as *OSS/Free drivers*. The kernel includes a few drivers, however, that fit outside of the OSS/Free framework.

- **Commercial OSS drivers** The original OSS driver source tree split. The basic drivers wound up in the Linux kernel, but the original developer has taken that core set and produced a separate tree with additional drivers, which are available as shareware.

- **The ALSA Drivers** The *Advanced Linux Sound Architecture* (ALSA) project is an effort to re-create Linux sound drivers in a way that its participants feel is technically superior to the OSS way.

The most popular boards are supported by all three driver projects, so you should have no trouble finding support if you have a common board. Some products, however, are supported by only one or two driver projects.

As a general rule, any of these drivers produces acceptable results, although the ALSA drivers tend to be the most difficult to install because they use an entirely separate source tree that you must compile in conjunction with the kernel you use. This task can be daunting, particularly if you use a development kernel, in which the sound-related interfaces are likely to change rapidly.

Linux Kernel Drivers

Most of the Linux kernel drivers are direct descendants of the OSS/Free drivers, and so this support is often referred to as *OSS/Free*. You compile the kernel sound drivers just as you compile any other kernel module, by selecting the appropriate items for compilation directly in the kernel or as modules. Figure 10.7 shows the basic kernel sound configuration options. You must select Y or M to the Sound card support option, and you must select Y or M to your individual sound card or sound card chipset's option. You might need to select two or more chipsets, particularly if you want both digital audio and MIDI support. For instance, you might need to select both the Crystal Semiconductor and Yamaha OPL-3 drivers, if your board contains both chipsets.

One very important option for the OSS drivers in conjunction with ISA cards is called *Persistent DMA buffers*. Because ISA cards can only directly address 16MB of RAM, it's vitally important that Linux be able to allocate buffers for these cards below 16MB of RAM. If you use your system for a while, this task might become impossible unless Linux preallocates appropriate buffers and keeps them active, whether or not you're using the sound card. The Persistent DMA buffers option enables Linux to do just this.

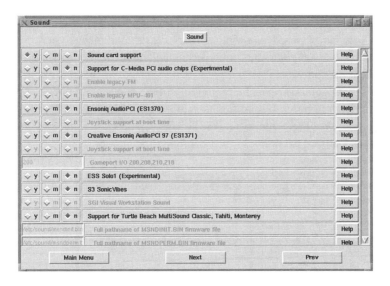

FIGURE 10.7

The list of sound cards and options is not ordered in a very helpful way, so you might need to take some time to locate your sound card.

The Commercial OSS Drivers

The commercial OSS drivers, available from `http://www.4front-tech.com`, are a shareware relation of the standard Linux drivers. The commercial drivers support more cards and come with some additional sound utilities. Of particular interest, a few sound card manufacturers don't release programming information except under non-disclosure agreements (NDAs). NDAs prevent the development of open source drivers, so the only hope of finding Linux drivers for such cards is in the commercial OSS offering. Even when a manufacturer releases specifications, Linux drivers often appear first in the commercial OSS drivers.

> **NOTE**
>
> As a general rule, I recommend avoiding hardware for which open source drivers aren't available. There are usually alternatives to such products, and it's better to support hardware manufacturers who support Linux by writing open source drivers or making specifications available to those who want to write them. If you already have a sound card from a manufacturer that doesn't release programming information, though, licensing the commercial OSS drivers is probably more cost-effective than buying a new sound card.

Installation of the commercial OSS drivers involves running an installation and configuration script included with the drivers. This script provides a text-based menu system (shown in Figure 10.8) to help you get your sound card drivers up and running quickly. In fact, it's often easier to configure the commercial OSS drivers than the standard kernel drivers. The commercial OSS drivers' configuration script helps you to set the various configuration options that might otherwise have to go in several different configuration files, such as /etc/isapnp.conf and /etc/conf.modules. The commercial OSS drivers handle these aspects of sound card configuration independently of the normal Linux configuration options.

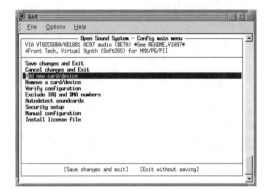

FIGURE 10.8

The commercial OSS configuration menu is simple but effective.

The commercial OSS drivers offer excellent compatibility with standard Linux sound utilities. The two sets of OSS drivers do, after all, share a common code base. Like the standard kernel drivers, the commercial OSS drivers include the SoftOSS software wavetable functionality. You must enable this feature as another sound card. (Figure 10.8 shows SoftOSS and a VIA 82c686 sound driver configured.)

One drawback to the OSS drivers is that, because they're available only in binary form, matching the driver to your kernel can be difficult. You must specify your kernel version when you download the driver, and the downloaded files include driver modules optimized for a variety of specific Linux distributions. If you need to recompile your kernel for some reason, or if you use a rare distribution that's not supported by 4Front, the installation scripts need to perform extra work, and are more likely to fail in their task of configuring drivers.

The ALSA Driver Project

The ALSA project (`http://www.alsa-project.org/`) provides an alternative sound driver architecture for Linux. To use the ALSA drivers, you must download and compile three separate packages:

- **alsa-driver** The ALSA driver files proper
- **alsa-lib** Libraries used by ALSA-enabled programs and utilities
- **alsa-util** Programs to use sound with the ALSA drivers

You compile each package much as you would other source code programs, by typing `./configure` and then **make install**. You should probably issue additional parameters to at least some of the configuration procedures, however, in order to add or remove support for features you do or do not need. Consult the INSTALL and README files that come with each package for details. You must also run the snddevices script that comes with the driver package in order to create appropriate ALSA sound device files in your /dev directory.

When the ALSA drivers are installed and the modules loaded, you can use your sound devices. You can compile the ALSA drivers with OSS compatibility support for digital audio functionality, and I recommend you do so. Many programs—particularly games and audio utilities that serve as adjuncts to desktop environments—assume that they'll be dealing with OSS-style audio drivers, so omitting this feature can reduce the utility of your sound system. You must explicitly load OSS compatibility modules for digital audio (snd-pcm-oss), MIDI (snd-seq-oss), and mixers (snd-mixer-oss) in order to use OSS-style audio applications. If you want to use software wavetable, you can use the TiMidity program with ALSA.

Sound Card Resource Allocations

Although the commercial OSS driver set includes utilities to help detect and configure sound cards, the kernel's OSS drivers and ALSA drivers rely upon manual configuration of the sound card in other ways. Two files are particularly important to this configuration:

- **/etc/isapnp.conf** This file contains configuration information for ISA PnP cards. I describe its configuration in detail in the section "ISA Bus" in Chapter 2. You only need to deal with this configuration file if you have an ISA PnP board. If you have a PCI sound card or an older jumper-configured ISA card, the card is configured automatically or through jumpers, respectively. In addition, the 2.3.x and later kernels include ISA PnP configuration features independent of the isapnptools utility package, for which /etc/isapnp.conf is the configuration file.

- **/etc/conf.modules**   You use this file to tell Linux kernel modules about the sound devices. For instance, if you've configured a sound card to use IRQ 7 in /etc/isapnp.conf, you might need to pass that same information to the driver module in /etc/conf.modules. A typical configuration might include lines like the following:

```
alias audio0 mad16
options mad16 io=0x530 irq=7 dma=0 dma16=1 cdtype=0 joystick=1
```

These options tell Linux to use the mad16 driver for the audio0 device, and that this device uses the resources specified on the second line.

> **NOTE**
>
> If you compile your sound drivers directly into the kernel, you don't configure them using the /etc/conf.modules file. Instead, you usually provide default values when you compile the kernel. You can modify these values, if necessary, by passing parameters to the kernel in the /etc/lilo.conf file or as options to LOADLIN.EXE.

Some Linux distributions include GUI configuration tools to help you configure these files. If you have access to such a tool, it can certainly help you configure your sound, but these tools also sometimes get things very wrong, so you might need to dig into the underlying text files to correct any problems.

The naming of Linux sound devices is mostly standardized, although there are variations on the standard themes. Typical sound devices include

- **/dev/audio**   This is the traditional digital audio device.
- **/dev/dsp**   This is an alternative method of accessing the sound device under Linux.
- **/dev/sequencer**   This is one of two MIDI device files in common use.
- **/dev/midi**   Not surprisingly, this is the other MIDI device file.
- **/dev/mixer**   The mixer device enables you to control the volume of sound, both from the sound card as a whole and from individual sources (MIDI, digital audio, audio CDs, and so on).
- **/dev/sndstat**   You can display the contents of this file (with cat /dev/sndstat or something similar) to find what sorts of audio devices are available on your system. This type of function is normally handled by the Linux /proc filesystem, but /dev/sndstat predates the /proc filesystem, and continues to exist for backward compatibility.

If you have more than one sound card, the second card takes on the preceding names, but with a 1 suffix. The ALSA drivers create these devices as well as alternative devices that use these device names, but with an a prefixed to the filename within /dev—for instance, /dev/amixer. These alternative devices use a different method of access to the underlying sound hardware, which the ALSA project programmers prefer to the OSS methods. The device major and minor numbers vary depending upon which driver set you use. The ALSA drivers, in particular, use their own major and minor numbers, independent of those used by the OSS drivers.

Sound file permissions need to be set in such a way that an ordinary user can access the sound card. In a multi-user environment, however, it's undesirable to give all users simultaneous access to the sound card. One malicious or ignorant individual could cause loud and obnoxious noises to play over the speakers for hours. Some distributions, such as Red Hat, attempt to get around this problem by using special scripts as part of the login process to set permissions on audio devices when a user logs in to the console (the keyboard at which the speakers are presumably located). Other distributions give all users blanket access to the audio devices, or restrict access to one group of users.

Linux Audio Utilities and Applications

Configuring sound drivers is all well and good, but by itself won't produce sound. To actually use your sound hardware, you must use audio applications of some sort. The commercial OSS and ALSA driver packages both come with a basic set of utilities, and Linux desktop environments such as KDE and GNOME are increasingly bundling GUI audio applications. There are also a wide variety of separate packages available for playing sound files. Finally, many applications that aren't strictly sound programs can use sound. Games, of course, fall into this category, but just about any program that cares to bundle a few sound files can use Linux's sound features.

Playing and Recording Digital Audio

In their most basic form, you can play and record sound files by using the /dev/dsp file directly. This procedure works with Sun's .au-format files. For instance, **cat testfile.au > /dev/dsp** plays testfile.au through the sound card's speakers. Similarly, **cat /dev/dsp > testin.au** records audio from the sound card to the file testin.au. (You'll need to press Ctrl+C to stop recording.)

> **NOTE**
>
> You might need to enable an appropriate input or output channel using a mixer application, described later, before access to raw audio devices will do any good.

At a somewhat higher level, you can use various text-mode utilities that include *play* in their names, such as `play`, `esdplay`, and `vplay`, to play and record sounds. These utilities include the capability to process a wider array of sound file formats than is possible by copying the file directly to an audio device file. When recording, these utilities can set options such as the bit size and sample rate.

For the easiest to use and most flexible playback and recording, though, it's best to use GUI utilities such as those included in the GNOME and KDE desktop environments, or standalone programs such as Sound Studio, shown in Figure 10.9. Programs such as these typically include controls that are easy to understand. The more sophisticated such utilities, including Sound Studio, include extensive editing features. These enable you to remove segments of a sound, paste one sound into another one, zoom into a small section of a sound, reverse a sound, and so on. Such programs are indispensable if you want to do serious sound editing—for instance, to manually remove pops from an LP record you're transferring to CD-R. Simpler utilities, such as KDE's `kmedia`, provide a subset of these features, which can be plenty if you just want to sample some sound files from your hard disk or record a quick voice memo.

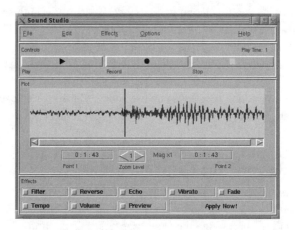

FIGURE 10.9

Sound Studio is unusually complete; many GUI sound applications provide much simpler controls—and less functionality.

Most general-purpose audio playback and recording utilities can handle simple sound formats such as Sun's `.au` and Creative Labs' `.wav`. More complex formats exist, however, many of which incorporate some form of compression. These formats generally require their own specialized players. For instance, Real Networks (`http://www.real.com`) supplies a Linux player for its popular RealAudio Web sound format. Various utilities exist to play the popular MP3 compressed music format. Kmp3 (http://area51.mfh-iserlohn.de/kmp3/) is a typical GUI MP3 player, but text-based utilities to play MP3 files also exist, such as mp3blaster (ftp://mud.stack.nl/pub/mp3blaster/).

Playing and Editing MIDI Files

Just as with digital audio, both text-based and GUI utilities exist to play MIDI files. One of the more popular text-based programs is playmidi, which is quite simple in its most basic mode—simply type **playmidi** *midifile.mid* to play *midifile.mid*. Of course, like most Linux commands, playmidi does support a large number of options. You can read about them in the playmidi man page. Two options deserve special mention, however:

- **-g** The -g option directs output to a Gravis UltraSound's internal MIDI synthesizer. One sound card isn't extraordinarily important, of course, but this feature becomes more important because the SoftOSS software wavetable features emulate a Gravis UltraSound. Therefore, you must use the -g parameter to playmidi when you want to use it in conjunction with SoftOSS.

> **NOTE**
>
> If you want to use the TiMidity application to play MIDI files using TiMidity's software wavetable, you can do so. I described TiMidity earlier in this chapter.

- **-e** The -e option directs output to external MIDI devices. You can use this option to play a MIDI file on an external keyboard, for instance. You also use this option to play a sound using wavetable MIDI on some sound cards that include wavetable MIDI support.

Various GUI MIDI players exist, in addition to the command-line variety. KDE includes a TiMidity-based MIDI player called kmidi, and TiMidity itself can be run in GUI mode, as described earlier in this chapter. If you don't want to use a TiMidity-based program, you don't need to do so. The xplaymidi program, for instance, adds a GUI interface to the playmidi command, as shown in Figure 10.10. Some GUI MIDI playback tools, including xplaymidi, add enough overhead that the timing of MIDI playback can be disrupted, particularly on a slow or heavily loaded computer.

Beyond mere MIDI playback lies MIDI editing. The prime MIDI editor (or *sequencer*, as this type of software is more formally known) for Linux is Jazz (http://www.jazzware.com), shown in Figure 10.11. A MIDI sequencer lets you change the notes, change the instruments, cut and paste music, and make other alterations to a MIDI score. You can even create a MIDI composition of your own from scratch. In essence, a MIDI sequencer is to MIDI files what a text editor is to ASCII files. If you want to pursue MIDI music for more than casual file playback, a MIDI sequencer is a must-have utility.

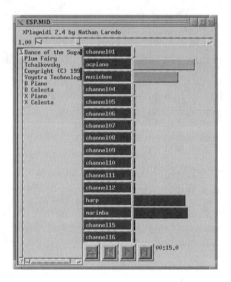

FIGURE 10.10

xplaymidi *shows what instruments a MIDI file contains, and uses a bar graph to display when these instruments are being used.*

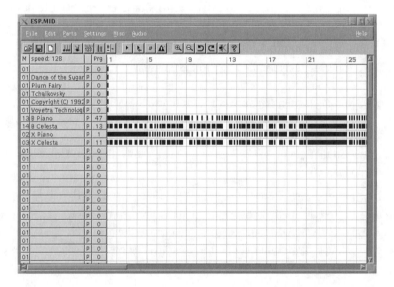

FIGURE 10.11

A MIDI sequencer enables you to edit a MIDI file much as you can edit an ASCII file or digital audio file.

CD Players

One aspect of sound under Linux that I've not yet described in great detail is that of playing audio CDs. All recent sound cards include input jacks mounted so that they can accept input from an internal CD-ROM drive. You can then play your audio CDs through your computer's speakers, but you need a CD player application to control the CD-ROM drive. Naturally, such utilities exist for Linux.

> **NOTE**
>
> Normally, playing music CDs does not entail *digital audio extraction* (DAE), as described in Chapter 7, "Optical Drives." Audio CD playing merely causes the CD-ROM drive to act just like an ordinary audio CD player, decoding music into analog form and sending the resulting signal to the sound card. The sound card then pipes the CD-ROM drive's input directly to the sound card's output jack. After being read from the CD, the music isn't processed digitally, and the computer's CPU is involved only insofar as the control program uses the CPU to update timer displays and so on. Therefore, playing audio CDs requires almost no CPU power; an 80386 CPU can do the task without causing a slowdown to other programs running on the computer.

A few basic text-mode audio CD players exist, such as `cdplayer` and `workbone`. These utilities let you play a CD under Linux even if you're not running X, but they're decidedly bare-bones programs. For a better user interface, it helps to move up to an X-based CD player, such as KDE's `kscd` (shown in Figure 10.12), GNOME's `gtcd`, or the independent `xplaycd`. These tools provide point-and-click access to CD controls, similar to those of dedicated audio CD players used with a stereo system. Computer-based CD playing offers certain advantages over using a stereo, however. For instance, note that in Figure 10.12, the artist (*Trout Fishing in America*), title of the CD (*Closer to the Truth*, which is truncated), and track title (*Dreaming*) all appear in the middle of the window. This feat is made possible by both local and Internet-based music databases, which the CD player can consult when you insert a CD. The CD player can even include options to open a Web browser to display music-related sites.

FIGURE 10.12
An X-based CD player provides all the amenities of a dedicated CD player and more.

Most Linux CD player applications assume that they'll have both read and write access to the
/dev/cdrom device file. You must therefore ensure that any user who will use the CD player
has this access, and that the file points to the actual CD-ROM device file, as described in
Chapter 7. The application does *not* need access to digital audio files (/dev/audio or
/dev/dsp), but you might need access to the mixer file (/dev/mixer) in order to control the
volume of the output sent to the speaker. In fact, in some case you might need to open a separate mixer utility in order to un-mute the CD channel or increase the overall system volume.

Linux Mixer Utilities

As you've gathered by now, sound cards provide many different inputs and outputs, including

- Digital audio output
- MIDI output
- CD audio input
- Line input
- Microphone input

Depending upon your sound card, you can have even more devices. For instance, some sound
cards support two separate line inputs. Even if your speakers have their own volume control,
it's often desirable to set the volume levels for various specific sound sources separately. For
instance, suppose you play a MIDI file and adjust the volume appropriately. You might then
want to play a CD, but need to adjust the volume again. When the system plays a sound to
inform you that you've got new mail, it might then be too soft to hear—or loud enough to disturb the neighbors! In order to set all your sound sources to reasonable volumes
simultaneously, Linux supports an application type known as a *mixer*.

It should be no surprise at this point that mixers come in both text-based and GUI varieties.
The text-based versions are most useful to set the system's volume to a default value whenever
you boot the computer. One of the most common such utilities is known as aumix, and you can
run it in any of three ways:

- By specifying volume levels for particular inputs and outputs on the command line
- In interactive mode, by typing **aumix** and then adjusting mixer levels using a text-based
  interface
- By specifying mixer values in a configuration file, either .aumixrc in the user's home
  directory or /etc/aumixrc

This final option is generally the way aumix is used. To do so, call it with the -L switch—that
is, **aumix -L**. The program then reads the configuration file, which looks something like this:

```
vol:80:80:P
synth:32:32:P
pcm:30:30:P
line:50:50:P
mic:16:16:R
cd:32:32:P
igain:75:75:P
```

Each line stands for one input or output (`vol` for overall system volume, `pcm` for digital audio, and so on), and is followed by the left and right channel volumes (on a scale of 0–99) and a code indicating whether the device is set for playing (`P`) or recording (`R`).

GUI mixer utilities also abound, of course. For instance, Figure 10.13 shows GNOME's `gmix` utility, which enables you to adjust the volume levels in a point-and-click manner. You can also mute individual channels and click the Lock button to adjust both right and left levels simultaneously.

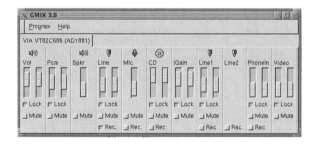

Figure 10.13

GUI mixers often feature icons and numerous buttons to enable and disable specific channels or features.

Unfortunately, there are several different mixer standards in common use. Most sound cards work with common utilities like `aumix`, `gmix`, or KDE's `kmix`, but sometimes you might need something more exotic. The ALSA drivers, for example, don't always work with the standard mixers. Fortunately, the ALSA utilities package includes its own mixers, so you need not go without this vital utility if you use the ALSA drivers. Even among the OSS drivers, though, specific cards sometimes require their own mixers. The `gmix` utility shown in Figure 10.13 supports multiple mixers, either for separate sound cards or as alternative means of accessing a single card.

Summary

Sound cards vary substantially in their features and in Linux support. Technology has improved substantially from the earliest 8-bit boards to today's PCI wavetable products. Linux drivers often lag slightly behind the very latest releases, but fortunately, the very latest products seldom offer such vast improvements as to make going with a somewhat older product a hardship. If you must have the latest board, check into the commercial OSS drivers, which frequently include drivers for more recent products than the standard kernel or ALSA drivers. Whatever product and drivers you purchase, the stable of Linux audio applications is wide enough for most users, even including sophisticated digital audio and MIDI editing programs. For day-to-day use, the set of mixers and audio file players that come with most Linux distributions is quite adequate.

Audio Input/Output

IN THIS CHAPTER

Chapter 10 covered sound cards, including various options that are required to obtain good sound reproduction from these devices. That chapter omitted one very important aspect of sound reproduction, however: what happens to sound before and after it reaches the sound card's electronics. The best available sound card will produce abysmal sound if it's matched with an abysmal pair of speakers. Likewise, when recording sound, a poor microphone can produce unintelligible speech even when the sound card's recording capabilities are excellent.

In addition to concerns of absolute quality of speakers and microphones, use of these devices in a computer setting poses unique challenges. For instance, speakers produce magnetic fields, and these magnetic fields can wreak havoc with magnetic recording materials and with other magnetically sensitive computer equipment.

Speakers and Headphones

Most sound card applications rely on sound output. Even if you want to record sounds, chances are you want to be able to play those sounds back to verify that they've been recorded accurately. You might also want to assess changes you make when you edit the sounds. Most computer users attach speakers to their computers, but headphones are an alternative for when you don't want to disturb others.

Speaker Designs

Most speaker sets designed for computers today use either two or three speakers. Speakers also use a variety of ancillary controls and components, such as cables, volume knobs, and so on. Understanding the options available in speakers can help you to avoid an inappropriate purchase.

Two- and Three-Piece Speakers

All modern sound cards are capable of stereo reproduction, in which sounds are recorded on two channels. A logical form for speakers, therefore, delivers them in pairs, as shown in Figure 11.1. Computer speakers range in size from cubical shapes of roughly 3 inches per side to roughly a foot tall with a footprint of about 6 inches square. As a general rule, the larger the speakers, the better the sound reproduction, but there are exceptions to this rule.

Most computer speakers are standalone units; that is, you position them on your desk independently of other components. Some speakers are designed to be mounted on a vertical surface, such as a computer monitor. These speakers typically come with Velcro fastenings to fasten the speakers to the monitor. Some are designed to mate with a specific monitor, and include appropriate attachment hardware for both the speakers and the monitor. A few go one step further: They're integrated into the monitor. Speakers that come built in to monitors are typically of low quality, unfortunately, and they add to the cost of the monitor. There's no reason you need to *use* speakers that come built in to a monitor, though. If you like a monitor *as a monitor*, you can always ignore its built-in speakers if you don't like them.

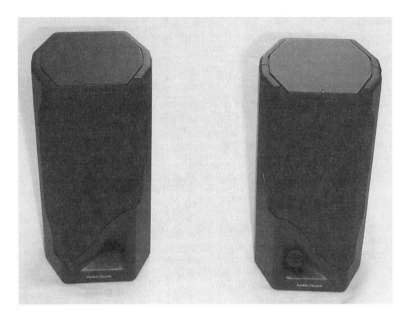

FIGURE 11.1
The traditional design for speakers uses one pair for stereo reproduction.

An alternative to the two-speaker design that's gained popularity in computer circles in the late 1990s uses three speakers for stereo sound reproduction. The human ear is good at localizing high-pitched (or *treble*) sounds, but not so good at locating the source of lower (*bass*) tones. The reproduction of bass tones, however, is the source of the increased size of higher-quality speakers. These tones require large speaker elements, known as *woofers* or *subwoofers*. If most of the bass tone reproduction is shifted into a third speaker, located between the two stereo speakers (which are now referred to as *satellite speakers*), those satellite speakers can be greatly reduced in size. A typical three-speaker system uses satellite speakers that are only about 2–4 inches on a side, and a subwoofer roughly 12-inch×8-inch×8-inch in size. Figure 11.2 depicts such an arrangement.

Which type of speaker should you get? There's no easy answer to this question. Both two- and three-speaker designs can achieve good sound reproduction; neither type is uniformly better than the other. The bulk of the higher-quality speaker sets marketed for computers in 2000, however, use three-speaker designs. The advantage of the three-speaker design is that it's less demanding of desk space. The satellite speakers are small and unimposing. The three-speaker system's subwoofer is quite bulky, however, so if under-desk space is limited, you might want to favor a two-speaker design. Another drawback to the three-speaker design is that it involves more in the way of cabling. A typical two-speaker design uses just two audio cables, one leading from one speaker to the computer and another leading from the first speaker to the second.

A three-speaker system, on the other hand, requires one additional cable to handle the sub-woofer. These speakers also sometimes use a fourth cable for a volume control.

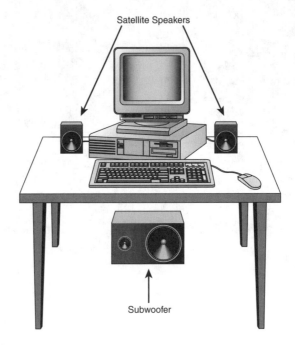

FIGURE 11.2

A three-speaker system places the bulkiest part of the speaker out of the way—typically under your desk.

Speaker Connectors and Options

Speakers for stereo systems generally use bare wire contacts or RCA plugs, as shown to the right in Figure 11.3. To simplify cabling and because of limited space on the backs of sound cards, however, computer speakers use 1/8-inch stereo jacks, as shown to the left in Figure 11.3. If you want to use stereo speakers that use the "wrong" type of connector for computers, adapters are commonly available from stereo shops and many computer stores.

Some USB-interfaced speakers have begun to appear on the market. These devices don't use the computer's sound card; instead, they use a combination of the computer's CPU and circuitry in the speakers themselves to produce sound. To use USB speakers in Linux, you must use a 2.3.x or later kernel, or a back-port of the USB drivers from these kernels to a 2.2.x kernel. Activate the USB Audio support option in the kernel configuration menu. I recommend against using USB speakers because they're so new. Conventional audio cards are much better supported in Linux.

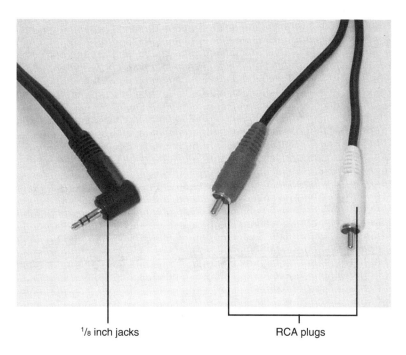

¹/₈ inch jacks   RCA plugs

FIGURE 11.3

RCA plugs (right) have long been used for connections between stereo components, whereas 1/8-inch jacks (left) are common on portable stereos and computer audio equipment.

Computer speakers must normally be *amplified*, which means that they include the capability to increase the volume of a signal. Many sound cards can't output a strong enough signal to drive an unamplified speaker. Along with the amplifier, most speakers include a knob or slider to let you control the volume of the sound. This control often resides on one speaker, but with three-speaker designs it's often on a cable that leads to the subwoofer. If your speakers lack a separate volume control, you can use a mixer application in Linux to control the volume. If you prefer something more tactile, you can purchase a separate volume control, as shown in Figure 11.4, which you insert between the speaker and the sound card. The knob in the middle of the short cable shown in the figure allows you to reduce the strength of the signal traversing the wire, and thus reduce the volume of the sound coming out of the speaker.

To power the amplifier, speakers require a power source. This is normally ordinary AC house current. Some speakers, though, provide an option to use batteries. Unless you're using the speakers with a portable computer, I recommend you use house current, because speakers can consume batteries quickly. Most battery-powered speakers either come with an AC adapter or include a jack for one. You can purchase a separate AC adapter at an electronics store.

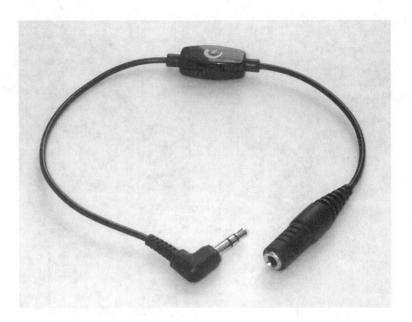

FIGURE 11.4

Add-on volume controls can be convenient if your speakers lack their own volume adjustment knobs.

Some speakers include controls that let you adjust the response of the speakers to different tones. For instance, there might be a switch that boosts the speakers' response to bass tones, or bass and treble adjustment dials. These controls can help you fine-tune a speaker for the best performance in a given room.

Shielded and Unshielded Speakers

One unusual characteristic of the area near a computer is the large number of objects that are sensitive to magnetic fields. Objects that can be damaged or malfunction in the presence of magnetic fields include

- **Removable disks**   Magnetic fields can erase data stored on floppy disks, Zip disks, LS-120 disks, and many other removable disk formats. Fortunately, neither magneto-optical disks nor CDs are affected by magnetic fields.

- **Backup tapes**   Backup tapes rely on the same recording technologies as do floppy disks, and so are just as sensitive to magnetic fields.

- **Monitors**   Traditional cathode-ray tube (CRT) monitors work by firing electrons from the rear of the picture tube to the front, where they strike phosphors that glow. Because electrons are charged particles, they're sensitive to magnetic fields. If you bring a magnet too close to a monitor, the image on the screen will become distorted. LCD monitors, such as those used in laptop computers, are not sensitive to magnetic fields.

Unfortunately, speakers work by the application of magnetic fields. The current from the sound card, amplified by the speaker or an external amplifier, causes changes in a magnetic field inside the speaker. These changes, in turn, cause vibrations in the membrane of the speaker, thus producing sound. A speaker can therefore potentially erase magnetic media and cause a monitor's display to go haywire.

Fortunately, speaker manufacturers are cognizant of these problems, and so they produce *shielded* speakers for use with computers. These speakers use layers of metal to block their magnetic fields, so they have little or no impact on nearby magnetically sensitive devices. Nonetheless, I recommend exercising some caution, even with magnetically shielded speakers. Don't place removable disks or tapes directly on or next to the speaker. If the speaker's shielding is inadequate and the speaker rests too close to the monitor, you'll see the difference, but you won't permanently damage the monitor, so you can adjust speaker/monitor distance as you see fit.

Most speaker manufacturers produce *unshielded* speakers in addition to their shielded models. These unshielded speakers can be electrically compatible with computer equipment, and they often cost less than their shielded counterparts. They're usually marketed for use with small or portable stereos. If at all possible, I recommend against using such unshielded speakers with computers, however, because of the great danger posed to your removable media. If you choose to use unshielded speakers with your computer, exercise extreme caution in where you store your magnetic media. Also, keep the location of the speakers relative to your monitor and the computer itself in mind. Removable media must be inserted into, and removed from, your computer to be of any use, so placing unshielded speakers too close to a computer can be a recipe for disaster.

How close is too close? For the sort of small speakers you're likely to use with a computer, 6–12 inches is probably adequate clearance, in my experience, but 24 inches doesn't represent an excessive safety margin. Keep in mind that the damage from a speaker's magnetic field can accumulate over time. Even if you've tested a floppy disk at 6 inches for a few minutes and found no damage, an exposure of days or weeks might destroy your data. Also, the higher the capacity of the media, the more sensitive it's likely to be to damage from magnetic fields. A floppy disk might not be damaged by a given exposure, for instance, but a Zip disk might become unreadable from the same exposure.

CAUTION

Don't forget non-computer speakers. Telephones, for instance, include their own speakers. So do the headphones you might use with a portable CD player. External modems often include speakers, although these might be shielded. Electric motors, such as those used in some mechanical clocks and various toys, can produce damaging magnetic fields, as well.

Headphones

Headphones can be a useful audio accessory in a variety of situations, such as

- You want to use your computer's sound card but don't want to disturb others around you, such as co-workers or family members.
- You want to get the best sound possible on a budget—headphones of a given price usually produce better sound than speakers of the same price.
- You enjoy the "super stereo" effect that headphones produce.
- You want to block out environmental noises while hearing your computer's sound output.
- You want to catch as many details as possible from the sound source—a feat that's easier with headphones than with speakers.

Tip

You might want to use your computer for detailed audio work, such as transferring old LP records to CD. If so, headphones can be useful for detecting minor audio defects. For instance, the pops that are endemic on LP records can be heard much more clearly on headphones than on speakers. You should therefore use headphones rather than speakers when tracking down and eliminating such flaws.

Caution

Don't turn up the volume on headphones in order to catch more details. It's easy to suffer permanent hearing loss as a result of listening to music (or computer sounds) at too high a volume over headphones. In fact, a good rule of thumb is to adjust the volume to a comfortable level and then turn it *down*, because people have a tendency to listen to music on headphones at too high a volume.

Headphones come in a wide variety of designs. There are, of course, numerous headphone classification schemes, but one convenient system breaks the designs down into three categories:

- **Over-the-ear**   These headphones surround the ear completely and can therefore serve as a partial barrier to outside noises. Over-the-ear designs are typically bulky, but can produce excellent sound quality. The pair of headphones on the right side of Figure 11.5 demonstrates an over-the-ear design.

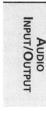
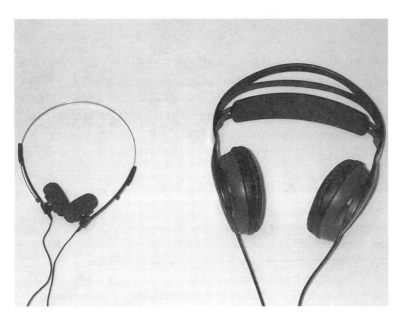

FIGURE 11.5

Headphones vary substantially in size, features, and sound reproduction quality.

- **On-the-ear**   This design places the headphone's speakers flat against the ear—or as flat as can be achieved given the geometries involved. On-the-ear designs range from compact models that are often used with portable stereos (such as the pair on the left in Figure 11.5) to larger designs suitable for use with a home stereo system. On-the-ear designs are usually lighter than over-the-ear models, and they don't block environmental noise as well. Sound quality ranges from poor to very good.

- **In-the-ear**   The smallest headphone speakers can fit partially inside the ear. Some of these models dispense with the band that connects the two speakers; instead, you insert one speaker into each ear like an earplug.

The type of headphone you choose is largely a matter of personal preference. More so than most computer products, headphone choice is a very personal matter. This is because the fit of headphones on the head and ears varies from one person to another. A comfortable fit for one individual might be excruciatingly tight for another.

Headphones generally require little in the way of amplification, and so don't normally need to be plugged into an AC outlet or use batteries. As with conventional speakers, however, headphones create magnetic fields and so can be damaging to magnetic media. Few headphones are magnetically shielded, so you must exercise caution in storing your headphones near your computer. Fortunately, the magnets inside headphones are correspondingly smaller than those in regular speakers, and so pose less risk to magnetic media at moderate distances.

Some headphones include volume controls, either on the sides or using a control in the headphone's cable. If yours doesn't include this feature, consider purchasing an in-line volume control, such as the one shown in Figure 11.4. You can also purchase splitters that allow you to connect both headphones and stereo speakers to the same computer at the same time. You can then don your headphones and power off the speakers whenever you want to use the headphones.

Understanding Frequency Response

Both headphones and speakers can be described in terms of their *frequency response* characteristics. Suppose you've produced or obtained a precise recording of a series of tones, covering the entire range of normal adult human hearing (20Hz–20,000Hz). If you play this series of recordings over an average speaker, chances are you'll perceive differences in the loudness of the different tones, although they were recorded at the same level. Switch speakers, and the pattern of differences can change. Recording the results with precision laboratory instruments can produce graphs similar to Figure 11.6. This graph is known as a *frequency response curve* —or rather, it's a *pair* of frequency response curves for two different products. On the whole, Product A is more accurate than Product B, because the bulk of Product A's curve lies close to the 100% line—the point at which the product produces precisely the output it should, given its input. To the extent that a speaker's frequency response curve lies close to the 100% point, it's considered to have a *flat* frequency response.

You'll sometimes see frequency response curves similar to those in Figure 11.6 in test reports of speakers in consumer and audiophile magazines. Most manufacturers don't make such graphs readily available. Instead, they report a frequency response *range*. This is the range of frequencies between which sound reproduction is at 50% or greater what it should be. For instance, one speaker might have a frequency response range of 30Hz–10,000Hz, and another might have a range of 20Hz–25,000Hz. The second is probably a better speaker, particularly at reproducing high notes, but the range alone doesn't tell you how the products performed in the wide middle ground. If the second speaker's reproduction fluctuates wildly, you might actually prefer the first speaker, especially if you seldom listen to music that pushes far beyond 10,000Hz.

The environment in which a speaker exists affects its frequency response curve. Furniture, wall hangings, carpets, floors, and so on can all affect a speaker's frequency response curve.

Similarly, the precise shape of your ear and skull can affect a headphone's frequency response curve. Indeed, part of our subjective experience of sound comes from the way sounds interact with the bones and tissues of our bodies on the way to our ears, so when measured apart from a human body, or a good simulation thereof, a good pair of headphones exhibits a frequency response curve that would be considered quite poor for speakers.

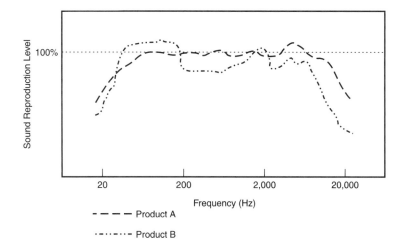

FIGURE 11.6

A frequency response curve lets you compare the quality of sound reproduction of two or more speakers or headphones.

Microphones

For most people, sound output is far more important than sound input. Nonetheless, microphones can still be an important part of your overall audio experience. This is particularly true if you want to use your computer to record your own music and then burn it onto a CD. For such an application, you'll need the best microphones possible. (In fact, for CD-quality recording, you're better off with specialized audio equipment, but a computer and its sound card can suffice in a pinch.) Even more modest uses sometimes require microphones. Computer telephony and videoconferencing, for instance, require audio input from microphones.

Unidirectional and Omnidirectional Microphones

One of the most important distinctions to understand between various microphone types is that between unidirectional and omnidirectional microphones. A *unidirectional microphone* picks up sounds from a narrow range of directions. Such microphones are very good for use in a noisy environment, because they won't pick up much of the noise from that environment—only your own voice. *Omnidirectional microphones*, on the other hand, pick up sound from a wide variety of directions. You might want to use an omnidirectional microphone if you want a single microphone to pick up the voices of several people gathered around the computer.

You can't tell a unidirectional from an omnidirectional microphone just by looking at the device, unless the information is printed on the microphone. There should be some indication of which type the microphone is on the product's packaging, however.

As a general rule of thumb, unidirectional microphones are better for use with computers, because most such uses involve input from a single individual. You might want to use an omni-directional microphone in some situations, though, such as recording a group conversation. Omnidirectional microphones that rest very close to your mouth might also serve well. Such microphones are typically less sensitive to noise; they rely upon proximity to your mouth to eliminate unwanted background noises.

Microphone Mounting Options

Microphones are available in a wide variety of mounts, including

- Handheld
- Stand mount
- Prop mount
- Head gear
- Lapel mount

Figure 11.7 shows a number of these mounting types. As a general rule, microphones that you wear tend to be convenient and unobtrusive if you sit at the computer using the microphone for long periods of time. Microphones that you leave on a desk, on the other hand, are often more convenient when you move around a lot, but they frequently do a poorer job plucking your voice out of a noisy environment.

Tip

The noise of a computer's fans and hard disks can overpower some microphones if you place the microphone too close to the computer. Be sure to put the microphone as far away from the computer as possible. For unidirectional microphones, it's also best if the computer does not lie in the microphone's sensitive range of angles.

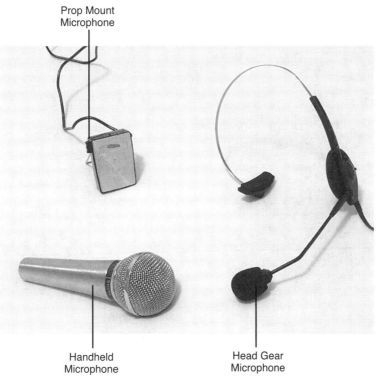

Prop Mount
Microphone

Handheld
Microphone

Head Gear
Microphone

FIGURE 11.7

Clockwise from bottom left: A handheld microphone can often convert to stand mount; a prop mount microphone can sit unobtrusively on a desk; and a head gear microphone can do an excellent job of picking one person's voice out of a noisy environment.

Selecting a Microphone for Your Needs

You must match a microphone to your sound card based upon a number of criteria, including

- **Stereo or mono** Most computer sound cards expect to receive stereo input from their microphones. Most microphones, however, are mono. Microphones marketed for computers simply use stereo connectors and pipe the same input into both channels. You can tell stereo from mono jacks by the number of black rings on the tips of the jacks. One ring indicates a mono device, and two indicates stereo. (Figure 11.8 shows a mono and a stereo connector for reference.) If you want to use two microphones to do stereo recording, you can use two mono microphones in conjunction with a mono-to-stereo adapter that merges two mono signals into a single 1/8-inch stereo jack. You should be sure that both microphones are well matched in their electrical characteristics, however, such as impedance.

FIGURE 11.8

A mono jack (left) has a single black ring at its tip, whereas a stereo jack (right) has two rings.

- **Impedance**   *Impedance* is a measure of resistance to current flow, and is measured in Ohms (Ω). Microphones vary substantially in their impedances—from 150Ω–20,000Ω or more. Sound cards vary in the range of impedances with which they work best, although most work best with low-impedance microphones—typically in the 150Ω–1,000Ω range.

- **Frequency response**   Like speakers, microphones can be described in terms of their frequency response curves or ranges. Using a microphone that's capable of a wider frequency response range than the sound card can handle isn't a problem, but using a poorer microphone results in a reduction in the quality of the recording, compared to what it might be with a better microphone.

- **Sensitivity**   This characteristic is measured in decibels (dB), and is usually a negative number. Higher sensitivities (that is, negative numbers closer to 0) generally result in louder input.

Unfortunately, finding the relevant specifications for a low-cost microphone can be difficult, and many sound card manufacturers fail to provide information on the relevant characteristics that they require in a microphone. You might therefore need to try several microphones, one after another, until you find a match.

Using a Home Stereo

It's sometimes desirable to link your computer and your home stereo. You might want to do this as a way to obviate the need for separate speakers for your computer, particularly if your stereo and its speakers are located within convenient distance to the computer. You might also want to use the two together to accomplish some specific goal, such as transferring cassettes or LP records to CD. Whatever the reason, linking your computer and stereo isn't a difficult task, but there are some pitfalls to be avoided.

TIP

If you want to use a stereo connection to listen to or record FM radio broadcasts, consider an FM radio card instead. I describe such hardware in the section "Radio and TV Tuners" in Chapter 13.

Directing Output to a Home Stereo

Most home stereos use RCA plugs for connecting components. In order to connect your computer's sound card output to a home stereo's input, therefore, you need two things:

- A set of free inputs on the home stereo. Note that a *phono input* is unsuitable for this task. Acceptable inputs might be labeled *tape*, *cassette*, *aux*, *TV*, or various other things, but never *phono*. The phono input is designed for a turntable, which has different electrical properties than all other inputs on the stereo system.

- A cable with a 1/8-inch stereo jack on one end and a pair of RCA plugs on the other. You can obtain such cables at an electronics supply store. Some sound cards ship with such cables.

Connecting the two components is a matter of plugging the cable in place. You can then use the front-panel controls on the stereo to listen to the computer's input, whatever it happens to be called.

If your stereo doesn't have enough inputs, you can purchase a switch of one sort or another. A simple switch box lets you select between two inputs. A more complex switch box can let you connect several devices with both inputs and outputs, and direct any given device's output to any other device's input. Figure 11.9 shows such a device, which has 16 RCA plugs on its back—two inputs and two outputs for each of the three devices and another stereo input/output pair for the monitor (the stereo receiver).

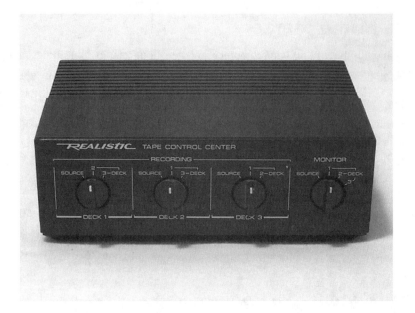

FIGURE 11.9

An audio switch box can let you connect your computer to an already maxed-out stereo system.

When you've connected your computer's audio output to your stereo, you must turn on the stereo whenever you want to hear sounds from your computer. You can then use both your Linux mixer, as described in Chapter 16, "Parallel and Serial Ports," and your stereo's volume control knob to adjust the volume of sound you hear. Depending upon the capabilities of your stereo, you might be able to tape record sounds coming from your computer or direct your computer's sound to speakers in another room.

Recording Stereo Input

One of the benefits of connecting your computer to your stereo is that you can digitally record music from the stereo. For instance, suppose you want to listen to a particular radio program, but you'll be away from home at that time. Rather than miss the broadcast, you can turn on the stereo and set up a Linux cron job to record the program at the appointed hour. In essence, you've turned your computer and stereo into a sort of audio VCR. Another possibility is to transfer old vinyl records and cassettes to CD.

In any event, connecting the stereo and computer requires the same sort of cable as is needed to listen to your computer's output through the stereo. Instead of connecting to the stereo's input jack, though, you connect to an output jack (such as one for a cassette); and instead of using the speaker output on the computer, you connect the stereo to the *line-in* jack.

> ## CAUTION
>
> Don't use the microphone input on the computer. Although this might produce sound, the electrical characteristics of microphone and line inputs are slightly different, so you won't get optimal results. On many sound cards, the microphone input is also an inferior input; it might support a frequency response range that's less than the frequency response range of the line-in jack.

After the connections have been made, you can follow these steps to record the stereo's audio input:

1. Set your stereo to direct an appropriate signal to the computer. If you use a switch box like the one shown in Figure 11.9, you might need to use it instead of, or in addition to, the stereo to select the desired input source.

2. Use a Linux mixer application to un-mute the line input, as shown in Figure 11.10.

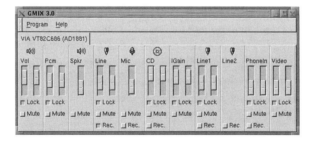

FIGURE 11.10

GNOME's gmix *is one of the better Linux mixers available when it comes to intuitive controls to select and un-mute an input source.*

3. Start your recording application and begin recording.

4. Stop recording after capturing a few seconds input, and check that the recording levels are OK. If they're not, adjust them using your mixer application and try again.

NOTE

If you set your recording level too low, you might be able to amplify the signal at playback by turning up the volume. This will also amplify background noise, however. If you set the recording level too high, the result is *clipping*—the digital recording stores a series of maximum or minimum values, which ends up producing a harsh, grating sound. In extreme cases, you might hear nothing but clicks in a severely clipped recording.

5. When you've adjusted your recording level to your satisfaction, begin recording in earnest, and stop whenever you're done.

TIP

Aside from turntables, the electrical requirements of most stereo equipment are standardized. You can therefore connect, say, a cassette recorder directly to your sound card's line input if you want to record a cassette, without going through the stereo system.

Avoiding Ground Loops

One problem you might encounter when you connect your stereo and your Linux computer is that of a *ground loop*. Many electronic devices, including desktop computers, are *grounded* in one way or another. For instance, the third prong on a computer's electric plug grounds the computer. The details of how a ground is achieved vary, but the result is the same: An electrical connection between the device and the ground—literally the earth outside your building. The ground serves as a safety feature; excess current can be dumped to ground when necessary. Surge protectors use this characteristic to protect the computer from power surges.

The problem arises when two or more *different* grounds are used by different components in an audio setup. When this happens, the result is a feedback loop that produces a 60Hz hum. (In North America, AC electrical supplies run at 60Hz. In Europe, it's 50Hz, so a ground loop creates a 50Hz hum.) Possible specific causes of this problem include

- **Using different electrical outlets**   Ideally, all the electrical outlets in a building are grounded at the same point. This isn't always the case, however, particularly if a building's electrical system has been expanded or modified over the years.

- **Improper electrical grounding**   If the grounding of your electrical system wasn't done correctly, you might get a ground loop because, in effect, a proper ground isn't available.

- **Ungrounded components**   Some components require grounding to function properly. Turntables, for instance, often include a special ground wire. Be sure it's connected to an appropriate point on your stereo.
- **Cable TV and TV antennas**   Cable TV systems and exterior antennas usually require their own grounds. As these are independent of your building's electrical system, they can cause ground loops. Note that the ground loop exists even when the TV isn't in use; all that's required is that the TV and stereo be linked in some way.

To eliminate a ground loop, you should try to eliminate its cause. For instance, plug all components into the same outlet, or unplug your TV's antenna connection to break a ground loop caused by that connection. Using a surge protector with cable TV protection can also help reduce or eliminate ground loops caused by that source.

Ground loops can sometimes cause a very subtle hum, so you might not hear it initially. It might become apparent when you listen to a CD you've created from the source, however, particularly if you use headphones for that listening. For this reason, I recommend checking for ground loops by recording a period of silence and listening to that recording with headphones and the volume controls turned up.

CAUTION

When you perform this test, be sure that no other sounds will play; with the volume turned up, a sound of normal volume can damage your headphones, and perhaps your own hearing as well!

If you can't completely eliminate a ground loop, you might be able to use software to do the trick after recording. I don't know of any Linux native software that performs this task, but the Windows program CoolEdit from Syntrillium (`http://www.syntrillium.com`) does work, and can run under WINE (`http://www.winehq.com`; check the WINE applications database for details).

Creating Clean Recordings of Music

One of the problems with digital recording under Linux is that such recording requires precision timing. Sound cards typically contain small or nonexistent input buffers, so if Linux can't get around to handling a given sample (say, because it's busy handling disk I/O associated with the previous batch of samples), the sample gets dropped. The result can be clicks or outright gaps in the recorded file. There are several steps you can take to reduce the odds of encountering such a problem:

- **Use a fast CPU.** The faster your CPU, the less likely it will be caught unable to juggle the recording and any other tasks you might have given it.

- **Use DMA disk transfers.** Direct memory access (DMA) transfer modes require little in the way of CPU supervision, and so can improve your odds of obtaining a clean recording. I describe DMA disk access in Chapter 5, "Hard Disks."

- **Use minimalist recording software.** Flashy GUI programs can be nice, but the overhead involved in dynamically updating displays can get in the way of recording audio accurately. A simple text-based program might do better.

- **Shut down unnecessary programs.** If you're running lots of programs, those programs' operations can get in the way of your recording. This is particularly true of CPU-intensive programs like `setiathome` (`http://setiathome.ssl.berkeley.edu`). In fact, all of the X Window System (X) can qualify as "unnecessary programs." If you normally boot to X, you can use the command **init** *n* to change to a text-only configuration. In this case, *n* is a *runlevel*—a number from 1–6 that represents what sorts of facilities are available. On most Linux distributions, *n* will be 3 for text-mode operation, but on some distributions it will be something else. You can find the current runlevel by typing `runlevel`.

- **Boost the recording priority.** The Linux `nice` program can be used to boost the priority of a process. To give your process maximal priority, use **nice -n -20 *program***. This command runs *program* with maximum priority (the value of `-20` is maximum priority). You might need to be `root` to use `nice` to increase a program's default priority.

If all these procedures fail to produce a clean recording, you might need to use DOS for your audio recording. For all its faults, as a single-tasking OS, DOS is inherently better suited to performing real-time tasks than is the multitasking Linux.

Special Considerations for LP Recording

Recording music from a vinyl record poses certain unique challenges:

- **Inputs** Unlike most audio components, a phonograph's outputs don't match the electrical characteristics required by a sound card's line input jack. You therefore must use an appropriate amplifier to handle the task. If you've already connected your computer to your stereo, this isn't a problem; but if you want to connect the turntable directly to the computer, it is. In this case, you can buy an inexpensive amplifier to serve as an intermediary.

- **Ground loops**   As mentioned earlier, turntables often include grounding wires to prevent ground loops. Be sure your grounding wire is connected to an appropriate point on your stereo.

- **Media defects**   Vinyl records are well known for their defects, which cause "pop" or "snap" noises. The best way to eliminate such defects is with an editor such as Sound Studio or Broadcast. You can use these editors to zoom in on the point of the defect and replace it with silence. Most such defects are so short that you never notice the silence in their place. Some Windows programs can automatically remove these defects, but I'm unaware of any Linux programs to do this task. I've been unimpressed with the results of automatic defect removal programs that I've tried.

- **Cartridge choice**   If you want to convert a collection of LP, 45 rpm, or 78 rpm records to CD, you probably want to use the best equipment possible. One of the most important characteristics of audio reproduction using vinyl technology is that of the *cartridge*—the part of the turntable that reads the record. These days, you're unlikely to find a good cartridge in your local Radio Shack store. Instead, you must shop at a specialty audio store. On the Web, Audio Advisor (`http://www.audioadvisor.com`) is one such retailer. Cartridges range in price substantially, but as a general rule of thumb, expect to pay $100 for a good one, or substantially more if you want the best possible reproduction.

Transferring music from records to CDs can be a time-consuming process, particularly because you shouldn't use your computer for anything else while doing the recording, lest you introduce gaps or noise from dropped samples. Nonetheless, if you have a cherished collection of music on vinyl that's not available natively in CD form, this transfer can be worthwhile.

Summary

Your choice of input and output devices for your sound card has a profound influence on the quality of the sound you hear and record. By the standards of home stereo systems, computer speakers tend to be mediocre in quality, but the best can produce reasonably good sound. For the best possible sound, you can connect your computer to your stereo. To do so, you must have a spare input on the stereo or use a switch box, and you might need to debug a ground loop problem.

For most people, input isn't as important as output, but for some purposes, input is indispensable. Microphones vary substantially in quality, but even many low-cost microphones are adequate for tasks such as voice annotation and Internet telephony. For recording music, you probably want to use your sound card's line input jack to connect to a stereo system. As with output to a stereo, ground loops can be a major problem in such a connection, and you might need to use a switch box to share a single tape deck output between a cassette recorder and your computer.

Video Cards

IN THIS CHAPTER

One of the trickiest products to purchase, from a Linux point of view, is a video card (a k a a *video board*). The video card marketplace changes rapidly, driven largely by increasing demand for complex graphics in Windows games. Most of these games aren't available in Linux, however, so Linux's needs are more modest. What's worse, the developers of XFree86, the GUI system most often used in Linux, have a hard time keeping up with the ever-changing video hardware market. As a general rule, therefore, Linux support for video cards lags a few months behind the state of the art.

This isn't to say that it's *difficult* to find a video card that's suitable for use in Linux. The problem is twofold, really:

- Without adequate research, it's easy to pick up a video card for which no XFree86 support exists. The odds are in your favor even if you randomly select a product from the store shelves, but less so than for most other products.

- If you've narrowed your choice to a few specific products based on non-Linux criteria, it can be difficult to track down which cards are well supported in Linux. Many manufacturers obscure important information, such as the chipsets they use, and it's not always obvious from the XFree86 documentation which specific products work and which don't.

This chapter exists to help you get around these problems.

Board Buses

One of the basic characteristics of a video card is the motherboard bus it uses. Video cards have been designed for just about every bus used on x86 computers. Most of today's cards use the AGP bus, although a few PCI bus cards are still available.

ISA Bus

ISA bus video cards were common on 80386 and early 80486 computers, but have become quite rare since then. The reason is simple: The ISA bus lacks the capacity for high-speed transfers that are needed by modern video displays. The ISA bus is capable of a theoretical maximum transfer rate of 8MB/s. A 1024×768 display rendered at 16 bits (65,536 colors) holds 1.5MB of data, meaning that such a display can handle a maximum of only 5.3 updates per second. Although this is adequate for updating text in a word processor's window, it's not adequate for complex games, whose displays frequently change substantially in a fraction of a second.

Because most ISA video card designs are so old, most are well supported in XFree86. Therefore, if you have an old 80386 or 80486 computer on which you want to run Linux, chances are you'll have no problems with the video card. In a pinch, you should also be able to use a video card scavenged from such a computer on a more sophisticated machine.

Some ISA cards are so old that they don't support video modes higher than 640×480 at 16 colors—the *Video Graphics Adapter* (VGA) resolution. Indeed, some ISA cards only work at still lower resolutions, and some don't support color graphics at all. Such video cards are adequate for running Linux in text mode, but not in X. In theory, you can run X at 640×480 or lower resolutions, but in practice this will be a very painful experience. Many Linux utilities assume screen resolutions of 800×600 or higher. I therefore don't recommend running X at less than 800×600 unless it's absolutely necessary.

VL-Bus

Seeing the need for higher video bandwidth than was available on the ISA bus, the *Video Electronics Standards Association* (VESA) developed a bus type known as the *VESA Local Bus* (*VL-Bus* or *VLB*). VL-Bus is capable of transferring 132MB/s on a 33MHz system bus. In the example of a 1024×768, 16-bit display, this translates to 88 complete redraws per second, which is fast enough for games.

VL-Bus video cards were quite common in the 80486 era, but are now quite rare because the VL-Bus itself has been displaced by the PCI bus. If you have a VL-Bus computer, though, locating a VL-Bus video card is your best bet if you need to replace or update your video card. Because of the scarcity of VL-Bus video cards, your best bet for locating such a card is probably on the used market. You can check Web-based auction sites or used computer stores for these boards.

As with the discontinued ISA bus boards, the lack of recent developments in VL-Bus boards means that XFree86 has been able to catch up on drivers. Most VL-Bus boards are supported by mature XFree86 drivers, so you'll have few problems with most boards. Of course, it doesn't hurt to check the compatibility of any given model before buying.

PCI Bus

The 32-bit *Peripheral Component Interconnect* (PCI) bus is capable of speeds that are identical to those of the VL-Bus, and the seldom-used 64-bit PCI bus can double those speeds. The PCI bus, therefore, is quite capable of handling high frame rates in video games and other applications that require rapid screen updates.

Soon after its introduction, the PCI bus attained the status of the preferred bus for video cards. It should therefore come as no surprise that PCI video cards are quite common today, although most new computers use the more advanced AGP bus. Nonetheless, you can purchase PCI video cards with fairly advanced chipsets. You should carefully check the XFree86 compatibility of any new PCI video card you buy.

AGP Bus

The *Accelerated Graphics Port* (AGP) bus is the currently preferred bus for video cards. Electronically, AGP is an extension of PCI, but AGP cards use a connector that's positioned differently than PCI connectors. You can't accidentally insert the wrong type of card in either an AGP or a PCI slot.

AGP comes in several different speed variants, the most common of which in 2000 are 2x and 4x. Even at the seldom-used 1x speed, AGP is capable of transferring data at twice the speed of PCI, so the speed of AGP at 2x or 4x is quite stunning—352 or 704 frames of 1024×768, 16-bit video per second. In practice, there's seldom a need for this sort of speed at this resolution, but AGP provides the potential for good speed at even higher resolutions. 3D graphics can also require high data transfer rates.

Today's fastest video cards are, not surprisingly, available exclusively on the AGP bus. Many of these cutting-edge cards don't work with XFree86. That's not to say that AGP cards in general are poor choices for use in Linux. The AGP bus itself is compatible with Linux, and many low-end and mid-range AGP video cards work fine with XFree86. Even some fairly advanced models can be made to work with Linux, although you might need to use experimental drivers or switch from XFree86 to a commercial X server.

Video Chipsets

Video cards rely on their chipsets to perform most of their functions. As with most other expansion cards, you need to locate Linux drivers by chipset more than by the specific brand and model of card. This fact can make shopping for the video card difficult, because most manufacturers don't trumpet the video chipsets they use. The manufacturers often prefer to present the illusion that they've designed and built everything on the video card themselves. (In fact, some manufacturers *do* design their own video chipsets, but others rely on chipsets that any video board manufacturer can purchase and use.)

Identifying a Board's Chipset

"Determining a Device's Chipset," in Appendix A, includes a discussion of how to discover what chipset a device uses. There are a few extra tricks to identifying video chipsets, however:

- **Magazine reviews**   Magazines sometimes include information on the chipset a product uses in their product reviews. You might therefore want to check product reviews on magazines' Web sites or in their print versions.
- **The Linux /proc/pci file**   If the video card is a PCI card, you might be able to locate information in the Linux /proc/pci file, which contains information on PCI devices. This approach won't help with ISA, VL-Bus, or AGP video boards, unfortunately.

- **lspci**   The lspci command, which you might want to use in conjunction with its -v parameter, displays information on PCI and AGP devices, including any PCI or AGP video card. This report might or might not give the name of the chipset used, however; it's possible it will give only the name of the video card itself.

- **SuperProbe**   The SuperProbe program is a utility that comes with XFree86. It's designed to probe and identify your video hardware, including the video card chipset, installed RAM, and RAMDAC (the component that converts digital data in the video card's RAM to analog output for the monitor). SuperProbe usually works well, but occasionally it crashes a computer or can't identify a chipset because the chipset is newer than the version of SuperProbe. Note that, unlike most Linux commands, SuperProbe is capitalized, and includes a capital P in its name, as well.

> **TIP**
>
> You can use the Linux-based identification methods even on a computer that doesn't have Linux installed on it. To do so, you must have a Linux emergency boot floppy. A Linux installation floppy might even do the trick. Boot with the Linux emergency floppy and run the appropriate command or check the appropriate file. Consult the Linux Bootdisk HOWTO for information on creating a custom boot disk. Many distributions come with boot floppies that can be used as emergency disks.

I recommend that you try two or more identification methods, because none is guaranteed to produce accurate or useful results. If your methods all converge on the same answer, you can be confident that you've identified the chipset correctly. If not, you should try more identification methods to resolve the uncertainty.

Popular Chipsets

The number of video card chipsets produced over the years is staggering. I cannot cover all the chipset manufacturers, much less all the products from each manufacturer. I can, however, provide an overview of the products that have been popular historically and that are commonly used today. The manufacturers of these chipsets include

- **3dfx**   3dfx (http://www.3dfx.com) has gained popularity of late with its Voodoo, Velocity, and Banshee series of video card chipsets. The company makes XFree86 servers available for many of these products at http://linux.3dfx.com. Support is also being added to the standard XFree86 releases.

- **ATI**   ATI (http://www.ati.com) is one of the most popular video card manufacturers. The company also produces its own chipsets. Most ATI chipsets end up in ATI video cards, but some are used in notebook computers and motherboards with integrated video support. Most ATI chipsets are well supported in XFree86, using the XF86_SVGA server, although there are also ATI-specific servers you might want to investigate.

- **Intel**   Intel (http://www.intel.com) has begun integrating video support into some of its motherboard chipsets, such as the 810. Intel has made a Linux XFree86 server for this chipset available at http://support.intel.com/support/graphics/intel810/ linuxsoftware.htm. Support will no doubt be integrated into standard XFree86 in the future. There are also a small number of video-only Intel chipsets, but these aren't very popular, at least not in 2000.

- **Matrox**   Matrox (http://www.matrox.com), like ATI, is a major video card manufacturer that also produces its own video card chipsets. Matrox uses most of its production in its own boards. For the most part, these products are well supported in XFree86 using the XF86_SVGA server.

- **NVIDIA**   NVIDIA's (http://www.nvidia.com) products are used on a large number of third-party video cards. Fortunately, many of these products advertise the chipsets they use—GeForce 256, RIVA TNT, RIVA TNT2, Vanta, or Quadro. NVIDIA is unusual in that it's an active Linux developer. It has released Linux XFree86 servers for many of its chipsets, and is working on OpenGL support for Linux.

- **Rendition**   XFree86 currently supports some Rendition (http://www.rendition.com) chipsets in the XF86_SVGA server. In early 2000, the chipsets' acceleration features were not well supported, so these products performed poorly, compared to other chipsets. This state of affairs is likely to change in the future.

- **S3**   S3 (http://www.s3.com) has long produced a line of high-performance video products. In mid-1999, S3 purchased video card manufacturer Diamond Multimedia (http://www.diamondmm.com), so the S3/Diamond combination now looks more like ATI or Matrox in terms of vertical integration. Nonetheless, third-party manufacturers continue to use S3 chipsets in their boards. S3 products are supported by various XFree86 servers, depending upon the product.

- **SiS**   Silicon Integrated Systems (SiS; http://www.sis.com.tw) mostly manufactures motherboard chipsets, but it also makes video card chipsets, and it integrates video card functionality into some of its motherboard chipsets. XFree86 support for many of these chipsets exists in the XF86_SVGA server.

- **Trident**   Trident's (http://www.tridentmicro.com) products have not traditionally been known for the fastest performance. Trident products are mostly used in other companies' video cards. SomeTrident chipsets have been incorporated into larger chipsets;

for instance, the Trident Blade3D chipsets is built into VIA's (`http://www.via.com.tw`) MVP-4 motherboard chipsets. Most Trident chipsets are supported by the `XF86_SVGA` server.

- **Tseng Labs**   Tseng Labs was a popular manufacturer of video chipsets in years gone by, but has since gone out of business. XFree86 supports most Tseng Labs chipsets using the `XF86_SVGA` server or the `XF86_W32` server.

> **NOTE**
>
> In X parlance, the *server* is the program that handles the display of information on the screen. Therefore, the terms *X server* and *X video driver* have very similar meanings. X as a whole includes more than a server for your video card. For instance, X includes libraries, fonts, and utility programs. Therefore, it's possible for a video card manufacturer to produce an X server that integrates into the XFree86 framework; the X server in this context is essentially just an X video driver. Commercial X servers, such as Accelerated-X and Metro-X, are a bit more complete, although they also sometimes rely upon libraries and utilities provided with XFree86.

In addition, several smaller companies produce, or used to produce, video chipsets, but most of these products have very small market share.

When you research video cards and video chipsets, you're likely to run across Windows benchmark programs. Take the results from these programs with a grain of salt. They don't really measure the hardware's speed—at least, not the *raw* hardware speed. Rather, they measure the combination of the hardware speed with the driver. Because the drivers in Linux are so different from the drivers in Windows, the speed of a product under Linux might not be closely correlated to its speed under Windows. There are X benchmark utilities available, such as `xbench`, and results of `xbench` run on an assortment of hardware are available on various Web sites, such as `http://charon.astro.nwu.edu/xbench/`. I recommend exercising caution in interpreting these results, though; your subjective impression of how fast a card is might not be accurately captured by a benchmark.

Checking for XFree86 Compatibility

It can sometimes be difficult to determine whether a chipset is supported by XFree86. There is a video card and chipset support list on the XFree86 Web site, at `http://www.xfree86.org/cardlist.html`, but it's decidedly incomplete. Another good official XFree86 resource is the documentation Web page, `http://www.xfree86.org/#support`. Click the version of XFree86 you want to use. The resulting Web page includes notes on the support for various chipsets and specific boards. If you're already running a system with

Linux, you can check the list that's presented as part of the XFree86 configuration program `xf86config`, which I describe in more detail later in this chapter.

As noted earlier, some manufacturers, such as 3dfx, Intel, and NVIDIA, provide X servers for at least some of their products. It's well worth checking both the card manufacturer's and the chipset manufacturer's Web sites in search of drivers. Some manufacturers, although they don't provide support themselves, include links to relevant information elsewhere.

In the Linux community, SuSE (`http://www.suse.com`) does a lot of work with X servers. You might want to search SuSE's Web site for the latest XFree86 servers. SuSE frequently makes these servers available before they're formally incorporated into XFree86.

3D Support

Many of the latest developments in video cards today focus on 3D graphics. This term doesn't refer to the sorts of displays seen in science fiction films, in which you can walk around the display and see something from all angles. Rather, it refers to a 2D representation of a 3D object or environment. 3D-capable graphics cards enable a program to specify the basics of the 3D design—an object's shape, color, texture, and so on—and the graphics card does much of the work of determining precisely how that object appears on the screen. This sort of function is very useful for games, engineering models, and so on.

3D Graphics Features

Generating realistic 3D graphics—particularly in real-time, as needed for 3D games—requires enormous computational effort. Characteristics that must be computed include a 2D image based on the 3D object, shadows, lighting effects, texture effects, reflections, transparency effects, and haze or fog effects.

The more of these effects that a given 3D chipset supports, and the better or faster a chipset implements these effects, the more realistic the resultant images or the faster they can be moved on screen. When a video card's chipset doesn't support a given 3D effect, either the software must implement the feature or it must be done without. If it's implemented in software, the computational costs on the computer can be burdensome, and can result in a degradation to overall system performance.

Most video cards sold today support at least minimal 3D operations. If you have an older card that doesn't support 3D features, and if you want these features, you can either replace the video card with a new one or add an expansion card. Most video cards manufactured in the past decade include an expansion connector (shown in Figure 12.1). You can attach a dedicated 3D graphics card to this connector. The dedicated card then handles 3D functionality, leaving normal 2D operations to the original card.

FIGURE 12.1
A video expansion connector lets you add specialized video features to an older video card.

The OpenGL 3D Specification

3D video hardware is useless without appropriate video software. In Linux, this software is provided by an implementation of Silicon Graphics' (SGI's) OpenGL specification. OpenGL is an *application programming interface* (API) —that is, a set of programming standards—to support 3D graphics operations. Just as X provides a set of APIs for ordinary 2D graphics manipulations, OpenGL serves that function for 3D graphics.

> **NOTE**
>
> OpenGL isn't the only 3D video API. The video card manufacturer 3dfx promotes Glide, which is an extended version of OpenGL available on many platforms. Microsoft promotes its own Direct 3D API, but Direct 3D isn't available for Linux. Therefore, if you intend to use only a video card under Linux, you can ignore any claims of Direct 3D support.

OpenGL is an unusual API in that it exists across platforms. Therefore, an OpenGL application written for one OS (for example, Windows) can be ported to another OS (such as Linux) with minimal fuss. OpenGL doesn't include all the features needed for an application, though, so it's still necessary to modify code for dialog boxes, disk accesses, and so on.

Like X, OpenGL is a network-aware API. This means that you can use a 3D application on one computer and use another computer to display the first computer's data. For example, you can use a very powerful Linux computer to create 3D models of buildings, but display those models using much less powerful computers equipped with suitable 3D graphics cards. The two computers need not even run the same OS. If you're used to dealing with X in a networked environment, this concept should be familiar.

Several different OpenGL implementations for Linux exist:

- **Mesa**   This implementation, available from `http://mesa3d.sourceforge.net`, is not officially an implementation of OpenGL for Linux. It is, rather, "very similar to… OpenGL," according to the Web site's opening page. Many OpenGL programs work quite well using Mesa, and it can be an acceptable replacement for OpenGL for many users.

- **Xi Graphics' 3D Accelerated-X**   Xi Graphics (`http://www.xig.com`) has released a version of its Accelerated-X commercial X server that includes OpenGL support. This product supports a variety of 3D graphics cards and includes code licensed from SGI.

- **Metrolink OpenGL**   Another competitor in the commercial X server market for Linux, Metrolink (`http://www.metrolink.com`) offers a package that includes the Metro-X server and an OpenGL implementation. Like Xi Graphics' product, Metrolink's OpenGL uses code licensed from SGI.

Whatever form of OpenGL you use, the result is an ability to create 3D images with relatively little programming effort. Figure 12.2 shows a simple example, produced by a demo program included with Mesa. OpenGL is likely to be used by many applications in the future, as more and more serious applications find uses for 3D graphics.

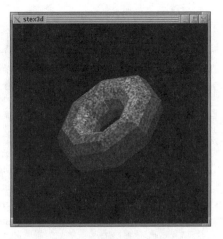

FIGURE 12.2
OpenGL lets you create 3D geometric images, animate them, and combine them with other images.

It's important to realize that OpenGL support for a video card is independent of X support for the same video card. A card might have very good 2D support in XFree86, Accelerated-X, or Metro-X, for instance, and have excellent 3D hardware, and yet have no OpenGL 3D support. Therefore, if 3D acceleration is important to you, it's vital that you check for support in both XFree86 (or a commercial X server) and your OpenGL implementation of choice.

Video RAM

In order to display an image on a monitor, a computer needs to provide a steady stream of information to the screen. Most monitors today have a *refresh rate* in the 70Hz–100Hz range at the resolutions at which the monitor is used, which means the monitor's display is completely redrawn 70–100 times per second. The video card must be able to provide a constant stream of data to the monitor. Consequently, the video card must have continuous access to the current image of the display. One of the reasons video cards exist at all is so that the video card can serve as a buffer between the computer and the monitor. Rather than deal with the logistical nightmare of providing access to a single image to both the computer's CPU and the video hardware, the video card serves as an intermediary between two banks of memory, as shown in Figure 12.3.

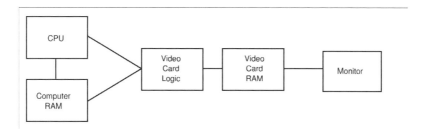

FIGURE 12.3
One of the functions of a video card is to create a pool of RAM apart from the system RAM in order to isolate the system RAM from video display–timing requirements.

This design leads to the need to consider a video card's RAM separately from the RAM used on a computer's motherboard. Using a video card with inadequate RAM can restrict the availability of high-resolution or high–color-depth video modes. Different video cards also support different types of video RAM, which vary in their speed characteristics, just as different types of motherboard RAM do.

Integrated Motherboard and Video RAM

The separation of video RAM from the motherboard's main memory store is literal for most desktop computers, which use video cards separate from the motherboard. This separation doesn't always occur, however. One of the main situations in which video and motherboard RAM are integrated is in motherboards that include video functionality on board.

When a single pool of RAM functions as both motherboard RAM and video RAM, the motherboard BIOS usually provides some means of specifying how much RAM is devoted to video functions. Typical choices today range from 2MB–16MB of RAM. If you devote, say, 4MB of RAM from 64MB total to video functions, then that 4MB will be treated as if it were separate, at least so far as the design of the chipsets involved allow. Linux will see only 60MB of main memory. Just as important, overall system performance can suffer, because access to the pooled RAM for video display purposes can slow access to RAM by the CPU.

Not all systems that include video support on the motherboard use a single pool of RAM for system and video use. Some of these designs include a dedicated area of RAM for the video functions. Such designs can provide slightly better performance than that of otherwise similar systems which use a pooled RAM area.

Types of Video RAM

As described in Chapter 3, "Memory," there are several varieties of memory available for motherboards, such as *fast page mode dynamic RAM* (FPM DRAM), *extended data out DRAM* (EDO DRAM), and *synchronous DRAM* (SDRAM). Similarly, there are several varieties of RAM that have been used over the years by video cards. The subtly different timing requirements of video hardware have led to a somewhat different stable of RAM types for video cards, however. There is some overlap between motherboard RAM types and video card RAM types, but as a general rule, the fastest video cards tend to use types of RAM that are optimized for the needs of video display hardware.

RAM types used in video cards include

- **FPM DRAM**   Many early video cards used the same FPM DRAM as was common on motherboards created at that time. Such RAM is inadequate to the demands of today's video display devices, however, and has fallen into disuse on video cards.

- **EDO DRAM**   Another RAM type that's been used on both motherboards and video cards, EDO DRAM is no longer used in most current designs.

- **VRAM**   *Video RAM* (VRAM) uses a *dual-ported* design, which means that it can be simultaneously accessed from two devices at once. This characteristic is helpful because it allows the video chipset access to the RAM at the same time the RAM is accessed by the circuitry that creates the image to be displayed on the monitor. VRAM is largely obsolete in today's video card market.

- **WRAM**   *Windows RAM* (WRAM) is a variant on the VRAM design aimed specifically at video card use. WRAM is seldom used in modern video cards.

- **MDRAM**   *Multibank DRAM* (MDRAM) is unusual in that it's built up of a large number of small components. This design allows a card to contain a peculiar amount of RAM, such as 2.5MB. If a display mode requires 2.5MB, most other RAM technologies would require that 4MB of RAM be installed on the video card to support that resolution. MDRAM was never very popular, and is rarely found on today's video cards.

- **SDRAM**   This memory technology is used on some high-performance video boards, as well as on motherboards.

- **SGRAM**   *Synchronous Graphics RAM* (SGRAM) is similar to SDRAM, but allows block writes that can speed up certain 3D graphics operations.

Other memory technologies are under development, and so this list will doubtless expand in the future. The type of memory installed in a card can have an influence on the card's performance, but memory type is not the only important factor. All things considered, the video chipset is more important, particularly under Linux, where video driver support can't be taken for granted.

Required Amounts of Video RAM

When displaying normal 2D images, the amount of video RAM required by a card is easy to compute. You can use this equation:

```
M = xres × yres × bpp / 8,388,608
```

In this equation, *xres* and *yres* are the horizontal and vertical sizes of the display (1024 and 768, for instance), and *bpp* is the number of bits per pixel (typically 8, 16, 24, or 32, for 256, 65,536, 16,777,216, or 4,294,967,296 colors, respectively). The resulting *M* value is the required RAM in megabytes. Table 12.1 presents several common combinations of display size, color depth, and the total required video RAM.

TABLE 12.1   Video RAM Requirements of Several Resolutions

Resolution	8 bpp	16 bpp	24 bpp	32 bpp
640×480	300KB	600KB	900KB	1.2MB
800×600	469KB	938KB	1.4MB	1.8MB

continues

Table 12.1 Continued

Resolution	8 bpp	16 bpp	24 bpp	32 bpp
1024×768	768KB	1.5MB	2.3MB	3.0MB
1280×1024	1.3MB	2.5MB	3.8MB	5.0MB
1600×1200	1.8MB	3.7MB	5.5MB	7.3MB

If you've examined ads for video cards, no doubt you have noticed that many of these products sport far more RAM than is required even for a huge 1600×1200 pixel display at a high color depth. Cards with 128MB are not uncommon, in fact. Why this discrepancy? The answer is 3D graphics. When handling 3D graphics, the video card takes over much of the task of *rendering* the images—that is, converting raw data such as object sizes, distances, and light sources into 2D images to be displayed on a monitor. These tasks are very computationally intensive. They also require a great deal in the way of RAM to support the computations. The video card must be able to store an assortment of information about objects' characteristics, intermediate computation results, and so on.

Some video cards can benefit from some extra RAM even when using 2D graphics. These cards can use special memory addressing modes to boost speed slightly, or might be able to store more than one screen of data at a time, which allows you to switch back and forth between screens quite quickly. Some of these functions require special support in your X server, however, and that support might not exist. One common use for extra RAM that is frequently supported is in a *virtual X desktop*. You can configure X so that it displays a desktop larger than your current video mode—for instance, 1024×768 when your monitor is running only 800×600. You can then pan the display so that you see an 800×600–sized portion of the large 1024×768 display. X can use the extra video memory to store the entire 1024×768 display, making the panning operation smoother than it would be if X had to redraw windows and other objects as you pan.

Tip

If you're not using all of your video card's memory on your current display resolution, you might be tempted to increase the bit depth to get some use from the RAM your card includes. Increasing your color depth unnecessarily slows down video display, however. Also, some programs, such as WordPerfect 8 and Netscape, have problems handling high–color-depth displays, particularly those with 24-bit modes. (32-bit sometimes causes problems, too.) For most users, a 16-bit display is quite adequate. An 8-bit display is usually inadequate, because X is far from frugal in allocating colors. An 8-bit display often runs out of colors very quickly, resulting in poor color options in some programs.

Some video cards support memory expansion, so you can buy a card with a small amount of RAM and expand that RAM at a later date. Unfortunately, RAM for such cards usually comes in proprietary formats, so it can be difficult to purchase RAM from anybody but the card's manufacturer. This results in grossly inflated prices for the RAM, even after the video card has become obsolete.

If you don't plan to make heavy use of OpenGL applications, there's little need to spend extra money on a video card that features huge amounts of RAM. 8MB will probably be plenty for any but the largest displays. If you want to use 3D graphics programs, though, you might want to get 32MB, 64MB, or even more on your video card.

XFree86

Any decision you make concerning the purchase of a video card is inextricably linked to XFree86. Although there are other X servers for Linux, XFree86 is the one that ships with all Linux distributions, and the alternatives are commercial products. Therefore, relying upon an XFree86 alternative seldom makes economic sense, because it can substantially increase the cost of Linux video support. In most cases, XFree86 is adequate.

Basic Design of XFree86

Linux's GUI environment is built up of several different layers. Many of the components that comprise each layer can be removed and replaced with equivalent components without disrupting the function of other layers of the system. Examples include

- **The X server**   The X server contains what is, in most OSs, called the *video driver*. The X server can be written for one specific video chipset or family of chipsets (such as the XF86_S3V server for S3's ViRGE series chipsets), or it can contain drivers for many unrelated chipsets (such as the XF86_SVGA server). The X server is the most important component of X when it comes to determining video hardware support.

- **X libraries**   X programs usually rely upon program *libraries*, which are routines that are potentially useful to any program of a certain type. XFree86 includes a set of libraries that are required by X programs.

- **The window manager**   A *window manager* controls the appearance of windows on the screen. Different window managers create different-looking drag bars, resizing controls, and so on. Window managers also handle the *desktop*—the background on which all windows reside. They usually include some means of launching programs from a pop-up menu. As a user, you can choose any of literally dozens of window managers for Linux. You can find out about many of the choices from http://www.plig.org/xwinman/.

- **X utilities**   XFree86 comes with a large number of small programs that help make X a usable environment. For instance, the xterm program creates a window in which a text-based Linux shell runs, as shown in Figure 12.4.

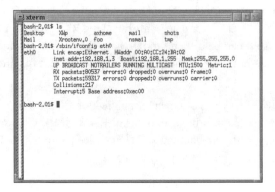

FIGURE 12.4

An xterm *window lets you type commands as if you were logged in to Linux using text mode.*

- **A Program's GUI toolkit**   Unlike the GUI environments of Windows, OS/2, and MacOS, X's GUI environment is quite sparse. Therefore, several *GUI toolkits,* or *widget sets,* have emerged. These packages provide tools for programmers to let them easily display and control features such as dialog boxes, menus, and scrollbars. Because the programmer of an application selects the GUI toolkit, this is one of the few features of the Linux GUI that you as an end user can't modify.

- **The desktop environment**   Since the late 1990s, two projects have been underway to develop complete *desktop environments* for Linux. These environments provide an integrated series of applications, including a window manager, a file manager, help utilities, xterm-like programs, and so on. The goal is to provide a single user-friendly environment with a consistent look and feel. The two projects are the *K Desktop Environment* (KDE; http://www.kde.org) and the *GNU Network Object Model Environment* (GNOME; http://www.gnome.org).

Most of these layers of software function independently of the X server and the underlying video hardware you use. You can use any GUI toolkit, window manager, or desktop environment on any video card, for instance, provided the X server supports the video card. Some of these tools make assumptions about the video hardware, however. Specifically, many X programs work best with large display sizes—at least 800×600, and occasionally 1024×768. Using a smaller screen can result in control windows that don't fit on the display. X's color allocation model works best when the system has many colors available—16-bit color depth or greater. You can use a less capable display, but you might need to use a virtual desktop that's larger than your physical screen, or suffer through poor color selections.

Locating an Appropriate Server

When you install X, or when you install a new video card in an existing system, you must select an appropriate server. In most Linux distributions, each server is shipped in a separate package. For instance, the XF86_SVGA server comes in the XFree86-SVGA-3.3.4-1.i386.rpm file in Caldera OpenLinux 2.3. This package contains only the XF86_SVGA program file and the associated man page.

The list of common video chipsets earlier in this chapter included information on the X servers that support many of these chipsets. For more specific information, you should consult the XFree86 Web page, and specifically the information at http://www.xfree86.org/#support. Here you'll find documentation for specific versions of XFree86. This documentation includes release notes for specific video card chipsets. You can find information here on what server to use for your video card.

In some cases, you might have a choice of using two different XFree86 servers. For instance, many chipsets in the S3 ViRGE family can use either the XF86_SVGA server or the XF86_S3V server. The former is a multipurpose server that works with many recent chipsets, whereas the latter is specific to the S3 ViRGE series. The more specific server is not necessarily the better one, however. The XFree86 project has been moving development away from separate servers and toward the monolithic XF86_SVGA server. This server might contain better acceleration or more features than a chipset-specific server.

As noted earlier, a few chipset manufacturers have developed XFree86 servers for their products. It's therefore worth checking the board manufacturer's and the chipset manufacturer's Web sites for such software. Also, the Linux distributor SuSE actively develops X servers for recently released products. You can find out more at http://www.suse.de/en/support/xsuse/.

Configuring XFree86 for Your Video Card

XFree86 configuration is something of a mysterious art. It sometimes proceeds smoothly, but other times results in serious hair pulling. With any luck, Linux will correctly detect and configure your card when you install the OS. If you're replacing an existing card on an already-installed Linux system, however, or if Linux didn't correctly identify your card during installation, you must configure XFree86 after installation.

> **CAUTION**
>
> If you replace a video card, be sure to configure your system *not* to start X automatically when it reboots with the new card. This task can be accomplished by editing the /etc/inittab file. Specifically, a line in this file reads something like id:5:initdefault:. The number (5, in this case) is the *runlevel*—a code indicating what set of services the system runs. On most Linux system, a runlevel of 5 corresponds to a full X startup, whereas a runlevel of 3 invokes a text-mode startup. Some Linux versions use different runlevels, though, and there are usually comments in /etc/inittab explaining the details. I recommend setting the runlevel to produce a text-mode boot when you change video cards. You can then test your new X configuration by running startx and, when you're satisfied with the results, change the runlevel back to a full GUI bootup. If you fail to make this change, it's likely that when you next start the computer, X will try to start, fail, then try to start again, fail, and so on. The result is that you won't be able to use the computer except from a network login.

There are several automated utilities available to help configure X. These utilities have names like xf86config or XF86Setup. Some of these utilities enable you to configure X by answering a series of questions in a text-mode screen, whereas others attempt to start X in a lowest-common-denominator VGA mode in order to let you use a GUI to configure X. Which utility works best for any given card is variable, so you might need to try two or more of these programs before you get a working configuration. You can check which ones are present on your system by using ls to search for appropriate filenames in the /usr/X11R6/bin directory, as in **ls /usr/X11R6/bin/*onfig***.

> **TIP**
>
> Configuring XFree86 frequently necessitates that you enter detailed specifications for your monitor. You should therefore have your monitor's manual at hand before you begin this configuration. If necessary, check your monitor manufacturer's Web site or technical support number for the horizontal and vertical refresh rates your monitor can handle.

At its heart, XFree86 configuration is handled almost exclusively through entries in a single configuration file, XF86Config. This file is generally located in the /etc or /etc/X11 directory. Like most Linux configuration files, it's plain text, and so can be edited in a text editor. The information it contains is tricky to define by hand, however, hence the configuration utilities.

As an example, you can run `xf86config` as `root` to configure X, following these steps:

1. Type **xf86config** to start the program. It displays a screenful of introductory information, to which you respond by pressing Enter.

2. The program displays several mouse protocols. Select the mouse type you're using by typing the appropriate number. For instance, 4 represents PS/2 mice.

3. Many X programs assume that a mouse has three buttons, but this isn't true of all mice. If yours has only two buttons, select **y** in response to the `Emulate3Buttons` prompt.

4. The program now prompts you for your mouse's device file. On many systems, `/dev/mouse` is a link to the appropriate file, but on others you might need to enter another filename, such as `/dev/ps2aux` for a PS/2 mouse or `/dev/ttyS0` for the first serial port.

5. Select your keyboard from the list of types, much as you selected your mouse.

6. Enter the horizontal monitor synchronization range, which is the range of horizontal frequencies your monitor can display. This information is normally printed in your monitor's manual, or you can use the associated resolution and refresh rates that `xf86config` provides. For instance, if you know your monitor can do 1280×1024 resolution at 85Hz, you can select option #10, `31.5 - 95.0`.

7. Enter the vertical synchronization range. This is similar to the horizontal synchronization range, but it's a different parameter. Enter this information from your monitor's manual.

8. When the program asks for some identification information for your monitor, enter anything you like here, so long as you don't include a quote character (`"`). This information is used only to help make the resulting `XF86Config` file more understandable to humans.

9. You can, if you like, look at a database of video cards. I recommend that you examine this database, because there's a good chance you'll find your video card in it, which can simplify configuration. When you find your card in the database, enter its number. `xf86config` presents summary information to confirm that you've entered the correct information.

10. Select the X server to use. In most cases, this will be option #5, which loads the server specified in the card definition database. You might want to choose another option to override this choice, however.

11. `xf86config` will ask whether you want it to modify the `/etc/X11/Xserver` file to point to the appropriate server file. In most cases, you want to respond **y** to this request.

12. Enter the amount of RAM installed on your card.

13. As with the monitor, `xf86config` prompts you for several strings to identify the video card.

14. For some (mostly older) cards, enter the RAMDAC used in those cards. This is the component that converts video data stored in the video card's RAM to a signal for the monitor. If you have a newer card, you can type **q** to skip this step; otherwise, you must locate and select the appropriate RAMDAC.

15. As with RAMDAC settings, the clock chip setting is something you don't need to set explicitly for most recent boards; press Enter to skip setting this value. If you've got an older board, you must track down this information.

16. `xf86config` can probe the card for clock settings. On most cards, this step is neither necessary nor recommended, so instruct the program not to do so by typing **n**. On some older cards, you should select **y** instead.

17. Set the default and other supported resolutions. Near the top of your screen you'll see a series of color depths and associated resolutions. You can set the default resolution for each color depth in turn by typing its number. When you type the number, you'll see a series of numeric codes for supported resolutions, such as *4* for 1024×768 and *5* for 1280×1024. Type a string of numbers for each video mode. For instance, typing **54** means that 1280×1024 is the default mode, but the server also supports 1024×768. Repeat this procedure for each color depth.

18. As a final security check, `xf86config` asks for confirmation that you want to overwrite the existing `XF86Config` file. If you reply **y**, then the old file will be replaced with the new one.

When you've finished writing the new `XF86Config` file, you can test the results by typing **startx** if you're running in text mode. (If you've reconfigured X while in X, you'll need to exit from X first.) With luck, X will start up without problems. If there are problems, you'll see an error message in the last few lines of text output. These error messages can be cryptic, but do point back to errors in the `XF86Config` file. One of the most common problems occurs when you specify incorrect horizontal or vertical refresh rate capabilities for your monitor. If X thinks your monitor can't handle any of your desired resolutions, X refuses to run, in order to avoid damaging your monitor. Another problem relates to the mouse device file; if it doesn't exist or points to nonexistent hardware, X will fail to run, or run with no mouse pointer available.

TIP

If your initial configuration doesn't work, I suggest you back up the `XF86Config` file and run a *different* X configuration utility. It's not uncommon for one configuration utility to succeed where another one fails. Even if both fail, you might learn enough from differing error messages and `XF86Config` file details to put together a working `XF86Config` file.

Instead of, or in addition to, running a new X configuration utility, you can edit the XF86Config file directly. As created by most configuration utilities, it's well commented, and you can find lines in it corresponding to each of the questions the xf86config configuration tool asked you. You'll also find lines containing *modelines*—detailed timing specifications for monitors. I discuss modelines in more detail in Chapter 14, "Monitors."

One modification to XF86Config that you're likely to want to make is to adjust the default color depth. X defaults to using 8-bit color, which is inadequate for most users. Near the end of the XF86Config file, you'll find one or more sections that begin with the keywords Section "Screen". Locate the one with the monitor information you entered into xf86config, and add the following line just before the first display subsection:

```
DefaultColorDepth 16
```

You can change the color depth from 16 to 24 or 32 if you like, but some programs have problems at these depths—particularly at 24. (This problem should be fixed with XFree86 4.0.)

Commercial X Servers

In most cases, XFree86 is a perfectly adequate X server for Linux users. There are, however, two commercial X servers that compete with XFree86, and there are times when one of these servers might be desirable.

Commercial X Server Options

The two commercial X servers for Linux are

- **Accelerated-X** From Xi Graphics (http://www.xig.com), this server is regarded as one of the fastest X servers available for many video cards. Xi Graphics adds support for new video cards somewhat faster than does the XFree86 team. A version of Accelerated-X that supports the OpenGL 3D API is also available. One unusual characteristic of Accelerated-X is that it allows programs to run at bit depths that don't match the screen's actual setting. For instance, Accelerated-X can tell a program that works best at 16 bpp that it's running at that depth when the screen is actually set to 24 bpp or 32 bpp.

- **Metro-X** This server, from MetroLink (http://www.metrolink.com), is generally not as fast as Accelerated-X. This server is distinguished by its support for touch screens, multi-screen configurations, and 3D input devices.

You can find more information about both these servers, including their supported video cards, on their respective Web sites. A demo version of Accelerated-X is available, so you can test it out on your hardware if you'd like to assess its suitability for your system.

Both Accelerated-X and Metro-X include GUI-based setup utilities that can help you to configure your system. Neither uses the same `XF86Config` file as does XFree86, so you can safely install and configure these servers without backing up your existing `XF86Config` file. You might need to adjust other files, however, if you try one of these commercial servers and then switch back to XFree86. For instance, some installations use a symbolic link from `/usr/X11R6/bin/X` to the actual X server in use, so you might need to change this to point to the correct server. Other installations create an entry in a configuration file, such as `/etc/X11/Xserver`, to point X to the appropriate server file.

When to Consider a Commercial Server

Most users have no need of a commercial X server. Even if you have a video card that's supported by Metro-X or Accelerated-X but not by XFree86, the cost of the commercial server might not be much less than the cost of a new video card, unless the card is very expensive. Nonetheless, under some circumstances it might make sense to buy a commercial X server:

- You need support for some feature, such as touch panel displays, that's not supported by XFree86 but that is supported by one of the commercial X servers.

- You do serious OpenGL work and find Mesa to be inadequate. Because both Xi Graphics' and MetroLink's OpenGL implementations ship with their X servers, you might as well use the commercial X server for maximum compatibility between the X server and OpenGL.

- You have an expensive video card that's not supported by XFree86, or which produces poor performance under XFree86. Of course, this reason is valid only if a commercial server supports your card better than XFree86 does.

Summary

Video card selection and configuration under Linux can be quite tricky. Information on XFree86 compatibility with various video cards and chipsets is available, but can be difficult to track down. Even identifying what chipset a board uses can be difficult, because manufacturers sometimes try to hide this information from their customers. Because the video card market changes so rapidly, XFree86 lags behind the latest developments in high-end video gear. When you have a video card, configuration can be tedious if your Linux installation doesn't handle the card properly.

Fortunately, although the video card market is a tedious one for the Linux user to navigate, most video cards *are* supported under Linux. The main trick is in tracking down the necessary information, and a few key Web sites are extremely useful in doing so.

Video Capture and AV Input Hardware

IN THIS CHAPTER

As the relevant technologies have progressed, the capabilities of computers have increased with respect to input and output of data directly understandable by humans. In 1980, the best computer printers for text mimicked the operation of typewriters and could not print graphics, whereas graphics-capable printers did a poor job rendering text. Today's laser and inkjet printers put the best printers of 1980 to shame in rendering both text and graphics. In other realms, input devices exist today that simply did not exist in 1980. This chapter is devoted to such input devices: digital cameras and video input devices. With these tools, you can use your Linux computer as a television, photo lab, and more.

> **NOTE**
>
> In some sense, another type of device deserves to be discussed along with digital cameras and video input: scanners. Scanners are complex enough, however, that I've given them their own chapter: Chapter 19, "Scanners."

More so than in most areas, Linux's support for digital imaging technology is crude. As a general rule, the best of the drivers are quite capable, but the best applications are still rough around the edges. Some application areas, such as videoconferencing, still lack much in the way of usable programs. This scarcity of applications will no doubt evaporate in the months and years to come, and even today Linux can be used for many image capture functions, as I describe in the following sections.

Types of Video Capture Hardware

The hardware I discuss in this chapter can be classified into two types:

- **Cameras**   You point a camera at a real-world object to obtain an image of that object. The image might be still or moving, depending upon the camera type.

- **Video capture**   Video capture devices allow you to view, capture, and digitally manipulate information from an external video source, such as a VCR or cable TV line.

The line between these devices can sometimes become rather blurred. For instance, it's possible to hook a video camera up to a video capture device and use the resulting combination much as you would a camera that interfaces more directly to the computer. Nonetheless, these devices have unique characteristics that make the distinction worth making, at least at the moment. The technology in this area is changing rapidly, so this distinction might become meaningless in a few years.

Cameras

Most people are familiar with cameras that have little or nothing to do with computers. From the disposable cameras found in supermarket checkout lines to professional gear costing thousands of dollars, cameras are everywhere. The migration of cameras to computers has produced two principal types: portable digital cameras that resemble their non-computer counterparts and cameras that are permanently tethered to the computer and can be thought of as an eye for the computer. This latter type of camera is generally known as a *WebCam*, because it's frequently used in conjunction with Internet applications, say to display the contents of a room on a Web page, updated at regular intervals.

> **NOTE**
>
> These two types of camera are largely distinct today, but there's some overlap. For instance, Creative Labs (`http://www.creative.com`) markets a model that converts between portable and WebCam functions.

Portable Digital Cameras

Portable digital cameras frequently resemble small 35mm cameras, as shown in Figure 13.1. Some models have more novel shapes, however. Rather than film, portable cameras use a light-sensitive device that converts light into electrical impulses, which the camera's circuitry can then store in some common graphics file format, such as JPEG or TIFF. You can then transfer the images to your computer via a serial or USB cable or by using a reader for the media used by the camera.

Portable digital cameras are marketed as complete or partial replacements for conventional film cameras. They frequently include the same sorts of features as film cameras, and these features should be evaluated much as you would evaluate the equivalent features in film cameras. They also possess features that are meaningless in reference to film cameras. Examples of both types of features include

- **Optical quality**   The lens used in a camera is a large part of what determines the picture quality. There's no simple rating scale for lenses, although consumer and computer magazines sometimes perform optical tests of digital cameras.
- **Zoom range**   Low-cost cameras usually don't include any zoom feature, but mid-range and high-end models usually have a lens that zooms. The wider the range, the more flexible the camera. On the downside, wide zoom ranges often distort images somewhat, particularly at the extreme ends of the zoom. A lens's magnification is measured by its

focal length, which is a number expressed in millimeters (mm), as in 55mm. The size of the image you see in a final photograph depends on both the lens's focal length and the size of the film or digital imaging plate inside the camera. Because a digital camera's imaging plate need not be the same size as a frame in a roll of 35mm film, a 35mm camera's zoom range isn't directly comparable to the zoom range of a digital camera. Indeed, even two digital cameras' zoom ranges might not be directly comparable. Most digital camera manufacturers, however, advertise a *35mm equivalent zoom range*, which is the zoom range of a 35mm camera that would produce the same image sizes as the digital camera does.

FIGURE 13.1

A portable digital camera resembles a conventional camera at first glance, but differs substantially internally.

NOTE

Many digital cameras include a *digital zoom* feature, in which the camera crops the image and then uses interpolation features to increase its size. Digital zoom produces a blurrier picture than does optical zoom, and so should not be considered a substitute for a true optical zoom, in which the lens changes the size of the image projected on the imaging plate.

- **Focus method**   Low-cost cameras use a *fixed focus* lens, which is permanently focused on a point that is a set distance from the camera. These cameras rely upon an optical characteristic known as *depth of field* to keep objects at greater and lesser distances than the fixed focus point in reasonably sharp focus. An *autofocus* camera, on the other hand, includes sensors that enable it to shift its focus to whatever object is in the viewfinder. Some cameras offer an override to this mode, or provide *manual focus*, in which you focus the camera by adjusting a control. Cameras with manual or autofocus differ in how closely they can focus upon an object.

- **Light sensitivity**   Film lightsensitivity is measured on a scale originally developed by the American Standards Association (ASA) but subsequently adopted by the International Standards Organization (ISO). Common film speeds for consumer film today are in the 100–400 ISO range, although both more- and less-sensitive films are available. Measuring a digital camera's light sensitivity is tricky because the characteristics of digital cameras are different from those of film. Nonetheless, manufacturers make the attempt. In 2000, most digital cameras have ISO equivalent ratings in the 100–200 range, although some are more sensitive than this. Most digital cameras have fixed ISO ratings, but a few can be adjusted to be more sensitive, at the cost of lower image quality.

- **Apertures**   Most cameras use a device known as an *aperture* to cut down the amount of light reaching the film or imaging device. Doing this is necessary in very bright light, to prevent overexposure. The range of apertures varies from one camera to another, and is measured in *f-stops*, as in f/4.5–f/16. The smaller the number the more light is admitted to the camera, so all other things being equal, you want an f-stop range that includes the smallest value possible.

- **Media type**   Most digital cameras use one of two media types: *Compact Flash* (CF) cards or *SmartMedia* cards. Both are small in size (Figure 13.2 shows a CF card next to a roll of 35mm film for scale) and can store up to tens of megabytes of data—enough for dozens or hundreds of photos at the resolutions used by most digital cameras. Both CF and SmartMedia cards are expensive, unfortunately. In early 2000, prices hovered around $2—4 per megabyte.

- **Resolution**   Digital camera resolution is often expressed in *megapixels*, or millions of pixels. For instance, a camera capable of recording 1280×960 images stores 1,228,800 pixels, or 1.2 megapixels. Digital cameras today range from 0.3 megapixels (640×480) to 2 megapixels or more (1600×1200 or larger). As a rule of thumb, if you expect to print your photos, you should purchase a camera capable of at least 1 megapixel resolution. Smaller resolutions might be acceptable for Web page images and other less-demanding applications.

- **Interface**   I describe interfaces in more detail later in this chapter. In general, a USB interface is preferred over a conventional serial interface, because the USB interface is faster. Using a PC card or SmartMedia adapter might be an even better way to retrieve images from your camera.

FIGURE 13.2

A CF card (right) can potentially hold more than a hundred images, and yet is smaller than a 36-exposure roll of 35mm film (left).

In 2000, digital camera technology is roughly equivalent in quality to 35mm cameras for most purposes, but only if you buy at the high end of the digital range. The more affordable mid-range and low-end digital cameras are acceptable for very casual use, but you can't produce high-quality printed enlargements from the images they produce. For specific tasks, of course, digital or film could have an edge. For instance, if you need to photograph objects in low light, film is usually superior. If you need to be able to take a picture and manipulate it on a computer within seconds, digital is the only way to go.

Linux includes support for many, but not all, digital cameras. I describe the software in more detail later in this chapter, but you might want to check the camera compatibility list maintained at http://www.gphoto.org for advice on what specific models work well with Linux, and via what interfaces.

NOTE

I took most of the photos in this book using the Kodak DC-240 digital camera, shown in Figure 13.1, and used the gPhoto software (described later in this chapter) to transfer the images to disk. Of course, black-and-white printed reproduction doesn't do this camera's images justice.

WebCams

Cameras that don't store their images, but rather transfer them directly to the computer, are frequently used for displaying real-time images on Web pages. For this reason, such cameras are often referred to as WebCams. Figure 13.3 shows a typical example, positioned next to a roll of 35mm film for scale. These devices are usually quite small and are designed to rest atop your computer or monitor, where they can capture your visage head-on as you use your computer. They vary substantially in shape and size, but they usually include some way to pivot their lenses up and down. They seldom incorporate much in the way of controls; usually just a status LED, one or two buttons, and a focus control.

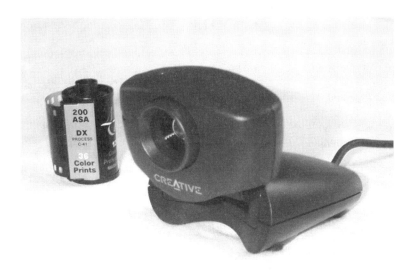

13

VIDEO CAPTURE
AND AV INPUT
HARDWARE

FIGURE 13.3

A WebCam is small and simple, and produces poor images compared to portable digital cameras.

WebCams can be evaluated by most of the same criteria I laid out for portable digital cameras; however, these devices are usually quite inexpensive and limited compared to their portable camera counterparts. For instance, most WebCams produce only 640×480 images, and they generally use crude manual focus mechanisms, such as a rotating ring around the lens. Because you probably intend to use a WebCam for rather limited purposes, these devices' limitations with respect to image quality are not extraordinarily important.

If you intend to use a WebCam for composing video email, creating audio/visual presentations, or similar functions, you must also have a sound card and microphone. I discuss these components in Chapters 10, "Sound Cards," and 11, "Audio Input/Output."

The software used to interface with a WebCam is different from that used to extract pictures from a portable digital camera. Under Linux, you use software developed for the Video for Linux interfaces (`http://roadrunner.swansea.linux.org.uk/v4l.shtml`) to access a WebCam. The Video for Linux interfaces are included in the Linux kernel. Software ranges from programs to grab individual "snapshots" to TV viewers (which can be used for live video image viewing and extraction from WebCams) to security camera applications.

Radio and TV Tuners

An alternative to cameras for video input comes in the form of audio/video input boards. These products usually include a TV tuner; the capacity to process raw video from a VCR, camcorder, or other device; and often an AM/FM radio tuner. These products vary along many of the same dimensions as do ordinary TVs and VCRs, such as

- **Number of channels**   Some tuners can handle more channels than others can, which is an important consideration if you want to capture video from a cable TV station with a high number.

- **Stereo**   Low-cost products process only mono sound, whereas more expensive products decode stereo sound.

- **Video inputs**   Some products accept only a coaxial cable input, which enables connection to cable TV systems or a VCR's antenna output. Others include RCA jacks or S-video inputs, for processing higher-quality signals. A well-outfitted card sports quite a wide array of input and output jacks, as shown in Figure 13.4.

- **Video signals**   Broadcast TV signals in North America follow the National Television Standards Committee (NTSC) convention, but signals in Europe and elsewhere follow the Phase Alternating Line (PAL) or Sequential Color and Memory (SECAM) standards. Some video decoder cards can handle all three standards, but others are more limited. Similarly, a few cards can receive AM or FM radio broadcasts, but others can't.

> **NOTE**
>
> Radio-only cards also exist. Oddly enough, these devices use the Video for Linux drivers and interfaces, although they aren't video devices at all. From a Linux driver and applications point of view, you can treat them as if they were TV cards, except that they produce no video image.

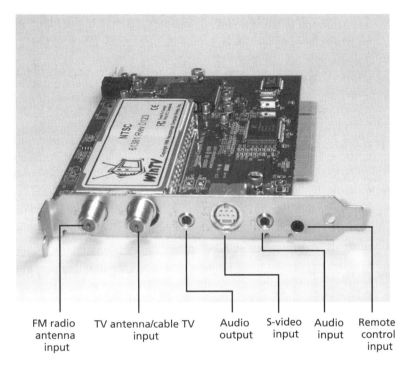

FM radio antenna input   TV antenna/cable TV input   Audio output   S-video input   Audio input   Remote control input

FIGURE 13.4

A video input card contains input jacks similar to those on a TV or VCR.

Products also vary in ways that don't correspond to features on conventional TVs or VCRs, such as

- **Interface method**   Most products use the PCI or ISA busses, but a few are external to the computer and interface via the USB port. Some internal products require the use of a video card's expansion connector, but others don't.

- **Resolutions**   Conventional NTSC, PAL, and SECAM broadcasts don't use precise digital resolutions. The video decoder products must therefore convert to a conventional computer resolution. The range of supported target resolutions varies from one product to another. Beyond 640×480 or thereabouts, however, little or nothing is gained in picture quality; only image size increases at higher resolutions.

TV tuners and video input devices rely upon the Video for Linux device drivers included with the kernel, and upon specialized TV viewing and video extraction tools described later in this chapter. Because these devices require such specialized drivers, it's critical that you check for compatibility of any given devices. The Linux kernel configuration utilities provide you with a list of video tuner chipsets that are supported, but you must locate manufacturers that use these devices. The Video for Linux Web site (`http://roadrunner.swansea.linux.org.uk/v4l.shtml`) includes pointers to some specific products, particularly those that use the popular BTTV driver (`http://www.metzlerbros.de/bttv.html`), which works very well for most people.

Video Interfaces

Video acquisition products use a number of interfaces, depending upon the device type and the design of the particular product. TV products generally use expansion cards, but sometimes use USB. Cameras use serial, parallel, or USB ports, or you can read files by exchanging media between the camera and your computer. Each of these interfaces has its unique benefits and problems.

Expansion Boards

Dedicated ISA or PCI expansion boards are used by TV products, but not by cameras. This design is generally best for handling real-time full-motion video. Consider a 640×480 NTSC video signal, sampled at 16-bit color depth. NTSC uses a 60Hz refresh rate, but that signal is *interlaced*, meaning that only half the picture is sent at a time; it takes two cycles to complete an image, for a total frame rate of 30 frames per second (fps). These figures combine for a total data transfer rate of 17.6MB/s. This value requires the speeds of an internal bus. In fact, even the ISA bus has only an 8MB/s maximum transfer rate, and so is theoretically incapable of handling real-time NTSC video. In practice, data compression or a reduced frame rate enables ISA TV cards to function, although PCI cards with their 132MB/s transfer rate are far better suited to the task.

If you want to use your computer to watch TV or acquire and edit video footage, I strongly recommend you purchase a PCI card for the task. Because PCI is more than capable of handling the bandwidth requirements, you won't have problems with choppy video or reduced quality as a result of your choice of video capture device. (Your other hardware components, such as your hard disk, must still be up to the task, of course, especially if want to save your videos to disk.)

USB Ports

Universal Serial Bus (USB) ports are an increasingly common interface choice for all varieties of video acquisition devices. In fact, all three video devices I discuss in this chapter—portable digital cameras, WebCams, and TV tuners—are available with USB interfaces. The suitability of these interfaces for each device type varies, however. As a general rule, USB makes an excellent interface for portable digital cameras, a good interface for WebCams, and a poor interface for TV video acquisition devices. The reason has to do with bandwidth. As I've just described, acquiring 30 fps video signals requires a great deal of bandwidth—17.6MB/s, in theory, although compression can reduce this value substantially. USB is only capable of a maximum speed of 1.5MB/s, however. Even with compression, therefore, you're unlikely to achieve more than 10–15 fps via a USB port.

A 10–15 fps rate can be acceptable for the sorts of video capture for which a WebCam is used, so the comparatively low data transfer rate of USB isn't such a hindrance to WebCams. When used to grab individual frames, the speed of USB is quite acceptable. In fact, USB is much faster than a conventional serial port and almost as fast as a parallel port. Therefore, USB is about the best external interface in common use, which makes it an excellent choice for interfacing to portable digital cameras, which are used to capture still images.

Linux's USB support is next to nonexistent in the 2.2.x kernel series, but the kernel developers have been busy writing USB drivers for the 2.3.x development kernel series, which will eventually be finalized in the 2.4.x kernels. Support for USB cameras—both portable digital cameras and many WebCams—is quite usable, even in the 2.3.x series kernels available in early 2000. You should check that drivers for your specific cameras exist, however, because not all devices are supported. Kernel support for USB TV acquisition cards is much rarer, which is another reason I recommend avoiding such products.

13

VIDEO CAPTURE
AND AV INPUT
HARDWARE

> **TIP**
>
> If you want to use a 2.2.x kernel and a USB device, you can patch your 2.2.x kernel source to include more recent USB support. Appropriate patch files are available from `http://www.linux-usb.org`. To find the latest development or stable kernels, check `http://www.kernel.org` or any major Linux FTP site.

> **NOTE**
>
> In the future, FireWire is likely to become a viable interface for all forms of video devices. Capable of up to 40MB/s—and likely higher in the future—FireWire is more than adequate for video transfer. At present, unfortunately, FireWire devices are rare, and Linux FireWire support is embryonic. In theory, SCSI could be used by external video capture devices, but SCSI is a rare interface for video devices.

Parallel Ports

Of the devices described in this chapter, only WebCams commonly use the parallel port. In theory, the best parallel ports can handle 2MB/s transfers, which is slightly better than USB's 1.5MB/s. The parallel port was, however, never intended for high-speed two-way communications, so you're less likely to achieve 2MB/s transfer speed via a parallel port than you are 1.5MB/s speed with USB. In addition, sharing a single parallel port between a camera and a printer can cause problems because the signals conflict. Adding an external removable disk drive, scanner, or other device to the mix only makes matters worse. USB, by contrast, was designed from the outset to handle multiple devices on a single port, and so is better able to handle the demands of several external devices.

If you're using the 2.2.x series Linux kernel, support for external parallel port cameras is better than for USB cameras. With the improvements in USB support in the 2.3.x development kernels, however, USB becomes a more viable option for WebCams in Linux. I therefore recommend using USB for most new purchases. Linux does support many parallel port cameras, however, so if you have one or if you prefer to avoid USB devices, a parallel port camera can be a viable choice. Be sure to check for compatibility of your specific camera, however, because not all parallel port cameras are supported.

Serial Ports

Among the devices discussed in this chapter, only portable digital cameras use the serial port. In fact, the Linux software used for transferring images from digital cameras (gPhoto, http://www.gphoto.org) works in precisely the same way for ordinary serial ports and USB ports.

The advantage of an ordinary serial port over a USB port is that the support for serial ports in Linux is much more mature than is support for USB ports. You're therefore less likely to run into problems with a conventional serial port. This is particularly true if you're using a 2.2.x kernel, in which USB support is virtually nonexistent. If you're using a 2.3.x development kernel, or a 2.4.x kernel after it's released, USB offers a major advantage over ordinary serial ports: speed. USB can transfer 1.5MB/s, but conventional serial ports are limited to 115,200 bps (or about 0.014MB/s). In practice, the speed difference isn't quite that great, but it's still substantial. Transferring photos from a digital camera via serial ports takes about half a minute per image, depending upon the camera, the resolution, and other factors. Performing the same transfer via USB takes only about 4 seconds per image.

Card Readers

Various devices exist to read the CF or SmartMedia devices used in digital cameras. Some of these are USB card readers, which in theory can work much like USB removable media drives in Linux (see Chapter 6, "Removable Disks"). Another option is to use a PC Card reader, such as exists on most laptop computers. A PC Card reader can also be added as an IDE device to desktop computers, in conjunction with an adapter card (see Figure 13.5). The CF or SmartMedia card slides into the PC Card adapter, and then the adapter and its payload slides into the PC Card reader. The resulting combination device can usually be mounted as an IDE drive. For instance, if you try this with a laptop, you'll probably see the CF card as /dev/hde, assuming you have the appropriate drivers installed. I describe PC Cards in more detail in Chapter 23, "Notebooks."

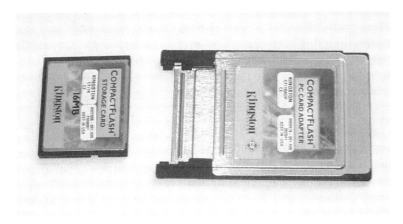

FIGURE 13.5

A PC Card adapter lets you mount a CF or SmartMedia card as if it were a removable disk.

CAUTION

CF and SmartMedia are electronically compatible, but are different sizes. Therefore, you need different adapters for each type. A CF adapter won't do you any good if you have a SmartMedia card. Some CF and SmartMedia cards ship with the adapters; for instance, the CF card and adapter shown in Figure 13.5 were sold in a single package.

Digital cameras use the FAT filesystem, so you can mount these devices with Linux's FAT filesystem drivers (types msdos, umsdos, or vfat, as you see fit). Details vary from one camera to another, but images are generally stored in one subdirectory, and the camera stores information for its own use in another. Most cameras use the JPEG format for their images, but a few use other formats (TIFF, for instance). These formats are almost always in common use and can be read directly by Linux graphics packages, such as the GIMP (http://www.gimp.org).

If you have a notebook computer or a PC Card reader on your desktop, transferring images via an adapter can be the quickest way to get the job done. This is particularly true if your camera supports only conventional serial interfaces, not USB. In this case, even a USB CF or SmartMedia reader can provide a substantial speed improvement over using gPhoto and a serial port. gPhoto, however, offers thumbnail views and other image manipulation tools that you might find helpful, as described later in this chapter.

Necessary Kernel Drivers

The kernel drivers that are required to use cameras and video input hardware are quite varied. As a general rule, you need both low-level drivers for your particular hardware or port and Video for Linux drivers. Sometimes the low-level drivers reside in the Video for Linux configuration area, however, and sometimes you don't need the Video for Linux drivers at all. You don't need these drivers to access a digital camera using gPhoto, for instance.

Some of the drivers you might need include

- **Video for Linux options**   The Video for Linux drivers are in a subsection of the Linux kernel configuration off the *Character devices* option set. Figure 13.6 shows the relevant window in a 2.3.43 kernel. If you're using a 2.2.x kernel, you'll see fewer devices, and if you're using a more recent kernel, you might see more devices. You should select Y or M to the main Video for Linux option, and then select Y or M for your video device. If you have more than one device, you can select them both and use them both, as described later. Even if your device is a USB device without a specific driver in this area, you must enable the main Video for Linux option.

- **I2C support**   In 2.3.x and later kernels, you might need to activate basic I2C support. This support, and various sub-options, are available from the Character devices option list. I2C is a bus developed to link video-related chips, so it's used internally by many video devices.

- **USB support**   If your video device uses a USB interface, you must activate appropriate USB support. I describe these options in more detail in Chapter 16, "Parallel and Serial Ports."

- **Parallel and serial support**   For parallel or serial devices, you should activate appropriate kernel options, as described in Chapter 16, "Parallel and Serial Ports."

FIGURE 13.6

The Video for Linux subsystem includes drivers for many devices.

After you've compiled your kernel, you might need to create appropriate device files for your video devices. This step isn't normally necessary if you're using a digital camera via the serial port, but it is for most other devices. Possible devices include

- **USB digital camera** If you've got a USB digital camera, you should create a digital camera device file. Consult the documentation for your digital camera driver for details on what device major and minor numbers to use, because these details have changed during the development of the USB drivers, and might change again.

- **TV card or WebCam** Most Video for Linux devices use the `/dev/video` device file, which has a device major number of 81 and a minor number of 0. If you have multiple devices, create multiple files (such as `/dev/video0` and `/dev/video1`), and increment the minor number for each additional device. Some Linux distributions ship with these devices predefined.

Note that there's no USB device file *per se*; instead, USB devices take over device files that are ordinarily used by other systems, or acquire entirely unique device files. Future USB video devices might conceivably require device files other than those I've outlined here, although anything that works through the Video for Linux framework is likely to use `/dev/video*`.

13

**VIDEO CAPTURE
AND AV INPUT
HARDWARE**

Supporting Applications and Utilities

Hooking your video devices to your Linux computer and compiling the kernel can occupy you for a few minutes, but chances are you want to *use* your video hardware in Linux. To do so, you need to use Linux video applications. You can find links to many such applications on the Video for Linux Web site (`http://roadrunner.swansea.linux.org.uk/v4l.shtml`) and the Video for Linux Resources Web page (`http://www.exploits.org/v4l/`). Current Video for Linux applications range from extremely crude to reasonably sophisticated.

Capturing Still Images

One of the simplest imaging tasks is that of recording a still image. There are two classes of programs for doing this: those that download images that have already been captured by portable digital cameras and those that capture an image from a WebCam or video capture card.

Using gPhoto with a Digital Camera

gPhoto (`http://www.gphoto.org`) is the most advanced Linux tool for interfacing to a portable digital camera. This program, which is shown in Figure 13.7, is still in beta test in early 2000, but is nonetheless usable, even with USB-interfaced cameras.

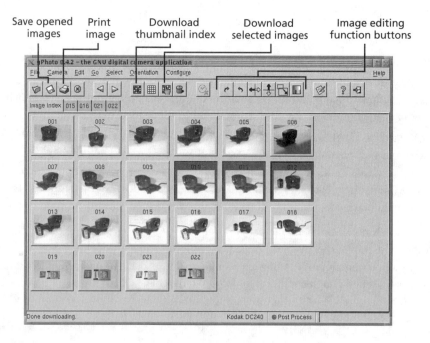

FIGURE 13.7

gPhoto can acquire thumbnail images from a digital camera, allowing you to select which images you want to download.

When you first start gPhoto, it asks for configuration information—namely, you must tell it what model camera you have and what device you're using. The program has no problems with USB devices, but provides no default USB device filename. If you use a USB camera, you must type its device filename by hand.

> **CAUTION**
>
> If you intend to use the USB interface, don't start gPhoto before you've created an appropriate USB device file. You should also connect your camera, turn it on, and set it to its computer connect mode before starting gPhoto, so that gPhoto can find the camera.

After gPhoto is configured and running, you can click the Download thumbnail index icon to acquire thumbnail images of all the photos stored in the camera, as shown in Figure 13.7. You can then select specific images and click Download selected images to download the files. Each picture has its own tab in the main window. You can click a tab to view the image at full resolution. You can then perform certain transformations on these images, such as rotating them, flipping them, or adjusting their brightness, contrast, and color values, as shown in Figure 13.8. When you're done, you can save one or all images by clicking the Save open image(s) button. You can also print an image by clicking the Print image button.

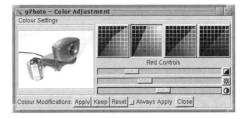

FIGURE 13.8
Image editing features let you adjust images that have incorrect color balance or exposure.

If you want to perform more extensive image editing, you can import the files downloaded by gPhoto into an image editing package, such as the GIMP (http://www.gimp.org). The GIMP offers very sophisticated tools for image manipulation, including everything offered by gPhoto plus much more. For more information on the GIMP, consult the program's Web site or a book such as Pruitt & Pruitt's *Sams Teach Yourself the Gimp in 24 Hours*, from Sams Publishing.

Grabbing Stills in Real Time with Video for Linux

One of the simplest ways to acquire still images from a WebCam is to use a program such as w3cam (`http://www.hdk-berlin.de/~rasca/w3cam/`). This program comes as source code and should compile smoothly on most systems. When compiled, the program `vidcat` is the one of interest. This program takes input from the `/dev/video0` device (or another device you specify via the `-d` parameter) and sends it to standard output—the command line, by default.

> **CAUTION**
>
> `vidcat` is designed to let you easily pipe its output to other programs, hence the default output to standard output. If you want to create a file from `vidcat`'s output, you must use output redirection (>) to redirect output, as in **`vidcat > image.jpg`**. If you fail to do this, `vidcat` fills your screen or `xterm` with gibberish.

A few parameters are particularly useful when used with `vidcat`, including

- **-s** Sets the size of the output image. The default is 320×240, but many video devices support 640×480 or even higher.
- **-f** Sets the output format—ppm, jpeg, or png.
- **-i** Sets the input channel—tv, comp1, comp2, or s-video. This option is only useful when `vidcat` is used in conjunction with a TV tuner card.
- **-q** Defines JPEG quality. The minimum, maximum, and default settings are 1, 100, and 80, respectively.
- **-d** Sets the input device, which defaults to `/dev/video`.

As an example, here's the command to create a 640×480 PNG file from `/dev/video1`:

```
vidcat -s 640x480 -f png -d /dev/video1 > image.png
```

`vidcat` is particularly useful if you want to perform an automated image scan—for instance, to take a picture every five minutes to place on a Web page, or to create time-lapse photography of a plant growing or some such. You can call `vidcat` from a cron job and forget about it unless and until you need to deal with the resulting images.

In some cases, you might want to use a more GUI-oriented program to capture images. In such a case, consider using a TV viewer. Such programs can work with WebCams, not just with TV cards, so that you can use such a program to take a snapshot of yourself at your computer, if you like. You need only locate an option to capture an image, which most such programs include.

Listening to Radio and Watching TV

Several radio and TV applications exist that support listening to, watching, and recording videos from these media. Examples include

- **XawTV**   This program, available from `http://me.in-berlin.de/~kraxel/xawtv.html`, is actually a small suite of applications, all of which can be accessed from the main program. The XawTV package includes a radio tuner for use on cards that include radio tuners, or on radio-only cards.

- **kWinTV**   This TV viewing application, available from `http://www.mathematik.uni-kl.de/~wenk/kwintv/index.html` and shown in action in Figure 13.9, is designed to integrate well into the KDE suite.

13

FIGURE 13.9
kWinTV and similar TV applications for Linux let you view and record TV broadcasts and videotapes under Linux.

Recording Sound and Live Video

XawTV and kWinTV both enable you to create an `.avi` file of a TV broadcast (or the images coming over a WebCam). You must choose an appropriate video recording command, and then set various options relating to frame rates, image size, and so on. As a general rule, XawTV does a better job recording video information than does kWinTV; the latter drops many more frames, especially on systems with low CPU power. For instance, in tests on a system with a Cyrix MII 333 (running at 266MHz), kWinTV dropped most frames, but XawTV captured most frames.

Another option for live video capture is to use a command-line tool. This option might be appealing if you want to use your computer as you might a VCR, to record a broadcast for playback at a later date or time. One such program is Vstream (`http://www.ee.up.ac.za/~justin/bttv/`). This program lets you record a stream of video to disk without an intervening GUI program. As such, it's more difficult to use than XawTV or some other TV-viewing utility, but it can produce superior results, and can be more convenient if you want to create an automated script or schedule a recording using Linux's cron facility.

> **Caution**
>
> Recording full-motion video consumes disk space at an alarming rate. Recall the calculations earlier, that TV video requires 17.6MB/s bandwidth. Recorded raw and without compression, that's the amount of disk space required—and the required speed of your hard disk. Many video recording programs can dynamically apply compression, which reduces the disk space and disk speed requirements, but increases the CPU speed requirements. You can also try reducing the frame rate or video image size to achieve better success recording video data.

Summary

Video and image capture hardware is a fast-growing field, spurred on by developments such as improving image capture technologies, increasing speed of Internet access, and a blurring of the line between computers and traditional home entertainment systems such as TVs and stereos. It's possible today to use your Linux computer as a photo editing and print station, a television, a security camera, and more. Linux drivers for the relevant hardware range from quite stable to experimental, but the overall state of drivers is good—if you stick to supported devices. Supporting software is less mature overall, but is likely to improve substantially as time goes on.

Monitors

IN THIS CHAPTER

Without monitors, most computers are next to useless. There are rare circumstances in which monitors aren't required. For instance, servers can run without monitors, although they're normally needed during installation; and blind individuals frequently use speech synthesis devices or Braille equivalents to monitors. For most people and purposes, though, a monitor is a necessity when using a computer. The monitor is also one of the components with which you interact most directly. A poor choice of monitor can lead to eye strain and headaches, so it's critical that your monitor be of high quality, particularly if you use it for more than an hour or two daily.

For the most part, your choice of monitor is independent of your OS. The characteristics that make for a good monitor in Windows or MacOS also make the monitor a good choice in Linux. You therefore don't need to apply any special Linux criteria in your selection of a monitor. Linux video configuration, however, requires that you know more about your monitor than you do to configure the monitor in Windows. I therefore include a section at the end of this chapter detailing how to obtain an optimal display from your monitor in Linux.

Monitor Technologies

There are two main technologies in common use today for monitors: *cathode ray tubes* (CRTs) and *liquid crystal displays* (LCDs). These technologies are radically different from one another, and you should understand these differences before making a purchase decision.

Cathode Ray Tubes

The principles at work in a CRT monitor are the same as those used in televisions since the 1940s, although modern computer monitors are substantially more sophisticated than the TVs of yesteryear, or even modern analog TVs. Today, CRT monitors for computers are most often found on desktop computer systems. CRTs are simply too large and heavy for use in portable computers.

Basic CRT Design

A CRT monitor's most prominent feature is the picture tube. At the back of the monitor is a component called the *electron gun* that fires electrons toward the glass screen at the front of the monitor (see Figure 14.1). This beam sweeps along the screen from left to right in a tiny fraction of a second—roughly 0.00002s, depending upon the display's resolution. The beam then turns off and begins again at a slightly lower point to paint the next line of the display, and so on. Once the monitor's displayed an entire image (which typically takes 0.01–0.02s), the beam shuts off and the process begins again from the top of the display.

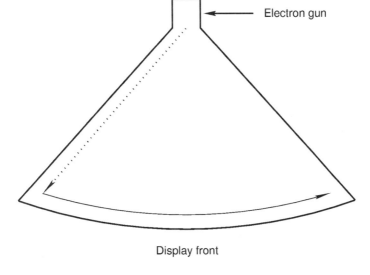

Electron gun

Display front

FIGURE 14.1

The electron gun fires a moving beam of electrons at the display to "paint" an image on the screen one line at a time.

The front of the display tube is coated with a phosphorous compound that glows when struck by the electrons from the electron gun. This coating is not uniform, however; it's broken into small units of red, green, and blue, which are arranged in patterns to allow the electron gun to strike each colored element precisely. To display a green object, the phosphor gun fires only when its electrons will strike the green phosphor element, for example. To display color other than red, green, or blue, colors are combined in various proportions. In this *additive* color scheme, white is a combination of all three colors, and black is the absence of all colors. (Paints and inks use a *subtractive* color scheme, by contrast, in which merging all the colors produces black.)

Persistence

Two factors combine to make the display appear steady and flicker-free to most people:

- **Phosphor persistence** Thephosphors used in monitors glow for a brief period after having been struck by the electron beam. Ideally, they glow precisely long enough to remain lit until struck again, but no longer. In practice, the glow fades over time, which is why you may see a faint afterimage of a bright object after you've moved it away from a dark background.

14

- **Human photoreceptor persistence**   The cells in your eyes that detect light also experience persistence. Where a monitor's phosphors continue glowing for a time after being struck by an electron beam, your photoreceptors continue firing electrical impulses to your brain after a light source has been removed. The human eye contains two broad classes of photoreceptors: *rods*, which are responsible for black-and-white vision, and *cones*, which are responsible for color vision. Rods are more common in your peripheral vision, and are generally more sensitive and have lower persistence.

> **TIP**
>
> As described later in this chapter, a monitor's refresh rate—how often the display is renewed—is one of its most important performance characteristics. If the refresh rate is too low, phosphor and photoreceptor persistence become insufficient, and you perceive flicker in the displayed image. You can detect this flicker most easily by looking slightly *away* from a monitor, so that you view it with your more sensitive rods. If you can perceive flicker in a display when you view it peripherally, you should adjust its refresh rate upwards, if possible. Failing to do so can result in headaches and eye strain when you use a monitor for a prolonged period.

Picture Tube Types

Two basic types of picture tube are in common use today:

- **Shadow mask**   In a shadow mask tube, a metallic screen lies between the electron gun and the front of the display. This screen is used to help keep the electron beam directed onto the proper color phosphors, without leakage onto nearby colors. Shadow mask technology is quite old, and results in a display that's curved both horizontally and vertically.

- **Aperture grille**   Sony invented the aperture grille design as an alternative to the shadow mask, and marketed the technology under the *Trinitron* name. These tubes use a series of fine wires strung vertically across the monitor instead of a shadow mask. This design allows a picture tube to be flat in the vertical direction, although the tube must still be curved horizontally. Today, aperture grille designs are available from several manufacturers, some of whom use Sony's Trinitron tubes and some of whom do not.

As a general rule, aperture grille designs are more expensive and produce brighter displays than do shadow mask designs. Shadow mask designs have traditionally had an edge in text display sharpness, but this is less true today than it used to be. Aperture grille designs suffer from the presence of one or two dark horizontal lines, a third of the way up from the bottom or down from the top of the screen. These lines are shadows cast by stabilizing wires that keep the aperture grille wires aligned.

I recommend you examine monitors of both types before deciding which you prefer, or if you have a preference. Many people like the brightness that's possible with aperture grille designs, and their curvature in only one direction can make them easier to align to reduce or eliminate reflections. On the other hand, some people find the dark lines cast by the stabilizing wires distracting, and the higher cost of aperture grille designs can be a problem.

Liquid Crystal Displays

LCDs use a fundamentally different technology from CRT displays. Instead of using a picture tube that fires electrons at the display, LCD technology uses special substances (the *liquid crystals* of the technology's name) that pass or block light to create different colors. The result is a display that's quite thin, as shown in Figure 14.2. Another advantage of LCDs is that they're completely flat.

FIGURE 14.2

The thinness and lightness of LCDs makes them ideal for use on notebook computers.

Fundamentals of LCD Technology

Light can be thought of as a wave phenomenon, much like ripples in a pond. Any given light wave is oriented in a particular direction; for instance, horizontally or vertically. Ordinary light (from the Sun, a light bulb, or a candle, for instance) is composed of light waves of all orientations. Various substances, however, including certain crystals, can block light waves of a given range of orientations. The result is *polarized* light, in which all the light waves are oriented in the same way (see Figure 14.3). Humans perceive polarized light no differently from ordinary light, but the polarization allows additional manipulations of the light.

FIGURE 14.3

A polarizing substance passes only light of a certain orientation.

An LCD works by using *two* polarizing elements. The first polarizes the light, and the second can be adjusted electrically to pass—or not pass—this already polarized light. For instance, if one filter polarizes light horizontally, and if a second filter is also set for horizontal polarization, the light passes through. If the second filter is set for vertical polarization, on the other hand, 100% of the light is blocked.

Color LCDs use three cells for each pixel—one cell each for red, green, and blue. In this respect, color LCDs resemble color CRT displays, so other video hardware and software doesn't need to be modified to handle color LCDs. Like CRTs, LCDs use an additive color scheme.

> **NOTE**
>
> An entirely different technology, *gas plasma displays*, are used in a few flat-panel monitors, such as some older Toshiba notebooks and flat-panel color TVs. Gas plasma displays are quite rare in notebooks and desktop displays in 2000, but they may become more common in the future.

Types of LCD Displays

In 2000, LCD displays fall into two broad categories:

- **Passive matrix**   Passive matrix LCDs are available in a wide variety of types, including monochrome and color, single- and dual-scan, and more. In a passive matrix design, each pixel on the screen is controlled by a pair of transistors corresponding to the pixel's X- and Y-coordinates. Each transistor is shared by all the pixels in its row or column, so the total number of transistors required is the sum of the horizontal and vertical resolutions—for instance, 1,400 for an 800×600 display. The transistors send an electrical pulse to a given pixel once per scan cycle. Most passive matrix screens sold today are used on low-end notebook computers, and are color dual-scan designs. The terms *dual-scan* and *high-performance addressing* (HPA) are synonymous, and refer to a design in which the display is split into two sections which function independently of one another. The result is a reduction in the time between pulses, and hence a brighter overall display. Twice as many transistors are required for a dual-scan display as for a single-scan display. Another term that is often applied to passive matrix designs is *supertwist numatic* (STN), which refers to a potentially great difference between the angle of the first polarizing crystal relative to the second. All of today's passive matrix displays qualify for the STN designation, although older displays might not.

- **Active matrix**   The active matrix design improves on the passive matrix design by using continuous voltage applied to each pixel by a dedicated transistor behind the panel. This design therefore requires more transistors—the product of the X- and Y-dimensions of the display, as in 480,000 for an 800×600 display. The larger number of transistors makes active matrix designs more expensive and more delicate than passive matrix designs, but the displays are brighter, quicker to respond, and more easily viewed from an angle than are passive matrix displays. Active matrix designs are used on most mid-range and high-end notebook computers and on most desktop LCDs. Another term that's often used to refer to these displays is *thin-film transistor* (TFT).

If you're after the best in image quality from an LCD screen, choose an active matrix model. These designs suffer less from the problems typically associated with LCD screens, particularly the range of angles at which a display can be viewed. They do cost more, however, and they consume more power than do passive matrix displays, which may be a concern in a laptop computer.

LCD Versus CRT

Compared to CRT displays, LCDs have the following advantages and disadvantages:

- Lightweight
- Thin
- Low power consumption
- Low electromagnetic emissions
- Low sensitivity to magnetic disturbances
- Larger viewable area for advertised size
- No geometric distortions
- Occasional "dead pixels"
- Narrow range of viewing angles
- Low contrast
- Single optimum resolution
- High cost

A few of these characteristics deserve additional comment. For instance, a CRT's advertised size is actually larger, by approximately 1–1.5 inches, than the actual viewable area. This is because a CRT's housing necessarily covers part of the CRT's measured size. By contrast, an LCD's advertised viewing area is much closer to the actual viewing area, because less of the LCD's area is covered. In both cases, the size is measured as the diagonal distance (say, from the lower-right corner to the upper-left corner). Thus, a 15-inch LCD panel is akin to a 16–17-inch monitor. When you shop for a monitor, therefore, you should take this discrepancy into consideration; compare 15-inch LCDs to 17-inch CRTs, for instance. Many monitors advertise both the CRT's size (including the unusable area) and the visible size.

LCD manufacturing produces occasional "dead pixels"—pixels that can't be tuned to pass light. Most LCDs you buy have two or three such pixels, which you can spot by turning the display completely white. You may run into a display with many more than this number of defective pixels, however, and you may want to return such a unit. In fact, the dead pixels are one reason for the high cost of LCDs; manufacturers must discard some displays because they contain too many dead pixels, and these discards drive up the price for the remaining units.

Because both passive and active matrix displays rely upon an unchanging number of transistors wired to specific pixels, an LCD's resolution is fixed. Notebook computers today typically have 800×600 or 1024×768 displays, but desktop LCD monitors add 1200×1024 to the mix. You cannot get a higher resolution from the monitor than its matrix allows, but you can set the monitor for a lower resolution. Doing so results in either a smaller image or an image in which multiple screen pixels correspond to a single display pixel. The latter produces images that tend to look blurry.

> **TIP**
>
> If you must run an LCD at a reduced resolution, try to use a resolution that's an even fraction of the display size. For instance, if you run a 1200×1024 display at 600×512, the result is precisely four monitor pixels in a 2×2 array devoted to each of the image's pixels.

Analog Versus Digital Displays

Two types of interfaces between video cards and monitors exist: analog and digital. In an analog display, the digital display data are converted into an analog form for transmission to the monitor. This analog form is similar in some ways to the form used by broadcast TV signals, although many details differ. In particular, this analog transmission involves precision timing of changes in the colors to be displayed. The video card controls the electron beam of a CRT, telling it to turn on or off each color at precise moments in time to match the beam's position on the screen. This technique works well for most CRTs, which are derived from the fundamentally analog technology used in broadcast TV standards.

> **NOTE**
>
> The new *high-definition television* (HDTV) standards are digital in nature, much like computer display data.

Digital displays, on the other hand, deliver data to the monitor in a digital format. Instead of relying upon precision timing to match the electron beam, the video circuitry sends digital data that precisely defines the status of each pixel on the display. This data is transmitted several times each second, just as with an analog display. As you might imagine, a digital interface is particularly useful for LCDs, which use a discrete method of addressing their pixels. Some older CRT forms used digital addressing, however, and some LCDs use analog signals. In the case of modern LCDs, the use of analog signals allows the display to be used in conjunction with conventional video cards designed for use with CRTs. The drawback is that the conversion from digital to analog and back to digital again can produce some artifacts in which pixels can flip back and forth between two states. For instance, if your screen displays a wide swath of green next to an area of red, with a sharp boundary between them, some pixels along that boundary might flicker between red and green color. As a general rule, therefore, LCD monitors work best with dedicated digital video cards. You must be especially cautious when purchasing such cards, in order to match the video card to the monitor. You must also be certain that the video card works in Linux, because if it doesn't, you may need to replace the monitor as well as the card. Most digital display cards use the same video chipsets that are used by conventional analog video cards, but it's best to try to locate information on Linux compatibility for the specific model of card, because the monitor interface circuitry may not match the expectations of XFree86.

Evaluating Monitor Quality

Once you've decided on the type of monitor you want (CRT or LCD) and the size you want, it's time to begin shopping for specific models. You can determine a lot about a monitor by examining its specifications, but in the end, it's your eyes that will be looking at a monitor, potentially every day for years to come. It's therefore critically important that you examine your monitor in person before buying it.

Checking Maximum Refresh Rates

One of the most important CRT monitor characteristics is its *refresh rate*, which is the rate at which the monitor re-draws the image on the screen. The refresh rate for the screen as a whole is generally given in Hertz (Hz), or number of times per second. Most monitors today are capable of refresh rates of up to 80–100Hz at the resolutions at which they typically run, and higher rates at lower resolutions.

> **NOTE**
>
> LCD screens also have refresh rates, but this characteristic isn't nearly as important for LCDs, because they don't suffer from flicker in the same way as do CRTs.

The overall screen refresh rate is actually determined by three characteristics in combination:

- **Maximum vertical scan rate**   In some sense this characteristic is the same as the overall refresh rate. It's the maximum number of times per second the monitor can move the electron beam from the bottom of the screen to the top and then back again. In most cases, however, the monitor's maximum vertical scan rate is far higher than the practical maximum refresh rate at a given resolution, because the next two factors come into play.

- **Maximum horizontal scan rate**   The horizontal scan rate is the speed with which the electron gun can display a single line, including a return to the start of the next line. This rate is much higher than the maximum vertical refresh rate, and is typically measured in kilohertz (kHz).

- **Lines of resolution**   The number of lines displayed on the screen is important because this characteristic, in conjunction with the maximum horizontal scan rate, usually determines the practical maximum overall refresh rate for a given monitor at a given resolution.

As an example, suppose a monitor has a 100kHz maximum horizontal scan rate, and you want to use a 1280×1024 display. Drawing 1024 lines at 0.00001s (100kHz) each takes 0.01024s. Stated in Hz, this is 98Hz, so the monitor's maximum overall refresh rate *at this resolution* is 98Hz. Reducing the resolution to 1024×768 produces a maximum refresh rate of 130Hz. If the monitor's maximum vertical scan rate is 125Hz, though, that will be the limit, despite the higher potential from the horizontal scan rate and lines of resolution at 1024×768.

NOTE

This example is somewhat simplified. In practice, not all of a display's vertical scan time can be consumed in drawing lines on the screen. A small amount of time must be spent moving the electron beam from the bottom of the display to the top. Therefore, rather than 98Hz at 1280×1024, the maximum refresh rate at this resolution might be 90Hz or 95Hz.

Most manufacturers make it easy to determine what a screen's maximum refresh rates are at common resolutions; they include this information in the specifications. This act saves you from having to make the computations yourself. In some cases, these statements round down to common refresh rates. For instance, the practical maximum refresh rate might be 88Hz, but the monitor manufacturer may quote 85Hz instead. If you're so motivated, you can modify X's configuration in Linux to gain back that extra 3Hz, although in most cases the result isn't worth the trouble.

If you want to use a resolution that's not been specified by the manufacturer, you must locate the horizontal and vertical refresh rates in the specifications and compute the value yourself. Alternatively, you can guess the value by using a resolution that's close to the one you want to use.

14

MONITORS

NOTE

Your video card must be able to support the resolution and refresh rate you've chosen. If your video card can't handle a given display mode, you may have to make do with a lesser display or replace the video card.

The preceding discussion applies to all CRT monitors in common use today. Very old monitors often used *fixed frequency* designs, in which the monitors could only synchronize to certain specific horizontal and vertical refresh rates. Such a monitor might only work at 640×480 (VGA) resolution, for instance. If you have a fixed frequency monitor, your choices for video resolution are quite limited. Such monitors are usually inadequate for modern Linux computers, but might be acceptable for use as backup displays or on servers that are seldom accessed using the console.

Dot Pitch and Maximum Resolutions

CRT displays are composed of large numbers of phosphor dots, as described earlier. These phosphors are smaller than the pixels that comprise the video display on a logical level, and just *how much* smaller they are is one of the important determinants of display quality. The size and spacing of phosphor dots is measured in millimeters (mm), and is referred to as *dot pitch*. This measure refers to the distance between the centers of phosphor dots. The smaller the dot pitch, the better. Typical monitors today have dot pitches in the 0.25mm–0.30mm range. I recommend purchasing a monitor with a dot pitch no greater than 0.27mm. In reality, the horizontal and vertical dot pitches are sometimes different, particularly for aperture grille monitors, but manufacturers usually quote the worse (higher) value. Assuming a uniform horizontal and vertical dot pitch of 0.25mm, a 19-inch screen (approximately 360×270mm viewable area) supports approximately 1440×1080 phosphor dots, which is enough to sustain the common 1280×1024 resolution. Driving this monitor to higher resolutions, such as 1600×1200, may be possible, but as this resolution uses more pixels than the screen has phosphor dots, image quality suffers. Specifically, the image looks blurry.

Most manufacturers quote maximum resolutions for their monitors that are a bit optimistic, if you compare the maximum resolutions to the monitor's dot pitch. For instance, many 19-inch monitors quote a 1600×1200 resolution, but by the preceding computations, this resolution stretches the limits of a 0.25mm dot pitch CRT. As a general rule of thumb, you should plan to use a monitor at a resolution that's one step down from the quoted maximum. For instance, plan on running a 19-inch monitor that can officially handle 1600×1200 at 1280×1024.

LCD monitors' resolutions are, as I described earlier, fixed by the number of transistors built in to their displays. This fact makes LCD monitors a poor choice if you have need to change resolutions frequently, as you might when designing Web pages or switching between games at modest resolution and work tasks at higher resolutions.

Viewing Angles

The range of acceptable viewing angles varies substantially between monitors, and particularly between different models of LCDs. This viewing angle range is measured in degrees. LCD monitors typically have fairly narrow viewing angles, as shown in Figure 14.4—most fall between 50° and 110°. By contrast, CRTs typically have viewing angles of 120° or so. As a general rule, active matrix displays feature much wider viewing angles than do passive matrix displays.

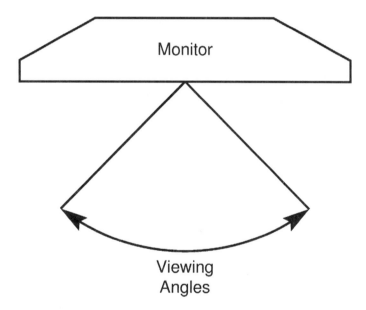

FIGURE 14.4

LCD monitors vary widely in their range of usable viewing angles.

All other things being equal, you want a monitor with a wide range of viewing angles. Of course, this characteristic is more important for some functions than for others. For instance, it may be critically important to have a monitor with a wide range of viewing angles if you expect to do presentations with it, or to work in a group of three or four people crowded around a single monitor. If you typically work alone and look straight into the display, on the other hand, this characteristic may not be so important to you.

With most displays, the range of horizontal viewing angles is symmetrical—that is, you can shift as far to the left as you can to the right before the image begins to fade or change in color. This isn't always true of the vertical range of viewing angles for LCD panels, however. This vertical range may not be identical to the horizontal range, and can be asymmetrical. Some LCD monitors include a pivot that allows the monitor to be tilted sideways, resulting in a display that's taller than it is wide (called a *portrait* display). An asymmetrical or narrow vertical range of angles can become important if you want to use the monitor in portrait orientation on a regular basis, because this vertical range becomes the horizontal range in portrait orientation.

CAUTION

Using a monitor in portrait orientation often requires support in your X server, and such support is rare in Linux. If you want to use a monitor in portrait orientation, you should carefully check for this support in your X server before you buy the display.

In-Store Checkout

It's important that you evaluate a monitor yourself before buying it. The characteristics that are important to a reviewer may not be important to you, and vice versa. Unfortunately, most computer stores feature eye-catching graphics on their display monitors, not the sorts of images that you'll be using on the display. We tend to look at graphics differently than we do text and icons, and these types of displays emphasize different aspects of a display's design. Therefore, if at all possible, I recommend locating a store that will hook a monitor up to a computer running a GUI environment, and evaluate the monitor in this context. It's not terribly important that the computer be running Linux; despite some cosmetic differences, the characteristics with which you're most concerned can be evaluated from any OS. You should, however, try to run the display at the same resolution and refresh rate you intend to use. Two monitors may perform quite similarly at 800×600, but show substantial differences at 1280×1024. A single monitor may perform quite differently at different resolutions, as well.

I recommend you look for certain specific characteristics in the monitors you evaluate in the store, such as

- **Sharpness**   How sharp are the images, particularly text?
- **Brightness**   The display should be bright, and the monitor should have controls that allow you to adjust the brightness within a broad range. You should also check that the brightness is even across the entire display. If the monitor is hooked up to a Windows computer, use the Display item in the Windows Control Panel to adjust the background color, as shown in Figure 14.5. Adjust the background color both to something light and to something dark, and judge how even the color is across the entire display.

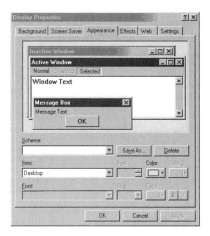

FIGURE 14.5

Select Desktop in the Item field, and then pick a new color in the Color field to change the desktop's color.

- **Contrast**   You should be able to adjust the contrast up or down, and fix it at a comfortable level.

- **Flicker**   Even at the same refresh rate, two CRT displays can produce different amounts of flicker because of differences in their phosphors. You should only try to evaluate flicker when the monitor is running at the refresh rate you intend to use. Look for flicker in your peripheral vision, when you look directly at a corner of the monitor, or slightly away from it.

- **Distortion**   Do rectangular shapes (such as windows) look rectangular? Do windows retain the same proportions as you move them around the screen? Monitors often contain controls to let you adjust for geometric distortion, so don't judge until you've located and adjusted these controls.

- **Color balance**   Do colors look reasonable? You might want to bring a high-quality digitized photo with you on a floppy disk to help judge color balance. Again, a monitor's controls often let you adjust this feature.

- **Misconvergence**   The electron beams fired by a monitor often miss their marks slightly, particularly in the corners of the display. This problem, called *misconvergence*, causes red or blue halos to appear around sharp lines.

- **Moiré**   Moiré patterns are patterns of apparent light and dark that emerge when two fine arrays of lines are placed atop one another. You can see moiré patterns by taking two window screens (the kind from a building's windows, not computer windows) and placing one atop the other. In computer monitors, moiré patterns are undesirable. You're unlikely to spot moiré in a store demo unless you bring a graphic file that's composed of

14

MONITORS

fine patterns, such as a checkerboard pattern where each square is one pixel in size. On a moiré-free monitor, such a display looks like a shade of gray. On a moiré-prone monitor, this pattern will appear uneven in brightness, and may shimmer if you move it around the display.

- **Screen flatness** Monitor manufacturers today strive to make their screens as flat as possible. LCD monitors have completely flat screens. Aperture grille displays are flat vertically, but curve in the horizontal dimension. Shadow mask displays curve both horizontally and vertically. For both aperture grille and shadow mask displays, the extent of the curvature varies from one model to another. Unfortunately, very flat screens have a tendency to suffer from other problems, such as misconvergence, although this correlation is far from perfect.

- **Control layout** The trend today is for minimalist controls—just two or three buttons, plus a power switch. A monitor with few controls can be confusing, but so can a wide array of tiny buttons with tiny labels. Spend some time with each monitor's controls and judge for yourself which one is easiest to use.

- **Dead pixels** LCD monitors often have pixels that simply don't work. Ideally, you want a monitor with no dead pixels, but you shouldn't expect to get such a monitor. Note that the number of dead pixels on a store's display monitor may not match the number on the device you purchase, so ideally you should check this out on the monitor you buy, not the display sample.

- **Size and weight** You can get size and weight information from most monitors' specification sheets, but it's useful to see them in stores. Monitors often take up more or less space as they're pivoted on their swivel bases, so be sure to take this fact into consideration if you have limited space for the monitor.

Unfortunately, you're not likely to be able to perform all these tests on any monitor until after you purchase it. For this reason, and because CRT monitors are so heavy—and therefore expensive to ship—I recommend buying monitors locally, and from a store with liberal return policies. If you bring a monitor home and find it's a dud, you can cart it back to the store without paying $50 or more to ship it back.

Checking Your Sample

You should perform all the preceding tests on the monitor once you've hooked it up to your own computer. If you're dissatisfied with the results of any test, you may want to research that aspect of monitor performance. It's possible that some minor adjustment could fix the problem. For instance, brightness, contrast, and color balance can all affect sharpness.

Unfortunately, monitors vary a lot from one sample to another. The monitor you saw in the store might or might not perform like the one you bring into your home or office. Geometric distortion, dead pixels, and other characteristics vary from one sample to another. In my experience, too, a large number of monitors suffer from flat-out defects—they flicker wildly (for reasons unrelated to refresh rates), don't turn on, emit loud noises, or otherwise perform badly. It's hard to offer specific advice on evaluating a monitor for such defects, so you should follow your own perceptions. If something seems *off* about a monitor you've just bought, try to pin down precisely what it is. Do a Web search on appropriate key words. Deja News (http://www.deja.com/usenet/) is a useful resource for locating discussions of defects in monitors. If you become convinced that your monitor is defective, return it for another sample of the same model, or a different model entirely.

Above all else, I recommend you set a high standard for performance from your monitor. Settling for a poor monitor can lead to eye strain, headaches, and a generally miserable existence as a result. With the possible exceptions of the keyboard and mouse, no other computer component is as important to your own health and well-being, so you shouldn't settle for a monitor that's sub-standard. Monitors cost more than keyboards and mice, too, so replacing a poor monitor some months down the road can be more of a strain on your budget.

Configuring XFree86

Most Linux distributions configure themselves for your monitor at installation time. This process is bound up with configuring XFree86 for your video card, and is described in Chapter 12, "Video Cards." If you replace your monitor, however, or if you want to fine-tune your configuration, you must modify your configuration. You can do so in one of two ways:

- **Re-run the configuration utilities**   Running the configuration utilities anew lets you enter the same sort of information you did initially. This approach is useful if you replace an existing monitor or if your initial configuration was incorrect. Some XFree86 configuration utilities—particularly the newer ones that are GUI-based, such as XF86Setup—let you quickly change one aspect of a configuration. Others, such as the old but reliable xf86config, make you configure *everything* from scratch.

- **Edit XF86Config by hand**   You can modify the XF86Config file in a text editor to adjust its settings. This approach can be faster than running through an entire configuration script if you know what you need to modify, and it allows you to configure non-standard video modes to get the most out of your monitor.

The rest of this chapter is devoted to this second approach. The XF86Config file is usually located in the /etc or /etc/X11 directory—some distributions use one location, others use the other. The structure and contents of this file are the same no matter what distribution you use. In most cases of upgrades to the monitor, simple changes suffice, so you may not need the more technical information presented here.

14

MONITORS

NOTE

Commercial X servers, such as Metro-X and Accelerated-X, use their own configuration files. These files contain the same sort of information as does the XF86Config file, but the details differ. Consult the documentation that came with your X server for details.

Basic XF86Config Structure

The XF86Config file is divided into several named *sections*, each of which controls some aspect of X function. These sections include

- **Files** Directories and files used by the server. Most importantly, you can set the *font path* here—where X looks for font files.
- **Keyboard** Options relating to the keyboard, such as its layout (U.S. 101-key, French, and so on).
- **Pointer** Information on the mouse (or other pointing device), such as its device file and protocol.
- **Monitor** Characteristics of the monitor, such as its supported refresh rates.
- **Display** Information on the display driver, such as the video card model, amount of RAM, and so on. Most modern cards and drivers require only very minimal Display sections, because the servers can query the cards directly for the relevant information.
- **Screen** Settings for the display, such as the screen size in pixels and the color depth.

Most of the settings I describe here fall in the Monitor section, although some appear in the Screen section. A single XF86Config file can contain multiple sections of any type—two or more Monitor sections, for instance. Each section begins with the keyword Section, followed by the section type in quote marks. Subsequent lines contain definitions relevant to that section. The section ends with the keyword EndSection. For instance, here's a sample Screen section:

```
Section "Screen"
    Driver      "accel"
    Device      "Mach 64"
    Monitor     "Iiyama"
    Subsection "Display"
        Depth       8
        Modes       "1024x768" "800x600" "640x480"
        ViewPort    0 0
    EndSubsection
EndSection
```

This section defines an 8-bit screen that runs at 1024×768 resolution using the ATI Mach 64 server (XF86_Mach64).

> **TIP**
>
> Many X configurations default to using 8-bit (256-color) displays. If your Screen section includes a 16-, 24-, or 32-bit color depth subsection, you can set that Screen display to use one of these definitions by default. Do this by including a line that reads DefaultColorDepth *n* (where *n* is the desired color depth in bits, such as 16) just before the Subsection "Display" line.

Setting Scan Rate Lines

You can specify a monitor's range of horizontal and vertical scan rates in the Monitor section. The relevant lines look like this:

```
HorizSync      27-115
VertRefresh    50-160
```

As you might guess, the first line sets the range of horizontal scan rates (in kHz), and the second sets the range of vertical scan rates (in Hz). You should be able to find appropriate values in your monitor's manual.

> **CAUTION**
>
> Don't set the refresh rate lines randomly or to values that you guess. If you set the rates incorrectly—particularly to values that are too high—XFree86 may try to run your monitor at too high a refresh rate. Most modern monitors are designed to ignore such signals, but some models—particularly older ones—can be damaged if you try to use a too-high refresh rate.

You do *not* directly set the overall refresh rate in XF86Config. Instead, XFree86 uses the horizontal and vertical refresh rates, in conjunction with your desired resolution and *modelines* (described shortly) to determine the maximum refresh rate your hardware can handle. XFree86 then uses that refresh rate automatically. This indirect method of setting the screen's refresh rate can be confusing at first, but XFree86's configuration method gives you an unusual degree of control over your video display, if you're inclined to modify the configuration.

> **TIP**
>
> If you've replaced a monitor with a more capable model, you might need do nothing more than adjust the horizontal and vertical scan rates in XF86Config. When you restart X, it will use the new values, and will adjust the overall refresh rate as appropriate. If you want to use a higher resolution with your new monitor, you should adjust the Modes line in the appropriate Screen section to list your new resolution first at the color depth you use, as well as adjusting the scan frequency lines.

Understanding Dot Clocks

If you don't want tocreate an unusual or custom video mode, there's no need for you to proceed further in this chapter. The remaining material is fairly advanced, and to use it, you'll need to experiment with your XF86Config file settings. This experimentation can be time-consuming and may not return enough to warrant the effort. If you really want to derive the most from your video hardware, however, read on.

A video card's *dot clock* is the maximum number of pixels it can output per second to a monitor, or the rate at which it actually sends data to the monitor. (The latter can be less than the former.) The dot clock is expressed in megahertz (MHz), which in this context is millions of pixels per second.

In most cases, the monitor's capabilities determine the maximum resolution or refresh rate, but if you use an underpowered video card, you may be unable to use a high refresh rate. For instance, suppose you have a monitor capable of 1280×1024 resolution at 100Hz. Multiplying these values together, the monitor displays about 131 million pixels per second—that is, it requires a video card capable of delivering a 131MHz dot clock. (The actual value is a bit higher than this, as will become clear shortly.) If your video card can only deliver a 120MHz dot clock, then you'll need to reduce the resolution or refresh rate.

You can determine your video card's maximum allowable dot clock by typing **X -probeonly** (or possibly **X --probeonly** on some older systems) when X is *not* already running. The result is a mass of information about your video hardware, including a line like the following:

```
(--) SVGA: Maximum allowed dot-clock: 220.000 MHz
```

This line reveals the maximum dot clock supported by your video card. Some video cards are limited to producing certain specific clocks, not just a maximum dot clock. On such cards, you'll see information on these permissible dot clocks, such as

```
(**) S3: clocks:   25.00   28.00   40.00    3.00   50.00   77.00   36.00   45.00
(**) S3: clocks:    0.00    0.00   79.00   31.00   94.00   65.00   75.00   71.00
```

If you choose to create a custom modeline, you must be sure that your modeline uses one of these specific dot clocks, else it won't work with your video card.

Creating a Custom Modeline

Chances are your XF86Config file contains several lines that look something like this:

```
Modeline        "1024x768"    65      1024 1032 1176 1344
➥768   771   777   806 -hsync -vsync
```

This line represents a way to carve up the available dot clocks into horizontal and vertical components. This line can be broken up into several sections, as follows:

- **"1024x768"**   Although this number represents the resolution, it's really just a label. When you create a Screen section, you specify a label for the desired resolution, and XFree86 searches for available modelines with this label. You could as easily call this resolution "MyRes" or just about anything else. Using the actual resolution is a convention that helps you locate the correct modelines.

- **65**   The dot clock. This resolution and refresh rate requires 65 dot clocks.

- **1024 1032 1176 1344**   This cluster of four numbers represents the horizontal resolution. The first number—1024—is the horizontal resolution in pixels. The second and third numbers represent where the *horizontal sync pulse* (which tells the monitor to begin a new line) begins and ends, and the fourth is the total *horizontal frame length* for a complete line.

- **768 771 777 806**   Thiscluster of four values is equivalent to the preceding four, but represents vertical resolution. In this case, there are 768 visible lines, with a vertical sync pulse starting at line 771 and ending at 777. The total number of lines, including invisible border area (often called the *vertical frame length*) is 806.

- **-hsync -vsync**   These are special flags. In this example, the polarities of the horizontal and vertical sync signals are set to negative. (Some monitors work best with negative sync signals, others with positive.) Other flags include interlace, which is used to set an interlaced video mode, and composite, which uses a composite sync signal. Chances are you won't need to use any of these options.

Creating a custom modeline isn't a matter of simply adjusting the values as you see fit, although minor adjustments along these lines may be successful. When you create a custom modeline, you should keep these rules in mind:

- The total number of pulses for both horizontal and vertical resolutions must be greater than the visible resolution. Typically, visible horizontal resolution is about 80% of the total number of horizontal pulses, and visible vertical resolution is about 95% of the vertical frame length.

- You need a certain amount of *guard time* on either side of the horizontal and vertical sync pulses. A good rule of thumb is 30 pulses for horizontal and 2 pulses for vertical. What works best with your monitor is definitely something you must determine through trial and error, however, unless you can locate documentation on this aspect of your monitor's design. The preceding example doesn't conform to these rules of thumb.

- Dot clock frequency divided by the monitor's horizontal scan frequency determines the number of horizontal pulses available, and hence the maximum horizontal resolution. Note that dot clocks are generally specified in megahertz, whereas horizontal scan frequencies are given in kilohertz, so if you divide the raw numbers, you must multiply by 1,000 to obtain a valid result. XFree86 reverses this computation to determine whether a modeline is usable for a given monitor; if the product of the dot clock and the number of horizontal pulses exceeds the monitor's horizontal scan frequency, XFree86 won't use the modeline.

- The screen's refresh rate is the dot clock frequency divided by the multiple of the horizontal and vertical frame lengths. In the preceding example, this value is 65,000,000 / (1344 × 806) = 60Hz. As with the horizontal scan frequency, XFree86 checks this value against the monitor's rated maximum horizontal sync frequency, and if the computed value exceeds the monitor's capabilities, XFree86 refuses to use the modeline.

- The horizontal frame length must normally be a multiple of 8. This limitation derives from characteristics of some video cards' hardware.

The following equation summarizes the relationship between dot clocks, refresh rate, horizontal frame length, and vertical frame length:

```
DCF = RR × HFL × VFL
```

DCF is the dot clock frequency in hertz, RR is the refresh rate in hertz, HFL is the horizontal frame length, and VFL is the vertical frame length. HFL is usually about 125% of the visible horizontal size of the display in pixels, and VFL is usually about 105% of the visible vertical size of the display in pixels. The key to designing a custom modeline is to ensure that DCF doesn't exceed your video card's capabilities, RR doesn't exceed your monitor's capabilities, and HFL times DCF (in hertz) doesn't exceed your monitor's horizontal refresh rate (in hertz). How you begin juggling these limitations depends on your priorities. For instance, if you want to achieve the maximum refresh rate at a given resolution, you can start with HFL and VFL values, then compute the maximum DCF given your monitor's capabilities. From there, it's a matter of experimentation to determine where best to place sync pulses.

Specifying a Monitor and Screen

The Monitor section used by XFree86 is determined by the Screen section. Each Screen section contains a line to identify the Monitor section with which it is associated, as in

```
Monitor "Iiyama"
```

This line specifies that the Monitor section called Iiyama will be used by this Screen definition. Many XF86Config files contain several Screen sections, though, so how does X determine which of these to use? The primary means is by choosing the section that matches the server that was called. For instance, many configuration programs produce Screen sections for VGA, mono, or other servers that aren't normally used. The X server knows to look for a Screen section that matches its capabilities. For instance, the XF86_Mach64 server would use the following Screen section, if it's present in the XF86Config file:

```
Section "Screen"
    Driver      "accel"
    Device      "Mach 64"
    Monitor     "Iiyama"
    Subsection "Display"
        Depth       8
        Modes       "1024x768" "800x600" "640x480"
        ViewPort    0 0
    EndSubsection
EndSection
```

The key point in determining what Screen section a server uses is the Driver line. The accel driver referred to in the preceding example is actually a reference to any of several specialized X servers. Another common driver is svga, which is used by the XF86_SVGA server.

Summary

Buying a monitor for use in Linux entails employing the same criteria you would use to buy a monitor for any other OS. Characteristics like monitor type (CRT or LCD), size, refresh rates, and supported resolutions all work largely the same in all OSs. Likewise, monitor quality issues such as sharpness and freedom from distortion are largely the same across OSs. Linux does provide more flexibility in monitor configuration than do most OSs, however. If you're willing to experiment with your XF86Config file's modelines, you can create a custom resolution or run your monitor at its highest available refresh rate for a standard resolution. If you're satisfied with one of the standard default resolutions, though, you need not edit the XF86Config file. Configuration scripts that were run when you installed XFree86 set it up with a range of typical resolutions and refresh rates.

14

MONITORS

Input/Output

PART

IV

IN THIS PART

Keyboards and Mice

IN THIS CHAPTER

The three computer components with which humans interact most directly are the monitor, the keyboard, and the mouse (or other pointing device). Chapter 14 described the features and configuration of monitors, and this chapter covers keyboards and mice. The monitor is an output device intended to relay information from the computer to you. The keyboard and mouse are the computer's principal human-input devices. Despite their radically different technologies, monitors and these input devices are related—taken together, they create a data-transfer loop between you and the computer.

> **NOTE**
>
> For brevity's sake, I often refer simply to *mice* in this chapter, and in others. In most cases, my comments apply to alternative pointing devices, as well as mice. When my comments apply only to mice, I use the term *conventional mice*.

As with monitors, a typical computer is useless without a keyboard. Servers can sometimes operate without keyboards, but it's difficult to install Linux without a keyboard. Furthermore, most x86 computers won't boot unless a keyboard is attached, so even for servers tucked away in a closet, a keyboard is a practical necessity. Mice aren't so critical; it's possible to run Linux without a mouse. A mouse is a practical necessity for using X, however, and few x86 computers today are sold without a mouse or equivalent pointing device.

The technologies used in keyboards are highly standardized, although some recent developments—particularly the expanding role of USB in computers—have altered the scene somewhat, leading to some Linux-specific concerns. Mouse technologies were never quite as uniform as those for keyboards, but Linux support is nonetheless quite good for mice. The growing popularity of USB mice does pose certain challenges for Linux. Linux works best with mice that have at least three buttons, a fact you should consider when choosing a mouse.

Port Types

Keyboards and mice interface with the computer proper through one of several different port types. Each type of port has unique characteristics, although some of them are closely related to one another. With the exception of USB ports, mice and keyboards use different types of ports.

Figure 15.1 shows the port block on the back of a modern ATX motherboard. This block contains all the different types of keyboard and mouse ports, plus a few extra ports that are used for other purposes, such as the parallel port. Older computers place their ports in a variety of locations, and some of these ports don't look like the ones in Figure 15.1.

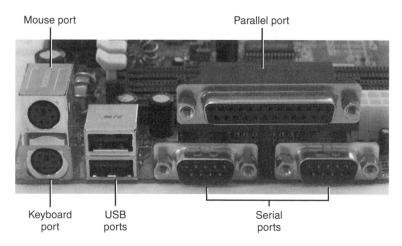

Mouse port   Parallel port

Keyboard port   USB ports   Serial ports

FIGURE 15.1
Most modern computers place their keyboard and mouse ports in the same block of external connectors.

Standard Keyboard Ports

Since the appearance of the original IBM PC, keyboards have used 5-pin DIN connectors. On AT-style motherboards (described in Chapter 2, "Motherboards"), the motherboard contains a connector for the 5-pin DIN keyboard plug. Some designs, however, have used a smaller *mini-DIN* connector, and this design has become standard with ATX and related motherboards. Because it was used on the IBM PS/2 computer, the mini-DIN design is sometimes referred to as a *PS/2 keyboard* port. Figure 15.2 shows both an older full-size 5-pin DIN connector (on the left) and an adapter that can be used to connect a full-size 5-pin DIN device into a newer mini-DIN motherboard.

Despite their physical differences, keyboards that use the old full-size 5-pin DIN connectors and those that use the newer mini-DIN connectors are electrically compatible. An adapter like the one shown in Figure 15.2 is very simple in design; it merely links connectors of differing sizes. You should therefore not be too concerned with the type of connector on a keyboard. In fact, many keyboards sold today come with appropriate adapters, and can be used with either type of motherboard out of the box.

CAUTION

Adapters like the one shown in Figure 15.2 have a tendency to fall out of their sockets in the computer, particularly when the computer is oriented as a tower. A better design uses a short cable between the full-size DIN connector and the mini-DIN connector. Unfortunately, this better design is rarer, so you might have to look harder to find it.

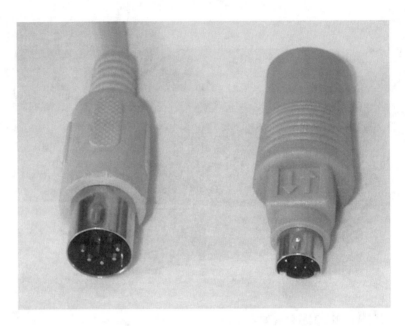

FIGURE 15.2

Older keyboards can be used with new motherboards by employing an adapter like the one shown on the right.

Although all modern keyboards that use the standard keyboard interface follow the same electrical and electronic characteristics, some very old keyboards are not compatible with today's designs. The earliest IBM PC and PC/XT computers, and many clones of these models, used a slightly different keyboard than did the subsequent IBM PC AT computer and its clones and descendants. Today's keyboards are therefore referred to as *AT keyboards*, whereas the older models are *XT keyboards*. You can't use an XT keyboard in a modern computer. A few models manufactured when both the XT and AT computers were available are compatible with both standards. These keyboards have a switch on the back or bottom to set compatibility with either standard. You can use these keyboards with modern computers; just be sure the switch is set correctly.

Linux includes support for standard keyboard ports, and you don't have to include any special kernel options to get this support.

PS/2 Mouse Ports

Modern ATX computers invariably include a mouse port modeled after the mouse port included on the IBM PS/2 computer. This port looks just like the mini-DIN keyboard port (refer to Figures 15.1 and 15.2). Because it was used on the PS/2 computer, this port is often referred to as a *PS/2 mouse port*.

> **NOTE**
>
> Most motherboards include one PS/2 mouse port and one PS/2 keyboard port. These ports are *not* interchangeable, though. You shouldn't plug a mouse into the keyboard port, or vice versa. Some notebook computers include a single combination mouse/keyboard port, so you can use *either* an external mouse *or* an external keyboard, but not both.

PS/2 mice almost always follow the same set of basic protocols, so you can swap PS/2 mice between computers without too much worry that they'll work. Recent *wheel mice*, however, which use wheels to facilitate scrolling, often require a somewhat different driver to provide access to their wheel features. I describe these issues later in this chapter, in "Configuring a Pointer in Linux."

Some mice come with adapters to let them function on either of two or more interfaces, such as serial and PS/2, or USB and PS/2. These adapters are often specific to one brand or model of mouse, so you might not be able to swap an adapter from one mouse to another.

The PS/2 mouse port consumes its own interrupt (IRQ 12). You can often disable this port—and therefore free IRQ 12—in the computer's BIOS, if you're not using a PS/2 mouse. Doing so can be worthwhile if you're short on IRQs and need a USB device for some other purpose. Switching from a PS/2 mouse to a serial mouse won't normally save an interrupt, because the serial port requires its own interrupt. (An exception would be if you use an advanced multiport serial card that consumes only one interrupt no matter how many devices are in use. Such cards are normally used only on systems that need many serial ports, such as computers used to accept many dial-in modem connections.) If you have some other device that you must configure for IRQ 12, however, switching from a PS/2 mouse to a serial mouse can make sense. The PS/2 port is very inflexible in its interrupt requirements, whereas you can often adjust the serial port's IRQs somewhat more.

BusMouse Ports

In the late 1980s and early 1990s, a type of mouse known as a *bus mouse* was mildly popular. These mice used their own specialized mouse port, which was typically handled on a plug-in ISA card. The bus mouse interface looks much like the interface for PS/2 mice, but it's electrically incompatible. You're unlikely to encounter a bus mouse on a modern computer, unless the mouse has been salvaged from an older computer.

Serial Ports

Conventional serial ports—more properly referred to as *RS-232* serial ports—were the most common way to attach mice to x86 computers through the mid-1990s. The serial port is a general-purpose port, and so can be used for many devices, albeit only one device per port. For this reason, most computers came with, and many still include, two RS-232 ports. Some computers, though, have only one RS-232 port.

Modern computers use 9-pin serial port connectors, as shown in Figure 15.1. Many older computers used at least one larger 25-pin connector, however. As with the full-size 5-pin DIN and smaller PS/2 keyboard connectors, adapters are available to connect 9-pin devices to 25-pin plugs, and vice versa. Figure 15.3 shows a 9-pin serial cable and a 9-pin-to-25-pin adapter. Despite the reduction in the number of pins, the 9-pin variety of serial port can be used for almost all the same tasks as can the 25-pin port; the additional 16 pins don't add any substantial functionality, and certainly nothing that's used by mice.

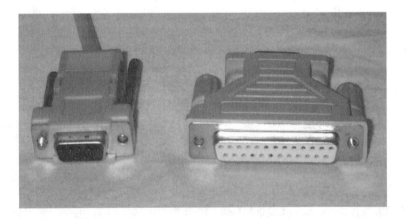

FIGURE 15.3

Serial connectors come in 9- and 25-pin varieties, and adapters let you convert from one type to another.

One of the reasons for the demise of 25-pin connectors on motherboards is the similarity of these connectors to 25-pin parallel port connectors. Serial and parallel ports differ in gender, however. On the computer side, parallel ports use a male connector on the cable and a female connector on the computer. For serial ports, this relationship is reversed. Because the cables used by serial mice are permanently attached to the mouse, you needn't be concerned with the gender of mouse cables on the mouse end.

A wide variety of serial mouse protocols have emerged over the years, the most common of these being Microsoft, Logitech, and Mouse Systems, each named after the company that originated the standard. Some mice support more than one protocol by use of a switch on the mouse's bottom or side. You select the mouse protocol you want to use at some point during Linux installation. If you choose the wrong protocol or change your mouse after installing Linux, you might need to adjust your XFree86 configuration, as described later in this chapter.

USB Ports

Universal Serial Bus (USB) is the latest craze in external device connectors. USB is substantially faster than RS-232 serial, which is a great boon for many applications. Mice and keyboards, though, require relatively little in the way of speed, so USB's speed improvements aren't terribly important for these applications. USB does have other advantages, though. Most importantly, all the USB devices attached to a computer (up to 127) consume a single interrupt. In theory, then, switching from a standard keyboard and PS/2 or serial mouse to USB devices can save you an interrupt, because you need only one interrupt rather than two for these devices. Unfortunately, the standard PC keyboard interrupt is so deeply engrained in the PC architecture that it's impossible to disable it on most computers, even when a USB keyboard is used instead. If you have other USB devices, however, such as a USB digital camera or modem, you might be able to save an interrupt by putting your mouse on the USB port, as well.

> **TIP**
>
> USB keyboards and miceare more common in the Macintosh market, so you might find a greater selection of these devices in the Macintosh section of your local computer superstore. Macintosh keyboards have slightly different keys than do PC keyboards, though. Specifically, Macintosh keyboards have no Windows key, and they have a Command key (imprinted with a cloverleaf design) instead of an Alt key. This difference is largely cosmetic. A bonus to buying a Macintosh USB keyboard is that Macintosh USB keyboards usually include a 2-port USB hub, which increases the number of USB devices you can attach to your computer. Macintosh USB mice should work fine on x86 hardware, but many of these devices have only one button, which is insufficient for Linux.

Linux's USB support is rudimentary at best in the 2.2.x kernels. The 2.3.x development kernels include support for many USB devices, so the 2.4.x kernel will almost certainly include stable USB support. Fortunately, USB keyboards and mice were some of the first USB devices to gain support in Linux, so these devices are well supported. Unfortunately, this support is still fairly new, so many x86 distributions don't support USB keyboards and mice during installation. If you want to use a USB keyboard or mouse, therefore, you might need to install Linux using conventional devices and then swap in the USB devices after you've installed Linux and perhaps recompiled the kernel. Fortunately, this situation is likely to improve in the near future, so you should check your distribution's list of supported hardware to see if USB devices are supported from the start.

One protocol supports all USB keyboards, and another supports all USB mice. You therefore don't need to deal with selecting a special protocol for each brand or model device. (You do need to select a USB keyboard's country codes, though.) The USB mouse protocol is modeled after that for PS/2 mice, so you can configure XFree86 just as you would for a PS/2 mouse, except that you specify a different device file.

USB connectors come in two varieties, known as Series A and Series B, both of which are shown in Figure 15.4. Motherboard USB ports normally accept Series A connectors, so this is the type you'll find on mice. Some external devices, such as scanners and printers, often use detachable USB cables, and these devices often have Series B connectors.

FIGURE 15.4

You'll find a Series A USB connector (left) on the end of a USB mouse or keyboard's cable. Series B connectors (right) are used on external devices that use detachable USB cables.

> ## Macintosh Mouse and Keyboard Ports
>
> Macintoshes have existed in a world of their own in terms of mice and keyboards for a long time. These computers have used the *Apple Desktop Bus* (ADB) to support both keyboards and mice. Ports of Linux to the Macintosh therefore support ADB devices natively.
>
> More recently, Apple has abandoned ADB in favor of USB. In fact, this shift has helped spur development of Linux USB support, especially for keyboards and mice. Versions of Linux for PowerPC computers come with sufficient USB support to use USB keyboards and mice from the start, and often to use additional USB components. If you have an iMac or another USB-enabled Macintosh, therefore, you shouldn't be concerned about Linux's USB support for your keyboard and mouse.

Keyboard Technologies

Keyboard technology is fairly simple and static, as computer technologies go. Most of the recent technological changes in keyboards have to do with their interfaces to the computer. Aside from the potential for problems if you get a USB keyboard, the most important technological differences between keyboards have to do with how the keyboards register key presses. The vast majority of keyboards on the market use one of two methods to accomplish this goal: mechanical switches or rubber dome membranes. There are also a number of less-used variants and alternative technologies.

Mechanical Key Switches

One method keyboards can use for registering key presses is to place an independent mechanical switch under every key. Most such switches work much like the switches on other electrical push buttons with which you're familiar, such as the buttons used to power on many computers or stereo components. A piece of metal in the movable portion of the switch completes an electrical circuit when the switch is depressed. The keyboard's circuitry detects this closed circuit and translates it into an appropriate signal to the computer. In order to have the key return to its original position after it's been depressed, mechanical switches usually include a spring. These components are normally all encased in a small package underneath the keys you see on your keyboard. Figure 15.5 shows two mechanical switches from which the keycaps have been removed. Locking the switch itself into a sealed box helps protect the sensitive components from dirt, thereby prolonging the switch's life.

FIGURE 15.5

Mechanical key switches are sealed against the environment to protect them from dust and other contaminants.

Mechanical key switches provide strong tactile feedback and long life. Keyboards of this type are often described as "crisp" or "clicky." This type of keyboard is available from NMB (http://www.nmbtech.com) and Alps (http://www.alpsusa.com), among others. Most people who have strong preferences about their keyboards prefer mechanical keyboards, although they can be hard to find. Mechanical keyboards are more expensive than the rubber dome designs that are more common.

Rubber Dome Keyboards

Most keyboards sold for x86 PCs today use a rubber dome design. Underneath the keys lies a rubber-like membrane formed into a dome. When you press a key, that action forces the rubber dome to collapse. Inside the dome lies a carbon contact, which completes an electrical circuit in much the same way that the switch in a mechanical keyboard completes a circuit. This arrangement is illustrated in Figure 15.6, which shows two rubber dome keyboard switches in cutaway side view, one depressed and one not. Because of the resiliency of rubber and similar compounds, rubber dome keyboards don't require springs.

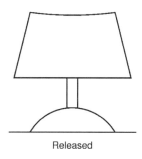 

Released   Depressed

FIGURE 15.6

The dome in a rubber dome keyboard collapses when you depress a key, then springs back to its normal position when you release the key.

Rubber dome keyboards vary substantially in their feel. Some have strong tactile feedback similar to that available in mechanical keyboards, although they're typically a bit quieter and not quite as crisp. Others have a much "mushier" feel. Touch typists generally object to keyboards that lack strong tactile feedback. Unfortunately, most new computers sold today include extraordinarily cheap rubber dome keyboards that provide little in the way of tactile feedback. If you purchase such a computer, you might want to replace its keyboard with a better mechanical model, or at least a higher-quality rubber dome keyboard. Fortunately, the keyboards all look the same to the computer, so you can replace a rubber dome keyboard with a mechanical switch keyboard without worry about compatibility with your computer.

One of the advantages of rubber dome keyboards is that they're resistant to dirt and liquids. Although I don't recommend trying it, I've heard of people running rubber dome keyboards through dishwashers to clean them, with no ill effects! Mechanical switch keyboards would almost certainly be damaged by such treatment, because water would likely seep into the switches, causing corrosion.

Miscellaneous Alternative Technologies

Some variants on the preceding keyboard types exist, including

- **Capacitive switch** These switches work on electromagnetic principles, detecting the change in capacitance as the components inside the switch move relative to one another. These switches use a spring to force the keycap back up after it's been depressed. Like purely mechanical switches, capacitive switches use mechanisms that are sealed against the environment, residing underneath plastic keycaps. Some of IBM's earliest PC keyboards used capacitive switch designs.

- **Foam element**   This keyboard type uses a piece of conductive foam at the bottom of a plunger to complete a circuit. Mechanically speaking, foam element keyboards are similar to mechanical switch keyboards, but the switch design uses foam rather than a metal switch. Like rubber dome keyboards, foam element keyboards tend to produce little in the way of tactile feedback. This design is rarely used today.

- **Membrane**   A membrane keyboard uses a flat or nearly-flat membrane atop a very shallow rubber dome. This one membrane replaces the many individual keys used in most other keyboard designs. The result is a keyboard that provides no or almost no tactile feedback and little or no key travel. These keyboards are therefore unsuitable for touch typing. Because they can be completely sealed, they're useful in harsh industrial environments. You're likely to see such keyboards on the cash registers at fast food restaurants.

NOTE

Rubber dome keyboards are often referred to as *membrane keyboards*, even by keyboard manufacturers. I use the term *rubber dome keyboard* to distinguish this type of keyboard from the flat membrane keyboards I've just described.

As a general rule, capacitive switch keyboards are some of the best available, at least in the judgment of most touch typists. Foam element keyboards are not highly regarded, and as already noted, membrane keyboards are unsuitable for serious typing tasks.

Keyboards with Extras

Some keyboards contain extra features that aren't strictly keyboard technology. Examples include

- Pointing devices
- Speakers
- Scanners
- Calculators

You can use some of these devices just as you would their equivalents in Linux. For instance, the built-in pointing devices (generally touch pads or TrackPoints) on some keyboards work just like ordinary pointing devices. Such keyboards generally include separate cables for the keyboard and additional hardware devices. In some cases, you must research drivers for the additional functions. In other cases, driver support is irrelevant because the device doesn't require drivers (as in speakers) or because it's not really a computer component (such as a calculator that functions independently of the computer as a whole).

Some keyboards include special nonstandard keys. These keys are usually designed to let you launch programs, control your speakers' volume, or perform other common functions more easily under Windows. Linux support for these unusual keys is generally lacking. In some cases, though, you might be able to map appropriate functions onto these keys. To do so, you must first determine whether the keys generate any events that are detectable by Linux. The xev program is particularly helpful in tracking down such events. This is an X program that tells you what X events are directed its way. For instance, launching xev and then pressing the *1* key produces the following output:

```
KeyPress event, serial 24, synthetic NO, window 0x4400001,
    root 0x25, subw 0x0, time 4075940102, (847,521), root:(922,780),
    state 0x0, keycode 46 (keysym 0x6c, l), same_screen YES,
    XLookupString gives 1 characters:  "l"

KeyRelease event, serial 24, synthetic NO, window 0x4400001,
    root 0x25, subw 0x0, time 4075940167, (847,521), root:(922,780),
    state 0x0, keycode 46 (keysym 0x6c, l), same_screen YES,
    XLookupString gives 1 characters:  "l"
```

Note that two events are generated: one for depressing the key, the other for releasing it. If this had been some special-purpose key on a keyboard, you could use this information to modify your X configuration to do something useful when the key is pressed. Such modifications can be tricky to implement, however, and many keyboards' special keys don't generate useful X events. I therefore don't recommend you buy such a keyboard in order to use these extra keys. If you already have such a keyboard, of course, you can use it as a normal keyboard without using the special keys.

One additional "extra" that deserves mention is the increasing trend towards *ergonomic keyboards*. These keyboards typically split the keys down the middle and rotate the left and right sections of the keyboard, the goal being to keep you from bending your wrists in a potentially injurious way as you type. Many ergonomic keyboards also raise the center of the keyboard, so that your wrists don't lie completely flat as you type. Other keyboards can use more radical designs. Most of these ergonomic designs are based on sound ergonomic *theories*, but the extent to which any given product can reduce repetitive-motion injuries is usually untested.

CAUTION

If you feel a constant and unusual tingling in one or more of your fingers, this can be a sign of a repetitive motion injury. You should consult a doctor about the problem. If your doctor recommends using an ergonomic keyboard, then by all means do so; but switching to an ergonomic keyboard might not be sufficient to prevent the problem from worsening.

Adjusting Keyboard Layout

You might need to adjust your keyboard's layout for any of a number of reasons. By *keyboard layout*, I don't mean the physical placement of the keys, but rather, what keys produce what actions. There are several reasons you might want to modify your keyboard's layout, including

- To gain access to keyboard features that are unique to your nation. Keyboards sold in Germany, for instance, have a slightly different mix of keys than do keyboards sold in the United States.

- To fix problems with keys that don't work as expected. For instance, word processors often use unusual key combinations, such as Shift+Tab, to perform functions. If whoever designed your default keyboard layout overlooked an important but unusual keystroke or mapped it incorrectly, you might need to adjust the layout to fix this problem.

- To create an unusual but desirable keyboard layout. For instance, some people prefer to use the Dvorak keyboard layout, which is optimized for better typing speed and less physical strain than is the more common QWERTY layout.

Unfortunately, adjusting your keyboard's layout entails different procedures for use in text mode than for use in X. You might therefore need to go through two parallel procedures rather than a single procedure to correct any keyboard problems you might have. It's also possible to configure Linux so that your keyboard works one way in text mode and another in X. This sort of configuration can be confusing and annoying—a keypress that works fine in a text-based program in an xterm in X might not work when you shut down X and work in text mode, for instance.

Keyboard Mapping Theory

When you press a key on your keyboard, several things happen:

- The keyboard sends a *scan code* to the computer. The scan code is an unprocessed representation of the key that was pressed. Depending upon the type of keyboard in use (QWERTY versus Dvorak; United States versus German; and so on), the same scan code might correspond to a different function or symbol.

- Some applications operate in *scan code mode*, and work on the scan codes as delivered by the keyboard. The kernel delivers scan codes directly to these applications.

- Other applications work on *key codes*, which have been parsed by the kernel into uniform codes no matter what type of keyboard is attached.

- Most text-mode applications don't work with either scan codes or key codes. These applications use codes that have been further parsed by Linux's terminal driver. I refer to these codes as *terminal codes*. The terminal driver takes key codes and converts them into a form that's uniform, not just across keyboards, but across wildly varying input devices, such as Telnet sessions or console logins.

- X works on scan codes and processes those scan codes in a way that's analogous to what happens for text-mode programs. In fact, text-mode programs run in an `xterm` window receive the same terminal codes they receive in text mode. Because the processing to get from scan codes to terminal codes is different, though, the keyboard mapping might be subtly—or wildly—different, as well.

It's possible to modify the keyboard layout at any step in this process. The most common points are in the mapping from key codes to terminal codes and in X's keyboard mapping from scan codes. Some keyboards are also programmable. If you have such a keyboard, you can reprogram it to produce a different set of scan codes. A few models, for instance, support remapping so that they produce the Dvorak layout natively.

Text-Mode Keyboard Layout

The principal method of setting the mapping from key codes to terminal codes in text mode is to use the program `loadkeys`. This program loads the specified keyboard map file and instructs the kernel terminal driver to use it for keyboard input. Linux distributions normally include a call to `loadkeys` in a configuration file. For instance, in SuSE 6.3, the file `/etc/rc.d/init.d/kbd` contains this call. In Caldera OpenLinux 2.3, the equivalent call is made in `/etc/rc.d/init.d/keytable`. Other distributions might place this call in other locations.

The trick to modifying a key map is to change which key map `loadkeys` uses. In the United States, most users configure their systems at installation to call an appropriate U.S. keymap. This key map file is probably called `us.map` and is buried in an obscure directory such as `/usr/lib/kbd/keymaps/i386/qwerty`. Of course, the Linux installation program handled setting up the details of the mapping, so you were probably unaware of these details. To change the key map, I recommend you locate the script or configuration file that specifies the key map file, and then change that file. In Caldera OpenLinux 2.3, for instance, the `/etc/sysconfig/keyboard` file contains the name of the key map file. You can change this definition to another predefined file, or you can change it to a file you create yourself. You can then copy and modify a key map file that's almost right.

A key map file consists of a series of lines like the following:

```
keycode   8 = seven          ampersand      braceleft       Control_underscore
```

This line lists four meanings of the key code. Which meaning is used depends on which modifier keys are used (Shift, Ctrl, or Alt on most keyboards, with additional options for left and right variants of these). Each modifier key has a value, as shown in Table 15.1. Which key meaning is used depends upon the sum of the modifiers. For instance, with no modifiers, the value is 0, so it's the 0th field—seven in the preceding example. With the Shift key pressed, the value is 1, so the value is ampersand. The Ctrl+Shift combination yields a value of 5, so the 6th field would be used. The preceding line includes only four fields, so in practice, this combination can be handled by individual programs as they see fit. Because the modifiers go up to 128, it's possible to have a *very* long line in the key map file—up to 256 entries.

TABLE 15.1 Modifier Keys Used in Key Map Files

Key	Value
Shift	1
AltGr	2
Ctrl	4
Alt	8
ShiftL	16
ShiftR	32
CtrlL	64
CtrlR	128

AltGr refers to the right Alt key. Shift and Ctrl refer to either Shift or Ctrl key, respectively, whereas these names with L *or* R *appended refer to the left or right keys only.*

If you want to modify just one or two keys, you can do so without adjusting your entire key map. You can do this using the keycode command, which takes the form:

```
keycode n = function
```

You must know the key code number and the function name in order to use this command. You can find the key code generated by a key by using the showkey command. Type **showkey** and the program displays the key codes generated by any key press you make.

X-Based Keyboard Layout

The principles of X keyboard layout adjustment are similar to those for text-based keyboard layouts, but some of the details differ. The basic keyboard layout selection is handled by the Keyboard section of your XF86Config file. This section should look something like this:

```
Section "Keyboard"
    Protocol "Standard"
    XkbRules "xfree86"
    XkbModel "omnikey101"
    XkbLayout "us"
    XkbVariant "nodeadkeys"
EndSection
```

This example sets the keyboard layout to use the us rules. You can change the layout by changing this code to another appropriate code, such as de for a German keyboard layout.

You can make adjustments to individual keys, or the entire mapping, by using the xmodmap command. To adjust an individual key's meaning, you can use the -e parameter to bind a key code to an action, as in

```
xmodmap -e 'keycode 23 = Tab'
```

To adjust a group of key bindings, you can place assignments like the one inside the quotes in the preceding example, one per line, in a file. You can then pass that file to xmodmap, as in `xmodmap xmodmap-bindings.txt`.

> **TIP**
>
> Many distributions are configured to run xmodmap and pass it the ~/.Xmodmap file when you log in. You can therefore place your adjustments in this file and not have to call xmodmap yourself.

Some Linux distributions configure the Backspace and Delete keys in a way that most individuals find confusing. You can alter their behavior by using the following xmodmap assignments:

```
keycode 22 = BackSpace
keycode 107 = Delete
```

Adjusting Key Repeat Rates

When you press a key, you get one instance of the associated character or action. If you keep the key held down, though, the computer begins repeating that key. By default, most Linux distributions set the key repeat rate to its maximum value, which is far too high for an average human to exercise much control over when the key stops repeating. To slow things down, you probably want to adjust the keyboard repeat rate. As with keyboard layouts, you do this differently for text mode and for X, although a text mode adjustment tends to carry over into X.

In text mode, you set the keyboard repeat rate using the kbdrate program. You call this program as follows:

```
kbdrate [-s] [-r rate] [-d delay]
```

The options are as follows:

- **-s**   This option specifies silent operation; the program doesn't report back its actions.
- **-r *rate***   Set the keyboard repeat rate to *rate* characters per second (cps). The default value on x86 hardware is 10.9 cps.
- **-d *delay***   Set the delay before the key begins repeating to *delay* milliseconds (ms). The default value on x86 hardware is 250 ms.

> **CAUTION**
>
> You can place a call to kbdrate in a startup script, such as /etc/rc.d/rc.local, to set the keyboard repeat rate whenever the computer starts.

In X, you can adjust the keyboard repeat rate using the AutoRepeat keyword in the Keyboard section, as in

```
AutoRepeat delay rate
```

The *delay* and *rate* values have the same meanings as they do with the kbdrate program.

Mice and Mutant Mice

The computer mouse was developed in the 1960s, but wasn't used much until the 1973 release of the Xerox Alto computer. The mouse wasn't popularized until the release of the Apple Lisa and Macintosh computers a decade later. Thereafter the mouse spread to a wide variety of computer systems, including x86 PCs. Today, all computers larger than a palmtop include a mouse or some alternative pointing device—and palmtop computers often use touch-sensitive screens that can be used in place of a mouse.

The range of options available in mice and competing pointing technologies today is quite wide. Fortunately, most of these options don't require special driver support, because the options relate to internal technologies that are transparent to software, or to ergonomic factors like the shape of the mouse. These are important considerations for you as a human purchaser of a pointing device, of course.

NOTE

I describe several popular pointing devices in the following pages, but I don't cover all the available pointing devices. If you happen upon an unusual pointing device, chances are it will work with Linux.

The Conventional Mouse

A conventional mouse, shown in Figure 15.7, is a device that's sized to fit in the palm of the hand. On its bottom is some sort of tracking mechanism—usually a ball that rolls against sensors that detect this motion, but sometimes an all-optical sensor grid. (I describe these technologies later in this chapter, in "Mouse Technologies.") On the top and sometimes on the sides of modern mice lie one or more buttons. Macintosh computers today ship with 1-button mice, but x86 PCs usually ship with 2- or 3-button mice. Some models include more buttons than this. Many modern mice include a *scroll wheel* in place of one button. This device can be spun like a wheel, and it's used to scroll text in windows. The scroll wheel can also usually be pushed like a button. If configured without special scroll wheel drivers, a scroll wheel works as a button in Linux, but the scrolling function isn't used. Even when used with special scroll wheel drivers, the scroll wheel requires configuration for applications or application types to use the wheel.

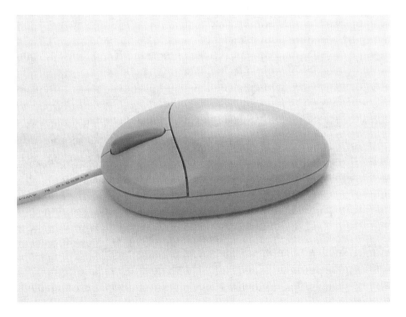

FIGURE 15.7

Mice vary substantially in design details, but the mouse shown here is typical of the breed.

15

KEYBOARDS AND MICE

The conventional mouse remains the most popular type of pointing device on x86 computers today. Most computer users are familiar with the operation of a mouse, and the mouse remains one of the most precise pointing devices available. Some criteria to consider when you purchase a mouse include

- **Interface**   Serial, PS/2, and USB are the most common mouse interfaces. All work fine with Linux, although you might need to upgrade your kernel to use a USB mouse.

- **Sensor technology**   As described shortly, mice use a variety of sensor technologies, and these have an influence on the mouse's performance.

- **Resolution**   Generally measured in dots per inch (dpi), resolution refers to how far you must move a mouse to achieve a given motion of the mouse pointer on the screen. Higher resolutions translate into greater pointer movement for a given physical movement. Alternatively, the tracking of the mouse on the screen can be adjusted downward with higher-resolution devices, yielding greater precision. You might therefore want to favor higher-resolution devices, particularly if you need to use the mouse for high-precision activities like manipulating graphics images.

> **TIP**
>
> If you find that your mouse doesn't track quickly enough, you can use the xset m *acceleration threshold* command to adjust the mouse's speed. Set *acceleration* to an integral value of 1 or more to speed up the mouse, and *threshold* to a number of pixels moved before the acceleration "kicks in." This pair allows you to move slowly when you move the mouse a short distance, which can be handy when positioning an object precisely. At the same time, an increased movement can benefit from acceleration.

- **Symmetry**   Some mice are symmetrical left-to-right, which means they're equally well (or poorly) suited for both left- and right-handed individuals. Others are shaped to fit a right or left hand. Left-handed individuals can have a hard time finding mice that are well suited to use with the left hand, because manufacturers often neglect the left-handed market.

- **General ergonomics**   No two people have hands that are precisely alike. It's therefore best to try a mouse before you buy it. Does it fit well in your hand? Are there awkward bulges? Do the buttons take too much or too little effort to depress? Only you can judge these factors.

- **Buttons**   X assumes that the mouse has three buttons. Because 2-button mice are so common, XFree86 includes an option to simulate the middle button when you simultaneously press both buttons on a 2-button mouse. This action can be awkward, though, so I strongly recommend you buy a 3-button mouse for use with Linux. Additional buttons might or might not be useful, but require additional effort to configure in any event.

- **Scroll wheel**   There's no reason to avoid scroll wheels for use with Linux, but configuring these devices requires extra effort.

- **Cordless mice**   Some mice use infrared technology to operate without a cord. This can be convenient at times, but if your desk is cluttered, the infrared beam can be blocked more easily than a cord.

Trackballs: Upside-Down Mice

One of the problems with the mouse is that the entire device must be moved in order to operate. Even if you set aside an appropriate amount of desk space, the mouse pointer on the screen has a tendency to get out of sync with the position of the mouse on the desk. The result is that you invariably run out of desk space in which to perform some operation. You must then pick the mouse up, move it, and continue the operation, sometimes while keeping the mouse button depressed. Some people's desks have a tendency to become so cluttered that setting aside space for a mouse can be a serious problem.

One solution is to use an upside-down mouse. Instead of placing a roller ball on the bottom of the mouse, the roller ball is placed on the top, where you manipulate it with one or more fingers. The result is known as a *trackball*, an example of which is shown in Figure 15.8. Mechanically, trackballs are much like mice; trackballs operate on the same types of mechanical, opto-mechanical, and optical sensors that mice use, as described shortly. Trackballs are physically quite different, however, and they vary substantially among themselves.

When you purchase a trackball, you should consider many of the same factors I outlined earlier with respect to mice. In addition, you should consider what fingers you use to manipulate the roller ball and buttons. The mouse shown in Figure 15.8, for instance, is designed for a right-handed individual to use his or her thumb to roll the ball, and the first three fingers to click the buttons. Other trackballs are designed so that the ball is manipulated by the index finger or a cluster of several fingers. You might like one type of trackball but detest another.

Touch Pads

One alternative to mice that's particularly common on notebook computers is the *touch pad*. This device is a small, flat pad, roughly 2–3 inches on a side. You touch the pad and move your finger about on it to move the pointer on the screen. Touch pads include one or more buttons that work just like mouse or trackball buttons. The touch pad shown in Figure 15.9, which is integrated into a notebook computer, includes two regular buttons and several auxiliary buttons to control various computer features. Such auxiliary buttons might or might not be usable in Linux.

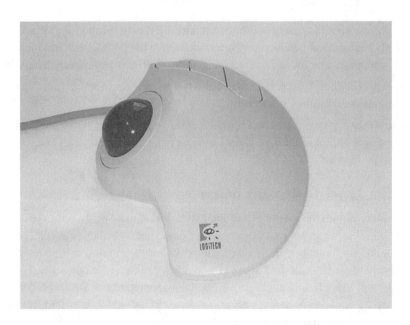

FIGURE 15.8

Trackballs allow you to move the on-screen pointer by rolling a ball that's accessible to one or more fingers.

FIGURE 15.9

Touch pads don't vary much in appearance, although different models place their buttons in different locations relative to the body of the pad.

Although touch pads are most commonly found on notebook computers, you can purchase touch pads for use with desktop computers. One common arrangement is a keyboard that includes a touch pad. These devices share one of the principal advantages of trackballs: They consume little desk space. They also require little in the way of cleaning, which makes them appealing for use in harsh environments. One drawback to touch pads is that they don't actually detect *touch*, in the sense of pressure. Instead, they sense the electrical characteristics of your finger. Therefore, they might not work if your finger is dirty, or if you're wearing gloves.

The IBM TrackPoint

The TrackPoint is a pointing device that's normally integrated into a keyboard. The device is a small pressure-sensitive stick with a rubber coating that protrudes between the *G*, *H*, and *B* keys. To move the pointer on the screen, you touch the TrackPoint device on the opposite side. For instance, to move the pointer left, you touch the right side of the TrackPoint. In this sense, the TrackPoint resembles the usual operation of a joystick. The TrackPoint differs from a joystick in three important ways, however:

- The TrackPoint doesn't move in response to the pressure you apply to it; only the onscreen pointer moves.
- The TrackPoint is positioned in the middle of the keyboard, which makes it unusually easy to manipulate if you're a touch typist who doesn't like moving your hand from the home row.
- The TrackPoint is much smaller than a joystick. In order to nestle in-between three keyboard keys, it must be smaller than those keys.

Like a touch pad, a TrackPoint has no moving parts and is resistant to dirt. Because it operates on pressure, it doesn't suffer from the sometimes erratic behavior that's common on touch pads. Like a trackball, a TrackPoint doesn't suffer from edge effects—there's no need to lift your finger and reposition it when you come to the device's edge, as you might have to do with a touch pad or mouse.

Despite these advantages, some people find TrackPoints to be awkward to use or difficult to control. The integration of the TrackPoint into a keyboard means that you might not get the optimum keyboard if you want to use a TrackPoint device. As with other pointing technologies, I recommend you try one before you buy it. Even if you're considering a TrackPoint-enabled keyboard for a desktop system, it might be easier to try the device on a notebook computer. IBM and Toshiba models are particularly likely to use TrackPoints.

15

KEYBOARDS AND
MICE

> **NOTE**
>
> IBM originally marketed a convertible mouse/trackball by the name TrackPoint. IBM subsequently sold the device I've just described under the names TrackPoint II and TrackPoint III, and other manufacturers use other names. The name *TrackPoint* has come to be used in references to these devices, and I follow that convention here.

Mouse Technologies

Mice and trackballs both rely on one of three basic types of technologies to sense motion of the mouse or ball:

- Mechanical sensors
- Opto-mechanical sensors
- Optical sensors

Each of these technologies has its unique advantages and disadvantages. Mechanical and opto-mechanical devices are quite similar to each other in most ways, so I describe them together. Purely optical devices have different performance characteristics.

TrackPoints, touch pads, and other pointing devices all use their own technologies. I briefly described the technologies used by touch pads and TrackPoints in their respective sections. Because mice and trackballs dominate the market, and because both devices come in varieties that use different technologies, I devote a more detailed description to those technologies.

Mechanical and Opto-Mechanical Devices

Most mechanical and opto-mechanical mice and all trackballs of these types use a small ball that rotates against two rollers in the body of the mouse or trackball, as shown in Figure 15.10. There's usually also a third roller that's used solely to stabilize the ball; no sensors are attached to this roller.

The mechanical and opto-mechanical designs deviate at this point. In a purely mechanical device, the rollers activate some form of mechanical sensor, whereas in opto-mechanical devices, an optical sensor is used. Most mice and trackballs sold today use an opto-mechanical design. In this configuration, the roller rotates a wheel that contains spokes through which light can pass. A small light source sends light through those spokes, and an optical sensor on the other side detects these light changes. This arrangement is depicted in Figure 15.11. Circuitry in the mouse can then combine the input from both rollers to determine in which direction the mouse or trackball is moving.

Rollers

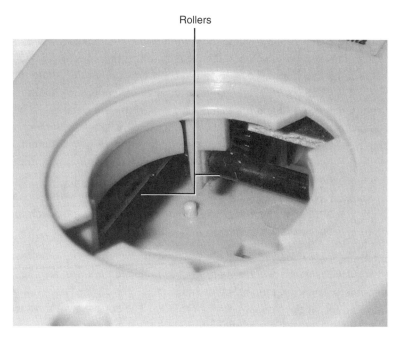

FIGURE 15.10

The rollers inside a mouse sense the movements of the ball that are associated with movements of the mouse against a desk.

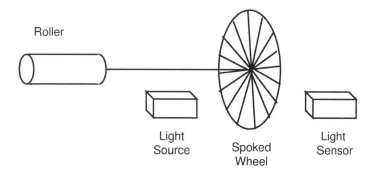

Roller

Light
Source

Spoked
Wheel

Light
Sensor

FIGURE 15.11

When the roller rotates in response to a mouse movement, the light beam's passage through the spoked wheel is interrupted, allowing the mouse to sense movement.

Mechanical and opto-mechanical mice and trackballs are fairly inexpensive to produce and yield acceptable results for most applications. They do have drawbacks, however. The most important of these is that they are quite sensitive to dirt. As the ball rolls on a desk or is turned by a human hand, it picks up dust, grit, and moisture. These have a tendency to transfer onto the rollers, which eventually become encrusted with the stuff. The result is that the mouse or trackball no longer moves smoothly. You might be able to feel this condition in your hand as you use the device, and you'll also see the result in a jerky motion of the pointer on the screen. In extreme cases, it can become nearly impossible to move the pointer in one direction or another. The solution to this problem is generally a thorough mouse cleaning, in which you remove the accumulated gunk from the rollers. All mice and trackballs feature a flap or ring you can open to remove the ball and clean the rollers. Sometimes a simple scraping with your fingernail will do the trick, but other times you might need to use cleaning chemicals. A cotton swab and rubbing alcohol can help loosen dirt from the rollers. No matter how you do it, remember to rotate the rollers so you clean their entire surfaces, not just whatever surface happens to be facing you. While you have the mouse open, you might want to clean the ball as well, although in my experience it's the rollers that usually cause problems.

For whatever reason, some mice and trackballs are more prone to develop problems than are others. Expensive devices aren't necessarily any better in this respect than are cheap ones. I've had expensive devices develop erratic behavior and a need to be cleaned almost daily, while inexpensive mice go for weeks without needing cleaning. The environment in which the mouse is used can play an important role in its reliability. Ideally, your work environment should be kept clean. You might want to invest in a mouse pad, which can help prevent dirt accumulation inside the mouse.

Optical Devices

Purely optical mice completely eliminate the need for moving parts in the mouse (aside from those in the buttons). They do this by using a light beam that bounces off a reflective surface underneath the mouse, as depicted in Figure 15.12. This surface must contain some form of texturing for the light sensor to detect, much as an opto-mechanical mouse detects changes in the light when the spoked wheel attached to a roller moves.

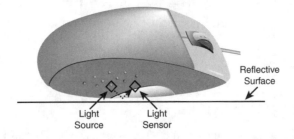

FIGURE 15.12

Optical mice use a light beam to detect movement against a surface.

Optical trackballs work in much the same way, but because the user turns a ball, optical track-balls don't eliminate the ball. Instead, the ball is covered in a pattern of dots, and instead of rollers, the trackball uses a sensor like the one used in an optical mouse.

Optical mice and trackballs offer advantages in reliability over mechanical and opto-mechanical designs. Because they don't rely on moving parts in their sensors, these devices' sensors aren't as likely to become clogged with dirt. These devices also aren't as likely to suffer from broken parts. Optical mice and trackballs do require occasional cleaning, however. An optical mouse typically uses felt pads as a buffer between its bottom and the desk or pad on which it rests, and these felt pads can accumulate dust over time, which increases drag. Similarly, the contact points on which an optical trackball's ball rests can accumulate dust and dirt. In extreme cases, an optical device's sensors might become clogged with dirt, which must be blown out. Such occurrences are quite rare, however. Cleaning optical devices is typically eas-ier than is cleaning mechanical and opto-mechanical devices.

Most optical mice suffer from a problem in that they require special mouse pads. These pads are reflective but are imprinted with a pattern of dots that the mouse uses to track movement. If you lose or damage the pad, the mouse becomes useless. A few optical mice, such as Microsoft's IntelliMouse Optical, can track on a wide variety of textured surfaces, such as blue jeans or wood-grain desktops. Because optical trackballs texture their balls, they don't require special pads.

In the grand scheme of pointing devices, optical mice and trackballs are fairly rare. Microsoft (`http://www.microsoft.com`) and Mouse Systems (`http://www.mousesystems.com`) manu-facture most of the optical mice available today, whereas Logitech (`http://www.logitech.com`) produces most of the optical trackballs available today. All three companies also produce conventional opto-mechanical devices.

Configuring a Pointer in Linux

Configuring Linux touse a mouse or other pointing device is typically something that you do when you install Linux. If you change your mouse device, or if you set it up incorrectly when you installed Linux, you might need to adjust your configuration. As with keyboard configura-tion, Linux uses separate settings for text-mode and X-based mouse operation. Both rely on the same underlying device files, however, so I'll start with that information.

Mouse Device Drivers and Files

To receive mouse input, you must activate one or more kernel modules, depending upon the type of mouse you're using:

- **PS/2 mice**   PS/2 mouse support is enabled in the *Mice* section of the Linux kernel con-figuration script, as shown in Figure 15.13. This section of the kernel configuration also includes support for a number of more exotic mouse types, including bus mice.

15

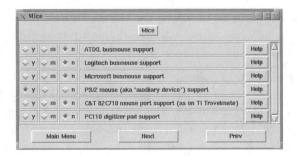

FIGURE 15.13

PS/2 mouse support requires its own specialized mouse driver.

- **Serial mice**   Serial mice use the normal Linux serial port drivers, which you activate by selecting the Standard/generic (dumb) serial support option in the Character devices configuration menu. If you've connected the mouse to a specialized multiport serial board, you must activate support for that type of board instead of, or in addition to, the conventional serial port support.

- **USB mice**   There are three mouse-related options in the Linux USB support kernel configuration area. The first is the USB Human Interface Device (HID) support option, which is used to support mice, keyboards, and other input devices. The second option is the USB HIDBP Mouse support, which provides support only for mice. You need only one of these two options. The third mouse option is titled Mouse support, and it allows a USB mouse to be accessed as if it were a PS/2 mouse. This is a desirable option because it makes USB mice usable by software (such as XFree86) that understands PS/2 mouse protocols. This last option also supports a suboption, Mix All Mice into One Device, which lets you connect multiple USB mice and have them all work through the same device file. If this option isn't selected, each mouse requires its own device file, and can be accessed independently. No matter what USB mouse-specific options you select, you must also enable basic USB support, including support for either UHCI or OHCI, as appropriate for your motherboard's USB controller.

Linux routes mouse input through a variety of device files, as summarized in Table 15.2. On most systems, /dev/mouse is configured as a symbolic link to the actual mouse device, such as /dev/psaux. Therefore, it's often possible to refer to /dev/mouse rather than the actual mouse device file. Doing so can be a useful mnemonic, but, as each mouse type is unique, it might not save you much effort in reconfiguring a mouse when you change from one type to another.

TABLE 15.2   Mouse Device Files

Mouse Type	Device Filename	Device Major Number	Device Minor Number
Serial	/dev/ttyS0	4	64
Serial	/dev/ttyS1	4	65
PS/2	/dev/psaux	10	1
Bus	/dev/logibm, /dev/inportibm, others	10	0, 2, others
USB	/dev/usbmouse	10	32 (and up)

Either of the two standard serial ports can be used for a mouse, or subsequent serial ports on computers so equipped. Normally only one USB mouse is used, but you can attach more than one, in which case you can configure the Linux kernel to merge all their inputs into one device or split them up, as mentioned earlier. In the second case, the device minor number for the second and subsequent mice is incremented, and you must create additional device files.

gpm for Text-Mode Operation

Linux allows you to use a mouse to cut and paste text when running in text mode. To do so, Linux uses a program called gpm. This program must be run as root, and is generally run from a startup script such as /etc/rc.d/init.d/gpm. If necessary, you can edit this startup file to modify gpm's behavior. If it doesn't start automatically on your system, you can add an entry to a startup file such as /etc/rc.d/rc.local.

The main parameters used by gpm are

- **-t** *type*   Specifies the mouse type. *type* can be any of several values, such as ps2 for a PS/2 mouse or ms for a 2-button Microsoft mouse. Type **gpm -t help** to see a complete list of the protocols gpm supports.

- **-m** *device*   Specifies the device file. The default value is /dev/mouse, so if that's a symbolic link to your actual mouse device, you can omit this parameter.

- **-k**   Kills any running gpm process.

- **-R** *type*   Repeats mouse actions into the /dev/gpmdata file, using whatever protocol you specify. (In theory, you can use any protocol supported by gpm with the -t *type* parameter, but some protocols aren't well supported.) The default protocol is msc (Mouse Systems). This option is sometimes helpful if running gpm in text mode interferes with X's mouse access. Rather than access the mouse directly in X, you can run gpm at all times and then access /dev/gpmdata as the mouse device in X.

Use of gpm after it's running is straightforward, and works much as cutting and pasting does in X:

1. Move the mouse to wherever you want to begin selecting text. As you move the mouse, you'll see an inverse video cursor on the screen; that's the mouse pointer.

2. Press and hold the left mouse button while you drag the mouse to select text.

3. Release the mouse button. This is gpm's cue to copy the selected text to its clipboard.

4. Position your text cursor—which is *not* necessarily the same as gpm's cursor—where you want to insert the cut text.

5. Click the middle mouse button to insert text. (If you have a 2-button mouse, you must *chord* the buttons—click them both at the same time.)

XFree86 Mouse Options

Mouse configuration in X is handled by the Pointer section, which looks something like this:

```
Section "Pointer"
    Protocol "Microsoft"
    Device "/dev/ttyS1"
    Emulate3Buttons
    Emulate3Timeout 60
EndSection
```

The preceding section configures a Microsoft-compatible 2-button serial mouse on /dev/ttyS1 (COM2: in DOS or Windows). The Emulate3Buttons line tells X to treat a chord of the mouse's two buttons as if it were a press of the middle button. The Emulate3Timeout 60 line tells X to tolerate 60 milliseconds (ms) of difference in the time of pressing the two buttons in doing the 3-button emulation; if the buttons are pressed more than 60 ms apart, they're treated as separate button presses. The default value is 50 ms. Mice with three buttons don't require the Emulate3Buttons or Emulate3Timeout lines.

X supports a large number of mouse protocols. Some of the more common of these include

- **BusMouse**   The old bus mouse protocol, used by many older mice that used dedicated interface boards.
- **IntelliMouse**   Microsoft's serial IntelliMouse protocol for mice with wheels.
- **IMPS/2**   Wheel mice that use PS/2 or USB interfaces.
- **Logitech**   Logitech serial mice, and compatibles.
- **Microsoft**   Microsoft serial mice, and compatibles.
- **MouseMan**   A more recent Logitech serial mouse protocol.

- **MouseSystems**   MouseSystems serial mice, and compatibles.

- **PS/2**   PS/2 or USB mice. This protocol works with wheel mice, but doesn't enable wheel functions. To enable wheel functions, use the IMPS/2 protocol instead. (The wheel's button functionality still works with the plain PS/2 protocol, however.)

X supports additional, more exotic mouse protocols. Check the XF86Config man page for a complete list.

> **NOTE**
>
> Don't assume that a mouse uses a protocol named after its manufacturer. Some Logitech serial mice, for instance, use the Microsoft protocol. All PS/2 mice use the PS/2 or IMPS/2 protocols, regardless of manufacturer.

If you have a wheel mouse, you must create custom configurations for each application or application type to map the wheel's movement onto useful actions. These configurations generally go in your ~/.Xdefaults file or an application-specific configuration file. As an example, here's what you add to ~/.Xdefaults to get programs that use the Athena widget set to recognize the scroll wheel:

```
!## Athena text widgets
*Paned.Text.translations: #override\n\
 Shift<Btn4Down>,<Btn4Up>: scroll-one-line-down()\n\
 Shift<Btn5Down>,<Btn5Up>: scroll-one-line-up()\n\
 Ctrl<Btn4Down>,<Btn4Up>: previous-page()\n\
 Ctrl<Btn5Down>,<Btn5Up>: next-page()\n\
 None<Btn4Down>,<Btn4Up>:scroll-one-line-down()scroll-one-line-down()
➥scroll-one-line-down()scroll-one-line-down()scroll-one-line-down()\n\
 None<Btn5Down>,<Btn5Up>:scroll-one-line-up()scroll-one-line-up()
➥scroll-one-line-up()scroll-one-line-up()scroll-one-line-up()\n\
```

The Web site http://www.inria.fr/koala/colas/mouse-wheel-scroll/ is dedicated to collecting useful configurations for Linux programs to enable them to use wheel mice features. This Web page also includes discussions of the quirks of specific wheel mouse models, so if you want to buy a wheel mouse and wheel functionality is high on your agenda, be sure to check this page for compatibility information.

Summary

There's very little about keyboard and mouse hardware that's likely to pose problems for Linux. The main caveat is that support for USB devices is still weak in stock Linux distributions for x86 computers. You might need to use a standard keyboard for installing Linux, or choose your distribution with an eye for USB support. Keyboards don't vary a lot in their features, although their underlying technologies do differ and impact the keyboard feel. Pointing devices, on the other hand, vary substantially in function, ranging from conventional mice to TrackPoints. Each technology has its advantages and disadvantages, as well as adherents and detractors. The key is to choose a pointer that's comfortable *to you*. Fortunately, pointers are inexpensive enough that you can probably afford to try several types—but be aware that the ergonomically superior models of any given type are usually the more expensive ones.

Parallel and Serial Ports

IN THIS CHAPTER

Traditionally, most external devices have interfaced to x86 computers through one of two types of port: an *RS-232 serial port* or a *parallel port*. Both ports are designed for general-purpose data communications, rather than for specific devices. Parallel ports have traditionally been used by printers, although in recent years these ports have taken on additional duties as a means of interfacing with external removable disk drives, WebCams, and so on.

These ports receive their names from their means of transmitting data. Serial ports use two data transmission lines, one in each direction. (There are also a number of control lines that aren't involved in the data transmission *per se* but that help regulate its flow.) On each line, data can be transmitted one bit at a time, so to transmit one byte (eight bits) worth of data, it's necessary to transmit the bits one after another—that is, in a *serial* manner. Parallel ports, by contrast, use eight data transfer lines, so it's possible to transmit an entire byte at once. The eight bits traverse the cable in *parallel* with one another.

All other things being equal, parallel ports are faster than serial ports, but parallel cables have more stringent length limits than serial cables. As technologies improve, it becomes possible to overcome both speed and cable length limits of the past. The latest form of serial port in use on x86 computers is known as *Universal Serial Bus* (USB). USB is substantially faster than the earlier RS-232 serial ports, and it's much more flexible. It's still very new, however, so Linux support for USB devices is still maturing. I use the term *serial port* to mean the earlier RS-232 serial port. USB's practical differences make it as different from RS-232 serial as is parallel port technology.

NOTE

Other types of ports, such as SCSI ports (see Chapter 9, "SCSI Host Adapters") and keyboard ports (see Chapter 15, "Keyboards and Mice"), can be classified as being parallel or serial in nature. In this chapter, I am concerned only with the parallel printer port, RS-232 serial, and USB.

Port Hardware Requirements

Parallel and serial ports both consume limited system resources—notably, interrupts and I/O ports. The specific interrupts and I/O ports used by specific serial and parallel ports is fairly well standardized, and is summarized in Table 16.1. I describe these requirements in greater detail shortly.

TABLE 16.1   Resources Used by Common Ports

Port	Device File	Device Major	Device Minor	Interrupt	I/O Port
First Serial	/dev/ttyS0	4	64	4	0x3f8–0x3ff
Second Serial	/dev/ttyS1	4	65	3	0x2f8–0x2ff
Third Serial	/dev/ttyS2	4	66	4[1]	0x3f8–0x3ff[1]
Fourth Serial	/dev/ttyS3	4	67	3[1]	0x2f8–0x2ff[1]
First Parallel	/dev/lp0[3]	6	0	7[2]	0x3bc–0x3bf
Second Parallel	/dev/lp1[3]	6	1	5[2]	0x378–0x37a
Third Parallel	/dev/lp2[3]	6	2	5[1,2]	0x278 –0x27a
USB	Variable	Variable	Variable	Variable	Variable

[1]*This standard assignment is shared, and might not work well under Linux. If possible, assign another resource to avoid problems.*

[2]*Use of an interrupt for parallel ports under Linux is optional.*

[3]*This is the device filename used to access a printer via a parallel port. Access to other parallel devices can be done through other device files.*

Interrupts

Interrupts (sometimes abbreviated *IRQs*, for *interrupt requests*) are used by devices to signal the computer that an important event has occurred, such as the receipt of data for processing. The x86 architecture allows for only 16 interrupts, numbered 0–15. One of these interrupts (number 2) is effectively unusable, because the x86 interrupt architecture uses two interrupt controllers, each of which can handle 8 interrupts. The second controller, which handles interrupts 8–15, requires an interrupt on the first controller to function, and the second controller uses IRQ 2 on the first controller for this purpose.

Each RS-232 serial port is assigned a standard interrupt number. Unfortunately, the standard assignment for ports beyond the second *shares* the interrupts between serial ports, as shown in

Table 16.1. Sharing interrupts in this way works acceptably in DOS, but requires special configuration in Linux. Therefore, if you purchase an internal modem or secondary serial port card, you should do one of three things:

- Disable an unused serial port on the motherboard and configure the internal modem to use its port number. For instance, you could disable /dev/ttyS0 (identified as COM1: in the BIOS) using your BIOS's setup routines, and configure the modem to take on this identity.
- Enable the Support for sharing serial interrupts option under Character devices in the Linux kernel configuration. Doing so enables you to use a shared interrupt for serial ports.
- Assign the new port an interrupt other than the standard one. For instance, you might give it IRQ 9. The add-on device will then become /dev/ttyS2 (and /dev/ttyS3, if it's a two-port serial card and you give the second card its own interrupt, as well).

If you need more than two or three serial ports, I recommend you use a multiport serial board. These products support running several serial ports on just one interrupt, but they require special drivers in Linux. Fortunately, the Linux kernel includes the necessary drivers to support several multiport serial boards, so you should check the kernel configuration options to find which boards are supported.

By default, most Linux distributions are configured to not use interrupts for printing on the parallel ports. Instead, the hardware is operated in *polling mode*, which consumes more CPU time but leaves the parallel port's interrupt available for use by other devices. If you want to switch to using an interrupt for a printer port, you can do so by copying the interrupt number to the /proc/parport/*n*/irq file, where *n* is the parallel port number. For instance, to change /dev/lp0 to use interrupt 7, issue the following command:

```
echo 7 > /proc/parport/0/irq
```

You can confirm that this action has had the desired effect by typing **cat /proc/interrupts** and checking that interrupt 7 is used by the parallel port driver. You should then check to be sure you can print. If this change causes problems, you can reverse it by echoing the value 0 to the /proc/parport/*n*/irq file.

NOTE

Linux kernels prior to 2.1.131 used a different method of configuring interrupt-driven printing. These kernels used a program called tunelp to do the job. I describe this program later in this chapter.

USB ports also require interrupts, but the interrupt assigned to USB ports varies substantially from one machine to another. Because most USB ports are PCI devices that are built in to the motherboard, it's usually not necessary to explicitly configure a USB port's interrupt.

I/O Ports

The term *I/O port* can be confusing, because it can refer either to an interface into which you can plug a device or to a small area of memory used by the x86 architecture to transfer data between the CPU and its devices. Serial and parallel ports, like other hardware, require access to certain I/O port ranges, as detailed in Table 16.1.

Like shared interrupts, shared I/O ports on serial ports can be a problem. You should be sure to change the I/O ports for such serial devices in much the same way as you change their inter-rupts—either disable a built-in device and let the add-on device take over the built-in device's settings, or assign an unused I/O port to the device. You can find a list of used I/O ports in Linux by typing **cat /proc/ioports**. This command produces output similar to the following:

```
0000-001f : dma1
0020-003f : pic1
0040-005f : timer
0060-006f : keyboard
0080-008f : dma page reg
00a0-00bf : pic2
00c0-00df : dma2
00f0-00ff : fpu
02f8-02ff : serial(auto)
0378-037a : parport0
03c0-03df : vga+
03f8-03ff : serial(auto)
0778-077a : parport0
da00-daff : eth0
```

You can use this list to select an appropriate free I/O port range. Be aware, however, that if a device hasn't been used recently, its assigned I/O ports might not appear in this list. You should therefore check the /proc/ioports file shortly after using every device you have on the com-puter.

Cabling Concerns

Except for internal modems, serial and parallel devices require cables. Figure 16.1 shows sev-eral types of serial and parallel cable connectors for reference. With the exception of the USB Series B and Centronics parallel port connectors, all these connectors plug into ports on the back of x86 computers. The USB Series B and Centronics parallel port connectors both con-nect to devices, such as printers, that interface via the USB and parallel ports, respectively.

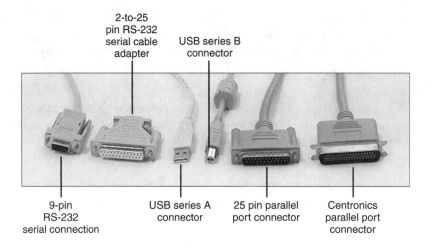

2-to-25
pin RS-232
serial cable   USB series B
adapter   connector

9-pin   USB series A   25 pin parallel   Centronics
RS-232   connector   port connector   parallel port
serial connection   connector

FIGURE 16.1

Serial and parallel cable connectors come in a wide variety of shapes and sizes.

Because cables are well standardized, there are few caveats when cable shopping. There are a few, however, including

- **IEEE 1284 parallel cables**   Many printers require cables that conform to the IEEE 1284 standards. These standards specify a minimum number of pins that must be connected for bidirectional communication. Some cheaper cables might not conform to the IEEE 1284 standards. Such cables often work with earlier printers, but not many later models.

- **Modem versus null modem cables**   A *null modem cable* is one that's designed to connect two computers via their serial ports. This cable must be wired differently than a cable to connect a computer to a modem (often called a *modem cable,* or a *straight-through cable*). With Ethernet so common, the need for null modem cables is slim, but these cables are still sold, so you should be careful not to buy one if you need a regular modem cable.

TIP

Null modem cables usually contain two 9- or 25-pin female plugs, whereas straight-through cables usually have one 9- or 25-pin female plug and one 25-pin male plug. You should generally go by the description on the cable's packaging, but if you have loose cables lying around, this rule of thumb can help you identify them.

- **Number of pins** Be sure the cables you buy have the correct number of pins. If they don't, you'll need an adapter like the one shown in Figure 16.1. These adapters can cost almost as much as a new cable.

Some cables use unusual connectors on the device end, in order to interface with unusual devices. Palmtop computers and digital cameras, for instance, often use extra-small connectors in order to save space. These cables tend to be expensive and difficult to find, so you should be careful not to lose or damage them.

A History of Ports in Linux

Throughout Linux's history, there have been some changes in its handling of ports. These changes can be relevant if you must deal with an earlier Linux distribution, or if you run across some outdated documentation.

Serial Port Devices

RS-232 serial port devices are accessed using the /dev/ttyS*n* device files, where *n* is a number from 0 up. Prior to the 2.2.x kernels, these devices could also be accessed using the /dev/cua*n* devices. These devices were the *callout* devices, which were used for dialing out with modems. The /dev/ttyS*n* devices, by contrast, were used for incoming connections, such as links to "dumb terminals."

The /dev/ttyS*n* and /dev/cua*n* devices both linked to the serial hardware, but the way they did so was subtly different. The existence of two access methods also posed problems in terms of controlling access to the serial hardware, because a program might not be able to tell that a device was already in use. Therefore, the /dev/cua*n* devices fell into disfavor, and it's recommended that you not use them. Support for /dev/cua*n* devices might be removed from the kernel in the future.

USB ports are handled in an entirely different way from RS-232 ports. RS-232 is intended as a one-to-one communications link—it connects one computer to one other device. If you have two RS-232 devices, you need two RS-232 ports on the computer to control both devices. USB, on the other hand, is a one-to-many bus. You can connect several USB devices to a single USB port. (You do need a USB *hub* to multiply the physical connectors to enable this type of connection, though.) As such, a single device file is inadequate to handle all USB devices. After all, if you've connected, say, a digital camera, a modem, and a mouse to your computer via USB, you need some way to uniquely identify each device. For this reason, Linux's USB support provides separate device files for each device. I describe the appropriate files for each USB device type in the appropriate chapters of this book.

> **NOTE**
>
> You can often connect more than one device to a parallel or RS-232 serial port by using a *switch box*. This box enables you to safely and quickly direct the port's traffic to and from one of two or more devices by pushing a button or turning a dial. Some switches can work the other way; you can use them to connect one printer to two or more computers. Today, this latter task is generally handled by networking the computers and enabling printer-sharing protocols, but a switch box can still sometimes be a useful tool.

USB support is a very recent addition to the Linux kernel. Only in the 2.2.x kernel series was USB support officially added, and it's still very primitive even late in the 2.2.x kernel series. The 2.3.x development kernels include much more extensive USB support, as described later in this chapter.

Parallel Port Devices

Through the 2.0.x kernels, the assumption in Linux was that parallel ports were used to interface with printers. As such, there was but a single parallel port driver. With the increasing popularity of parallel-port devices such as Zip drives, scanners, and WebCams, it became desirable to break the parallel port driver into two parts: a low-level parallel port driver and a higher-level driver to handle the needs of specific devices. In the 2.2.x kernel, therefore, there are several parallel port kernel options, including

- **General setup, Parallel port support**   This option is the core parallel port support. You *must* enable it (using either the Y or M option) to use any parallel port device. Enabling this feature is not sufficient to use a parallel port device, however. This option also has a couple of suboptions relating to the types of parallel-port hardware supported. For x86 systems, the *PC-style hardware* option is what you want to use.

- **Block devices, Parallel port IDE device support**   Enable this option, and whatever suboptions are appropriate, to use most disk-like devices that connect to the parallel port. I describe the details in the chapters devoted to each of these devices.

- **SCSI support, SCSI low-level drivers, IOMEGA parallel port**   There are actually two variants of this option for different varieties of Iomega Zip drive. You must also enable basic SCSI support to use these drives.

- **Character devices, Parallel printer support**   This is the option you enable to use printers that connect to the parallel port.

- **Character devices, Video for Linux**   Some drivers on this menu relate to parallel-interfaced WebCams.

> **NOTE**
>
> Most of these devices actually use their own device files; the /dev/lp*n* files are used mostly by the parallel-printer support.

There was a change between the 2.0.x kernels and the 2.2.x kernels in the way the /dev/lp*n* devices were assigned to hardware. In the 2.0.x kernels, *n* was matched to hardware on a hard-wired basis according to the cable connectors port (shown in Table 16.1). In 2.2.x, the first parallel port found becomes /dev/lp0, regardless of its cable connectors port, and subsequent parallel ports are assigned subsequent numbers.

Adding a Port

Most motherboards today include one parallel, two RS-232 serial, and two USB ports. Some motherboards trim this back to one RS-232 or one USB port, particularly on compact and notebook computers. If you find your port selection to be inadequate, you can add additional ports by plugging an expansion card into your computer.

Adding a Standard Expansion Card

In the 80486 era and before, serial and parallel ports usually came on ISA cards. A typical card included two serial ports, one parallel port, and a joystick port. Some also included an IDE port and a floppy port. Today, cards that carry one or two serial ports, one or two parallel ports, or a combination of these are readily available. There are also USB port cards that enable you to add USB support to computers that lack this feature.

> **TIP**
>
> If you have an old computer gathering dust, you might want to pry out its serial/parallel port card rather than buy a new card. These old cards can actually be easier to configure for Linux than new cards that use ISA PnP features—if you have the old card's documentation.

Modems

Traditionally, internal modems have consisted of two components on a single expansion card: a conventional serial port and a modem. Electronically, these two devices functioned together just like a serial port and an external modem. You install and configure such cards much as you would a third or replacement RS-232 serial port. More recently, *software modems* have become available. (These devices are often called *WinModems*, but that term is a trademark of 3Com, and so should be applied only to 3Com products.) Software modems omit much of the circuitry of both the serial port and the modem, and instead rely on specialized drivers to function. These drivers have not been available for Linux until recently, and even now, support for software modems is spotty at best. Software modem drivers typically configure the modem to look and work much like a serial port, but the serial port no longer exists. For more information, check Chapter 18, "Modems," or the Web site `http://www.linmodems.org`, which contains the latest information on support for a wide variety of software modems.

Serial Ports

Assuming you're adding a traditional serial port or an internal modem that includes a serial port, you should pay attention to the type of *Universal Asynchronous Receiver/Transmitter* (UART) it includes. The UART is a critical part of an RS-232 serial port, and the model UART included on a board determines its capabilities. UART types include

- **8250**   This UART was used on early x86 computers, but has been largely abandoned. It performs poorly by today's standards.
- **16450**   This chip is an improved version of the 8250. It owes most of its improvement to a 1-byte transmit/receive buffer, which reduces the chance that data will be lost to incoming data.
- **16550**   This chip is pin-compatible with the 16450, but it expands the size of the transmit/receive buffer to 16 bytes. Although 16 bytes might not sound like much, it's enough to substantially improve the UART's reliability. The original 16550 was buggy, unfortunately, and so is no better than a 16450. The 16550A and later revisions are more useful.
- **16650 and 16750**   Some companies have produced 16550-compatible UARTs that include larger buffers—typically 32 or 64 bytes. These chips are normally sold under the *16650* and *16750* names, respectively.

In practice, most UARTs in modern motherboards are built in to the motherboard's chipset, so there really is no 16x50 chip installed. The same is often true of boards that include serial ports along with a parallel port; a single chip handles the functionality of two 16x50 UARTs and the parallel-port circuitry. Many companies produce UARTs compatible with the models I've listed previously, but National Semiconductor originated the design. Even when a board includes separate UART chips for each serial port, the chips might or might not have been manufactured by National Semiconductor, and they might or might not bear the model numbers I've specified. UARTs from other manufacturers should be detected correctly by Linux, however.

Parallel Ports

Today, parallel ports come in three main varieties:

- **SPP** The *standard parallel port* (SPP) is the design that's been used for years. Originally intended only for transmitting data at rates of up to about 150KB/s, the SPP is not well suited to handling input. By performing some clever programming, though, an SPP can handle input at up to about 50KB/s.

- **EPP** The *enhanced parallel port* (EPP) was introduced in late 1991 as a way to achieve both faster speeds and better input modes on a parallel port. These ports can handle a maximum data transfer rate of 2MB/s. There are actually two EPP variants in common use. One is known as EPP 1.7, and the other is sometimes referred to as EPP 1.9, although it's more properly considered part of the broader IEEE 1284 standard. Both variants have similar capabilities.

- **ECP** The *enhanced capabilities port* (ECP) is another parallel port standard, which was introduced in 1992. Like EPP, ECP supports high-speed transfers. Unlike EPP and SPP, ECP consumes a *direct memory access* (DMA) channel, which can cause conflicts with other devices. ECP can therefore be more difficult to configure than EPP. IEEE 1284 includes both EPP and ECP.

Today's parallel port cards support both EPP and ECP modes, so chances are you'll get both of these on any expansion card you buy. If you salvage a card from an old 80486 or earlier computer, however, the card might support only SPP mode. Given the higher speeds of EPP and ECP modes, these are clearly preferable, particularly if you use a device that requires high rates of data transfer, such as a high-resolution color printer or an external removable disk drive.

Multiport Cards

A *multiport card* includes several ports—usually several RS-232 serial ports. They're most commonly used by Internet service providers (ISPs) to link potentially dozens of dial-in modems to a single computer, or to provide access to a single computer from several "dumb terminals" run over serial lines. There are two basic configurations possible for multiport serial cards:

- **Extended "dumb" serial ports** Some cards use what is essentially the same serial port architecture used on traditional systems, but with more than the usual 1–4 ports per card. You can enable support for such boards in the Linux kernel by using the Support more than 4 serial ports and Support for sharing serial interrupts options in the Character devices kernel configuration menu, shown in Figure 16.2. (You must enable Extended dumb serial driver options to get to these options, and you might also need the Support special multiport boards option, as well.)

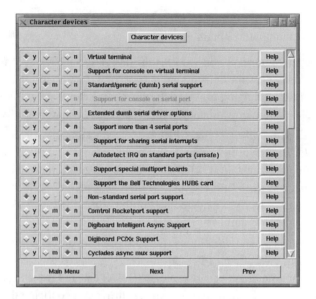

FIGURE 16.2
Serial and parallel cable connectors come in a wide variety of shapes and sizes.

- **Nonstandard serial ports** Several products are available that provide several serial ports on a single card and interrupt. Linux supports these products through options available when you enable the Nonstandard serial port support feature in the Character devices kernel configuration menu. Note that you must select the specific product you're using in order to get support for that product.

As a general rule, a nonstandard serial port is a better choice than an extended dumb serial port when you need more than three or four serial ports. These nonstandard serial port cards were designed with an eye toward supporting multiple devices, whereas the extended dumb cards are extensions to standards that weren't designed with large numbers of ports in mind.

ISA and PCI Cards

As with many other expansion cards, when you add a serial or parallel port card, you must choose between the earlier Industry Standard Architecture (ISA) bus and the later Peripheral Component Interconnect (PCI) bus. None of the serial or parallel busses discussed in this chapter strain the limits of the ISA bus, so you'll see no performance gain in your bus accesses if you choose the PCI bus.

Even most serial and parallel ports on motherboards are actually treated as ISA devices. Therefore, if you buy a PCI expansion card, you'll be treading ground rarely explored by

Linux users. PCI serial and parallel port cards do work with Linux, but I can't promise that *all* PCI devices work. If you choose a PCI board, therefore, I recommend that you do so from a store that has a liberal return policy.

Configuring Linux for Multiple Ports

Adding serial or parallel ports to Linux sometimes poses configuration problems, particularly when your system is short on interrupts. Some cards, and particularly earlier ones, require configuration by jumpers. Other cards use ISA *plug-and-play* (PnP) features, or are PCI cards that are configured by the BIOS. You can also use an assortment of Linux features to help configure your ports for optimal use.

If your card is an ISA PnP device, you should read the isapnp man page or the "ISA Bus" section of Chapter 2 to learn how to configure your new card in Linux. ISA PnP configuration can sometimes be a bit tricky, so many people prefer to use jumpered cards. A few ISA modems support both PnP and jumpered configuration; you set a jumper to tell the card to use other jumpers or an ISA PnP configuration.

Using `tunelp` and the `/proc` Filesystem to Tune a Parallel Port

Earlier in this chapter, I mentioned the use of the /proc filesystem to enable or disable the use of an interrupt by the parallel port. Specifically, you write the interrupt number (or 0 to disable use of interrupts) to /proc/parport/*n*/irq, where *n* is the port number. You can also use other files in this directory to learn more about your current configuration. For instance, you can display the contents of /proc/parport/*n*/hardware to learn about your parallel port hardware:

```
$ cat /proc/parport/0/hardware
base:    0x378
irq:     none
dma:     none
modes:   SPP,ECP,ECPPS2
```

The tunelp utility can be used to adjust the handling of the printer specifically, but not other parallel-port devices. Some of its more important options include

- **-i** *irqnum*   Sets pre-2.1.131 kernels to use the specified interrupt number. This option has no effect on more recent kernels.

- **-t** *time*   Specifies the time, in *jiffies* (hundredths of a second), that the system waits before trying to send a character if the first attempt fails. Setting this value low (say, to 0) results in faster printing, but greater CPU load. Setting the value high (say, to 500) can result in slow printing but low CPU load.

- **-c** *chars*   The number of times the kernel tries to send a character to a printer before it pauses for *time* jiffies (set with the -t *time* option). This value should be set to 1 if you use interrupt-driven printing. The recommended value for polling printing is 120, although you might need to adjust it up or down to obtain optimum results with any given printer.

- **-a** *[on | off]*   Causes the system to abort (*on*) or not (*off*) when there's an error, such as a paper jam. For most systems, you want to set this value to off, but if the printer is unattended, on might be preferable.

- **-T** *[on | off]*   Tells the kernel to trust or not trust an interrupt when using interrupt-driven printing. Some printers work better with this option set to on, and others work better with it set to off.

As an example, you might issue the following command:

```
tunelp /dev/lp0 -t 10 -c 1 -T on
```

This command tells the system to send just one character before pausing for 10 jiffies should that attempt fail, and to trust the state of the interrupt over other printer availability indications. It applies these options to the first parallel port.

Using setserial to Tune an RS-232 Serial Port

You can use the setserial program to adjust a number of serial port options, most of them fairly obscure. On most systems, the kernel automatically configures the serial port at boot time, but setserial enables you to override that configuration. A few of its options include

- **port** *portnum*   Sets the port number; for instance, 0x3f8 for the first serial port (/dev/ttyS0)

- **irq** *irqnum*   Sets the interrupt number; for instance, 4 for the first serial port

- **uart** *uarttype*   Sets the UART type; for instance, 16550A for a 16550 revision A or later

- **autoconfig**   Attempts to automatically configure the serial port

You can check the setserial man page for further information on this command. In most cases, you won't need to use it, but you might in some cases. For instance, you might have an unusual UART that's been misidentified by the kernel, in which case you can issue a command such as **setserial /dev/ttyS0 uart 16550A** to get it working correctly.

Configuring USB Devices

Each USB device requires its own device file. For instance, if you have a USB mouse and a USB digital camera, each of those devices must have its own dedicated device file, such as

`/dev/usbmouse` and `/dev/camera`, respectively. The details of what these devices are called and what their device major and minor numbers are vary substantially from one device type to another. Some USB devices require unusual device files, but others latch onto other Linux drivers and use more common device files. For instance, USB removable media drives are accessed as if they were SCSI devices.

USB configuration is changing rapidly in the 2.3.x kernel series. It's done through the USB drivers kernel configuration area. Here are some points to understand about this configuration:

- You *must* enable the first option, Support for USB.
- There are two basic low-level USB hardware types, UHCI and OHCI. You must include a driver for whichever type of USB hardware your system supports. Intel and VIA chipsets use the UHCI system, whereas most other chipsets use the OHCI driver. There are two UHCI drivers available, so if one causes problems, you can try the other.
- You must include support, either compiled into the kernel or as a module, for each USB device type you want to use, such as printers, scanners, and so on.

Because USB support is so new, the details of USB kernel configuration are likely to change before the release of the first 2.4 kernel. Indeed, chances are there will be active development of USB throughout the 2.4 kernel's lifetime, and the 2.5.x development kernels and following stable kernels will be substantially different. Consult `http://www.linux-usb.org` for the latest information on USB support in Linux.

USB: The Future of External Ports?

USB is a fairly new technology, and it functions in a way that's fundamentally different from the way traditional RS-232 serial and parallel ports function. The differences reside not so much in the nature of the low-level serial hardware, but in its multidevice nature, which has required substantial changes to the Linux kernel. USB is also a *hot-swap* technology, meaning you can safely install and remove USB devices while the computer is turned on. (This is *not* true of traditional RS-232 serial and parallel ports, although you might get lucky when swapping components.) These differences have implications for Linux that deserve extra consideration.

In 1998, USB devices were extremely rare. In 2000, they're becoming common. USB is moving into territory that has hitherto been the domain of RS-232 and parallel port devices. A few USB devices even compete against SCSI devices, but USB devices are much slower than their SCSI counterparts.

USB has certain advantages over both RS-232 serial and parallel ports, including

- **Multidevice design**   USB was designed to handle several devices—up to 127, in fact. Neither serial nor parallel ports were designed for this feat, although many non-printer parallel-port devices accomplish the job through clever hacks. In the end, this advantage comes down to one of reduced resource use on the host computer. If you want to run a printer, a scanner, a modem, and a mouse via USB, only one interrupt is required. If you used two separate parallel ports and two serial ports, you'd need from two to four interrupts.

- **Hot swapping**   USB's capacity to safely handle attaching and detaching devices makes it very desirable from a consumer point of view. This is a feature that's taken the Linux kernel programmers some time to implement, though, because Linux doesn't like to see its devices mysteriously vanish.

- **Speed**   At a theoretical maximum speed of 1.5MB/s, USB is far faster than RS-232 serial ports (0.014MB/s top speed on typical x86 hardware). EPP or ECP parallel ports can best USB at 2MB/s, but the difference isn't very dramatic. Keep in mind, though, that USB's speed is shared among all devices.

Comparing USB to RS-232 and parallel ports, USB's main drawback is its comparative newness. This drawback is particularly important in Linux, because Linux's USB drivers are still evolving, and driver support for specific USB devices is spotty in the late 2.3.x kernels. This situation will likely improve in time, however. All things considered, USB will likely become more important as an interface for low-speed devices.

Note that I said USB *will likely* become important for *low-speed* devices. High-speed devices such as hard disks and even the faster removable disks require more speed than USB can provide. The *FireWire*™ protocol (also known as *IEEE 1394,* or *i.Link*) is more suited to high-speed external devices. FireWire might merge with the existing SCSI protocols and take over for high-speed external devices. At the moment, however, FireWire devices are quite rare, and Linux's FireWire support is even more limited than its USB support. No doubt this situation will change as 2000 wears on and moves into 2001 and beyond.

Summary

RS-232, USB, and parallel ports represent vital links between your computer and a wide variety of external devices. Printers, modems, scanners, cameras, and other devices all interface through these ports. Because of the importance of these ports, they're included as standard equipment on all modern motherboards. In some cases, however, the ports included on the motherboard can be inadequate. You might need to connect two parallel-port printers or three

RS-232 serial devices, for instance. In such cases, you can add additional ports to expand your system's capabilities. There are limits to the number of ports that a computer can sustain, however, particularly when you use conventional ports. Using ISA (Industry Standard Architecture) serial cards enables you to add many more serial ports. In many cases, USB offers a superior solution when you need to connect several external devices because a single USB port can support up to 127 USB devices.

Network Hardware

IN THIS CHAPTER

Desktop computers can be powerful tools. You can write documents, perform simple or complex computations, maintain databases of vital information, and so on. These functions are extremely useful, but an entirely new realm of computer utility exists when isolated computers are linked together. These linked computers are referred to as a *network*, and creating a network involves both hardware and software.

In theory, you can create a computer network using generalized communications ports, such as parallel or serial ports (discussed in Chapter 16, "Parallel and Serial Ports"). In practice, however, these ports are less than ideal for creating a network, so most networks use specialized hardware. In a pinch, you can use parallel or serial ports for networking, and there's one specialized case in which this is the norm: using modems to connect to the Internet via an Internet service provider (ISP). Chapter 18, "Modems," discusses this topic, including both conventional analog modems that typically use a serial port and the newer cable and Digital Subscriber Line (DSL) modems, which generally interface through the type of networking hardware I describe in this chapter.

Atop the networking hardware lies a set of software programs that implement the *network stack*. Each layer of the network stack communicates with the layer above or below it. The lowest layer communicates with the network hardware, and the highest layer communicates with the user. In many cases it's possible to swap out one layer of the stack and insert a different version of that layer to achieve different results. For instance, you can swap out drivers for one type of network card in exchange for another type. This change doesn't affect the performance of the network applications, such as Netscape Navigator.

There are many different types of networks possible, and I can't begin to cover the subtle differences between them. If you want to learn more about networking, you might want to consult a book on the subject, such as my *Linux: Networking for Your Office* (Sams Publishing, 2000).

Ethernet Adapters

The network hardware that goes into the computer is known as a *network interface cards* (NICs). Today, most small networks use *Ethernet* as the hardware type, and so NICs are often called *Ethernet cards*, *Ethernet NICs*, or something similar. Ethernet isn't the only type of networking hardware available, however. Alternatives such as Token Ring and LocalTalk are still popular in some environments, and more exotic hardware is available and might even be required in some cases. As a general rule, if you're putting together a small network of between two and a few dozen computers, Ethernet is the way to go. If you want to connect your computer to an existing network, you should consult with whoever maintains that network to determine what type of network hardware to buy.

CAUTION

Unless your network administrator specifically mentions Linux compatibility, don't assume that the hardware he or she recommends is Linux compatible. Although most Ethernet hardware is Linux compatible, some more exotic hardware might not be. This is particularly true of internal network cards for cable and DSL networks.

Speed Considerations

Ethernet comes in several different varieties, which are summarized in Table 17.1. Each type of Ethernet has its advantages, but for most new networks, the extra speed afforded by 100BaseT makes it the variety of choice. I describe the different types of cabling later in this chapter, in "Cabling Choices."

TABLE 17.1   Varieties of Ethernet

Ethernet Type	Cable Type	Maximum Cable Length	Maximum Speed
10Base2	Thin coaxial	607 ft.	10Mbps
10Base5	Thick coaxial	1,640 ft.	10Mbps
10BaseT	Category 3, 4, or 5 twisted-pair	328 ft.	10Mbps
100BaseT	Category 5 twisted-pair	328 ft.	100Mbps
1000BaseT	Category 5 twisted-pair	328 ft.	1,000Mbps
1000BaseSX	Fiber-optic	1,804 ft.	1,000Mbps

NOTE

The *2* and *5* in *10Base2* and *10Base5* refer to their respective maximum cable lengths in hundreds of meters. The *T* in *10BaseT* and *100BaseT* refers to twisted-pair cable. The *10* and *100* in the Ethernet names refers to the maximum speed in megabits per second.

Broadly speaking, two types of Ethernet adapter are commonly available today:

- **10Mbps**   These boards support all the 10Mbps varieties of Ethernet. Today, they usually include connectors for 10Base2 and 10BaseT, although you can use an adapter to connect 10Base5 cabling if necessary.
- **10/100Mbps**   These boards support both 10Mbps and 100Mbps speeds. They normally support only twisted-pair cabling. Figure 17.1 shows a typical 10/100Mbps NIC.

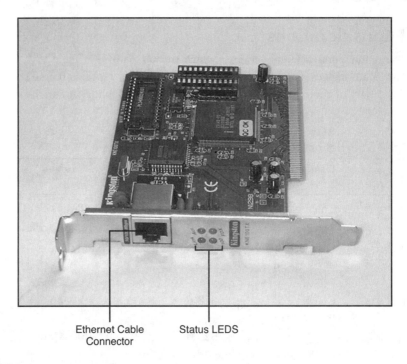

Ethernet Cable   Status LEDS
Connector

FIGURE 17.1

A typical NIC includes one or more cable connectors and some activity LEDs.

NOTE

A few NICs are capable of using *only* 100Mbps protocols. These boards are quite rare, though. Most 100Mbps NICs also support 10Mbps speeds. The 1,000Mbps devices, which also go by the name *gigabit Ethernet*, are not common on workstations today. They're more commonly used to connect high-demand servers to a network by means of a switch or router.

If you're building a new network or connecting to an existing twisted-pair network, I recommend you get a 10/100Mbps NIC. Even if your network can't now use the full 100Mbps speed, the 10/100 NICs don't cost substantially more than their 10Mbps-only counterparts, and the existence of 100Mbps-capable NICs can make it easier to upgrade your network speeds in the future.

Mixing 10- and 100Mbps hardware usually works well, although in some cases you might get only 10Mbps speeds, even between two 100Mbps-capable devices. Specifically, if you use a hub to connect your computers, all your devices default to the lowest speed supported by all your computers. If you use a switch instead of a hub, on the other hand, you'll get 100Mbps transfers between those components that support the higher speed, and 10Mbps only when one computer supports only the lower speed. I describe the differences between hubs and switches in more detail later in this chapter, in "Hubs and Switches."

Ethernet works by encapsulating data in *frames*, which the NIC sends over the network cable. A typical frame contains about 1.5KB of data. When two computers link directly to one another, or when you use a switch to connect computers, the computers can transmit and receive data at the same time. This is known as *full duplex* operation. A 100Mbps Ethernet card operating in full duplex mode can theoretically send data at 100Mbps while it simultaneously transmits at the same speed. When you use a hub or coaxial cable, however, this isn't possible, so you can send at 100Mbps or receive at 100Mbps, or split the speed, as in 50Mbps sending and receiving. This is known as *half duplex* operation. In this configuration, too, there's an increased possibility of *collisions*. A collision occurs when two computers attempt to send data at the same time. As when two people talk at the same time, it becomes impossible to discern either signal. When an Ethernet card detects a collision, it pauses for a random but brief period of time and tries again. The other sender does the same. Because both pause for a random period of time, it's unlikely that their frames will collide again. Because of the need to retransmit, collisions can slow down Ethernet speed, particularly on networks that see a lot of traffic.

ISA and PCI Adapters

Today, the vast majority of Ethernet adapters sold use either the Industry Standard Architecture (ISA) bus or Peripheral Component Interconnect (PCI) bus. A few boards sold during the 80486 era used the EISA bus or the VL-Bus, but these products are quite rare today. ISA's theoretical maximum speed is 5MB/s, or 40Mbps, expressed in typical network speed terms. This fact means that ISA bus NICs are adequate for 10Mbps networks, but not for 100Mbps networks. Consequently, 100Mbps ISA NICs are rare, although a few such models do exist. Because of the ISA bus speed limitations, ISA bus 100Mbps NICs can't take full advantage of 100Mbps network speeds, but they are faster than 10Mbps NICs.

If you're building a 100Mbps network, I recommend that you purchase PCI NICs. Exceptions to this rule can involve

- **Older computers**   If you have an old 80486 or earlier computer that doesn't support PCI, you naturally can't buy a PCI NIC for the computer. You might nonetheless want to seek out a 100Mbps-capable ISA NIC, because using a mix of 10- and 100Mbps boards can reduce your overall network's performance. Alternatively, use a 10Mbps NIC but make sure you use a switch rather than a hub to link your computers.

- **Low-speed interfaces**   Sometimes you need a single 10Mbps interface even on a 100Mbps network. For instance, if you use a Linux computer as a router between a network in your home or office and a cable or DSL modem, chances are the NIC that connects to the cable or DSL modem doesn't need 100Mbps speeds. For such a low-speed application, an ISA NIC is perfectly adequate. There's no reason to *favor* an ISA NIC for such an application, unless you're short on PCI slots.

- **Existing hardware**   If you have an existing ISA NIC and your situation doesn't require better speed than that card can provide, you might as well use it. PCI NICs can be quite inexpensive, though (as low as $15 or so from some vendors), so even a small reason to buy a PCI NIC can be enough to recommend doing so.

One other advantage of PCI NICs over ISA models is that the PCI devices tend to consume less in the way of CPU time than do the ISA NICs. Therefore, even when 10Mbps speeds are all you'll achieve, a PCI NIC is usually a better choice than an ISA model.

Supported Linux Ethernet Chipsets

Like other expansion cards, Ethernet boards rely upon their chipsets to do most of the work. Linux drivers for these products are also written for particular chipsets. As a result, you might need to determine what chipset your Ethernet card uses before you can use it in Linux. Appendix A, "Linux Device Drivers," covers this topic in detail. Fortunately, most Ethernet adapter manufacturers today include Linux drivers on their Web sites or on the floppy disks that come with their products. These drivers are typically just the normal Linux drivers for the chipset, but their inclusion makes it easy to determine which driver you need—you just examine the drivers included by the manufacturer and select the appropriate option during Linux installation.

In some cases, the driver included with the kernel might not support the latest version of a chipset. In these cases, you might need to obtain an updated driver or use the driver included with the board. Follow the directions that come with the updated driver to compile and install it.

Ethernet adapters are, as a class, one of the best-supported types of hardware in Linux. You can almost always find a driver for an Ethernet board. Some of the more popular boards and chipsets available today include

- **3Com 3c59x and 3c905b series**   These chipsets are used in 3Com's EtherLink XL series boards and on a few third-party products. They use the 3c59x Linux driver.

- **DEC Tulip 21x4x series**   Digital Equipment Corporation (DEC) produced a popular series of Ethernet chipsets that was used on a large number of DEC and third-party products, many of which were quite inexpensive. When DEC folded, Intel bought the Tulip design, and a few products still ship with Tulip chips from Intel. These products use the Linux tulip driver.

- **Intel i82557/i82558 series**   These chipsets are used almost exclusively on Intel's EtherExpress Pro 100B board. Some motherboards use this same chipset, and so work with the same Linux drivers, the eepro100.

- **NE2000 clones**   When ISA Ethernet cards were the rage, National Semiconductor produced a board called the *NE2000*. It became quite popular, and many manufacturers cloned it. Most of these clones work with the Linux ne driver. There are even NE2000 clones for the MCA (ne2) and PCI (ne2k-pci) busses.

- **RTL8129**   RealTek's RTL8129 chipset has become fairly popular among low-cost boards from several manufacturers. It uses the rtl8129 driver in Linux.

- **Tulip clones**   Several manufacturers, including PNIC and Macronix, have produced clones of the popular Tulip chipsets. Boards based on these products generally work well with the Linux tulip driver, and are quite popular because of their low cost. Some of these boards are new enough that they require an updated driver or kernel version 2.2.14 or later, however.

- **VIA Rhine**   VIA produces an Ethernet chipset known as the *Rhine* that's been used in a number of low-cost PCI Ethernet boards. These products use the via-rhine driver.

As a general rule, any of these products works acceptably under Linux. If you need the best performance, though, you should probably favor an Intel, 3Com, or Tulip-based product, because these boards perform best under heavy network loads. NE2000 clones are particularly likely to produce poor throughput under heavy loads, and so should be avoided for servers.

You should not take the preceding list to be even remotely comprehensive. Many more products are available than I can list here, and most of them work well under Linux. For details, consult the Linux kernel configuration menus or the hardware compatibility list for your distribution.

17

NETWORK HARDWARE

Non-Ethernet NICs

Some of the principles I've laid out for Ethernet adapters also apply to other network proto-cols. For instance, other types of NIC are available in PCI and ISA varieties, and the PCI vari-ety is generally preferable, especially if the theoretical maximum network speed approaches or exceeds ISA's 5MB/s (40Mbps).

As a general rule, I don't recommend you use anything but Ethernet for a new local network. Ethernet's popularity ensures that you'll get good prices on Ethernet hardware and be able to find support for any Ethernet networking problems you encounter. If you must hook your com-puter up to an existing network that uses another protocol, though, it might be simpler to use that protocol directly.

If you need to substantially expand an existing network, you have two choices:

- Expand the existing network using its own protocols. For instance, you might expand a 10-computer Token Ring network to 20 computers by using Token Ring directly in the new computers.
- Create two subnetworks, one of which uses the old protocol and one of which uses Ethernet. This approach is more complex, but has its advantages, such as higher speed if the old protocol is slower than 100Mbps. You'll need a dedicated router or a computer with one Ethernet and one alternative protocol NIC to link the two subnetworks.

You should probably consult a networking book or a networking consultant to help you decide which approach to take.

Token Ring

IBM developed Token Ring technology to provide networking on small computers. There are two speeds of Token Ring available: 4Mbps and 16Mbps. Token Ring networks link their com-puters in a logical ring, as shown in Figure 17.2. Before it transmits data, a computer waits to receive a *token* from its neighbor. When the computer receives the token, it transmits the token along with a packet of data to its other neighbor. The neighbor computer then passes on the data, if required, and so it goes until the data reaches its intended recipient. Because only one computer at a time is allowed to transmit data, Token Ring networks don't suffer from collision problems, as can Ethernet networks.

In terms of hardware, Token Ring networks use a hub-like device and twisted-pair cables, so Token Ring hardware closely resembles that of 10BaseT or 100BaseT Ethernet. The Token Ring's ring is implemented inside the hub.

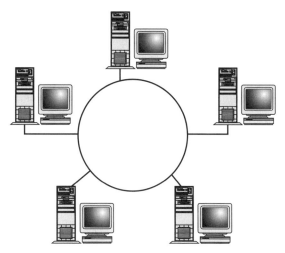

FIGURE 17.2
The closed loop of a Token Ring network lets the token cycle endlessly through the network.

Linux includes support for several Token Ring adapters, under the Network device support, Token Ring devices kernel configuration option. Linux's Token Ring support is much weaker than its support for Ethernet, however, so you should be sure to thoroughly investigate driver support for any Token Ring boards you might consider.

One particularly useful source of information for Token Ring users is the Linux Token Ring HOWTO document, which should come with your distribution. As of early 2000, this document had not been updated since 1998, however, so some of its information is geared towards 2.0.x-series and even earlier Linux kernels.

LocalTalk

When Apple introduced its expensive LaserWriter printer in the mid-1980s, it needed some way to network the printer so that small offices could justify the printer's high price. The result was a protocol called *AppleTalk*. That name originally applied to both the hardware and the software, but eventually the hardware acquired its own name: *LocalTalk*. Nonetheless, there are still occasional references to the hardware by the name *AppleTalk*.

By today's standards, LocalTalk is quite primitive and slow. Its maximum speed is 2Mbps—one-fifth the speed of 10Mbps Ethernet, and one-fiftieth (1/50) the speed of modern 100Mbps Ethernet. The original LocalTalk cabling was a proprietary design and limited in length to 1,000 feet in a bus topology (described shortly). Although LocalTalk is an Apple technology, another company, Farallon, introduced a product called PhoneNET that allows LocalTalk to traverse ordinary telephone wires. PhoneNet also extends LocalTalk's cabling range to 3,000 feet.

Because of its very low speed, I don't recommend using LocalTalk unless you must. If you must connect a Linux computer to a LocalTalk network, you might be able to get it to work in one of two ways:

- **Linux LocalTalk support**   The Linux kernel includes support for two x86 LocalTalk boards, in the Network device support, Appletalk devices kernel configuration menu. These boards are difficult to find, though, and LocalTalk networks frequently aren't configured for the protocols used on the Internet as a whole.

- **LocalTalk/Ethernet bridges**   Separate hardware products exist to link LocalTalk and Ethernet networks. For instance, the Asante (`http://www.asante.com`) AsanteTalk lets you connect eight LocalTalk devices to an Ethernet network.

LocalTalk poses an additional challenge to Linux: It's almost always used with the AppleTalk file- and printer-sharing protocols. Most Linux networking occurs through the Transmission Control Protocol/Internet Protocol (TCP/IP) networking stack, but AppleTalk uses a separate stack. The Netatalk program (`http://www.umich.edu/~rsug/netatalk/`) allows Linux to use the AppleTalk protocols to serve files or printers on a Linux computer to Macintoshes, or to print to Macintosh printers using AppleTalk protocols. (You can read more about using Netatalk in my book, *Linux: Networking for Your Office*, Sams Publishing, 2000.)

> **NOTE**
>
> The AppleTalk protocols aren't limited to LocalTalk networks. Recent Macintoshes no longer include LocalTalk support; instead, they include Ethernet adapters. These Macintoshes use AppleTalk over Ethernet. You can safely mix Macintoshes and x86 PCs on the same network; the AppleTalk and TCP/IP networking stacks don't interfere with one another.

Exotic Adapters

Linux includes support for a number of more exotic network protocols, including

- **Cable and DSL modems**   Some cable and telephone companies use internal modems to link subscribers' computers to their cable and DSL networks. Linux support for these products is rare, but a handful are supported. I discuss this matter in more detail in Chapter 18.

- **FDDI**   Fiber Distributed Data Interface (FDDI) is an alternative to Ethernet for high-speed local networks. It's rarely used, but Linux does support a few FDDI cards.

- **HIPPI**   High Performance Parallel Interface (HIPPI) provides access speeds of 800Mbps or 1,600Mbps, depending upon the variety. It's generally used to link clusters of computers or supercomputers over distances of dozens or hundreds of meters.

- **Wireless networking**   A number of wireless networking protocols are gaining in popularity. Linux supports several of these, but you should check the kernel configuration options to be sure Linux supports any given product before you make a purchase.

- **Multiport cards**   A few manufacturers, including Intel (`http://www.intel.com`) and Adaptec (`http://www.adaptec.com`), offer cards with two or more Ethernet ports. These ports are independent, so you can use them to connect a single computer to two or more networks. In most cases, using multiple NICs is less expensive, because these multiport cards are costly. If you're running short on slots, though, and need to connect a computer to two or more networks, these devices can be quite convenient. They're configured just like ordinary Ethernet NICs; each product registers as two or more separate devices.

- **Gigabit Ethernet**   Beyond 100Mbps Ethernet lies 1,000Mbps, or 1Gbps, Ethernet. This technology is still fairly new, but Linux adds support for several gigabit Ethernet cards in the 2.3.x kernel series.

- **Dial-up networking**   Many individuals and small businesses connect to the Internet through dial-up accounts with local ISPs. These accounts typically use the Point-to-Point Protocol (PPP), or occasionally the Serial Line Interface Protocol (SLIP), via a modem. Linux supports both protocols. There are also a number of implementations of PPP over Ethernet (PPPoE) for Linux. This protocol is becoming popular on DSL networks. See `http://www.rodsbooks.com/network/network-dsl.html` for information on several PPPoE implementations for Linux.

As a general rule, when you compile support for an exotic network interface into your kernel, you can then use that hardware in conjunction with the normal Linux TCP/IP stack, including client programs such as Netscape Navigator and server programs such as Apache. If the network to which you're attaching is linked to the Internet, you can then communicate with any Internet-connected computer in the world, regardless of the network hardware used on that computer.

Cabling Choices

To a large extent, the cabling you use is determined by the type of network to which you're connecting. You can't use LocalTalk cables on an Ethernet network, for instance. If you're building a network from scratch, you might need to decide not just what type of network cards to buy, but what type of cabling. This is particularly true of 10Mbps Ethernet, which supports two types of Ethernet cabling—coaxial and twisted-pair. Understanding the differences between these cable types can be important even if you're connecting a computer to an existing network. An error in connecting your computer can cause problems to other users of the network, so it's important that you do the job correctly. Table 17.1 summarizes some of the characteristics of these cabling types.

Network Topologies

The arrangement of cables between computers cannot be random; it must follow specific rules. These rules are determined by the network technology, and the result is referred to as the network *topology*. Three topologies are in common use on small networks today:

- **Bus** A *bus* topology links each computer to two others, except for the computers at the ends of the bus. The result is a chain of computers, as depicted in Figure 17.3. The coaxial Ethernet technologies and LocalTalk use bus topologies.

FIGURE 17.3
The bus of a bus topology links all the computers in a line.

- **Ring** A *ring* is much like a bus topology, except that the bus loops back on itself. The result is depicted in Figure 17.2. The *ring* portion of *Token Ring* derives from the fact that Token Ring uses this topology in its hubs.

- **Star** A *star* topology links all the computers to a central point, as shown in Figure 17.4. This central point is a networking device known as either a *hub* or a *switch* in Ethernet networks. (The differences between hubs and switches are discussed later in the chapter.) Twisted-pair Ethernet networks use the star topology. Token Ring networks are wired in the same way; the ring of these networks is implemented internally to the Token Ring hub.

If you examine Table 17.1, you might think that the star topology twisted-pair networks suffer relative to their coaxial cable counterparts in terms of the size of the network that's supported. This isn't usually the case, however. The cable length limit for the coaxial technologies refers to the entire length of the bus, whereas the cable length limit for twisted-pair Ethernet refers to the length of the cable from *one* device to the hub. Therefore, unless the computers are strung out in a straight line, the star topology and twisted-pair cabling actually allow you to connect computers over a wider area than do the coaxial technologies. In fact, even in a straight line, twisted-pair wins over thin coaxial, because if you place a hub at the midpoint of the line, cables can extend from the hub 328 feet in *each* direction, for a total linear extent of 656 feet, which is slightly greater than the 607-foot limit of thin coaxial cabling.

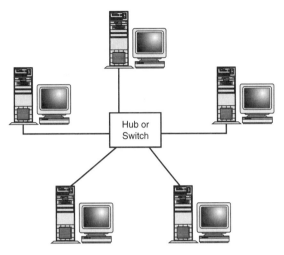

FIGURE 17.4
All network traffic passes through the central device in a star topology network.

Coaxial Cabling

Coaxial cabling looks much like the cabling for cable TV installations. For Ethernet, it comes in two varieties: thin and thick. Those adjectives describe the most obvious difference between the types of cable. How you hook a computer up to each variety also varies:

- To connect a computer to a thin Ethernet cable, you must cut the cable and attach each of the cut strands to a BNC T-connector, as illustrated in Figure 17.5. You can then attach the BNC connector to the jack on the Ethernet card.

- To connect a computer to a thick Ethernet cable, you use a *vampire tap*. This device allows you to tap into the thick Ethernet cable without cutting it.

Thin Ethernet's T-connectors tend to cause problems, for a couple of reasons:

- Adding a computer requires temporarily cutting the Ethernet cable. This cuts off two parts of the network from each other, and the lack of termination in each half can cause problems even within each segment. With any luck, this disruption only lasts a minute or two, but on a large network on which computers are routinely added and removed, this can be a serious problem.

- If the cable is given a solid yank, it can break free of the T-connector, thus causing network disruptions. This can happen accidentally as furniture is moved around, or potentially even as a computer user shifts his or her legs under a desk.

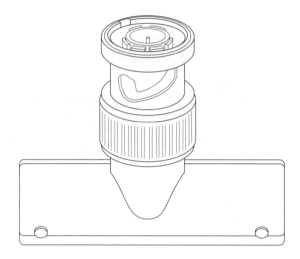

FIGURE 17.5

A BNC T-connector lets you link a computer onto a thin coaxial Ethernet bus.

Thick Ethernet tends to cause fewer problems than does thin Ethernet, but the thick variety is more difficult to string and use. All in all, coaxial Ethernet cabling is a poor choice for new installations. It's trouble-prone, requires use of half duplex transmissions, and can only be used at up to 10Mbps speeds. If you need to add one or two computers to an existing coaxial Ethernet network, you might as well use this technology. For a new network, though, or for major expansions of an existing one, you're probably better off with twisted-pair cabling.

Twisted-Pair Cabling

Twisted-pair cabling gets its name because of the fact that it uses pairs of thin wires twisted around each other, as shown in Figure 17.6. The twisted-pair cabling used in Ethernet networking uses four such pairs, in fact. The twisting provides a degree of resistance to extraneous signals, and therefore helps extend the length of cables that can be created using this technique.

Ethernet twisted-pair cabling uses RJ-45 jacks on each end, shown in Figure 17.7. These jacks resemble those on ordinary telephone cords, except that they're wider. These cables come in a variety of colors, and you can use this fact to help differentiate your cables. If you use a different color cable for each cable you plug into a hub, you can easily trace cables to their matching computers.

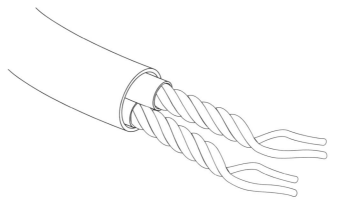

FIGURE 17.6
Twisting pairs of wires helps eliminate interference from radios and other cables.

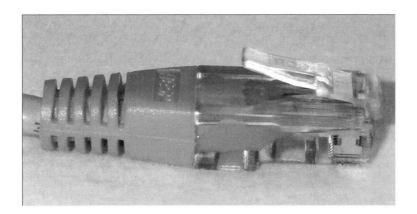

FIGURE 17.7
The connector on a twisted-pair cable resembles those used on telephone cords.

Twisted-pair cabling comes in a variety of *categories*. The higher the category, the cleaner the signal delivered by the cable. 10BaseT networking requires cabling of category 3, 4, or 5, whereas 100BaseT networking requires category 5 cables.

TIP

Even if you intend to use only 10Mbps speeds, purchase category 5 cables. This will greatly simplify your life if and when you decide to upgrade to 100Mbps speeds—particularly if you run cables in ways that would be time-consuming to replace.

> **CAUTION**
>
> If you run cabling between rooms or floors, particularly in a business setting, you might need to pay attention to your locality's fire codes. For instance, you might need to purchase Ethernet cables that are fire-resistant, run them through sealed conduits, or take other special precautions. If you're in doubt, contact a network consultant or electrician.

One final advantage of twisted-pair cabling over coaxial cabling is in the ease with which you can add and remove computers. Because twisted-pair cabling uses connectors much like those on telephone wires, you can simply snap a cable into the hub or switch on one end and a computer on the other, and you're set up. The other computers on the network aren't disrupted by this activity, as they are when you add a computer to a thin coaxial network. What's more, if a cable is damaged or gets yanked out of its connector, only one computer's network service is disrupted, which makes diagnosing the problem much easier than it would be with coaxial cabling.

Telephone Wiring Kits

With the increase in popularity of home networking, many companies have introduced Ethernet kits that are designed to be used over ordinary telephone wiring. Most home telephone wiring configurations include at least two pairs of wires. The better installations use twisted-pair wiring, but in many homes, the wiring isn't twisted and so is subject to greater interference than is common with Ethernet cabling. In any event, a single telephone line requires only one pair of wires, no matter how many extensions you have. The remaining pair or pairs can be used by a low-speed home network.

Such networks typically work at speeds of 10Mbps or lower. (2Mbps is common.) They typically use Ethernet cards that have been modified in various ways to support ordinary telephone wires rather than Ethernet cables. You should therefore be careful, if you decide to buy such a kit, to buy one that can be used with ordinary Linux Ethernet device drivers.

Hubs and Switches

If you use twisted-pair Ethernet cables, you must link your computers in one of three ways:

- **Using a crossover cable**   A *crossover cable* is wired in such a way that two computers can communicate directly. If you want to network only two computers, you can link them directly using a crossover RJ-45 cable. Doing so has the advantage that the NICs can communicate in full duplex mode, which will probably increase the networking speed. It also saves you the cost of a hub or switch.

- **Daisy-chaining**   If you place two NICs in most of the computers, you can use a series of two-computer links using crossover cables. Such a setup requires extra effort to configure, however, and it requires that all the computers be turned on to work. I don't recommend you attempt such a setup in most cases. (This can be an acceptable way to link two different *types* of network, however. For instance, you can use a computer with both an Ethernet and a Token Ring card to link these two sub-networks into one larger network.)

- **Using a hub or switch**   These devices allow you to link two or more computers in a star topology. This is the usual way to set up a small Ethernet network today. It's also a requirement if you want to link together more than two computers using twisted-pair cabling—at least, assuming you don't want to use an awkward daisy-chaining scheme.

Your choice of a hub or switch has a substantial impact on the way your network performs. Although they can be used in much the same way, hubs and switches have different performance characteristics. There are also differences within each category, so you should understand something of these differences before you buy a hub or switch.

The Difference Between Hubs and Switches

Hubs and switches perform similar functions: They both sit in the center of a star topology network and thereby link several computers together. Unless the device is marked as a hub or switch, you can't normally tell them apart from their appearance. Both are fairly nondescript boxes that contain several RJ-45 jacks and some LEDs. Figure 17.8 shows a typical hub. The smallest hubs and switches support about four computers, but higher-end models support many more.

Hubs and switches differ primarily in the way they connect the computers on a network. Hubs are comparatively simple devices that echo any incoming packet out to all the other devices, as shown in Figure 17.9. This feature means that every computer on the network must wade through all the traffic on that network. For instance, in Figure 17.9, when `polk` sends data to `pierce`, the computers `tyler`, `monroe`, and `madison` must also examine the same packets. Fortunately, Ethernet frames include *media access control* (MAC) addresses, which uniquely identify Ethernet cards. The processing load on the network's computers of having to examine all frames is therefore extremely low, because frames can be accepted or rejected on the basis of the MAC address. In fact, in most cases the computer's CPU need not be involved in the process at all; the NIC can handle the task alone. The distribution of data to all computers on the network does mean that collisions are more-or-less inevitable, particularly on large or heavily used networks.

FIGURE 17.8

Hubs and switches vary in size and shape, in part to accommodate differing numbers of connections.

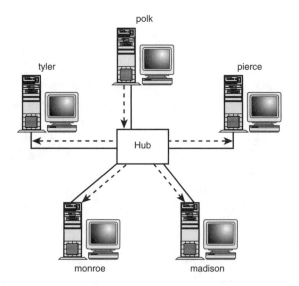

FIGURE 17.9

A hub passes network traffic destined for a single computer (indicated by the dashed lines) to all machines.

A switch, by contrast, is smarter than a hub. A switch can examine the MAC addresses of the Ethernet frames it receives and forward the frames on to only the intended recipient. This situation is illustrated in Figure 17.10. The result is less network congestion and less chance of collision. For instance, if polk transfers data to pierce, as shown in Figure 17.10, while tyler transfers data to monroe, there need be no collision. This is despite the fact that both polk and tyler transmit at the same time—a situation which *would* cause a collision with a hub.

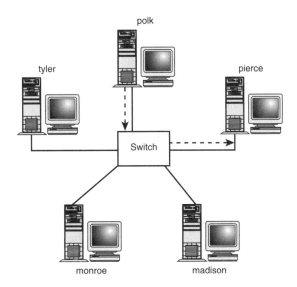

FIGURE 17.10
A switch forwards data only to the intended recipient computer.

Switches offer the following additional benefits over hubs:

- Because of the one-to-one link allowed by a switch, computers linked by a switch can communicate using full duplex, which further increases throughput, particularly when two computers exchange data in both directions.

- The one-to-one link established by a switch lets two computers communicate at their fastest possible speed, even when that speed is faster than is supported by other computers attached to the switch. Hubs, by contrast, force all computers to run at the slowest supported speed. For instance, suppose madison in Figures 17.9 and 17.10 has a 10Mbps NIC, but all the other computers have 100Mbps NICs. In this case, polk and pierce can only transfer data at 10Mbps when a hub is used, whereas they can transfer data at 100Mbps when a switch is used.

- Because Ethernet frames normally go only to the recipient computer, switches make setting up a *sniffer* on one computer ineffective at retrieving data from other computers on the network. This feature is a major security benefit on networks on which individual computers might be compromised in one way or another. On the other hand, it can be a minus if you want to perform network diagnostics.

All in all, then, switches are superior devices. Why would anybody buy a hub? In a word, cost. Hubs have traditionally cost less than switches. Since 1998, though, the costs of hubs and switches have equalized somewhat. Hubs still cost less than switches, but the difference is less than it used to be.

If you have a small network (say, fewer than half a dozen computers) and don't require the absolute best in speed, a hub can be an acceptable device. If you need the best performance possible, though, or if your network is large or hosts a lot of traffic, a switch is a better choice.

> **TIP**
>
> Some devices have some hub-like and some switch-like characteristics. For instance, there are hubs that include two banks of connections, with switch-like communication between the two banks. Such devices can be very useful in reducing network traffic or supporting networks with a mix of 10- and 100Mbps NICs, without going for full switches. Such devices blur the line between hubs and switches, which complicates buying. You should be sure you get a full switch if that's what you want, and not a hybrid device.

Hub and Switch Features

Hubs and switches both vary in a number of features. A few additional features apply only to switches. Examples of features you should consider in switches or both devices include:

- **Speed**   Ethernet hubs and switches are commonly available in 10Mbps and 100Mbps speeds. Most models sold today can automatically detect and use the appropriate speed, but some older models require you to flip a switch to set the appropriate speed. If you use a 10Mbps hub or switch, your network can't run faster than this, even if you have category 5 cabling and 100Mbps NICs on all your computers.

> **CAUTION**
>
> Some companies sell network kits that include a hub, two or three NICs, and appropriate cables. A few of these products advertise themselves as being 10/100Mbps kits, but they ship with 10Mbps hubs. If you buy a 10/100Mbps kit, be sure it includes a 100Mbps-capable hub as well as 100Mbps-capable NICs and category 5 cables.

- **Number of ports**   The number of ports on a device determines the number of computers it can link. Few hubs or switches have fewer than four ports, but many support more—sometimes many more. Small home and office configurations seldom need more than a dozen or so ports, but large installations can need many more. Specialized rack-mount switches are often used for such configurations.

- **Uplink port**   An *uplink port* allows you to link two hubs or switches together to increase their capacity or their geographic range. For instance, suppose you've got five computers in each of two rooms 40 feet apart, and you want to network all ten computers. You can buy two hubs or switches, each with an uplink port. Put one hub or switch in each room and run an Ethernet cable between them. When you connect the computers to their local hubs, the result is that all ten computers can see each other, as if they were connected to a single hub or switch. You can achieve a similar effect by using a crossover cable between ordinary ports on hubs or switches that aren't equipped with uplink ports.

- **LEDs**   Most hubs and switches feature activity LEDs that help you diagnose problems. These LEDs don't vary a lot in their utility, but you might want to check for this feature in any event.

- **Noise**   Some hubs, and especially some switches, have fans that can be noisy. Other devices have quieter fans or no fans at all.

- **Special features**   Some devices include special features that can be of interest to those who use DSL or cable modems to connect to the Internet. These devices support the *Dynamic Host Configuration Protocol* (DHCP) or PPPoE protocols used by many cable and DSL providers. They can also support features similar to Linux's IP masquerading to let several computers share a single IP address. In fact, these devices are often more like routers than hubs or switches, and they're often sold as such. A *router* is a device that's more sophisticated than a switch, and it's used to link one network to another.

- **Throughput**   Throughput is important for switches, but isn't normally a variable for hubs. Suppose you have a six-port 100Mbps switch. In theory, this switch can support three connections between pairs of computers, each of which can transfer up to 200Mbps of data (100Mbps in each direction), for 600Mbps total data throughput. In practice, most switches limit their throughput in one way or another, so you might not be able to achieve this level of performance. You should definitely check the throughput levels supported by any switch you buy, to ensure it's adequate for your anticipated needs.

- **Number of switched connections**   As noted earlier, there are hybrid hub/switch devices available. To be sure of what you're buying, you should check that a device that advertises itself as a switch really is a full switch.

17

NETWORK HARDWARE

Selecting the Hub or Switch That's Right for You

The main decisions you face in buying a hub or switch are whether you want a hub, a switch, or a hybrid device; and how many ports you need. Switches are, as I've said, superior to hubs in most respects, so if you find the price differential isn't exorbitant, I recommend you buy a switch, or at least a hybrid device. For a small and low-bandwidth network, however, a hub might be adequate.

I recommend you buy a hub or switch with at least two ports more than you need in the near future. For instance, if you have three computers and expect to buy a fourth in a month or two, get a hub or switch with at least six ports. Doing so makes it less likely that you'll need to replace or supplement your port in the near future.

Don't feel compelled to purchase the same brand hub or switch that you used for any NICs on your network. Brand-to-brand incompatibilities between network components are extremely rare. My own home network, for instance, uses a Linksys hub and NICs (or built-in Ethernet ports) from Linksys, Kingston, NDC SOHOWare, D-Link, and Apple. These devices are all compatible with one another.

Basic Linux Network Configuration

When you've got a network card, it's time to configure Linux to use that card. Most of the effort involved in this configuration can be done when you install Linux—if your card is installed at that time, and if you know how your network is set up. If you add a card later, or if your network configuration changes, you might need to reconfigure all or some of Linux's network settings. Although I can't provide an absolutely complete set of directions for network configuration, I can provide an overview of the basics.

Linux Kernel Configuration

As with many other hardware components, configuration of network cards begins with the kernel. There are three main kernel network configuration areas: Networking options, Network device support, and Ethernet (10 or 100Mbit). (Starting in the 2.3.x kernels, this final section has become a sub-section of the *Network device support* menu.) There are also a few menus relating to more obscure network devices, such as LocalTalk board drivers.

Networking Options

The *Networking options* menu, shown in Figure 17.11, provides options for a variety of general-purpose networking features. For instance, it is here that you enable support for TCP/IP networking or other network stacks, such as AppleTalk. These options don't relate to the low-level network hardware *per se*; instead, they cover the protocols that network utilities use.

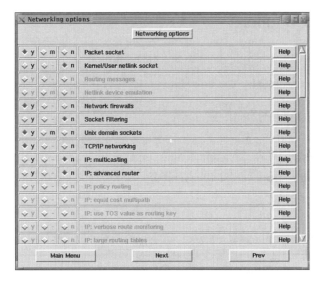

FIGURE 17.11

Use the Networking options menu to set TCP/IP and other network stack options.

The number of options in this menu is fairly substantial. Some of the more critical options include

- **TCP/IP networking**   You normally want to enable this option. Note that you cannot enable TCP/IP networking as a module; you must compile it directly into the kernel.

- **Firewall options**   Network firewalls and IP: firewalling must both be set to Y if you want to use the computer as a firewall.

- **The IPv6 protocol**   The next great leap in Internet technology is IPv6, which will allow many more computers to be on the Internet than is possible today. IPv6 is still quite rare, but this feature will become important in the future.

- **The IPX protocol**   IPX is the name of the networking stack used on Novell networks. Enable this option if you want your Linux computer to participate in such a network.

- **AppleTalk DDP**   Enable this option if you want your Linux computer to use Netatalk to serve files and printers on a Macintosh network, or to print to Macintosh printers.

There are many details you can set, particularly for TCP/IP networking. Most basic networking books, including my own *Linux: Networking for Your Office*, cover these options in greater detail.

17

NETWORK
HARDWARE

Network Device Support

The Network device support kernel configuration menu lets you enable support for a variety of non-Ethernet devices. Some highlights from this menu include

- **Network device support**   You must select Y to this option if you want to use network hardware. Note that this is true even if you want to use only Ethernet hardware, which you must then enable in a different menu.

- **PPP (point-to-point) support**   Enable this option if you intend to use a modem to connect to the Internet. Most such connections use PPP, which this option implements.

- **SLIP (serial line) support**   SLIP is a predecessor to PPP, and is still used by a few ISPs. It's also used by diald, which lets Linux automatically dial an ISP when it detects outgoing traffic.

This menu also contains options for a few exotic types of networking hardware, such as FDDI and HIPPI devices. In the 2.3.x and later kernels, you activate support for specific Ethernet devices from a sub-menu accessed from this menu.

Ethernet Devices

You can enable support for your specific Ethernet board from the Ethernet (10 or 100Mbit) menu, shown in Figure 17.12. Unfortunately, it can be difficult to locate specific devices on this menu because its organization reflects opportunistic growth over the years. Some boards are categorized in one way, whereas others are grouped in other ways. For instance, 3Com, Western Digital, and Racal-Interlan cards each have their own categories. Some ISA cards are grouped under Other ISA cards, and some EISA, VL-Bus, and PCI cards appear under the EISA, VLB, PCI and on board controllers option. Still other cards are uncategorized. As a result, you might need to hunt a bit to locate your Ethernet board's chipset.

Loading the Driver

The easiest way to load your Ethernet driver in most cases is to build it directly into the kernel. When you do this, the kernel normally detects the hardware at boot time. You can check to see if this has happened by issuing the command **dmesg | grep eth** shortly after booting the computer. If your kernel has detected your hardware, you'll see something like this in response:

```
eth0: Macronix 98715 PMAC rev 32 at 0xda00, 00:80:C6:F9:3B:BA, IRQ 9.
eth1: VIA VT3043 Rhine at 0xdc00, 00:80:c8:fa:3b:0a, IRQ 10.
eth1: MII PHY found at address 8, status 0x782d advertising 05e1 Link 0000.
```

In this example, two NICs are installed. One (eth0) uses a Macronix 98715 chipset (which is a Tulip clone chipset). The other (eth1) uses a VIA VT3043 Rhine chipset.

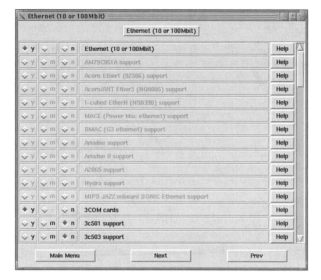

FIGURE 17.12

The Ethernet (10 or 100Mbit) menu is organized somewhat haphazardly.

If you haven't compiled a driver into the kernel, you must tell Linux about the driver in some other way. One way is to manually load the driver using the insmod or modprobe commands. For instance, use **modprobe ne** to load the ne (NE2000) driver. Chances are you don't want to do this manually every time you start your computer, though. In this case, you can add a line or two to your /etc/conf.modules or /etc/modules.conf file to tell Linux about your hardware. For instance

```
alias eth0 ne
options ne io=0x240
```

These lines tell Linux to use the ne driver for eth0, and to look for the card at I/O port 0x240. The second line might be required for some ISA cards, but shouldn't be necessary for most PCI NICs. If you have more than one Ethernet card, you can add a similar line or lines for each card. After you've added these lines, Linux should automatically detect and load your kernel modules when it boots.

Bringing Up the Interface

After you've loaded your NIC's driver, you can activate the interface. Unlike most hardware, you don't access a network card through a device file entry in the /dev directory. Instead, you tell the kernel to associate a network device with a particular IP address by using the ifconfig command. This command has the following syntax:

```
ifconfig interface [options] address
```

The *interface* is the network interface, such as eth0 for the first Ethernet card. You can set various Ethernet options with the optional *options* parameters. The *address* is a four-number IP address, such as 192.168.33.2, which should be provided to you by your network administrator. If you're setting up a small home network, you can use addresses in a reserved private network address range, such as 192.168.*x.x*. For instance, here's a basic command to activate an Ethernet interface:

```
ifconfig eth0 up 192.168.33.2
```

One potentially vital option is the netmask option. The term netmask is short for *network mask*, and it splits the network address space into a range for the network address and a range for the computer address. For instance, 192.168.33.0 is a network address, and .2 is a machine address within that network. The Internet is structured in such a way that addresses have certain default splits. If your network is broken up in this default manner, you don't need to specify the netmask. If not, though, you must do so by using what looks like an IP address. Converted to binary, a value of *1* in this address indicates that the equivalent bit is part of the network address, whereas a value of *0* indicates that the bit is part of the machine address. For instance, 255.255.255.0 indicates a Class C address, in which the final byte is the machine address. An example of the netmask option in use would be:

```
ifconfig eth0 netmask 255.255.255.128 up 192.168.33.2
```

If you used this command on a local network, you could have only 126 computers on the network, rather than 254 in the normal Class C 192.168.33.*x* network. This sort of split isn't normally worthwhile for a private network, but large organizations and ISPs often use this technique to assign subnetworks to departments or other organizations to which they sell the addresses.

You should consult the ifconfig man page for more information on this command. After you issue this command, you should be able to verify that the interface is up and running by typing **ifconfig** without any parameters, or with the name of the interface only. For instance

```
$ ifconfig eth0
eth0      Link encap:Ethernet  HWaddr 00:80:C6:F9:3B:BA
          inet addr:192.168.33.2  Bcast:192.168.33.255  Mask:255.255.255.0
          UP BROADCAST RUNNING MULTICAST  MTU:1500  Metric:1
          RX packets:12 errors:0 dropped:0 overruns:0 frame:0
          TX packets:7 errors:0 dropped:0 overruns:0 carrier:0
          collisions:0
```

Used in reporting mode, ifconfig shows vital network statistics for one or more interfaces. In this case, it shows the MAC address (the string of six hexadecimal numbers after HWaddr), the IP address, and assorted statistics on packets received and sent.

Setting the Route

In order to send network traffic, your computer must know to what interface data should be sent. If you only have one Ethernet card, it might seem obvious what interface to use, but it's not quite that simple. Every Linux computer supports a network interface known as the *loopback* device, which refers to the host computer itself. This interface is locked to the 127.0.0.1 IP address, and is configured automatically. You might also use PPP dial-up networking or have a second NIC. For these reasons, you must set up a *routing table,* or *route*, which is a set of rules for the transmission of network traffic.

Routing for a Local Network

Suppose that you're setting up a local network on one interface (let's call it eth0). You want traffic destined for computers on this interface to go through eth0, but you want other traffic to go through another interface, such as a PPP dialup link or another Ethernet board. In order to configure eth0, you use the route command, which has the following basic syntax:

```
route add | del target [gw gateway]
```

To add a route, you use the add parameter and specify the target address or addresses. For instance

```
route add 192.168.33.0
```

In this example, I've specified an address that ends in .0, which is an indication that this is a network address, not just an address for a single computer. In this case, the system sends all data for the 192.168.33.x network through this route. Because you've already bound eth0 to 192.168.33.2 (using the ifconfig command), Linux can determine that this route is associated with the eth0 device.

Setting the Default Route

Most networked computers have at least two routes: one for the loopback device, and one for everything else. The "everything else" entry sends data through a *router,* or *gateway,* computer. The router knows how to send data on to computers on the Internet at large. Thus, your computer doesn't need to know how to access, say, 63.69.110.75; it simply sends all requests for this—or any other address for which it doesn't have a more explicit route—to the gateway system. You set the default route using the gw option to the route command. For instance

```
route add 0.0.0.0 gw 192.168.33.100
```

The 0.0.0.0 IP address is shorthand for any address. You can use default in place of this number, if you like. The 192.168.33.100 address in this example is the IP address of your network's router. You can obtain this address from your network's administrator.

> **NOTE**
>
> When you start a dial-up PPP session, the pppd program automatically adds appropriate routes to direct your Internet traffic.

As with ifconfig, you can use the route command without any options to examine the status of your routing table. On a simple network configuration, the result might look something like this:

```
Kernel IP routing table
Destination     Gateway          Genmask          Flags Metric Ref    Use Iface
192.168.33.0    *                255.255.255.0    U     0      0        0 eth0
127.0.0.0       *                255.0.0.0        U     0      0        0 lo
default         192.168.33.100   0.0.0.0          UG    0      0        0 eth0
```

The routing table is arranged from most- to least-specific addresses:

- **192.168.33.0**   This address is for a small network (a *Class C* network). Chances are all the computers on this network are linked to the computer more-or-less directly, on the same coaxial cable or connected to the same hub or switch.

- **127.0.0.0**   This is the loopback network. In reality, there's just one computer on this network (the host computer itself), but Linux configures the route as if it were a large (*Class A*) network.

- **default**   The default route sends data through the 192.168.33.100 gateway machine, for anything that doesn't match either of the two preceding destinations.

After you've set the default route, you should be able to access any computer on the network, albeit only by IP address. To use the more familiar computer names, such as www.macmillanusa.com, you must configure your system to use a DNS server.

Setting the DNS Server

The Internet relies on the *Domain Name System* (DNS) to resolve computer names into the IP addresses upon which TCP/IP networking relies. Your network administrator can provide you with the names of your network's DNS servers. You can then add these IP addresses, and perhaps your default domain, to the /etc/resolv.conf file, as in

```
# Default domain:
domain threeroomco.com
# Additional networks to search:
search tworoomco.com room2.threeroomco.com
# Nameservers:
nameserver 192.168.33.101
nameserver 192.168.33.102
```

The domain line specifies the domain in which the computer resides, and the search line specifies one or more domains the computer searches so that you don't need to provide a complete computer name. For instance, if threeroomco.com has computers called polk and tyler, and if tworoomco.com has the computers elizabeth and henry, you can specify any of these computer names without their corresponding domains and you'll get back the correct IP addresses. The nameserver lines, as you might guess, specify the addresses of the nameservers. You can have up to three nameserver lines in the /etc/resolv.conf file.

Automatic Configuration with DHCP

Many networks use DHCP to make configuration of most systems easier. DHCP allows a network administrator to store most of the information I've just described on a central DHCP server computer. If your computer is on a network that uses DHCP, you still need to load the appropriate kernel driver, but the computer can obtain its IP address, set its route, and set appropriate nameservers automatically. Depending upon your Linux distribution, you use either the dhcpcd or dhclient command to accomplish these tasks. To use these tools manually, type the program's name followed by the interface you want to configure, as in

dhclient eth0

If an appropriate server exists on your local network, it passes back appropriate information, and Linux configures itself using that information. Both dhcpcd and dhclient support several additional parameters, so you should check their man pages for more information.

GUI Network Configuration

Many Linux distributions include GUI tools to aid in network configuration. For instance, Figure 17.13 shows linuxconf, which comes with the Red Hat and Mandrake Linux distributions. You can use these tools to set most or all of the Linux network configuration options. The details of how these tools work vary substantially from one distribution to another, unfortunately.

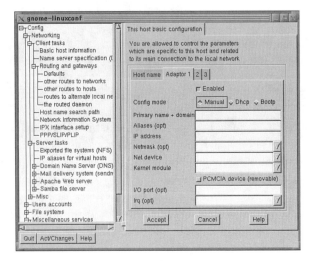

FIGURE 17.13
GUI configuration tools help you configure networking options in Linux.

Summary

Linux's development has been inextricably tied to the Internet. Without the Internet, the many individuals who have contributed to Linux would find it difficult to collaborate. It's therefore appropriate that Linux's support for networking hardware is excellent. This is particularly true in the realm of the most popular networking technology for x86 computers: Ethernet. Ethernet comes in many forms, most of which are very similar at the level of the TCP/IP stack and even at the driver level. Linux therefore doesn't need to know anything about the non-NIC Ethernet peripherals you buy, such as hubs and switches. You do, however, have to tell Linux a little about the logical structure of your network, in terms of routes to local computers, and a route to the gateway you use to communicate with the rest of the Internet. You should consult your network administrator to obtain this information. If you're setting up your own network, you should read appropriate Linux HOWTO documents or a good book on Linux networking.

Modems

IN THIS CHAPTER

Although most large businesses are wired for high-speed Internet access, most homes and even many smaller businesses are not. The individuals and organizations so affected typically rely on modems to make Internet access a reality. Modems are also useful tools for other types of access. You can use them to dial up a Linux computer to perform text-mode operations, for instance, even without involving full Internet access. They're also useful for sending and receiving faxes, and sometimes even for receiving voice mail.

The word *modem* is actually an acronym, standing for *modulator-demodulator*. The origin of this term lies in the fact that a conventional telephone modem modulates digital data into an analog form, and demodulates analog data from the phone line into digital form. Today, conventional telephone modems are extremely common, but other types of modems are starting to become popular. These are *Digital Subscriber Line* (DSL) and cable modems; they permit much higher transfer rates over telephone wires and cable TV systems, respectively. These devices function in fundamentally different ways than do conventional telephone modems, however. In fact, the term *modem* isn't technically accurate when applied to them. Some people and companies therefore refer to them by other terms, such as *ADSL Network Terminator* (ANT) or *Data Service Unit* (DSU). The word *modem* is most commonly applied to these devices, however, and I call them modems in this chapter.

Telephone Modems

Telephone modems plug into an ordinary telephone jack using ordinary telephone cord. They can then dial telephone numbers just like a telephone, but in most cases it's expected that they'll connect to another telephone modem on the other end. The two devices go through a *handshake* period, in which each device communicates its capabilities, and they settle on a set of protocols to govern their communications. Thereafter, a data link exists, and the data one computer sends to its modem appears as input to the other computer. Figure 18.1 illustrates this arrangement.

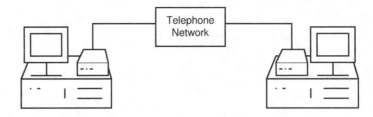

FIGURE 18.1

A modem uses the telephone company's wires as a networking medium.

The fact that telephone modems work over ordinary telephone lines makes them an extremely useful tool for networking, because there's no need to lay specialized network cables. On the other hand, modems are slow as networking technologies go. In early 2000, the fastest analog modems use the v.90 protocol, which permits a theoretical maximum speed of 56Kbps downstream—substantially less than competing technologies allow. (Even this theoretical maximum speed isn't attainable in practice, for reasons I describe later in this chapter.) If you spend a lot of time online, a telephone modem also poses the problem that you can't use the phone line for voice calls while using the modem. Many businesses and even home users therefore obtain a phone line that's dedicated to modem use, which raises the cost of Internet access.

Modem Technologies

Modems can be classified in several different ways—by speed, by the supported error-checking and compression protocols, by whether the modem is internal to the computer or uses a separate external box, and by whether the modem incorporates all its features in its hardware or requires special software to operate. I describe each of these classifications in turn.

Modem Speeds

Some of the earliest modems operated at 300 bits per second (bps). Many of these devices didn't interface to the phone line as modern devices do, through a telephone jack. Instead, these modems used an audio coupler; you fitted a telephone handset into the modem. The modem contained a microphone near the phone handset's earpiece and a speaker near the telephone's microphone. The modem then generated audio tones to do its work. Fortunately, such crude modems are museum pieces today. All modern modems use direct electrical links to your building's telephone wiring.

Each modem speed, from 300 bps upwards, follows a standard. Table 18.1 summarizes the modem standards that have been in common use over the past two decades. Most modems implement all the major standards up to a given point. For instance, you can use a modern v.90 modem to communicate with a much older 300 bps model, if the need arises.

TABLE 18.1 Modem Speed Standards

Protocol	Upstream Speed (bps)	Downstream Speed (bps)	Duplex
Bell 103	300	300	Full
CCITT v.21	300	300	Full
Bell 212A	1,200	1,200	Full
ITU v.22	1,200	1,200	Half
ITU v.22bis	2,400	2,400	Full
ITU v.23	1,200	75	Full

continues

TABLE 18.1   Continued

Protocol	Upstream Speed (bps)	Downstream Speed (bps)	Duplex
ITU v.29[1]	9,600	9,600	Half
ITU v.32	9,600	9,600	Full
ITU v.32bis	14,400	14,400	Full
v.32fast[3]	28,800	28,800	Full
ITU v.34	28,800	28,800	Full
ITU v.34[2]	33,600	33,600	Full
K56Flex[3]	56,000	33,600	Full
x2[3]	56,000	33,600	Full
ITU v.90	56,000[4]	33,600	Full

1 The v.29 standard is used mainly by fax machines and by modems when sending or receiving faxes.
2 The original v.34 specification only supported up to 28,800 bps, but a revised version of the standard, which used the same name, supports up to 33,600 bps speeds.
3 The protocols v.32fast, K56Flex and x2 were not approved standards in the same sense as are the ITU standards. These protocols were promoted by various companies before v.90 (or v.34, in the case of v.32fast) was finalized.
4 The v.90 standard permits 56Kbps transmission speeds, but Federal Communication Commission (FCC) regulations limit the speed in the United States to 53Kbps.

NOTE

The term *baud* is sometimes used in reference to modem speeds. This term refers to the number of modulations per second. When the number of bits transmitted per modulation is one, then baud and bps values are equivalent. Most modem encoding standards, however, send more than one bit per modulation, so baud and bps values are different. For this reason, the term *baud* has fallen into disuse. When it is used, it's often used incorrectly as a synonym for *bps*.

As you can see from Table 18.1, modem speeds have increased dramatically from the early Bell 103 protocol. Today's v.90 modems are nearly as fast as can be supported by standard telephone wires using the range of tones supported by voice lines. Work is underway on a protocol that might be called *v.90+* or *v.92*, which might increase the upstream speed past 33.6Kbps, and perhaps cut the time required to negotiate a connection. This new protocol is unlikely to increase the downstream speed past its current 56Kbps limit, however.

Most of the protocols in Table 18.1 use *symmetrical* speeds —transmission speed is the same as receiving speed. Two protocols, however, use *asymmetrical* speed systems. Most importantly, this is true of the fastest speed: v.90. This protocol requires that one modem have a special digital connection to the phone line. This connection is made by *Internet Service Providers* (ISPs), so you don't need to concern yourself with it unless you want to run a 56Kbps dial-up system. The 56Kbps speed of v.90 is also more theoretical than real, for two reasons. First, FCC regulations limit the speed to 53Kbps in order to avoid interference with other peoples' phone lines. Second, most phone lines contain small flaws that reduce the speed below 53Kbps. In practice, you're very lucky to get a speed of more than 45Kbps or so with a v.90 modem, and many users find themselves able to connect at only 40Kbps or thereabouts.

> **TIP**
>
> If you don't already have a v.90 modem but do have a v.34 modem, you can test your line to see if it's capable of handling v.90 speed. You can do this by using a terminal program such as `minicom` or `seyon` to dial 1-847-262-6000. The computer that responds asks for your first and last names. Reply `line` and `test`, respectively. The system then informs you if the line from which you called can support v.90 speeds. Note, however, that you might not achieve *good* v.90 speeds even if your line passes the test. For instance, you might routinely connect at 36Kbps–40Kbps. These speeds are v.90 speeds, but they might not be worth the bother to upgrade from v.34.

Error Correction and Data Compression

All modern modems support an assortment of error correction and data compression protocols. These protocols detect and correct errors to ensure an accurate stream of data, and can compress data that's transmitted over the phone line. Examples of these protocols include

- **MNP 1–4**   Microcom developed several error correction protocols that are known as *Microcom Networking Protocols* (MNP) 1–4.

- **v.42**   This is a more sophisticated error correction scheme than the MNP protocols, and it includes a fallback to MNP 4. Therefore, an MNP 4 modem can establish an error correction link with a v.42 modem.

- **MNP 5**   Microcom's MNP 5 is a data compression standard that allows for up to 2x compression of data.

- **v.42bis**   This protocol allows for up to 4x compression on highly-compressible data, such as text. Although v.42bis is not backward-compatible with MNP 5, nearly all v.42bis modems also include support for MNP 5.

All modern telephone modems support both v.42 and v.42bis, but older devices might not do so. Error correction is vitally important to modern modem operation. Without it, PPP links tend to become unstable and fail after a few minutes of operation. Data compression is less vital, because PPP includes optional data compression algorithms of its own. Some of the error correction techniques, such as v.42, actually provide a small amount of compression by themselves. This is because the error correction protocols package several bytes of information into one unit that's transmitted without the control bits that normally accompany the data.

You should generally set your serial port's speed at about twice the speed of the modem's connection, if you expect to use a compressed connection and transmit highly compressible data. For instance, using a v.90 (56Kbps) modem, set your serial port speed to 115,200 bps. Although some compression protocols claim a greater maximum compression than 2x, it's unlikely that you'll achieve such a high rate of compression. In fact, you might receive none if you transfer highly compressed files like tarballs.

NOTE

Most x86 serial ports can only handle a port speed of up to 115,200 bps. Therefore, you can't set the port speed to higher than 2 times theoretical connect speed with a v.90 modem. Because *actual* connect speed is lower than 56Kbps, however, a 115,200 bps port speed is often about 2.5–3 times faster than the actual connect speed.

Internal and External Modems

Modems for x86 computers have traditionally been serial port devices. That is, they connect to the computer through a serial port (see Chapter 16, "Parallel and Serial Ports"). It's therefore logical that modems be external peripherals, as shown in Figure 18.2. These devices use a serial cable to connect to one of your computer's serial ports. They also require a separate power cable. These devices vary substantially in size and shape.

Other models are *internal* devices. These are ISA or PCI cards that have external connectors for telephone cords. They look much like any other expansion card. Traditionally, internal modems have contained all the circuitry of external modems plus the circuitry of a serial port, and so they're indistinguishable from external models from a software point of view. Since the late 1990s, however, *software modems* have become increasingly popular. These devices eliminate some of the hardware in favor of special drivers. I describe them in greater detail shortly. For the moment, we'll consider only traditional *controller-based* internal modems, which contain all the usual modem circuitry.

FIGURE 18.2
An external modem is typically a rectangular box that can sit next to or on top of a computer.

Each variety of modem has its advantages and disadvantages. Benefits of external modems include

- **Portability**   You can easily unplug an external modem from one computer and move it to another computer. Doing this with an internal model is also possible, but takes more effort.

- **Freedom from interference**   The interior of a typical computer's case is filled with various types of electromagnetic and radio interference, which can sometimes cause poor performance in a modem.

- **No slots required**   External modems don't consume any slots in your computer, unless you need to add a serial port to accommodate the modem.

- **Simpler configuration**   The need to add a serial port or reconfigure an existing one for internal modems can be a nuisance. External modems are simpler to configure because most Linux distributions include support for the two standard serial ports by default.

- **Independent power switch**   You can easily power off an external modem by flipping its power switch or, at worst, by unplugging it from your electrical outlet. This can sometimes be important if the modem is malfunctioning—either dialing numbers erroneously or failing to respond at all. Powering the device off and then on again often fixes such problems.

- **LEDs**   External models usually feature a bank of half a dozen or so LEDs that indicate the modem's status. These LEDs can be extremely useful in diagnosing problems.

18

MODEMS

On the other hand, the benefits of internal models include

- **Zero footprint**   As internal devices, internal modems don't consume any desk space.
- **Reduced cable clutter**   Although all modems require at least one cable for a connection to the telephone outlet, external devices also require a serial cable and a power cable. Internal devices require neither of these.
- **No serial port required**   If you're currently using both your external serial ports, an internal model frees you from having to buy a separate serial port card or using an external serial port switch box.
- **Reduced cost**   Internal modems typically cost less than do external modems.

This final item is the deciding factor for many purchasers; internal modems are quite popular. This is particularly true on new computers, which frequently include a modem. (Some of these actually include the modem on the motherboard.)

You can use either internal or external modems under Linux. Aside from issues of configuring an internal modem's serial port, their configuration and use is exactly the same. (See Chapter 16 for a description of configuring a new serial port.)

USB Modems

External modems are beginning to abandon the traditional RS-232 serial port in favor of the USB port. This process is far from complete, so you can still buy external RS-232 serial modems. If you're in the market for a new modem, this is the safest route to take in most cases.

If you must buy a USB modem for some reason, you'll need to use the USB support from 2.3.x or later kernels. These kernels include a driver for USB modems that use the *Communication Device Class Abstract Control Model* (CDC-ACM) interface. This driver requires device files with major number 166 and minor numbers from 0 up. Filenames for these devices typically take the form /dev/ttyACM*n*, where *n* is a number from 0 up.

Not all USB modems support the CDC-ACM protocols, so you should shop carefully. You can check http://www.linux-usb.org for the latest on USB information for Linux, including a database of information on hardware compatibility.

Software and Controller-Based Modems

Telephone modems are essentially specialized computers. These computers are designed exclusively to convert digital to analog data, and vice versa. As x86 CPU speeds have increased over the years, it's become possible for the computer's CPU to perform some of the computational tasks traditionally performed by the modem. In such an arrangement, the modem still requires some hardware, but the modem's hardware can be much simpler, and therefore much less expensive, than the hardware for a conventional modem.

Various terms have come into being to describe both older modems and the new software varieties. The new software-driven modems can be called *software modems*, *controllerless modems*, or *WinModems*, although the last is actually a trademark of 3Com and so should only be applied to certain 3Com models. Software modems for which Linux drivers exist are sometimes called *LinModems*. Old-style modems are usually referred to as *conventional modems* or *controller-based modems*.

Software modems have traditionally been scorned by the Linux community for two reasons:

- **Specialized driver requirements** Software modems can't work with normal Linux serial port drivers. Instead, they require specialized drivers that have only started to become available in late 1999. Even in 2000, many software modems simply don't work in Linux.

- **CPU load** Because software modems rely on software to perform tasks normally performed in hardware, these modems rob you of some CPU time. This can be a serious problem on comparatively slow computers, such as 100MHz Pentiums. On modern 500MHz or faster machines, this problem is less important.

Despite their poor favor in the Linux community, software modems do have a few advantages, including

- **Low cost** Software modems cost very little to manufacture, and so their retail price can be quite low. I recently heard of a software modem selling for $25 with a $20 rebate offer, for instance.

- **Small component size** Because of their simplicity, software modem components can easily fit into space-limited board designs, such as those for notebook computers.

- **Programmability** In theory, software modems can support future standards and even entirely unanticipated functions merely by updating the software. In practice, Linux support for the devices is so slim that this is more of a *potential* advantage than a real one.

All in all, I recommend you avoid software modems whenever possible. Linux driver support for these modems is in its early stages, and some of these drivers are available only in binary form, which means they might stop working with future kernels if the manufacturer loses interest in maintaining the driver. In some cases, you might have little choice in the matter. For instance, almost all notebook computers sold today include software modems. You can buy PC-Card or external serial port modems to replace the built-in models, but you'll find it easier to use the built-in software modem, if that's possible.

18

MODEMS

Software modems are available as internal models only. The computations required to implement a software modem require the high speed of an ISA or PCI slot. You can usually identify a software modem by checking the requirements panel on the modem's box. If it lists a Pentium CPU or Windows among its minimum requirements, it's almost certainly a software modem. If the box lists an 80486 or earlier CPU, or DOS, OS/2, or Linux among its minimum requirements, chances are it's a controller-based modem. (If the box lists a Pentium CPU and mentions Linux but not DOS, it might be a software modem for which Linux drivers are available.) External modems are almost always Linux compatible. The main exceptions are some USB modems. As described in the sidebar, "USB Modems," earlier in this chapter, some of these devices work with Linux's USB drivers, but some don't.

If you have a software modem, you might as well look for Linux drivers before you attempt to replace it. The Web site http://www.linmodems.org has the latest information on software modems under Linux, including links to drivers, information on software modem chipsets, and miscellaneous additional information.

> **NOTE**
>
> A few internal modems have been released based on IBM *Mwave* chips. These products usually support both modem and sound card functionality. They aren't software modems in the same sense as are most software modems, because the Mwave chip performs the usual modem processing functions. Mwave products do rely upon specialized drivers to load the modem processing code, however, and so don't work under Linux. There have been some abortive attempts to write Linux drivers for Mwave devices, but none has yet borne fruit.

Extra Modem Features

All modems sold today support conventional data traffic using the v.90 protocol (or possibly only some earlier protocol, if it's an older model in a closeout bin). Additional features supported by anywhere from a few to the vast majority of modems include

- **K56Flex**   K56Flex was a 56Kbps modem protocol that predated v.90. It was used by a variety of modem manufacturers, led by the modem chipset manufacturer Rockwell. Some ISPs still support K56Flex, but I don't recommend buying a K56Flex modem unless it also supports v.90.

- **x2**   Like K56Flex, x2 was a 56Kbps protocol that predated v.90. This protocol was used mostly in U.S. Robotics (USR) modems (USR has since been bought by 3Com). As with K56Flex, I only recommend buying an x2 modem if it also supports v.90.

- **Fax features** The capability to both send and receive faxes is standard on modern modems. As a general rule, you should look for a modem that supports Class 2.0 fax protocols, which impose the least overhead on the sending applications. In Linux, programs such as mgetty+sendfax (http://alpha.greenie.net/mgetty/) or HylaFax (http://www.hylafax.org/) handle sending and receiving faxes. Unfortunately, most of these programs are far less user-friendly than are their Windows equivalents. Matters are improved somewhat by fax front-end programs like GFax (http://www.gmsys.com/gnome-gfax.html), which provide an easy-to-use GUI atop the underlying fax software.

- **Voice features** Some modems support voice functionality. You can use these modems as speakerphones, answering machines, or voicemail systems. Linux support for these devices exists, but is extremely crude compared to the user-friendly Windows voicemail programs for the same hardware. The main Linux package for voice modems is vgetty (http://alpha.greenie.net/vgetty/index.html). This is a variant of the mgetty+sendfax package.

Using Modems for PPP Internet Connections

You can use a modem to connect your Linux computer to the Internet using the *Point-to-Point Protocol* (PPP). Most Linux distributions today include tools to help you manage a PPP dial-up account. For instance, the *K Desktop Environment* (KDE), which is the default desktop on many Linux installations, includes a program called kppp, shown in Figure 18.3. When you click the Setup button in the main window, you get the kppp Configuration window shown in the foreground. You can enter information on your PPP account in this window much as you would enter information in a Windows PPP dialer. When you're done, you can connect to your ISP by clicking the Connect button in the main kppp window. Other GUI PPP dialers function in a similar fashion, although the details differ.

Depending upon the authentication method you use, you might need to take one additional step: You might need to add your username and password to the /etc/ppp/pap-secrets or /etc/ppp/chap-secrets file, depending upon whether your ISP uses PAP or CHAP authentication. These files are readable only by root, and they contain your sensitive passwords. An example is

```
# client      server  secret              IP addresses
rodsmith      *       password
```

This sample file allows the user rodsmith to log in to a PPP server using the password password. In most cases you want to leave the *server* field set to an asterisk (*), which allows a login to any server. If you're assigned a static IP address by your ISP, you can enter it in the final IP addresses field; otherwise, leave that field blank.

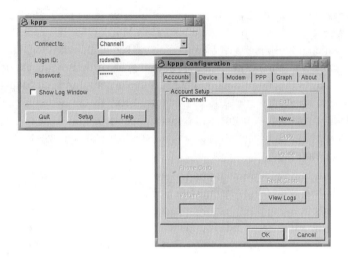

FIGURE 18.3
The kppp *program is a typical PPP GUI dial-up utility.*

Null Modem Cables

Sometimes you need to connect two computers together via their serial or parallel ports. This can be an inexpensive way to network the two computers, or it can be a way to use one computer as an inexpensive terminal for another. For instance, you can use an old 8088 computer as a terminal for a much more capable Linux box. This can be a good way to use Linux's multiuser capabilities. Precisely how you make these connections depends on whether you want to use a serial or parallel port for this purpose.

Serial Null Modem Cables

The easiest way to use a serial port for connecting two computers is to purchase a *null modem* cable or an adapter to turn a conventional modem cable into a null modem cable. Figure 18.4 shows both a null modem cable and a null modem adapter. The null modem cable closely resembles an ordinary RS-232 serial cable, except that both connectors are female, which is unusual in conventional modem cables. For modern x86 computers, both ends use 9-pin connectors, but if you want to link a computer that uses a 25-pin serial connector, one or both ends might need to have 25 pins.

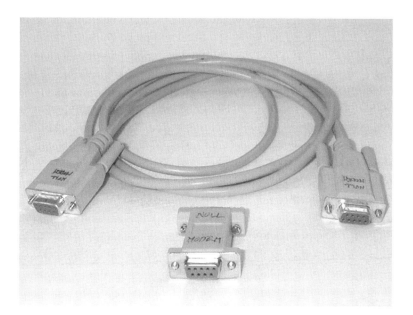

FIGURE 18.4

Null modem cables look very much like ordinary cables, so I recommend you label them as null modem devices, if they aren't so labeled when you buy them.

> **NOTE**
>
> You might occasionally run into a serial null modem cable on which one end uses a specialized connector. For instance, cables of this sort come with many palmtop computers. You can use these cables to link the palmtop to your Linux computer, and then use the Linux computer via a terminal program or a PPP link.

Precisely how you configure your Linux computer to work with the null modem cable depends on what you want to do with it. In most cases, you must modify the /etc/inittab file. This file should have a number of lines that look something like this:

```
# Run gettys in standard runlevels
1:12345:respawn:/sbin/getty tty1 VC linux
2:2345:respawn:/sbin/getty tty2 VC linux
3:2345:respawn:/sbin/getty tty3 VC linux
4:2345:respawn:/sbin/getty tty4 VC linux
5:2345:respawn:/sbin/getty tty5 VC linux
6:2345:respawn:/sbin/getty tty6 VC linux
```

These lines run the getty program, which handles the text-mode login: prompt. Each instance of getty in the preceding example is linked to a different Linux *virtual console*, identified by the tty*n* number on each line. You should add a similar line for any additional function you want to perform with the serial port. For instance, if you want to use another computer as a *dumb terminal*, which provides only text-mode access, you could add a line like the following:

```
S0:2345:respawn:/sbin/getty ttyS0 VC linux
```

This line allows for a 19,200 bps connection to /dev/ttyS0 via a null modem cable. The computer you use as a dumb terminal could be an old-style terminal (such as a DEC VT-100) or it could be a PC, Macintosh, palmtop, or some other system running a terminal program.

> **NOTE**
>
> Linux distributions differ in the details of how they provide login access. Specifically, there are several different variants on the getty program, such as getty, mingetty, and mgetty. Each of these programs has different capabilities. For instance, mingetty can't handle serial port access, so if your distribution uses mingetty, you might need to use getty or mgetty instead of mingetty to use a terminal connected to a serial port with Linux. You can continue using mingetty on the virtual console devices.

In some cases, you might need to replace the call to /sbin/getty with a call to some other program. For instance, if you want to use the serial port for a PPP connection, you would use pppd in place of getty. You can also use more advanced getty-like programs, such as mgetty, to handle real modems for dial-in access or fax reception.

For the most part, serial ports aren't a very efficient communication method. The maximum serial port speed of 115Kbps is simply too low compared to the speeds that are possible with Ethernet (10–100Mbps) or other networking technologies. Therefore, serial ports aren't much used for serious networking. They can be very useful for limited text-mode logins, though.

PLIP for Parallel-Port Networking

Parallel ports, like serial ports, can be used with a sort of null modem cable. The term *null modem cable* isn't generally used in reference to parallel ports, however. Under Linux, the primary use of parallel-port, computer-to-computer communication is as a low-cost network interface. Because every x86 computer manufactured in recent years has a parallel port, you can connect any two arbitrary computers without adding additional hardware to either computer. You do need a special parallel cable, however.

You can use a Turbo LapLink (aka *null printer*) cable, which you might be able to find at a computer store, in low-speed mode (*mode 0*). A better solution is to create a custom cable that can support higher-speed (*mode 1*) transfers. To create such a cable, you need two 25-pin male connectors, a length of 25-conductor cable, and some experience in wiring custom cables. If you lack this experience, you might want to seek out somebody who possesses it. Table 18.2 shows the wiring connections for the custom cable.

TABLE 18.2   High-Speed PLIP Cable Pinouts

Computer 1	Computer 2
1	11
2	2
3	3
4	4
5	5
6	6
7	7
8	8
9	9
13	17
14	12
16	10
18	15
25	25

18

MODEMS

In Linux, parallel-port networking is referred to as *Parallel Line Internet Protocol* (PLIP). You must enable support for this protocol in the Linux kernel configuration, in the *Network device support* kernel configuration menu. After you've activated this support, you can use the parallel port as a network device with the `plip0` network device name (or possibly `plip1` or `plip2` if the computer has multiple parallel ports).

Because the parallel port is capable of 2MB/s speeds, PLIP is at least theoretically competitive with 10Mbps Ethernet. In practice, the parallel port is seldom as fast as Ethernet. Because Linux is the only OS to implement PLIP, this form of networking might not always be useful. You can also link only two or three computers directly in this way. You can find more information on PLIP in the `/usr/src/linux/Documentation/network/PLIP.txt` file and in the NET-3-4 HOWTO, which comes with all Linux distributions.

ISDN Modems

One technology that competes with conventional analog telephone service is *Integrated Services Digital Network* (ISDN). ISDN works by providing one or two 2-way, 56Kbps digital links over ordinary telephone wires. The promise of ISDN is that these two links can be managed in an intelligent way, to provide voice and data service at the same time. For instance, you can download data at 56Kbps while using the phone and, when you hang up the phone, your data transfer rate can double.

ISDN never became very popular in the United States, but it has enjoyed some popularity in Europe. Linux supports a variety of ISDN network cards. To use these, you must activate the cards in the *ISDN support* kernel configuration menu. Some ISDN adapters also connect to the computer through the serial port, much like conventional telephone modems. These devices work much like regular modems, including Linux PPP access methods.

In the United States, ISDN service is usually more expensive than competing DSL or cable service, and it provides lower data transfer rates. It's therefore not generally a very cost-effective means of providing Internet access. ISDN can be used at greater distances from your phone company's central office (CO) than can DSL, however, so it might be your only option if you are so located and have no suitable Internet access through a cable TV company. One DSL variant, *IDSL*, is based on ISDN technology and might be available where other forms of DSL are not.

> **NOTE**
>
> Telephone companies operate several COs in most major cities. The CO serves as a central control point for telephone service. Your phone lines lead, directly or indirectly, to the CO. From there, your telephone traffic goes on to telephone centers for broader regions. The distance a telephone line traverses between the CO and your building is critically important in determining the quality of your telephone service, particularly for advanced services such as ISDN and DSL.

To learn more about Linux's ISDN support, consult `http://www.isdn4linux.de/`.

DSL Modems

I mentioned earlier that v.90 telephone modems come very close to the theoretical limit of data transmission speed over conventional voice telephone lines. Although this is true of *voice* telephone frequencies, ordinary copper telephone lines can carry much higher frequencies than humans can hear. Using these frequencies, it's possible to transmit data at much higher speeds.

The result is a technology known as *Digital Subscriber Line* (DSL). DSL has been available in some areas since 1998, if not earlier, but only in late 1999 and 2000 has the technology begun to take off. It seems likely that DSL will be one of the major methods of providing high-speed Internet access to homes and small businesses for the first few years of the 21st century. In 2000, its main competitor is Internet access through cable TV systems. I describe this alternative later in this chapter, in the section "Cable Modems."

Aside from higher speed, one of the major advantages of both DSL and cable service is the possibility of *always-on* access. Unlike connecting to the Internet using a conventional telephone modem and PPP, DSL and cable technologies enable your computer to be connected to the Internet at all times, so there's no delay in accessing the Internet. This feature also makes it technically feasible to run servers on your own computer, although some ISPs forbid this practice and some implement their service in a way that makes it impractical to run your own servers.

Understanding DSL Technology

Conventional telephone service (often referred to as *plain old telephone service*, or *POTS*) transmits the frequencies most often used in human speech—roughly 300–3,300Hz. Conventional telephone modems extend this range by only about 200Hz. DSL, on the other hand, uses an entirely different range of frequencies—typically about 4,000–1,100,000Hz. It's therefore possible to use DSL on the same wires that provide POTS to your home or office. In practice, though, many DSL installations use separate lines, either because existing lines are of poor quality or because local phone companies don't like sharing the line with a third party that provides DSL service. (The courts have ruled that phone companies must share lines, but implementing this ruling might take some time.)

Types of DSL Technology

There are several variant DSL technologies available:

- **ADSL**   *Asymmetric DSL* (ADSL) is the most popular type in the home marketplace. This form of DSL takes its name from the fact that upstream speed is much slower than downstream speed. For instance, an ADSL line might provide 640Kbps downstream but only 90Kbps upstream (or *640/90 service*, as it's often called). This discrepancy works well for most home users, who mostly browse the Web and download data; but it's not so good for businesses, which often run high-volume servers. There are two modulation techniques in common use for ADSL service, *Discrete Multi-Tone* (DMT) and *Carrierless Amplitude and Phase Modulation* (CAP). You needn't be too concerned about which method your DSL provider uses. There's a general trend toward DMT, though, so if you get CAP service you might be required to upgrade your modem at some point. ADSL speeds range from 384/90 to 7,100/1,500 (the upper end of this scale is highly variable depending upon your provider). Prices range from about $40/month to more than $100/month, depending upon the speed, ISP, level of service, and so on. ADSL service can generally be obtained only within about 18,000 feet of your telephone company's CO.

- **G.Lite** *G.Lite*, which is also known as *ADSL Lite*, is a variant of ADSL. The key selling point of G.Lite is that it obviates the need for a telephone company technician to visit your home. In most DSL installations, a technician installs a *splitter* on your line at the point where the phone line enters your building. This splitter breaks up the DSL and voice signals and puts them on separate lines in your building, so that you don't hear a high-pitched whine on your phone and so that your use of the telephone doesn't interfere with the DSL service. Alternatively, some providers run entirely separate lines to your building to provide DSL. In G.Lite, by contrast, the DSL provider sends you DSL *microfilters* to be used at every phone, so in theory a technician need not visit your home, which saves cost. (This arrangement is illustrated in Figure 18.5.) Unfortunately, many homes have substandard phone wiring, so a service call is required in many cases even with G.Lite. G.Lite speeds are also capped at about 1,500Kbps downstream.

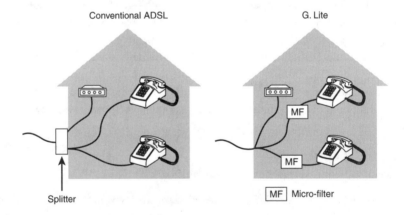

FIGURE 18.5

G.Lite replaces an external splitter with a series of internal microfilters.

- **SDSL** *Symmetric DSL* (SDSL) provides the same speed in both directions. SDSL is generally marketed to business users, and it usually costs more than does ADSL service—usually $100–$300 per month. SDSL speed typically ranges from about 144Kbps to 1500Kbps. SDSL uses different modulation techniques than does ADSL, and works out to 11,000 feet or so from the CO. Like ADSL, it's usually installed with a single splitter at the point of entry to a building.

- **HDSL** *High-bit-rate DSL* (HDSL) is much like SDSL, but uses *two* pairs of wires to increase the overall data capacity. HDSL is fairly rare in today's marketplace.

- **IDSL**   *ISDN-based DSL* (IDSL) uses ISDN technology to deliver symmetric DSL service at speeds of 128–144Kbps. This speed is low compared to other DSL technologies, but it can be used at distances of up to 38,000 feet. IDSL service typically sells for $100–$300/month.

- **xDSL**   This isn't a separate type of DSL; it's simply a term that refers to any variety of DSL service.

The preceding summary of DSL technologies should be taken as a rough guideline. For various reasons, many providers limit DSL speed or won't install at distances near the limits I've outlined here. There are also more exotic forms of DSL that might be available in your area, although ADSL (and its G.Lite variant), SDSL, and IDSL dominate the marketplace.

DSL Authentication

DSL providers, like other ISPs, need some way to authenticate their users. There are three methods in common use:

- **Static IP addresses**   Some providers assign each user one or more static IP addresses. You then enter this information into your Linux system as if you were connecting to an Ethernet network. Static IP addresses are great if you want to run a server, but they're the least secure form of authentication. It's often possible for another DSL user to "hijack" your DSL IP address. If this happens, you might find yourself unable to use your DSL service.

- **DHCP**   The *dynamic host configuration protocol* (DHCP) is a means for ISPs to assign IP addresses dynamically. A server that the ISP maintains keeps a record of IP addresses available, and assigns them to computers as they come online. DHCP can be configured to use your Ethernet card's *media access control* (MAC) number as authentication, so it's somewhat more secure than is a static IP address. It's also possible for an ISP to assign a given customer the same IP address every time the customer boots the computer. Most DSL ISPs don't work in this way, though, so you might get a new IP address every time you boot. Configuring Linux to use DHCP is simple, as I described in Chapter 17, "Network Hardware."

- **PPPoE**   *PPP over Ethernet* is the latest craze in the DSL world. This protocol uses PPP to authenticate computers, but over a DSL modem rather than a conventional telephone modem. The 2.2.x and 2.3.x kernels don't include support for PPPoE, but there is work underway to integrate PPPoE into the kernel. In the meantime, several alternative PPPoE implementations for Linux exist. Links to many of these are at `http://www.rodsbooks.com/network/network-dsl.html`. PPPoE is the most secure of the authentication methods currently in use, but also the least convenient for Linux users. Most PPPoE implementations assign a new IP address every time you boot the computer, so PPPoE is a poor choice if you want to run a server. Some ISPs provide a fixed IP address via PPPoE, typically for a higher price than a random IP address.

18

MODEMS

For Linux use, I recommend you try to locate an ISP that uses static IP addresses or DHCP, at least until Linux's PPPoE support makes its way into the kernel. PPPoE schemes *can* be made to work, but they're more trouble, and they often require that you initialize the account using Windows. If you don't dual-boot your computer between Windows and Linux, using PPPoE might therefore be a major problem. (After the account is configured, there's no need to reboot Windows, so you can eliminate it from your computer and use only Linux if you like.)

Types of DSL Modems

DSL modems come in two basic varieties: internal and external. For the most part, internal DSL modems are useless under Linux, because they lack drivers. I know of only one internal modem for which DSL drivers currently exist, the Diamond 1MM. A link to the driver for this board exists on `http://www.rodsbooks.com/network/network-dsl.html`. Other internal DSL modems will no doubt be supported in the future, however.

External DSL modems come in a variety of shapes and sizes. In general, they're somewhat larger than conventional telephone modems, but they otherwise look similar. Figure 18.6 shows a typical external DSL modem. Like telephone modems, DSL modems usually include a number of status LEDs, an ordinary telephone jack, and a jack for an external power brick. Unlike telephone modems, DSL modems don't include RS-232 serial ports. Instead, these devices interface through Ethernet or USB ports.

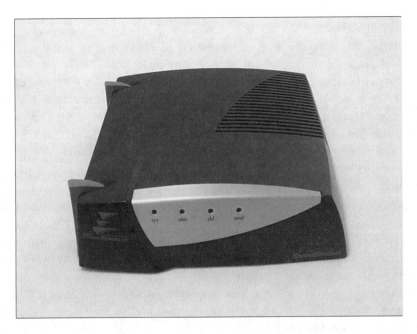

FIGURE 18.6

DSL modems look much like conventional telephone modems.

For use in Linux, I strongly recommend you use an external DSL modem that uses an Ethernet interface. These devices enable you to treat a DSL connection as if it were an ordinary Ethernet connection. In fact, it *is* an ordinary Ethernet connection. To use such a modem, you must have an Ethernet card. Because DSL speeds are usually well below 10Mbps, a 10Mbps Ethernet card is sufficient. A 10/100Mbps card is also usable, however. Given that the price difference is so small, you might as well use a 10/100Mbps NIC, unless your ISP provides you with a 10Mbps NIC as part of the installation package.

Some external DSL modems interface via the USB port. This is a suboptimal arrangement, particularly in Linux, because driver support is so weak and because high-speed USB devices tend to chew up a fair amount of CPU time. If you find yourself with a USB-interfaced DSL modem, check `http://www.linux-usb.org` to locate the latest information on drivers that might support it. You'll need to use a 2.3.x or later kernel, or apply a USB back-port to a 2.2.x kernel.

Most DSL modems function as network *bridges*. This means that they pack up any Ethernet frames they receive and send them out over the telephone wire using a DSL encoding method. When the data reaches your ISP, the DSL encoding is stripped away and the raw Ethernet frames sent by your system are decoded and sent on their way. More advanced DSL modems function as *routers*. A router is more advanced than a bridge, and can often be programmed to not pass certain types of Ethernet frames, or to process the frames in one way or another. For instance, some DSL routers can handle the PPPoE encapsulation that some DSL ISPs use. If you use such a device, you can configure your computer just as you would if your ISP gave you a static IP address. The DSL router then converts your data into PPPoE form and sends it on its way. If your chosen ISP uses PPPoE, therefore, you might want to look into the possibility of using a DSL router rather than a DSL bridge. You'll pay more for a router, however.

Most DSL providers include a DSL modem in the installation cost for the service. From time to time, providers run installation specials in which you pay a very low cost for installation, including the hardware. It's therefore generally best to use whatever DSL modem your ISP provides. If you decide to buy another one, be sure to check that it's compatible with your ISP's service. Because there are so many forms of DSL—including two major modulation techniques for ADSL alone—it's easy to buy a modem that can't be used with your ISP's service.

18

MODEMS

> **TIP**
>
> With the exception of G.Lite devices, you won't find DSL modems in most computer stores. Nonetheless, there are cases where you might need to buy one. For instance, you might have an internal model and want to switch to Linux. You can often find external DSL modems on Internet auction sites such as eBay (`http://www.ebay.com`). Be very careful when buying, though; you don't want to wind up with a DSL modem that's incompatible with your ISP's DSL protocols.

Obtaining Information on DSL Service in Your Area

There are three companies with whom you must deal when you obtain DSL service. They are

- **Your regional phone company**   Your local phone company provides the physical wiring from your site to the phone company's CO. In most areas, the phone company holds a monopoly on this service, so you *must* deal with them, although in some cases only indirectly.

- **A DSL provider**   Various companies, including most regional phone companies and third parties such as Covad (`http://www.covad.com`) and Northpoint (`http://www.northpoint.net`), provide DSL connectivity. The DSL provider rents space in the phone company's CO and operates the DSL circuit on the line provided by the phone company. The DSL provider then passes the DSL traffic from the CO to your chosen ISP.

- **An ISP**   The ISP provides your connection to the Internet proper. Without the ISP, you wouldn't be able to communicate with any interesting computers. The ISP usually also offers email access, space for a personal Web page, access to Usenet news, and possibly other services.

In some cases, two or three of these companies can be the same. This is particularly true when you order DSL service through your local phone company—but the phone company is usually big enough that it breaks itself into divisions which communicate amongst themselves much as if they were separate companies.

In most cases, you initiate DSL service by contacting a DSL ISP. The DSL ISP then contacts its DSL provider, which in turn arranges for your local phone company to run a line to your home or piggyback a DSL carrier onto your existing phone line. Depending upon the type of service you request and from whom, you might have between zero and two visits from the phone company or the DSL provider before you get service. If problems arise, additional visits might be necessary.

How do you find a DSL ISP, though? The single best resource for locating a DSL ISP is DSL Reports, `http://www.dslreports.com`. This site features extensive user reviews of assorted DSL ISPs, a DSL locator, information on DSL modems by brand and model, a security test suite, and more. You can even enter your address and phone number into a form on this page and receive back the distance to your phone company's CO and a listing of ISPs that can provide service to you.

CAUTION

Take DSL Reports' CO distance estimate, and therefore its availability information, with a grain of salt. This estimate is based on database entries of CO locations, street maps, and so on. The actual distance is based on how telephone cables are strung in your neighborhood, and could be substantially greater than what DSL Reports indicates. DSL Reports' databases might also be in error, resulting in an *over*-reporting of the distance from you to your CO. Even DSL ISPs sometimes report availability incorrectly.

TIP

If you believe you're closer to your CO than DSL Reports—or a would-be ISP—claims, don't give up! Some people have better luck with another ISP—ideally one that uses a different DSL partner than the first. In some neighborhoods, it's also possible that one phone line takes one route to a building, whereas another takes another route. Therefore, some badgering sometimes results in action even when the initial attempt to acquire DSL service fails.

In addition to checking with DSL Reports, you might want to consult with your neighbors and co-workers. You might find their experiences informative, particularly with respect to installation quirks that might be local in nature.

When you contact the ISP, I recommend you make it clear that you run Linux. The best ISPs have no problems with users running Linux. Many don't forbid Linux, but they also don't support the OS. Although this might not sound very bad initially, it can be a major problem if you call to report a problem but are denied help because of your choice of OS. A few ISPs are actively hostile towards Linux, and might forbid your using it. Although not as bad as Linux hostility, many DSL ISPs—particularly those who market their service towards residential users—forbid running servers on DSL-connected computers. Most Linux distributions run several servers by default, so you might be running a server and not even know it. It's often desirable to intentionally run one or two servers on DSL-connected computers. For instance, you might want to run a *secure shell* (SSH) server, so you can log into your home system from work. You should know what your ISP allows and forbids before signing up for service.

> **CAUTION**
>
> The fact that most Linux distributions run several servers by default is a potential security problem. I strongly recommend that anybody who runs a Linux computer that's connected to the Internet for more than the briefest periods investigate Linux security. A good book on this topic is *Maximum Linux Security*, (Sams Publishing, 1999).

Cable Modems

Two technologies are competing for consumers' attention with respect to high-speed Internet access: DSL and cable. Some of the highlights of the differences between these technologies include

- DSL runs over telephone lines, whereas cable runs over cable TV lines.
- In most localities in which DSL is available, you have a choice of many ISPs. In most localities in which cable is available, you can only use one ISP.
- DSL provides a dedicated line at least as far as the CO, whereas cable is a shared medium. I discuss this issue in greater detail shortly.
- DSL is capable of top speeds that are usually slower than those of cable systems. (The shared nature of cable reduces the importance of this benefit, however.)
- DSL prices are more variable and, usually, higher than cable prices. Cable Internet access typically costs $30–$60/month.
- The number of homes that can be served by DSL is smaller than the number that can be served by cable, because the loop-length limits on DSL restrict its use in many rural and even suburban areas. Cable doesn't suffer from these limits.
- The number of businesses that can be served by DSL is greater than the number that can be served by cable, because business districts aren't usually wired for cable TV access.

Many of the issues involved in cable modem access are the same as those for DSL access. For instance, it's theoretically possible to use static IP addresses, DHCP, or PPPoE with cable modems, just as it is for DSL. In practice, most cable ISPs use DHCP, whereas static IP addresses and PPPoE dominate the DSL arena.

Understanding Cable Modem Technology

Internet access via cable TV infrastructure uses technologies that are very different from those that provide DSL access. The physical cabling is, of course, quite different, but the differences go deeper than this.

Shared Bandwidth

Cable TV technology allows for the distribution of very large amounts of data. A typical cable TV system provides about 750MHz of bandwidth, and each channel consumes about 6MHz. The first channel (2) consumes the frequency range from 50–56MHz, channel 3 consumes 56–62MHz, and so on. This pattern yields a total capacity of more than 100 channels.

Internet access using this system works by devoting one channel to digital data distribution. DSL systems work by using a mere 1MHz frequency range, so with 6MHz in a single cable TV channel, it might seem that cable TV systems have the edge in speed. This is true in some sense, but cable's advantage is reduced or eliminated by the fact that this 6MHz of bandwidth is *shared*.

When you tune in a particular cable TV station to watch your favorite show, that same signal is viewable by your neighbors. The same is true of the digital Internet data coming over the cable. If you and your neighbor both download large files, you must *share* that 6MHz of bandwidth. The more customers a cable company signs up for Internet access, the more people will share the available bandwidth and the slower the access becomes. The cable company doesn't pre-carve the bandwidth, however, so the slowdown varies with actual use. For instance, at 4:00 a.m., chances are that few people are using the network, so if you download the latest Linux distribution at that time, you'll probably get a blazingly fast download. Try the same thing at a peak hour—say, 8:00 p.m.—and performance will be less stellar, because you'll be competing against your neighbors reading their email and cruising the Web.

Your cable company can split up a neighborhood into several independent network segments, however, so if the network becomes too crowded, it's possible to relieve the congestion. When this happens, the channel devoted to Internet access carries entirely different signals in the different segments.

Like cable service, DSL service also becomes combined at some point. This combination occurs further from the subscriber in the case of DSL. Figure 18.7 illustrates this difference. Suppose that four of the five computers in the left group of the cable network shown in Figure 18.7 are downloading large files, and that one of the five in the right group is doing the same. This arrangement produces, at that moment, speed disparity between those two groups of subscribers. If the equivalent computers in the DSL network are downloading files, all the users experience the same speed.

One other aspect of the shared nature of cable connections deserves mention: security. Because you and your neighbors receive the exact same signals, it might be possible for your neighbors to snoop on your network traffic in a cable modem network. In practice, this isn't usually the case, because most cable companies encrypt traffic in such a way that a subscriber's cable modem only decodes the data destined for that modem. It's also possible to misconfigure a DSL network such that one subscriber receives another's traffic. You should definitely ask about encryption used on your cable company's network if you consider using a cable modem.

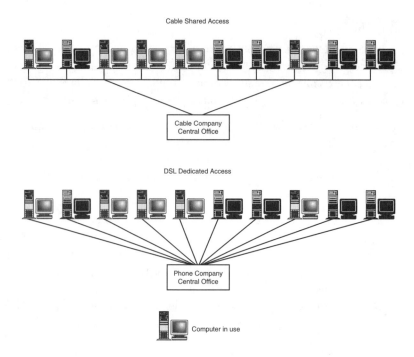

FIGURE 18.7

Minute-to-minute differences in network use have a greater influence on cable networks than on DSL networks.

CAUTION

Just as with DSL, you should read up on Linux security issues if you connect a Linux system to a cable network. *Maximum Linux Security*, from Sams, is a good resource with which to start.

One-Way and Two-Way Systems

I said earlier that cable networks typically devote one channel's bandwidth to Internet traffic. This isn't always entirely true. Most cable modem systems today devote either *two* channels to this traffic, or devote one full channel and some spare bandwidth that can't otherwise be used for TV signals. The second channel or spare bandwidth is dedicated to upstream traffic. (This same bandwidth segment is often used for cable TV services that require upstream data transmission, such as pay-per-view movie ordering.) The main channel is used only for downstream traffic. Such systems are *two-way* cable networks. They provide full Internet connectivity through the cable TV system.

A few cable networks don't provide full connectivity. On these systems, one channel is devoted to downstream traffic, but there's no provision made for the return signal. Instead, you must use a conventional telephone modem to send your return traffic. This is referred to as a *one-way* cable network. This sort of hybrid cable modem/telephone modem system lacks many of the advantages of the better cable networks, and Linux software to support these networks is rare in early 2000. Fortunately, these systems are quite unusual. You should ensure that your cable company provides full two-way service before signing up.

> **NOTE**
>
> Internet access via satellite dish is becoming moderately popular, particularly in remote areas. Like one-way cable networks, this access requires a separate dial-up line for the upstream traffic.

Interfacing the Modem to Your Computer

Most cable modems are external devices that both look and work much like external DSL modems (refer to Figure 18.6). These devices include a coaxial input for the cable connector, an RJ-45 Ethernet jack for linking the device to your computer, and a jack for an external power brick.

Configuring Linux for a cable modem configuration usually works much like configuring Linux for any other Ethernet connection—you set the static IP address and related information provided by your ISP or configure your system to use DHCP to obtain this information automatically. Unlike DSL systems, few cable ISPs use PPPoE, so chances are you won't need to deal with PPPoE configuration. This could change in the future, however.

A few internal cable modems exist. Like internal DSL modems, these devices require special drivers, which are rare in Linux. One device that's supported in the 2.3.x and later kernels is the General Instruments Surfboard 1000, which is a one-way cable modem. You can activate support for this device in the *Network device support* kernel configuration menu.

Most cable ISPs rent the cable modem, much as cable companies rent set-top boxes for decoding cable TV signals. Some cable companies, however, offer a lower monthly rate if you buy a cable modem. You'll need to decide for yourself which approach is better for you.

The Linux Cable Modem Mini-HOWTO document (`http://www.oswg.org/oswg-nightly/Cable-Modem.html`) contains detailed configuration information for many cable ISPs. You should consult this document if you have trouble configuring your new cable service under Linux.

Obtaining Information on Linux-Friendly Cable Systems

Unfortunately, most cable companies provide no choice in ISPs; you must use the ISP with which the cable company partners. In a few communities, you might have choice in the form

18

MODEMS

of two or more competing cable companies, and in fewer communities, you might have a choice of ISPs through a single cable company. You'll need to research these matters yourself.

Most cable ISPs are Linux-neutral, meaning that they allow you to use Linux, but provide no support in the event of problems. As with DSL ISPs, this can be a major drawback, particularly if you don't dual-boot your cable-connected computer between Linux and Windows. You should be sure to ask your would-be ISP how it handles service calls from customers who run Linux.

A few ISPs are actively hostile towards Linux, and won't connect service if you run Linux. If you find your provider falls into this category, you might need to look at DSL rather than cable service, or run a Windows computer as a gateway, if the ISP doesn't forbid such an action.

The Cable Modem Mini-HOWTO (`http://www.oswg.org/oswg-nightly/Cable-Modem.html`) includes information on many cable modem ISPs. This HOWTO includes more in the way of practical configuration information than hints about ISPs' Linux-friendliness. Nonetheless, you might find it useful in determining if your cable company's ISP is worth dealing with.

Summary

Modems provide an increasingly vital link between your Linux computer and the outside world. Most homes today connect to the Internet through a conventional telephone modem, using PPP or occasionally SLIP. Telephone modems are also useful for non-PPP dial-up connections to an assortment of computers, and as a means to send and receive faxes on your computer. The main Linux compatibility issue with telephone modems is in avoiding Windows-only software modems. The simplest way to do this is to get an external model, but some internal modems are still controller-based, and therefore useful under Linux. An increasing number of software modems also have Linux drivers, although a true controller-based modem is usually superior.

As the need for high-speed Internet access increases, a growing number of individuals and businesses are relying upon DSL and cable modems for their Internet connectivity. In most cases, you configure Linux to use these devices as if the computer were hooked up to an Ethernet network. As a general rule, you should avoid internal and USB-interfaced DSL and cable modems, but all Ethernet-based products work fine with Linux.

Even if you have a DSL or cable modem and appropriate Internet access through this device, you might want to keep a conventional telephone modem. The telephone modem can serve as a backup device in case your DSL or cable service goes down, and it can also be useful for sending and receiving faxes, and possibly also as an answering machine if your telephone modem is voice-capable.

Scanners

IN THIS CHAPTER

Scanners are increasingly important in many businesses, and even for personal use. These devices are optical input tools, much like digital cameras (see Chapter 13, "Video Capture and AV Input Hardware"), but scanners are designed to input images from flat sheets of paper, often at very high resolutions. Today, scanners with resolutions of 600 dots per inch (dpi) are considered bottom-of-the-line. Scanning an 8.5×11-inch sheet of paper with such a scanner yields an image that's 5,100×6,600 pixels in size—far larger than the 640×480–3,000×2,000 resolutions that are common in digital cameras. The high resolution of scanners means that they can be used to accurately reproduce textual documents. Combined with a printer (see Chapter 20, "Printers") or a modem with fax capability (see Chapter 18, "Modems"), a scanner can serve as a stand-in for a photocopier or outgoing fax machine, respectively. Because modern scanners invariably support color, you can create color copies if you have a color printer. Even without these adjuncts, you can use a scanner to digitize paper documents, your child's artwork, or family photos.

Understanding Scanner Technology

Most scanners work by reflecting light off of an object and detecting the reflected light with a *charge-coupled device* (CCD). Stated this broadly, scanners are no different from digital cameras. In practice, scanners usually take longer to form an image because their CCDs can't take in the entire image at once. Instead, the scanner builds up the image as its CCD views one part of the page after another. Precisely how the scanner shifts its point of view varies from one device to another. These variations form the basis of the major classifications of scanners.

Flatbed Scanners

The most popular type of scanner today is the *flatbed* scanner, so called because it uses a flat imaging surface, very similar to that of a photocopier (see Figure 19.1). Most flatbed scanners sold today support scanning 8.5×11-inch sheets of paper, or possibly slightly larger sizes, such as 8.5×14-inch (legal size). The scanners themselves are therefore slightly larger than this, although most units aren't larger by much.

The route taken by light within a flatbed scanner is actually quite circuitous, as shown by Figure 19.2. This design is fairly complex—it involves three mirrors (two of which must pivot in precisely controlled ways), a lens, a CCD, and a moving light source. When you use a flatbed scanner, you can usually spot the light source moving its way down the page, even with the lid closed. This action is much like the scanning action on a photocopier. In both technologies, the device images a portion of the document at a time. Photocopiers use a rotating photosensitive drum similar to that in a laser printer, but scanners use a light-sensitive CCD array.

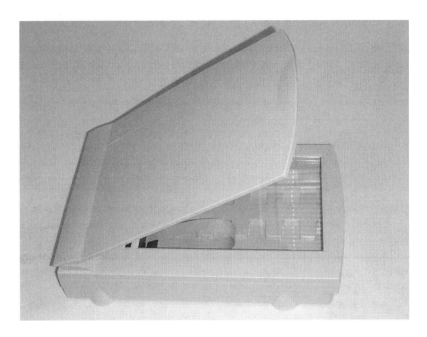

FIGURE 19.1

You place a document to be scanned on a flatbed scanner's flat glass plate, as if the scanner were a photocopier.

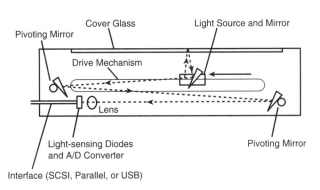

Light Path from Light Source to A/D Converter

FIGURE 19.2

Flatbed scanners are more expensive than other consumer scanners in part because they require several precision moving parts.

Characteristics of flatbed scanners that are important to most consumers include

- **Size**   Flatbed scanners are larger than most other consumer-oriented scanners. Because you typically lift the lid to insert a sheet of paper, you can't stack other items atop these devices, so they consume their desk space quite thoroughly.

- **Quality**   Flatbed scanners produce higher-quality scans than do most other types of scanner. This is largely because they scan at higher resolutions than do most other scanner types.

NOTE

Most scanners today advertise two resolutions: *raw* and *interpolated*. The latter is higher, and relies upon software in the device's drivers to break a single scanned pixel down into multiple pixels. For instance, the interpolation might take two adjacent pixels, one black and one white, and create from them a series of pixels of various shades of gray. Interpolation works well when scanning color graphics, but it's less useful when scanning text or line art.

- **Diverse media options**   You can scan standard 8.5×11-inch sheets in flatbed scanners, but you can also scan smaller documents (such as photos printed from conventional film, half-sheets, and so on), pages from books, and so on. Some models even come with attachments to help produce good scans of film negatives or slides. With most models, you must scan each original individually. Some models have sheet feeders that let you scan several documents automatically.

- **Diverse interface options**   Flatbed scanners come in SCSI, parallel-port, and USB varieties.

On the whole, if you want a scanner for use in Linux, a flatbed scanner is probably your best bet. These devices are common, well supported, and produce very good results for most uses.

Sheet-Fed Scanners

A flatbed scanner keeps the document stationary and moves internal components to scan the entire surface of that document. Sheet-fed designs reverse this relationship; they keep the scanner elements stationary and use rollers to move the document through the scanner. This design is common on fax machines, and computer scanners that use this design closely resemble fax machines in their capabilities.

Characteristics of sheet-fed scanners include

- **Size** Sheet-fed models can be quite small. In fact, some designs are small enough to fit into a briefcase or portable computer tote bag. Because of their small size, these devices are often integrated into other components, such as keyboards and printers.

- **Quality** Most sheet-fed scanners don't deliver the high resolutions for which flatbed scanners are known. Also, if a sheet jams or slips while being scanned, the result can be a scan that's stretched out or otherwise corrupt. For many purposes, though, sheet-fed scanners produce acceptable results.

- **Limited media options** Sheet-fed scanners are limited in the sizes and types of media they can accept. You can't scan a book with these devices, for instance—at least, not without destroying the book in the process. They usually can't handle thick cardboard or very small originals, either.

- **Limited interface options** Most sheet-fed scanners use the parallel port for interfacing to the computer. A few newer models use the USB port, however. Because these ports aren't as well supported for scanning in Linux as the SCSI port, these devices often don't work very well in Linux.

On the whole, sheet-fed scanners can be useful if you only want to scan loose sheets of paper, or if you want a compact scanner for a space-hungry office or to accompany a notebook computer when you travel. You should be particularly careful to investigate Linux compatibility of these devices, however.

Hand Scanners

Another type of scanner is known as the *hand scanner*. These devices are small handheld devices. Instead of using a motor to move a mirror and light source, or to drive the paper through the scanner, these devices rely upon *you* to provide the motor—you must drag a hand scanner down a sheet of paper to be scanned. This feature leads to many of this device type's characteristics:

- **Size** Hand scanners are even more compact than most sheet-fed scanners. They're often smaller than this book, in fact.

- **Quality** Hand scanners really fall down in the quality department. The devices seldom deliver higher than 300 dpi scans. What's worse, their reliance on a human to move the device in a steady way often produces poor scans. A minor variation in the speed at which you drag the scanner can produce stretched-out and scrunched-up parts of a scan. If you inadvertently move the scanner horizontally as you drag it vertically, the result is a wavy-looking scan. If you need to scan something that's wider than the scanner's head, you might need to patch together two separate scans, which might not match perfectly.

- **Flexible media options**   Because hand scanners are hand-held, you can scan more things with them than you can with most other scanner types. For instance, you can scan your home's wallpaper pattern if you like. You can also scan a book and do less damage to it than would be likely if you used a flatbed scanner.
- **Limited interface options**   Most hand scanners use either the parallel port or proprietary ISA-card interfaces. These interfaces severely limit the options for Linux use of these devices.

Hand scanners are very rare in today's marketplace, so you might need to hunt or resort to the used market if you really need one. Unless you have a need to scan delicate books or exotic materials that you can't scan with a flatbed scanner, you should probably bypass a hand scanner in favor of a flatbed or sheet-fed device. In some cases, you can use a high-resolution digital camera in place of a hand scanner, but a digital camera is likely to be more expensive.

Exotic Types

In addition to the preceding scanner types, several more exotic devices exist. These scanners serve professional or other specialized functions. They're usually quite expensive. They include

- **Slide and negative scanners**   Some scanners are designed exclusively to scan 35mm or other film negatives and slides. These devices typically support very high resolutions, back-lighting, and other features that are important for this function.

TIP

Photofinishers often offer film scanning services, so you can use them to scan a few—or many—negatives or slides. You can usually obtain your scanned images on Photo CD or floppy, or via the Internet.

- **Photo scanners**   Photo scanners are specialized scanners designed for scanning 5×7-inch or smaller photographic prints. Prints have been enlarged from negatives or slides, and therefore contain less detail than the original negatives. Photo scanners thus have much lower resolutions than slide or negative scanners.
- **Drum scanners**   Drum scanners are very high-end devices. They can scan as high as 8,000 dpi and produce a wider range of colors and shades of gray than can typical flatbed scanners. To use these devices, you mount an original on a cylinder, which the scanner then spins at high speed past imaging sensors.

Flatbed scanners can perform the same functions as can negative/slide and photo scanners, but sometimes not as well. In particular, flatbed scanners usually can't scan slides or negatives as well as can a dedicated unit. Photo scanners are of interest mainly to save space when you want to scan an existing collection of photographs, or new photographs you take with a conventional film camera.

Multifunction Units

Scanners often appear in devices that perform additional functions. The most common combination is one of scanner and printer. Such devices can often function as photocopiers, even when the computer is turned off. Some models also include fax capabilities, so you can send and receive faxes as well. A few scanners include nonprinter functionality instead of these features. For instance, there are a few scanner/keyboard combinations available.

Multifunction units can be a great way to save space in a crowded office, but they do have their drawbacks. Prime among these is the fact that Linux support for multifunction devices is often lacking. You should carefully investigate Linux support for each function provided by the device. For instance, in a multifunction scanner/printer, check for scanner support (as described later in this chapter) *and* check for printer support (on `http://www.picante.com/~gtaylor/pht/printer_list.cgi`, as described in Chapter 20). You should also check to be sure that the device doesn't need special drivers to support what ought to be standalone features, such as making photocopies in a scanner/printer.

Another drawback to multifunction devices is that they often don't produce results that are as good as separate devices might produce. They might support lower resolutions or be slower than separate devices. This is particularly true of creating photocopies, compared to a dedicated photocopier. Rather than using normal photocopier technologies, combination units scan in a normal scanner way and then print in a normal printer way. That combination is likely to be slower than a standalone photocopier.

Scanner Interfaces

Scanners typically use one of three interfaces: the SCSI port, the parallel port, or the USB port. In most cases, the SCSI port is the best port for scanning in Linux, although USB is becoming a more viable option.

19

> **CAUTION**
>
> The interface port isn't the only factor in determining which devices are compatible with Linux. I describe Linux compatibility later, in the section titled "Linux Scanner Drivers."

SCSI Interfaces

The Small Computer System Interface (SCSI) is the best interface for scanners under Linux. Most scanners use the 8-bit (25- or 50-pin) Narrow SCSI format. Modern SCSI scanners usually support at least Fast SCSI-2, although they don't need the 10MB/s speed of which Fast SCSI-2 is capable. (A 24-bit, 1,200-dpi scan of an 8.5×11-inch page consumes 385MB, and so could be passed over a 10MB/s SCSI connection in 38.5 seconds. This is faster than most scanner mechanisms can produce an image of this size.) Even if scanners don't normally saturate a SCSI bus, the SCSI bus's speed is an improvement over the 1.5MB/s of USB or the 2MB/s of the parallel port. When a manufacturer offers the same basic mechanism in both SCSI and parallel or USB varieties, the SCSI version is typically about twice as fast as the other versions.

Most SCSI scanners use 8-bit, 25-pin interfaces. Most modern SCSI adapters, though, provide only a single 68-pin external connector. This combination can make interfacing the scanner to modern SCSI host adapters difficult, because 68-pin-to-25-pin SCSI cables are extremely rare. The task can be accomplished with a 68-pin-to-50-pin cable and a 50-pin-to-25-pin adapter, such as the one in Figure 19.3.

FIGURE 19.3
Adapters can be very helpful in linking mismatched SCSI components.

Another option is to use a second, less-powerful SCSI host adapter for the scanner than you use for Wide SCSI hard disks. (This idea also works with some other non-disk devices.) In fact, many SCSI scanners come with SCSI host adapters, although these adapters are usually *very* low-end, and might produce slower performance than you can get from even inexpensive Fast SCSI-2 host adapters. Some bundled SCSI adapters are also unsupported in Linux. Of course, if you don't use SCSI hard disks, you probably don't need a powerful Wide adapter, so a SCSI card that supports only Narrow devices is just fine.

Parallel-Port Interfaces

The parallel port has long been a favorite of scanner manufacturers, because it's the fastest external port that's available on the vast majority of x86 computers. Unfortunately, it's a less-than-ideal port from a Linux perspective because so few parallel-port scanners can claim support in Linux. Most of these devices use proprietary protocols that require unique drivers, and manufacturers are often unwilling to provide the necessary programming information to Linux programmers.

Assuming you have a Linux-compatible parallel-port scanner, you can attach the device using a special cable, or you can attach another device to the scanner, so you can use both the scanner and a printer on the same parallel port. Mixing additional devices is sometimes possible, but tricky. It might be possible to use a given parallel-port scanner in conjunction with a parallel-port CD-ROM drive, for instance, but only if the CD-ROM drive is attached directly to the computer, and the scanner attaches to the CD-ROM drive. A reversal of this order might cause one or both devices to fail. These interactions are invariably device-specific, so I can't provide any rules for deciding which device to attach first, except to say that you mightneed to experiment.

> **TIP**
>
> You can use a parallel-port switch box to attach two or more devices to one parallel port if you don't need to use both devices at the same time. You can then switch between the scanner, printer, and any other parallel-port devices you have by flipping a switch or pushing a button. Another alternative is to add one or two extra parallel ports, as described in Chapter 16, "Parallel and Serial Ports."

On the whole, I must recommend against getting parallel-port scanners. They're slower than SCSI devices and more trouble-prone, plus Linux support is slim. If you've already got a parallel-port scanner, though, you might as well check to see if it's supported and, if it is, try to get it working. (I describe Linux scanner drivers, including how to find them, in more detail shortly.)

USB Interfaces

The Universal Serial Bus (USB) is starting to replace the parallel port as the favorite interface of low-end scanner manufacturers. The USB port is almost as fast as the parallel port (1.5MB/s versus 2MB/s), and it's free of the sharing problems associated with the parallel port.

The big problem with USB interfaces as far as Linux is concerned is the lack of standardization in USB protocols for scanners. Many USB scanners therefore use proprietary commands, so every device requires its own driver. A few of these drivers exist, and the list of supported USB scanners will doubtless grow over the course of 2000 and 2001. Nonetheless, it's *vital* that you check compatibility at `http://www.linux-usb.org` and `http://www.mostang.com/sane/` before buying a USB scanner. Of course, if you want to buy a USB scanner and write a driver for it, that's great!

If you run a 2.2.x kernel, another problem with USB is the fact that USB support in the 2.2.x kernel is minimal at best. You must upgrade to a 2.3.x or later kernel, or apply a back-port of more recent USB support to the 2.2.x kernel, in order to use USB scanners in Linux.

Linux Scanner Drivers

Linux scanner support is provided by drivers from two locations: the Linux kernel and the SANE (*Scanner Access Now Easy*) software package. The kernel drivers provide low-level access to the interface hardware, such as a SCSI host adapter. These drivers need not be configured for specific scanner models. The SANE drivers, on the other hand, must support specific devices or scanner standards used by specific devices.

Necessary Kernel Drivers

The kernel drivers you need depend upon the device type: SCSI, parallel-port, or USB, as described here:

- **SCSI**   SANE relies upon SCSI generic support to function with SCSI scanners. You can activate this option from the *SCSI support* kernel configuration menu (shown in Figure 19.4). You must also enable basic SCSI support and support for your specific SCSI host adapter.
- **Parallel port**   SANE directly supports very few parallel-port scanners. There are drivers available for a few parallel-port scanners that work with SANE, though. The requirements for these drivers vary somewhat, but in general, you must enable the *General setup, Parallel port support* kernel configuration option.
- **USB**   If you have a USB scanner, you must activate basic USB support, including support for UHCI or OHCI interfaces (whichever your motherboard uses). In addition, you must enable the *USB Scanner support* option in the *USB support* menu.

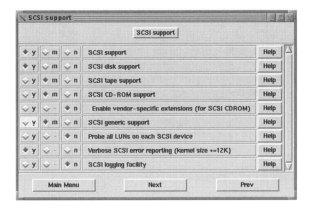

FIGURE 19.4
SCSI generic support enables programs to access SCSI devices that don't fit into the categories of disks, CD-ROMs, or tape drives.

NOTE

Most of these USB options aren't present in standard 2.2.x kernels. You must use a 2.3.x or later kernel or apply patches to the 2.2.x kernel in order to use theseoptions. 2.2.x kernel patches are available from `http://www.linux-usb.org`, and the latest kernels can be found at `http://www.kernel.org` or most Linux archive FTP sites.

These kernel drivers aren't enough to get your scanner working, though; they're only enough to get programs talking to the scanner. As with printers, much of the real work of controlling the device rests with a separate program. In the case of scanners, this program is known as SANE.

SANE Software

Scanner Access Now Easy (SANE) is a set of protocols and programs that enable you to access a scanner's features under Linux. In many respects, SANE is analogous to Ghostscript for printers. The goal of the SANE project is to provide a uniform interface to all scanner hardware. This goal is similar in concept to that of the TWAIN interface in the Windows world. SANE differs from TWAIN, however, in that SANE separates the low-level drivers from the user interface. TWAIN tightly integrates the two, so all programs that use a scanner use the same interface. This fact makes SANE at least potentially more cross-platform than TWAIN, and it allows for network scanning—using a scanner connected to one computer through software located on another computer.

Figure 19.5 illustrates the relationship between the various hardware and software components in a SANE-driven scanning system. SANE's mediation means that you can change a scanner (and hence a SANE driver) at will, and continue to use your scanning software just as you had before the change.

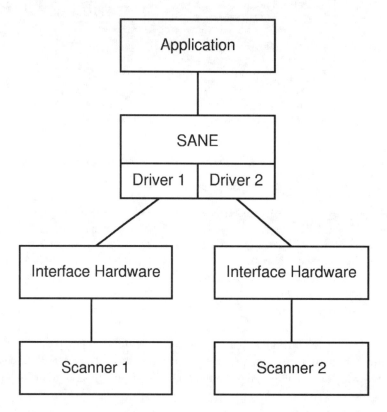

FIGURE 19.5

SANE presents a uniform face to applications that can use a scanner.

Because SANE is the component that most directly communicates with the scanner, it's here that you need to look for drivers. The SANE project includes support for most SCSI scanners, a handful of parallel-port scanners, and a growing number of USB scanners. You can find SANE drivers for some devices from third parties, but tracking them down can be difficult. In fact, your efforts might be in vain. In general, it's best to use a device whose drivers come with SANE.

In addition to scanners, SANE includes early support for Video for Linux devices (see Chapter 13). You can therefore use applications that support SANE to capture images from WebCams, TV tuners, and the like. Likewise, SANE directly supports a few WebCams and digital cameras, even without Video for Linux.

Locating Linux-Compatible Scanners

It's vitally important that you thoroughly research any scanner model you're considering before making a purchase. There are several potential sources of information on specific scanners, including

- **The SANE home page**   The SANE home page, `http://www.mostang.com/sane/`, includes a listing of supported devices. Some scanners have drivers that aren't officially part of the SANE project, though, so this list is incomplete. If possible, stick with a scanner that's listed directly, because it might be easier to configure than one that requires a driver separate from the main SANE distribution.

- **The Linux USB home page**   The USB development home page, `http://www.linux-usb.org`, includes listings of supported USB devices. This page has more complete information on some USB scanners than is on the SANE home page.

- **The USB scanners home page**   There's a Web page devoted entirely to USB scanners, at `http://www.buzzard.org.uk/jonathan/scanners-usb.html`. This page includes the most comprehensive information on USB scanner support in Linux, including links to information on projects that are underway but far from complete.

- **Usenet news postings**   If you can't find mention of a particular scanner anywhere else, try Usenet news. The Deja News Web site (`http://www.deja.com/usenet/`) is a particularly useful resource in tracking down postings about a wide variety of topics. Try typing in your scanner's make or model along with a keyword such as `sane` or `linux`. For instance, you might type **umax and 1220u and (linux or sane)** to find posts about the UMAX 1220U scanner under Linux.

19

SCANNERS

CAUTION

Some of the scanner drivers you find on the Web might be incomplete or very buggy. If you want to use your scanner for serious work, I recommend you avoid such projects and instead buy a scanner with mature support. Only try a development scanner driver if you want to contribute to development or if you already own the hardware and are desperate to get it working.

Scanner Applications for Linux

Most of the time you spend using scanners in Linux is spent working with scanner applications. The SANE package comes with some basic text-mode and GUI scanner tools. It's also possible to access SANE-driven scanners from other applications, such as the GIMP.

Scanner Back Ends

A SANE scanner *back end* is a SANE driver for a particular scanner. You select the back end in different ways in different programs. To find out what back ends you have available on your system, type **scanimage --list-devices**. The result is a list of the SANE back ends, as in

```
device 'mustek:/dev/scanner' is a Mustek MFC-06000CZ flatbed scanner
device 'pnm:0' is a Noname PNM file reader virtual device
device 'pnm:1' is a Noname PNM file reader virtual device
```

This output reveals that there are three scanner devices. The first is a *physical* scanner, but the second and third are *virtual* scanners. You can use these devices to "scan" some graphics files, even if you don't have a real scanner. You might use this feature to adjust the image's brightness or contrast without loading up a full graphics package to do the job.

If you don't see a scanner that you know you have attached to your computer, you can try editing the dll.conf file, which probably resides in /etc/sane.d or /usr/local/etc/sane.d. Most SANE installations are configured to use the dll meta-back end, which enables SANE to dynamically load additional back ends. (If your system doesn't use the dll back end, you must reconfigure SANE whenever you switch from one device to another.) The dll.conf file consists of a series of lines, each of which lists a specific back end. For instance, the file might look like this:

```
# enable the next line if you want to allow access through the network:
net
mustek
pnm
```

The first line, which starts with a pound sign (#), is a comment, and is ignored by SANE. Subsequent lines each list a back end. Many SANE configurations come with the pnm back end disabled. You can enable this back end by uncommenting the pnm line. If SANE can't find hardware to match a given back end, it ignores the line in dll.conf that specifies the back end, so extraneous dll.conf entries do no harm. When it comes time to scan, you specify a device by using the name reported by the scanimage --list-devices command. For instance, you could use the pnm:0 device to scan a file, or mustek:/dev/scanner to scan with the Mustek scanner.

Scanner device names begin with the name of the back end, as in pnm or mustek. Each back end includes some way to name specific devices. For the pnm back end, devices are numbered 0 and 1. (These are essentially identical.) The mustek back end uses a device filename (as in /dev/scanner). There can be several layers of labels for a scanner device. The network back end uses this feature, as described shortly.

Network Scanning

The net device enables network scanning. For instance, suppose you have two computers on a network, lili and ronald. The computer lili has a scanner attached to it, but ronald does not. Nonetheless, you want to scan a document directly into an application on ronald. You can accomplish this task by running an appropriate scanner server on lili and specifying the network device when you run the scanner software on ronald. You must perform several steps to get this configuration to work:

1. Add the SANE service name to /etc/services on the computer to which the scanner is attached (lili in the example). This line should read

   ```
   sane 6566/tcp # SANE network scanner daemon
   ```

NOTE

Some distributions might already include the SANE service name in /etc/services, so check for it before you add it.

2. Add an entry to the scanner host system's /etc/inetd.conf file to launch the SANE server when it's called, like this:

   ```
   sane  stream tcp nowait saned.saned /usr/sbin/saned saned
   ```

   This line assumes that there's a saned user and a saned group. You might want to change the saned.saned part to another user and group. If you set these options to root.root, you might introduce security problems, because a bug in saned might allow Internet undesirables access to your computer. You might also need to change the location of the saned binary to match its location on your computer.

3. Edit the `saned.conf` file, which should be in the same directory as the `dll.conf` file, to include a list of hosts that are allowed to access the scanner. For instance, you might add the following lines to `lili`'s `saned.conf` file to allow `ronald` and `renee` to access the scanner:

```
ronald
renee
```

   In some cases, you might need to use complete hostnames. For instance, you might use `ronald.pangaea.edu` instead of `ronald`.

4. Restart the `inetd` server. On most systems, you can do this by typing **`/etc/rc.d/init.d/inet restart`**, although some distributions do things differently.

5. On the client computer (`ronald` in this example), edit the `net.conf` file (in the same location as the `dll.conf` file) and add the name of the computer to which the scanner is attached (`lili` in this example, or a complete hostname, such as `lili.pangaea.edu`). You can add a list of scanner hosts—each name on its own line—much as you can add a list of allowed clients in the server's `sane.conf` file.

6. On the client computer, be sure the `net` device is active in the `dll.conf` file.

Network scanning is now configured. You can access the network scanner by using `net`, the hostname, and the scanner device on the host as the scanner device. For instance, instead of `mustek:/dev/scanner`, you would use `net:lili:mustek:/dev/scanner` to access the `mustek:/dev/scanner` device on the host `lili`.

> **TIP**
>
> You can use a network scanner even on a single computer. This trick can be handy in working around restrictions on devices. For instance, you might want to restrict access to the low-level hardware devices to certain users, but allow others to use the scanner. If you use a network scanner protocol, the server can run with sufficient privilege to access the hardware, and then pass the results to less-privileged users.

Scanner Front Ends

SANE comes with several scanner *front ends*—that is, programs that can access the scanner. A front end can be either a dedicated scanner program, or an add-on or feature of a more general program. Examples of scanner front ends include

- **scanimage** This program, which I introduced earlier as a means to locate scanner devices, is actually a basic scanner program for Linux. You can use it to create a PNM graphics file from a scanner. For instance, typing **scanimage --device=mustek:/ dev/scanner > image.pnm** image.pnm program> image.pnm>creates the image.pnm graphics file from the mustek:/dev/scanner device. Many scanner devices support device-specific parameters you can pass to scanimage. For instance, the pnm devices, which read from a file, require the --filename=*file.ext* parameter to tell the back end what file to read.

- **xscanimage** This program provides an X-based interface to SANE, as shown in Figure 19.6. Each device's interface contains somewhat different options.

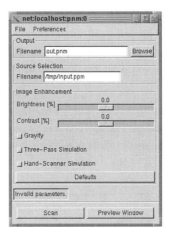

FIGURE 19.6
GUI scanner utilities provide you with easy-to-use sliders and buttons to adjust scan brightness and other features.

- **The GIMP** The *GNU Image Manipulation Program* (GIMP) is a powerful and popular Linux graphics program. The GIMP accepts *plug-ins*—small programs written by a variety of authors that extend the GIMP's capabilities. SANE comes with a plug-in for the GIMP that enables the GIMP to acquire images directly from a scanner.

- **GOCR** The *GNU Optical Character Recognition* (GOCR; see http://altmark.nat.uni-magdeburg.de/~jschulen/ocr/) is an early attempt at OCR software for Linux. This software takes a graphical input file and creates a textual output file. GOCR doesn't actually accept input directly from a scanner; you must scan to a file and then feed the results through the program. I mention it here because OCR is one of the more interesting applications of scanners. Compared to OCR software for Windows, GOCR is primitive, but it might improve over time.

19

SCANNERS

- **OCRShop** This commercial package costs between $99 and $3,295, depending upon your scanner model and use (personal, nonprofit, or corporate). This program, unlike most Linux scanner applications, does *not* work through SANE, so its list of supported scanners doesn't match that of SANE. It's built on Caere's (http://www.caere.com) OmniPage OCR technology. You can find out more from Vividata's OCRShop Web page, http://www.vividata.com/ocrshop.html.

As Linux's scanner support continues to mature, and as Linux grows in popularity, more SANE-enabled applications are likely to arrive on the scene. Check the main SANE Web page at http://www.mostang.com/sane/ for the latest information.

Summary

As a general rule, flatbed scanners are the most flexible type of scanner available for most uses. These devices consume a great deal of desk space, however, so you might prefer a sheet-fed or hand scanner, particularly if you want a scanner to accompany you when you take a laptop computer on the road.

Linux support for scanners is variable. Linux works with most SCSI scanners, an increasing number of USB scanners, and a few parallel-port scanners. Linux support for scanners comes largely in the form of the SANE project, which provides a uniform programming interface for application developers.

Printers

IN THIS CHAPTER

The "paperless office" was a vision of the 1970s and early 1980s. With the advent of personal computers on every office worker's desk, people thought there would be a decreasing need for paper documents. Unfortunately for many trees, this vision is far from becoming reality, and will likely remain remote for years. The reason is simple: Computers—through printers—make it *easier* to produce paper documents than ever before.

Linux includes good support for printers. Linux's printer support, unlike support for most other devices, doesn't lie so much in the Linux kernel as it does in a separate program, known as *Ghostscript*. I describe Ghostscript later in this chapter. First, though, it's necessary to understand more basic information about printer technology, such as the assorted methods used to print and the types of interfaces and printer languages available.

Types of Printer Hardware

The goal of a printer is to place text or images on a sheet of paper. Over the years, manufacturers have developed quite a few technologies to accomplish this goal. Physical contact with an intervening inked ribbon, squirting ink, and photocopier-like technologies have all been common. Each of these technologies has its merits and its flaws. If you're in the market for a printer, one of the first decisions you should make is which of the many printing technologies you want to embrace.

Laser Printers

Laser printers are the current favorite form of office printer. These printers work on principles similar to those of photocopiers. They also traditionally require a fair amount of computing power in the printer itself, although some recent models change this fact.

Basic Laser Printer Technology

Laser printing centers on the printer's *drum*, which is a light-sensitive cylinder. A laser printer imparts an electrostatic charge on the drum. When exposed to light, the drum's electrostatic charge changes. A laser and mirror assembly "paints" an image of the document to be printed on the drum, which simultaneously rotates. As the drum rotates, it's brought near a reservoir of *toner*, which is a static-sensitive plastic powder. The toner sticks to the drum in the areas that have been struck by the laser's light. Further rotation of the drum brings it into contact with paper, which has also been charged, so the toner is drawn from the drum onto the paper. The paper is then heated in a *fuser* assembly to a high-enough temperature to melt the toner, which quickly cools and sticks to the paper. Additional components then return the drum surface to its original state, and the process begins again. Figure 20.1 illustrates this process.

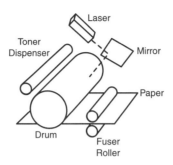

FIGURE 20.1
A laser printer's innards use a number of precision components operating in concert to produce a legible image.

A variant on the laser printer is the *LED printer*, which uses a bank of *light emitting diodes* (LEDs) in place of the laser and mirror shown in Figure 20.1. Aside from anything having to do with lasers, everything I write in this chapter about laser printers applies to LED printers, as well. In fact, many people refer to LED printers as *laser printers*, despite the fact that there's no laser in an LED printer. The term *page printer* is sometimes used to refer to both types of printer.

Most laser printers include the drum assembly in a sealed package along with the toner. Because the drum eventually wears out, this arrangement allows for easy replacement of the drum when the toner runs out. Other models have separate drum units and toner supplies. With these, the drum is typically designed to last longer, but it's more expensive than the drum/toner units of other models. When you compute the estimated operating costs of a laser printer, be sure to consider both the toner and (if it's separate) drum cartridges.

CAUTION

Laser printer toner cartridges are not usually interchangeable. Also, some firms offer recycled toner cartridges or toner cartridge refill kits. The more reputable firms rebuild their toner cartridges, but some companies do a poor job when refilling toner cartridges with new toner. Refill kits are likely to be of poor quality. I therefore suggest you proceed with caution when using recycled cartridges. Be sure to find out how much effort the firm employs in checking and, if necessary, replacing worn components.

The process of printing a page in a laser printer is very timing-sensitive. If the mechanism stops mid-page, the part of the page in the fuser assembly can become scorched, and the images burned on the drum can degrade. Therefore, laser printers have traditionally begun printing only after receiving a complete page's data, which is stored in the printer's RAM. This fact, and the need to compute an image quickly from the provided data, means that laser printers have traditionally included fairly powerful computers. In fact, early laser printers were often more powerful computers than the computers they served.

At 300×300 dots per inch (dpi), the minimum resolution for laser printers, an 8.5×11-inch sheet of paper requires slightly more than 1MB of RAM to describe. If the resolution is doubled, to 600×600 dpi, the RAM required quadruples, to 4MB. High-end laser printers today support 1,200×1,200 dpi resolutions, which require 16MB of RAM. Most laser printers today support data compression technologies that can reduce RAM requirements, but compression doesn't always work optimally. Printers that rely on compression can sometimes run out of RAM when processing complex pages, such as photos. When printing text, less RAM is required, because the printer can store the text as ASCII codes, and create bitmaps for these ASCII codes one line at a time. Under Linux, however, text printed to PCL laser printers is printed as if it were a graphic, so you might need more memory under Linux than you do under Windows.

> **NOTE**
>
> Some laser printers sold since the mid-1990s use minimal RAM, and instead rely on quick data transfer from the host computer. These models typically use nonstandard printer languages, and so aren't useful under Linux.

Color laser printers work much like black-and-white models, but they use three toner colors, and the imaging process is correspondingly more complex. For this reason, color laser printers are more expensive than black-and-white models, and they're usually bulkier and cost more to operate.

Characteristics of Laser Printers

Laser printer technology gives rise to many of the characteristics that define laser printers' role in the marketplace. These characteristics include

- **High purchase price**   Compared to inkjet printers, laser printers cost a lot to buy. Prices range from $200 for a bare-bones model to several thousand dollars for high-end printers. For use in Linux, you'd do best to avoid the low end; plan on spending at least $400.

- **Low operating costs**   Laser printer supplies typically cost less on a per-page basis than do inkjet supplies. Typical laser printer costs are $0.01–$0.03 per page for toner, plus paper and electricity.

- **Excellent text printing quality** The quality of laser printers is unsurpassed for printing text, except by high-end typesetting equipment. Earlier laser printers (those that can only produce 300×300 dpi resolution) are surpassed by modern inkjet printers, however.

- **High print speed** Even low-end laser printers today produce print speeds of 6 pages per minute (ppm) or higher. Workgroup printers can print at up to 40 ppm. Most laser printers print at the same speed no matter what resolution you choose, although a few models slow down a bit at their highest resolutions. Laser printer speed statistics are usually somewhat optimistic, but not as much as speed estimates for inkjet printers.

- **Media insensitivity** Print quality from laser printers doesn't vary as much from one type of paper to another as does the print quality from inkjet printers. This fact means you can often get by with less expensive paper for laser printers than you can with inkjets.

- **Water-resistant printing** Laser printer toner doesn't smear when it gets wet. It can, however, come off on some plastics.

This set of characteristics makes laser printers an excellent choice for many business uses. Most businesses' printing needs center around production of text—reports, invoices, letters, and so on. For the same reasons, you might want to consider a laser printer if you use your Linux computer at home for business. For situations in which text quality and print speed are less important, but color output is important, inkjets are a good alternative to laser printers.

Inkjet Printers

Inkjet technology is fundamentally different from that of laser technology. Nonetheless, there are certain similarities. For instance, both work by creating tiny areas of light, dark, or color on a page. These pixels combine together to form letters or images. As a general rule, inkjet technology is aimed at home users, whereas laser technology serves businesses.

Basic Inkjet Printer Technology

Inkjet printers rely on tiny drops of ink to print. The printer contains a *print head* with dozens of tiny nozzles out of which the ink is forced. The print head moves back and forth across the surface of the paper, and the paper is advanced after every pass. This arrangement is illustrated in Figure 20.2.

Like laser printers, inkjet printers convert text or graphics into bitmaps. Because the technology doesn't involve heat applied to the paper or rotating drums that can lose their charges, an inkjet printer can print part of a page, pause, and then continue printing. Therefore, inkjets don't normally need to have an entire page's worth of data before they begin printing. Although inkjets do often have some memory and processing capability, they don't need as much of these commodities as laser printers do.

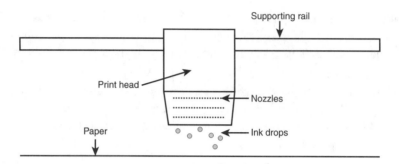

FIGURE 20.2

An inkjet printer works by spraying ink onto the paper in precisely controlled patterns.

> **NOTE**
>
> A few inkjet printers support the PostScript printer language, which I describe later in this chapter. PostScript-equipped inkjets need memory and processing power similar to that in laser printers.

Most inkjets sold since the mid-1990s support color printing. A typical color printer supports four separate inks: cyan, magenta, yellow, and black. This system is often referred to as *CMYK printing*, after the names of the colors. (*K* is used for *black* to avoid confusion with *blue*.) Most CMYK printers use two ink cartridges: one for black and one for cyan, magenta, and yellow. This arrangement enables you to replace the black ink separately from the color inks. A more flexible system uses separate ink cartridges for each color, which allows for still less wasted ink.

A few printers—mostly earlier models—used no separate black cartridge. These *CMY* devices produce nearly black text by combining all four of the color inks, which tends to be costly and slow. Some models support separate black and color ink cartridges, but allow you to use only one cartridge at a time, which can be awkward. Some of the latest models add additional ink colors, which can improve the quality of color reproduction.

Most inkjet printers combine the ink nozzles into the print cartridges themselves. This design means that a clogged nozzle need not be an expensive repair proposition; you can simply replace the cartridge. A few printers, most notably Epson models, use a higher-quality, nondisposable printhead that contains the ink nozzles. If a serious clog develops on such a printer, you might need to take the printer in to be serviced to clear the problem. Some Canon models take a hybrid approach, and use separate disposable ink cartridges and printheads.

Characteristics of Inkjet Printers

The technology of inkjet printers determines the advantages and disadvantages of this breed of printer. These include

- **Low purchase price** Inkjet printers tend to be inexpensive. Prices start at about $100, and even the most expensive units seldom cost more than $2,000.

- **High operating costs** Inkjet printer supplies typically cost more on a per-page basis than do laser printer supplies. Typical inkjet costs are $0.03–$0.10 per page for ink, plus paper and electricity. The cost of a high-density color page is likely to be about 10 times that of a page of text, because dense graphics consume more ink. Inkjets often use less electricity than do laser printers.

- **Good text printing quality** Given high-quality paper, modern inkjets can meet or exceed the print quality that can be obtained from an older 300dpi laser printer. Few inkjet printers can match the quality of modern 600dpi–1,200dpi laser printers, though.

NOTE

The ink from inkjets tends to spread slightly on paper, whereas toner stays put better. Therefore, an inkjet usually produces slightly blurrier text at a given resolution than does a laser printer of the same resolution. Poor paper quality can worsen this effect.

- **Low print speed** Most inkjet printers claim print speeds in the 2ppm–12ppm range. These claims are usually based on very optimistic assumptions, however, such as low-quality, black-and-white printing. Unlike laser printers, inkjet speed varies a lot with factors such as the printer's resolution and whether or not you're printing color.

- **Media sensitivity** The extent to which ink spreads upon hitting the paper varies a lot from one paper to another. You're generally best off buying paper that's marketed for inkjet printers, although there's a lot of variability even in that market. For the best results from graphics, buy special coated inkjet papers which cost $0.10–$1.00 per page. For text, less expensive inkjet papers will do as well, but these papers usually cost a bit more than multipurpose or laser printer paper.

- **Water-sensitive printing** The inks used in inkjet printers are, by and large, water-soluble. They therefore smear or run if the paper gets wet. Some manufacturers use water-resistant inks. The key word here is *resistant*. These inks are not waterproof; they simply smear less than do other inks.

On the whole, inkjet printers are a good choice for many homes. The lower purchase price and the ability to print in color are very important for the typical consumer. Speed and text print quality aren't as important for most home users as they are for business users.

Some businesses, and even some home users, can benefit from having two printers: a fast laser printer for high-quality text output and an inkjet printer for producing color pages. Given the low cost of inkjet printers, this strategy provides maximum flexibility at minimal cost.

Other Printer Technologies

A wide variety of other printer technologies exists. Some of these technologies have been popular in the past. Others represent niche markets today, or they offer fewer compromises on one point of performance or another when compared to laser printers or inkjets. These technologies include

- **Daisy wheel**   Daisy wheel printers work much like typewriters of years past. They use circular wheels, on which raised mirror-image letters appear. Between this print wheel and the paper lies an inked ribbon. The print wheel is spun and struck against the paper to form an image of a letter. Although popular in the 1980s, daisy wheel printers are all but extinct today.

- **Dot-matrix**   Dot-matrix printers use an array of pins and an inked ribbon to create images on the paper. These pins are combined into images of characters as the printhead moves across the page. Dot-matrix printers are rare today, but they continue to hold onto a niche market because they can print multipart forms.

- **Dye sublimation**   This technology, which also goes by the name *thermal dye transfer*, uses ribbons that contain dyes. The printhead on these devices heats the dyes into a gas, which then sticks to the paper. These printers produce excellent color output, but they're slow and expensive, both in initial purchase price and in ongoing operating costs.

- **Thermal wax transfer**   Thermal wax transfer printers work much like inkjet printers, except that the printer heats and squirts colored waxes rather than inks. Print quality and speed generally fall between those of inkjets and dye sublimation printers. Some models support both thermal wax transfer and dye sublimation modes.

- **Plotters**   A few devices print by placing a pen on a piece of paper and dragging it about. These devices are known as *plotters*, and they excel at producing straight lines at any angle. They're often used in drafting applications, such as creating blueprints.

Chances are you already know whether you need one of these specialized printer types, because they're well known in the professions that use them. If you're uncertain, you should probably consult your co-workers.

Be sure to investigate Linux compatibility with any printer you buy. This need is particularly acute with these oddball printer types, because they might not use the normal printer languages, for which Ghostscript drivers exist.

Choosing a Printer Interface

As external devices, printers need to interface with your computer through one of the computer's external interfaces. The most popular printer interface method has traditionally been the parallel port, but USB and Ethernet ports are both gaining in popularity. Some printers offer RS-232 serial port interfaces, as well, but these interfaces are quite slow for modern printer uses, and so aren't often used.

Most printers come with a fixed set of interfaces—or more properly, *an interface*, because most printers support only one interface. Some mid-range and high-end printers include the capability to add an interface. The most common application of this capability is to add an Ethernet port to a printer in order to turn it into a workgroup printer that doesn't require its own print server.

Parallel-Port Printers

For many years, the vast majority of printers sold for x86 computers have used the parallel port. As a result, this port is often referred to as the *printer port*. It should come as no surprise, therefore, that the parallel port is an excellent choice for connecting printers to x86 computers.

The cable used to connect a printer and computer via the parallel port is shown in Figure 20.3. This cable has different types of connectors on its two ends. The connector on the left in Figure 20.3 is a 25-pin male connector that attaches to the computer's parallel port. Printers use an entirely different type of connector—a *Centronics* connector, shown on the right in Figure 20.3.

The parallel port's speed is very good. This fact, combined with the fact that a parallel port is standard equipment on all modern x86 computers, makes the parallel port an excellent choice for a printer interface. To get the best possible speed, both your computer and your printer must support an advanced parallel-port standard, such as ECP or EPP (see Chapter 16, "Parallel and Serial Ports").

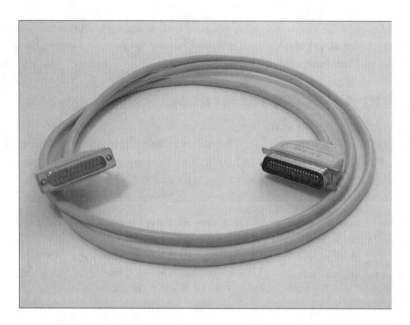

FIGURE 20.3

Printer cables use different connectors on the printer and computer ends.

Because most computers come with precisely one parallel port, it's possible to connect precisely one printer to the computer. If you want to connect more than one printer, you have several options:

- **Install additional parallel ports**   Adding a parallel port card enables you to connect two parallel-port printers. The practical limit on parallel ports for x86 computers is three devices, so you might not be able to fulfill all your needs this way if you want to use a Linux computer as a print server for more than three printers.

- **Use a switch box**   A parallel-port *switch box* lets you connect two or more parallel-port devices to a single parallel port. Switch boxes require manual intervention, though—you need to turn a dial or press a button to direct output to a given printer. This limitation might be acceptable for a desktop computer, but not for a print server.

- **Use additional port types**   There's no law that says you can use only one type of printer interface. You can have a parallel printer and a USB printer connected to a single computer, for instance.

The parallel port is my first choice for a printer interface for use in Linux. There are specific circumstances in which other ports are desirable, though.

To access a parallel-port printer, you write data to the `/dev/lp`*n* device files, where *n* is a number between `0` and `2`. You normally specify the port in the `/etc/printcap` file, as described later in this chapter.

Serial-Port Printers

Most x86 computers come with two RS-232 serial ports. A few printers support printing through the serial port instead of or in addition to printing through a parallel port.

Because the serial port is limited in speed to 115Kbps, the serial port isn't a good choice of printer port. This is particularly true for printers that accept bitmaps as input, which describes all non-PostScript printers under Linux. For instance, a 600×600 dpi black-and-white page requires 4MB to describe completely. At 115Kbps, this page takes 4.75 minutes to send to the printer. This sort of speed is unacceptable. I therefore recommend that you use a serial port only when the printer uses PostScript. Most Linux programs output PostScript natively, and unless you print bitmapped graphics, a PostScript print job is likely to be much shorter than a non-PostScript print job. That 4MB page, for instance, might have come from a 100KB PostScript file. This 100KB file would take just 7 seconds to transfer to the printer at 115Kbps.

To use a serial port for a printer under Linux, you access the printer on the regular serial port device files—`/dev/ttyS`*n*, where *n* is the port number, from 0 up. Most motherboards support two serial ports, and you can add more if you need them, as described in Chapter 16, "Parallel and Serial Ports."

USB Printers

Printers that communicate via Universal Serial Bus (USB) started to become popular in 1999. At a maximum speed of 1.5MB/s, USB is a reasonable choice for a printer interface.

Like parallel printer cables, USB printer cables use different connectors at the computer and printer ends, as shown in Figure 20.4. The Series A connector on the right attaches to the computer, whereas the Series B connector on the left plugs into the printer.

The main problem with USB printers in Linux is that support for USB is so new. USB printers are supported in 2.3.x and later kernels. You need to activate the *USB Printer support* option in the USB kernel configuration menu to use a USB printer. You must then create an appropriate USB printer device file. The conventional name for USB printer devices is `/dev/usblp`*n*, where *n* is a digit from `0` up. (Some distributions place all USB device files in the `/dev/usb` subdirectory.) These devices use device major number 180 and device minor numbers from 0 up. If your distribution doesn't already have appropriate devices, you can create them with commands such as

```
mknod /dev/usblp0 c 180 0
```

20

PRINTERS

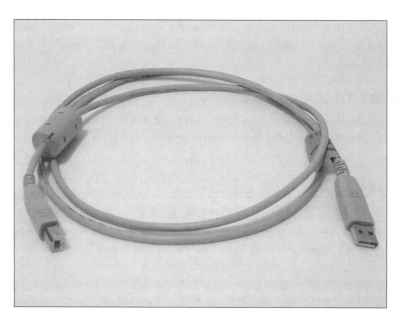

FIGURE 20.4

USB printer cables are the same as USB cables for scanners and many other USB devices.

You must change the final character (0, the device minor number) and the device filename if you need to create more than one USB printer device. Some distributions require specific ownership and permissions on printer device files. You might therefore want to check the ownership and permissions on /dev/lp0 and adjust /dev/usblp0 to match, using the chown and chmod commands. After it is created, you can use the USB printer device file in your /etc/printcap file, just as you would the device file for a parallel-port or serial-port printer.

Ethernet Printers

Some printers—particularly high-end laser printers—support the Ethernet interface. You can plug such printers into your local network and print to them using network printer protocols such as lpd. This feature is particularly useful for printers that are shared on a network, because printers with Ethernet interfaces don't need a print server. If you want to have several printers accessible on your network, scattered around several locations, this capability can be very convenient.

There are a few critical pieces of information you should consider in any Ethernet-interfaced printer:

- **Ethernet speed**   As described in Chapter 17 ("Network Hardware"), Ethernet comes in both 10Mbps and 100Mbps varieties. Ideally, your Ethernet printer should support both speeds. A 10Mbps-only printer can, in some situations, slow down a 100Mbps network to 10Mbps speeds.

- **Ethernet cable type**   Three types of Ethernet cables are in common use: *thick coaxial*, *thin coaxial*, and *twisted-pair*. Be sure your printer supports the type of cabling you use, or at least check on the availability of adapters.

- **Configuration tools**   Network printers need to be configured for their network access, the same as other devices. For instance, they need 4-byte IP addresses. The printers might need to be configured in other ways, as well. In most cases, you can enter an IP address using controls on the printer, but more advanced configuration can be relegated to tools run on other computers. Be sure you can run any such tools on Linux or on some other OS you have available on your network.

- **Print protocols**   Most UNIXes (including Linux) rely natively on a network printing protocol called `lpd`, whereas Windows computers use SMB/CIFS, Netware networks use IPX/LPX, and Macintosh computers use AppleTalk. Fortunately, Linux can use any of these protocols.

Even if your printer doesn't support Ethernet directly, you can buy small standalone print servers. These devices work much like a Linux computer running print server software, but they're small and comparatively inexpensive—usually $100–$300. They include an Ethernet jack and one or more printer ports (usually of the parallel variety). Some include extra features. For instance, many high-end Ethernet print servers can function as hubs or switches.

You should consider the same factors in print servers that you consider in Ethernet ports built into a printer, such as the network protocols the device supports. Some support just one or two protocols, but others support a wide range.

To access a network printer, you use whatever network printing protocol the printer supports. For instance, if the device supports `lpd`, you use the `rm=` and `rp=` parameters in `/etc/printcap` to tell Linux where the printer is.

Printer Languages

A printer takes as input a string of data and produces as output a page of text or graphics. Most printers can accept raw ASCII as input, but in order to produce sophisticated effects such as

20

multiple fonts or graphics, something more is required. Printer manufacturers have therefore developed printer *languages*, which are ways of encoding data such that the printer can produce good-looking results. The simplest printer languages are very crude; they consist of little more than special codes that precede characters in order to alter the appearance of those characters. Others are sophisticated computer programming languages. Printer languages that fall into this latter class are often referred to as *page description languages* (PDLs).

Some printers support only one language, but others support two or more languages. Multilanguage printers are particularly common among mid-range and high-end laser printers, which frequently support both PostScript and PCL (Printer Command Language, described later in the chapter). Most of these devices can automatically detect what printer language is being used, but some earlier models require hints in the form of special escape codes.

PostScript

Adobe's (http://www.adobe.com) PostScript was the first sophisticated PDL. This is particularly true for Linux use, because most programs that print in Linux output either ASCII or PostScript. Therefore, PostScript printers require no drivers or special treatment; the Linux printing system can take program output and dump it directly to the printer port.

When a program prints PostScript to a non-PostScript printer, the *Ghostscript* program intervenes. Ghostscript converts PostScript into a format that can be understood by non-PostScript printers. Doing so chews up CPU time and RAM, however, so printing to a non-PostScript printer is generally slower than printing to a PostScript printer with similar specifications.

> **NOTE**
>
> Ghostscript converts PostScript data into a bitmap, which is then sent to the printer. Therefore, features such as a large selection of built-in fonts are generally useless under Linux, unless the printer supports PostScript.

Because PostScript is such a complete language, it requires more in the way of onboard printer capability than do most other printer languages. This fact raises the cost of PostScript printers. So does the fact that Adobe charges fairly high licensing fees for PostScript. The high cost of genuine PostScript has created a market for an assortment of PostScript clones. Since the late 1990s, major companies such as Hewlett-Packard and Lexmark have begun to abandon genuine Adobe PostScript in favor of clones. In years past, PostScript clones often did a poor job of handling PostScript files, but most recent implementations are quite good. Nonetheless, if you regularly create unusual or demanding PostScript output, you should carefully investigate the capabilities of any printer's PostScript interpreter. Ideally, you should take sample files to a computer store and have them printed on any printer you're considering. The Usenet newsgroup `comp.lang.postscript` is also a helpful resource. Fortunately, most Linux programs create pretty basic PostScript code, which should print on just about any PostScript printer.

PostScript is most often found on laser printers that cost $600 and more. A handful of high-end inkjet printers also support PostScript. These PostScript-enabled inkjet printers have memory and CPU requirements similar to or greater than the requirements of PostScript laser printers. (An inkjet printer might need more memory to handle PostScript because color images require more memory to process than do black-and-white images.) Most PostScript printers ship with enough RAM for basic functionality, but printing complex documents often requires more RAM. As a general rule, therefore, I recommend adding sufficient RAM to at least double the memory in most PostScript printers. PostScript printers generally accept RAM in the form of SIMMs or DIMMs. These memory modules can be the same as those used on motherboards, or they might use unusual or proprietary formats.

Some printers are advertised as supporting PostScript, but a closer look at the fine print reveals that the support comes in the form of a Windows PostScript emulator. This works much like Ghostscript in Linux. As such, this feature is useless in Linux, because Ghostscript either supports the printer already or it doesn't; the Windows software doesn't change that equation. Some printers don't come with PostScript by default, but accept a PostScript add-on card. Unlike a Windows-based software interpreter, a PostScript add-on card turns a printer into a PostScript model. These add-on cards sometimes install like RAM, in SIMM or DIMM sockets. A few models put the PostScript interpreter in a cartridge you can insert into the printer without using tools.

PostScript has gone through several different revisions, known as *levels*. The most important PostScript features, such as scalable fonts, support for graphics and text on the same page, and so on, have been present in PostScript since Level 1. Most Linux programs also produce Level 1 PostScript code. Many PostScript clones today emulate Level 2, often with some extensions from Level 3, which Adobe introduced in 1997. Level 3 (and many Level 2 implementations) supports TrueType fonts in addition to PostScript fonts.

PCL

Hewlett-Packard was one of the first companies to sell laser printers in the x86 marketplace. HP used its *Printer Command Language* (PCL) in these printers. HP originally developed PCL for use in daisy wheel and inkjet printers; the first version to appear in laser printers was PCL 3. Over the years, HP has added more and more features to PCL, to the point that today it's almost as powerful as PostScript. Table 20.1 summarizes the changes in PCL over time.

20

TABLE 20.1   PCL Versions

Version	Introduction	LaserJet Models	Features
3	1984	LaserJet, LaserJet Plus	Full-page formatting
4	1985	LaserJet Series II	Downloadable macros; additional fonts
4e	1989	LaserJet IIP, IIP Plus	Compressed fonts and graphics
5	1990	LaserJet III series	Outline (scalable) fonts and vector graphics
5e	1992	LaserJet 4 series and some 5 series	600dpi printing; additional fonts
5c	1994	Color LaserJet series	Color extensions
6	1996	LaserJet 5, 5se, 6 series, 4000 series, 5000 series	Faster graphics; 1200dpi printing
XL	1996	LaserJet 6P, 6MP	Additional graphics commands; smaller file sizes

HP uses PCL in both its laser printers and many (but not all) of its inkjet models. The inkjet printers usually implement a subset of the full PCL functionality.

PCL has become so successful that most laser printer manufacturers support it on their printers. This fact makes supporting laser printers fairly simple, because one set of drivers supports a wide variety of printers. (Some low-end models use strange proprietary protocols, however, as I describe shortly.)

When buying a PCL printer, pay attention to the PCL version the printer emulates. In particular, if you get a 600dpi printer, be sure the printer supports PCL 5e or later. PCL 5 and earlier printers support printing at up to only 300dpi. Some 600dpi printers support PCL 5 or earlier, but require special Windows drivers to work at 600dpi. You should generally avoid such printers.

A few Linux programs, such as ApplixWare (http://www.applix.com), can produce PCL output. Most Linux programs, however, produce PostScript. To use a PCL printer, therefore, you must use Ghostscript to convert most Linux programs' PostScript output into a form that the printer can understand. I describe this process shortly.

As with PostScript printers, most PCL printers come with RAM that's only marginally adequate. I recommend doubling or tripling the RAM in most PCL printers. The need for increased RAM is particularly acute if you print bitmapped graphics, because these graphics files typically don't compress as well as does text.

If you're in the market for a laser printer, my first recommendation is to buy a PostScript model. If PostScript printers are too rich for your blood, though, a PCL printer is my second—and final—choice. Some laser printers use other protocols, but they're generally very difficult to get working acceptably under Linux.

ESC/P and ESC/P2

In the 1980s, dot-matrix printers were the most popular type of printer on small computers. Among dot-matrix printers, Epson dominated the market. Epson developed a simple printer language, known as *ESC/P*, for its dot-matrix printers. ESC/P commands could set fonts, adjust margins, or send an encoded bitmap graphic, among other things.

Like HP's PCL, Epson's ESC/P language was widely copied. If you need to use a dot-matrix printer with Linux, I strongly recommend you ensure that the printer understands ESC/P. Ghostscript can output to ESC/P, so you can produce good output from Linux on an ESC/P printer.

When Epson began producing inkjet printers, it refined ESC/P and called it ESC/P2. Epson's inkjet printers all use ESC/P2, although each printer speaks a slightly different dialect of the language. Fortunately, Ghostscript handles most ESC/P2 variants equally well.

Unlike ESC/P, ESC/P2 hasn't been widely copied. Most non-Epson inkjet printers use other languages—some high-end models use PostScript, some use PCL, and others use their own proprietary languages.

Other Languages

A large number of proprietary printer languages exist, for example:

- Many early dot-matrix printers used their own languages. Some of these are supported by Ghostscript.
- Canon inkjet printers use a proprietary Canon language. Most of these printers are supported by Ghostscript.
- Most Lexmark inkjets use a proprietary Lexmark language, although a few use PostScript, and Lexmark laser printers use PCL or PostScript. Unfortunately, there are no Ghostscript drivers for Lexmark's inkjet language.

20

PRINTERS

- Some Hewlett-Packard inkjets use a proprietary system known as the *Printing Performance Architecture* (PPA). There's limited support for some subvarieties of PPA. Other Hewlett-Packard inkjets and most Hewlett-Packard laser printers use PCL.

- Smaller inkjet printer manufacturers occasionally go their own way, but more often they emulate another manufacturer's language—most often PCL.

If it's not clear from a printer's box or Web site what language it uses, you should assume it's a proprietary language that's not supported by Linux.

Windows-Only Printers

In the mid-1990s, manufacturersbegan introducing low-cost laser printers that shipped with ridiculously small amounts of RAM and anemic processors. These printers relied upon special bidirectional Windows 3.1 (and later Windows 95 and 98) drivers to feed data to the printer at a precisely controlled rate. These printers work in Windows, but they're boat anchors in all other OSs. Some of the more polite names applied to these printers include *WinPrinter*, *GDI Printer* (after Windows' Graphics Device Interface subsystem), and *host-based printer*.

A few printers are host-based at 600dpi, but have enough RAM and CPU to support 300dpi printing in more conventional ways. These printers typically support PCL 5 or earlier, but require Windows to print at 600dpi.

Linux's printing system isolates Ghostscript, which does the conversion from PostScript to a printer's native language, from the low-level, parallel-port drivers. Therefore, writing reliable Linux drivers for host-based printers is an extremely difficult proposition.

The logic behind host-based printers, and the reason for pessimism concerning Linux drivers for these printers, doesn't apply to inkjet printers. Most inkjet printers don't have extensive RAM or processor support to begin with, and their timing needs aren't as critical as are those for laser printers. The difference between a supported inkjet printer and an unsupported one is simply that nobody has written a Ghostscript driver for the unsupported printer. Likewise, a few laser printers aren't technically host-based printers, but they use proprietary and undocumented protocols and therefore aren't supported in Linux. None of this should be taken to mean that writing drivers for unsupported conventional printers is an easy task. As I've said, some of the protocols used are undocumented, and might in fact be quite complex. Writing such drivers is not a trivial undertaking.

By whatever name, you should avoid Windows-only printers. For information on support for specific printers, check the Printing HOWTO Support Database at `http://www.picante.com/~gtaylor/pht/printer_list.cgi`. This is the single most valuable resource for anybody in the market for a Linux printer.

> **NOTE**
>
> If you're using a Linux computer exclusively as a print server for Windows computers, you might be able to serve a printer that can't otherwise be used from Linux. You must load the printer's native drivers on the Windows client computers and export the printer as a "raw" queue—that is, without filtering the print jobs through Ghostscript. This procedure works for Windows-only printers that don't have any unusual timing requirements, but it doesn't work with most host-based printers.

Using Printers in Linux

In most OSs, printer drivers serve as an interface between an application and a printer. Communication can go both ways in this arrangement. For instance, a printer driver can inform an application that the printer supports wide margins. This isn't the case in Linux. In Linux, applications produce PostScript output, usually without features that tailor the output for specific printers. If your printer supports wide margins, you must find some way to convince your application of this fact.

Because most printers sold for the x86 market are *not* PostScript printers, Linux includes a utility, Ghostscript, that converts between PostScript and an assortment of other printer languages. In effect, Ghostscript takes over many of the roles of a printer driver in other OSs, although Ghostscript doesn't communicate back to the application what a printer's capabilities are.

In addition to Ghostscript, Linux computers implement a printer queue system. This queue holds the output from an application until the printer becomes ready. The queue then feeds the job through Ghostscript or some other program, if necessary, and passes the result on to the printer.

Understanding Linux Printer Queues

Most Linux installations use a printer queue system known as `lpr`, named after one of its component programs. To print using this system, a user or program calls `lpr` and passes to it the name of a file to print. Optionally, it also passes various parameters, such as the name of a printer, for instance,

```
lpr -Pepson example.ps
```

This command prints the file `example.ps` to the printer queue called `epson`. The `lpr` printing system includes a second program, known as `lpd`. This program is a *daemon*, which processes files in the queue according to rules outlined in the `/etc/printcap` configuration file, which I

20

PRINTERS

describe shortly. The usual action is to pass the file through one or more *filters*, which can convert the file into a format that the printer can understand. For instance, a filter might pass the file through Ghostscript. lpd then passes the result of the filter process to the printer's port. The system's use of print filters lets you create queues that can automatically handle a wide variety of file types.

The key to configuring a printer in Linux is the /etc/printcap file. This file contains one entry for each printer queue. The entries look something like this:

```
epson:\
        :lp=/dev/lp0:\
        :rm=:\
        :rp=:\
        :sd=/var/spool/lpd/epson:\
        :mx#0:\
        :sh:\
        :if=/var/spool/lpd/epson/printfilter:
```

The preceding entry defines a printer queue called epson. All but the last line of this entry ends in a backslash (\) character. This character is a "line continuation" character—technically, each /etc/printcap entry occupies one line, but formatting in this way is awkward. Important options in /etc/printcap include

- **lp=**   This line defines the line printer device—/dev/lp0 in this example.
- **rm=**   The name of a remote print server that hosts the printer. If you use a print server or a printer with an Ethernet interface, you enter its machine name or IP address here.
- **rp=**   The name of a print queue on a remote print server.

NOTE

You can define *either* a local printer device via an lp= line *or* a remote printer device via rm= and rp=. You can omit options relating to one or the other device type. I left both options in the preceding example to show that both are possible.

- **sd=**   This is the device's spool directory—the directory where lpr places files you want to print.
- **mx#**   This is the maximum job size, in kilobytes. Note that a pound sign (#) is used in place of an equal sign (=) for this option.

- **sh**   Include this option if you want to suppress header pages. Without this option, lpd prints a header page that identifies the individual who queued the print job.

- **if=**   This line identifies the input filter. Most distributions use a script in the spool directory to call the filter with appropriate options to process a print job. If you omit this line, lpd won't use a filter; it passes the results directly to the printer.

Much of the tricky part of configuring the printer comes in setting up the print filter. There are several "smart filter" packages available for Linux. Most Linux distributions ship with their own filter packages, so you shouldn't need to install anything special to get a filter working with your printer queue.

In fact, most distributions include printer configuration utilities that help you set up all the details of both the /etc/printcap file and the printer filter configuration, including Ghostscript options. For instance, Figure 20.5 shows the printer configuration area of Caldera's COAS utility. You can select options using drop-down option buttons or type entries directly into data fields, as appropriate. The details of GUI printer configuration utilities vary from one distribution to another; for instance, Red Hat uses a program called printtool for this task.

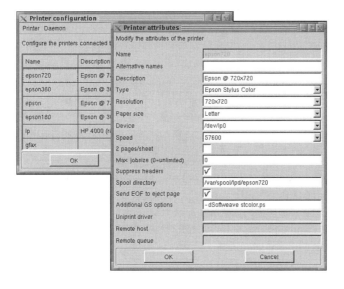

FIGURE 20.5

GUI printer configuration utilities usually let you select your printer by model, set a few options, and not cope with the details of Ghostscript or printer filter configuration.

20

PRINTERS

Understanding Ghostscript Drivers

To delve more deeply into Linux printer configuration, it's necessary to understand more about Ghostscript. Ghostscript is essentially a third-party implementation of PostScript. Unlike the third-party PostScript interpreters you find in many printers, Ghostscript runs on your computer. You can use it to view PostScript files on your screen or to print PostScript files on non-PostScript printers. You can find the latest version of Ghostscript, including complete documentation, at `http://www.cs.wisc.edu/~ghost`.

> **Note**
>
> Ghostscript comes in two forms. One, Aladdin Ghostscript, is the latest version. Aladdin Ghostscript is free for most uses, but cannot be included in any package for which money is charged without paying license fees to Aladdin. After a given version of Aladdin Ghostscript has been out for a while, the company changes its license to the GNU General Public License (GPL), which permits wider distribution. For this reason, Linux distributions ship with GNU Ghostscript, as this older version is called. In most cases, GNU Ghostscript is adequate, but if you want the latest features, you must obtain Aladdin Ghostscript from its main Web site or from some other site.

Ghostscript includes a large number of drivers for an assortment of printers, displays, and graphics file formats. These drivers must be compiled into the Ghostscript binary file, so to save space, most binary versions of Ghostscript omit some of the drivers. You can find out which drivers your version includes by typing **gs – help**. This results in output that includes a list of drivers with names such as `epson`, `laserjet`, `stcolor`, `pcx256`, `pngmono`, and `pdfwrite`.

Unfortunately, the Ghostscript device names can be somewhat cryptic, so you might need to consult some helpful resource to learn what device to use with your printer. The single most helpful such resource is the Printing HOWTO Support Database at `http://www.picante.com/~gtaylor/pht/printer_list.cgi`. This Web site includes a search engine that lets you find comments on specific models of printer, including the Ghostscript driver you need to use with a given printer.

If you find that your binary of Ghostscript doesn't include support for your printer, you must locate another binary of Ghostscript or compile your own. The latter is an extremely tedious proposition, so I recommend you hunt for a binary that includes the appropriate support. Check the Ghostscript binaries at `http://rufus.w3.org/linux/RPM/` or `http://www.debian.org/distrib/packages` for RPM or Debian packages, respectively. I've also found the binary RPMs of Ghostscript 5.10 at `http://www.users.dircon.co.uk/~typhoon/` to be very complete, although now that Ghostscript 6.0 is out, this source might not be as appealing.

TIP

If you find that you must recompile Ghostscript from scratch, you should read the instructions that come with the source code *completely*. Ghostscript is particularly tricky to configure to recompile, so it's important that you understand the process fully before you begin.

You can check basic Ghostscript functionality by passing the program a PostScript file. (Several sample PostScript files come with Ghostscript, typically in the /usr/share/ ghostscript/*x.yz*/examples directory, where *x.yz* is the Ghostscript version number.) You must specify an output filename, the driver to be used, and various other options, as follows:

```
gs -dNOPAUSE -dBATCH -q -r100x100 -sDEVICE=png256 -sOutputFile=test.png test.ps
```

This command creates a PNG file called test.png from the test.ps input file. You can view test.png in a Linux graphics program such as the GIMP. You can change the device driver name and resolution (the -sDEVICE= and -r options, respectively) to match your printer. You can then send the file directly to your printer device, as in

```
cat test.pcl > /dev/lp0
```

If this results in a good printout, you can configure your printer queue to use Ghostscript with these options.

Using Ghostscript in a Linux Printer Queue

The simplest way to configure Linux to use Ghostscript is to use your distribution's printer queue configuration tools, such as Caldera's COAS or Red Hat's printtool. If you needed to hunt down a new Ghostscript driver, though, chances are your distribution's tools aren't set up to handle that printer, so you might need to edit configuration files by hand. I recommend you start by creating a printer queue using a printer driver that you don't use. You can then edit this configuration to use the correct driver.

You might need to track down the configuration files, which can be a tedious process. Your starting point is /etc/printcap and its if= line. The file listed on this line is usually a script that calls a filter program. This script might call other scripts or include Ghostscript options directly. You should try to track down these scripts or configuration files. One of them will contain the Ghostscript options, which you must modify. For instance, Caldera places information on the printer drivers to be used in files in the /etc/sysconfig/printers directory. In Red Hat, equivalent information appears in the /var/spool/lpd/*queuename*/postscript.cfg file, where *queuename* is the name of the printer queue.

In most cases, there's no need to use Ghostscript if your printer includes PostScript capability. In these cases, the Linux printer queue passes PostScript files to the printer unaltered. In a few cases, though, particularly with earlier PostScript clones, the printer can't handle some PostScript files. In these cases, you might want to configure a queue using the `pswrite` Ghostscript driver. This driver converts, odd as it might sound, PostScript to PostScript. The output PostScript, however, is a huge bitmap, just as the output to other printer types is. This bitmap might be easier for a printer to handle than the original PostScript file would be.

Summary

Printers are necessary adjuncts to most computer systems. As a general rule, Linux works well with mid-range and high-end printers. Low-end printers sometimes cause problems, however, because they often use proprietary protocols for which no Linux driver exists. It's therefore important that you check for compatibility of any given printer at `http://www.picante.com/~gtaylor/pht/printer_list.cgi`.

When you've got a printer that you know is compatible with Linux, the easiest way to configure it is usually through a GUI tool that came with your distribution. In some cases, however, you might need to manually configure your queue using your distribution's print filter or another print filter, such as MagicFilter. These tools automatically identify files of particular types and pass them through appropriate conversion programs, such as Ghostscript, so that they can print correctly on your printer.

Prebuilt Systems

PART V

IN THIS PART

Store-Bought Non-Linux Systems

IN THIS CHAPTER

This and the next two chapters cover complete computers. This chapter is devoted to the most common type of computer—desktop computers that come preinstalled with Windows. Most such computers can run Linux, although you might need to hunt for drivers or replace one or more specific components (such as a software modem or sound card) for which no Linux drivers exist.

As a general rule, if you want to buy a new computer to run Linux, it's best to buy a computer that comes preinstalled with Linux. I describe such systems in Chapter 22, "Linux Workstations." The lower cost of non-Linux systems and their ready availability from local computer stores are often enticing, however. In addition, if you want to run both Windows and Linux, a computer preinstalled with Windows might require no less effort to configure than a computer preinstalled with Linux. Some vendors will preinstall both OSs, though, which can save you some effort.

NOTE

To learn more about configuring a computer to run multiple OSs, read my book, *The Multi-Boot Configuration Handbook*, from Que.

Evaluating the Hardware

When you're deciding what computer to buy, your main task is to evaluate the hardware. You should be concerned with three main factors:

- Linux compatibility
- Hardware quality
- Ease of hardware upgrades

Of course, you must also deal with less-hardware-related issues, such as cost, purchase convenience, and aesthetics. Some of these factors vary with the type of manufacturer, but others vary between specific manufacturers or between different models from a single manufacturer.

Types of Manufacturers

PC hardware manufacturers vary along two main dimensions:

- **Manufacturer size**   Manufacturers range in size from hobbyists who sell a few computers to their friends and neighbors to multinational corporations. As a general rule, the small and mid-sized companies are likely to use standard components and allow you to customize your order by specifying particular components. These companies also usually offer better prices than the large megacorporations. Large firms are likely to use at

Store-Bought Non-Linux Systems

CHAPTER 21

557

21

STORE-BOUGHT
NON-LINUX
SYSTEMS

least some custom-made components, which can sometimes cause problems down the road.

- **Distribution channel**   You can buy some computers at "brick and mortar" retail outlets, whereas others you purchase online or over the phone. (I refer to the second as *mail-order* vendors, although the U.S. Postal Service is seldom involved.) Local retailers are frequently more convenient than mail-order firms, particularly because buying locally enables you to see a computer before you buy. Mail-order retailers often charge less than the local variety, however. Sometimes you can purchase a computer either by mail or in person.

Table 21.1 summarizes the characteristics of various combinations of these two dimensions. My breakdown of manufacturers into three size categories is somewhat arbitrary. In deciding which route to take, you should consider how important customizations, quick delivery, manufacturer reputation, and ease of return are to you.

TABLE 21.1   Characteristics of Manufacturers and Retailers

Manufacturer Size	Local Retailer Services/Considerations	Mail-Order Retailer Services/Considerations
Small	Quick delivery of custom-made computers. You can often discuss your needs in depth with the person who'll build the machine. Retailer and manufacturer are usually the same. *Example:* "Mom & Pop" computer store.	Longest wait to obtain a finished computer, wide selection of customization options. Retailer and manufacturer are usually the same. *Example:* small online shop.
Medium	Quick delivery of computer with a limited range of customization options. Retailer and manufacturer are usually the same. *Example:* CompUSA or Micro Center house brand.	Typically supports online option system to help you construct an "ideal" system. Retailer and manufacturer are usually the same. *Example:* large mail-order "custom-build" shop.

continues

TABLE 21.1   Continued

Manufacturer Size	Local Retailer Services/Considerations	Mail-Order Retailer Services/Considerations
Large	Walk into the computer store and walk out with a computer within minutes; few customization options. *Example:* IBM or Compaq bought at local store.	Longer wait than when buying locally, but retailer might offer lower price or wider selection of customization options. *Example:* IBM or Compaq bought by mail, or Dell.

Non-x86 Computers

You can run Linux on many non-x86 computers. As a general rule, you must shop more intently for these computers, than for x86-based computers. Some manufacturer-specific tips on buying non-x86 models include

- **Apple Macintosh**   Check a major PowerPC Linux distribution's Web site, such as `http://www.linuxppc.com` or `http://www.yellowdoglinux.com`, to determine which specific Macintosh models are compatible with Linux on the PowerPC.

- **Alpha-based Systems**   Compaq (`http://www.compaq.com`) offers several machines based on its Alpha CPU. Compaq explicitly supports Linux on some of these computers. A variety of third-party manufacturers also offer Alpha-based systems, generally running Linux. Check `http://www.linux.org/vendors/systems.html` for a list of companies that sell these computers, as well as x86-based Linux systems.

- **Sun Systems**   Most of Sun's (`http://www.sun.com`) computers use SPARC CPUs. These machines typically ship with Solaris, but are usually capable of running Linux.

High-end, non-x86 computers can be a good buy when you're looking for a machine with absolutely top-of-the-line performance, because many of these CPUs are faster than the best x86 CPUs. You aren't guaranteed to get better performance with these computers, though.

Checking for Linux Compatibility

After you narrow your choices down to a few computers, you should begin investigating the computers' capability to run Linux. Among x86 computers, you rarely need to be concerned with the CPU or motherboard. Your choice of CPU and motherboard are important in determining your overall system speed, but Linux seldom has problems with specific models. In terms of Linux compatibility, you should focus on other components, in particular:

- **Video hardware**   Find out what video chipset the computer uses, and then check this against the supported video hardware in XFree86 (`http://www.xfree86.org`). Chapter 12, "Video Cards," covers this matter in detail.

- **SCSI host adapter**   Most x86 computers sold today do not include SCSI adapters. If you want this feature, you should be sure that the SCSI host adapter is supported in Linux. Chapter 9, "SCSI Host Adapters," covers this matter in detail.

- **Modem**   Most x86 computers that include modems ship with software modems, many of which are unusable in Linux. Read Chapter 18, "Modems," and ask any vendor about this matter explicitly.

- **Sound card**   Most sound cards are supported in Linux. Find out what audio chipset a computer uses, and then research Linux support for that chipset. Chapter 10, "Sound Cards," covers this matter in detail.

- **USB**   If the computer uses a USB keyboard or mouse, I recommend you bypass it or ask for the older AT-style keyboard and a PS/2 mouse. Although you can use USB keyboards and mice in Linux, the support is still fairly new. Chapter 15, "Keyboards and Mice," covers this matter in detail.

> **NOTE**
>
> The preceding advice about USB devices applies to distributions based on most 2.2.x kernels. When distributions based on 2.4.x kernels become common, USB keyboards and mice will become much less troublesome. A few distributions today include USB support sufficient to handle keyboards and mice, so if you're really tempted by a system that uses these devices, check your favorite distributions for support details.

- **Network cards**   Make sure any network card included in the computer is Linux-compatible. Linux support for network cards is excellent, as described in Chapter 17, "Network Hardware," but a quick check into the matter is worthwhile.

- **Printers**   Retailers often offer bundles of computers with printers. Unfortunately, these bundles often include very low-end printers for which no Linux drivers exist. You should be cautious, and read Chapter 20, "Printers," before buying such a bundle.

Most other common components don't present any Linux compatibility troubles. A few components, like TV tuner cards and scanners, might require checking, but they're seldom included with new computers. Likewise, some older devices like obsolete CD-ROM drives with proprietary interfaces might cause problems, but you won't find these in new computers.

You might be perfectly happy with a computer even if one or two components aren't Linux-compatible. For instance, you might buy a computer with a Linux-incompatible modem but not need the modem because you use a cable modem for your Internet access. If the component is an inexpensive one, such as a modem, you might also be willing to replace it.

Evaluating Hardware Quality

Determining whether the hardware is of high quality is something that's very difficult to do. If you're considering a computer from a major manufacturer, you might be able to find some information from customer satisfaction surveys conducted by computer or consumer magazines. You might also be able to find reports from individuals by searching Deja News (`http://www.deja.com/usenet/`).

Beyond checking for previous users' experiences in these ways, you can ask the vendor for certain information, such as

- **Component brand names**   If the vendor uses components from major manufacturers, you can be more confident of the quality of the computer than if no-name clones are in use. This isn't an absolute rule, though; some name-brand components are low in quality, and some no-name clones work fine.

- **Burn-in period**   Particularly if you buy from a small or mid-sized company, ask whether the computer undergoes a *burn-in period*, in which the manufacturer runs the computer uninterrupted for some period of time—typically a day or two. If any problems manifest themselves in this time, the manufacturer can fix them before shipping the computer.

- **Visual examination**   If you buy locally, examine the computer yourself. Does the case look like it's high quality, as described in Chapter 4, "Case and Power Supply?" Have the vendor let you look inside. Are cables and wires routed neatly or scattered about in a chaotic fashion? If you know enough to check these matters, look for proper connection of major devices.

- **Overclocking**   One particularlyimportant item to check is whether the CPU is running at its correct speed. Some manufacturers sell CPUs that are run at faster than their rated speeds. This practice is known as *overclocking*, and it frequently works well, up to a point. Unfortunately, it also sometimes fries the CPU. Most CPUs are labeled as to their speed. For instance, Figure 21.1 shows a Cyrix M-II 333 CPU, which bears the *333* model number. Cyrix CPUs use model numbers that are higher than their clock speeds.

The speed of this model is marked as *75MHz Bus 3.5x*—75×3.5 is 262.5MHz, which is the correct speed for a Cyrix M-II 333. Unfortunately, checking for overclocking entails removing the CPU fan, which is a nuisance. Disreputable firms often remove the original markings and replace them, which can make it very difficult to spot an overclocked CPU. Even if the CPU's markings haven't been intentionally altered, they might be worn away by friction when installing the heat sink, as has happened to some extent to the CPU shown in Figure 21.1.

FIGURE 21.1
CPUs generally bear speed markings.

Unfortunately, computer quality is something of a hit-or-miss proposition, particularly for mail-order computers. You might not know that you've bought a "lemon" until you've had the computer for a month or more.

Checking for Ease of Upgrade or Replacement

Many prebuilt computers, particularly those from large manufacturers, use highly integrated motherboards. These motherboards often include features such as video, sound, Ethernet, and modem functions. Although these motherboards are convenient for the manufacturer and reduce the cost of the hardware, they might make it more difficult to upgrade the computer. Although you can probably disable one or more of these built-in components, it's possible that the functionality will interfere with its replacement. Just as important, these computers often include fewer slots than their counterparts that use separate boards. This might not be apparent if the manufacturer advertises the number of *free* slots. For instance, consider two computers. One has integrated video, sound, and modem features on its motherboard, and comes with three PCI slots and one ISA slot. The other computer has video, sound, and modem features on separate cards—an AGP card for the video and PCI cards for the sound and modem. This computer's motherboard has one AGP slot, five PCI slots, and one ISA slot. The number of *free* slots is the same on both computers, but if you decide to replace, say, the sound card, the number of free slots on the second computer remains the same, whereas it drops by one for the first computer. Worse, if you need to replace the video card, you can't use an AGP board for the first computer, because it lacks an AGP slot. If you consider a computer that has extensive functionality built in to the motherboard, you should at least investigate Linux compatibility of each of these integrated components very thoroughly to be sure you won't need to immediately replace them.

Some of the largest x86 computer manufacturers use components that have non-standard mounting requirements. For instance, these machines might not use industry-standard ATX motherboards. Some use strange faceplates that make it difficult or impossible to install third-party CD-ROM or floppy drives. I recommend you avoid any computer that uses non-standard components because, should the component break or should you want to upgrade it in the future, you'll pay exorbitant prices to replace the component.

Obtaining Technical Support

It's very likely that, sooner or later, you'll need support for any computer, whether you buy it at your local computer superstore, from a mail-order outfit, or build it yourself from parts. If you've bought a prebuilt system that came with Windows installed, you might find yourself shunned by the manufacturer if you mention Linux. There are some ways to reduce the magnitude of this problem.

Contacting the Manufacturer

If possible, you should leave Windows installed on any computer that came with Windows. If you remove Windows completely, chances are that, if and when you call the manufacturer with a problem, you'll be told they can't help you because you're not running a supported OS. If you can dual-boot into Windows, however, you'll be able to perform whatever steps it takes to convince the customer service representative that the problem is real, and not caused by Linux.

> **TIP**
>
> If possible, don't even mention that you've reconfigured the computer to run Linux in addition to Windows. Of course, if your problem really does appear to be Linux-related, you might have no choice in the matter. I also don't recommend you lie about it if you're asked. If you're convinced that the problem isn't Linux-related, you might save yourself some grief by not mentioning Linux. Otherwise, Linux might become the technician's target.

Before you contact the manufacturer, collect some basic information on the problem and on the computer. You might be asked for a serial number, and chances are the customer service representative will want you to read some information from Windows configuration utilities. Therefore, if the computer boots at all, have it running Windows when you call.

Internet Newsgroup Support

One of the best forms of support for Linux is the Linux newsgroups. Most of these newsgroups fall under the `comp.os.linux.*` hierarchy, as in `comp.os.linux.networking` or `comp.os.linux.hardware`. For video-related support, you might also want to check the X newsgroups, `comp.windows.x.*`. There are also newsgroups devoted to specific devices, such as `comp.dcom.modems` and `comp.periphs.printers`. Some of these are dominated by Windows users, and so are less useful as a Linux resource.

When posting a question about a specific model of computer, you should include specific information, such as

- **Relevant hardware** Don't assume that *anybody* will know what hardware your model includes. The fact that you have a MegaComp 2553 means *nothing* to 99.9% or more of the readership of any newsgroup. If you have a problem with a specific feature of the computer, you *must* locate information on what chipset that feature uses.

- **Linux version** Include information on both what distribution you use (such as Red Hat 6.2 or Corel 1.0) and what kernel you're running (such as 2.2.14 or 2.3.50). You might also need to include information on relevant additional software. For instance, if your problem is printer-related, post the version of Ghostscript you're using.

- **Steps taken to correct the problem** You're much more likely to get a good response if you can provide some evidence that you've done some troubleshooting of your own before posting. Have you read any relevant HOWTO documents? (They're available at `http://www.linuxdoc.org` and are included with all distributions.) Does the problem exist in both Linux and Windows? Have you done an appropriate Deja News search?

Before you post, you should search for similar problems on Deja News (`http://www.deja.com/usenet/`). This site archives Usenet News postings, and enables you to search through both recent and older postings for keywords.

Installing Linux

Installing Linux on a computer that already contains Windows entails providing Linux with disk space. One way to achieve this goal is to purchase a second hard disk. You can then devote one disk to Windows and another to Linux. If you don't want to purchase a new hard disk, though, you must re-allocate disk space used by Windows so that Linux can use that space. The easiest way to do this is to remove Windows entirely. If you want to keep Windows as well as Linux, however, you must find a way to shrink the Windows installation so that you can install Linux.

> **NOTE**
>
> Some Linux distributions can install themselves in a Windows partition, thus obviating the need to repartition the hard disk. I recommend you not use this option, however. Linux's disk performance suffers when it's installed in this way, and it's generally not as reliable as an installation to a dedicated Linux partition. With the ready availability of tools to repartition, as I describe shortly, there's very little reason to install Linux to a Windows partition.

Removing Windows

If you want to devote the computer entirely to Linux, you can remove Windows from the machine. The simplest way to do this is to use whatever partitioning tools your Linux distribution provides during installation. For instance, Figure 21.2 shows the partitioning tool from the Corel Linux 1.0 installation. To remove the FAT-32 partition on which Windows resides, you click its name (`/dev/hda1`) and then click Delete. You can then select the entire hard disk (`/dev/hda`) and click Add to create new Linux partitions.

Precisely how you perform these actions varies from one Linux distribution to another, so the details of the preceding description might not apply to your distribution. The basic principles are the same, though.

Some distributions include options that cause the distribution to automatically take over the entire hard disk. This feature can be convenient if you want to quickly install Linux with whatever default partitioning scheme the distribution favors. But if you want finer control, you should select the customized partitioning options.

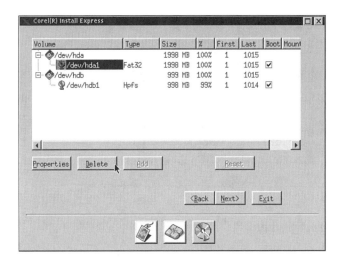

FIGURE 21.2
Most Linux distributions enable you to remove and add partitions during installation.

For more details on Linux installation consult your distribution's documentation or a book on the distribution you want to use.

Shrinking Windows

If you want to keep Windows on the computer, the best option available is to use a partition resizing program to shrink the Windows partition to make room for Linux. Several such programs are available, including

- **FIPS**   The First Nondestructive Interactive Partition Sizing (FIPS) program is a simple DOS utility that can break a FAT partition into two partitions. To use it, you must boot your computer into DOS mode. FIPS is useful, but limited in many ways. Its user interface is crude, and it can only split one primary partition into two parts. You can't use FIPS to increase the size of a partition or to work on non-FAT partitions, as might be required if your new computer comes with Windows 2000. Most Linux distributions come with FIPS, which is an open source program.

- **PartitionMagic**   The PartitionMagic program, shown in Figure 21.3, is a very flexible partition resizer. You can use it to shrink, grow, move, copy, create, and delete FAT, NTFS, HPFS, and ext2fs partitions. Version 5.0 can handle Windows 2000's NTFS 5, but earlier versions can only work with previous versions of NTFS, used by Windows NT 4.0 and earlier. If you want to maintain a multi-OS computer, PartitionMagic is well worth having. It's commercial software, available from PowerQuest (`http://www.powerquest.com`).

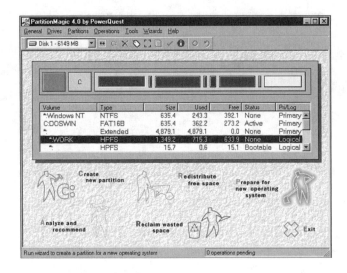

FIGURE 21.3

PartitionMagic provides an easy-to-use interface on advanced partition manipulation tools.

- **System Commander 2000**   V Communications (`http://www.v-com.com`) offers two products that compete with PartitionMagic: System Commander 2000 and Partition Commander. The former is more complete; it can resize FAT, NTFS, and ext2fs partitions, whereas Partition Commander can only resize FAT partitions. Neither product can handle OS/2's HPFS partitions. System Commander 2000 includes a very capable boot loader, so you can select between many OSs installed on a single computer. Like PartitionMagic, these are commercial products.

- **Ranish Partition Manager**   This program, available from `http://www.users.intercom.com/~ranish/part/`, is a shareware partition manager that's roughly comparable to Partition Commander in its capabilities. It can resize FAT partitions, but it can't move them, and it can't handle Linux ext2fs partitions.

- **Linux installation utilities**   Linux Mandrake 7.0 includes partition resizing capabilities in its installation routine. You can resize FAT or Linux ext2fs partitions during installation, which can greatly simplify the installation procedure.

Some distributions, such as Corel Linux 1.0 (`http://linux.corel.com`) and SuSE Linux 6.3 (`http://www.suse.com`), insist on creating their own Linux partitions. Others, such as Linux Mandrake 7.0 (`http://www.linux-mandrake.com`), are happy to install in existing Linux partitions, such as those you might create in PartitionMagic. If you're uncertain about what your distribution requires, you should leave blank space for Linux, rather than creating partitions.

> **CAUTION**
>
> I strongly advise you to completely back up your Windows installationbefore shrinking its partition. Although partition-shrinking programs are typically reliable, problems do occasionally occur. Of course, if you've just received the computer, you might be able and willing to recover the system from an emergency recovery CD. Be sure you've got a recovery CD before proceeding, though. Some PC manufacturers omit this CD in order to save manufacturing costs.

Obtaining a Linux Distribution

Depending upon your definition of *major*, Linux is available from three, or up to a dozen, major Linux vendors. Each vendor takes a Linux kernel and a large assortment of key Linux programs, bundles them together with an install program, and distributes this bundle. The resulting package is known as a Linux *distribution*. Most distributions are available in a variety of ways:

- **As an Internet download**   You can obtain most distributions from Internet download sites, such as `ftp://sunsite.unc.edu/pub/linux/distributions` and Linuxberg (`http://tzo.linux.tucows.com/distribution.html`). The easiest way to get Linux in this way is to download a CD-ROM *image file* and burn that to a CD-R, which you can then use to install Linux. (You must use an option in your CD-R software called Create CD from Image File or something similar.) When you download Linux in this way, you get no technical support from the distribution vendor.

- **On a low-cost CD-ROM**   Many Linux retailers, such as Linux Mall (`http://www.linuxmall.com`) and CheapBytes (`http://www.cheapbytes.com`), sell Linux on CDs that cost $1–$3. Even counting a typical $5 shipping cost, you can therefore get a Linux distribution—or even two or three of them—for under $10. As with a version downloaded from the Internet, you get no technical support or printed documentation when you obtain Linux in this way.

- **As an accompanying CD-ROM to a book**   Many introductory Linux books come with a Linux CD-ROM. Magazines also occasionally ship Linux on CD-ROMs. Buying Linux in this way can be a good way to learn the OS because of the accompanying book. On the downside, publishing delays usually result in books on shelves that are a version or two behind the latest Linux distribution. You also typically get no technical support with such packages.

- **In an official package**   You can buy an official boxed set of a Linux distribution, complete with technical support and a printed manual. These boxed sets typically sell for $30–$150, although you can sometimes find them for less. Most include a few extra commercial programs, such as limited versions of PartitionMagic or office programs such as WordPerfect. If you want official support, or if you want to support Linux packagers financially, this is the way to get Linux.

Which Linux should you get? That's an often-asked question, and a difficult one to answer. The best distribution for one person might be the worst for another. Some of the more popular distributions, and their advantages and disadvantages, include

- **Caldera eDesktop 2.4**   Caldera's (`http://www.caldera.com`) distribution, formerly known as *OpenLinux* and now going by the *eDesktop* and *eServer* names, is targeted towards businesses, but is perfectly usable by home users, as well. Caldera has one of the best installation procedures available. It's a reasonably stable and complete distribution but, if you need to install a large number of packages from third parties, you might have problems. Many third-party packages come as Red Hat Package Manager (RPM) files, and assume that they're installing on a Red Hat system. Although Caldera uses the RPM file format, some RPM packages don't work well with the distribution.

- **Corel Linux 1.0**   Corel's (`http://linux.corel.com`) distribution is the newest major Linux distribution. It's got a very good installation routine and can be fairly easy for new Linux users, but it's rough around the edges. It installs many servers by default, which is a serious security problem for systems that are connected to the Internet. Corel Linux is based on Debian, but is much easier to use.

- **Debian Linux 2.1**   Debian (`http://www.debian.org`) is unusual in that it's not distributed by a commercial entity. It's known for being extremely robust and complete, but its installation procedure is extremely difficult for new users. The next version, which might be available by the time you read this, should have a better installation routine. Debian originated the Debian package format, which is also used by Corel Linux.

- **Linux Mandrake 7.0**   This distribution, available from `http://www.linux-mandrake.com`, is an offshoot of Red Hat Linux. Mandrake comes with a good installation routine, including partition resizing capabilities. Most RPM packages install cleanly on Mandrake.

- **Red Hat Linux 6.2**   Red Hat (`http://www.redhat.com`) has long been the dominant Linux distribution. Its installation routine isn't as slick as are some others, but it's reasonably easy to administer. Because it's so popular, it's easy to find Red Hat help on Usenet newsgroups.

Store-Bought Non-Linux Systems

CHAPTER 21

569

21

STORE-BOUGHT
NON-LINUX
SYSTEMS

- **Slackware 7.0**   Slackware (`http://www.slackware.com`) is the oldest surviving major Linux distribution. It uses neither RPM nor Debian packages, which means it can be difficult to add and remove packages from the OS. Like Debian, Slackware shuns GUI configuration screens, so it's best for experienced UNIX administrators.

- **SuSE 6.4**   SuSE (`http://www.suse.com`) originates in Germany. It's an RPM-based distribution, and is somewhat more compatible with Red Hat RPMs than is Caldera, but less so than Mandrake. Its configuration tools are not quite as sophisticated as are those of Red Hat, Mandrake, Caldera, or Corel, but it's better than Debian or Slackware in this respect. The commercial version of SuSE is distinguished by being available either on several CD-ROMs or on a single DVD-ROM. It comes with an unusually wide selection of software.

If you're new to Linux and have Linux-using friends or colleagues, you might want to use whatever distribution your friends or colleagues use. That way, you'll have an easier time getting support from these individuals. If you're a lone new user, I recommend you start with Caldera, Corel, Mandrake, or Red Hat, because these are the easiest for a new user to install and configure. If you want to dive in without the "crutches" of GUI configuration tools, Debian would be my choice, although Slackware also deserves praise.

Running a Linux Installation

Today, most Linux distributions come on bootable CD-ROMs. You can insert the CD-ROM in the drive, turn on the computer, and the installation routine starts up—if your BIOS is configured to boot from the CD-ROM drive. Details differ from one BIOS to another, but you can typically adjust this detail by entering the CMOS setup utility by pressing a key such as F2 or Delete early in the boot process. You can then locate and adjust the boot order option so that the CD-ROM drive comes first, as shown in Figure 21.4. If booting from the CD-ROM drive doesn't work for some reason, you can usually create a boot floppy disk or start the installation from DOS or Windows. Consult your distribution's documentation for details.

The details of Linux installation vary substantially, but as a general rule they proceed through several steps:

- **Basic configuration**   The installation routines ask what language to use, what sort of keyboard and mouse you have, and so on. Distributions sometimes also ask you about SCSI host adapters and Ethernet cards.

- **Package selection**   You must tell the system what programs to install. Increasingly, distributions offer simple options, such as *desktop system* or *server configuration*. These options select a large number of packages. Other distributions, such as Debian 2.1, require that you select packages on a more fine-grained basis, or offer such selection as an "advanced" installation option.

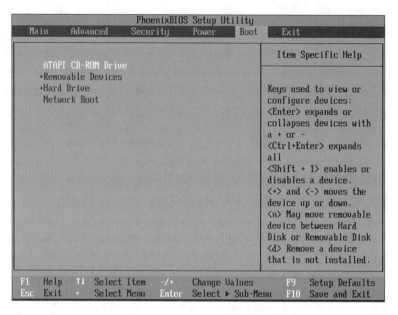

FIGURE 21.4
Modern BIOSs enable booting from a CD-ROM drive.

- **Partitioning**   Distributions invariably provide some way for you to identify what partitions or free space you want to use. Figure 21.2, for instance, shows Corel Linux's partitioning screen.

- **Package installation**   The installation process itself usually requires little or no user intervention. The installer simply installs the packages you've selected on the computer.

- **X configuration**   Most distributions run a utility to help you configure the X Window System (X) for your hardware. In my experience, this is the single most-troublesome part of a Linux installation, because the process sometimes fails in one way or another.

TIP

If you're given the choice, tell the installer *not* to start X when Linux boots. If the X configuration doesn't work, the computer can lock itself into a cycle of trying to start X, and you'll be unable to use the computer except by logging in from a network connection. You might be able to fix this problem by typing `linux single` at the LILO `boot:` prompt when you boot. The system then boots up into single-user mode, without running X, and you can edit the X configuration to fix the problem. After you've installed Linux and convinced yourself that X works correctly, you can edit your `/etc/inittab` file to start Linux directly into X, as described in Chapter 12, in the section called "Configuring XFree86 for Your Video Card."

Store-Bought Non-Linux Systems

CHAPTER 21

571

21

STORE-BOUGHT
NON-LINUX
SYSTEMS

- **Miscellaneous configuration**   Most distributions let you configure additional aspects of the system. For instance, you might be asked whether you want to install a printer or configure your system's networking settings.

- **Reboot**   After the system's done installing everything, it typically reboots and starts Linux.

These steps might or might not occur in precisely the order I've outlined here. For instance, you might be asked to configure a printer or Ethernet adapter before you configure X. Most distributions step you through all these procedures during installation, though.

If you run into problems installing Linux, you have two choices:

- **Try another distribution**   Sometimes one distribution works on a computer, but another doesn't. The most common issues are support for very new hardware components, such as recent video cards or SCSI host adapters. If you want to try another distribution, try to find one that was released more recently than whatever distribution you've tried first.

- **Look for help**   You can check the Linux newsgroups, the distribution's Web site, your Linux-using friends, or any other resources you can think of to try to find help.

Obtaining a Refund for Windows

The license terms for Microsoft's Windows include language stating that, if you don't agree with the terms of the license, you can return the product for a refund. Therefore, if you buy a computer with Windows preinstalled, remove Windows, and install Linux in its place, you might be able to return the Windows CDs for a refund on the price of the Windows software. Note that I said you *might* be able to do this. The way the license is written, it's the PC manufacturer who's responsible for handling the refund, and most PC manufacturers are not overjoyed at the prospect of handling refunds for unused Windows licenses. Individuals attempting to obtain such a refund have met with varying degrees of success. For more information on this topic, check `http://dmoz.org/Computers/Software/Operating_Systems/ Microsoft_Windows/WinRefunds/`, which has a large number of links to press articles, user discussions, success stories, and so on.

CAUTION

You shouldn't apply for a refund if you intend to dual-boot your computer between Linux and Windows, unless you already have an *unused* copy of Windows you can install on the new computer.

Rather than buy a Windows computer and then struggle to obtain a refund, it's generally better to buy a computer with Linux preinstalled, or at least without an OS installed at all. (Many of the small- and mid-sized PC manufacturers will build a computer without an OS installed.) Linux machines are typically harder to find than Windows-based computers, but they're not unobtainable. Chapter 22 covers this topic in more detail.

Summary

If you're in the market for a new computer, one option is to purchase a machine that was never designed to run Linux, but to run Linux on it anyhow. Most computers can work in this way, although you might have to replace one or two components, such as a software modem or sound card, to get it to work. If you buy a computer from a vendor that will build a system to your specifications, you can ensure that it has adequate hardware from the beginning. You must do some research on basic Linux hardware, particularly video cards, SCSI adapters, and sound cards, if you don't want to be stuck with a machine that runs Linux poorly, if at all.

After you've got your computer, you'll need to spend some time preparing it to run Linux and installing the OS. This task is no different from installing Linux on a system you've had for some time. The task can be safer because, if you make a mistake that wipes out Windows, you can probably recover Windows to its immediate post-installation state by running a recovery CD provided by the computer's manufacturer.

Linux Workstations

IN THIS CHAPTER

If you're in the market for a computer on which you intend to run Linux, the simplest way to ensure hardware compatibility is to purchase the computer from a vendor who sells computers preconfigured with Linux. By doing this, you shift responsibility to the vendor to research specific components, check for strange interactions, and even install Linux in a reasonable way. This can be a great time-saver, although it does have its drawbacks. For instance, if the vendor you select barely understands Linux, that vendor can make mistakes. Letting the dealer configure your Linux system also means that you won't learn as much about Linux installation and configuration. Finally, you're likely to pay more for a computer that's preconfigured with Linux than for an equivalent machine sold with Windows installed. This might seem odd, given that Linux costs less than Windows, but the reason is that you're paying for a greater level of expertise on the part of the manufacturer. In many cases, Linux computers also contain more expensive hardware than do Windows systems that appear similar at first glance. For instance, many Linux computer dealers use SCSI hard disks, rather than EIDE drives, which both raise the cost and improve performance.

Many of the considerations when you buy a computer preinstalled with Linux are the same as those when you buy a computer that comes preinstalled with Windows. You might therefore want to read Chapter 21, "Store-Bought Non-Linux Systems," to learn about these issues. I refer to specific sections of Chapter 21 throughout this chapter.

Locating a Linux-Aware Vendor

If you want to buy a computer with Linux preinstalled, your first challenge is in locating a suitable vendor. At the moment, you're unlikely to find Linux computers for sale in the local computer superstore, although this could change in the future. Instead, you'll need to buy through mail order or at a more specialized local store. Locating such sources of supply can be tricky if you don't know where to look. Fortunately, a few resources can be very helpful in locating Linux-aware computer retailers.

Major National Computer Companies

There are a few names that consumers associate with new computers: IBM, Compaq, Dell, Gateway, and others. These manufacturers invariably feature Windows on their most popular models, and those are the ones you'll find on most computer store shelves. Some of these manufacturers, however, offer Linux on some of their computers. These Linux-equipped machines are typically sold as servers, and so have very powerful processors, lots of hard disk space, and other high-end features. If you want a truly well-equipped desktop system, there's no reason you couldn't use one of these "servers" as a workstation. Some specifics include

- **IBM**   In 1999 and 2000, IBM dramatically increased its support for Linux, including contributing to some Linux development efforts and porting some of its products to Linux. IBM now offers Linux on some of its NetFinity servers, and has embarked on a program to ensure Linux compatibility for most of its hardware. For more information, check `http://www-4.ibm.com/software/is/mp/linux/`.

- **Compaq**   Compaq offers Linux as an option on some of its Proliant servers. The company also sells computers based on the Alpha CPU line it acquired from DEC, and Linux is available on some of these computers. For more information, check `http://www.compaq.com/products/servers/platforms/` and `http://www.digital.com/alphaserver/`.

- **Hewlett-Packard**   The company best known for its printers also sells computers, and offers Linux on some of its servers. Check `http://internetsolutions.enterprise.hp.com/linux/` for more information.

- **Silicon Graphics**   Best known for its high-powered UNIX workstations, Silicon Graphics (SGI) offers a line of x86-based Linux workstations as well. You can read more at `http://www.sgi.com/servers/1400/1overview.html`.

- **Dell**   Dell offers Red Hat Linux preinstalled on a number of its computers. Linux information is scattered about on its Web site; go to `http://www.dell.com` and do a search on *Linux* to locate relevant pages.

In most cases, you must purchase these Linux-equipped computers directly from the company, or special-order them through a computer retailer. These models aren't typically on display in local stores. As Linux grows in popularity, though, this might change. Other major computer manufacturers might also begin to offer Linux preinstalled on some of their models.

Large companies that sell Linux as an option typically invest in testing their hardware with Linux, so you can be reasonably sure that the hardware works well with Linux. Some of these companies have invested in Linux driver development or other open source programming projects to further the usability of Linux on their hardware.

One of the biggest advantages of buying from a major non-Linux company is that you have that company's support. This is particularly true if you buy an expensive server system, because such computers often come with good support packages. You can be reasonably certain that a major company like this won't fold any time soon, leaving you with an "orphaned" machine. On the other hand, these manufacturers sometimes use nonstandard hardware, which can be difficult or expensive to upgrade or replace.

Linux Specialty Vendors

One of your best bets for locating a computer with Linux preinstalled is to purchase from a specialty Linux vendor. These companies specialize in building Linux computers. They can therefore generally be trusted to produce computers that work well under Linux. Most of these companies are small enough that they can't invest in Linux development, but a few, such as VA Linux (`http://www.valinux.com`), can do so.

Most Linux specialty stores sell x86-based Linux computers. Some offer Linux installed on other processors in addition to, or instead of, x86 CPUs. The most common non-x86 CPU used is the Compaq (formerly DEC) Alpha CPU, which is very well suited to high-performance computing tasks, particularly those that require heavy floating-point computations. (The special effects for the film *Titanic* were done with a farm of Alpha-based computers running Linux.) Non-x86 computers do have their drawbacks, however, including an inability to run binaries compiled for the more mainstream x86 version of Linux. This fact can be important if you want to run commercial software such as WordPerfect or ApplixWare.

Most Linux specialty stores operate on a mail-order basis. This can make it difficult to evaluate hardware's quality before you buy, but you can still ask some questions to help ensure you get a good product. Read the section "Evaluating Hardware Quality" in Chapter 21 for more information. Of course, if you find a local shop that specializes in Linux, you can check the hardware in person before you buy, which can make buying a good product much easier.

You can find a list of vendors who sell Linux computers at `http://www.linux.org/vendors/systems.html`. Linux magazines such as *Linux Journal* and *Linux Magazine* also sport ads from these companies. I've listed several of them in Appendix B, under the heading "Computer Manufacturers."

Local Computer Assemblers

Many small computer shops build computers around a set of hardware choices, but will build a computer to your specifications within that range of hardware. Some will also add one or two custom components; for instance, if you want a specific video board, the store will order it for your computer. Some of these shops are willing to install Linux on a computer, although they usually install Windows.

If you want to buy locally but also want a computer with Linux preinstalled, such local assemblers might be your only choice. The main drawback to such shops is that they might or might not know much about Linux. They therefore might or might not provide optimal hardware for Linux. On the other hand, because they are local, you can go in and examine the hardware yourself before buying it, which is a luxury you don't have in the case of mail-order, specialty Linux retailers.

> **TIP**
>
> You may want to read key chapters of this book—particularly Chapters 9, "SCSI Host Adapters;" 10, "Sound Cards;" and 12, "Video Cards," before buying a Linux system from a dealer with less-than-perfect Linux expertise. The Linux Hardware Compatibility HOWTO document (`http://www.linuxdoc.org/HOWTO/Hardware-HOWTO.html`) may also contain useful information.

Locating local stores that install Linux can be difficult. You might need to check your telephone directory and call several computer stores before you find one. You can also check local computer publications, which might have an ad or two for preinstalled Linux systems. If you're lucky, one of the Linux specialty shops discussed in the preceding section might be local to you, in which case you might be able to buy in person rather than over the Internet.

Evaluating the Hardware

One of the primary reasons for purchasing a computer that comes with Linux installed is to avoid having to research every individual component in detail. Nonetheless, it's often beneficial to check out the hardware that a vendor proposes including in a computer, or check the manufacturer's quality control in other ways. In fact, you might want to read the section "Evaluating Hardware Quality" in Chapter 21, because the advice presented there applies equally well to computers designed to run Linux. When the manufacturer knows about Linux, though, you should hold the hardware to a higher standard. There's no excuse for including, say, a software modem with no Linux drivers in a computer that runs Linux. There are a few other items you might want to consider in a computer that runs Linux from the start.

Design Considerations

You might be willing to live with some peculiarities in a computer that's designed for Windows. You shouldn't have to deal with these minor annoyances in a computer that's designed from scratch to run Linux, though. Some examples of differences you might find between Linux and Windows computers include

- **Linux keyboards** A few manufacturers have begun to produce keyboards with a Tux penguin logo, rather than a Windows logo, on the keys that are normally identified as Windows keys. These keyboards function the same as conventional keyboards, but if the computer is to be used only in Linux, why put a Windows logo on the keyboard? (I don't recommend sacrificing keyboard quality to get a Linux keyboard, though; this improvement is purely aesthetic, whereas carpal-tunnel syndrome is far more serious.)

- **No-compromises chipsets** Some components work in Linux, but suboptimally. For instance, a sound card's Linux drivers might not support its wavetable features, or a video card might not deliver optimum speed. You might be willing to put up with such a component in a computer designed for Windows, but a competent Linux computer vendor won't use such components. Unfortunately, I can't provide pointers to all the suboptimal components that exist, because the marketplace is so dynamic and the number of such components is quite large. Specific chapters of this book provide advice on the types of features you should consider, though.

- **100% Linux compatibility** Ask the vendor if *every* component in the computer works with Linux. Some smaller dealers might try to take an existing design, slap Linux on the hard disk, and sell it as a Linux computer. Although this approach can work quite well if the components are well chosen, it can be a problem if the original design includes components for which no Linux drivers exist, like many software modems.

- **Optimum disk performance** Linux can benefit from SCSI hard disks more than Windows can, so you might want to give serious consideration to buying a computer that uses SCSI. This isn't to say you should reject an EIDE-based system, particularly if you want a low-end computer. If a dealer doesn't even offer a SCSI option, though, be wary, because this indicates that the dealer sells only low-end systems, and therefore might not be familiar with Linux's performance capabilities and requirements.

- **CPU choice** Most Linux systems use Intel, AMD, or VIA/Cyrix CPUs. Many Linux vendors offer systems built around other CPUs, particularly Alpha systems. You might want to consider such computers for high-end work, but be aware that you'll lose something in compatibility. Commercial programs such as Corel's (`http://linux.corel.com`) WordPerfect Office 2000 usually don't work on most non-x86 platforms, although there are exceptions to this rule. Even if you don't want a non-x86 system, a vendor who offers such systems probably knows more about Linux's hardware requirements than a vendor who doesn't.

Of course, if you feel compelled to dig into the details of a computer's configuration in great detail, you lose one advantage of buying a preconfigured Linux system—letting the dealer do the homework on components. On the other hand, if you're considering just one or two preconfigured machines, you'll need to investigate many fewer components than you would if you wanted to design a computer from scratch.

Determining the Vendor's Familiarity with Linux

You probably don't want to buy a computer from a vendor who's only slightly familiar with Linux. Such a dealer might make suboptimal hardware choices, and might also install Linux or accompanying software strangely or in a way that will cause problems in the future. You can probably get a good idea of a dealer's level of Linux expertise by asking a few questions, such as

- **What version of Linux, and why that one?**   Ask what Linux distributions the dealer offers, and why. Be wary of a reply like "We use distribution *X* because it's the best." As I outlined in the section "Obtaining a Linux Distribution" in Chapter 21, there is no single best Linux distribution; every one has its advantages and disadvantages.

- **What partitioning options do you offer?**   A serious Linux vendor should allow you to specify any partitioning scheme you like. A dealer with little or no experience might offer just one or two configurations, or might respond in a way that indicates confusion about the question.

- **Why do you use component *X*?**   Ask about one or two components that are particularly important to you personally or that can cause problems in Linux, such as video cards or sound cards. Does the response match what you read on Usenet newsgroups and any relevant Linux Web sites? (You can search for recent Usenet news postings about a component on `http://www.deja.com/usenet/`.) Be particularly wary if the dealer refers to reviews in mainstream computer magazines, which seldom consider Linux compatibility. Windows benchmarks are particularly unreliable for predicting Linux performance.

- **What do you suggest for peripheral *X*?**   Even if the dealer doesn't offer peripherals such as printers or scanners, a knowledgeable Linux shop should have some idea about what works well and what doesn't. Compare the dealer's response to the listings on appropriate Linux hardware Web sites, such as `http://www.picante.com/~gtaylor/pht/printer_list.cgi` for printers or `http://www.mostang.com/sane/` for scanners.

- **What Linux support do you offer?**   If the dealer offers post-sale Linux support, this is a good thing. Some dealers might not offer Linux support after the sale, or might rely on a third party to offer that support.

- **How long have you been offering Linux?**   The longer a firm has been installing Linux on its computers, the better they're likely to understand its capabilities and requirements. You might also express this question in terms of how *many* Linux computers they've sold.

22

LINUX
WORKSTATIONS

TIP

If the dealer also sells Windows-based systems, try to ask these questions of a dealer's Linux expert. A salesperson might not be familiar with the details of Linux systems, but that doesn't mean that the expertise doesn't exist elsewhere in the company.

You can also look for information on a dealer from other customers. You can ask about mail-order specialty Linux dealers on a Usenet newsgroup like comp.os.linux.hardware. For recommendations of local stores, you might ask your friends or colleagues. If there's a Linux user group in your area, you might ask about local Linux retailers at a user group meeting.

Evaluating the Software

Presumably you're considering buying a system with Linux already installed in order to save the time and effort it would take to install Linux. You should be sure, therefore, that you get the software you want on the computer to begin with. There's little point, for instance, in buying a computer that comes with Linux Mandrake if you really want to run Debian Linux. Similarly, many Linux hardware vendors optionally install additional Linux software, much as many Windows hardware vendors install extra Windows software packages. You should investigate all the software options provided by any vendor before making a purchase.

> **NOTE**
>
> If you want or need to reinstall Linux on a Linux workstation, you can almost certainly do so. With the possible exception of some non-x86 computers, you'll probably have no problem installing another distribution, if you decide you don't like the distribution with which the computer initially shipped. You should be sure to check that the dealer hasn't used any strange components that might cause problems should you change distributions. For instance, a dealer might install a software modem along with an appropriate Linux driver, which would require extra effort to configure after you reinstall Linux.

Linux Distributions

I provide a rundown of many of the current Linux distributions in Chapter 21, in the section "Obtaining a Linux Distribution." If you're unfamiliar with Linux, just about any of the major distributions will serve your needs well. Debian and Slackware are two possible exceptions to this rule, because neither comes with extensive GUI configuration tools. If you're already familiar with Linux, you might want to favor a vendor that ships the same distribution you've used in the past. If you buy a system that runs another distribution, you might be puzzled by the differences between the distributions. This is particularly true with respect to configuration features. For instance, Red Hat and Mandrake both use the linuxconf tool for system administration, shown in Figure 22.1. SuSE, on the other hand, uses the text-based YaST, shown in Figure 22.2. Other distributions use other configuration tools.

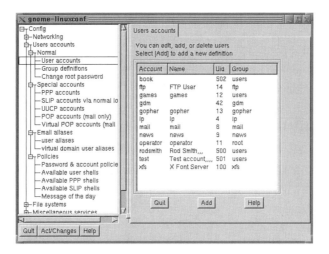

FIGURE 22.1

Red Hat's linuxconf *is an extensible configuration tool used by the Red Hat and Mandrake distributions.*

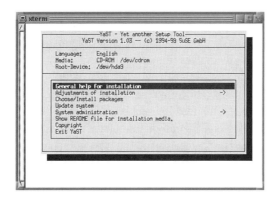

FIGURE 22.2

SuSE's YaST is not as flashy as is linuxconf, *but it provides access to a similar set of options.*

You should ask the vendor whether it uses the full commercial version of a distribution or a freely-available version. If the former, you should get a set of installation CDs, a manual, and support from the publisher. If the latter, be sure that the vendor at least gives you a Linux installation CD. Some might include extra printed documentation—either a printout of some set of documents that come in electronic form with Linux or a Linux book that covers a distribution.

Larger vendors might occasionally modify a standard distribution in some way. For instance, a vendor might include updated packages released since the distribution appeared. Others might modify the login screen to display the vendor's name. The former is generally desirable, because security-related bugs can and do appear now and then. It's best to get a distribution that doesn't require immediate updates to be safe.

Additional Linux Software

If the vendor uses a full commercial release of a distribution, the vendor might install any additional software that comes with that distribution. For instance, the Deluxe version of Corel Linux 1.0 ships with the full version of WordPerfect 8.0. If the vendor doesn't install such packages, you might need to install them yourself, if you want them.

No matter what distribution a dealer uses, the dealer has the option of including additional software with the computer. Packages such as WordPerfect and StarOffice are popular productivity tools you might want to use. A commercial X server, such as Accelerated-X or Metro-X, can be useful if the computer uses certain video cards with weak support in XFree86. System maintenance utilities such as the Backup and Recovery Utility (BRU) can be useful additions to a new computer package.

Some vendors might offer ancillary packages of open source programs. For instance, the dealer might include a CD-ROM with archives of popular Linux FTP sites. In most cases, the vendor won't install the software from these CD-ROMs, because doing so would consume exorbitant amounts of disk space. Having the software on a CD-ROM can be quite convenient, though, particularly if you don't have high-speed Internet access. If you don't get such a CD-ROM with your computer, you might consider buying one from a Linux retailer such as Linux Mall (`http://www.linuxmall.com`) or CheapBytes (`http://www.cheapbytes.com`). You can usually get an archive of Linux software delivered to your door for less than $10 from such dealers.

Fortunately, most Linux distributions ship with a very wide array of software, including programs such as word processors, spreadsheets, drawing programs, Web browsers, games, and backup packages. Some of these programs might not be installed by default, however. So, if there's a specific program you want, you might want to ask the vendor if it's installed in the standard package.

You should ask how much disk space the standard installation consumes. Although it can be convenient to have a large selection of software preinstalled, such a configuration can consume a great deal of disk space. You might prefer a leaner configuration to start with, and install additional packages as you need them.

Non-Linux Software

You might need to run non-Linux programs in addition to Linux programs. Examples include

- **Microsoft Windows** Many dealers will configure computers to boot both Linux and Windows. You should be able to specify how much disk space you want devoted to each OS. Also, be sure you get the version of Windows you want; Windows 98 and Windows 2000 are very different OSs in many ways. (Microsoft is preparing an update to Windows 98, called *Windows Millennium Edition*.)

- **DOS boot floppy** A DOS boot floppy can be a convenient thing to have. Many boards that use flash BIOSs, including motherboards, frequently use DOS utilities to update those BIOSs. Similarly, there are often DOS-based diagnostic programs for many hardware components. A FreeDOS (http://www.freedos.org) boot floppy is a trivial addition to any Linux system. If a vendor doesn't provide this feature, I recommend you obtain one yourself from the FreeDOS Web site. Alternatively, you can use an old copy of some other DOS, such as MS-DOS or PC-DOS.

- **Windows programs** If you want a dual-boot system, you might be able to add Windows software into the mix, such as Microsoft Office 2000 or WordPerfect Office 2000 for Windows.

- **Additional OSs** Some dealers will install more exotic OSs on your computer, such as OS/2 or BeOS.

- **Multi-OS utilities** PowerQuest's (http://www.powerquest.com) PartitionMagic is a particularly useful utility for maintaining a multi-OS computer. So is V Communications' (http://www.v-com.com) System Commander 2000.

If you intend to use Linux as your primary OS, some of these non-Linux programs are decidedly "icing on the cake." If features like Windows and Windows office suites are extremely important to you, you might want to consider buying a computer designed for Windows instead of a Linux computer. On the other hand, buying from a dealer who's competent to install both OSs can certainly save you some time and effort.

Obtaining Technical Support

One of the advantages of buying a computer that comes with Linux is that the vendor should support the computer after you've installed Linux. Windows-based computer manufacturers, by contrast, frequently deny any responsibility for problems after you install Linux (or any other unsupported OS, for that matter). If you don't want to live without technical support, therefore, a computer that hosts Linux to begin with can be a good buy.

The Vendor's Support Policy

You should check the details of the vendor's support policy before you buy. Some dealers—particularly small computer shops that mostly build Windows machines—offer little or nothing in the way of Linux-specific support. At a minimum, you should accept a willingness by the store to replace a suspect component within the warranty period without your having to install Windows to prove that there's a problem. The more familiar a store is with Linux, the more likely it is that the store will be able to provide competent support for the hardware when it's running Linux.

Some vendors rely on third parties, such as the distribution's support or contracted Linux consultants, to provide Linux support. Most Linux distributions come with very limited support, however, even in their boxed versions. These distributions typically include *installation* support, but as the computer's vendor has already installed Linux, this installation support won't do you much good. Therefore, if the vendor says that Linux support comes from the distribution maintainer, query further. Make sure that the vendor includes an extended support option in the price of the computer.

Larger firms and those that specialize in Linux frequently provide more in the way of Linux-specific support. You might be able to call and ask how to reconfigure your X server, for instance, and get an intelligible and correct answer. Some of these firms also offer technical support databases online, so you can pose your question in a Web form and—if you're lucky—get a helpful link or two.

Internet Newsgroup Support

As with many other things related to Linux, Usenet newsgroups can be a great form of support for Linux computers. You can use a newsreader such as Knews (shown in Figure 22.3) or the newsreader that comes with Netscape Communicator to read Usenet newsgroup postings on a wide variety of topics. You should follow the directions that come with your newsreader to configure it. You'll need to know the name of your Internet service provider's (ISP's) news server to use a newsreader.

Several newsgroups are potentially of interest to purchasers of Linux computers. These include

- **`comp.os.linux.hardware`**   This is potentially the most relevant newsgroup for people who buy Linux computers. Any Linux hardware-related topic is fair game here.
- **Other `comp.os.linux.*` groups**   Other groups in the `comp.os.linux.*` hierarchy can be relevant for specific components or topics. For instance, `comp.os.linux.networking` is a good place to post network-related questions.
- **X groups**   The `comp.windows.x.*` newsgroups are a good place to ask questions about configuring XFree86, or any other X server, to work with your hardware.

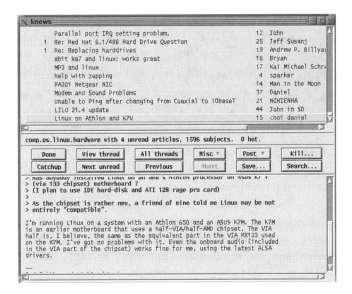

FIGURE 22.3
A newsreader lets you participate in Internet-based discussions on a wide variety of topics.

- **Data communication groups**   The comp.dcom.* newsgroups are devoted to data communication (hence *dcom*)—in other words, modems and similar devices. Many postings in these groups don't refer to Linux specifically, but Linux discussions do occasionally crop up in these groups.

- **CD-R groups**   The comp.publish.cdrom.* groups are devoted to discussions of CD-R technologies. Again, these groups aren't devoted to Linux, but Linux-related discussions are welcome.

- **PC hardware groups**   The comp.sys.ibm.pc.hardware.* hierarchy exists to facilitate discussion of x86 hardware. Specific groups are devoted to chipsets, video hardware, hard disks, and so on. This hierarchy is another that's not Linux-specific, but still useful.

- **Computer peripherals groups**   The alt.comp.periphs.* hierarchy isn't carried by all ISPs, but it contains a number of helpful groups devoted to various peripheral devices, such as printers, scanners, and motherboards. There's a smaller, but equally helpful, hierarchy called comp.periphs.*. These hierarchies are not Linux-specific, but you can post Linux-specific questions.

- `comp.lang.postscript`   This group is devoted to discussion of PostScript. It can be useful when you want to research PostScript printers for use by Linux. Again, Linux isn't the only OS used by readers of this group, but Linux questions are welcome.

- **Distribution-specific newsgroups**   Many distributions, including Red Hat, Caldera, Debian, and Mandrake, have their own newsgroups. Some of these are in the `alt.*` hierarchy; others are in the `linux.*` hierarchy. Corel maintains a set of newsgroups for its products on its own news server, `cnews.corel.com`. You must enter that name rather than your ISP's normal news server name to access these newsgroups.

When you post a question about your Linux computer to a newsgroup, include more than the manufacturer's name and model number. For the most part, the names of the manufacturer and model don't mean much to most readers. Instead, you should post details about the hardware that's giving you problems or about which you have a question. For instance, if you want to know how to add support for a new Ethernet card, you should include the make, model, and chipset of that card in your post. It's also often helpful to include the name and version of the Linux distribution you're using, and your kernel version. If you've taken any steps to resolve a problem, summarize them.

Usenet news can be a great way to get support. In fact, due largely to this forum, the Linux Internet community won the 1997 InfoWorld Best Technical Support award (`http://www.infoworld.com/cgi-bin/displayTC.pl?/97poy.supp.htm`).

Summary

Buying a computer with Linux preinstalled can be a great way to get up and running quickly with Linux. This approach can be particularly helpful if you need to buy many computers; for instance, if you need to set up an office with a dozen or more Linux machines. As with buying a computer that comes pre-installed with Windows, however, you can't be guaranteed of getting good hardware when you buy a Linux machine. You should therefore check out the hardware as much as you can before you buy. In addition, because Linux expertise is rarer than Windows expertise in the computer assembly business, you should investigate a dealer's Linux credentials. You might be better off installing Linux yourself if the vendor doesn't understand the OS well enough to do a competent job. Fortunately, there's a wide selection of competent dealers who sell computers with Linux preinstalled, and that selection is likely to increase in the future as Linux grows in popularity.

Notebooks

IN THIS CHAPTER

Desktop computers are very useful tools, but they suffer from a major problem for some functions: They're too large. There are many situations in which you might want to work at a computer, but can't use a desktop computer because it's too bulky.

It's for situations like this that portable computers of various types have been developed. The most common types of portable computers are known as *notebooks* or *laptops*. These devices are large enough to host a standard-sized keyboard and a liquid crystal display (LCD) of 10–15 inches. They also usually have a hard disk, CD-ROM drive, and floppy drive. Figure 23.1 shows a typical notebook computer.

FIGURE 23.1

A notebook computer is a bit smaller than a typical briefcase, and so is portable enough for many purposes.

Two excellent resources for information on running Linux on a notebook are `http://www.cs.utexas.edu/users/kharker/linux-laptop/` and `http://home.snafu.de/wehe/index.html`. The first of these sites includes links to a large number of other sites that report individuals' experiences running Linux on specific models of notebook computer. Both sites include additional information and general-purpose notebook links.

NOTE

Computers still smaller than notebooks exist. These *palmtop* computers have tiny or no keyboards, and usually rely upon touch-sensitive LCD screens for some or all input. Linux has been ported to a few of these devices, but it's not really usable on most. Samsung has developed a Linux-based palmtop. See `http://www.sem.samsung.com/eng/product/digital/pda/` for more information. The Web site `http://www.linux.org/projects/ports.html` has links to sites hosting ports of Linux to a wide variety of hardware, including palmtops.

A Comparison to Desktop Systems

Most notebook computers are sold with Windows preinstalled, so much of Chapter 21, "Store-Bought Non-Linux Systems," applies to these computers. If you look hard enough, you can find a few notebook computers with Linux preinstalled. Some of the dealers listed at `http://www.linux.org/vendors/systems.html` offer such computers.

Notebook computers have their own peculiarities compared to desktop systems. Most of these aren't particularly relevant to Linux, as compared to any other OS, but you should be aware of them nonetheless. A few notebook oddities do affect Linux operation or the selection of a computer for use with Linux, so you should pay particular attention to these areas.

CAUTION

The single most important thing to remember when buying a notebook computer is that it's often impossible to replace specific subsystems. It's therefore critically important that you fully investigate Linux support for all a computer's major components before you buy the computer.

Central Processing Unit

A computer's central processing unit (CPU) consumes a fair amount of the system's power. Most CPU manufacturers offer special low-power versions of their CPUs for use in notebooks. These CPUs are usually smaller and slower than desktop CPUs of similar cost, and occasionally they lack some of the more advanced features of desktop CPUs. None of these factors affects Linux compatibility, however.

In early 2000, notebook computers typically feature Intel Celeron, Intel Pentium-II, Intel Pentium-III, and AMD K6-2 CPUs. The fastest CPUs typically aren't available on notebook computers because of heat dissipation and power consumption issues. Notebook CPU speeds increase over time, but so do desktop CPU speeds, so the performance gap remains.

The Transmeta (http://www.transmeta.com) Crusoe CPU is an x86-compatible CPU that's been developed with portable devices in mind. It features very low power and heat dissipation requirements, so it appears to be well suited to use in notebooks. As I write this, however, the Crusoe is very new, and has yet to appear in many notebook computers.

Memory

Most notebook computers come with a certain amount of RAM soldered directly onto the system's motherboard. These systems usually feature a single socket for a memory upgrade SIMM or DIMM. These memory modules often use proprietary designs, although many of the latest computers have begun to settle on a standard laptop DIMM format, known as *SO-DIMM*. You should be extremely cautious when buying a memory upgrade; a DIMM that works in one computer might not work in another. Some online memory retailers include a memory selection system in which you specify what model computer you own, and the system locates the appropriate memory upgrade for you.

Some notebooks, instead of using a fixed amount of RAM soldered to the motherboard, use two SIMM or DIMM sockets, one of which contains memory when shipped from the factory. You can then replace the existing memory if you need to do so. For instance, you might upgrade a computer from 32MB to 96MB by adding a 64MB SO-DIMM, and later replace the original 32MB module with a 128MB module to bring your total RAM to 192MB.

Hard Disk

Modern notebook computers invariably use 2.5-inch EIDE hard disks. These devices are smaller and more expensive than their 3.5-inch cousins in desktop computers. Because of space constraints, laptop computers seldom include space for a second hard disk. When that option is available, it's usually a bay into which you can put a CD-ROM, floppy, or hard disk; you can't have all three installed at once.

There are no special Linux considerations for a notebook computer's hard disk. You should, however, make sure that Linux supports the motherboard chipset's direct memory access (DMA) disk access methods, as described in Chapter 5, "Hard Disks." If Linux doesn't support the chipset's DMA mode, you should still be able to use the disk under Linux, but you might not get the best possible speed out of it.

SCSI hard disks are virtually unheard-of in the notebook computer world. There are, however, a few SCSI PC Card adapters, so you can add external SCSI hard disks if you purchase a SCSI PC Card for which Linux drivers exist.

Removable Storage Media

Most notebook computers come with a floppy drive and a CD-ROM drive. Some models include these devices as removable components, so you can use only one at a time. On others, the drives are permanently attached to the computer, so you can use both at the same time. The latter design is preferable from a Linux point of view, because it can simplify installation. Most Linux installation CD-ROMs are bootable, however, and today most notebook computers support booting from bootable CD-ROMs, so this feature isn't as important as it once was.

An increasing number of notebook computers offer Zip or LS-120 drives as an option. Some include an LS-120 drive instead of a conventional floppy drive. Others let you remove a floppy or CD-ROM drive and slide the additional drive into the computer. Even if your computer doesn't support these options, you can add a removable media drive that interfaces through a parallel or USB port. SCSI devices are also an option if you use a SCSI PC Card. Chapter 6, "Removable Disks," discusses many of these options in detail.

Video Hardware

Video hardware is critically important to a Linux notebook computer purchaser. Because this hardware can't be replaced and is so basic to using a notebook computer, I recommend that you place video hardware compatibility at the very top of your list of things to investigate before purchasing a notebook computer. *Do not* buy a notebook computer unless you've found solid documentation about the capability of XFree86 (or, if you like, a commercial X server) to handle the computer's video chipset.

In order to save space, many notebook computer manufacturers use video chipsets that are integrated into the main motherboard chipset. For instance, the VIA MVP-4 chipset includes Trident Blade3D graphics support, and is used on many notebooks that use AMD K6-2 CPUs. There's no reason to avoid notebooks that use heavily integrated components like this, so long as you're sure that Linux supports all the chipset's integrated features, or at least the ones that are important to you.

Notebook computers come with integrated LCD screens. Low-end models frequently use passive matrix displays, usually at 800×600 resolution. Mid-range models use active matrix 800×600 displays, and high-end machines use 1024×768 active matrix panels. The active matrix designs consume more power than the passive matrix designs, but the result is a display that's brighter and viewable from a wider range of angles. Because so many Linux programs assume that the screen is at least 1024×768 in size, the larger display is unusually important in Linux. (For more information on LCD technologies, see Chapter 14, "Monitors.")

Serial, Parallel, and USB Ports

Most notebook computers have just one serial, one parallel, and one USB port, although some have two USB ports. One serial port is usually adequate because modern notebook computers include a built-in pointing device and usually a built-in modem. If you need additional ports, you might be able to use a USB hub or a serial or parallel switch box to accomplish the task. These devices sometimes require access to AC power, however, so you should consider your needs and shop appropriately.

Some notebook computers include one or two ports for PS/2 keyboards and mice. One-port models usually accept *either* a keyboard *or* a mouse, but not both.

TIP

If you want to add a full-size keyboard and mouse to your notebook computer, consider USB devices. Keyboards sold for the Macintosh market can be particularly convenient because they usually include a two-port hub, so you can connect three USB devices (including the keyboard) to a single USB port. Some high-end notebooks support *docking station* functions, in which you slide the notebook into a device that provides several additional ports, and sometimes even hard disks or other devices. You can use a notebook in conjunction with a docking station to provide functionality equivalent to a notebook and a separate desktop computer, but this combination can be more convenient because you need to maintain only one configuration.

PC Card Ports

PC Cards are small credit card-sized devices that slide into a notebook computer. (Figure 23.2 shows a typical PC Card device.) The PC Card bus is electronically very similar to an EIDE bus, but a PC Card bus is used for devices that attach to ISA or PCI busses on desktop computers—Ethernet adapters, SCSI adapters, modems, and so on. PC Card devices can be inserted into and removed from a computer quite easily; no tools are required, and the case need not be opened. It's therefore possible to swap a PC card device in and out much as you would a floppy disk. Linux supports a wide variety of PC Card devices.

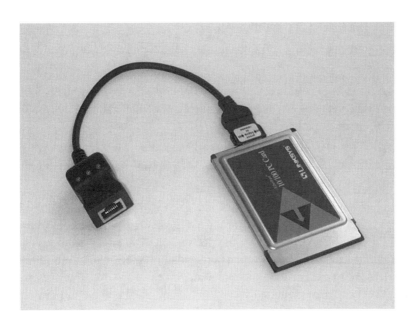

FIGURE 23.2
PC Card devices are very thin, so they often use short cables to provide connectors, as in the Ethernet jack on this PC Card Ethernet adapter.

> **NOTE**
>
> *PC Card* used to be named after the organization that originated the standard, the *Personal Computer Memory Card International Association* (PCMCIA). Most Linux documentation continues to use this name for the technology. Most manufacturers, however, now use the term *PC Card* instead. I follow this convention in this book.

PC Card Hardware

PC Card slots typically reside on one side of the computer. You slide the PC Card device into the computer much as you would a floppy disk. If all goes well, when the device locks in place, Linux detects it and loads the appropriate drivers. You can then use the device without further ado.

There are several varieties of PC Card connectors:

- **Type I**   Type I PC Cards are no thicker than 3.3mm. They're typically used for memory devices.
- **Type II**   Type II PC Cards can be up to 5.0mm thick. They're typically used for modems, Ethernet adapters, and other non-memory, all-electronic devices. Type II cards are today's most commonly used type.
- **Type III**   These PC Cards can be up to 10.5mm thick. They're generally used for devices with moving internal components, such as hard disks. Type IIIcards are quite rare.

Each of these types of PC Card is the same width and length. As a result, you can use a Type I card in a Type II or III slot, or a Type II card in a Type III slot. Most notebook computers have one or two PC Card slots. A typical configuration includes two slots, one of which supports only a Type I device, the other of which supports either a Type I or a Type II device. Because PC Card devices are so easily added and removed, you can own several devices and swap them in and out of the computer as required.

In addition to the preceding physical form factors, there are several different electronic and logic standards for PC Cards:

- **PCMCIA 1.0**   Defines the Type I and Type II form factors, as well as the basic characteristics of PC Cards
- **PCMCIA 2.0–2.1**   Define the Type III form factor, ATA interface, and assorted other advanced features
- **PC Card standard**   Further refines the PCMCIA 2.0–2.1 standards, adding support for 32-bit operation, 3.3-volt support, and other features

You can learn more about these form factors and standards, as well as variant technologies such as CardBus and SmartMedia, at `http://www.pc-card.com`.

NOTE

You can add a PC Card adapter to a desktop system. As a general rule, there's no reason to do so, because PC Cards are more expensive than equivalent devices in ISA or PCI card format. If you can share devices between a desktop and notebook computer, however, it might make sense to add a PC Card slot to a desktop system.

Linux PC Card Support

The 2.2.x kernel series includes essentially no support for PC Card devices. Instead, a separate package of kernel modules is available from the Linux PC Card site, `http://pcmcia.sourceforge.org`. You can obtain these drivers and install them separately from the kernel. When installed, these drivers work as if they were normal kernel modules. In the 2.3.x kernel, drivers for some PC Card devices exist in the main kernel. PC Card Ethernet adapter support, for instance, exists in the Network device support, PCMCIA network device support kernel menu. For other uses, such as PC Card hard disk support, you must still acquire the separate PC Card support package.

PC Cards are designed to be *hot-swappable*—that is, you can insert or remove them when the computer is powered on. This fact presents certain challenges to Linux, which tends to assume devices won't disappear unexpectedly. Therefore, PC Card support in Linux requires special software. This support is provided by a feature known as *Card Services*, which is available from the Linux PC Card site. When installed, Card Services controls PC Card access through files in the `/etc/pcmcia` directory. There's a script in this directory for each type of PC Card— for instance, `network` and `ide`.

> **NOTE**
>
> Devices such as palmtop computers and digital cameras frequently use *Compact Flash* (CF) or SmartMedia cards for storage. These devices are *not* hard disks, but they can look like PC Card EIDE hard disks when coupled with an appropriate adapter. You can therefore use Linux's PC Card support to access these storage media. You can use this feature to read images you've recorded with a digital camera because these devices use the FAT filesystem.

Fortunately, most Linux distributions ship with PC Card support enabled by default. You therefore don't normally need to be concerned with starting Card Services yourself.

When you insert or remove a PC Card, Card Services runs the appropriate script in `/etc/pcmcia`. This script shuts down or starts up whatever functions are required for the device. For instance, when you insert a PC Card Ethernet adapter, Card Services loads the PC Card's kernel driver and then activates the Ethernet interface, including assigning its IP address, setting a default route, and so on. When you eject that Ethernet card, Card Services shuts down the interface, removes the interface's routing table entries, and so on.

The Importance of Audio/Video Support

When you buy a desktop computer, you almost always have the option of replacing trouble-some components. For instance, if your video card doesn't work to your satisfaction, you can remove it and install another card. Some desktop systems support some features through chipsets built in to the motherboard, but you can usually disable these features and install a separate card to handle these functions. Not so with notebooks. Because of the severe space constraints, notebook computers don't include conventional ISA or PCI slots. To some extent you can use a PC Card or possibly an external device to work around non-functional integrated components, such as a modem. Sound and video, however, can be virtually impossible to replace. It's critically important that any notebook computer you purchase use a video chipset that's supported by XFree86 or a commercial Linux X server. You might or might not consider sound support to be so critical but, if you do, you must be equally sure that Linux supports your computer's sound hardware.

Locating Support for Your Hardware

Fortunately, most notebook manufacturers make it clear what video hardware they use. Ads for notebook computers typically include this information. Because the video support is integrated into the motherboard, the ads usually specify the video chipset that's in use. This is precisely what you need to know to locate a Linux driver, as described in Chapter 12, "Video Cards," and Appendix A, "Linux Device Drivers."

Sound chipsets are not always advertised quite as clearly as are video chipsets. Many manufac-turers merely report that their notebooks have "SoundBlaster-compatible" sound, or they trum-pet the manufacturer of the *speakers*, but don't mention who makes the sound chipset in use. In some cases the sound chipset is integrated into the motherboard chipset, and isn't well known to consumers. Many notebook computers sold in 2000 that use VIA chipsets, for instance, incorporate sound support from the VIA 82c686a, which is incorporated into some of VIA's recent motherboard chipsets.

In the case of both video and audio chipsets, you can usually find what the computer uses if you can access the computer when it's running Windows. To do so, open the System item in the Windows Control Panel, as shown in Figure 23.3. Click the Device Manager tab and then click the plus signs next to the Display adapters and Sound, video and game controllers items to reveal the video and audio chipsets used by the computer. In the case of the computer used to create Figure 23.3, the display adapter is a Trident CyberBlade i7, and the audio support comes from a VIA PCI audio controller.

Of course, if you want to find what hardware a notebook computer uses *before* you buy it, this method requires that you have access to the computer. Most local computer stores run display samples of notebook computers, so you can usually check the hardware before you buy. This might not be possible for mail-order hardware, however. In this case, you might need to rely on the sales staff or some other resource. The Linux on Laptops Web page (`http://www.cs.utexas.edu/users/kharker/linux-laptop/`) is particularly useful in this respect. This Web page includes links to a large number of descriptions of Linux systems run on a wide variety of notebook computers. Many of these individual pages include links to the `XF86Config` files that the maintainers use. You can then download these files and use them yourself if you buy the same or a similar computer, thus saving you some time and effort configuring XFree86.

FIGURE 23.3
The Device Manager tab in the Windows System Properties dialog box can reveal the chipsets used by a notebook's audio and video hardware.

If you buy a new notebook that's not listed on one of these pages, you can do others a great favor by putting together a Web page describing your experiences and submitting it for inclusion on the Linux on Laptops page. Even a brief description stating that the computer works, and specifying your distribution, can be helpful.

When you know what chipsets a notebook computer uses for audio and video features, you can go looking for support for those chipsets. Chapters 10, "Sound Cards" and 12 can help you in this respect, as can Appendix A. In brief, though, you should check several Web sites and other resources for information:

- **The Linux on Laptops Web page**   If the computer you're considering is listed on this page, you can generally find the information you need there.

- **The Linux kernel configuration options**   Check the Linux kernel sound configuration options for standard support for your sound hardware.

- **The Shareware OSS site**   Check `http://www.4front-tech.com` for information on commercial Linux sound drivers.

- **The ALSA site**   Check `http://www.alsa-project.org` for information on the *Advanced Linux Sound Architecture* (ALSA) drivers.

- **The XFree86 site**   Check `http://www.xfree86.org` for information on video support in XFree86. You might need to dig a bit on this site to find the information you require.

- **The SuSE site**   SuSE (`http://www.suse.com`) contributes a lot to the XFree86 project, and often makes early versions of its XFree86 drivers available from its own site.

- **The Accelerated-X site**   Accelerated-X, from Xi Graphics (`http://www.xig.com`), is a commercial alternative to XFree86.

- **The Metro-X site**   Metro-X, from MetroLink (`http://www.metrolink.com`), is another commercial alternative to XFree86.

If you think it's *likely* that you can make a notebook's hardware work under Linux, but you're not positive you'll succeed, you might still consider buying the computer. I recommend doing so only from a store with a good return policy, however. If you think you might need to use software with which you're not familiar, you might want to try that software on a desktop system, if possible, before buying the notebook. For instance, if your target notebook's sound chipset is supported by ALSA but not by the standard kernel drivers, you might want to try ALSA on another system, simply to familiarize yourself with it.

Replacement Hardware

If your video chipset doesn't work under XFree86, you might still be able to use the computer in text mode. To use X programs, you'll need to link the computer to a network and use an X server running on another computer. That's not very convenient for a notebook, but it might be acceptable in a pinch.

If your audio chipset doesn't work under Linux, your options are somewhat broader, although still not good. Two possibilities are

- **USB speakers**   These devices don't work through a standard sound card; instead, the sound card functions are included in the speakers themselves. You'll need to lug the speakers around with you wherever you go, or at least wherever you want sound support. You'll also need to use a 2.3.x or later kernel, or apply a back-port of the 2.3.x USB support to a 2.2.x kernel.

- **PC Card sound card**   There are a small number of PC Card sound cards on the market. Most of these aren't well supported in Linux, however. For the latest information, check `http://pcmcia.sourceforge.org/ftp/SUPPORTED.CARDS`, which has links to information on supported PC Cards and projects to add new support. As with USB speakers, you'll need to carry around a set of conventional external speakers.

> **NOTE**
>
> Many notebook computers include 1/8-inch jacks for speakers or headphones. Therefore, if your internal sound card works fine but you don't like the quality of speakers, you can use separate speakers or headphones. If you want portable speakers, you should be sure to get a model that supports operation on battery power, not just wall power.

Input/Output

Most input/output devices on notebook computers function much like their counterparts on desktop systems. A few comments are in order concerning specific devices, however:

- **Ethernet**   Most notebook computers don't come with Ethernet built in. If you have a built-in Ethernet adapter, be sure it's adequate to your needs. I don't recommend buying a new notebook with built-in 10Mbps-only Ethernet, because 100Mbps speeds are now common. 10/100Mbps PC Card Ethernet adapters are common, and most are well supported in Linux. Check `http://pcmcia.sourceforge.org/ftp/SUPPORTED.CARDS` for details on specific models.

- **Modem**   Most notebook computers today come with built-in modems. Unfortunately, most of these modems are software modems, many of which have no Linux support. What's worse, manufacturers do not generally advertise what modem chipsets they use, so you might have no clue what you're getting until you get the machine. If you can check the computer in a store, though, the Modem item in the Windows System Properties dialog box (refer to Figure 23.3) can be helpful. Check `http://www.linmodems.org` for information on software modems supported under Linux. Fortunately, PC Card modems are fairly common, and many of these are not software modems, so you can bypass a software modem if necessary. Be sure to check that the PC Card modem is supported in Linux, though, because some are software modems. You can also use a conventional external RS-232 serial modem or a Linux-supported USB modem. Most such devices require wall power, however, and they're bulkier than a PC Card modem.

- **Keyboard and mouse**   Many notebook computers have a connector for PS/2-style keyboards and mice. You can also use USB devices on notebooks that are equipped with USB ports.

Power Management Software

Notebook computers come with nicked-cadmium (NiCd), nickel metal hydride (NiMH), or lithium ion (LIon) batteries. As a general rule, NiCd batteries aren't used on modern notebooks, although you might find them on older models. Today's low-end models generally use NiMH batteries, whereas higher-end devices use LIon batteries. LIon batteries have higher capacities and suffer less from "memory" effects than do NiMH batteries.

> **CAUTION**
>
> There's little standardization in notebook computer batteries. A battery designed for one computer usually doesn't work in another. The main exceptions are in closely related computers from the same manufacturer.

In order to make batteries last as long as possible, most notebook computers implement a number of power-saving features. These features generally require communication between the hardware and the OS, and these features are often mediated by the BIOS. In Linux, they're implemented through the *Advanced Power Management Daemon* (APMD) package. The main APMD site for Linux is `http://www.worldvisions.ca/~apenwarr/apmd/`.

Linux Kernel Options

APMD requires a number of kernel options to function properly. You can activate these options in the General setup kernel configuration menu. Specific options you should consider include

- **Advanced Power Management BIOS support**   This option is required. Without it, none of the other options are available.

- **Enable PM at boot time**   Responding Y to this option enables most power management features. For instance, with this option enabled, the computer enters a power-saving sleep mode after a certain period of time.

- **Make CPU Idle calls when idle**   This option can sometimes improve power savings slightly, by putting the CPU in a low-power mode if it's not been used for a while.

- **Enable console blanking using APM**   If you regularly work in text mode, enable this option. It tells the system to blank the screen using APM BIOS calls, which can save battery power. If you don't enable this option, the screen goes blank, but it's still powered.

- **Power off on shutdown**   Enable this option to have the computer power itself off when you shut it down with a command such as **shutdown now -h**. If you don't enable this option, you'll need to use a manual power-off procedure, such as holding down the power switch for several seconds.
- **RTC stores time in GMT**   If your notebook computer runs *only* Linux, you might want to store the system time as *Greenwich Mean Time* (GMT), which is the norm for UNIX systems. This procedure can cause glitches for power management, however, unless you enable this feature. If you choose to keep your hardware clock set to local time rather than GMT, you should set this option to N.

You might also need to use some of the other APM support options. Most of the remaining options are workarounds for bugs in various APM BIOSs, or are specialized options for rare situations.

Most Linux distributions come with a reasonable array of APM kernel options enabled. You therefore might not need to adjust these options. You should keep them in mind if and when you recompile your kernel, however.

The APM Daemon

APMD interfaces with the APM BIOS in order to provide APM services in Linux. Most Linux distributions ship with APMD configured to behave in a reasonable manner for both notebook and desktop systems, so you probably don't need to adjust your APMD configuration. If you do want to adjust the configuration, you can edit the timeout values in your computer's BIOS. How you enter the BIOS varies from one computer to another, so consult your documentation on this detail.

You can manually query the APM configuration and issue APM commands using the apm program. Typing **apm** by itself produces a status report on the battery power, and typing **apm -s** puts the computer into *suspend mode*. In suspend mode, the computer consumes a small trickle of power, but the hard disk is powered down, the display is turned off, and the computer is generally dormant. You can wake the computer up again by pressing a key. Many computers include a special keystroke to enable suspend mode.

There are assorted X-based interfaces to APM functions, such as kapm (part of the KDE package) and xapm (which comes with some APMD packages). These interfaces provide a constant on-screen indication of the status of the battery. They can also sometimes suspend the system.

Hard Disk Power Conservation

A notebook computer's hard disk accounts for a large part of its power consumption. You can use the hdparm utility to configure the hard disk to go into a low-power mode after a specified period of time, as described in Chapter 5. To summarize, you issue the hdparm command with the -S parameter in order to tell the system to power down the hard disk after a specified period. Table 23.1 summarizes the meanings of the -S parameter. As an example, **hdparm -S 24** powers down the hard disk after 120 seconds (2 minutes).

TABLE 23.1 hdparm -S Options for Hard Disk Spindown Times

Values	Meaning
0	Energy-saving power-down disabled (drive is always fully active).
1–240	Multiples of 5 seconds; for instance, 6 means 30 seconds.
241–251	1–11 units of 30 minutes, for times ranging from 0.5–5.5 hours.
252	21 minutes.
253	Vendor-defined timeout value.
255	21 minutes and 15 seconds.

If you regularly use your notebook computer on battery power, it's important that you find a good hard disk power-down time for the way you use the system. If the period is too long, you'll waste battery power needlessly on keeping the hard disk spinning. If the period is too short, you'll end up being annoyed by the delays when the system awakens the hard disk. Because every individual's usage patterns are different, you'll have to experiment to find a good value.

NOTE

Linux systems tend to access the hard disk more than Windows systems do. For instance, Linux maintains various *log files* (located in the /var/log directory tree), in which it stores important system events, such as logins, server activity, and so on. Even if you aren't actively using the computer, it's possible that various daemons and other background processes will perform disk accesses, thus resetting the clock on the hard disk power-down timer. Likewise, these events can cause the hard disk to spring to life even if you're not using the computer.

Summary

It's possible to run Linux on many modern (and not-so-modern) notebook computers. In fact, Linux can use advanced notebook-centric features such as APM and PC Cards, thus providing a good notebook experience. You must be unusually cautious when you choose a notebook computer, however, because it's difficult or impossible to replace certain critical hardware components on a notebook computer. Prime among these is the video chipset, but the sound chipset is also quite difficult to replace. Therefore, before you buy a notebook, I strongly recommend that you check on hardware compatibility before buying. If you can't find reports from existing Linux owners of a given model, learn what chipsets the notebook uses, particularly for video and sound, and thoroughly investigate those chipsets with respect to Linux support. These steps can save you hours of grief or the need to return the computer.

23

NOTEBOOKS

Appendixes

IN THIS PART

Linux Device Drivers

IN THIS APPENDIX

Locating device drivers for Linux can be a challenging task. Most hardware manufacturers don't advertise Linux support for their hardware, in part because the manufacturers themselves don't support Linux. Lack of manufacturer support for Linux doesn't mean that the hardware doesn't work in Linux, however. It does usually mean that you must dig a bit to find out if Linux supports the hardware and, if so, where to find appropriate drivers. This appendix presents an in-depth examination of the process of finding drivers for a device. Information on specific devices, including useful Web sites and peculiarities of device types, appears in the relevant chapters of this book. This appendix is best used if you haven't found drivers after an initial check, and need to dig deeper.

Determining a Device's Chipset

For most expansion boards, including video, sound, Ethernet, SCSI, and software modem boards, the key to locating Linux drivers is knowing what chipset the device uses. The *chipset* is one or more chips on the product that provide most or all the board's core functionality. Most hardware manufacturers purchase chipsets from other manufacturers, and then slap the chipsets on circuit boards and sell the product under their own names. Although the design of the circuit board and additional features such as ROMs can make a difference in the performance of the product, it's the chipset for which a Linux driver is written.

For some products, the chipset isn't terribly important. Some of these, such as most serial- and parallel-port cards, use highly standardized chipsets, so there's no need to locate special drivers. (Multiport serial cards are an exception to this rule.) Other devices, such as printers and scanners, are complex enough that compatibility is described in terms of characteristics other than a chipset, such as the *printer language* used by a printer. Some of the chipset-determination procedures I'm about to describe can be useful for these devices, but, in general, you should try to locate drivers based on these devices' model numbers. Check the relevant chapters in this book for details.

As a general rule, the chipset is important for devices you plug into an ISA or PCI slot. For external devices, you should look for drivers based on the device model number or type. Most disk devices (hard disks, floppy disks, CD-ROM drives, and so on) work through a controller in a motherboard or on an expansion card. The disk devices themselves almost never require device-specific drivers.

Asking About the Chipset

People often overlook what is, in hindsight, the most obvious course of action. In the case of identifying a device's chipset, this is generally asking the manufacturer about it. You might not need to actually walk into an office or place a phone call to do this. Manufacturers often make chipset information available on their Web sites or in documentation. In my experience, manufacturers of video cards are most likely to do this, but manufacturers of other devices might do it, too.

Unfortunately, some manufacturers treat the chipsets they use as if they were trade secrets. You can sometimes still extract information from other people, but by asking people *other than* the manufacturer. The contributors to Usenet newsgroups devoted to Linux hardware, or to particular types of devices, can be good people to start with. I recommend searching on Deja News, `http://www.deja.com/usenet/`, before posting a message. It's stunning how frequently questions about the chipsets used particular products come up in frequently visited hardware newsgroups.

In some cases, manufacturers *change* the chipsets used on their products without altering the name of the product. You might therefore find that you get a product that's different from what you expect, particularly if you base your expectations on just one or two responses to a Usenet news posting, or to knowledge gleaned from a friend or co-worker. I therefore recommend looking for several responses to a chipset query before making a purchase.

Physical Examination

One way to determine what chipset a board uses is to examine the device. There are usually one or two chips on the board that are distinguished by their large size. These chips are usually the components of the chipset. For instance, Figure A.1 shows an ISA sound card. Its main chip is located near the center of the board. Figure A.2 shows a close-up of this chip, so you can more easily read its markings. This chip is clearly identified as an AMD InterWave chip, part number AM78C201KC.

> **NOTE**
>
> On most expansion cards, the chipset is composed of a single chip. Motherboard chipsets often include two or more chips, as do the chipsets on some older products. Some devices—particularly sound cards—use two separate but interlocking chipsets. Motherboards that include audio, video, or other non-standard functions often do so by placing independent chipsets on the same motherboard. Some motherboard chipsets incorporate these extra functions, however, which can reduce manufacturing costs.

As a general rule, the chipset name or part number appears in the first line or two of text printed on the chip's surface. Sometimes subsequent lines can be important, however, so if you're in doubt, I recommend you write down everything you see on the chip. Likewise, if you see two chips that are roughly the same size, write down whatever is printed on both of them.

A

LINUX DEVICE DRIVERS

FIGURE A.1

As the chip or chips that provide most of a board's functionality, the chipset components are larger than most others on the circuit board.

Some board manufacturers place stickers over their main chipset parts, as if to lay claim to the chipset. You can safely peel away such stickers to discover whatever's printed on the chip. If you see a clear window underneath the sticker, though, replace the sticker. Such windows appear on some older *erasable programmable read-only memory* (EPROM) chips. Such chips store important data, such as a motherboard's BIOS. If you expose them to ultraviolet light, you'll erase that data. The sticker is present to prevent accidental erasure. EPROMs are rare on modern components, however; they've been largely replaced by the more sophisticated *electronically erasable PROMs* (EEPROMs), which have no clear windows.

CAUTION

Some chipsets—particularly those on high-performance motherboards and video cards—run at fast enough speeds that they require special cooling. These chipsets typically come with heat sinks attached, much like small CPUs. If the heat sink is glued onto the chip, *do not* attempt to remove it! Doing so might damage the chip, or cause damage later when it overheats.

FIGURE A.2

Chipset markings typically contain cryptic part numbers and often company names or logos.

Some manufacturers remove the chipset makers' name and part number from a chip and replace it with their own. If you see the board maker's name silkscreened on a chip, there's a good chance this is what's happened. Some large manufacturers, however, such as Intel, genuinely produce both expansion cards and the chips that go on those cards.

Unfortunately, the names and part numbers printed on chips can sometimes be cryptic. You might need to do a Web search to discover what these chips are. Try entering any names or part numbers you've found on the chip into search engines, such as those at http://www.yahoo.com or http://www.excite.com. The Deja News site, http://www.deja.com/usenet/, can also be a useful search tool. Don't try just the complete part number, but also try truncated versions of it. For instance, instead of `AM78C201KC`, try `AM78C201` and `78C201`. (In the case of the InterWave chip depicted in Figure A.2, the string `InterWave` is most likely to produce helpful results.)

A

Checking Probes in Windows

If the computer runs Windows, you can often find useful information about the chipsets on assorted devices by double-clicking the System icon in the Windows 95 or 98 Control Panel. The System Properties dialog box, shown in Figure A.3, will open. Click the Device Manager tab. You can then expand any device category you like to discover what hardware the device uses. For instance, Figure A.3 shows that the computer uses a Trident CyberBlade i7 video card, a VIA bus master IDE controller, and a Lucent DF software modem.

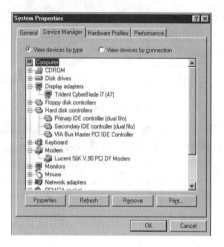

FIGURE A.3
The Windows 95/98 System Properties dialog box can reveal a lot about the hardware installed in a computer.

Other OSs often contain similar means of revealing the installed hardware. For instance, Windows 2000 provides this functionality through its Device Manager, which you can access from the System Properties dialog box in the Control Panel (see Figure A.4).

One trouble with locating chipset information from a running OS is that the information you find in this way might or might not uniquely identify the chipset. Basically, the information you see in the System Properties dialog box comes from the device's driver. As such, if a manufacturer distributes its own driver, the manufacturer can present its own name in the System Properties dialog box, rather than the name of the chipset manufacturer. This is less likely to be the case if the device uses a driver installed from the OS instead of a driver provided by the manufacturer.

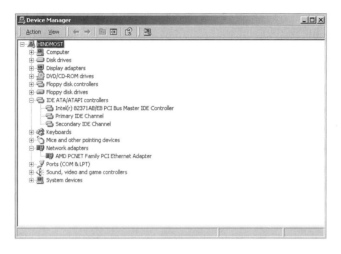

FIGURE A.4
Windows 2000 presents much the same information as does Windows 95/98 about hardware, but in a slightly different form.

Checking Device Driver Files for Windows

You can examine device driver files for Windows, or for some other OS, for clues concerning the chipset used by the underlying hardware. Unfortunately, there are no guarantees about where you might find relevant information. Possibilities include the following:

- **Filenames**   Driver filenames occasionally include clues concerning the device chipset names. Try doing an Internet search on these filenames (sans extensions) to see if anything turns up.

- **Text file contents**   The contents of text files, such as .inf files, can include chipset names. These names can appear in comments or in device description lines.

- **Binary file contents**   You can use the Linux strings command to extract any plain ASCII that's present in binary driver files. These files can contain a chipset's name. Unfortunately, you'll have to wade through a lot of irrelevant strings before you come across a chipset name.

One of the problems with extracting device identification information from existing drivers is that it's not always obvious what the chipset name or number is, even when you're looking directly at it. As a general rule, chipsets are identified by numbers, often preceded by a letter or two as a shorthand for the manufacturer name. These numbers sometimes include a *C* embedded within them. The number string is also often terminated by one or more letters. The

A

LINUX DEVICE
DRIVERS

InterWave chip depicted in Figure A.2 fits this description. Other chipsets don't bear all these characteristics. For instance, the MX98715 is a Macronix Ethernet chipset. This part number lacks an embedded *C* and trailing letters, but otherwise fits this description. If you're lucky, you'll only find a few possible strings in the driver files you examine.

Locating Drivers in the Linux Kernel

As a general rule, you want to look for a driver in the Linux kernel after you have identified a device's chipset. In some cases, you might want to search for a driver using the methods I'm about to describe when you've only identified *potential* chipset names or numbers. For instance, you might have two or three strings you've extracted from visual identification, the Windows System Properties dialog box, or examination of Windows device driver files. You can look for each potential name in turn.

Broad Classes of Driver Support

One method of locating a driver is to start a kernel configuration session and browse the available drivers. You can begin a configuration session with one of three methods, each of which requires that you use a shell prompt in the Linux kernel directory (usually `/usr/src/linux`):

- `make config`   This method runs a configuration script that asks you about each configuration option in turn. This method is extremely tedious, especially if you want to search for a device driver.

- `make menuconfig`   This procedure starts a text-based kernel configuration menu. You can use the cursor keys, the Enter key, the Tab key, and so on to move around in the menu structure to select configuration options. This method is generally easy to use, and is my preferred method of configuring a kernel from a text-mode login, Telnet session, and so on.

- `make xconfig`   This method starts an X-based kernel configuration session, as shown in Figure A.5. `make menuconfig` and `make xconfig` are quite similar in their features, but the latter is usually more convenient if you're running X.

NOTE

In comparison to the 2.2.x kernel menu, shown in Figure A.5, the 2.3.x kernel menu consolidates some categories as subcategories of other options, thus reducing clutter on the main menu.

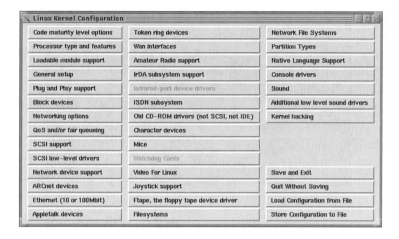

FIGURE A.5
The Linux 2.2.x kernel configuration menu has many option categories.

When you select a specific category of hardware, such as Ethernet (10 or 100Mbit), you get a new menu that displays choices relevant to that class of hardware, as shown in Figure A.6. As a general rule, this menu names hardware based on the chipsets' most common names. These names can be numeric part numbers, such as *dc21x4x*, or "nicknames," such as *Tulip* or *Rhine*. Sometimes an option isn't available until you've selected another option. In most cases, you can click the Help button (or choose the Help item if you use `make config` or `make menuconfig`) to read a description of what the driver or option does (see Figure A.7). This description sometimes includes additional information on the chipsets for which a driver can be used.

Searching for chipset support by browsing the Linux kernel is fairly inefficient, but it can be quite informative. By reading a variety of help items or even just browsing device names, you can familiarize yourself with Linux's capabilities and supported devices. If you subsequently do more research to find a driver, you might recognize a name from your previous kernel configuration option browsing, and therefore locate a driver.

Using `grep` to Find a Driver

Linux includes a tool that's very useful for finding a file that contains a particular string: `grep`. This tool is very powerful, but for the purposes of this discussion, its syntax is fairly simple:

```
grep [-r] searchstring files
```

A

LINUX DEVICE
DRIVERS

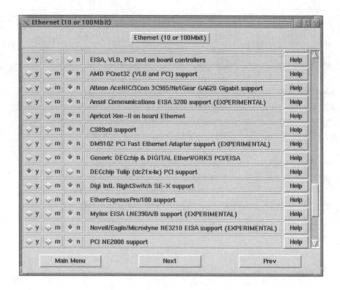

FIGURE A.6

Each kernel configuration submenu includes a list of specific drivers or kernel options.

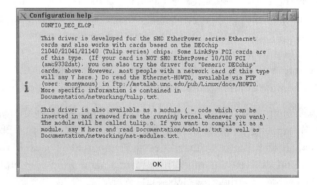

FIGURE A.7

Kernel configuration help often provides useful clues about what a driver or option does.

You should consult the grep man page for more information on additional grep options. The specific components of this command that I've highlighted here are

- **-r** The optional -r parameter tells grep to perform a recursive search. If you omit this parameter, grep doesn't search subdirectories. If you include this parameter, the program searches all subdirectories specified by the *files* parameter.

> **NOTE**
>
> The `-r` parameter is a recent addition to grep's repertoire. If you try this parameter and it doesn't work, you might need to update your version of grep.

- ***searchstring*** The string for which you're searching. For instance, if you want to find drivers for the InterWave chipset, you might use *InterWave*, *Interwave*, or *interwave* as a search string. You might need to try several variants, including strings with variant case, before you find a match. If you want to find a string that includes a space, enclose the *entire* search string in quotation marks.
- ***files*** The files and directories you want to search. From the /usr/src/linux directory, you might want to use drivers as the *files* parameter, at least if you use the -r parameter. You can use wildcards such as ? and * to search a group of files or directories.

I recommend you search the /usr/src/linux/drivers and /usr/src/linux/Documentation directories for any likely chipset names or numbers. In the case of numbers, you might want to omit leading and trailing letters, because these are often omitted in chipset documentation. As an example, suppose you have in your hands an Ethernet board that uses the MX98715 chipset I mentioned earlier. You might perform the following search:

```
$ grep -r 98715 drivers/
drivers/net/tulip.c:  { "Macronix 98715 PMAC",
drivers/net/tulip.c:  { "Macronix 98715 PMAC", 256, 0x0001ebef,
```

(The search returns several additional hits in the drivers/net/tulip.c file.) You can check the tulip.c file for more details, but the gist is clear: The MX98715 is a clone of the DEC Tulip chipset, and is supported by the tulip.c driver file. You can then go into the Linux kernel configuration menus and enable support for the relevant driver, which is visible in Figure A.5. (The menu options usually bear some resemblance to the driver filename. If they don't, check the help option for all the drivers; there should be some clue there.)

Tracking Down Experimental and Third-Party Drivers

If you've got a particularly new or unusual board, you might have little choice but to use an experimental or third-party driver. Some of these drivers come with the Linux kernel, but require you to select Y to the Code maturity level options, Prompt for development and Incomplete code/drivers. Other experimental drivers, though, *do not* come with the Linux kernel. You must track these drivers down in other ways, which can be a challenge. You must then either compile them separately or integrate the changes into your kernel and recompile the kernel.

Web-Based Sources for Driver Information

Specific chapters of this book include information on popular clearinghouses for drivers for specific devices. There are a few general-purpose Web sites, as well as sites that are particularly important for specific types of devices. These include the following:

- **The Linux kernel site** `http://www.kernel.org` is the official site of the Linux kernel. You won't find non-kernel drivers on this site, but you will find the latest kernels, including *development* kernels. In Linux kernel development, kernels with even second numbers (such as 2.0.3 and 2.2.14) are considered *stable*. Kernels with odd second numbers (such as 2.1.7 and 2.3.48) are *development* kernels. Development kernels are at least potentially unstable, but they usually contain more drivers than stable kernels. You therefore might want to check a development kernel for new or updated drivers.

- **The Linux Hardware Components site**   Check `http://www.linux.org/hardware/components.html` for a list of companies that make Linux drivers available, and a list of projects related to Linux hardware development. Some, but not all, of these links lead to new and experimental drivers that aren't present in the kernel.

- **The ALSA Project site**   The Advanced Linux Sound Architecture (ALSA) project is dedicated to producing an alternative set of sound drivers for Linux. This project's Web site is located at `http://www.alsa-project.org`. The ALSA drivers are officially beta-test and therefore experimental, but in practice they're quite stable, on the whole.

- **The OSS site**   4Front Technologies (`http://www.4front-tech.com`) offers a set of shareware sound card drivers for Linux. Most of these Open Sound System (OSS) drivers aren't really experimental, but they are alternatives to the usual Linux drivers.

- **The Linux USB site**   `http://www.linux-usb.org` is the official home of USB development for Linux. In the 2.2.x kernels, USB support is minimal. The 2.3.x kernels include more in the way of USB support, and this site documents these developments. You can also obtain a port of the 2.3.x USB drivers to a 2.2.x kernel from this site. After 2.3.x stabilizes into 2.4.x (which is expected by the end of 2000), USB development will no doubt continue in the 2.5.x kernel series. Chances are the Linux USB site will then make 2.5.x USB drivers available for 2.4.x kernels.

- **The LinModems site**   `http://www.linmodems.org` is the best site for information on, and drivers for, software modems.

- **SuSE X servers**   SuSE develops XFree86 drivers, and usually offers these drivers from its Web site, at `http://www.suse.de/en/support/xsuse/`, before they're available from XFree86. As a general rule, the drivers SuSE makes available are quite stable.

- **SANE drivers**   Linux scanner support comes from the *Scanner Access Now Easy* (SANE) project, which is hosted at `http://www.mostang.com/sane/`. Check here for pointers to experimental SANE drivers. The Linux USB site, mentioned earlier, also has links to SANE drivers for USB scanners.

- **Ghostscript drivers**   Most Linux distributions ship with GNU Ghostscript, which is typically a few months behind the latest version of Aladdin Ghostscript. You can update from `http://www.cs.wisc.edu/~ghost`. You can also find information on this site about unofficial Ghostscript drivers. Another extremely useful site is `http://www.picante.com/~gtaylor/pht/printer_list.cgi`, a site that contains a database of printers, including pointers to unusual Ghostscript drivers.

With any luck, one of the preceding links will take you to the information you need. If not, check the chapter on the relevant device. I've included many URLs for driver development projects throughout this book.

> **CAUTION**
>
> Experimental drivers can be extremely dangerous. A bug in a driver can crash your computer, corrupt data on your hard disk, or otherwise cause serious problems. Many of the drivers you'll find at the preceding sites are quite stable, but some aren't. Exercise caution when you use any experimental driver.

Checking with the Manufacturer

An increasing number of manufacturers support Linux, either directly by sponsoring driver development or indirectly by distributing Linux drivers written by others. Sometimes the manufacturer merely makes available drivers that already come with the Linux kernel, but other times the drivers are patched or are more recent versions than those that come with the kernel. If you're having trouble with a standard driver, it's worth trying the driver provided by the manufacturer. At the very least, it's worth checking to see if it's the same driver that comes with the kernel. If not, that might indicate a patch by the manufacturer to improve compatibility or performance.

You should check with both the board manufacturer and the chipset manufacturer; one might provide drivers, but the other might not. Appendix B, "Hardware Manufacturers," provides contact information for many hardware manufacturers. The Web site `http://www.linux.org/hardware/components.html` also provides links to many hardware manufacturers that provide Linux drivers for their products.

A

LINUX DEVICE
DRIVERS

Using Experimental Drivers

Experimental and commercial drivers come in several basic forms:

- **Independent source code**   Some drivers, such as the ALSA drivers, come as source code trees, independent of the main Linux kernel source code. To use these drivers, you extract their packages and compile the drivers as if they were a non-driver software package. When you type `make install`, however, the drivers install themselves in your kernel modules directory, `/lib/modules/a.b.c`, where `a.b.c` is your kernel version. You can then load the drivers as if they were normal kernel modules. This approach doesn't normally allow you to include the driver in the kernel file itself, however; you *must* use the driver as a module.

- **Kernel source tree patch**   Some drivers come as a set of patches to the normal kernel tree. To use these drivers, you change to the Linux kernel directory and then issue a command such as `patch -p0 < patch-filename`. You then reconfigure and recompile your kernel. Depending upon the driver, you might be able to use it as a module, as part of the kernel proper, or both. Some simple driver replacements only require you to replace one or two files in the kernel source tree, rather than use a patch file.

- **Binary-only distribution**   Some drivers, such as the shareware OSS drivers and Lucent's software modem driver, come only as binary code. These drivers normally come with an installation script and are used only as modules. They're more likely than source code drivers to break when you upgrade to a new kernel version.

- **Non-kernel drivers**   Some devices don't use kernel drivers. For instance, XFree86 for video displays, Ghostscript for printers, and SANE for scanners all require drivers in the form of non-kernel programs. These drivers might need to be compiled directly into the relevant program, or they might work independently. Check the relevant documentation for details.

It's critically important that you read and follow the directions included with experimental or other non-standard drivers. The usual way to distribute Linux drivers is through the kernel, so separately distributed drivers are all non-standard by definition. As such, there is no standard way to apply patches. Each project is different.

Contributing to Driver Development

Linux is a community effort. When Linus Torvalds made the earliest versions of the Linux kernel available, other programmers looked upon the software as a living thing which could grow only through their participation. Without the contributions of these many other programmers, Linux today would not be very useful. Linus Torvalds, by himself, almost certainly could not have written the drivers for the dozens of SCSI cards, Ethernet cards, sound cards, and so on that today comprise the kernel. One way to "pay" for the free Linux kernel is to give back currency in the form of your own programming efforts. Of course, if you're not a programmer, you might not be able to do this, but even in this case there are ways you can contribute, as described later in the section, "Non-Programming Contributions."

Resources for Kernel Developers

If you're interested in contributing to the development of one or more core drivers—for a filesystem, EIDE controller, Ethernet card, or other low-level hardware—you want to write for the Linux kernel. You might want to investigate any of several resources:

- **Existing kernel source code**   Sooner or later, you'll need to dig into existing kernel source code. You might be able to use an existing device driver as a model for your own code. If you want to fix a bug, you'll have to work from the existing code. Even before you begin coding, you might want to check out the source code to get a feel for its style and structure. If you want a guided tour of the kernel code, Scott Maxwell's *Linux Core Kernel Commentary* (Coriolis, 1999) might help you.

- **The `linux-kernel` mailing list**   Major Linux kernel developers subscribe to this mailing list. If you want to join, send email to `majordomo@vger.rutgers.edu`. The email should include the line `subscribe linux-kernel` *`your_email@your_ISP`*, where *`your_email@your_ISP`* is your email address.

CAUTION

The `linux-kernel` mailing list is *very* high-volume. It's been known to top 6MB of messages in a week.

A

- **Kernel Traffic Web site**   You can find summaries of discussions on the `linux-kernel` mailing list `http://kt.linuxcare.com/kernel-traffic/index.epl`. Unless you're *very* serious about Linux kernel development, checking this site on a regular basis is probably a wiser move than subscribing to `linux-kernel`.

- **Kernel programming classes**   Many colleges and universities offer classes on OS kernel development. Enrolling in such a class can be a good way to learn about the issues involved in kernel development. Some of these classes rely on the Linux kernel as a model, but others don't.

- **Kernel programming books**   There are a few books on the market that cover Linux kernel programming, such as *Linux Kernel Internals* (Addison-Wesley, 1997) and *The Linux Kernel Book* (John Wiley & Sons, 1998). Other books that cover UNIX driver development or OS kernels in general can also be useful.

Linux kernel development isn't a task you should undertake as your first programming project. If you already know how to program in C, though, it doesn't take much additional skill to delve into the Linux kernel. Doing the job *well* might take additional effort, but *starting* is easy. Developing or modifying a Linux kernel driver can be a great way to refine your programming skills.

> ## CAUTION
>
> The Linux kernel contains a great deal of code that's absolutely critical to the proper functioning of your computer. Developing a kernel driver can therefore be a potentially dangerous proposition. If you're serious about learning kernel programming, I recommend you do it on a spare system that contains no critical data. That way, if your driver damages the Linux installation, you won't lose any truly important files.

In addition to—or instead of—direct kernel programming, you might want to contribute to a related project. For instance, if you want to develop sound drivers, you can contact the ALSA Project developers. Aside from ALSA, most unofficial kernel-level drivers are small projects devoted to just one device or feature. Sooner or later, the main kernel tends to swallow smaller kernel-level projects.

Resources for Non-Kernel Projects

Various non-kernel projects exist, and most of these projects welcome donations of your programming talents. Examples include

- **XFree86**   If you want to fix, expand, or write a new video card driver, contact the XFree86 project (`http://www.xfree86.org`).

- **Printer drivers**   You can develop a new driver for a printer, and contribute it to Ghostscript (`http://www.cs.wisc.edu/~ghost/`). Unlike most Linux driver development, Ghostscript development is fairly centralized. The way in which Ghostscript is released (first under a comparatively restrictive license and then under the GPL) means that you might need to sign away certain rights if you want your driver to be incorporated into the main Aladdin Ghostscript package.

- **Scanner drivers**   Contact the SANE project (`http://www.mostang.com/sane/`) to contribute scanner drivers. A number of SANE drivers are available as add-ons to the main SANE package, so you can contribute scanner drivers without close coordination with the main project.

Because the drivers for most non-kernel devices don't have privileged access to the hardware, writing such device drivers presents less potential for serious crashes than writing kernel drivers does. For instance, if your new Ghostscript driver fails, you're likely to just print one or more sheets of gibberish, not crash your computer. X, however, has somewhat closer access to the hardware than do most non-kernel drivers. It's also possible to drive a monitor at too high of a refresh rate, thus damaging it.

Non-Programming Contributions

Even if you have no programming skills or no inclination to write drivers or other Linux programs, you can contribute to Linux development. There are several ways you can do this:

- **Buy retail Linux distributions.**   Most Linux vendors contribute to Linux development. Therefore, when you buy a retail Linux distribution, some of the purchase price goes towards Linux development. To a lesser extent, you can help by purchasing hardware and software from companies that support Linux. For instance, suppose you're considering two Ethernet adapters, both of which have support in Linux. If one manufacturer has helped Linux development in some way and the other hasn't, buy the first product.

> **TIP**
>
> You can sometimes find acknowledgement of help from hardware manufacturers in a driver's source code or documentation files. XFree86 maintains a list of donors on its Web page, http://www.xfree86.org/sponsors.html.

- **Donate money.**   Some of the non-profit open source software organizations accept cash donations. You can give money to help XFree86, Inc. or the Free Software Foundation (FSF), for instance. Such donations buy hardware, pay for Internet connectivity, and sometimes even pay salaries for hired programmers.
- **Donate equipment.**   Instead of selling or throwing away old equipment, donate it to an interested developer. Such a donation could be something as informal as giving a device for which no Linux drivers exist to somebody who's expressed an interest in writing drivers. You can also donate equipment (supported or not) to organizations like XFree86, Inc. or the FSF. *All* driver developers need hard disks, RAM, monitors, and other hardware components.
- **Provide feedback.**   If you encounter a bug in a driver, write a *polite* email to whoever is responsible for that driver. (You can usually find the maintainer's email address in the relevant source code file.) Try to include relevant information, such as exact information on your hardware and details of how and when the problem occurs. If you can provide

A

LINUX DEVICE
DRIVERS

information that helps the developer fix a bug, you will help not only yourself, but anybody else who might encounter that bug. Likewise, if a new driver or feature makes your life easier, consider writing a thank you note to the developer. Such messages can help keep a programmer motivated.

Linux has grown substantially over the past few years, both in terms of the OS's user base and in terms of the size of the Linux kernel. The increased size of Linux, in both these senses, requires continued support from the Linux community. Therefore, if you want to see Linux continue to thrive, you should seriously consider contributing to the however you are able.

Summary

In many cases, Linux installs itself to a computer and works with the computer's hardware without any special effort on your part. In some cases, however, you must track down unusual drivers in order to get some component to work. Doing this can take some effort and perhaps even ingenuity, because many small driver projects lurk in out-of-the-way locations on the Web. The first step, however, is usually to identify the device's chipset. With that information, you can at least search for the driver in an intelligent way. Web sites, including search engines such as `http://www.yahoo.com` and `http://www.deja.com/usenet/`, can be powerful tools when you want to locate a driver. So can some commands included with Linux, used in conjunction with the Linux kernel source code.

Hardware Manufacturers

IN THIS CHAPTER

This appendix lists many of the larger manufacturers of computer hardware components. Because the number of firms that sell hardware is quite large, this appendix's list is necessarily incomplete. I list both chipset and complete board manufacturers, where applicable.

The structure of this appendix roughly mirrors the structure of the book, progressing from CPUs through to complete systems. There are a few exceptions. For instance, I don't list memory suppliers, because many people consider memory to be a commodity, and, in fact, it's often sold generically, without a brand name attached. I've included a section on Linux retailers at the end of the appendix.

Central Processing Units

The CPU lies at the heart of every computer. AMD, Intel, and VIA produce x86 CPUs—the sort with which Linux was originally developed. Compaq produces the Alpha CPU, which was originally designed by DEC. Motorola produces the PowerPC CPU, which is used in Apple Macintosh computers, as well as a few others.

Advanced Micro Devices (AMD)
One AMD Place
P.O. Box 3453
Sunnyvale, CA 94088-3453
408-732-2400
http://www.amd.com

Compaq Computer Corporation
P.O. Box 692000
Houston, TX 77269-2000
800-231-0900
http://www.compaq.com

Intel Corporation
2200 Mission College Blvd.
Santa Clara, CA 95054-1537
408-765-8080
http://www.intel.com

Motorola, Inc.
Microprocessor and Memory Technology Group
3501 Ed Bluestein Blvd.
Austin, TX 78762
512-895-2000
http://www.mot.com

VIA Technologies
1045 Mission Court
Fremont, CA 94539
http://www.via.com.tw

Motherboards

Many manufacturers produce motherboards, so this section is necessarily incomplete. Some of the entries in this section are for motherboard manufacturers, but others are for motherboard chipset makers and BIOS distributors.

ABIT Computer Corporation
46808 Lakeview Blvd.
Fremont, CA 94538
510-623-0500
http://www.abit-usa.com

Acer Laboratories, Inc. (ALi)
Pacific Technology Group
4701 Patrick Henry Drive, Suite 2101
Santa Clara, CA 95054
408-764-0644
http://www.ali.com.tw

American Megatrends, Inc. (AMI)
6145-F Northbelt Pkwy.
Norcross, GA 30071
770-246-8600
http://www.ami.com

ASUS Computer International
721 Charcot Ave.
San Jose, CA 95013
510-739-3777
http://www.asus.com

Award Software International
777 E. Middlefield Rd.
Mountain View, CA 94043
650-237-6800
http://www.award.com

Diamond Flower, Inc. (DFI)
135 Main Ave.
Sacramento, CA 95838
916-568-1234
http://www.dfiusa.com

Elitegroup Computer Systems
45401 Research Ave.
Fremont, CA 94539
510-226-7333
http://www.ecsusa.com

EPoX Computer
531 East Jamie Ave.
La Habra, CA 90631
714-680-0898
http://www.epox.com

First International Computer (FIC)
980-A Mission Court
Fremont, CA 94539
510-252-7777
http://www.fica.com

Gigabyte Technology
18305 Valley Blvd., Suite A
La Puente, CA 91744
626-854-9338
http://www.giga-byte.com

Intel Corporation
2200 Mission College Blvd.
Santa Clara, CA 95054-1537
408-765-8080
http://www.intel.com

Jaton Corporation
556 S. Milpitas Blvd.
Milpitas, CA 95035
408-942-9888
http://www.jaton.com

OPTi, Inc.
3393 Octavius Drive
Santa Clara, CA 95045
408-486-8000
http://www.opti.com

Phoenix Technologies, Ltd.
Refer to *Award Software International*

Silicon Integrated Systems (SiS)
240 N. Wolfe Rd.
Sunnyvale, CA 94086
408-730-5600
http://www.sis.com.tw

B

HARDWARE
MANUFACTURERS

SOYO Tek, Inc.
41484 Christy St.
Fremont, CA 94538
510-226-7696
http://www.soyo.com

Supermicro Computer, Inc.
2051 Junction Ave.
San Jose, CA 95131
408-895-2000
http://www.supermicro.com

Tekram Technologies
11500 Metric Blvd., Suite 190
Austin, TX 78758
512-833-6550
http://www.tekram.com

Tyan Computer Corporation
1753 S. Main St.
Milpitas, CA 95035
408-956-8000
http://www.tyan.com

Unicore Software, Inc.
1538 Turnpike St.
North Andover, MA 01845
978-685-6468
http://www.mrbios.com

VIA Technologies
1045 Mission Court
Fremont, CA 94539
http://www.via.com.tw

VLSI Technology, Inc.
(A division of Philips Semiconductor)
1109 McKay Drive
San Jose, CA 95131
408-434-3000
http://www-us.semiconductors.
philips.com/vlsi/

Cases and Power Supplies

Cases and power supplies arecritically important for the reliability and future expandability of your computer, yet they're often treated as commodities. You can usually track down the manufacturer of these components, if you like.

American Power Conversion (APC)
132 Fairgrounds Rd.
West Kingston, RI 02892
401-789-5735
http://www.apcc.com

Astec America, Inc.
5810 Van Allen Way
Carlsbad, CA 92008
760-930-4600
http://www.astec.com

Best Power
P.O. Box 280
Necedah, WI 54646
608-565-7200
http://www.bestpower.com

Elitegroup Computer Systems
45401 Research Ave.
Fremont, CA 94539
510-226-7333
http://www.ecsusa.com

Enlight Corporation
15-16, Ting Hu Rd.
Ta-Kang, Kwei-Shan
Taoyuan, Taipei
Taiwan, R.O.C.
`http://www.enlightcorp.com`

In-Win Development/Astra Data Inc.
891 S. Azusa Ave.
City of Industry, CA 91748
626-913-6822
`http://www.in-win.com`

NMB Technologies, Inc.
9730 Independence Ave.
Chatsworth, CA 91311
818-341-3355
`http://www.nmbtech.com`

PC Power & Cooling
5995 Avenida Encinas
Carlsbad, CA 92008
760-931-5700
`http://www.pcpowercooling.com`

Superpower Supply, Inc.
10675 East Rush St.
South El Monte, CA 91733
626-455-0777
`http://www.spower.com`

Tripp Lite Manufacturing
1111 West 35th St.
Chicago, IL 60609
773-329-1777
`http://www.tripplite.com`

Hard Disks

A handful of companies dominate the hard disk marketplace. These manufacturers occasionally shift, leave the business, or merge; but others often step in to take the place of the exiting firms. Some companies resell under their own names products from the major manufacturers. This practice is particularly common for external SCSI drives.

Fujitsu Computer Products of America
2904 Orchard Drive
San Jose, CA 95134-2009
800-626-4686
`http://www.fcpa.com`

International Business Machines (IBM)
New Orchard Rd.
Armonk, NY 10504
914-499-1900
`http://www.ibm.com`

Maxtor Corporation
211 River Oaks Pkwy.
San Jose, CA 95134
408-432-1700
`http://www.maxtor.com`

Quantum Corporation
500 McCarthy Blvd.
Milpitas, CA 95035
408-894-4000
`http://www.quantum.com`

Seagate Technology
920 Disc Way
Scotts Valley, CA 95066
714-641-2500
`http://www.seagate.com`

Toshiba America, Inc.
9740 Irvine Blvd.
Irvine, CA 92718
714-583-3926
`http://www.computers.toshiba.com`

B

HARDWARE
MANUFACTURERS

Western Digital Corporation
8105 Irvine Center Drive
Irvine, CA 92618
714-932-5000
http://www.westerndigital.com

Removable and Optical Disks

This category includes a wide variety of devices, including floppy drives, CD-ROM drives, CD-R drives, and high-capacity removable-media drives. Most of the manufacturers in this section make at least two or three different types of removable-media drives. I've also included in this section several large manufacturers of removable-drive media.

Acer America Corp.
2641 Orchard Pkwy.
San Jose, CA 95134
408-432-6200
http://www.acer.com

ASUS Computer International
721 Charcot Ave.
San Jose, CA 95013
510-739-3777
http://www.asus.com

Castlewood Systems, Inc.
7133 Koll Center Pkwy., Suite 200
Pleasanton, CA 94566
925-461-5500
http://www.castlewood.com

Creative Labs
1901 McCarthy Blvd.
Milpitas, CA 95035
800-998-1000
http://www.creative.com

Fujitsu Computer Products of America
2904 Orchard Drive
San Jose, CA 95134-2009
800-626-4686
http://www.fcpa.com

Hewlett-Packard Company
3000 Hanover St.
Palo Alto, CA 94304-1185
650-857-1501
http://www.hp.com

Imation
1 Imation Place
Oakdale, MN 55128
612-704-4000
http://www.imation.com

Iomega Corporation
1821 West Iomega Way
Roy, UT 84067
801-778-1000
http://www.iomega.com

JVC Information Products
5665 Corporate Drive
Cypress, CA 90630
714-816-6500
http://www.jvc.com

Maxell Corporation of America
22-08 Route 208
Fair Lawn, NJ 07410
800-533-2836
http://www.maxell.com

Maxoptix Corporation
3342 Gateway Blvd.
Fremont, CA 94538
510-353-9700
http://www.maxoptix.com

Mitsumi Electronics Corporation
5808 W. Campus Circle Drive
Irving, TX 75063
214-550-7300
http://www.mitsumi.com

NEC Technologies, Inc.
1414 Massachusetts Ave.
Boxborough, MA 01719
978-264-8000
http://www.nec.com

Panasonic Communications & Systems
2 Panasonic Way
Secaucus, NJ 07094
201-348-7000
http://www.panasonic.com

Philips Consumer Electronics
P.O. Box 14810
One Philips Drive
Knoxville, TN 37914
423-521-4316
http://www.magnavox.com

Plextor
4255 Burton Drive
Santa Clara, CA 95054
408-980-1838
http://www.plextor.com

Sony Corporation of America
Sony Drive
Park Ridge, NJ 07656
800-326-9551
http://www.ita.sel.sony.com

TDK Corporation of America
12 Harbor Park Drive
Port Washington, NY 11050
516-625-0100
http://www.tdk.com

Teac America, Inc.
7733 Telegraph :contact informationRd.
Montebello, CA 90640
213-726-0303
http://www.teac.com

Toshiba America, Inc.
9740 Irvine Blvd.
Irvine, CA 92718
714-583-3926
http://www.computers.toshiba.com

Verbatim Corporation
1200 WT Harris Blvd.
Charlotte, NC 28262
704-547-6500
http://www.verbatimcorp.com

Tape Backup Drives

This section lists the major tape backup device manufacturers, as well as major tape media manufacturers.

Exabyte Corporation
1685 38th St.
Boulder, CO 80301
303-442-4333
http://www.exabyte.com

Fujitsu Computer Products of America
2904 Orchard Drive
San Jose, CA 95134-2009
800-626-4686
http://www.fcpa.com

Hewlett-Packard Company
3000 Hanover St.
Palo Alto, CA 94304-1185
650-857-1501
http://www.hp.com

Maxell Corporation of America
22-08 Route 208
Fair Lawn, NJ 07410
800-533-2836
http://www.maxell.com

OnStream
1951 S. Fordham St.
Longmont, CO 80503
303-772-9000
http://www.onstream.com

Quantum Corporation
500 McCarthy Blvd.
Milpitas, CA 95035
408-894-4000
http://www.quantum.com

Seagate Technology
920 Disc Way
Scotts Valley, CA 95066
714-641-2500
http://www.seagate.com

Sony Corporation of America
Sony Drive
Park Ridge, NJ 07656
800-326-9551
http://www.ita.sel.sony.com

TDK Corporation of America
12 Harbor Park Drive
Port Washington, NY 11050
516-625-0100
http://www.tdk.com

Teac America, Inc.
7733 Telegraph Rd.
Montebello, CA 90640
213-726-0303
http://www.teac.com

Tecmar Technologies, Inc.
1900 Pike Rd.
Longmont, CO 80501
303-682-3700
http://www.tecmar.com

Verbatim Corporation
1200 WT Harris Blvd.
Charlotte, NC28262
704-547-6500
http://www.verbatimcorp.com

SCSI Host Adapters

Some of the companies listed here produce SCSI chipsets; others use chipsets to produce SCSI host adapters. Other companies produce both chipsets and complete products. Many of these companies produce EIDE controllers in addition to SCSI host adapters.

Adaptec
691 S. Milpitas Blvd.
Milpitas, CA 95035
408-945-8600
http://www.adaptec.com

ASUS Computer International
721 Charcot Ave.
San Jose, CA 95013
510-739-3777
http://www.asus.com

BusLogic
See *Mylex Corporation*

Initio Corporation
2205 Fortune Drive, Suite A
San Jose, CA 95131-1806
408-577-1919
http://www.initio.com

LSI Logic, Inc. (formerly Symbios)
1551 McCarthy Blvd.
Milpitas, CA 95035
408-433-8000
http://www.lsilogic.com

Mylex Corporation (formerly BusLogic)
34551 Ardenwood Blvd.
Fremont, CA 94555-3067
510-796-6100
http://www.mylex.com

Promise Technology
1460 Koll Circle, Suite A
San Jose, CA 95112
408-452-0948
http://www.promise.com

QLogic Corporation
26650 Laguna Hills Drive
Aliso Viejo, CA 92656
949-389-6000
http://www.qlogic.com

SIIG, Inc.
6078 Stewart Ave.
Fremont, CA 94538-3152
510-657-8688
http://www.siig.com

Tekram Technologies
11500 Metric Blvd., Suite 190
Austin, TX 78758
512-833-6550
http://www.tekram.com

Sound Cards

Many small companies produce sound cards based upon the chipsets of other firms. The most common chipsets include those made by Cirrus Logic/Crystal Semiconductor, ESS, and OPTi. Increasingly, sound functionality is being moved into the motherboard chipsets, although this practice is still far from universal.

Acer America Corp.
2641 Orchard Pkwy.
San Jose, CA 95134
408-432-6200
http://www.acer.com

Cirrus Logic, Inc./Crystal Semiconductor
3100 W. Warren Ave.
Fremont, CA 94538
510-623-8300
http://www.cirrus.com

Creative Labs
1901 McCarthy Blvd.
Milpitas, CA 95035
800-998-1000
http://www.creative.com

ESS Technology, Inc.
48401 Fremont Blvd.
Fremont, CA 94538
510-492-1088
http://www.esstech.com

Intel Corporation
2200 Mission College Blvd.
Santa Clara, CA 95054-1537
408-765-8080
http://www.intel.com

International Business Machines (IBM)
New Orchard Rd.
Armonk, NY 10504
914-499-1900
http://www.ibm.com

Jaton Corporation
556 S. Milpitas Blvd.
Milpitas, CA 95035
408-942-9888
http://www.jaton.com

OPTi, Inc.
3393 Octavius Drive
Santa Clara, CA 95045
408-486-8000
http://www.opti.com

Roland Corporation, U.S.
5100 S. Eastern Ave.
Los Angeles, CA 90040-2938
323-890-3700
http://www.rolandus.com

Turtle Beach
See *Voyetra-Turtle Beach, Inc.*

VIA Technologies
1045 Mission Court
Fremont, CA 94539
http://www.via.com.tw

Voyetra Turtle Beach, Inc.
5 Odell Plaza
Yonkers, NY 10701-1406
800-233-9377
http://www.voyetra-turtle-beach.com

Yamaha Corporation of America
6600 Orangethorpe Ave.
Buena Park, CA 90620
714-522-9011
http://www.yamaha.com

Audio Input/Output

Many companies produce speakers, headphones, and microphones. For use with a computer, you're best off with speakers designed for computers, because they're more likely to be adequately shielded to protect sensitive magnetic media from harm.

Altec Lansing Technologies, Inc.
Route 6 & Route 209
Milford, PA 18337
800-258-3288
http://www.altecmm.com

Bose Corp.
The Mountain
Framingham, MA 01701-9168
508-879-7330
http://www.bose.com

Cambridge SoundWorks
311 Needham St.
Cambridge, MA 02464
617-332-5936
http://www.cambridgesoundworks.com

Creative Labs
1901 McCarthy Blvd.
Milpitas, CA 95035
800-998-1000
http://www.creative.com

JVC Information Products
5665 Corporate Drive
Cypress, CA 90630
714-816-6500
http://www.jvc.com

Logitech, Inc.
6505 Kaiser Drive
Fremont, CA 94555
510-795-8500
http://www.logitech.com

NMB Technologies, Inc.
9730 Independence Ave.
Chatsworth, CA 91311
818-341-3355
http://www.nmbtech.com

Labtec Enterprises, Inc.
1499 SE Tech Center Place, Suite 350
Vancouver, VA 98683
360-896-2000
http://www.labtec.com

Philips Consumer Electronics
P.O. Box 14810
One Philips Drive
Knoxville, TN 37914
423-521-4316
http://www.magnavox.com

Radio Shack
300 West Third St., Suite 1400
Ft. Worth, TX 76102
817-415-3200
http://www.radioshack.com

Sony Corporation of America
Sony Drive
Park Ridge, NJ 07656
800-326-9551
http://www.ita.sel.sony.com

VideoLogic Systems
6980 Corte Santa Fe
San Diego, CA 92121
888-336-1198
http://www.videologic.com

Yamaha Corporation of America
6600 Orangethorpe Ave.
Buena Park, CA 90620
714-522-9011
http://www.yamaha.com

Video Cards and Chipsets

The video card marketplace changes *very* rapidly, even by computer standards. Five years ago, the list of companies in this section would be quite different than what appears here today. As with many other sections, some of these firms produce chipsets, others produce complete products, and some produce both. Since the late 1990s, there has been an increasing trend towards *vertical integration*—one company producing both chipsets and cards.

3D Labs
480 Potrero Ave.
Sunnyvale, CA 94086
Phone: 408-530-4700
http://www.3dlabs.com

3Dfx
4435 Fortran Drive
San Jose, CA 95134
Phone: 408-935-4400
http://www.3dfx.com

ATI Technologies, Inc.
33 Commerce Valley Drive East
Thornhill, ONT L3T 7N6 CANADA
905-882-2600
http://www.atitech.ca

Cirrus Logic, Inc.
3100 W. Warren Ave.
Fremont, CA 94538
510-623-8300
http://www.cirrus.com

Creative Labs
1901 McCarthy Blvd.
Milpitas, CA 95035
800-998-1000
http://www.creative.com

ELSA, Inc.
1630 Zanker Rd.
San Jose, CA 95112
408-961-4600
http://www.elsa.com

Gigabyte Technology
18305 Valley Blvd., Suite A
La Puente, CA 91744
626-854-9338
http://www.giga-byte.com

Jaton Corporation
556 S. Milpitas Blvd.
Milpitas, CA 95035
408-942-9888
http://www.jaton.com

Matrox Graphics, Inc.
1025 St. Regis Blvd.
Dorval, PQ H9P 2T4 CANADA
514-969-6300
http://www.matrox.com

nVidia Corporation
1226 Tiros Way
Sunnyvale, CA 94086
408-617-4000
http://www.nvidia.com

Trident Microsystems
189 N Bernado Ave.
Mountain View, CA 94043
650-691-9211
http://www.tridentmicro.com

VideoLogic Systems
6980 Corte Santa Fe
San Diego, CA 92121
888-336-1198
http://www.videologic.com

Video Capture and AV Input Hardware

This section presents manufacturers of a wide variety of video products: portable digital cameras, WebCams, and TV tuner cards. Many companies produce more than one type of product.

Agfa Corp.
100 Challenger Rd.
Ridgefield Park, NJ 07660
201-440-2500
http://www.agfa.com

Canon USA, Inc.
One Canon Plaza
Lake Success, NY 11042
516-488-6700
http://www.canon.com

Casio, Inc.
570 Mt. Pleasant Ave.
Dover, NJ 07801
973-361-5400
http://www.casio-usa.com

Creative Labs
1901 McCarthy Blvd.
Milpitas, CA 95035
800-998-1000
http://www.creative.com

Eastman Kodak Company
Rochester, NY 14650
888-375-6325
http://www.kodak.com

Epson America, Inc.
3840 Kilroy Airport Way
Long Beach, CA 90806
562-276-7202
http://www.epson.com

Fuji Photo Film USA, Inc.
Attn: Consumer Information Services
P.O. Box 7828
Edison, NJ 08818-7828
800-800-3854
http://www.fujifilm.com

Hauppauge Computer Works, Inc.
91 Cabot Ct.
Hauppauge, NY 11788
516-434-1600
http://www.hauppauge.com

Hewlett-Packard Company
3000 Hanover St.
Palo Alto, CA 94304-1185
650-857-1501
http://www.hp.com

Intel Corporation
2200 Mission College Blvd.
Santa Clara, CA 95054-1537
408-765-8080
http://www.intel.com

Kensington Technology Group
2855 Campus Drive
San Mateo, CA 94403
650-572-2700
http://www.kensington.com

Kodak
Refer to *Eastman Kodak Company*

Logitech, Inc.
6505 Kaiser Drive
Fremont, CA 94555
510-795-8500
http://www.logitech.com

Mustek, Inc.
121 Waterworks Way, #100
Irvine, CA 92618
949-790-3800
http://www.mustek.com

Nikon Inc.
1300 Walt Whitman Rd.
Melville, NY 11747-3064
631-547-4200
http://www.nikonusa.com

Olympus America, Inc.
Two Corporate Center Drive
Melville, NY 11747-3157
631-844-5000
http://www.olympus.com

Sony Corporation of America
Sony Drive
Park Ridge, NJ 07656
800-326-9551
http://www.ita.sel.sony.com

UMAX Technologies, Inc.
3561 Gateway Blvd.
Fremont, CA 94538
510-651-4000
http://www.umax.com

VideoLogic Systems
6980 Corte Santa Fe
San Diego, CA 92121
888-336-1198
http://www.videologic.com

Monitors

Monitors are a fairly narrow product category, although with the increasing popularity of LCD monitors, the technology is splitting into two tracks. Most manufacturers that make LCD screens also make conventional CRT displays.

Acer America Corp.
2641 Orchard Pkwy.
San Jose, CA 95134
408-432-6200
http://www.acer.com

CTX International
18501 San Jose Ave.
City of Industry, CA 91748
626-709-1045
http://www.ctxintl.com

Hewlett-Packard Company
3000 Hanover St.
Palo Alto, CA 94304-1185
650-857-1501
http://www.hp.com

Hitachi America, Ltd.
2000 Sierra Point Pkwy.
Brisbane, CA 94005
650-589-8300
http://www.hitachi.com

Hyundai Electronics America
3101 N. First St.
San Jose, CA 95134
408-232-8000
http://www.hei.co.kr

KDS USA
12300 Edison Way
Garden Grove, CA 92641
714-379-5599
http://www.kdsusa.com

MAG Innovision
20 Goodyear
Irvine, CA 92618
949-855-4930
http://www.maginnovision.com

Mitsubishi Display Devices America, Inc.
2401 Portico Blvd.
Calexico, CA 92231
760-357-7330
http://www.mitsubishi.com

NEC Technologies, Inc.
1414 Massachusetts Ave.
Boxborough, MA 01719
978-264-8000
http://www.nec.com

Panasonic Communications & Systems
2 Panasonic Way
Secaucus, NJ 07094
201-348-7000
http://www.panasonic.com

Philips Consumer Electronics
P.O. Box 14810
One Philips Drive
Knoxville, TN 37914
423-521-4316
http://www.magnavox.com

Princeton Graphics
2801 South Yale St.
Santa Ana, CA 92704
714-751-8405
http://www.princetongraphics.com

Sharp Electronics Corporation
Sharp Plaza
Mahwah, NJ 07430-2135
201-529-8200
http://www.sharp-usa.com

Sony Corporation of America
Sony Drive
Park Ridge, NJ 07656
800-326-9551
http://www.ita.sel.sony.com

Tatung Company of America, Inc.
2850 El Presidio St.
Long Beach, CA 90810
310-637-2105
http://www.tatungusa.com

Toshiba America, Inc.
9740 Irvine Blvd.
Irvine, CA 92718
714-583-3926
http://www.computers.toshiba.com

ViewSonic
381 Brea Canyon Rd.
Walnut, CA91789
909-869-7976
http://www.viewsonic.com

Keyboards and Mice

Many manufacturers sell both keyboards and mice, but a few sell only one type of device. Most manufacturers of mice also produce mouse substitutes, such as trackballs. There are a huge number of manufacturers of very low-cost keyboards and mice; this section lists only some of the best-known or highest-quality manufacturers of these devices.

Acer America Corp.
2641 Orchard Pkwy.
San Jose, CA 95134
408-432-6200
http://www.acer.com

ALPS Electric
3553 N. First St.
San Jose, CA 95134
408-432-6000
http://www.alpsusa.com

Belkin Components
501 West Walnut St.
Compton, CA 90220
800-223-5546
http://www.belkin.com

Creative Vision Technologies, Inc. (formerly Northgate)
110 Hamel Rd.
P.O. Box 14
Hamel, MN 55340
612-478-6446
http://www.cvtinc.com

International Business Machines (IBM)
New Orchard Rd.
Armonk, NY 10504
914-499-1900
http://www.ibm.com

Kensington Technology Group
2855 Campus Drive
San Mateo, CA 94403
650-572-2700
http://www.kensington.com

KeyTronic Corporation
P.O. Box 14687
Spokane, WA 99214
509-928-8000
http://www.keytronic.com

Logitech, Inc.
6505 Kaiser Drive
Fremont, CA 94555
510-795-8500
http://www.logitech.com

Macally
5101 Commerce Drive
Baldwin Park, CA 91706
626-338-8787
http://www.macally.com

Maxi Switch, Inc.
2901 East Elvira Rd.
Tucson, AZ 85706
602-294-5450
http://www.maxiswitch.com

Maxoptix Corporation
3342 Gateway Blvd.
Fremont, CA 94538
510-353-9700
http://www.maxoptix.com

Microsoft Corporation
One Microsoft Way
Redmond, WA 98052-6399
425-882-8080
http://www.microsoft.com

Mitsumi Electronics Corporation
5808 W. Campus Circle Drive
Irving, TX 75063
972-550-7300
http://www.mitsumi.com

Mouse Systems
2605 E. Cedar St.
Ontario, CA 91761
909-923-3510
http://www.mousesystems.com

NMB Technologies, Inc.
9730 Independence Ave.
Chatsworth, CA 91311
818-341-3355
http://www.nmbtech.com

Wacom, Inc.
1311 SE Cardinal Court
Vancouver, WA 98683
800-922-9348
http://www.wacom.com

Network Hardware

Network hardware ranges from network interface cards (NICs) to hubs and switches to specialized devices like print servers. Most companies that sell one type of networking hardware sell an entire line of devices. Most of the companies listed here sell complete boards and devices, but a few sell networking chipsets.

3Com Corp.
5400 Bayfront Plaza
P.O. Box 58145
Santa Clara, CA 95052-8145
Phone: 408-764-5000
http://www.3com.com

Asante Technologies, Inc.
821 Fox Lane
San Jose, CA 95131-1601
800-662-9686
http://www.asante.com

Belkin Components
501 West Walnut St.
Compton, CA 90220
800-223-5546
http://www.belkin.com

Boca Research, Inc.
1601 Clint Moore Rd.
Boca Raton, FL 33487-2747
561-997-6227
http://www.bocaresearch.com

Cisco Systems
170 West Tasman Drive
San Jose, CA 95134-1619
408-526-4000
http://www.cisco.com

D-Link
53 Discovery Drive
Irvine, CA 92618
714-788-0805
http://www.dlink.com

B

HARDWARE
MANUFACTURERS

Hewlett-Packard Company
3000 Hanover St.
Palo Alto, CA 94304-1185
650-857-1501
http://www.hp.com

Intel Corporation
2200 Mission College Blvd.
Santa Clara, CA 95054-1537
408-765-8080
http://www.intel.com

Jaton Corporation
556 S. Milpitas Blvd.
Milpitas, CA 95035
408-942-9888
http://www.jaton.com

Kingston Technology Corporation
17600 Newhope St.
Fountain Valley, CA 92708
714-435-2600
http://www.kingston.com

Lantronix
15353 Barranca Pkwy.
Irvine, CA 92718-2216
714-453-3990
http://www.lantronix.com

Linksys
17401 Armstrong Ave.
Irvine, CA 92614
949-261-1288
http://www.linksys.com

NDC Communications, Inc.
265 Santa Ana Court
Sunnyvale CA 94086
408-730-0888
http://www.ndclan.com

Netgear
4401 Great America Pkwy.
P.O. Box 58185
Santa Clara, CA 95052-8185
408-988-2400
http://www.netgear.com

SMC Networks, Inc.
350 Kennedy Drive
Hauppauge, NY 11788
516-435-6000
http://www.smc.com

SOHOware
Refer to *NDC Communications, Inc.*

VIA Technologies
1045 Mission Court
Fremont, CA 94539
http://www.via.com.tw

Xircom
2300 Corporate Center Drive
Thousand Oaks, CA 91320
805-376-9300
http://www.xircom.com

Modems

Most modems sold today are telephone modems—they use an ordinary telephone line to connect to another computer. An increasing number of devices, however, are Digital Subscriber Line (DSL) or cable modems, which use dedicated telephone lines or a cable TV hookup, respectively. Many companies produce more than one type of modem. Most of the companies listed here produce end-user products, but a few specialize in modem chipsets that go into those products.

3Com Corp.
5400 Bayfront Plaza
P.O. Box 58145
Santa Clara, CA 95052-8145
Phone: 408-764-5000
http://www.3com.com

Alcatel
1000 Coit Rd., CHB
Plano, TX 75075
972-519-3000
http://www.alcatel.com

Boca Research, Inc.
1601 Clint Moore Rd.
Boca Raton, FL 33487-2747
561-997-6227
http://www.bocaresearch.com

Cisco Systems
170 West Tasman Drive
San Jose, CA 95134-1619
408-526-4000
http://www.cisco.com

Creative Labs
1901 McCarthy Blvd.
Milpitas, CA 95035
800-998-1000
http://www.creative.com

D-Link
53 Discovery Drive
Irvine, CA 92618
714-788-0805
http://www.dlink.com

Efficient Networks, Inc.
4849 Alpha Rd.
Dallas, TX 75244
972-852-1000
http://www.efficient.com

Global Village Communication
(A subsidiary of Boca Research)
1601 Clint Moore Rd.
Boca Raton, FL 33487
561-997-6227
http://www.globalvillage.com

Jaton Corporation
556 S. Milpitas Blvd.
Milpitas, CA 95035
408-942-9888
http://www.jaton.com

Lucent, Inc.
600 Mountain Ave.
Murray Hill, NJ 07974
908-582-8500
http://www.lucent.com

Multi-Tech Systems
2205 Woodale Drive
Mounds View, MN 55112-9907
800-328-9717
http://www.multitech.com

Rockwell Semiconductor Systems
4311 Jamboree Rd.
Newport Beach, CA 92660-3095
714-221-4600
http://www.rockwell.com

Westell Technologies, Inc.
750 N. Commons Drive
Aurora, IL 60504
800-323-6883
http://www.westell.com

Zoom Telephonics
207 South St.
Boston, MA 02111
617-423-1072
http://www.zoomtel.com

B

HARDWARE
MANUFACTURERS

ZyXEL Communications, Inc.
1650 Miraloma Ave.
Placentia, CA 92870
800-255-4101
http://www.zyxel.com

Scanners

A few companies dominate the scanner marketplace. Most scanners sold today are flatbed models, but a few sheet-fed or other specialized scanners are available. Multi-function units (generally a scanner with a printer and sometimes a modem) are also popular.

Acer America Corp.
2641 Orchard Pkwy.
San Jose, CA 95134
408-432-6200
http://www.acer.com

Agfa Corp.
100 Challenger Rd.
Ridgefield Park, NJ 07660
201-440-2500
http://www.agfa.com

Canon USA, Inc.
One Canon Plaza
Lake Success, NY 11042
516-488-6700
http://www.canon.com

Epson America, Inc.
20770 Madrona Ave.
Torrance, CA 90509-2842
310-787-6300
http://www.epson.com

Fujitsu Computer Products of America
2904 Orchard Drive
San Jose, CA 95134-2009
800-626-4686
http://www.fcpa.com

Hewlett-Packard Company
3000 Hanover St.
Palo Alto, CA 94304-1185
650-857-1501
http://www.hp.com

Microtek
3715 Doolittle Drive
Redondo Beach, CA 90278
800-654-4160
http://www.microtek.com

Mustek, Inc.
121 Waterworks Way, #100
Irvine, CA 92618
949-790-3800
http://www.mustek.com

UMAX Technologies, Inc.
3561 Gateway Blvd.
Fremont, CA 94538
510-651-4000
http://www.umax.com

Visioneer
34800 Campus Drive
Fremont, CA 94555
510-608-6300
http://www.visioneer.com

Xerox Corporation
Xerox Square
Rochester, NY 14644
203-968-3000
http://www.xerox.com

Printers

Most printers sold today are either laser printers or inkjet printers. A handful of companies
dominate the printer market, with another handful occupying niche positions.

ALPS Electric
3553 N. First St.
San Jose, CA 95134
408-432-6000
http://www.alpsusa.com

Brother International Corporation
100 Somerset Corporate Blvd.
Bridgewater, NJ 08807-0911
908-704-1700
http://www.brother.com

Canon USA, Inc.
One Canon Plaza
Lake Success, NY 11042
516-488-6700
http://www.canon.com

Citizen America Corporation
2450 Broadway, Suite 600
Santa Monica, CA 90404
310-453-0614
http://www.citizen-america.com

Compaq Computer Corporation
P.O. Box 692000
Houston, TX 77269-2000
800-231-0900
http://www.compaq.com

Eastman Kodak Company
Rochester, NY 14650
888-375-6325
http://www.kodak.com

Epson America, Inc.
20770 Madrona Ave.
Torrance, CA 90509-2842
310-787-6300
http://www.epson.com

Fujitsu Computer Products of America
2904 Orchard Drive
San Jose, CA 95134-2009
800-626-4686
http://www.fcpa.com

Hewlett-Packard Company
3000 Hanover St.
Palo Alto, CA 94304-1185
650-857-1501
http://www.hp.com

Kodak
Refer to *Eastman Kodak Company*

Lexmark
740 New Circle Rd.
Lexington, KY 40511
606-232-2000
http://www.lexmark.com

B

HARDWARE
MANUFACTURERS

NEC Technologies, Inc.
1414 Massachusetts Ave.
Boxborough, MA 01719
978-264-8000
http://www.nec.com

Okidata
532 Fellowship Rd.
Mount Laurel, NJ 08054
609-235-2600
http://www.okidata.com

Panasonic Communications & Systems
2 Panasonic Way
Secaucus, NJ 07094
201-348-7000
http://www.panasonic.com

QMS, Inc.
P.O. Box 81250
One Magnum Pass
Mobile, AL 36689
800-523-2696
http://www.qms.com

Tektronix, Inc.
See *Xerox Corporation*

Xerox Corporation
Xerox Square
Rochester, NY 14644
203-968-3000
http://www.xerox.com

Computer Manufacturers

Where many other equipment categories in this appendix are somewhat incomplete, this category is *spectacularly* incomplete. It sometimes seems there's a small computer shop on every street corner in America. In this section, therefore, I list some of the larger manufacturers and some of those that are well known in the Linux community. For a more complete listing of Linux computer manufacturers, see http://www.linux.org/vendors/systems.html.

Acer America Corp.
2641 Orchard Pkwy.
San Jose, CA 95134
408-432-6200
http://www.acer.com

Apple Computer, Inc.
1 Infinite Loop
Cupertino, CA 95014
408-996-1010
http://www.apple.com

AST Research, Inc.
16225 Alton Pkwy.
Irvine, CA 92618
714-727-4141
http://www.ast.com

Atipa Linux Solutions
6000 Connecticut
Kansas City, MO 64120
800-360-4346
http://www.atipa.com

Cobalt Networks, Inc.
555 Ellis St.
Mountain View, CA 94043
650-623-2500
http://www.cobalt.com

Compaq Computer Corporation
P.O. Box 692000
Houston, TX 77269-2000
800-231-0900
http://www.compaq.com

Dell Computer Corporation
1 Dellway
Round Rock, TX 78682
512-338-4400
http://www.dell.com

Emperor Linux
Smyrna, GA 30082-6408
888-651-6686
http://www.emperorlinux.com

Gateway
P.O. Box 2000
610 Gateway Drive
North Sioux City, SD 57049
605-232-2000
http://www.gateway.com

Hewlett-Packard Company
3000 Hanover St.
Palo Alto, CA 94304-1185
650-857-1501
http://www.hp.com

International Business Machines (IBM)
New Orchard Rd.
Armonk, NY 10504
914-499-1900
http://www.ibm.com

MicroWay, Inc.
Research Park
Box 79
Kingston, MA 02364
http://www.microway.com

NEC Technologies, Inc.
1414 Massachusetts Ave.
Boxborough, MA 01719
978-264-8000
http://www.nec.com

Penguin Computing
965 Mission St., Suite 600
San Francisco, CA 94103
888-736-4846
http://www.penguincomputing.com

Silicon Graphics, Inc. (SGI)
1600 Amphitheatre Pkwy.
Mountain View, 94043
650-960-1980
http://www.sgi.com

Sun Microsystems, Inc.
901 San Antonio Rd.
Palo Alto, CA 94303
650-960-1300
http://www.sun.com

Sony Corporation of America
Sony Drive
Park Ridge, NJ 07656
800-326-9551
http://www.ita.sel.sony.com

Toshiba America, Inc.
9740 Irvine Blvd.
Irvine, CA 92718
714-583-3926
http://www.computers.toshiba.com

Tuxtops, Inc.
1253 Lakeside Drive
Suite 300
Sunnyvale, California 94086
408-739-9457
http://www.tuxtops.com

VA Linux Systems
1382 Bordeaux Drive
Sunnyvale, CA 94089
877-825-4689
http://www.valinux.com

B

HARDWARE MANUFACTURERS

Linux Hardware and Software Retailers

For the most part, the companies in this section don't manufacture their own hardware. (There are a few partial exceptions; for instance, CompUSA has its own store brand components and sells computers under its own name.) Instead, these firms sell hardware and software. Some are built around Linux. Others, such as CompUSA and CDW, are general-purpose computer retailers who happen to carry some Linux products.

CompUSA, Inc.
14951 N. Dallas Pkwy.
Dallas, TX 75240
800-266-7872
`http://www.compusa.com`

Computer Discount Warehouse (CDW)
200 N. Milwaukee Ave.
Vernon Hills, IL 60061
800-726-4239
`http://www.cdw.com`

eLinux
2555 W. 190th St.
Torrance, CA 90504
877-395-4689
`http://www.elinux.com`

Indelible Blue, Inc.
3209 Gresham Lake Rd., Suite 135
Raleigh, NC 27615
800-776-8284
`http://www.indelibleblue.com`

LinuxMall
P.O. Box 460190
Aurora, CO 80046-0190
800-234-7813
`http://www.linuxmall.com`

Linux System Labs
49884 Miller Ct.
Chesterfield MI 48047
810-716-1704
`http://www.lsl.com`

Micro Warehouse
535 Connecticut Ave.
Norwalk, CT 06854
800-547-5444
`http://www.warehouse.com`

INDEX

SYMBOLS

opto-mechanical mice, 426, 428

Orange Book CDs, 196

orientations, portrait (monitors), 390

OSs
exchanging media, 184-189
multi-OS utilities, 583

OSS (Open Sound System)
drivers, 300-302
Persistent DMA buffers, 300
Web site, 618

output, directing to home stereos, 327-328

over-the-ear headphones, 320

overclocking CPUs, 560-561

P

packages
alsa-driver, 303
alsa-lib, 303
alsa-util, 303
CPUs (central processing units), 22
hfsutils, Web site, 188
isapnp, PnP configuration, configuring cards, 41
mtools, 187-188
ziptool, 172, 174

page description languages (PDLs), 542

page printers, 531

PAL (Phase Alternating Line), 364

palmtop computers
SmartMedia cards, 595
touch-sensitive screens, 420
Web site, 589

Palmtop CPU, 14

Panasonic Communications & Systems, 631, 639, 646

panels, cases, 116-117, 121

Parallel Line Internet Protocol (PLIP), 497

parallel ports, 66, 183, 368
2.2.x kernel options, 442
adding, 443, 445
cable connectors, 439, 441
device files, locating, 215
devices, 183, 442-443
drives, kernel options, 181-182
ECP (enhanced capabilities port), 445
EPP (enhanced parallel port), 445
expansion cards, adding, 443
hardware requirements, 436-437
I/O, 439
interfaces, 176-177, 202, 239-240, 519
IRQs (interrupt requests), 437-439
ISA (Industry Standard Architecture) cards, 446-447
Linux, configuring for multiple ports, 447-449
modems, adding, 443-444
multiport cards, 445-446
notebooks and desktops, comparing, 592
null modem cables, 496-497
parallel
PCI (Peripheral Component Interconnect) cards, 446-447
PLIP (Parallel Line Internet Protocol), 496-497
printers, accessing, 537-539
scanners, kernel drivers, 520
SCSI supporting, 272
SPP (standard parallel port), 445
tuning, 447-448

parallel support, kernel drivers, 370

parameters
-k (gpm program), 431
-m device (gpm program), 431
-r, 616
-R type (gpm program), 431
-S, 161-162
-t type (gpm program), 431
gpm program, 431
tar, 250
vidcat, 374

parity, 86, 91

partial CAV (partial constant angular velocity), 204

partition #1 or partition #4, removable disks, 184

Partition Commander, 566

partitioning
disks, SCSI host adapters, 275
hard disks, 138, 140-142
removable disks, 184

PartitionMagic program, Web site, 565

partitions
FAT-32, removing, 564
hard disks, 138-141, 159
swap, 79
Windows, Linux, installing, 564

parts numbers, chips, 90

passive matrix, LCDs (liquid crystal displays), 383

patch files, Linux Web site, 367

PC Cards, 46, 178, 592-595, 598

PC hardware newsgroups, 585

PC Power & Cooling, contact information, 129, 629

PCI (peripheral component interconnect), 282
bus, 44-45, 271, 337
cards, 284, 446-447
chipsets, 299
devices, non-x86 computers, 100
expansion boards, 366
PnP, 45
Ethernet, 457-458

PCL (Printer Command Language), 543-545